AF552383

PEACE, LOVE, *and* PEPPER SPRAY

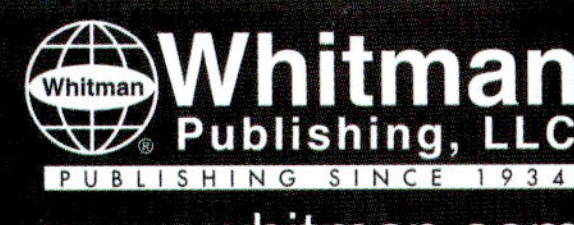

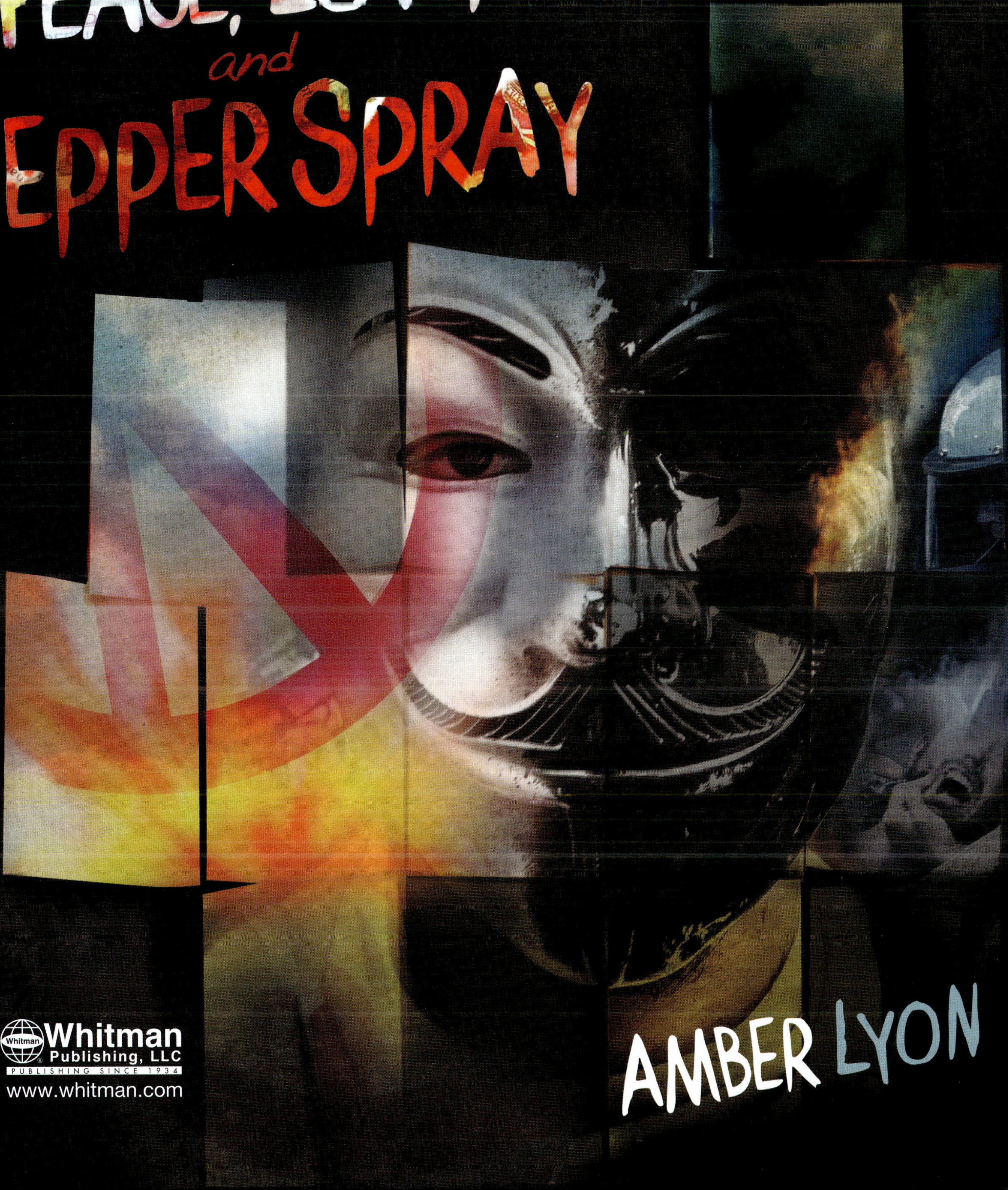

www.whitman.com

AMBER LYON

PEACE, LOVE, and PEPPER SPRAY

www.whitman.com

3101 Clairmont Rd. • Suite G • Atlanta, GA 30329

Correspondence concerning this book may be directed to the publisher, Attn: Peace, Love, and Pepper Spray, at the address above.

ISBN: 0794838030
Printed in China

Scan this QR code to browse
Whitman Publishing's full catalog of books.

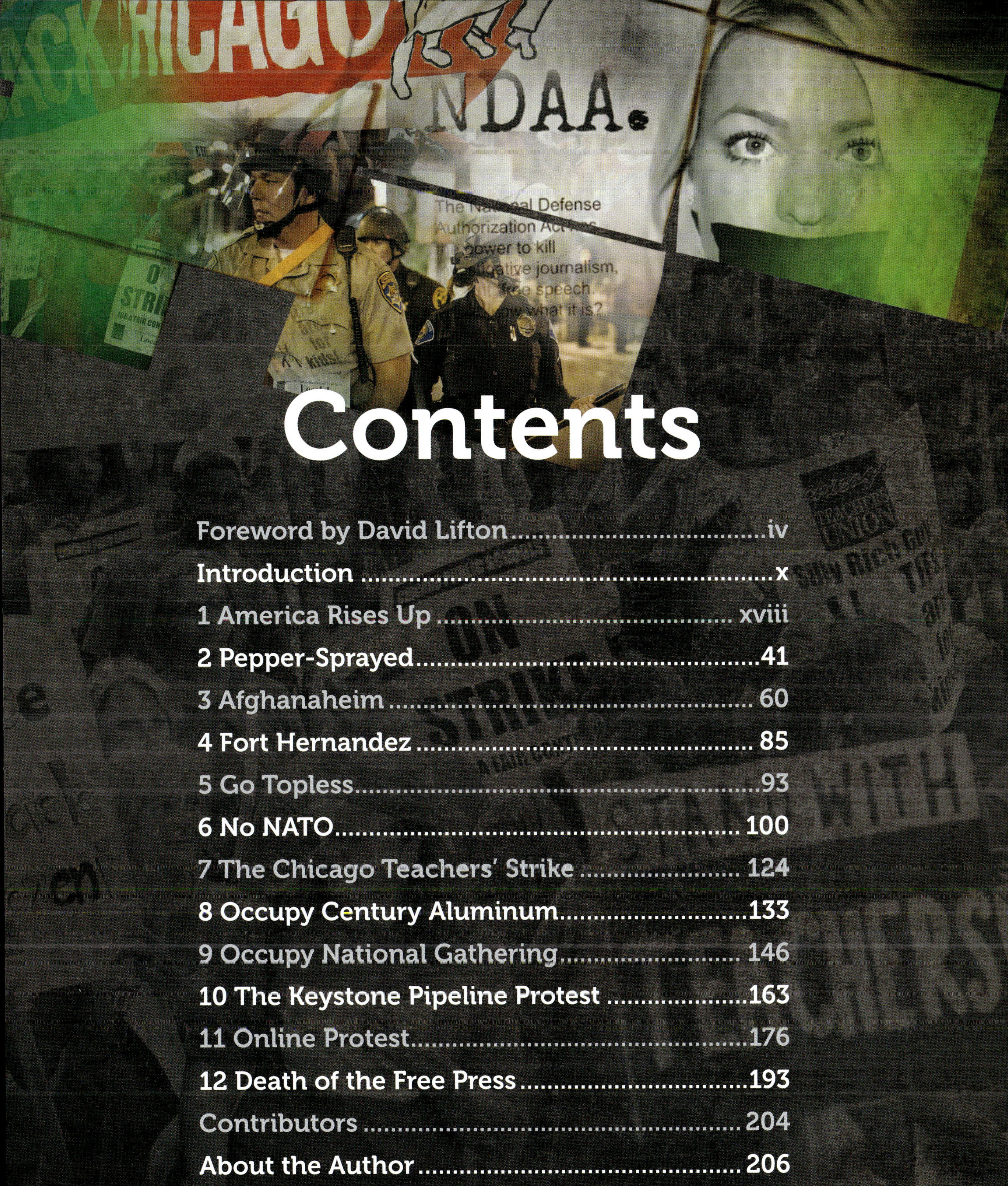

Contents

FOREWORD

DAVID LIFTON

The First Amendment to the United States Constitution protects the rights of American citizens to speak freely, assemble peacefully, and petition the government. From the protests that led to the Revolutionary War to the demonstrations sparked by the issues of today, the desire to make, as the Founding Fathers said, "a more perfect Union," is a notion rooted deep in the American character.

Regardless of ideology, many of the freedoms taken for granted today could not have been possible without the work of citizens who were willing to stand up—and in some cases risk and even give their lives—for the causes in which they believed.

PRE-REVOLUTIONARY PROTESTS

The need for the right to protest stems from America's days as a colony. In the years leading up to the Revolutionary War, the colonists repeatedly spoke out against the tyranny of British rule. The most famous of these protests—and arguably the most famous protest in American history—was the Boston Tea Party.

In May 1773, the British Parliament passed the Tea Act, which imposed an additional tax on tea imported into America by the British East India Company, which controlled the legal sale of all tea in the colonies. The colonists had long let it be known that, as British citizens, they had no right to be taxed without representation in Parliament. The Declaration of Rights and Grievances of 1765 expressed their disapproval in writing. However, these objections were ignored by the home country, and the taxation continued.

Protests against the Tea Act in most of the major port cities led ships containing the tea to return to Britain or to allow tea to rot rather than being unloaded. But in Boston a standoff with the governor, who demanded that the tax be paid, caused the colonists to act.

On the evening of December 16, 1773, members of a group called the Sons of Liberty, some dressed as Mohawk warriors, boarded the three ships and threw all the tea into the harbor.

In response, Parliament passed the so-called Intolerable Acts, which closed Boston Harbor and sought to exert greater control over the dissent coming from the colonies, especially Massachusetts. The acts united the colonies in opposition and eventually forced the beginning of the Revolutionary War.

WHISKEY REBELLION

The American obsession with protesting higher taxes didn't end following independence from Britain. In 1791, needing to pay off the national debt, the government imposed a tax on whiskey produced in America. Farmers in western Pennsylvania, who occasionally turned their excess grain into whiskey for an additional source of income, felt this unfairly affected their profits.

For the next two years, resistance to the tax grew, occasionally reaching the level of threats and even riots against the authority of the tax collectors. By the summer of 1794, the situation had become so bad that President George Washington had to organize a militia of approximately 13,000 citizens from throughout the mid-Atlantic region.

The display of force by the federal government caused the insurrection to collapse before the army had reached its destination. Those arrested for their participation in the Whiskey Rebellion were eventually either acquitted or pardoned by President Washington. The tax was repealed by Thomas Jefferson's administration shortly after he became president in 1801.

SLAVE REBELLIONS

At the heart of all of America's protests is the people's belief that they have the right to determine their own freedom. Although America was founded on the principle that "all men are created equal," that concept wasn't extended to everybody in practice.

Slaves had been rebelling in America against their captivity since as early as 1526 in San Miguel de Gualdape, a Spanish colony believed to be near Winyah Bay, South Carolina. On August 21, 1831, Nat Turner, a slave living in Southampton County, Virginia, led an armed rebellion against his oppressors. He and his fellow slaves broke into houses, killing nearly 60 whites and freeing their slaves.

Within two days, the rebellion had been quashed by a militia, who captured the escaped slaves, 55 of whom were executed for their participation. With help from white civilians, the militia then killed approximately 200 blacks in a two-week spell before being ordered to stop.

Turner, a devout Baptist who believed he was on a mission from God, went into hiding but was found three months later. He was tried and hanged for leading the rebellion. Following the rebellion, the Virginia General Assembly passed legislation that restricted the education, both secular and religious, of slaves, a move that was repeated throughout the South.

THE LABOR MOVEMENT

As America further industrialized, job creators looked to maximize their own profits. Unfortunately, this was often at the expense of their own workforce, which was largely composed of immigrants, many of whom were women and children. Wanting fair wages, shorter hours, and safe working conditions, employees began forming unions.

From the years following the Civil War to the Great Depression, workers in the garment, railroad, textile, and mining industries gave themselves strength in numbers to fight against their own exploitation. Their strikes were often met by force, which ranged from goon squads hired by their bosses to attack picket lines to the National Guard or federal troops, when national interests were at stake.

A year after the Triangle Shirtwaist Factory Fire of 1911, in which 146 people were killed, the U.S. Department of Labor was created to protect the rights of American workers and put and end to sweatshops. Many of the benefits enjoyed by a large percentage of Americans today, including paid vacation, health insurance, overtime pay, and the 40-hour week, could not have been possible without the labor movement. Minimum wage, occupational safety, and child labor laws have also been enacted over the years.

WOMEN'S SUFFRAGE

By the middle of the 19th century, women were beginning to organize to advance the cause of women's suffrage. The movement picked up steam after the Civil War, when the 15th Amendment extended the right to vote to black men, but still overlooked women of all races.

Susan B. Anthony and Elizabeth Cady Stanton drafted an amendment to the Constitution in 1878 that would right this wrong. It was defeated in the Senate and the movement lost steam for the next 30 years.

In the winter of 1913, activists marched from New York to Washington, D.C., determined to create awareness of the movement. The day before Woodrow Wilson's inauguration as president, more than 5,000 women marched down Pennsylvania Avenue in protest. Unfortunately, many male spectators flooded the streets and verbally and physically harassed the women while the police did nothing.

The mistreatment of the women helped garner public support for their cause. Beginning in 1917, the National

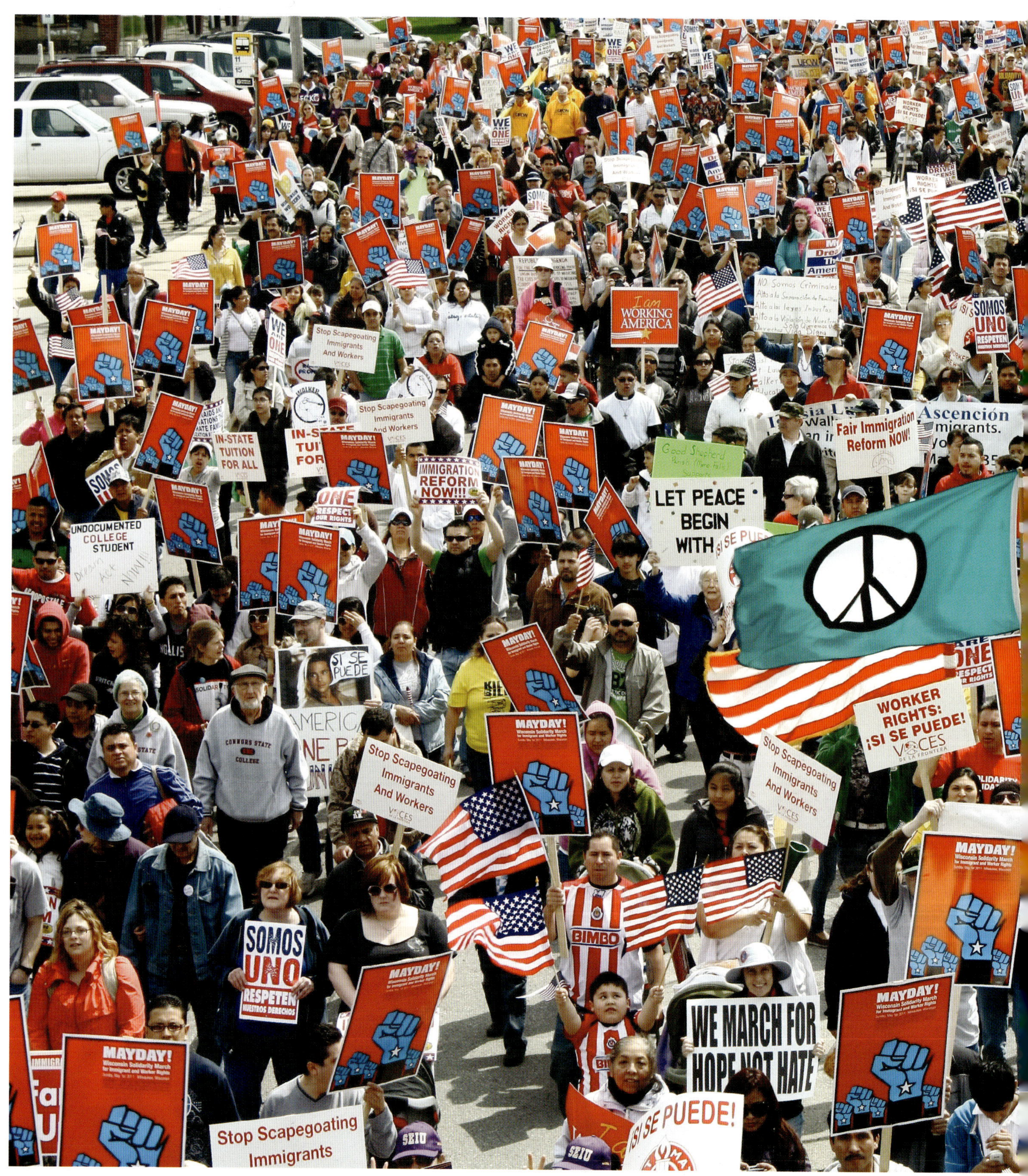
MAYDAY!
Stop Scapegoating Immigrants And Workers
I am WORKING AMERICA
UNDOCUMENTED COLLEGE STUDENT
IN-STATE TUITION FOR ALL
IMMIGRATION REFORM NOW!!!
LET PEACE BEGIN WITH
Fair Immigration Reform NOW!
Ascención
SOMOS UNO RESPETEN
WORKER RIGHTS: ¡SI SE PUEDE! VOCES
WE MARCH FOR HOPE NOT HATE
¡SI SE PUEDE!
BIMBO
Stop Scapegoating Immigrants
SEIU

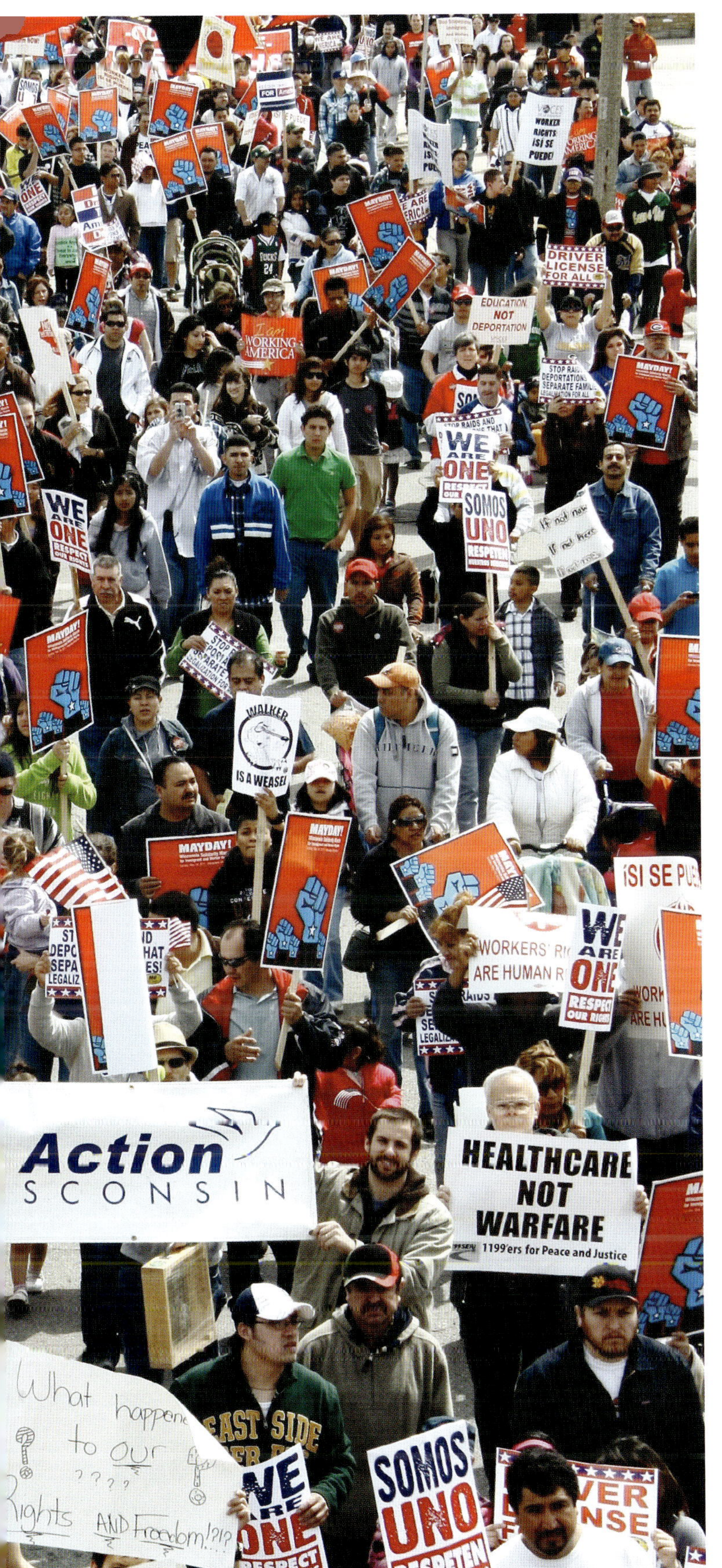

Women's Party, led by Alice Paul, staged nonviolent protests in front of the White House. Paul and other "Silent Sentinels" were eventually arrested and jailed. The publicity forced Wilson, who had long been against women's suffrage, to change his mind.

The president pressured Congress to pass the proposed amendment, which finally happened in 1919. One year later, the 19th Amendment to the Constitution was ratified by the states. It read simply, "The right of citizens of the United States to vote shall not be denied or abridged by the United States or by any State on account of sex. Congress shall have power to enforce this article by appropriate legislation."

CIVIL RIGHTS

Following the post–Civil War Reconstruction era, "Jim Crow" laws, which codified segregation, were passed throughout the South. The suppression caused many blacks to exist as second-class citizens and face harassment, or move north, where conditions were slightly better.

The landmark *Brown v. Board of Education* case of 1954 saw the Supreme Court unanimously declare the phrase "separate, but equal," which had been used since 1896 to justify segregation, to be unconstitutional for public schools. Despite the decision, the South was slow to follow the Court's orders and desegregate, thus ushering in the Civil Rights Movement.

On December 1, 1955, Rosa Parks, an African American woman in Montgomery, Alabama, was arrested for refusing to give up her seat on the bus to a white man. Local civil rights leaders, led by Dr. Martin Luther King Jr., organized a boycott by blacks of Montgomery's bus system. King and other leaders were jailed for their actions, and their houses and several black churches were firebombed.

Despite the violence from the opposition, the boycott continued as the courts weighed in on the legality of segregation. A year after the boycott began, the Supreme Court ruled that black passengers had the right to sit anywhere they desired. The victory instantly turned King into a leading national voice in the burgeoning movement, and he became the first chairman of the newly formed Southern Christian Leadership Conference (SCLC).

The Greensboro Sit-Ins

Civil rights organizations such as the Congress of Racial Equality (CORE) and the SCLC began challenging the status quo with a series of nonviolent protests. In 1960, four students in Greensboro, North Carolina, arranged a sit-in at the lunch counter at Woolworth's department store, which was for whites only.

Over the next few days, the number of protesters grew, which attracted the attention of whites, who harassed the students. Despite the provocation, the men remained peaceful, and the national publicity caused other sit-ins and boycotts to spring up at segregated lunch counters across the region. After more than five months, Woolworth's ended its discriminatory policy.

Freedom Riders

Despite several Supreme Court decisions, private interstate bus lines traveling through the South in 1961 remained segregated. In response, CORE began the Freedom Rides, in which men and women, black and white, rode side by side and with at least one black passenger in the front in defiance of the policy. The rides were scheduled to leave Washington, D.C., on May 1 to travel to New Orleans for a civil rights rally on May 17.

They encountered some resistance along the East Coast, where openly defiant riders were arrested and several were beaten. But as they reached Alabama, the Ku Klux Klan, with the support of sympathetic local law enforcement, retaliated in numbers. Mobs attacked the buses as they reached Anniston, where one bus was firebombed, and Birmingham.

The riders decided to fly to New Orleans following the riot, but the rides resumed following the rally and continued through the summer. After being pressured by Attorney General Robert Kennedy, the Interstate Commerce Commission finally implemented a policy to enforce the anti-segregation laws.

"I Have a Dream"

On August 28, 1963, the Civil Rights movement coalesced, as six civil rights groups came together to organize the March on Washington for Jobs and Freedom. One hundred years after the Emancipation Proclamation, more than 250,000 people of all ethnicities from across the country converged on the Lincoln Memorial to make a statement that segregation and discrimination must end.

The march featured speeches from the heads of the six groups and from Catholic, Jewish, and Presbyterian leaders. African American opera star Marian Anderson, who had famously sung on the steps of the Lincoln Memorial in 1939, sang the National Anthem. Gospel great Mahalia Jackson sang Clara Ward's "How I Got Over," and folk singers Bob Dylan, Joan Baez, and Peter, Paul and Mary performed songs of protest. Many actors, including Harry Belafonte, Charlton Heston, Sidney Poitier, and Marlon Brando, joined the contingent in support.

But the true star of the afternoon was Dr. King. His "I Have a Dream" speech, considered to be among the finest in American history, articulated the need for racial equality with an eloquence that hadn't been heard before. King was named *Time* magazine's "Man of the Year" for 1963 and was awarded the Nobel Peace Prize a year later.

Less than a year after the Great March on Washington, President Lyndon B. Johnson signed the Civil Rights Act. The law, proposed by President John F. Kennedy in 1963, outlawed racial and sexual discrimination in public and private institutions.

"Bloody Sunday"

While the Civil Rights Act made it illegal to deny the right to vote on the basis of race, it did not ban poll taxes, literacy tests, or grandfather clauses that had long been used to disenfranchise blacks. Voter registration drives in the South throughout the Civil Rights Era were met with resistance and hostility.

In February 1965, an African American man was killed by a state trooper during a drive in Marion, Alabama. A march from Selma to Montgomery, a distance of 50 miles, was planned for Sunday, March 7, in order to confront Governor George Wallace about the shooting. Led by John Lewis of the Student Nonviolent Coordinating Committee (SNCC), a group of approximately 600 men and women volunteered. As they crossed the Edmund Pettus Bridge out of Selma, they were met by state troopers demanding that they turn around. The marchers weren't even given time to state their case before the police attacked them with nightsticks and tear gas. Lewis suffered a fractured skull during the beating.

A week after "Bloody Sunday," President Johnson sent the Voting Rights Act to Congress. The bill, which removed all barriers designed to prevent citizens from voting, overwhelmingly passed both the Senate and the House.

Since 1986, Lewis, who was also beaten during the Freedom Rides, has represented Atlanta in the U.S. House of Representatives. In 2011, he was awarded the Presidential Medal of Freedom by President Barack Obama for his lifetime of service to the country.

THE VIETNAM WAR

By the time of Dr. Martin Luther King Jr.'s assassination in 1968, he was speaking with greater frequency in opposition to the war in Vietnam. In addition to its inherent immorality, he felt war was also a drain on financial resources that could be better used to fight poverty and social injustice in America.

The anti-war movement began in the mid-1960s, mostly on college campuses with students burning their draft cards. As the war escalated, so did the protests. President Johnson ended his bid for reelection in March 1968 when he realized his pro-war stance was increasingly unpopular within the Democratic Party. This decision was made a month after newsman Walter Cronkite, known as "The Most Trusted Man in America," noted on the *CBS Evening News* that the war was a stalemate.

At the Democratic National Convention in Chicago that summer, demonstrators clashed with law enforcement all week. On the second-to-last night of the convention, the police attacked the protesters and tear-gassed the crowd in Grant Park in front of national television cameras.

The organizers of the protests, dubbed the "Chicago Eight," were arrested for their actions, and their trial received publicity for the contempt for the judicial system shown by the defendants. Five of the members were found guilty of crossing state lines with the intent to start a riot. Their convictions were thrown out on appeal in 1972.

KENT STATE

Following President Richard M. Nixon's decision to invade Cambodia in April 1970, students at Ohio's Kent State University staged a demonstration. On the night of April 30, the scene grew ugly, and there was widespread property damage throughout the city of Kent. The next day, the Ohio Army National Guard was called in to try to keep the peace.

On May 4, following a day and a half of escalating tensions, the National Guard moved to shut down a protest by launching tear gas canisters into the crowd. Many students dispersed, but the Guardsmen followed them to a football field, where they repeatedly pelted the Guardsmen with rocks. The Guardsmen marched back up a hill, as if to retreat.

When they reached the top, 28 of the troops turned and fired their weapons. In 13 seconds, between 61 and 67 shots were fired. Four students were killed, two of whom were only walking between classes rather than protesting, and another nine were wounded.

Unlike with other protest movements, it's hard to calculate the influence of the protests on the decision to end American involvement in Vietnam in August 1973. But the anti–Vietnam War protests that raged for nearly a decade helped change public opinion and democratically unseat a president, is undeniable.

GAY RIGHTS

On June 28, 1969, the Stonewall Inn, an unlicensed, mob-run gay bar in New York's Greenwich Village, was raided by the police, a common practice at the time. Patrons and onlookers who gathered outside the bar on Christopher Street, fed up with police harassment over the years, fought back as the bar's employees and patrons were removed from the premises. Chants of "Gay Power!" rose from the crowd during the melee.

A riot squad was called in, and the protestors mocked them by playing up gay stereotypes, which led the officers to charge the crowd and beat them with nightsticks before the streets were cleared for the night. The events were repeated over the next few days, and it was considered a victory for New York's gay community in the way that they stood up to the police and how the uprising drew attention to the discrimination faced by homosexuals.

Gay activist groups were formed in New York in the wake of Stonewall to address issues of discrimination and harassment, and gays across the country began to come out of the margins of society. A year later, the anniversary of Stonewall was celebrated with the country's first Gay Pride parade, and many cities followed suit soon thereafter.

In 1999, on the 30th anniversary of Stonewall, the site of the uprising was designated a national landmark by the U.S. Department of the Interior as the place where the gay rights movement began. In his second inaugural address, President Obama referenced Stonewall as a key moment in the struggle for equality.

The phrase "All political power is inherent in the people" is written in many state constitutions. Throughout American history, people of all stripes have joined together to wield that power in the fight for equality and justice. The spirit of those activists can be found in the protests of today, and their actions will continue to inspire future generations of American citizens.

INTRODUCTION

PEPPER-SPRAYED

My eyes were streaming and my airways were burning. Each time I desperately tried to gasp for air, it made me cough and choke even more. I was being directly shot at with pepper balls. As they shattered on the ground around me, the acrid rounds infused the air with capsicum, turning it into a gaseous poison. As a correspondent for CNN I'd covered many war zones, but this one was not in some far-flung corner of the globe—it was in my own backyard in Anaheim, California.

It was the summer of 2012, and I was at a protest in the shadow of Disneyland in California. Local residents were mourning the tragic and unnecessary loss of members of their community and expressing their anger and disgust at the police department's trigger-happy brutality. Months before, an incident at the University of California, Davis, in northern California had shocked the world when images of a police officer pepper-spraying peaceful student protesters

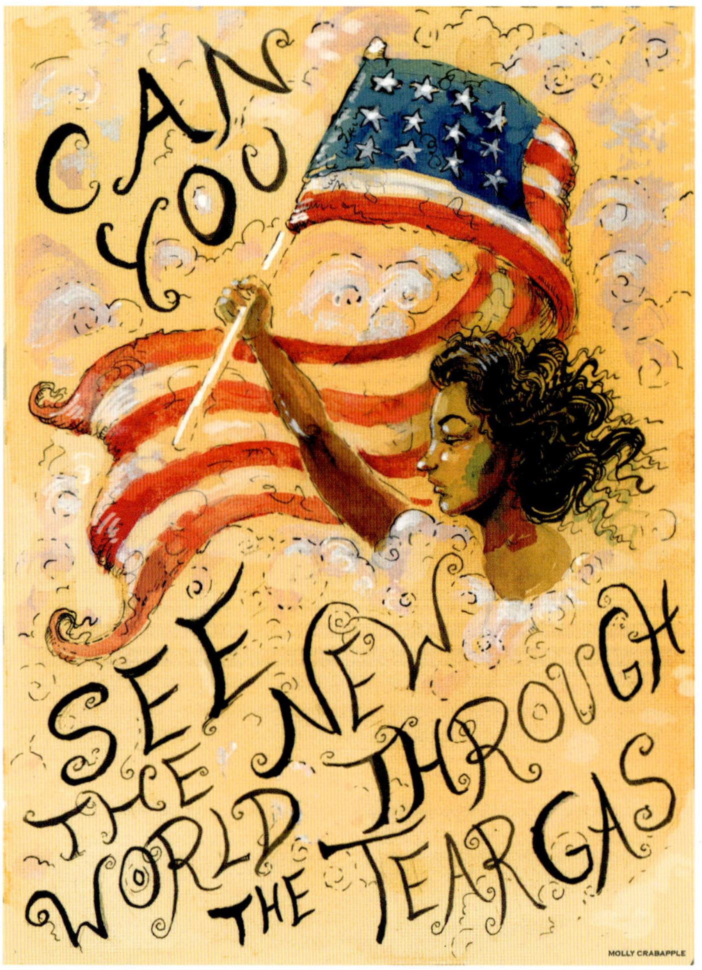

MOLLY CRABAPPLE

emerged on the internet. Now, the use of such weaponry by agents of the United States government had become commonplace, such treatment of American citizens an accepted reality. But then, much had happened in the intervening year . . .

A TALE OF TWO SQUARES

As a correspondent working for CNN, I'd reported from Tahrir Square in Egypt in March 2011. President Hosni Mubarak had resigned a month earlier, but the people of Egypt continued to gather in Cairo's now-infamous public plaza to protest daily and to voice their discontent with the economy and an increasingly militarized regime. Mubarak's fall taught the people of Egypt that ordinary individuals working together could rise up and defeat a corrupt government and its military machine. Using technology to coordinate a populist uprising like never before, they'd won their revolution, and they weren't going to stop until they were able to mold Egypt into the kind of country they deserved.

For the protesters, the daily shouting and marching were cathartic; for me, the passion was infectious. As the people of the Middle East and North Africa took their fate into their own hands and protest fever spread across the region—through Libya, Tunisia, and Bahrain—I kept wondering when the energy of the Arab Spring would spread to the United States. The people here deserved change too.

And then the occupation of Zuccotti Park began on September 17. It seemed as if a dragon that had been slumbering since the '60s was finally beginning to stir. The waking masses gathered in the spiritual home of corruption, the core of the U.S. financial system, to stare those who had ruined this country in the face, to let the bankers know they might have escaped our justice system but they couldn't escape our wrath.

Zuccotti Park was a place of chaos when I arrived in November 2011, shortly before the police raid that would obliterate the round-the-clock encampment. As one who rarely follows rules, I found the chaos welcoming and refreshing. Wall Street had suits, skyscrapers, and Mercedes. The denizens of Zuccotti Park had mismatched clothing, drums, and tents. Zuccotti Park—or Liberty Plaza, to give the quasi-public space its precorporate "non-slave" name—was one big fuck-you to conformity and corruption. And I loved it.

As a journalist who had spent the past decade reporting from the frontlines both at home and abroad, attending countless soldiers' funerals, and having witnessed too many families being kicked out of their foreclosed homes, it was with a sense of relief that I watched the American people rise up. They were standing up for their rights, for equality, and for justice, against a system that had failed them. They'd quite simply had enough.

THE WHOLE WORLD WAS WATCHING . . . BUT NOT ON CABLE TV

I'd done my first Occupy-related report for CNN in October 2011, when the story of Iraq war veteran Scott Olsen made national headlines—making it something the cable news network couldn't ignore. Olsen, who had survived two tours of duty physically unscathed, had been seriously injured by a police projectile at Occupy Oakland. A long night of protest had degenerated into a pitched battle between Occupiers and police, which had been caught on camera by the ever-present live-streamers. The moment Olsen was struck in the head—a blow that fractured his skull—had been captured from multiple angles by citizen journalists using their smart phones, and the world had been watching online via the various live streams. This event galvanized the movement. Olsen was a war hero, and the incident put the Oakland Police Department's decades-long record of brutality and corruption under the microscope—and ultimately helped place the entire police department under court control.

FINDING FREEDOM BETWEEN POLICE LINES

I was laid off from CNN along with dozens of my colleagues in April 2012 when the network dissolved its investigative journalism and documentary unit. For me, the layoffs were a blessing in disguise, since they got me out of my contract. I grabbed my camera and headed to Chicago to photograph the NATO protests in May. I was drawn to the protests. I had to go.

The NATO protests were my first as an independent journalist. I felt as if duct tape had been ripped from my mouth, as if a collar and leash had been removed from my neck. Having escaped my mainstream media bondage, I felt freer than I've ever felt in my career.

Thousands of protesters from all across America took to the streets of Chicago to voice their anger at the U.S. government and NATO for misleading the public in the run-up to the Iraq war and continuing to do so in order to justify American's occupation of the oil rich region. The main march on May 20th was led by a group of veterans, which included Olsen. The procession was scheduled to end near the McCormick Convention Center, where President Barack Obama was meeting with other world leaders. There the veterans planned to give speeches before symbolically throwing back their medals.

The massive march was heavily policed from the outset. Officers dressed in riot gear and armed with an intimidating selection of handcuffs, zip ties, batons, and both less lethal and completely lethal weaponry lined the streets and boxed protesters in at both ends. After being allowed to march from the staging area in Grant Park through the streets of the city, protesters were met by a heavy police blockade that kept them several miles away from the entrance to the summit. The intense presence of aggressively attired and overtly armed officers heightened tensions and aggravated the protesters, who simply wanted their voices to be heard by NATO's leaders.

Unable to move forward and trapped by police on all sides, the veterans gave their speeches and threw their medals at an intersection where they'd effectively been kettled. Afterward, with nowhere to go and no way to escape, those at the front nearest the lines of police became crushed by marchers still entering the area from the rear. Dispersal orders were given; however, since there was no clear dispersal route offered, panic set in. As a result, scuffles broke out between the trapped protesters and the police who were blocking their exit.

At this point, trapped myself, I got caught in a skirmish that erupted around me. I'd like to extend my deepest

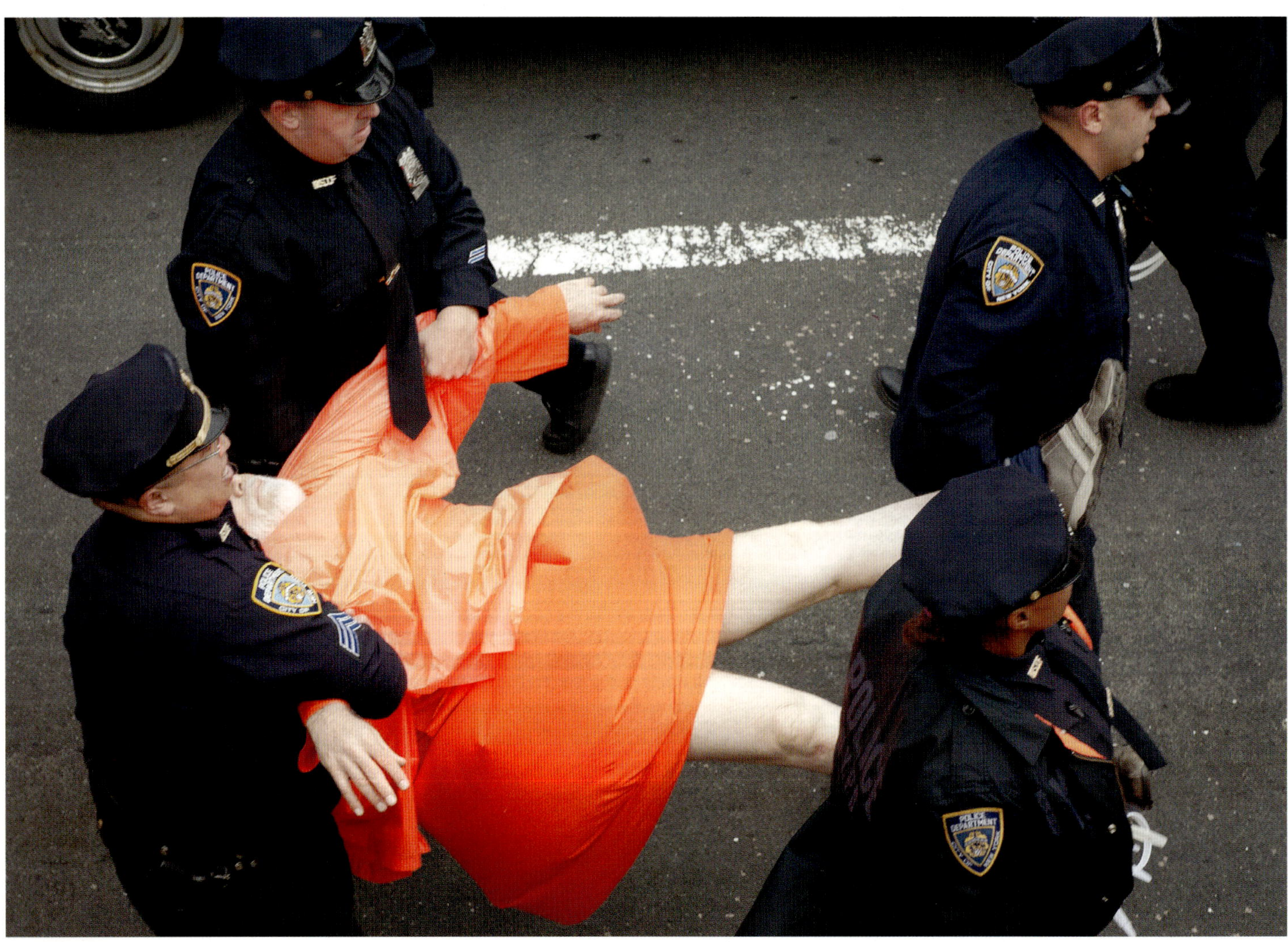

thanks to the unidentified protester who saved my camera and the memory chip within it, enabling the publication of this book.

I'd positioned myself at the front of the heaving mass so I could shoot the veterans' ceremony, which was intended to mark the culmination of the march. Shortly afterward, I somehow became sandwiched between the dense crowd of protesters and a formation of baton-wielding police. When the wall of protesters lurched towards the wall of police I was knocked to the ground, and a pile of people began to fall on top of me.

As I was falling toward the cement, I held my camera out in front of me to keep it from smashing. At that moment, a female protester grabbed it and tucked it protectively against her chest. I hit the ground with a thud and was beginning to have trouble breathing as more and more protesters landed on top of me. Through the tangle of arms and legs above me, I caught a glimpse of the woman. Each time she tried to stand up, she was knocked back down and repeatedly hit by a police officer who kept slamming his baton into her body. Instead of using her arms to break her fall or shield herself from the blows, she selflessly held tightly onto my camera, holding it close to her chest.

When I was eventually able to pull myself out from underneath the mass of toppled bodies, I reached out to the woman and helped her up. Her shirt was torn, her bra exposed, and she had multiple cuts on her arms, which were bleeding profusely. She handed me back my camera, which she'd managed to preserve without a scratch on it. I couldn't believe this stranger had sacrificed her bodily safety to help me.

"I don't know how to thank you. I am shocked," I said.

"No, thank you," she replied. "We need you to document this."

We hugged and parted ways. I never saw her again.

COMING FULL CIRCLE: ECHOES OF TAHRIR IN AFGHANAHEIM

Despite my brush with the long baton of the law in Chicago, the harsh reality of the rapidly increasing state of police militarization in this country didn't really hit home until I was photographing the spontaneous anti-police-brutality uprisings in Anaheim, California. During the course of my career I'd visited numerous war zones around the world, but I'd never been directly shot at until I covered these protests just a few miles from my Los Angeles home.

Residents there were outraged after Anaheim Police officers shot and killed Manuel Diaz, an unarmed 25-year-old man, in broad daylight. Diaz's crime? Running away when police approached him. Just one day after the Diaz killing, police gunned down 21-year-old Joel Mathew Acevedo, who was also unarmed. The shootings further increased the disconnect between the majority-Hispanic community and the majority-white police force.

When a group of protesters refused to disperse from outside Anaheim's City Hall, a bottle was thrown from the crowd toward police. The police response to this was incredible: they began shooting rubber bullets, foam projectiles, and pepper balls indiscriminately into the crowd, which included women and children. A female casualty of this shocking assault limped down the street as blood flowed from two beanbag wounds on the back of her leg. Blood covered the head of a dazed male pedestrian who told me he'd been struck by a police projectile while walking home from work.

At one point I recall standing on a busy main road shooting photos of a dumpster that was on fire when a wall of police began to shoot beanbag rounds at me. At first I froze in shock, but then quickly ran and hid between two nearby U-Haul trucks to avoid being struck. These police projectiles are called "less lethal" rather than "nonlethal" for a reason: if you get hit in the wrong place with one, they can still be deadly. I'd witnessed and reported on cases of people dying after rubber and beanbag bullets had been deployed, so I was fully aware of their deadly potential.

After two minutes crouched behind the trucks, and fearing an ankle strike, I emerged with my hands in the air yelling "Press!" As the wall of officers with guns continued marching toward me, one officer said, "Don't you know how to cover a riot? You need to stand back there," pointing to a group of journalists corralled behind a police line.

When you're behind the police line it's nearly impossible to document injuries. I believe I was deliberately shot at by these officers in an effort to intimidate me and stop me reporting from within the crowd. Judging by the carnage I saw, I could understand why they didn't want me witnessing and photographing the injuries they'd caused.

As a journalist, my supreme duty is to serve as a watchdog on authority and document the response of those in power to those exercising their First Amendment rights. I refuse to allow the police to treat me and other journalists as propaganda puppets. Despite the risks, I continue to report from

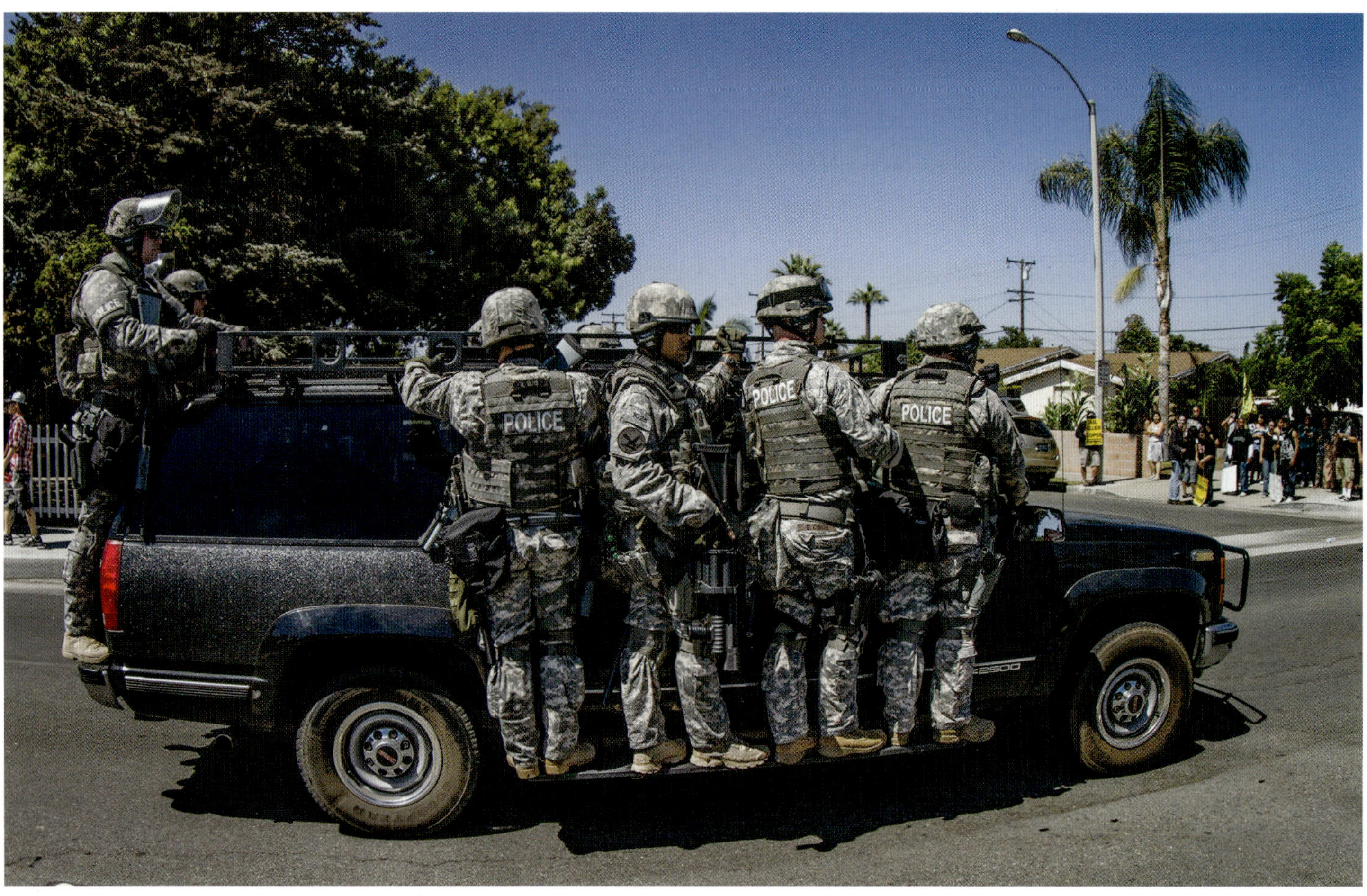

within crowds of protesters and will not let the authorities dictate what I am able to shoot by forcing me to stand behind their arbitrary lines.

With the Anaheim community still up in arms, days later I returned to the area to cover another anti-police-brutality march. This one was headed toward Disneyland, which is often referred to by locals as the Tragic Kingdom due to the tarnished American Dream it now represents. During this protest, I witnessed police on horseback with wooden swords in their hands attempting to corral protesters onto the sidewalk.

I was balancing my need to get decent shots with my desire not to get trampled on by the police horses when something caught my eye that forced me to stop in my tracks. The sight had a similar effect on almost everyone around me. Coming down the street towards us were numerous open-backed trucks, each carrying a dozen or so camo-clad soldiers. I felt as if I had returned to the streets of Egypt. How could this be happening in the United States? As the trucks neared, I realized it was police officers dressed in military attire, and not soldiers. That knowledge gave me little comfort since it was indicative of a terrifying escalation of police department modus operandi.

When the images I'd shot of the camo-clad cops went viral across the net, Anaheim earned the nickname "Afghanaheim." As a result, I was expecting public uproar. Instead, because of mainstream media censorship of the events—a phenomenon I had witnessed firsthand while working at CNN—there was none. The absence of an appropriate level of outrage in the aftermath of Afghanaheim made it clear to me that the militarization of the police had become an accepted norm in the United States.

Thanks to the collusion of police PR departments and corporate media outlets, who both had a vested interest in the elimination of dissent, Occupiers and protesters in general had been portrayed as untrustworthy transients at best and terrorists at worst. Successfully demonized by the mainstream media, the unquestioning masses were told they needed protecting from the very people who were fighting to protect their rights. As a consequence, the public was sold a package of intimidation tactics that are now being regularly used against protesters and journalists who dare to seek out the truth.

AN ENDING AND A NEW BEGINNING

As the summer neared its end, we headed into election season. In years past there'd been big demonstrations at both the Democratic and Republican national conventions. However, reporting from the DNC in Charlotte, North Carolina, at the beginning of September, I found that protesters of any sort were by and large conspicuous by their absence.

Being a movement born of a generation that felt completely disenfranchised and betrayed by the American political system, Occupy had opted out of party politics. As the debates raged on TV and in the media, Occupy therefore struggled to find relevance as the November 2012 presidential election approached. But that wasn't the only factor that caused it to lose steam.

Occupy's encampments across the nation had been raided, and its permanent canvas homes were gone. The movement was also mired by incessant infighting, though it was impossible to tell how much of this truly came from within. Extensive surveillance and infiltration of Occupy have been well documented, and there have been several cases of protesters being entrapped (in Cleveland, Portland, and Chicago, among other cities). Law enforcement agencies and the government got the high-profile prosecutions and the resulting headlines they needed to successfully demonize the movement in order to protect and preserve the status quo. But alongside the losses also came numerous wins.

Though I felt the forces of infiltration at work even at my local Occupation in downtown Los Angeles, which at times seemed to get steered inexplicably in the wrong direction, a four-month-long satellite encampment outside a foreclosed home in Van Nuys, dubbed "Fort Hernandez," could definitely be chalked up as a success. It not only brought massive mainstream media attention to the problems surrounding subprime mortgages, but also shone the spotlight on the impossible-to-navigate federal loan modification program, which had failed to provide the intended relief.

Another offshoot of the Occupy movement, Strike Debt, also successfully raised awareness for the problems arising from loans. The organization managed to win high praise from respected publications such as *Forbes* and has provided both symbolic and tangible relief with its Rolling Jubilee. The so-called People's Bailout, the Rolling Jubilee program has so far raised hundreds of thousands of dollars, which has enabled Strike Debt to buy millions of dollars' worth of medical debt for a fraction of its face value, with the sole purpose of forgiving it.

Meanwhile, Occupy the SEC, another affinity group born out of Occupy Wall Street, has earned similar respect from the financial press for its articulate 325-page critique of the banking and securities industry. The group is also doing something our government has failed to: holding those directly responsible for the financial collapse to account. On February 27, 2013, Occupy the SEC filed a lawsuit in a New York district court against the individuals and government agencies that failed in their duty to protect the interests of the American people.

JUSTICE COMES TO THOSE WHO WAIT

And there's been more progress made within the legal system, seemingly against all the odds. Occupy Wall Street (OWS) protesters have walked free from New York courts on at least two separate occasions after photographic evidence, which was brought to light with the help of citizen journalists and a cameraman from alternative media outlet *Democracy Now!*, directly contradicted police testimony. Alexander Arbuckle was acquitted on charges of disorderly conduct in May 2012, and Michael Premo was found not guilty of felony assault charges in the first OWS-related case to come before a New York jury on February 28, 2013.

It was also noteworthy that charges against five Occupy Boston protesters were unexpectedly dropped on February 8, 2013, just three days before their trial was scheduled to start. Frustrated that they were denied their day in court, the Massachusetts chapter of the National Lawyers Guild, which was representing the defendants, subsequently issued a statement saying that they believed that the Suffolk County district attorney's decision amounted to "an acknowledgment of the unconstitutionality of the arrests and criminal charges that had been brought against hundreds of Occupy Boston participants." Unfortunately, the majority of these protesters had already been pressured into taking pleas.

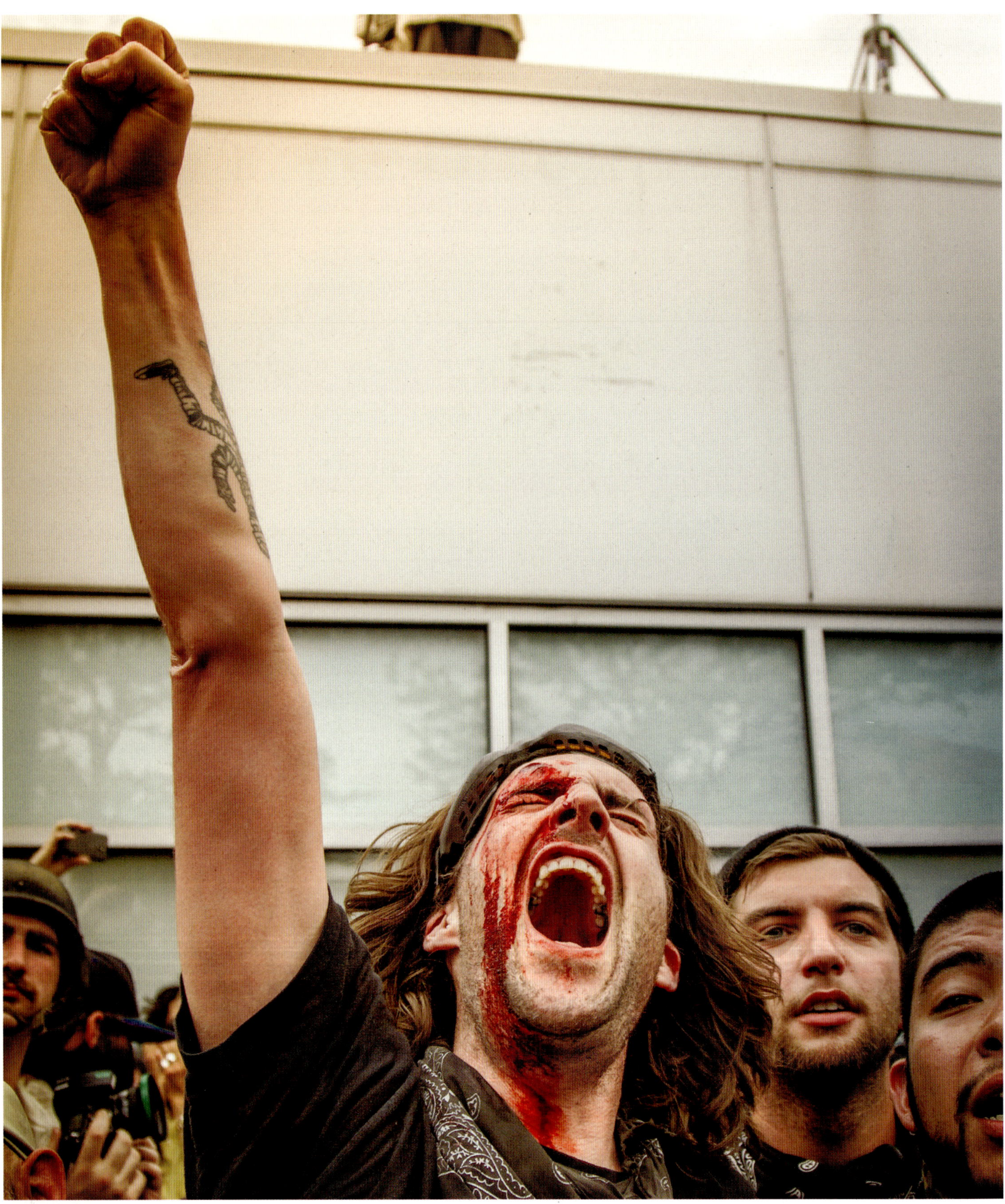

Indeed, across the nation, those who were brave enough to roll the dice and insist on their day in court have frequently been rewarded by the justice system, much to the chagrin of overzealous prosecutors. It's become increasingly apparent that juries are unwilling to punish protesters for standing up to the man. In March 2012, five protesters in Seattle were found not guilty of trespassing, even though they had undeniably occupied a Chase Bank. Similarly, in March 2013 a dozen Occupy Philadelphia protesters—including Dustin Slaughter, a contributor to this book—were found not guilty in a Court of Common Pleas after a jury decided their sit-in at a Wells Fargo bank served the greater good. After presiding over the case, Judge Nina N. Wright Padilla even asked the defendants to approach the bench so she could personally shake each of their hands. She also went on record as saying they were the "most affable group of defendants" she's ever come across. This character assessment is clearly at odds with how many in our government would like to portray those who dare to challenge the system.

THE KNOCK-ON EFFECT

Beyond the wins in court—and the shifting opinions of those in the jury pool—this wave of next-generation protest has changed the national dialogue and emboldened those engaged in more traditional struggles. For example, in February 2013, for the first time ever executives of the Sierra Club, America's oldest grassroots environmental organization, engaged in an act of civil disobedience. The Sierra Club's president, Allison Chin, and executive director, Michael Brune, were among 48 people arrested after they chained themselves to the White House gates to protest the construction of the Keystone XK pipeline. (The construction project is a highly contentious endeavor that will save the oil companies an estimated $2 billion per year by bringing cheap Canadian Tar Sands oil to Texas refineries—at great environmental cost.)

This act of civil disobedience was significant not only because it went against the historically staid organization's policies, which dictate that all affiliated protests should remain within the confines of the law, but also because it sent a wider message. In crossing the legal line, the organization's leadership was acknowledging that our flawed democracy no longer bends to the will of the people but to the will of corporations that have purchased control. With the land of the free having been bought, Chin and Brune appear to have reconciled their consciences with the fact that it's not always possible to work solely within the system to effect radical change, even if it's clearly in the interest of the majority of the people. In this post–Citizens United society, which puts a greater emphasis on the personhood of corporations than that of actual living, breathing people, this rationale for radicalization will probably have increasing impact.

Whether you care about economic and social justice, or equality when it comes to topless sunbathing, the beauty of protest is that anyone can do it—all it takes is passion and a little coordination. Although the Occupy movement has dissipated, it gave us new organizing tools, served as the antidote to apathy that America desperately needed, and engaged the passions of a significant swathe of the population like never before. It gave Walmart's warehouse workers the courage to go on strike for the first time in the company's history and inspired many progressive unions to try to harness the tactics and energy that the movement unleashed. Though the idea that anything that was "of" Occupy could be co-opted was anathema to many occupiers, the adoption of the movement's central ideas by the mainstream may ultimately be its greatest lasting legacy. One thing's for sure: protest in America will never been the same. I only hope that the threat of pepper spray will never prevail over the voice of the American people.

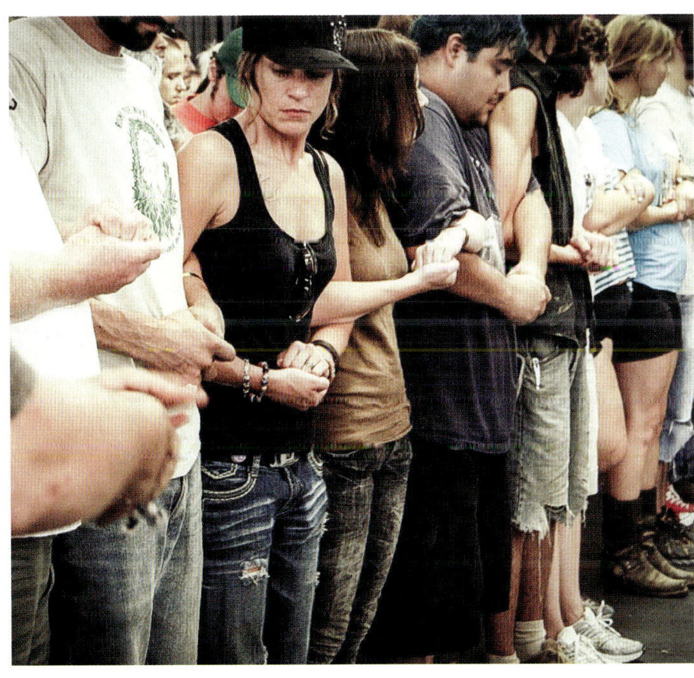

America Rises Up

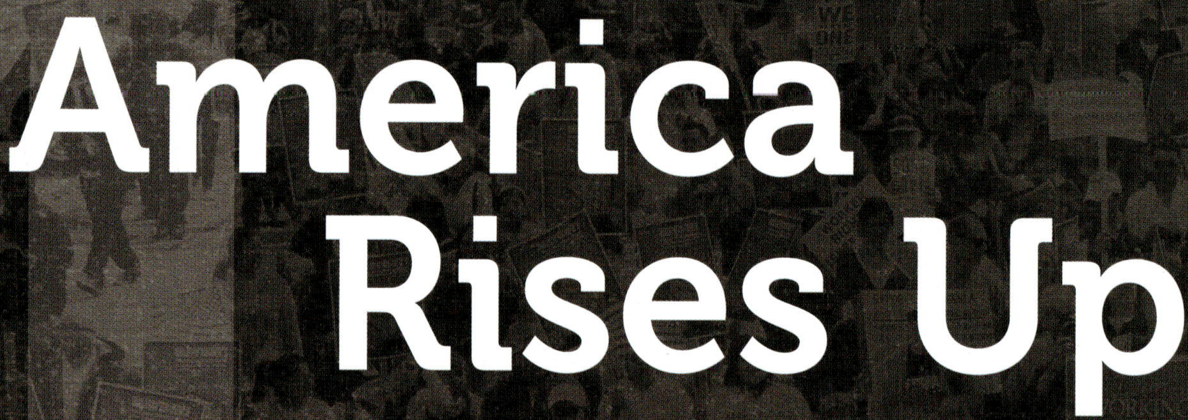

Freedom of speech is one of the rights that Americans cherish. U.S. citizens and residents from all sides of the political spectrum united to seize the opportunity to stand up for the First Amendment, taking action to promote the causes they believe in and call for change where they feel injustice is being done. Illustrated here are some vivid examples of Americans rising up to make their voices heard—and make a difference.

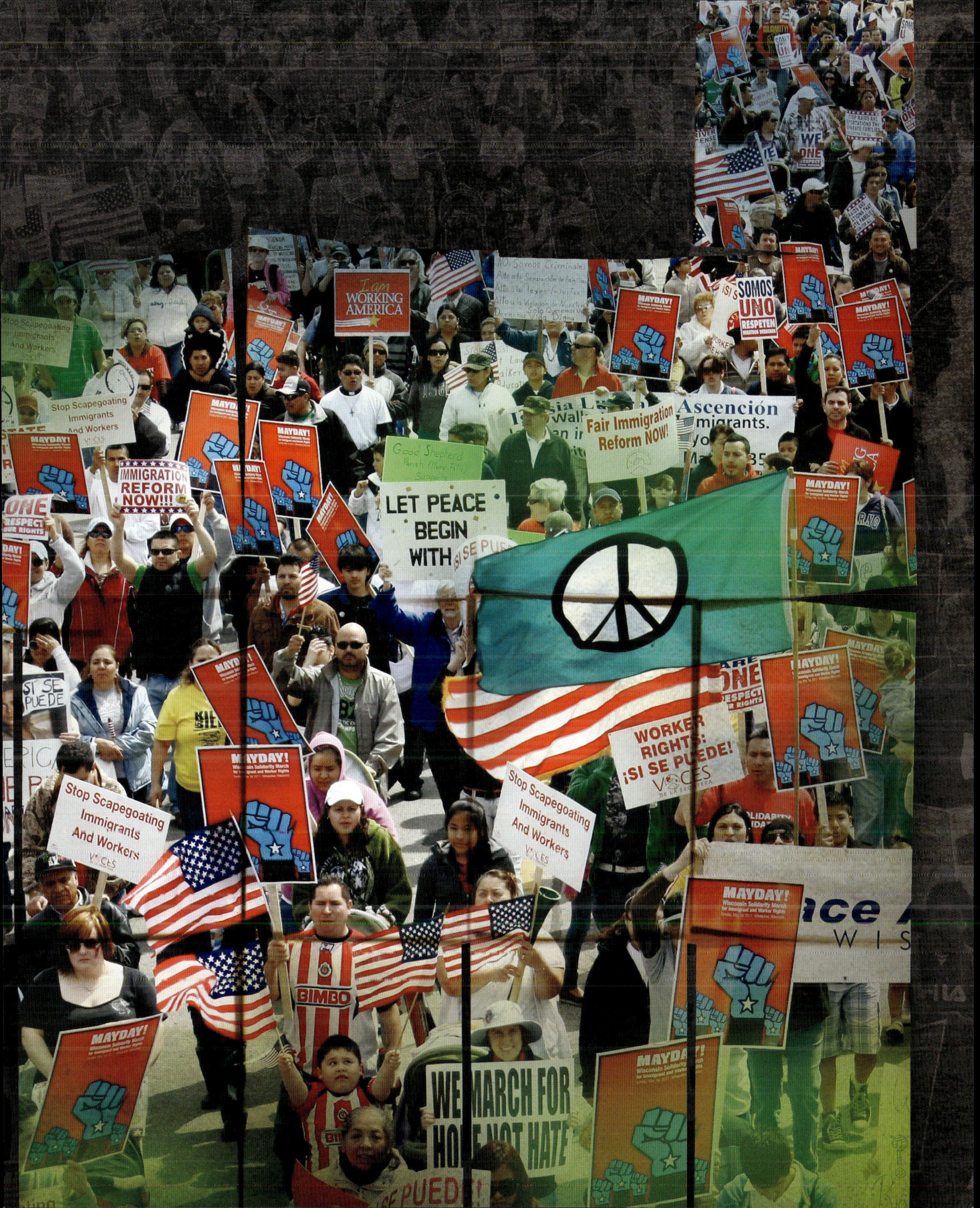

I am WORKING AMERICA
MAYDAY!
Stop Scapegoating Immigrants And Workers
IMMIGRATION REFORM NOW!!!
LET PEACE BEGIN WITH
Fair Immigration Reform NOW!
Ascención
SOMOS UNO RESPETEN
WORKER RIGHTS: ¡SI SE PUEDE!
VOCES
BIMBO
WE MARCH FOR

Ride for Justice

On July 4, 2012, a group of two dozen or so undocumented mothers, fathers, students, and DREAM Act supporters from Arizona, Texas, Colorado, and New Mexico boarded a bus in Phoenix—dubbed the "UndocuBus"—to highlight the plight of those living in the United States without visas or citizenship statues. The UndocuBus's destination was North Carolina, where the passengers hoped to make the silent minority's voice heard at the Democratic National Convention held in Charlotte on September 4 through 6. The group lived up to their slogan "No Papers, No Fear" when 10 of their members were arrested for blocking traffic near the entrance to the DNC. Fortunately for those involved, immigration officials decided not to detain the group. They hoped their act of civil disobedience would bring attention to anti-immigrant legislation and put pressure on President Barack Obama to support the DREAM Act (Development, Relief, and Education for Alien Minors), which provides a path to legal residency for individuals who entered the country as minors. Around 400,000 immigrants are deported each year, which amounts to well over 1 million since Obama took office. In the words of the No Papers, No Fear website, "We can't wait for anyone else any longer. We've come too far to allow this country to be turned back."

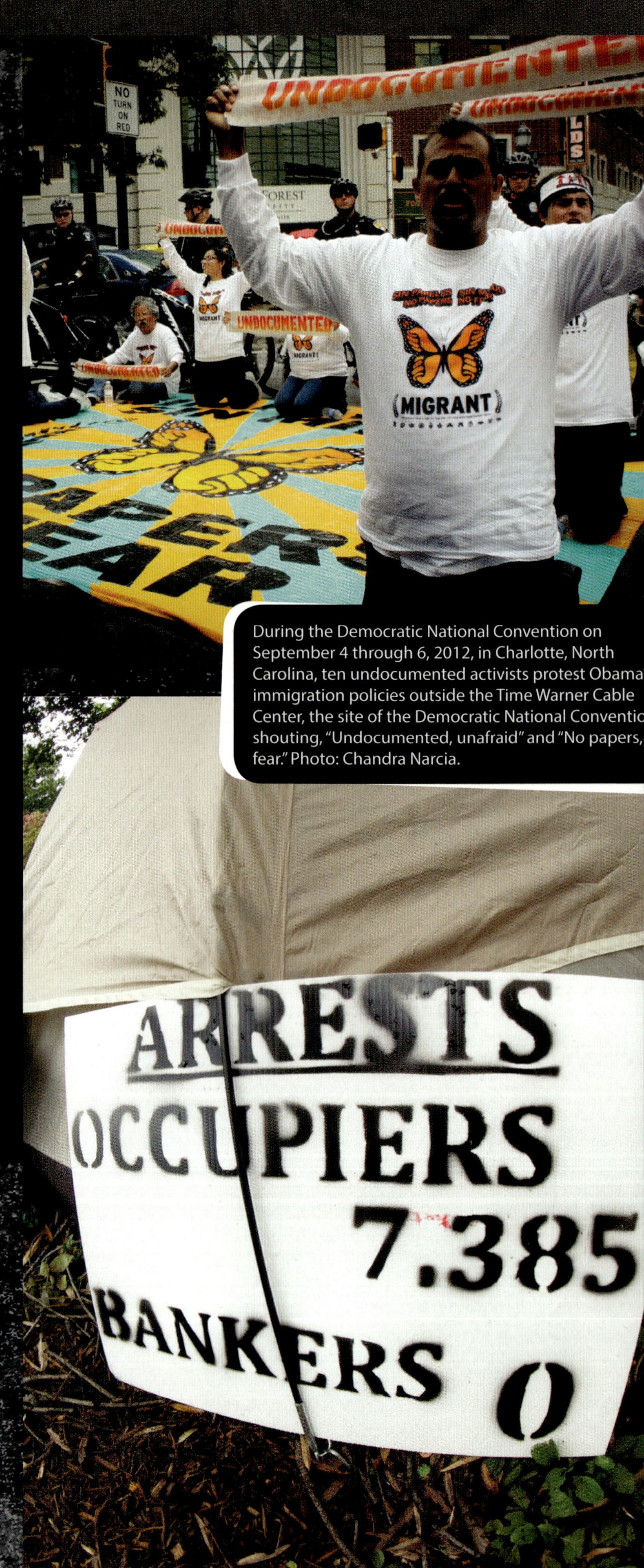

During the Democratic National Convention on September 4 through 6, 2012, in Charlotte, North Carolina, ten undocumented activists protest Obama immigration policies outside the Time Warner Cable Center, the site of the Democratic National Conventic shouting, "Undocumented, unafraid" and "No papers, fear." Photo: Chandra Narcia.

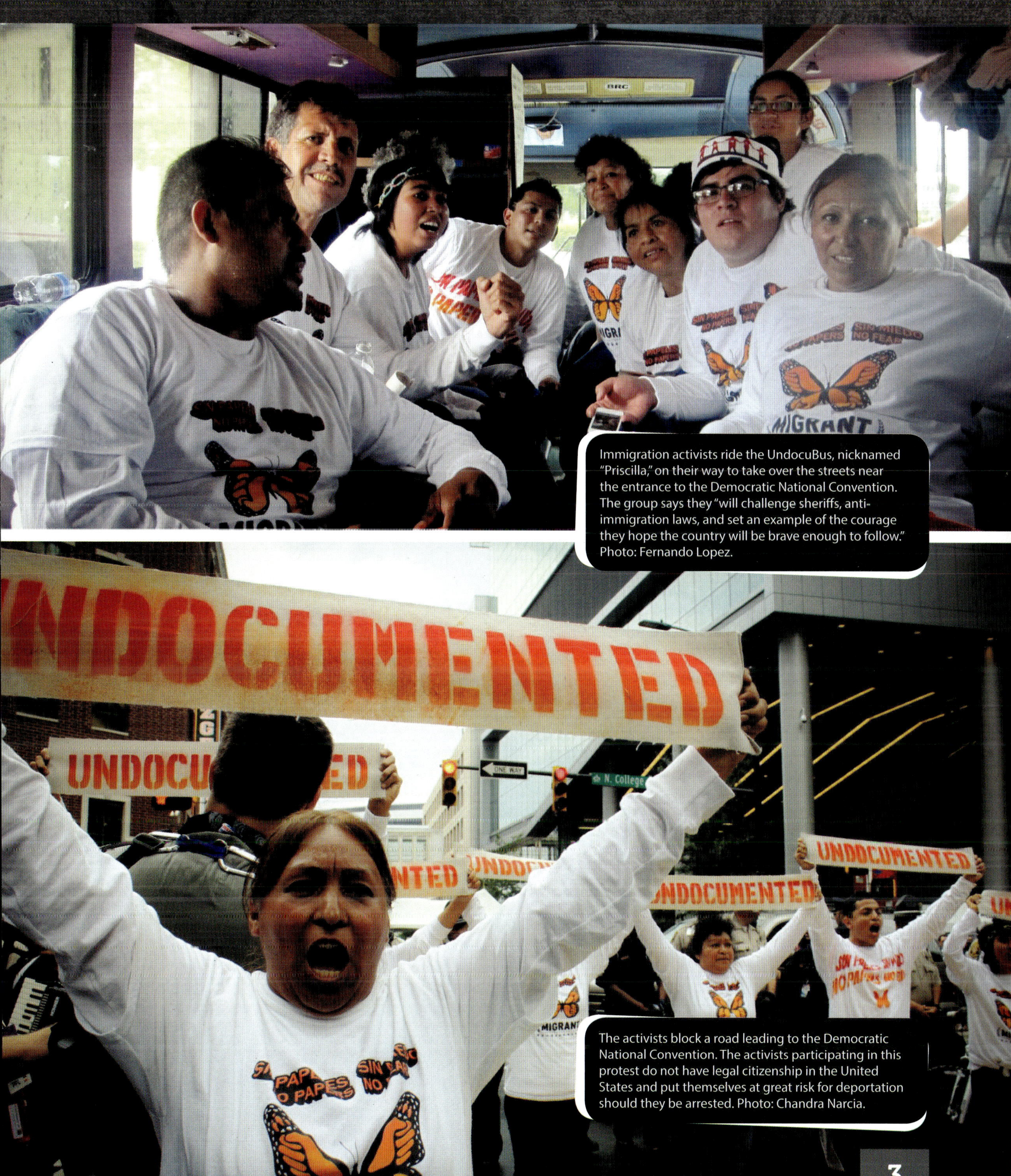

Immigration activists ride the UndocuBus, nicknamed "Priscilla," on their way to take over the streets near the entrance to the Democratic National Convention. The group says they "will challenge sheriffs, anti-immigration laws, and set an example of the courage they hope the country will be brave enough to follow." Photo: Fernando Lopez.

The activists block a road leading to the Democratic National Convention. The activists participating in this protest do not have legal citizenship in the United States and put themselves at great risk for deportation should they be arrested. Photo: Chandra Narcia.

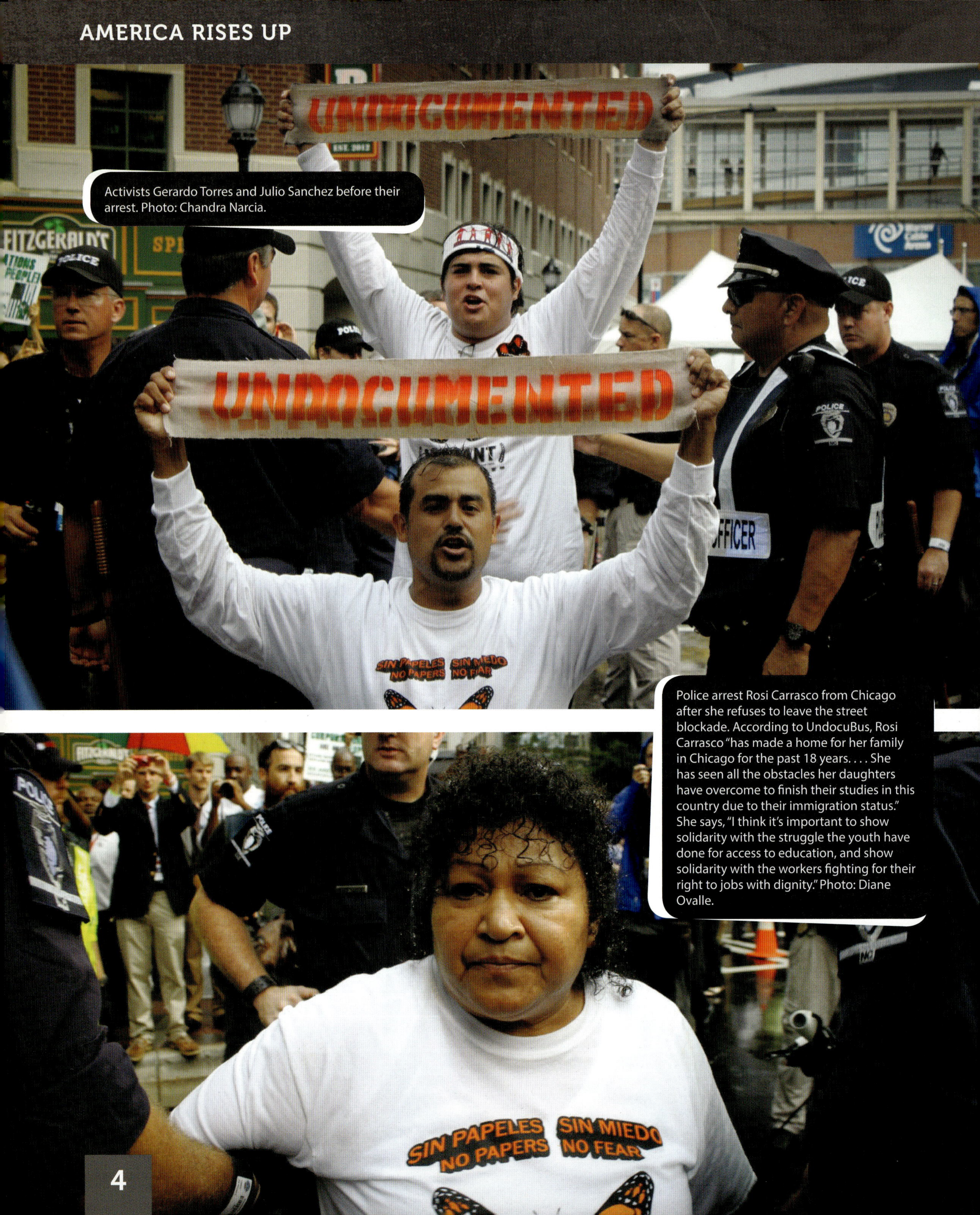

Activists Gerardo Torres and Julio Sanchez before their arrest. Photo: Chandra Narcia.

Police arrest Rosi Carrasco from Chicago after she refuses to leave the street blockade. According to UndocuBus, Rosi Carrasco "has made a home for her family in Chicago for the past 18 years. . . . She has seen all the obstacles her daughters have overcome to finish their studies in this country due to their immigration status." She says, "I think it's important to show solidarity with the struggle the youth have done for access to education, and show solidarity with the workers fighting for their right to jobs with dignity." Photo: Diane Ovalle.

Police prepare to load activist Eleazer Castellanos into the paddy wagon. Castellanos moved from Nogales, Sonora, to Tucson, Arizona, in 1996. A former computer programmer, he now works as a day laborer. He says, "I am going on the bus to come out of the shadows, to make the president hear our community's voice, and so that we can move forward and make all of our lives better. We all deserve jobs with justice and dignity." Photo: Diane Ovalle.

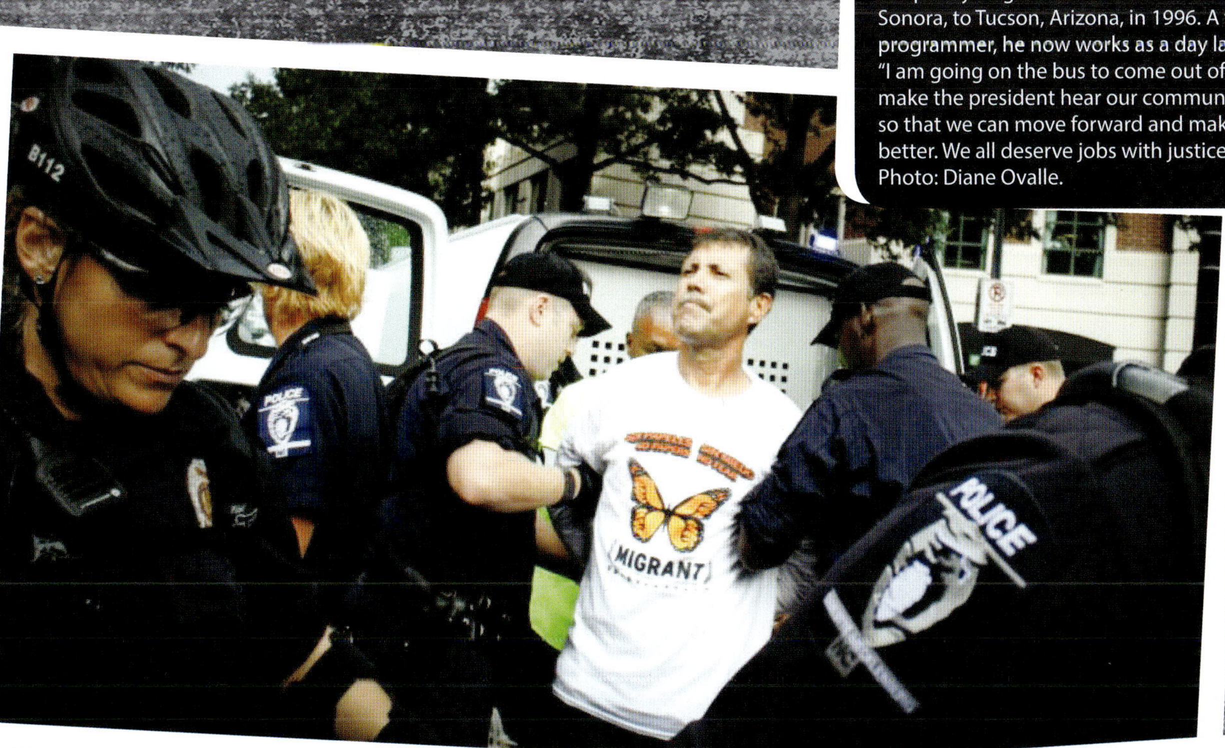

Police carry away Martin Unzueta, an immigrant from Chicago, who left Mexico seeking better educational opportunities for his children. The executive director of a nonprofit organization devoted to workers' rights, he is on the bus because "I want other communities to hear our stories of how we have helped to organize and support workers in Chicago, and the necessity for each community to protect the rights we have at work. We need to learn to use the tools we do have to defend these rights." Photo: Diane Ovalle.

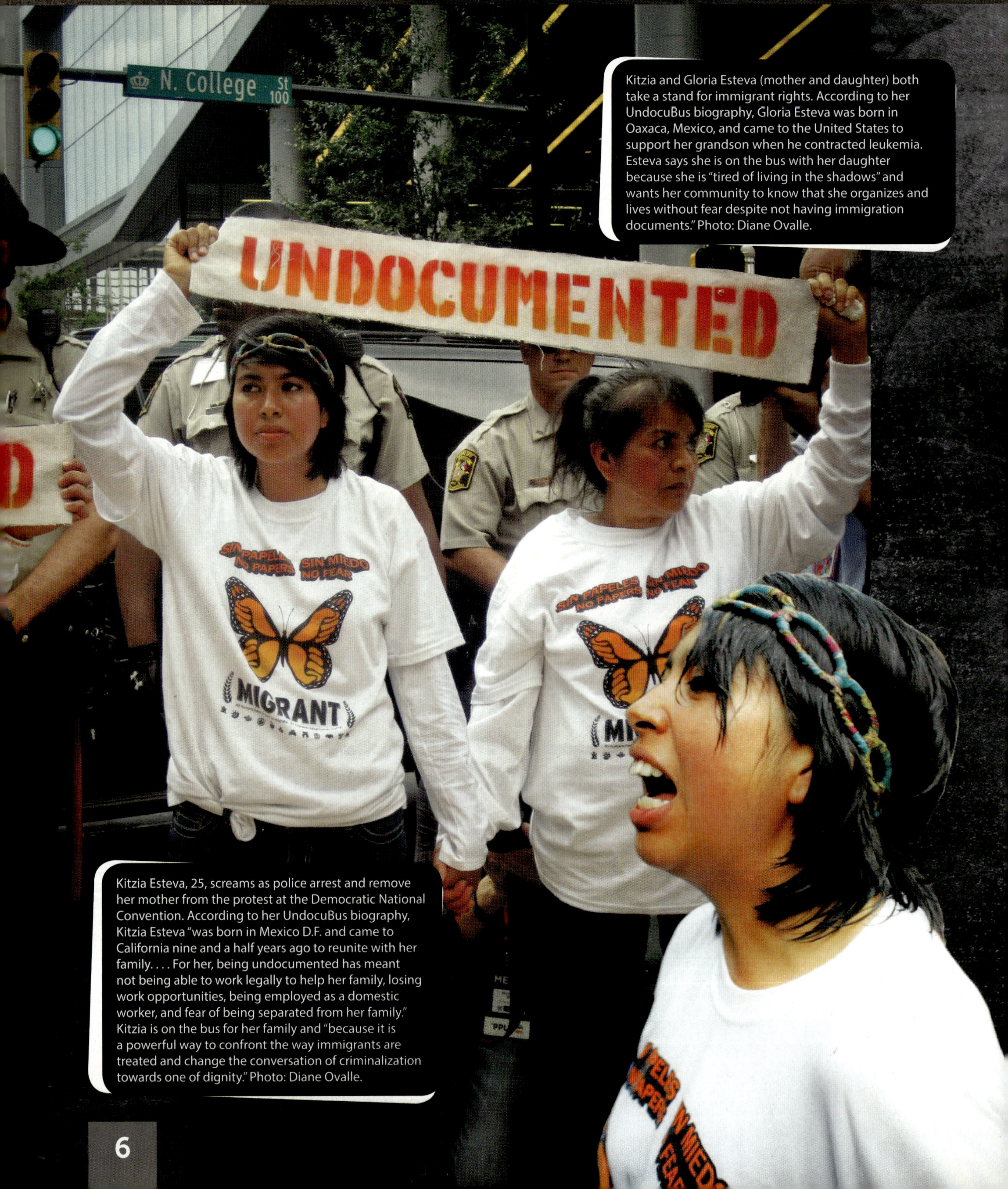

Kitzia and Gloria Esteva (mother and daughter) both take a stand for immigrant rights. According to her UndocuBus biography, Gloria Esteva was born in Oaxaca, Mexico, and came to the United States to support her grandson when he contracted leukemia. Esteva says she is on the bus with her daughter because she is "tired of living in the shadows" and wants her community to know that she organizes and lives without fear despite not having immigration documents." Photo: Diane Ovalle.

Kitzia Esteva, 25, screams as police arrest and remove her mother from the protest at the Democratic National Convention. According to her UndocuBus biography, Kitzia Esteva "was born in Mexico D.F. and came to California nine and a half years ago to reunite with her family. . . . For her, being undocumented has meant not being able to work legally to help her family, losing work opportunities, being employed as a domestic worker, and fear of being separated from her family." Kitzia is on the bus for her family and "because it is a powerful way to confront the way immigrants are treated and change the conversation of criminalization towards one of dignity." Photo: Diane Ovalle.

Democratic National Convention

The Democratic National Convention protests united the Occupy, immigration, pro-choice, pro-life, anti–gay rights, pro–gay rights, and environmental protesters under the common belief that the U.S. government, whether Democrat or Republican, is failing everyday Americans. The protesters are united in the belief that the two-party system is a distraction and that corporations, banks, and the military industrial complex are running the country and will continue to do so regardless of which party gets elected.

Two gay men kiss in front of a group of conservative anti-abortion protesters.

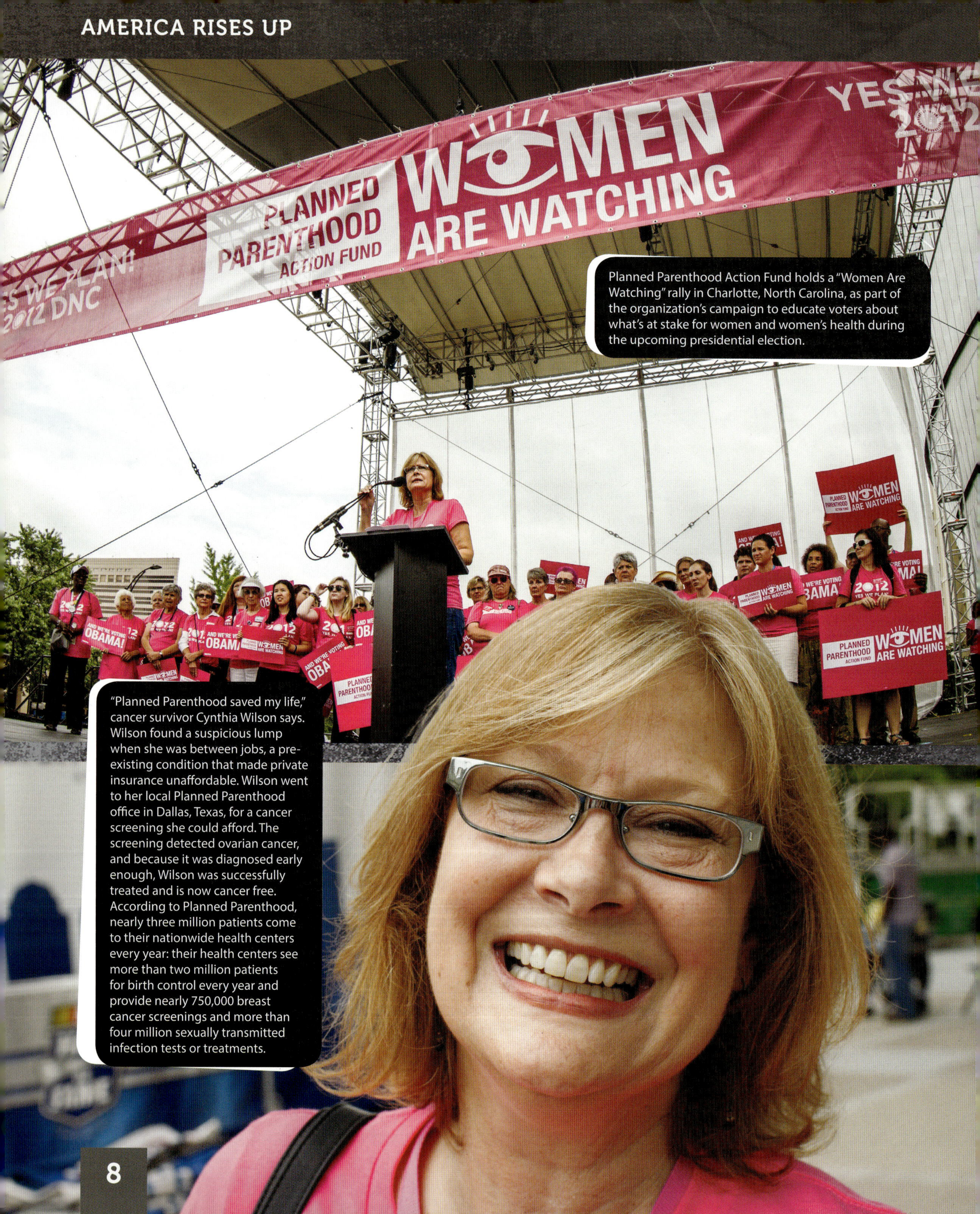

Planned Parenthood Action Fund holds a "Women Are Watching" rally in Charlotte, North Carolina, as part of the organization's campaign to educate voters about what's at stake for women and women's health during the upcoming presidential election.

"Planned Parenthood saved my life," cancer survivor Cynthia Wilson says. Wilson found a suspicious lump when she was between jobs, a pre-existing condition that made private insurance unaffordable. Wilson went to her local Planned Parenthood office in Dallas, Texas, for a cancer screening she could afford. The screening detected ovarian cancer, and because it was diagnosed early enough, Wilson was successfully treated and is now cancer free. According to Planned Parenthood, nearly three million patients come to their nationwide health centers every year: their health centers see more than two million patients for birth control every year and provide nearly 750,000 breast cancer screenings and more than four million sexually transmitted infection tests or treatments.

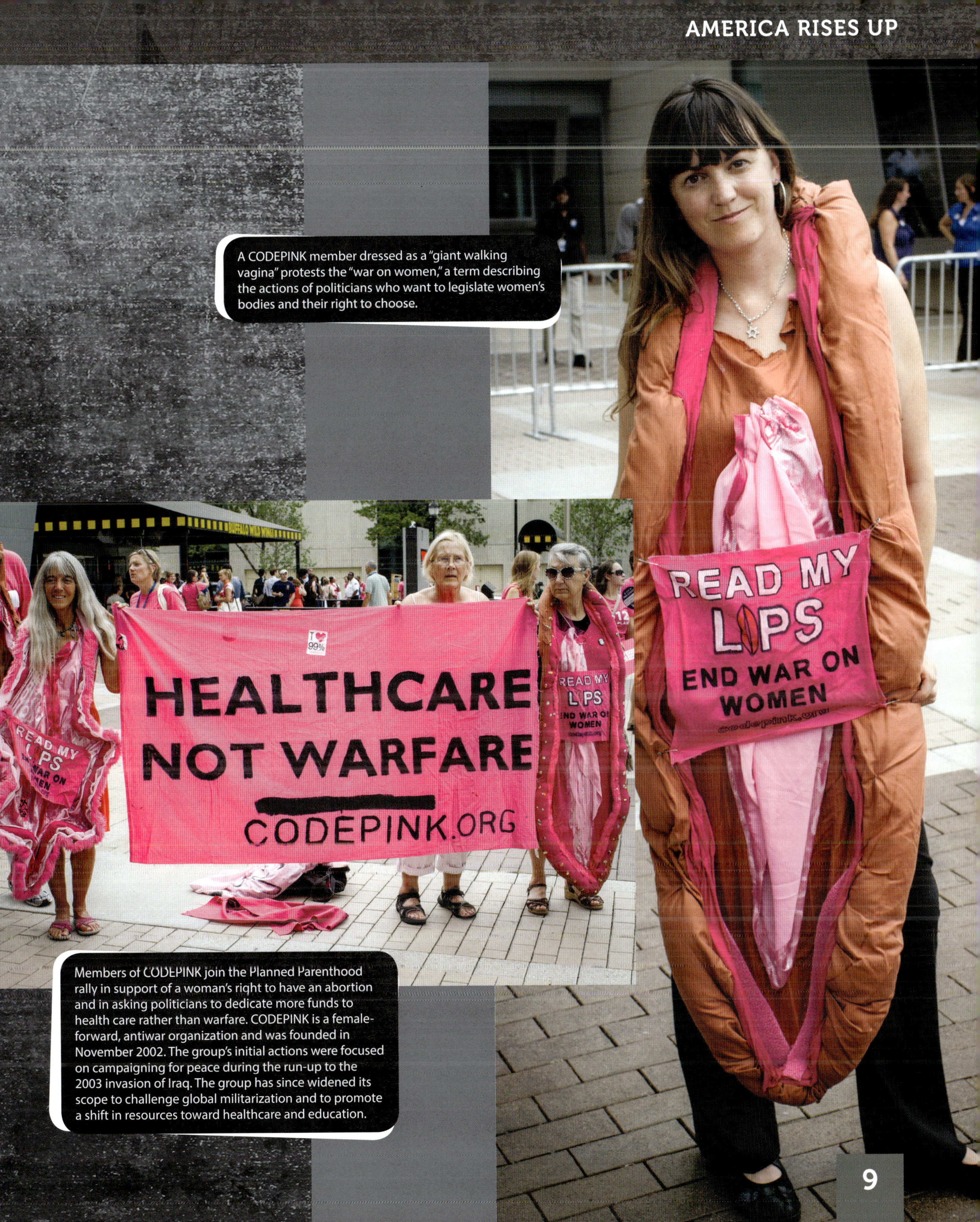

A CODEPINK member dressed as a "giant walking vagina" protests the "war on women," a term describing the actions of politicians who want to legislate women's bodies and their right to choose.

Members of CODEPINK join the Planned Parenthood rally in support of a woman's right to have an abortion and in asking politicians to dedicate more funds to health care rather than warfare. CODEPINK is a female-forward, antiwar organization and was founded in November 2002. The group's initial actions were focused on campaigning for peace during the run-up to the 2003 invasion of Iraq. The group has since widened its scope to challenge global militarization and to promote a shift in resources toward healthcare and education.

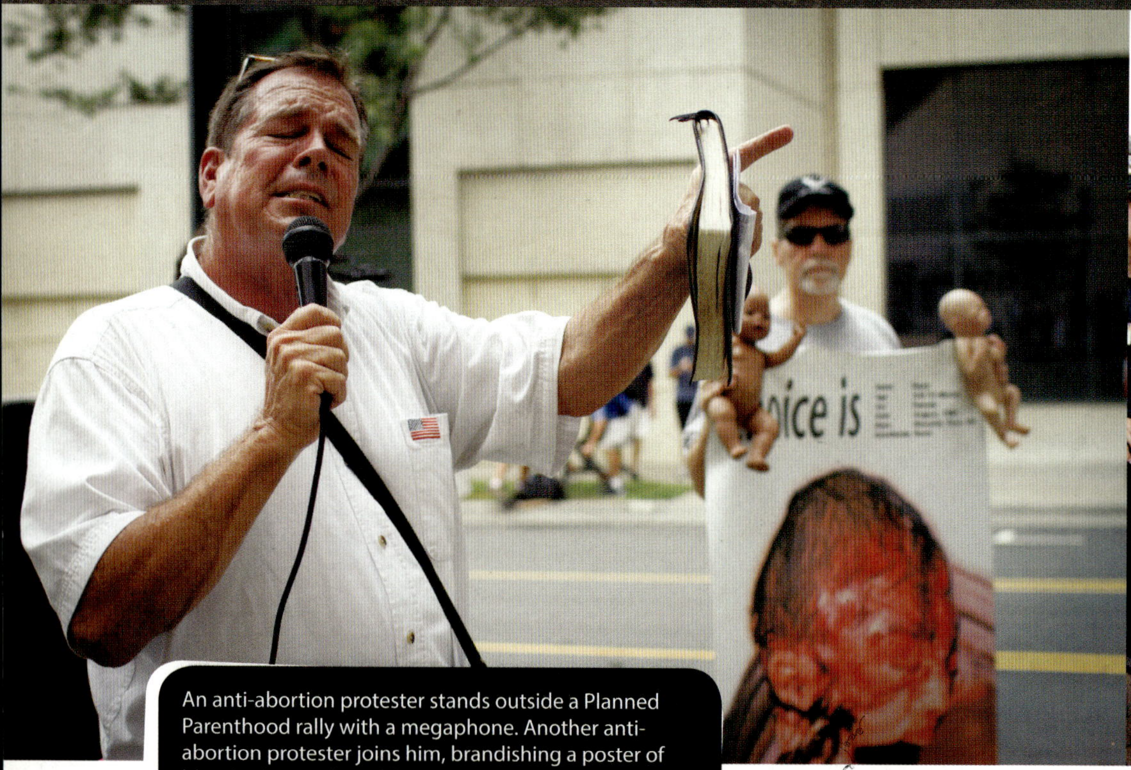

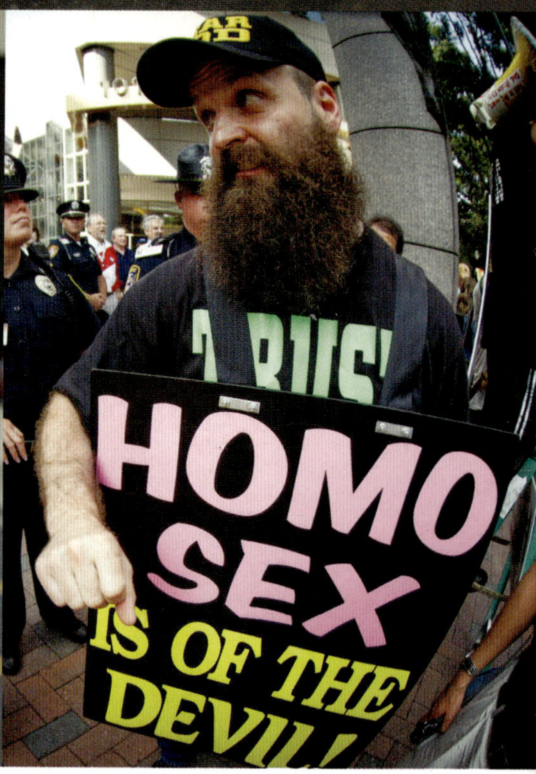

An anti-abortion protester stands outside a Planned Parenthood rally with a megaphone. Another anti-abortion protester joins him, brandishing a poster of bloody, dismembered fetuses.

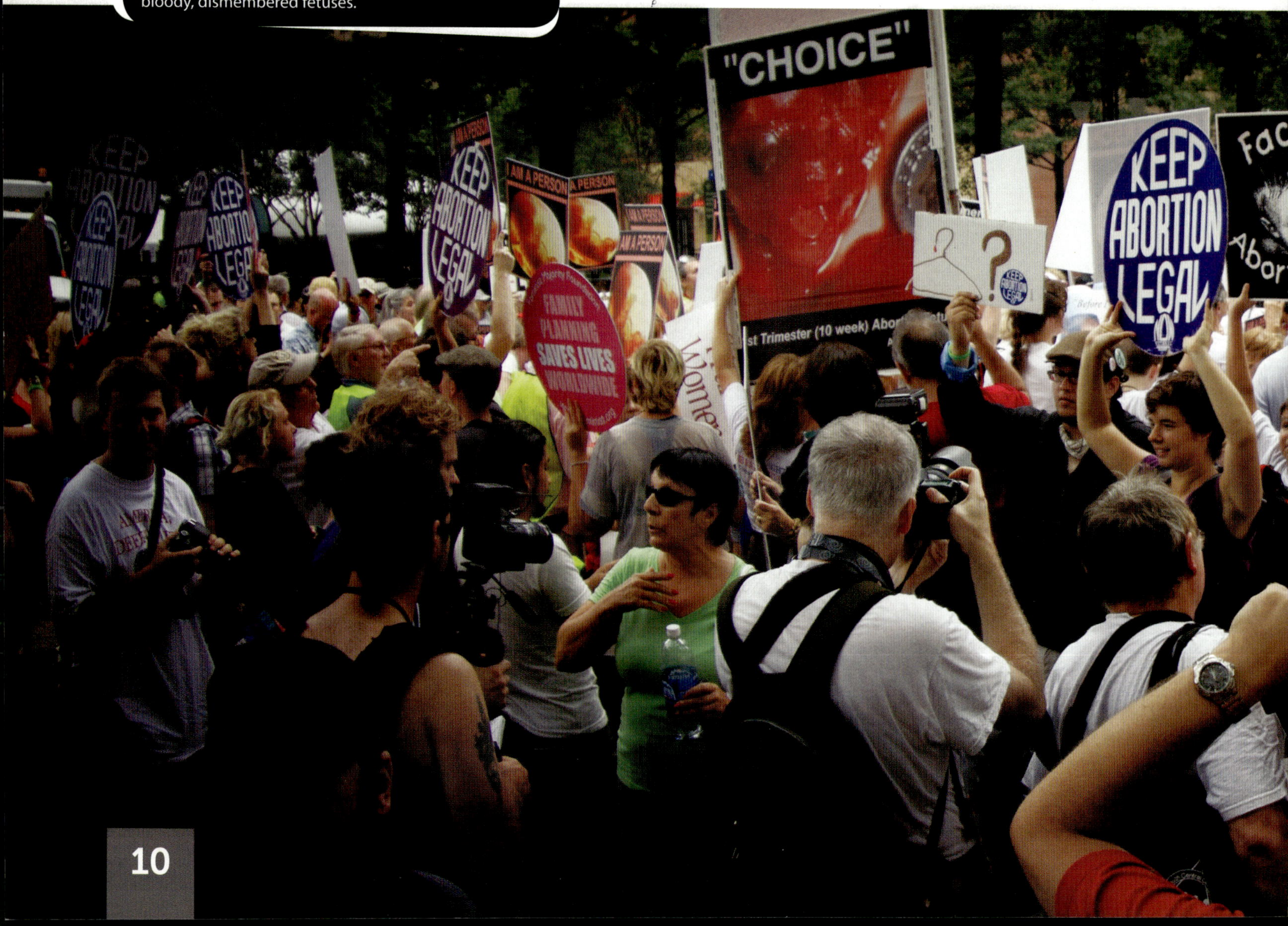

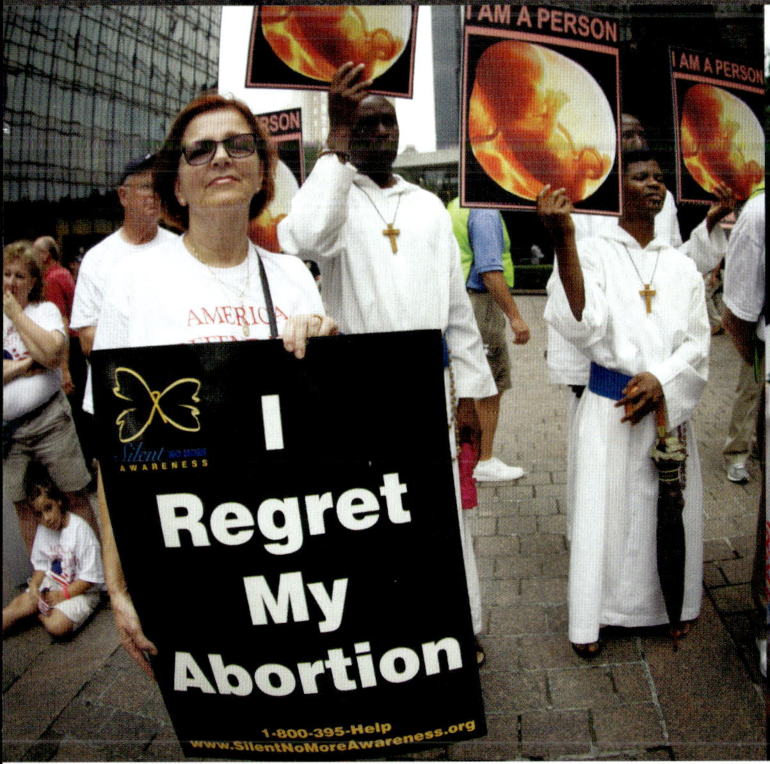

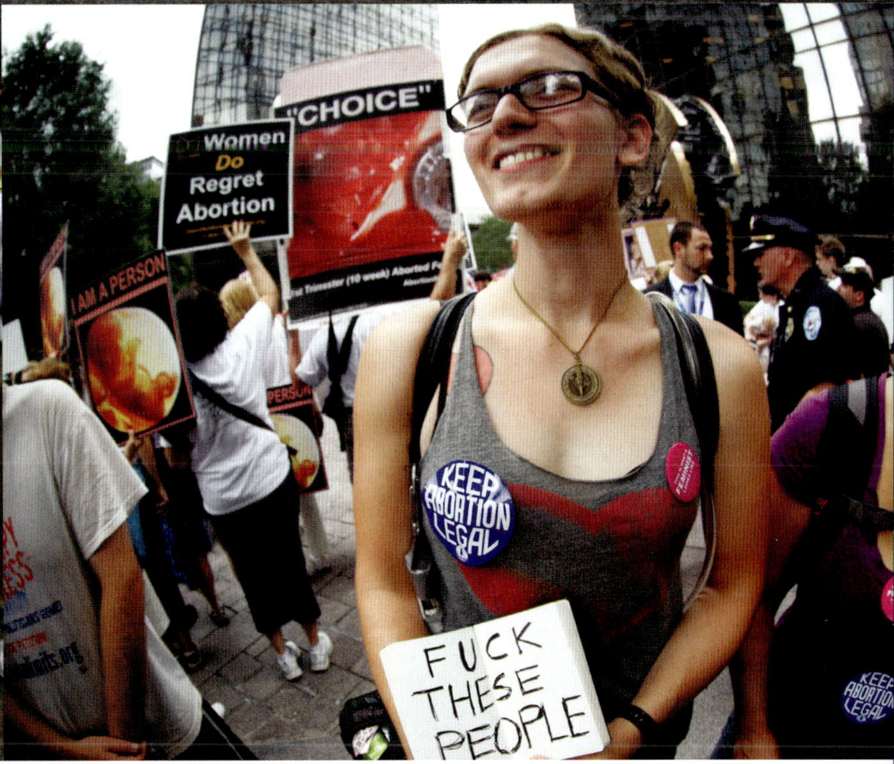

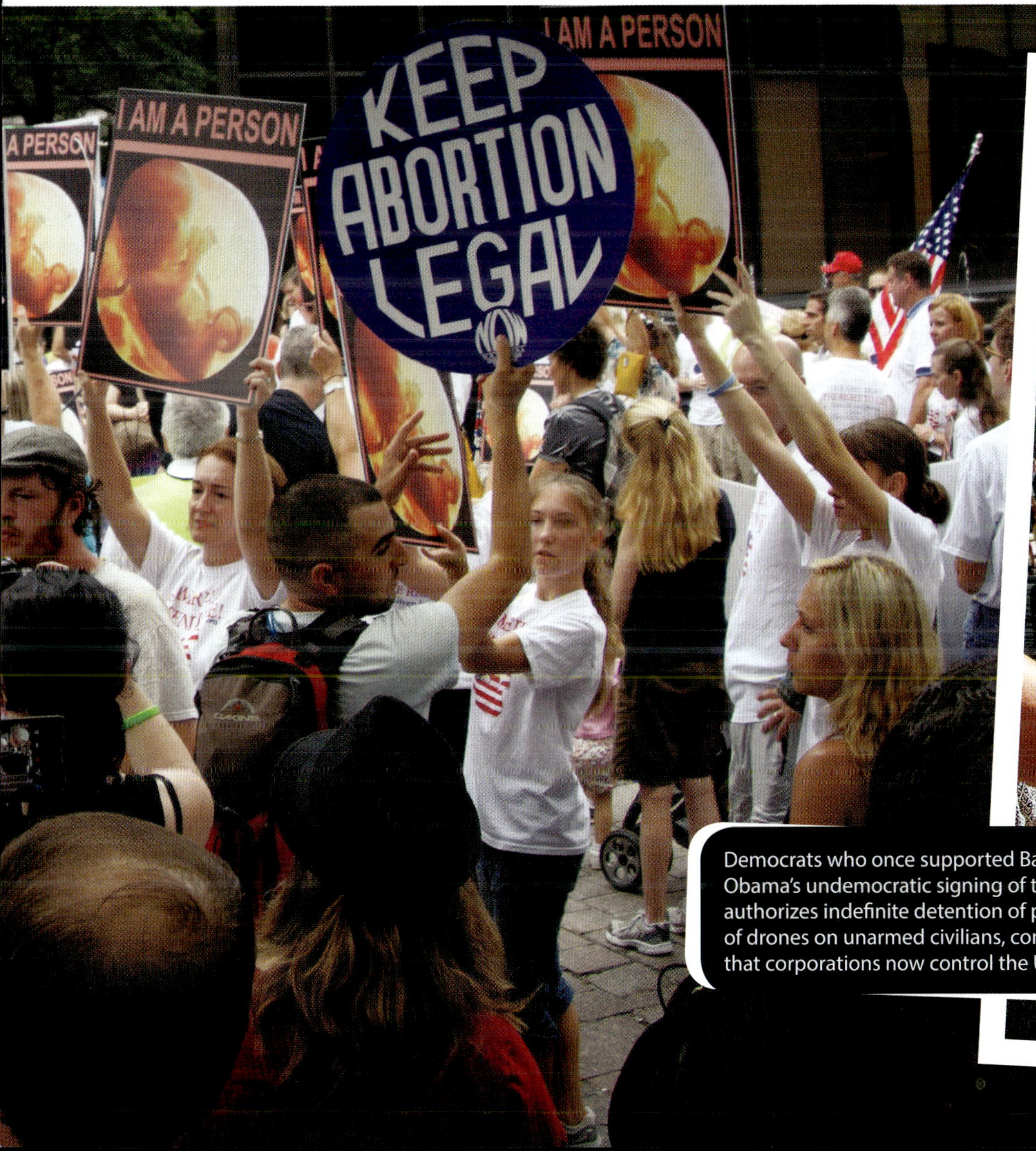

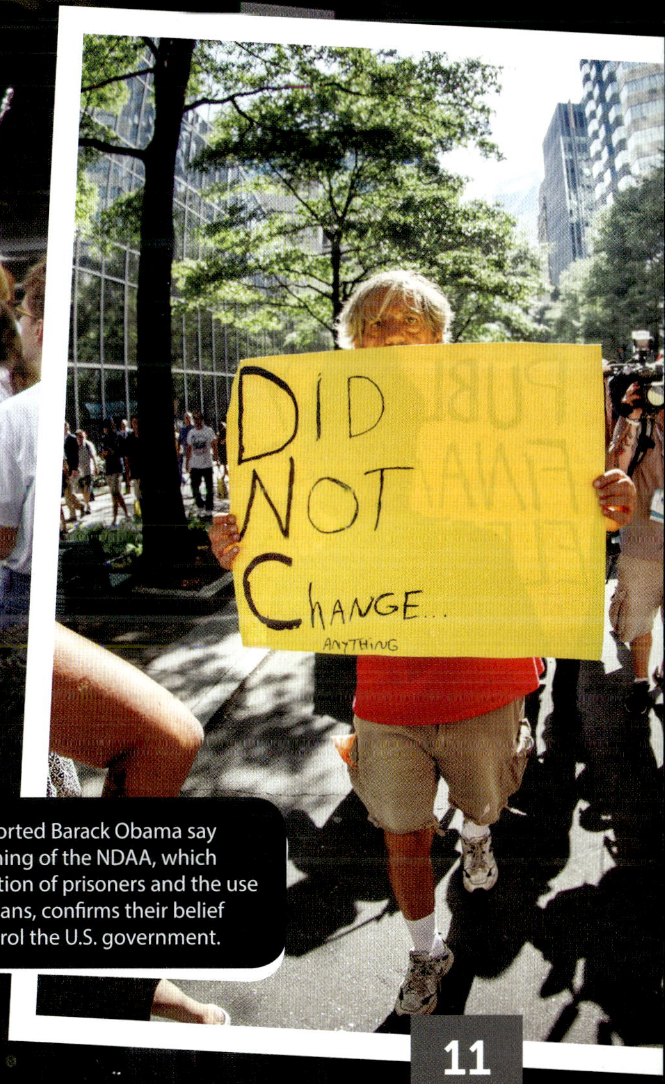

Democrats who once supported Barack Obama say Obama's undemocratic signing of the NDAA, which authorizes indefinite detention of prisoners and the use of drones on unarmed civilians, confirms their belief that corporations now control the U.S. government.

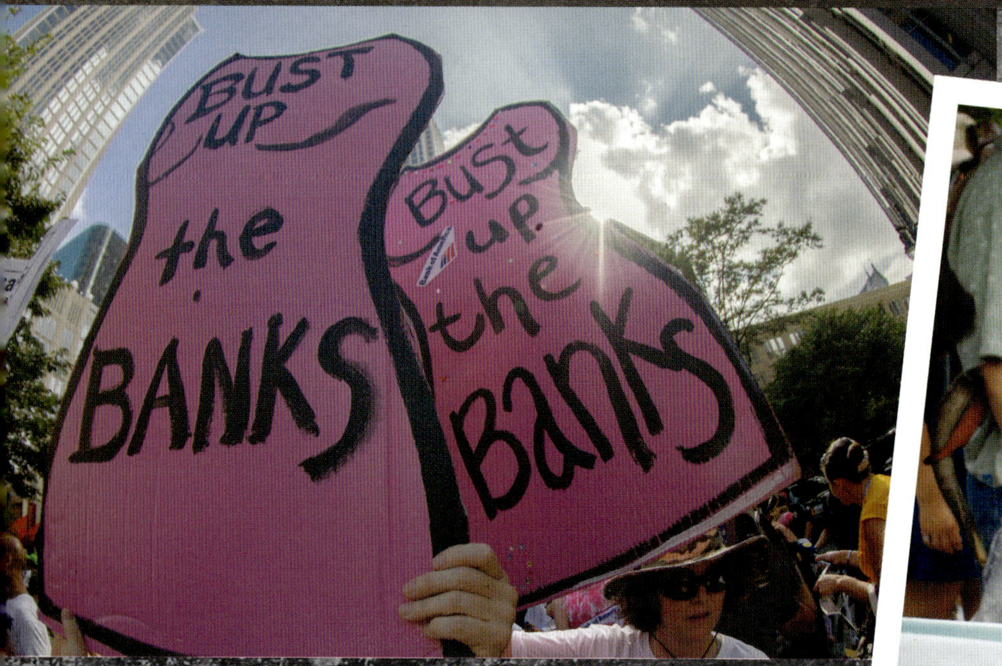

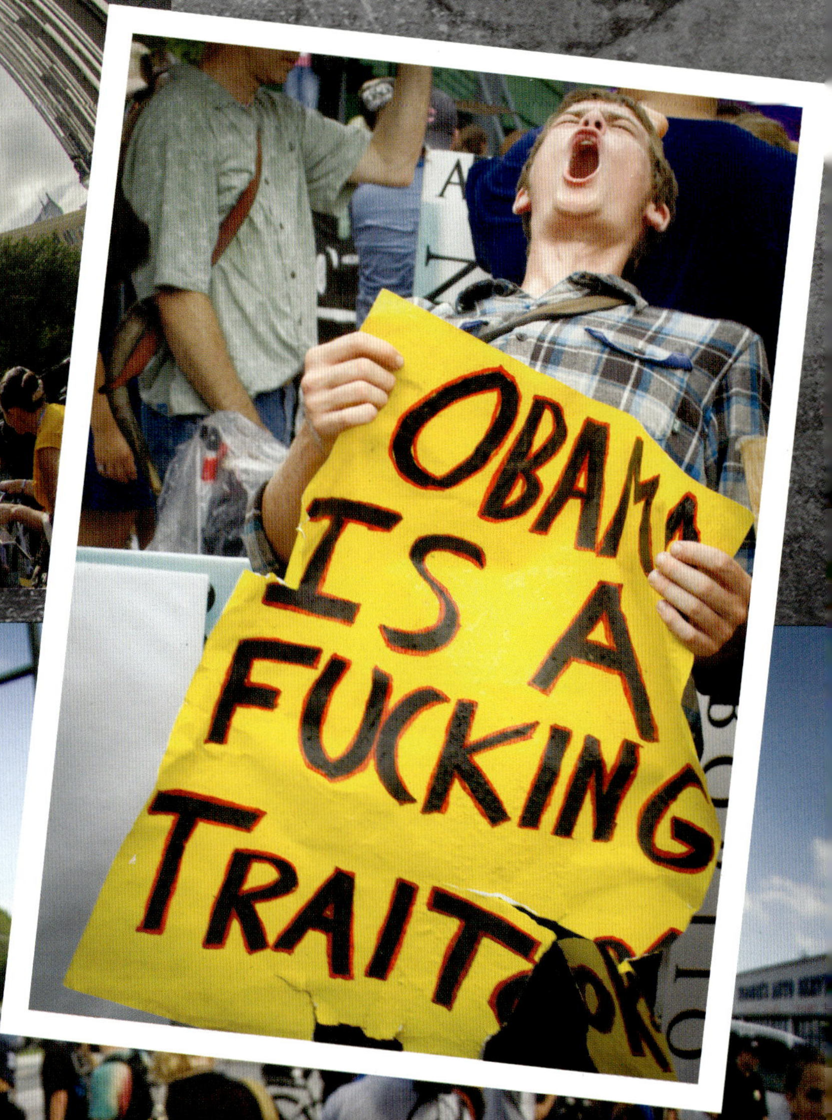

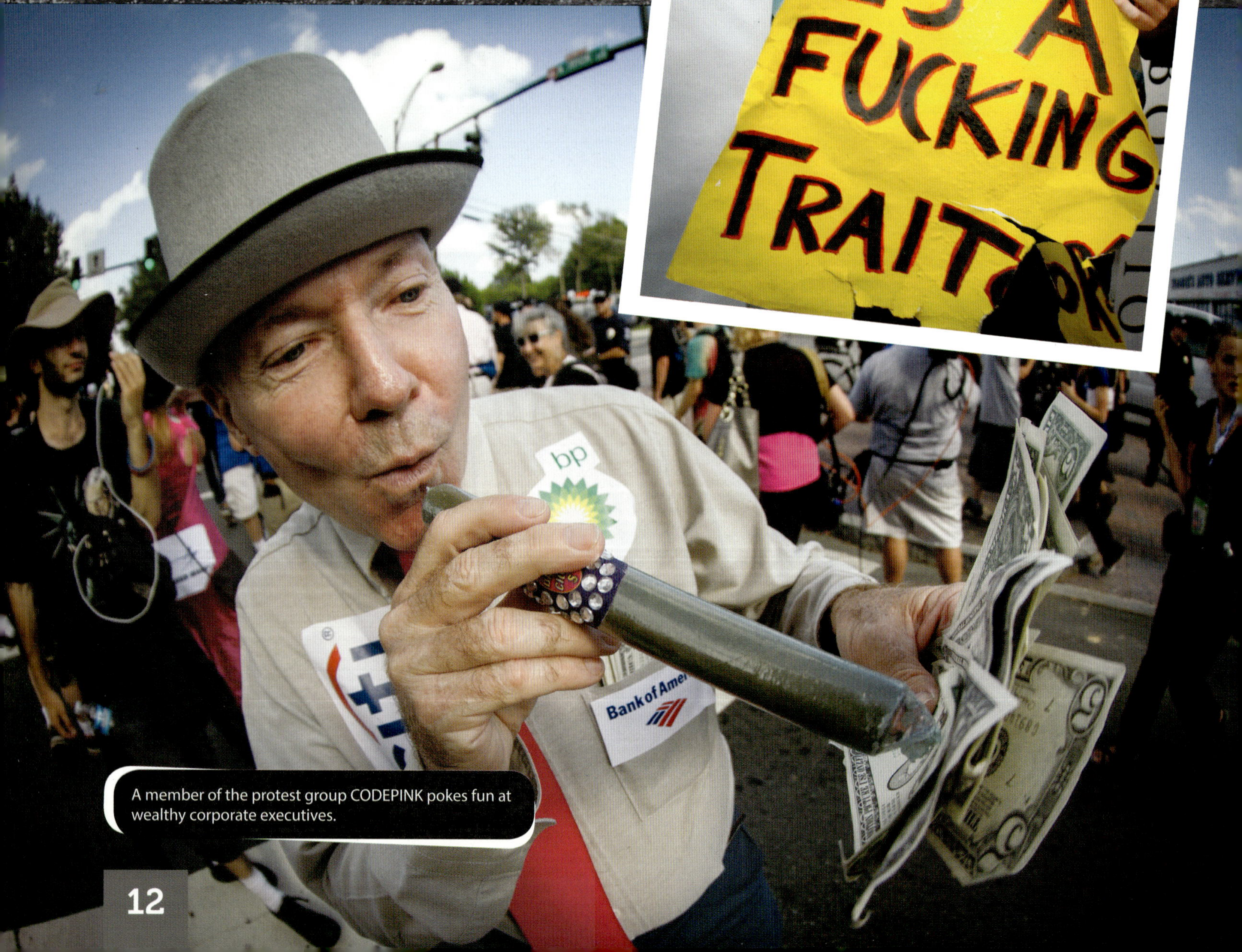

A member of the protest group CODEPINK pokes fun at wealthy corporate executives.

Bank Protests

Emergency payments were made to banking institutions by the U.S. government under the Emergency Economic Stabilization Act of 2008 in response to the subprime mortgage crisis. While billions of dollars were used to keep banks that were crippled by toxic debt from failing, these financial institutions continued to foreclose on families, many of whom were perceived by the public as being victims of corrupt lending practices. Public resentment toward banks was amplified as the CEOs of these ailing institutions continued to be rewarded with extravagant bonuses. The outrage culminated on September 17, 2011, when hundreds of people descended on New York's financial district to protest corporate greed and the disproportionate influence of the affluent minority over America's democratic process. $700 billion in taxpayer dollars was initially allocated to aid global financial institutions who were labeled "too big to fail." The funds were doled out to the banks by the Troubled Asset Relief Program (TARP). The top recipients were Citigroup, Bank of America, AIG, JP Morgan Chase, and Wells Fargo, who each received between $25 and $45 billion.

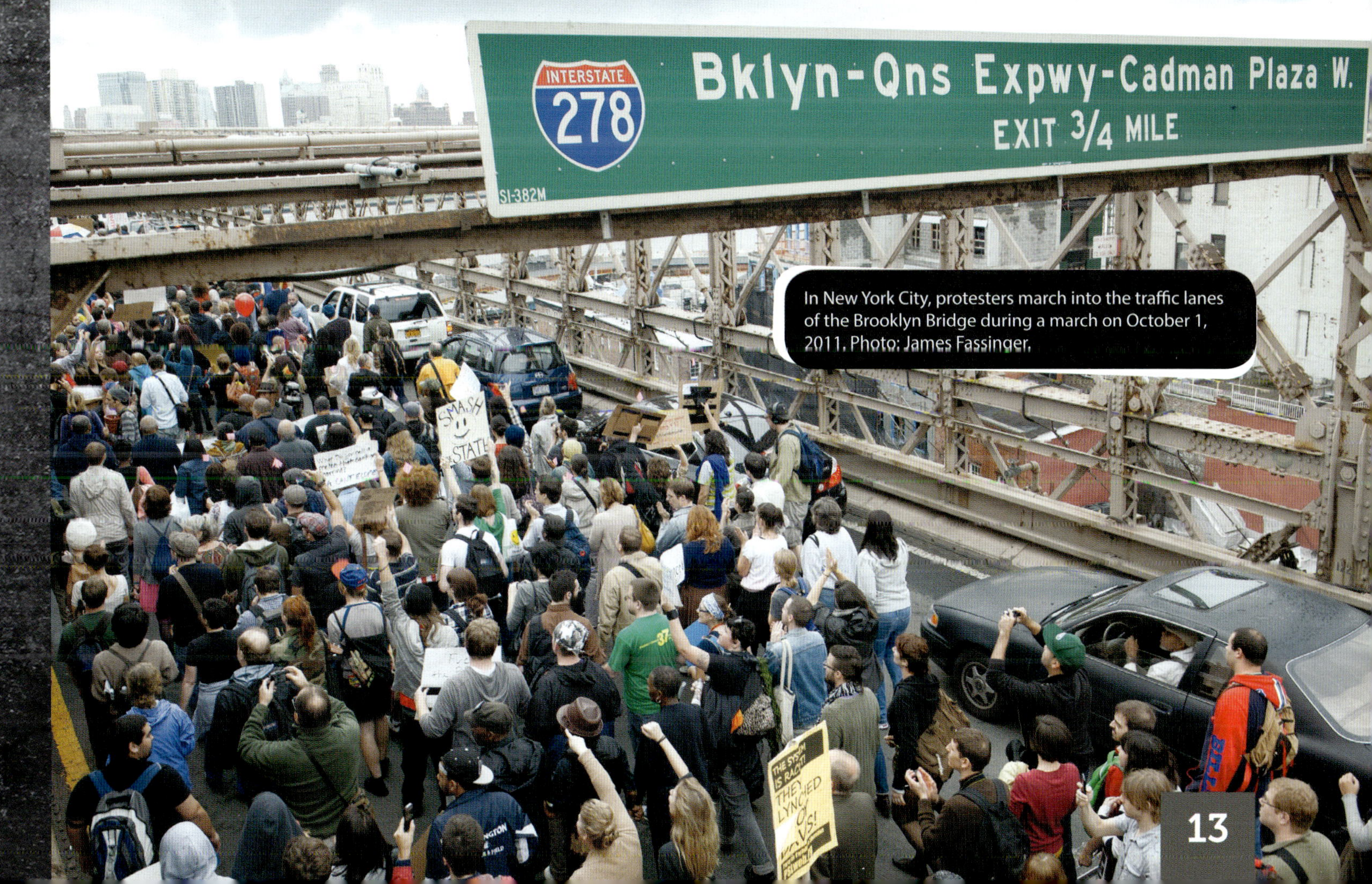

In New York City, protesters march into the traffic lanes of the Brooklyn Bridge during a march on October 1, 2011. Photo: James Fassinger.

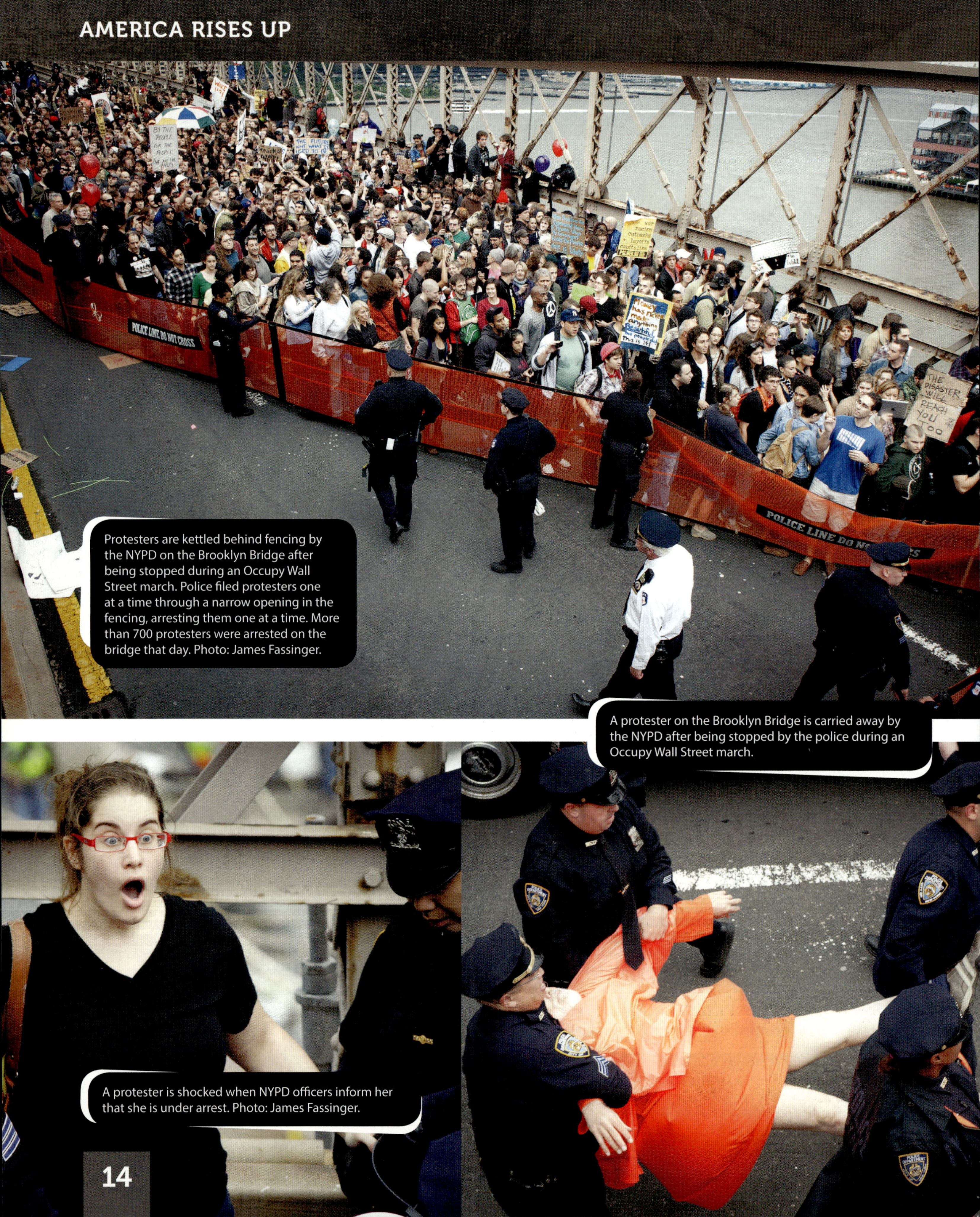

Protesters are kettled behind fencing by the NYPD on the Brooklyn Bridge after being stopped during an Occupy Wall Street march. Police filed protesters one at a time through a narrow opening in the fencing, arresting them one at a time. More than 700 protesters were arrested on the bridge that day. Photo: James Fassinger.

A protester on the Brooklyn Bridge is carried away by the NYPD after being stopped by the police during an Occupy Wall Street march.

A protester is shocked when NYPD officers inform her that she is under arrest. Photo: James Fassinger.

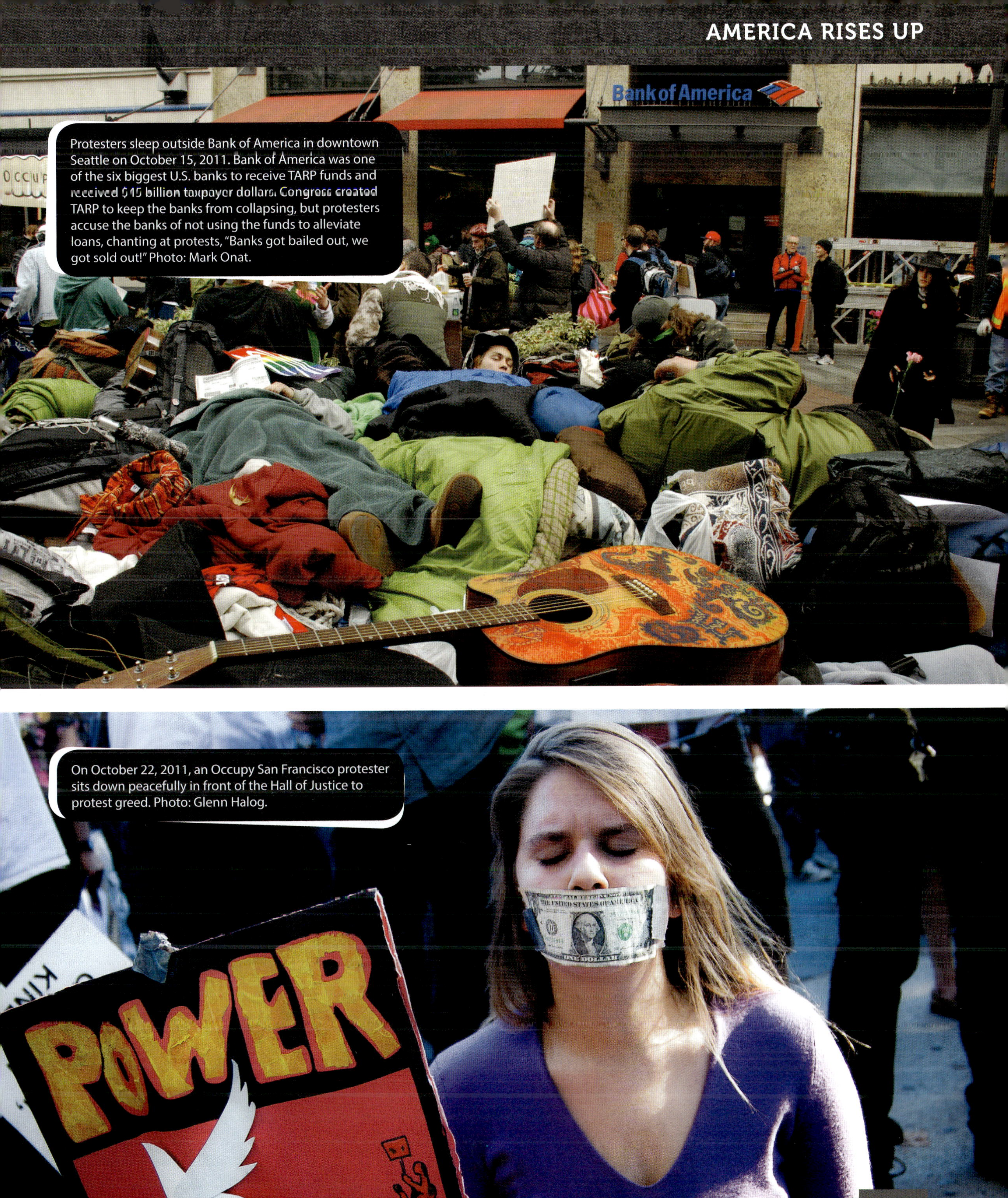

Protesters sleep outside Bank of America in downtown Seattle on October 15, 2011. Bank of America was one of the six biggest U.S. banks to receive TARP funds and received $15 billion taxpayer dollars. Congress created TARP to keep the banks from collapsing, but protesters accuse the banks of not using the funds to alleviate loans, chanting at protests, "Banks got bailed out, we got sold out!" Photo: Mark Onat.

On October 22, 2011, an Occupy San Francisco protester sits down peacefully in front of the Hall of Justice to protest greed. Photo: Glenn Halog.

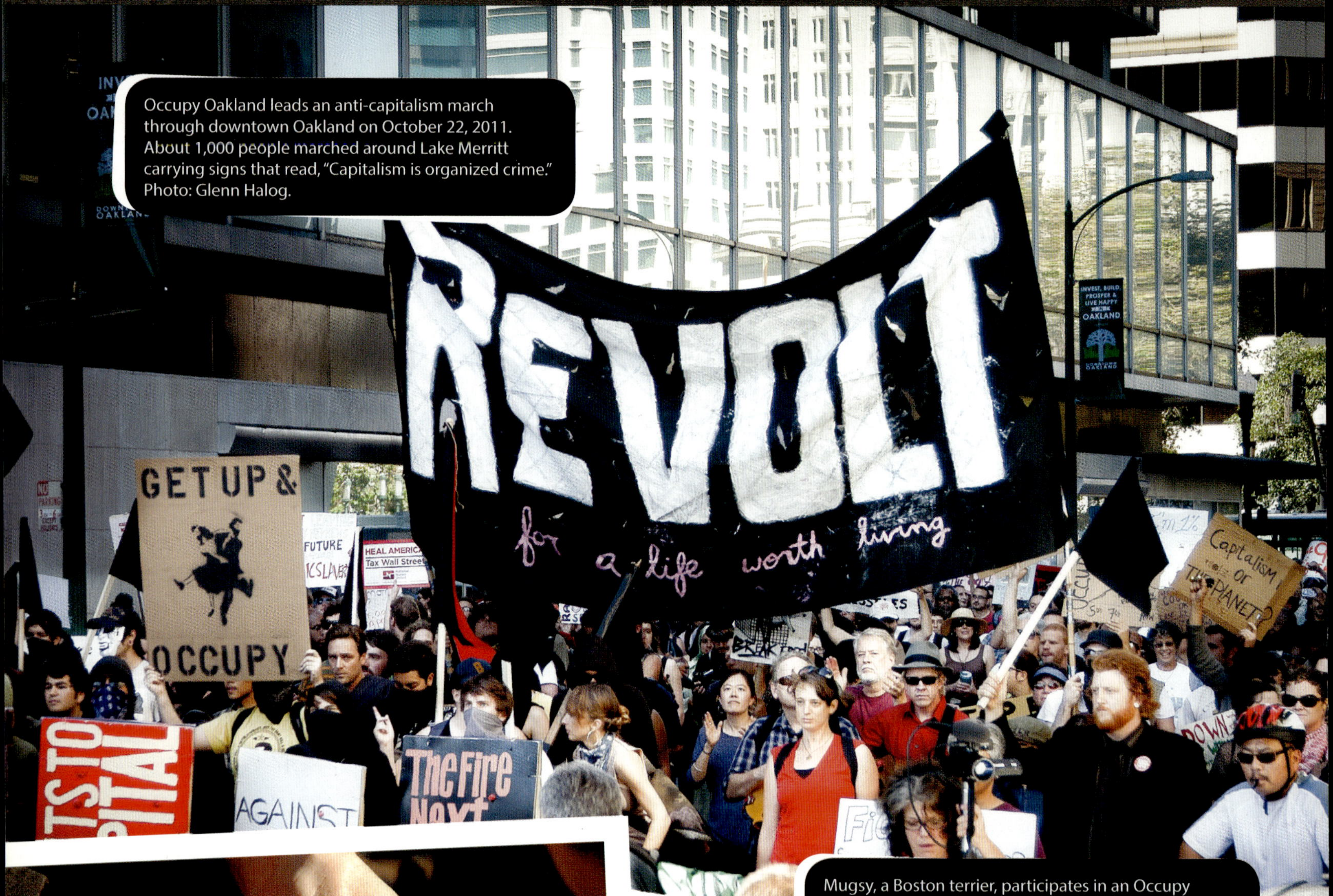

Occupy Oakland leads an anti-capitalism march through downtown Oakland on October 22, 2011. About 1,000 people marched around Lake Merritt carrying signs that read, "Capitalism is organized crime." Photo: Glenn Halog.

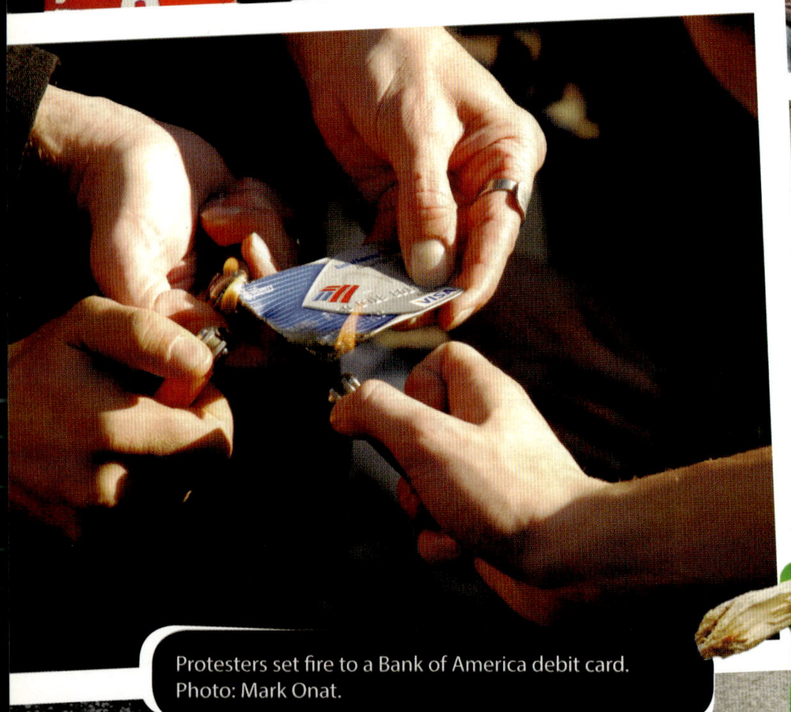

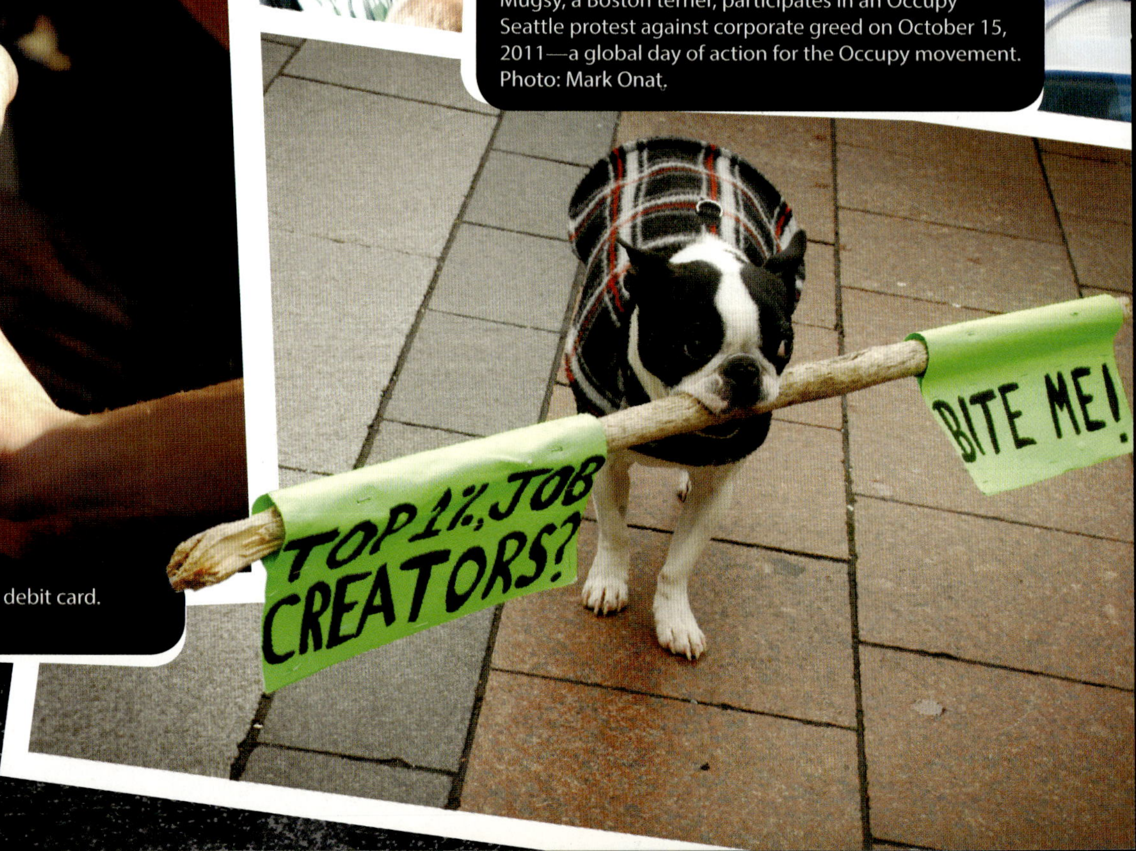

Mugsy, a Boston terrier, participates in an Occupy Seattle protest against corporate greed on October 15, 2011—a global day of action for the Occupy movement. Photo: Mark Onat.

Protesters set fire to a Bank of America debit card. Photo: Mark Onat.

Activist Profile

Name: Lucky Tran
Age: 29
City: New York City
Protesting since: September 2011 (for OWS)
Affiliation: Occupy Wall Street
Twitter handle: @luckytran (though I generally Tweet from various OWS accounts including @illuminator99, @occupytownsq, and @allinthered)

What happened in your life that motivated you to attend your first protest? I was a six-month-old refugee from Vietnam, and my father's first job in Australia after immigrating was as a refugee and social worker. This meant that from a young age I was always at rallies for refugee and immigrant rights. In fact I even won an award from the Refugee Association at the age of six for public speaking on these issues. Since then I have always cared about creating vibrant communities and addressing inequality in society.

How have you been protesting? At Occupy, I started out in the outreach working group. Since then I've been heavily involved in several projects: Occupy Town Square, which is a project that aims to reclaim public space by having regular events in neighborhoods all around the city that capture the self-organizing, participatory spirit of community, discussion, and mutual aid that was found in Zuccotti; the Illuminator, which is a mobile guerilla projection van that challenges the corporate visual space with light art and messaging; and recently I've been organizing with All in the Red, which is a creative affinity group that is inspired by powerful student movements in places like Quebec, Mexico, and Chile but focuses on educational issues and student debt in the U.S.

Have you ever been pepper-sprayed, injured, or arrested while demonstrating? If so, what happened? I have been arrested on a student debt–focused march for trying to prevent my fellow protesters from being run over by aggressive drivers. The NYPD here are highly militarized and trained to actively suppress the movement, using very violent and often illegal means to stop protests. Despite this, there is a wonderful amount of courage and solidarity in the movement, and protesters here refuse to be intimidated by an army that serves special interests.

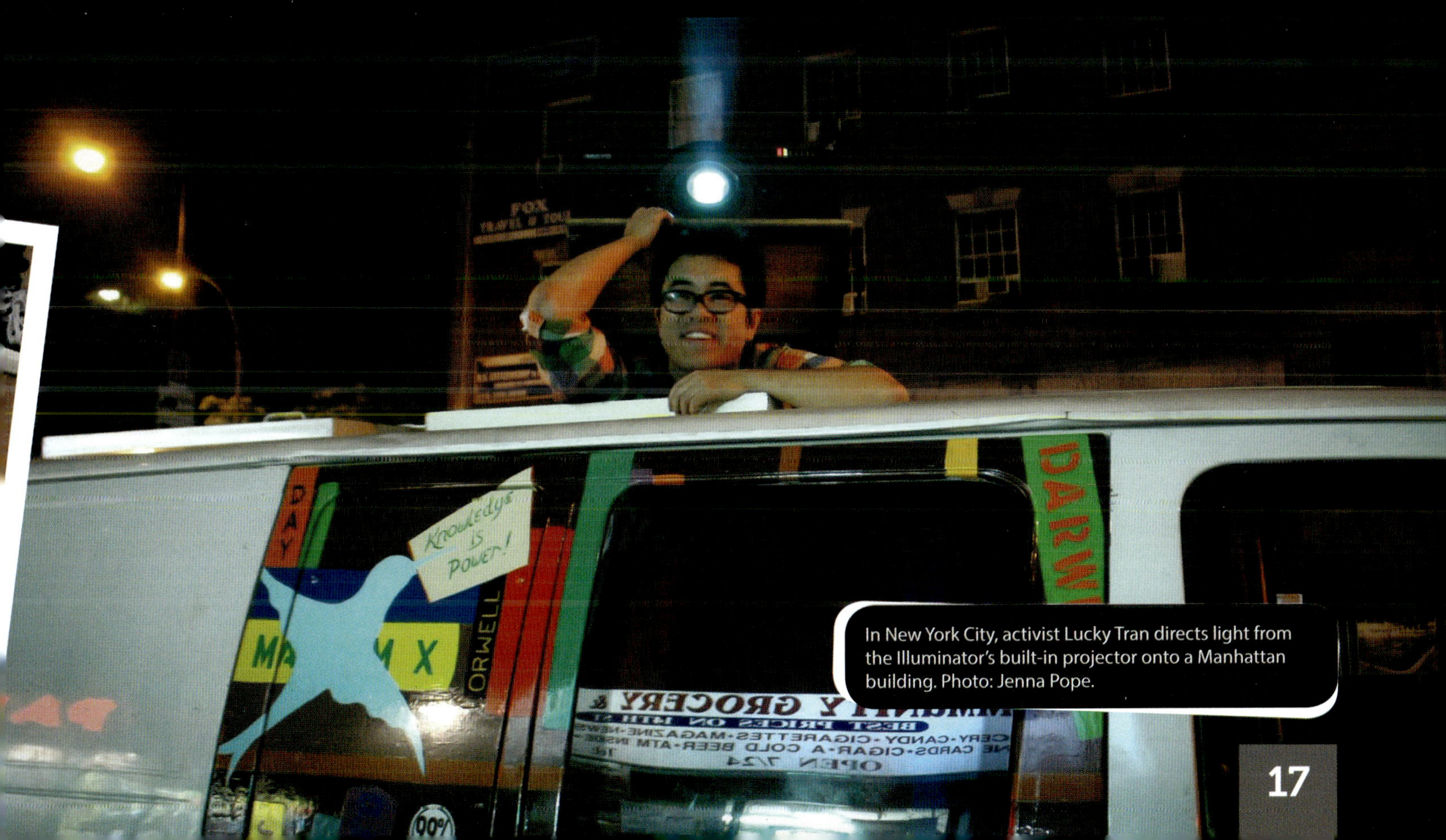

In New York City, activist Lucky Tran directs light from the Illuminator's built-in projector onto a Manhattan building. Photo: Jenna Pope.

Have your efforts resulted in change? I believe that any act of personal engagement generates change through conviction. The biggest barrier is in leaping out of a state of apathy or false comfort. Occupy is such an amazing movement because more than stimulating minor policy changes or similar appeasements, the greatest legacy of all projects is that they create a strong network of engaged activists who spend every drip of time when they finish their day job, not in front of the television or hanging out in a bar, but in striving for social and economic justice. It's that shift in personal commitment and community participation that is the most transformative thing about the movement.

What's the most egregious mainstream misconception about protesters? That protesters only complain and therefore are less valued members of society. It is true that it is important for protests to call out the source of injustices in society, because if you do not understand the causation then you cannot fix things. However, most of the time activists actually are discussing and implementing solutions or alternatives to current problems. For instance, Occupy has created temporary autonomous zones where mutual aid is practiced in public space, put out a manual on debt resistance, and created a strong, democratized media network.

When will you be satisfied, stop protesting? I believe that protest and being an activist is an essential component of citizenship in a society, and therefore one must never disengage from these commitments. In absence of a utopic universe there will always be injustices that require citizens to be concerned about and work hard towards correcting. It is the greatest tragedy of modern life that we can cocoon ourselves into a life of consumption and dehumanize the important struggles that occur all around us.

Favorite quote: "Words are cheap. The biggest thing you can say is 'elephant.'" —Charlie Chaplin

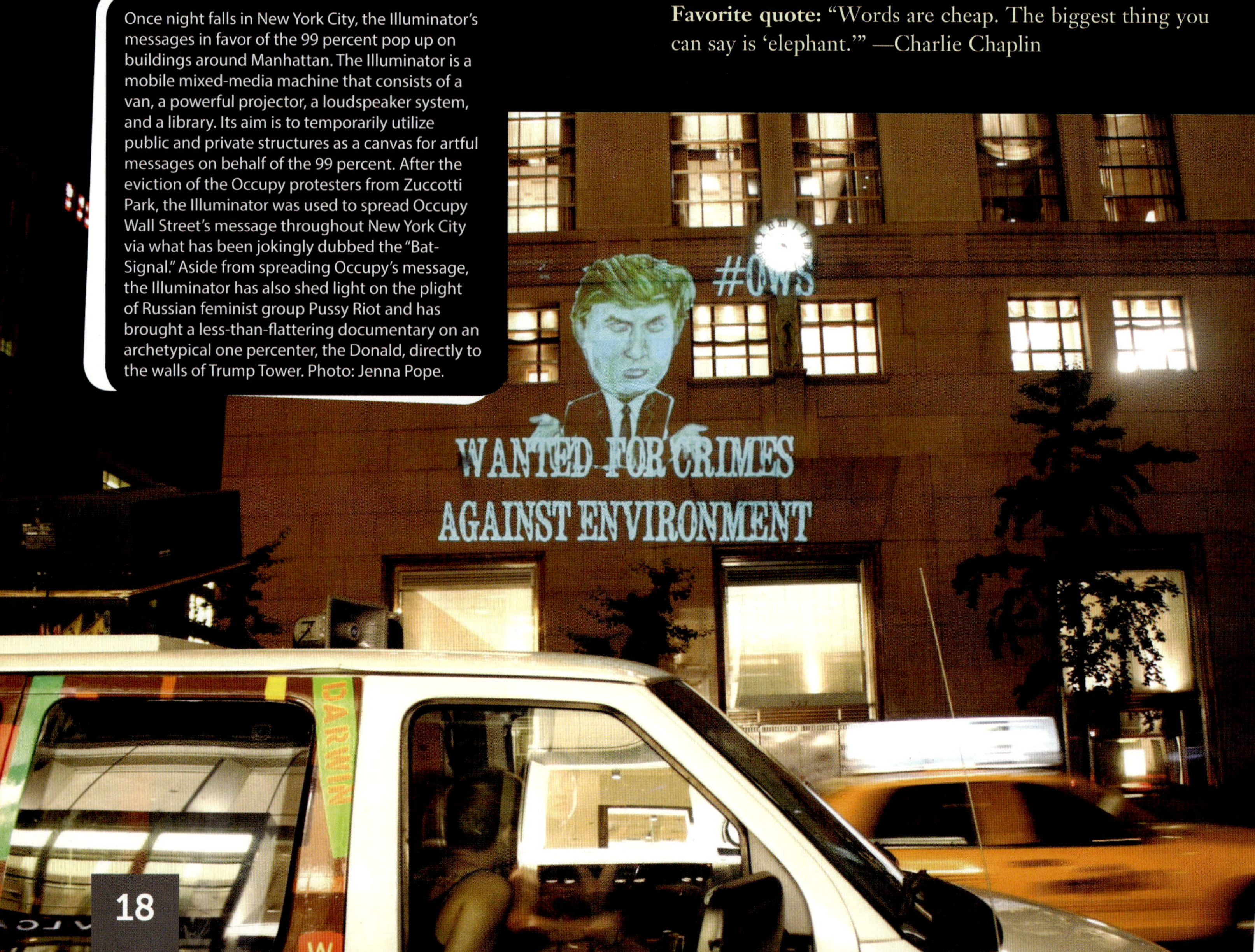

Once night falls in New York City, the Illuminator's messages in favor of the 99 percent pop up on buildings around Manhattan. The Illuminator is a mobile mixed-media machine that consists of a van, a powerful projector, a loudspeaker system, and a library. Its aim is to temporarily utilize public and private structures as a canvas for artful messages on behalf of the 99 percent. After the eviction of the Occupy protesters from Zuccotti Park, the Illuminator was used to spread Occupy Wall Street's message throughout New York City via what has been jokingly dubbed the "Bat-Signal." Aside from spreading Occupy's message, the Illuminator has also shed light on the plight of Russian feminist group Pussy Riot and has brought a less-than-flattering documentary on an archetypical one percenter, the Donald, directly to the walls of Trump Tower. Photo: Jenna Pope.

Activist Profile

Name: Vermin L. Supreme
Age: 62
City of Dreams: The Internet Machine
Activated as an activist/peoples' candidate: in earnest since 1986
Affiliations include: The Free Pony Party, misinformed citizens bureau, VP candidate: Rent is Too Damn High Party, Evil Twin Booking Agency, Rainbow Family of Living Love and Light, Seeds of Peace Collective
Twitter handle: @verminsupreme

What happened in your life that motivated you to attend your first protest? "Darn shame," I thought, tossing aside a several month old copy of *Mother Jones* magazine. Then, one full week after reading all about its alleged and apparently exaggerated demise, David Mixner's magical, wayward love child, the Great Peace March for Global Nuclear Disarmament, rolled into the parking lot of the Baltimore Colts' beloved Memorial Stadium. Five thousand strong, it was an entire mobile city of "peaceful, loving people" with a rolling infrastructure to match, an amazing sight. Water trucks, school buses of many functions, multi-grade schoolhouses on wheels, mobile mimeograph media centers, a library, kick-ass kitchens, Porta-Potty trailers,

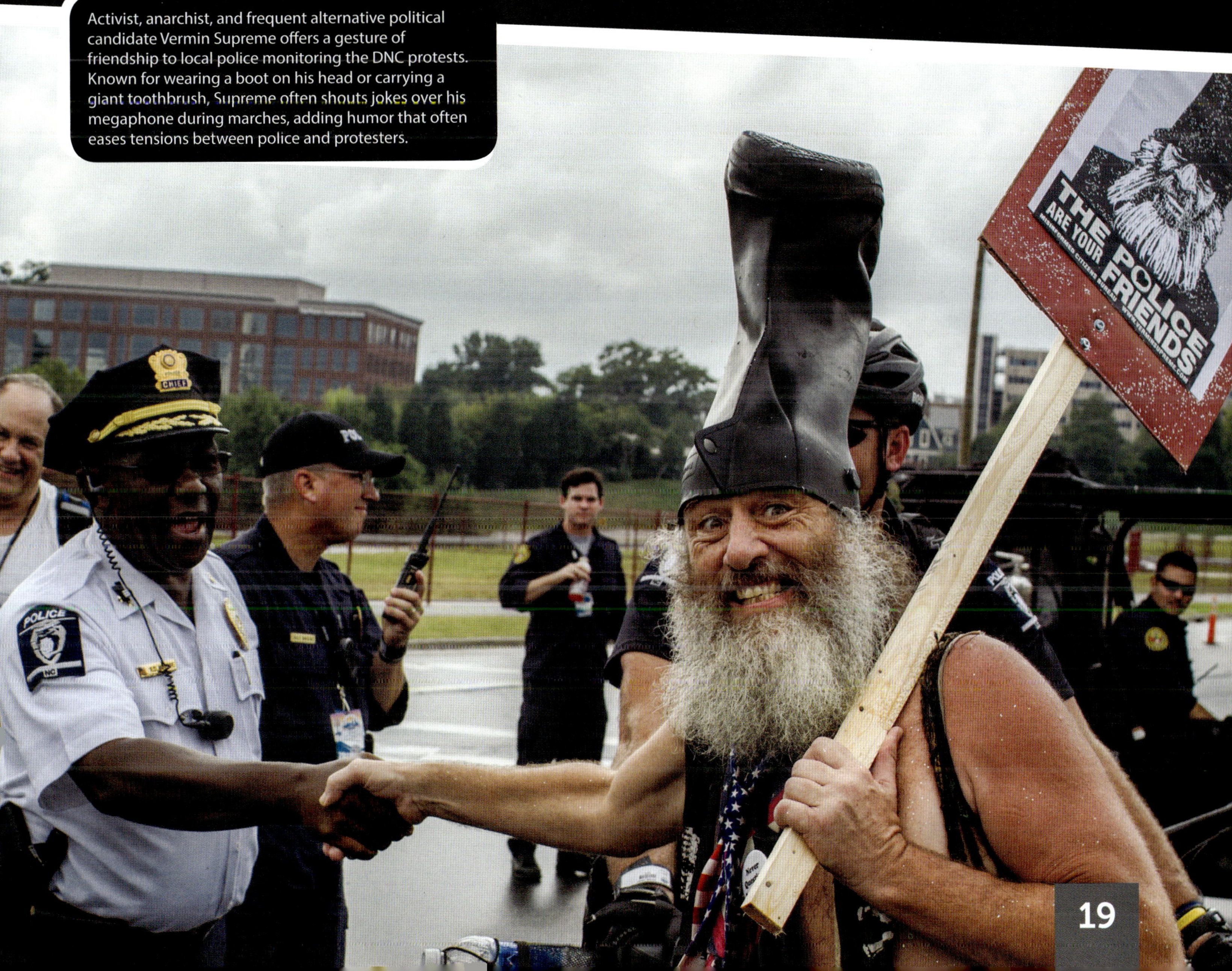

Activist, anarchist, and frequent alternative political candidate Vermin Supreme offers a gesture of friendship to local police monitoring the DNC protests. Known for wearing a boot on his head or carrying a giant toothbrush, Supreme often shouts jokes over his megaphone during marches, adding humor that often eases tensions between police and protesters.

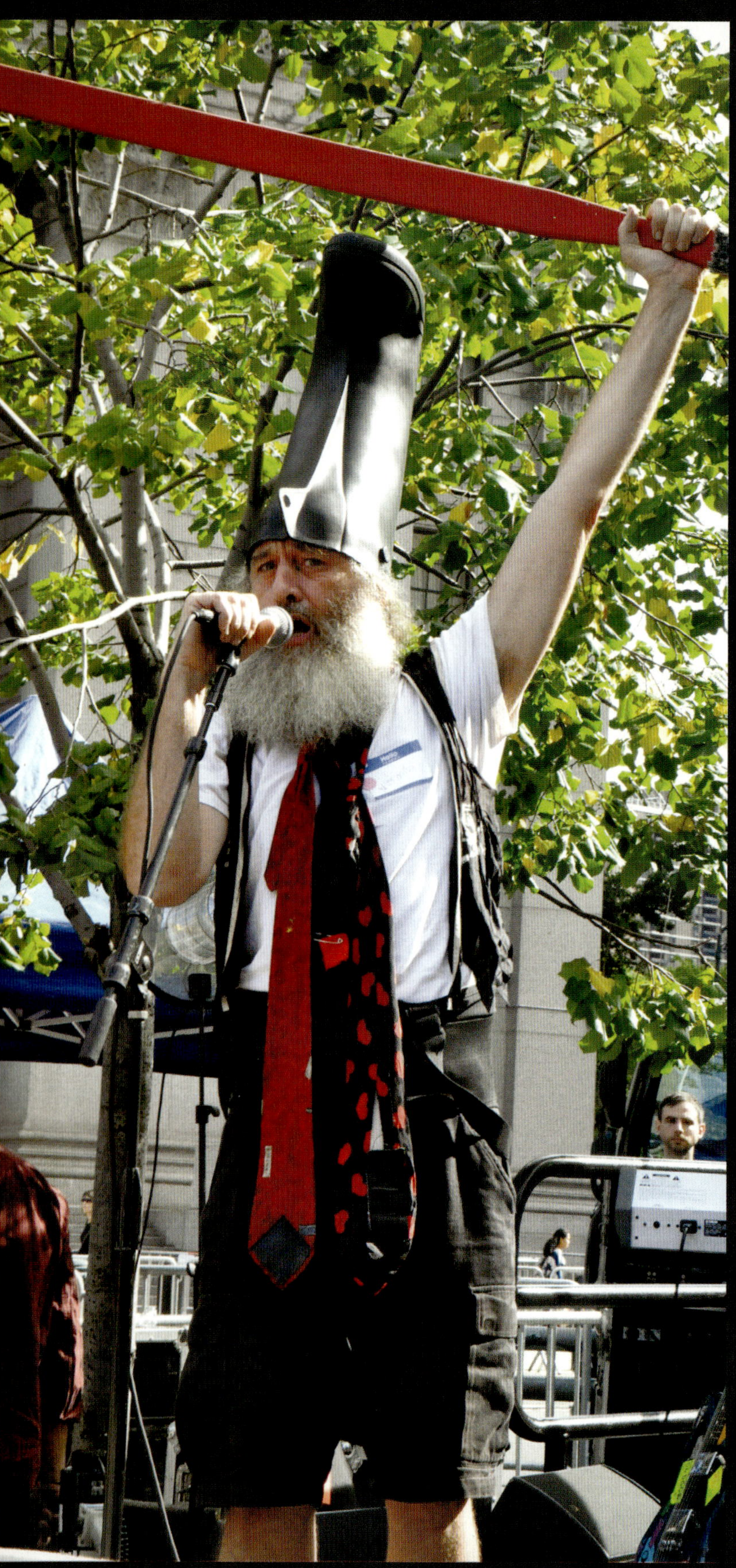

honey trucks, repair shops, semi-trailer trucks hauling the marchers' two-milk-crate luggage allotment, were just a portion of the flotilla. This Peace City had its own functioning consensus-based decision-making bodies, daily town meetings, a ceremonial mayor, and its own zip code.

Inspired, I walked the blocks to the nearest thrift store to buy a change of clothes and a sleeping bag. Then I joined the march on its final miles to D.C. It was there that I met a group of marchers that intended to continue the marching. They formed a collective and found funding to purchase some of the leftover GPM equipment, including Porta-Potty, water, and kitchen trailers. These were logistical components required in moving hundreds of people down the road. The group was called Seeds of Peace (Kitchen) and exists to this day. I left Baltimore that day and became a traveling activist, walking hundreds of miles for peace, participating in national political convergences, joining the annual gatherings of the rainbow family, and meeting my wife of 25 years along the way.

How have you been protesting? *Protesting* seems to me to be a bit of a media-based pejorative term. As a citizen I am actively engaging with the existing political system, on behalf of myself and my constituents, by exercising my rights of free assembly and speech.

Over the years, I have developed a multi-pronged approach to amplifying my voice in order to maximize my effectiveness as an activist.

One bit of political pop culture that I have exploited is taking on the role of a fringe presidential candidate. For over 20 years, in the media and in the streets, I have presented myself as such. My camPain occurs in the real world in real time, reacting to fluid unscripted situations, interacting with candidates and voters, media and police, Secret Service, etc. In order to present my critique I have accessed ballots and voter's guides, and debates, recently placing third in the 2012 New Hampshire Primary. I have attracted more attention nationwide than most of the 400+ candidates running for president any given cycle. By wearing a boot on my head and focusing on my core issues of zombie preparedness, mandatory toothbrush laws, time-travel research, and free ponies, I have gained a sizable voter base.

Another area in which I have found a happy place is that tense space that exists between demonstrators and riot police. In order to reduce the risk of police-on-protester violence and avoid crowd panic, I have been developing a communication strategy. I have been using a bullhorn to fill that space with reassurances and humorous patter, in order to dispel fear. Offering relevant information and updates to the crowd and reaffirming the right of the assembled helps create confidence and reduces anxiety. By reading to officers from crowd control manuals, the vacuum is filled, basic expectations for police conduct are reaffirmed and defined. This technique has de-escalated many a situation that may have otherwise turned from bad to worse.

Have you ever been pepper-sprayed, injured, or arrested while demonstrating? If so, what happened? Poked in the gut with a nightstick in LA DNC. Repeatedly tear gassed in Quebec WTO. LRADded in Pittsburgh G20. Mass arrested in NYC WEF, suffered handcuff neuropathy. Unlawfully arrested on Wall Street. Unlawfully arrested in Boston. Unlawfully arrested at LA DNC. Unlawfully arrested in a national forest for distributing my own campain material. Unlawfully arrested in a national forest for reciting the First Amendment. I have settled lawsuits with the NYPD and LAPD.

Have your efforts resulted in change? There have been changes. For example: overwhelming shows of force and intimidation, infiltration, and entrapment. Creation of an overarching surveillance state. Coordinated federal responses in crushing occupy encampments. The increasing militarization of police forces. The criminalization and demonization of dissent. The loosening of Posse Comitatus. There has been an ongoing series of experiments and tactics by police (most recently S17 NYPD snatch squads) designed to prevent, discourage, and frighten the people from speaking and assembling. These are very serious threats to democracy. Constant agitation is a key force for change in society. That, ALEC, and the Koch brothers. Citizen pressure helped to end the war in Viet Nam. Women gained the vote. The civil rights movement demanded and fought for equality. Other minorities continue the struggle for their rights. Laws against child labor laws were enacted. The eight-hour five-day work week became possible only after ferocious labor struggles. It was Malcolm X and the Panthers that made MLK's demands seem moderate. The road to Ponytopia will not be easy. There will be hardships. Not all of us will make it. The groundwork for a pony-based economy is being laid today. We are in it for the long haul. We fight for the children. We fight for the ponies. Victory is ours. Let us ride our ponies into the future.

What's the most egregious mainstream misconception about protesters? That they are somehow a separate class of citizens. That they are not informed. That they are not honorable and admirable for acting for what they believe in. That they somehow deserve punishment for exercising their First Amendment rights. That the threat of minor vandalism justifies such overwhelming threats of violence against peaceful demonstrators. That they don't have better things to do.

When will you be satisfied, stop protesting? When you can pry my cold dead fingers from my bullhorn of truth. Struggle is forever. We are fighting for what is left of the future. The planet is poisoned. The economy is failing. The government response is to ratchet up the security apparatus and demonize anarchists. I will not stop defending my friends and family from this government.

Favorite quote: "To be GOVERNED is to be watched, inspected, spied upon, directed, law-driven, numbered, regulated, enrolled, indoctrinated, preached at, controlled, checked, estimated, valued, censured, commanded, by creatures who have neither the right nor the wisdom nor the virtue to do so. To be GOVERNED is to be at every operation, at every transaction noted, registered, counted, taxed, stamped, measured, numbered, assessed, licensed, authorized, admonished, prevented, forbidden, reformed, corrected, punished. It is, under pretext of public utility, and in the name of the general interest, to be place under contribution, drilled, fleeced, exploited, monopolized, extorted from, squeezed, hoaxed, robbed; then, at the slightest resistance, the first word of complaint, to be repressed, fined, vilified, harassed, hunted down, abused, clubbed, disarmed, bound, choked, imprisoned, judged, condemned, shot, deported, sacrificed, sold, betrayed; and to crown all, mocked, ridiculed, derided, outraged, dishonored. That is government; that is its justice; that is its morality." —Pierre-Joseph Proudhon, *General Idea of the Revolution in the Nineteenth Century*, translated by John Beverly Robinson (London: Freedom Press, 1923, 293–294)

Anti–Police Brutality March

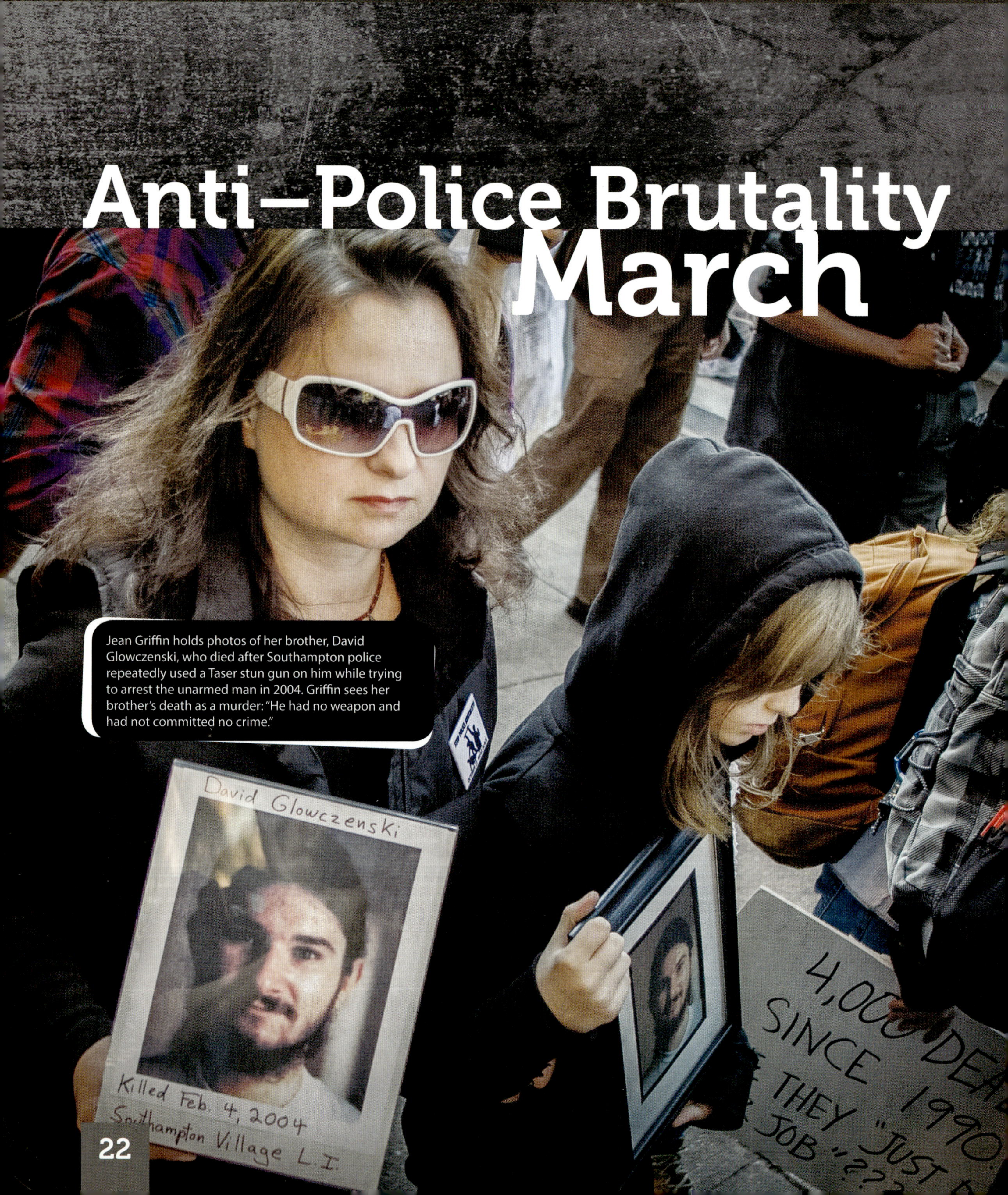

Jean Griffin holds photos of her brother, David Glowczenski, who died after Southampton police repeatedly used a Taser stun gun on him while trying to arrest the unarmed man in 2004. Griffin sees her brother's death as a murder: "He had no weapon and had not committed no crime."

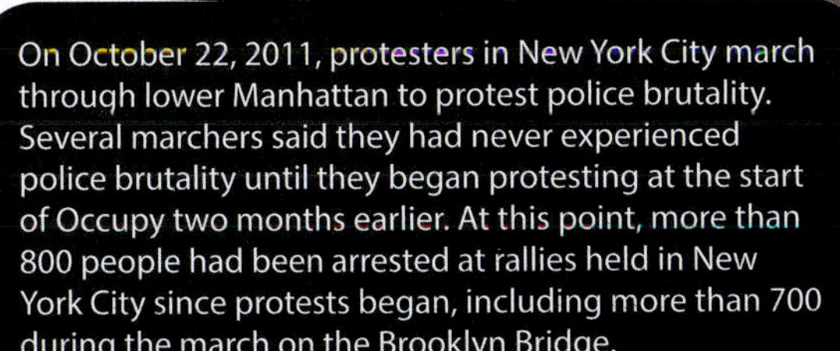

On October 22, 2011, protesters in New York City march through lower Manhattan to protest police brutality. Several marchers said they had never experienced police brutality until they began protesting at the start of Occupy two months earlier. At this point, more than 800 people had been arrested at rallies held in New York City since protests began, including more than 700 during the march on the Brooklyn Bridge.

Protester Mesiah Hameed marches against police brutality. The protesters chanted, "NYPD KKK, how many kids have you killed today?"

According to the New York City Police Department's Annual Firearms Discharge report, 24 people were shot by NYPD officers in 2011, and nine were killed as a result. That number is down from its peak in 1971, when NYPD officers killed 93 people.

Walmart Worker Uprising

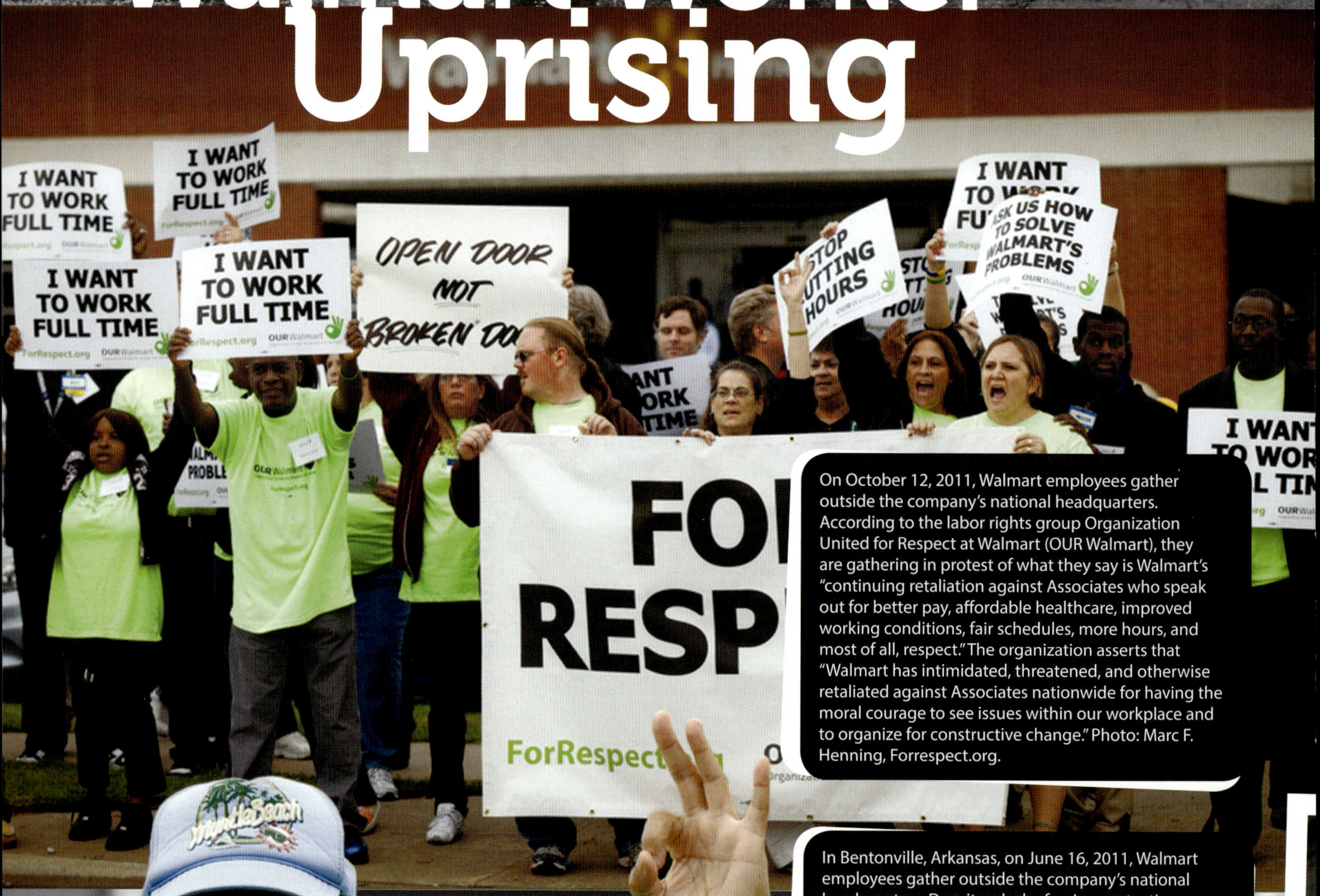

On October 12, 2011, Walmart employees gather outside the company's national headquarters. According to the labor rights group Organization United for Respect at Walmart (OUR Walmart), they are gathering in protest of what they say is Walmart's "continuing retaliation against Associates who speak out for better pay, affordable healthcare, improved working conditions, fair schedules, more hours, and most of all, respect." The organization asserts that "Walmart has intimidated, threatened, and otherwise retaliated against Associates nationwide for having the moral courage to see issues within our workplace and to organize for constructive change." Photo: Marc F. Henning, Forrespect.org.

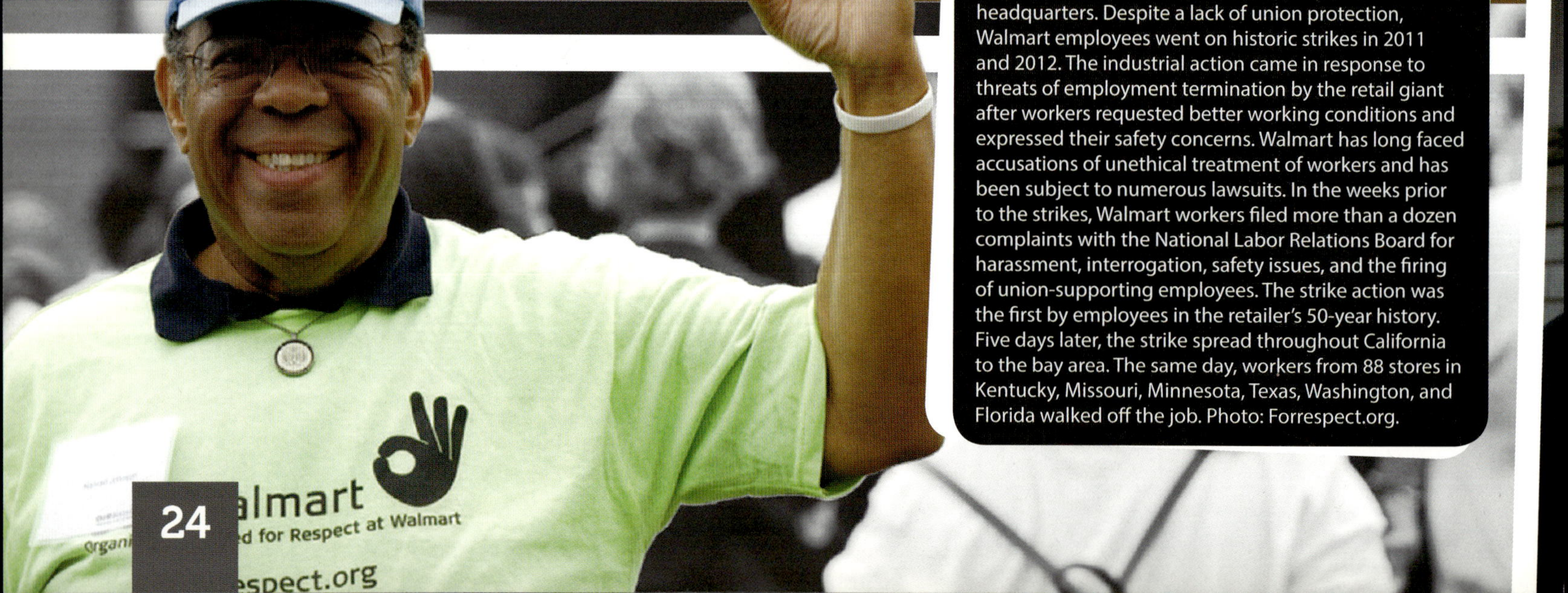

In Bentonville, Arkansas, on June 16, 2011, Walmart employees gather outside the company's national headquarters. Despite a lack of union protection, Walmart employees went on historic strikes in 2011 and 2012. The industrial action came in response to threats of employment termination by the retail giant after workers requested better working conditions and expressed their safety concerns. Walmart has long faced accusations of unethical treatment of workers and has been subject to numerous lawsuits. In the weeks prior to the strikes, Walmart workers filed more than a dozen complaints with the National Labor Relations Board for harassment, interrogation, safety issues, and the firing of union-supporting employees. The strike action was the first by employees in the retailer's 50-year history. Five days later, the strike spread throughout California to the bay area. The same day, workers from 88 stores in Kentucky, Missouri, Minnesota, Texas, Washington, and Florida walked off the job. Photo: Forrespect.org.

Bank Transfer Day

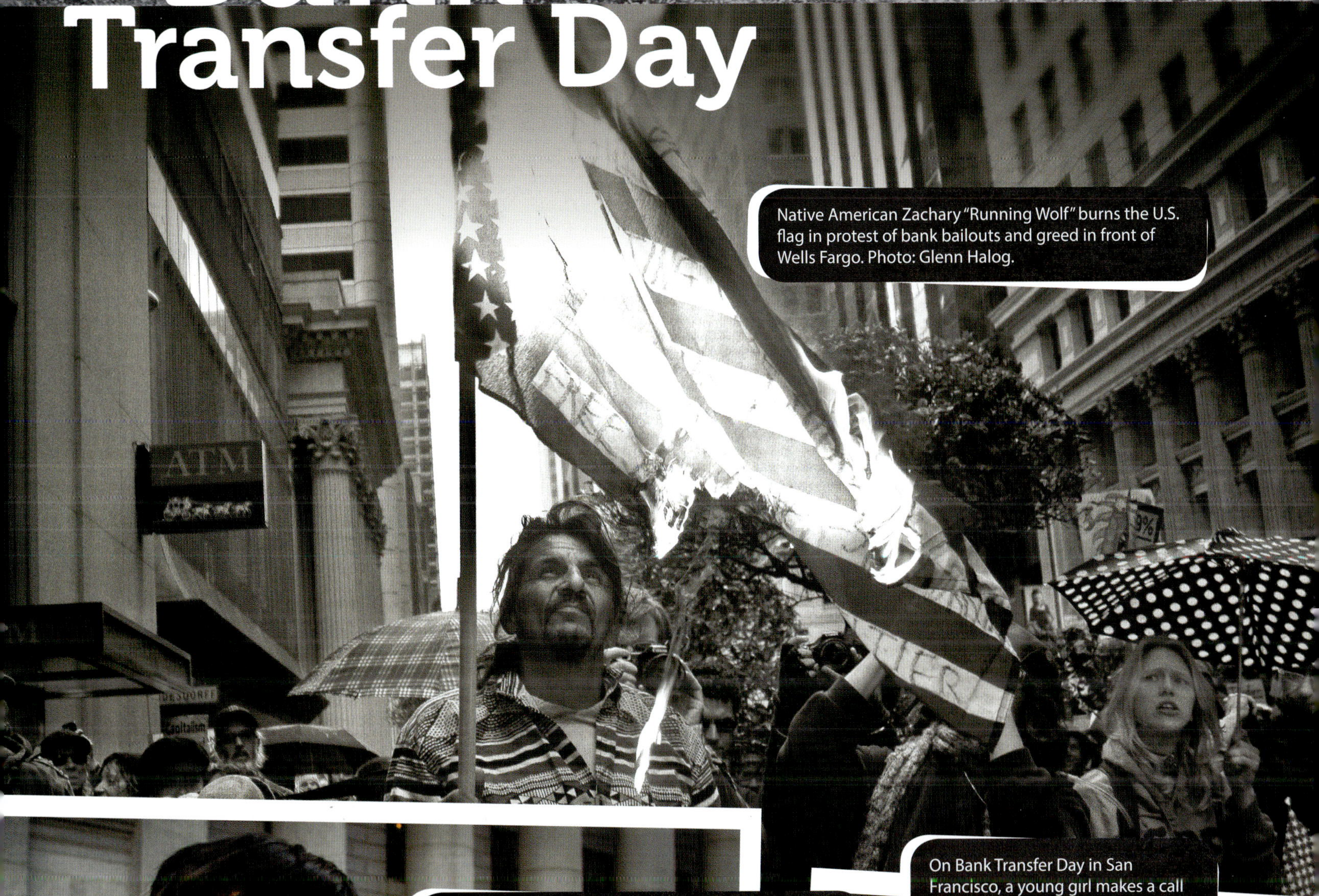

Native American Zachary "Running Wolf" burns the U.S. flag in protest of bank bailouts and greed in front of Wells Fargo. Photo: Glenn Halog.

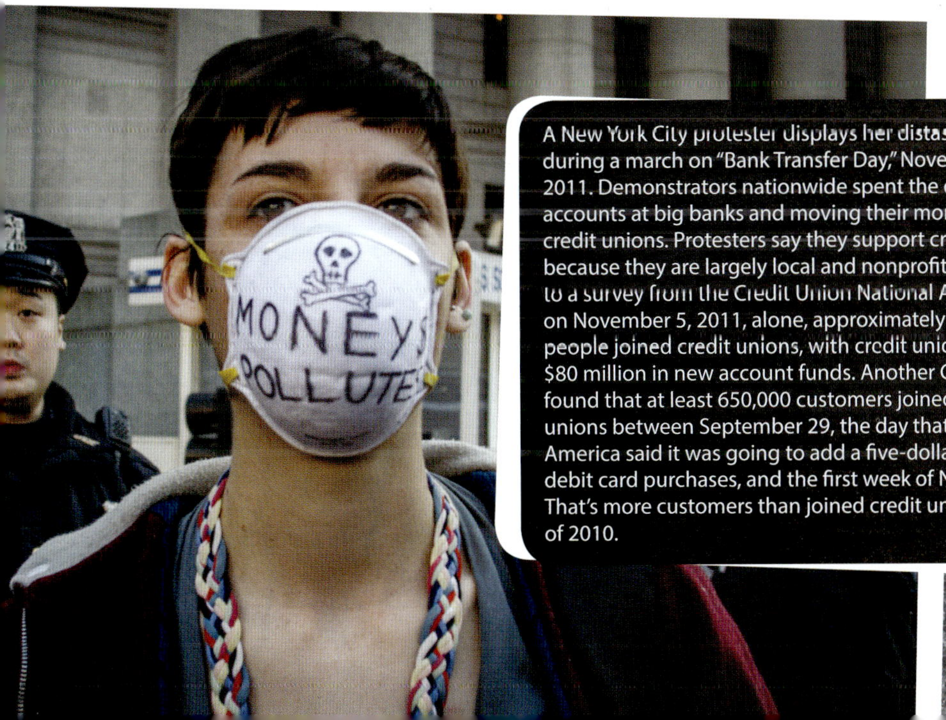

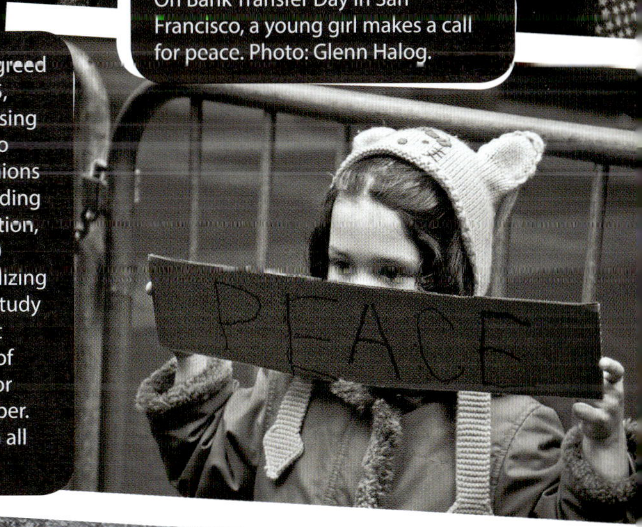

On Bank Transfer Day in San Francisco, a young girl makes a call for peace. Photo: Glenn Halog.

A New York City protester displays her distaste for greed during a march on "Bank Transfer Day," November 5, 2011. Demonstrators nationwide spent the day closing accounts at big banks and moving their money into credit unions. Protesters say they support credit unions because they are largely local and nonprofit. According to a survey from the Credit Union National Association, on November 5, 2011, alone, approximately 40,000 people joined credit unions, with credit unions realizing $80 million in new account funds. Another CUNA study found that at least 650,000 customers joined credit unions between September 29, the day that Bank of America said it was going to add a five-dollar fee for debit card purchases, and the first week of November. That's more customers than joined credit unions in all of 2010.

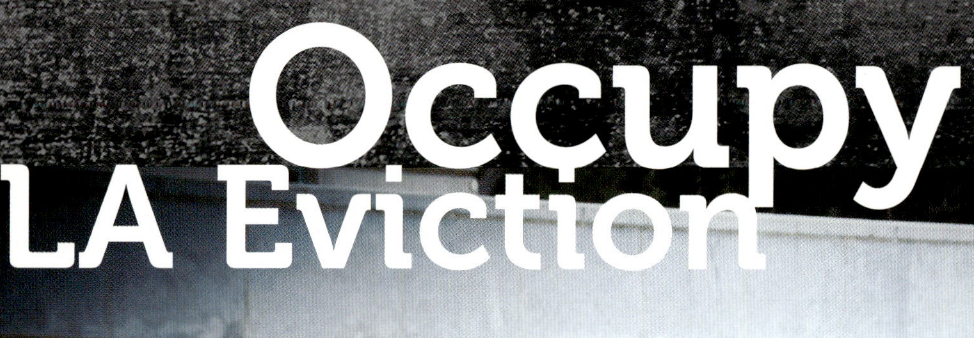

Occupy LA Eviction

On November 30, 2011, in Los Angeles, California, a city worker drags a tent belonging to the evicted Occupy L.A. encampment to throw it into the dumpster. In pre-raid negotiations with the LAPD, members of Occupy L.A. had requested that any tents and supplies vacated by occupiers and confiscated by police be given to the homeless. It was therefore another sign of betrayal when perfectly good tents were tossed into the trash by city workers during the early morning cleanup after the raid. Photos: Nicole Powers.

A protester's gas mask lies among the ruins of the Occupy L.A. encampment.

Bikes, backpacks, and tents lie in the rubble of the Occupy L.A. encampment. All were thrown away by city cleaning crews.

Oakland Occupy Events

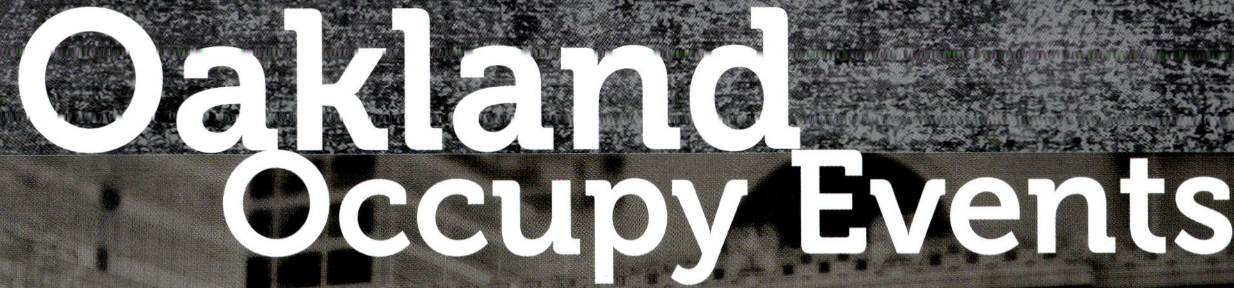

On October 14, 2011, in Oakland, California, Occupy Oakland sets up encampment in front of City Hall at Frank Ogawa Plaza, which the occupiers renamed "Oscar Grant Plaza" after a man who was fatally shot by police in 2009. Photo: Glenn Halog.

On the day of action, thousands of protesters marched to the Port of Oakland and blocked traffic coming in and out, effectively shutting America's fifth-busiest port down. Photo: Quinn Norton.

Members of Occupy Oakland in California called for a general strike on November 2, 2011. Several unions expressed their support, including Service Employees International, the United Brotherhood of Carpenters, the Oakland Education Association, and the International Longshore and Warehouse Union. Though none of the labor organizations officially went as far as endorsing a general strike, they did encourage members to take personal days off work to show solidarity. Photo: Quinn Norton.

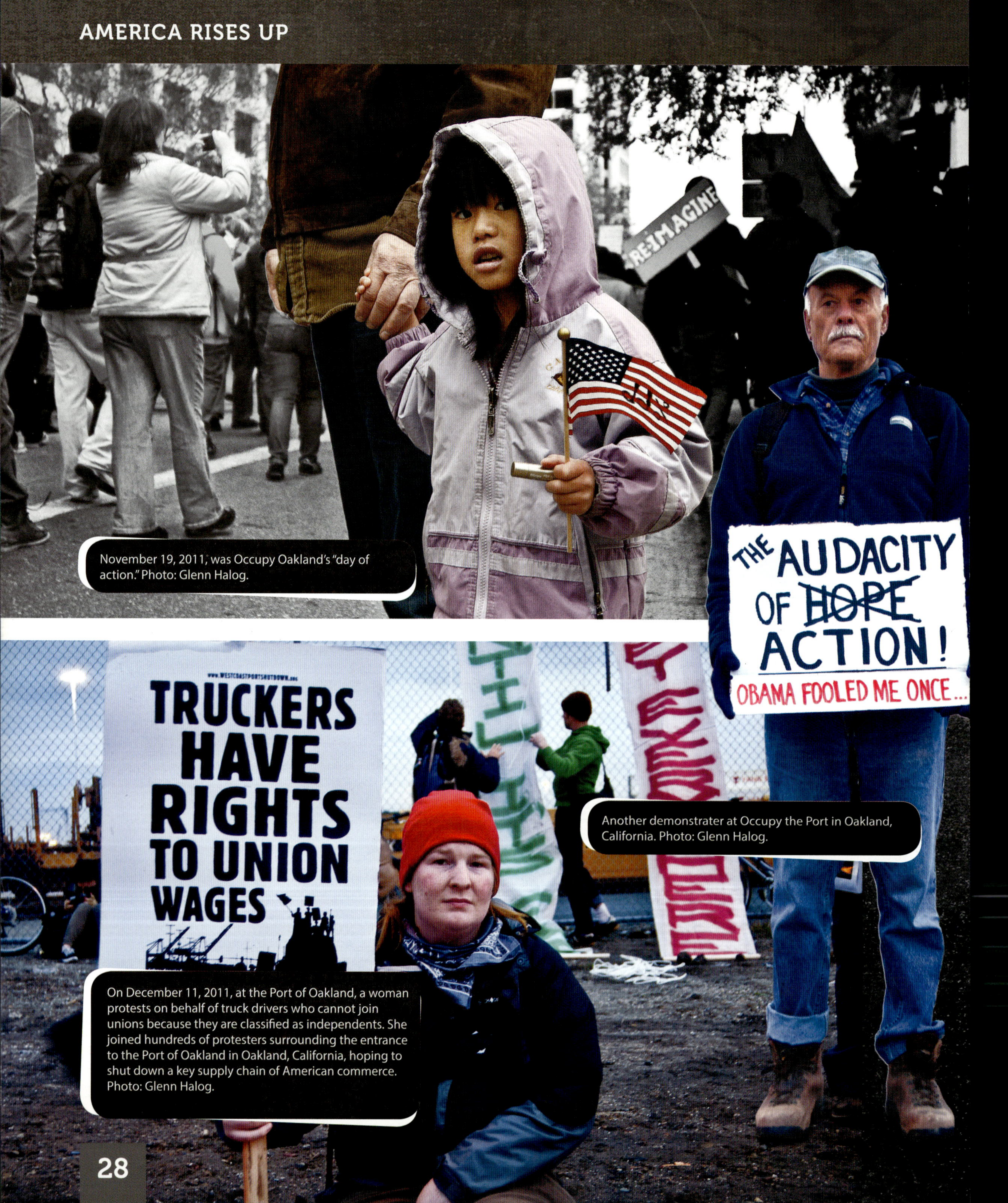

November 19, 2011, was Occupy Oakland's "day of action." Photo: Glenn Halog.

Another demonstrater at Occupy the Port in Oakland, California. Photo: Glenn Halog.

On December 11, 2011, at the Port of Oakland, a woman protests on behalf of truck drivers who cannot join unions because they are classified as independents. She joined hundreds of protesters surrounding the entrance to the Port of Oakland in Oakland, California, hoping to shut down a key supply chain of American commerce. Photo: Glenn Halog.

Million Hoodie March

On March 27, 2012, in Los Angeles, California, a little boy attends one of the nationwide protests that took place after the killing of Trayvon Martin. Trayvon Martin was a 17-year-old African American high school student who was shot and killed on February 26, 2012, while walking through a suburban Florida neighborhood at night. The shooter, George Zimmerman, a 28-year-old man of South American descent, was the neighborhood watch coordinator of a gated community in Sanford, Florida, where Martin was temporarily residing. Zimmerman claimed self-defense, and the police initially declined to prosecute. Seeking to put pressure on Florida's Attorney General, Martin's mother created a Change.org petition that called for Zimmerman's arrest. Nearly 2.3 million signatures were collected. After intense media coverage focused on possible but unproven racial motivations for the shooting, supporters began a social-media campaign on Twitter using the hashtag #millionhoodies, a reference to the hoodie Martin was wearing at the time of the incident. The protests subsequently spilled out onto the street, with "million hoodie marches" occurring in multiple cities. On July 13, 2013, Zimmerman was acquitted of second degree murder and manslaughter charges. The verdict spurred public outcry and nationwide protests on the part of many who felt justice had not been served. Photos: Amber Stephens.

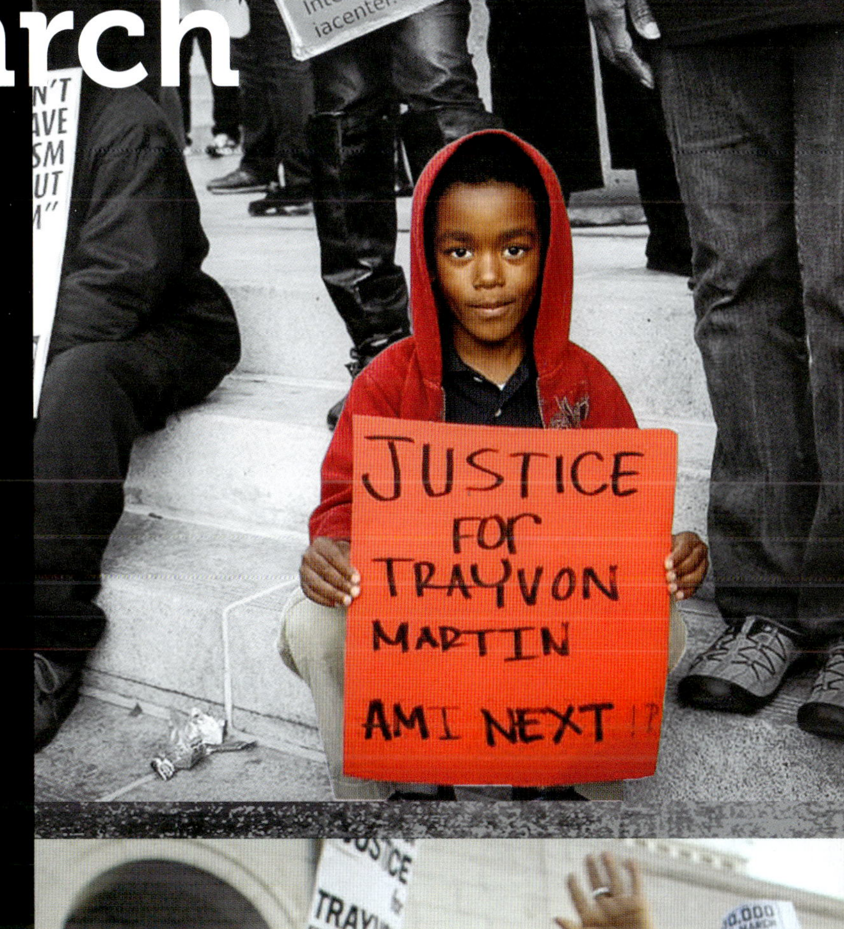

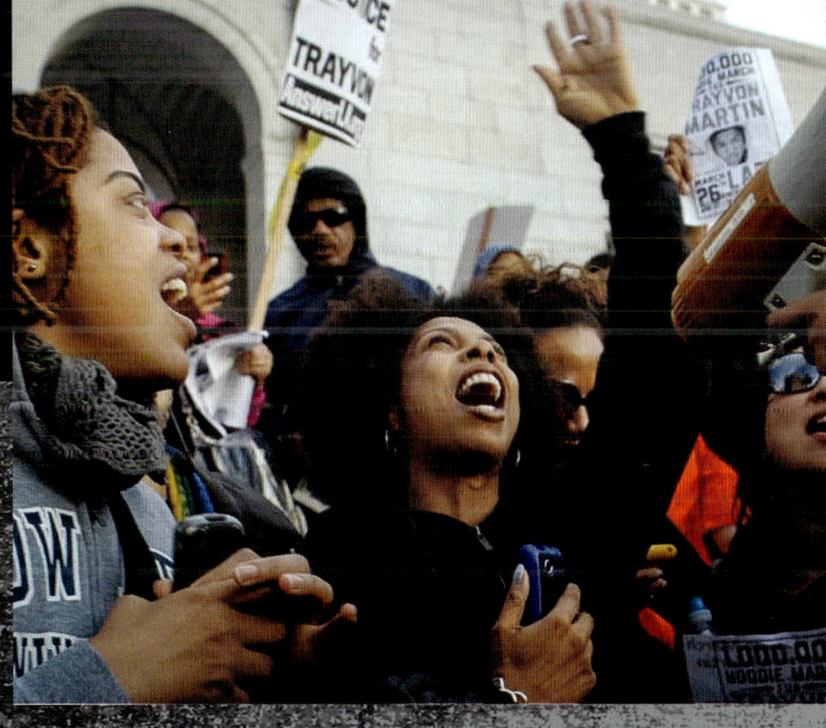

May Day Protest

May 1 is a national holiday in many countries. Dubbed International Workers' Day, it honors the organized labor movement. It is somewhat ironic that although International Workers' Day commemorates those that were massacred by police in 1886 at a rally in Chicago in support of workers striking for an eight-hour day, it is not recognized as a public holiday in the United States. The Occupy movement therefore chose May 1 as a day of action to highlight the widening gap between those who work for a living and those who don't need to work. Occupiers also hoped to use the day to raise awareness for the rights fought for by unions that are under attack.

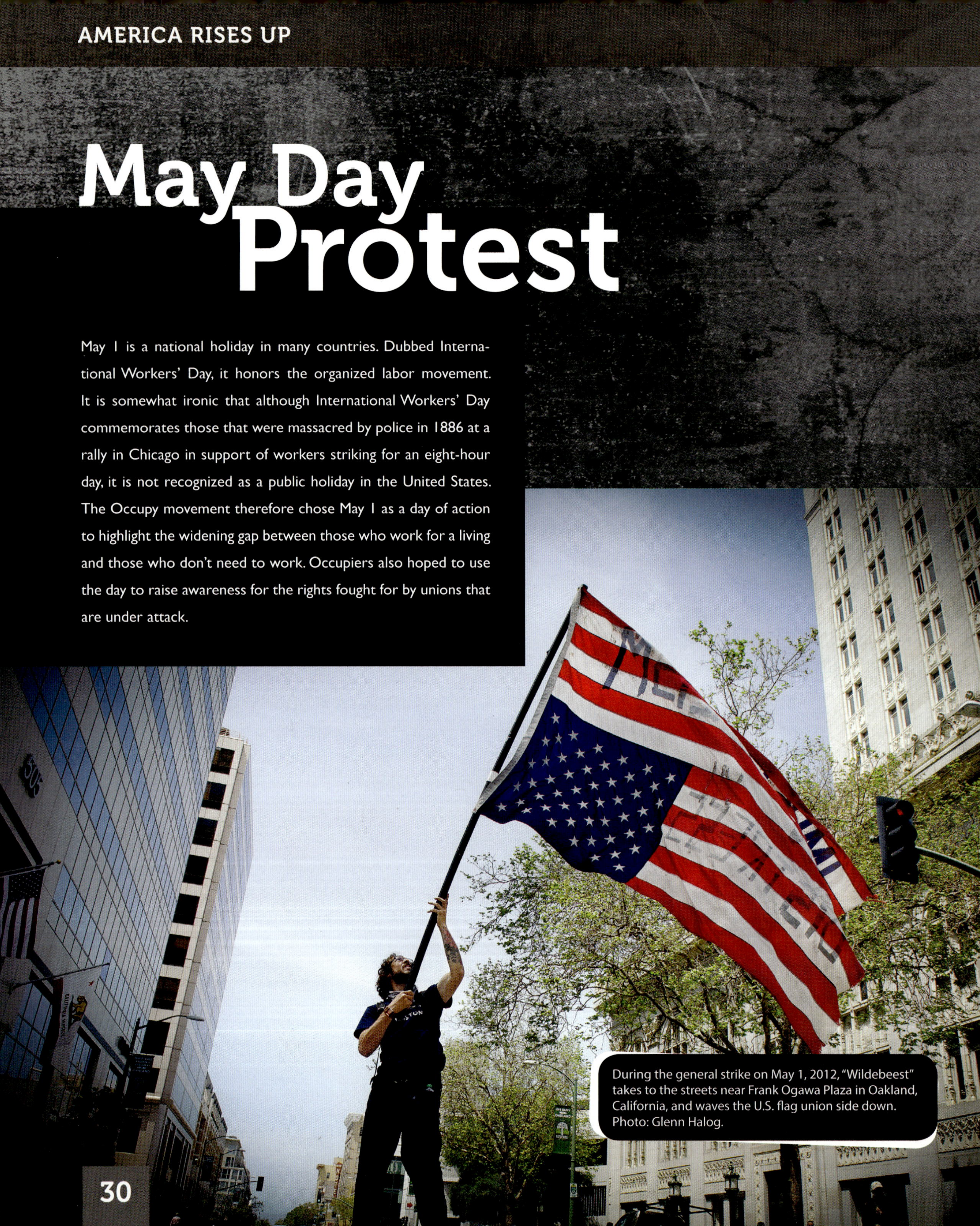

During the general strike on May 1, 2012, "Wildebeest" takes to the streets near Frank Ogawa Plaza in Oakland, California, and waves the U.S. flag union side down. Photo: Glenn Halog.

Bilderberg Protests

The Bilderberg protests took place May 31 through June 3, 2012, in Chantilly, Virginia. The first meeting of the Bilderberg Group took place in 1954 at the Hotel de Bilderberg near Arnhem in the Netherlands. The well-connected Polish political advisor Joseph Retinger is credited as being a key player in the foundation of the group. Retinger also helped found the European Movement, which was responsible in part for the creation of the European Union. The aim of the Bilderberg Group is to host off-the-record discussions to foster stronger transatlantic bonds. Each year around 120 invited guests gather at a different location, which is expressly chosen for its ability to provide privacy. Those selected to participate in the Bilderberg conferences normally include heads of state, prominent politicians, and captains of industry. The secretive, behind-closed-doors nature of the meetings are a cause for concern for many, who feel such cabals of the rich and powerful can circumvent prescribed instruments of democracy. The 2012 Bilderberg conference, which took place between May 31 and June 3 at the Westfields Marriott in Chantilly, Virginia, therefore attracted protesters demanding greater transparency. Photos: Edmond Maurice Peyroux.

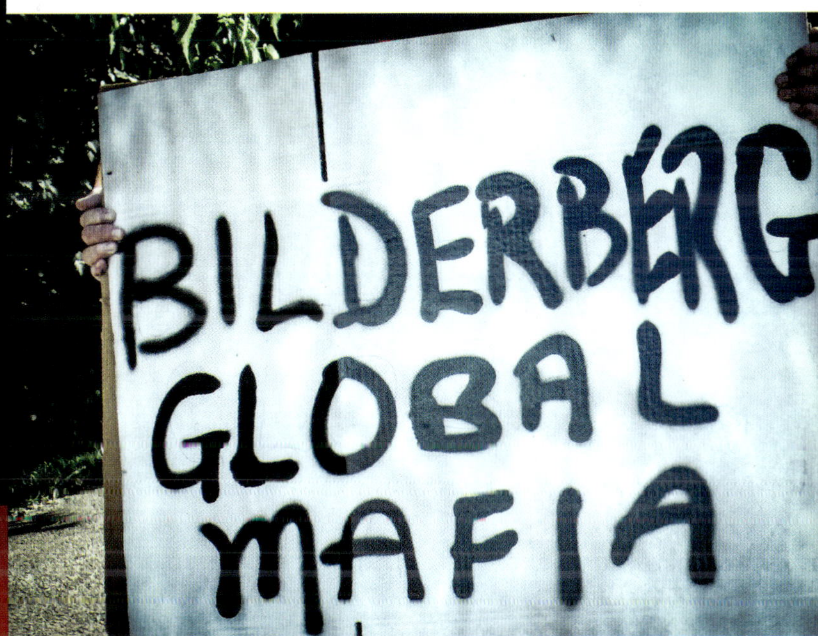

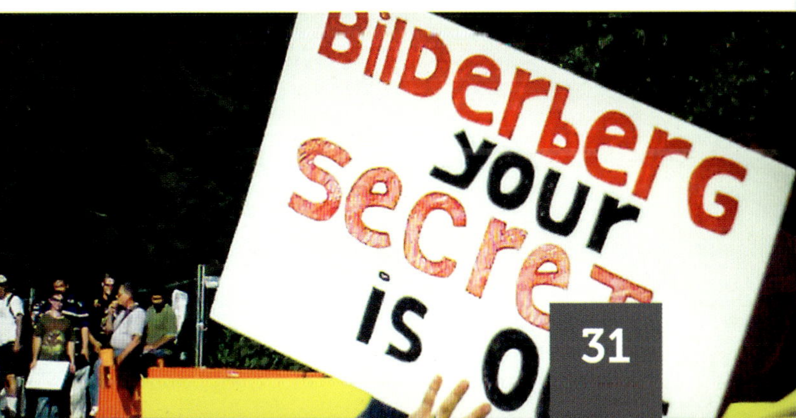

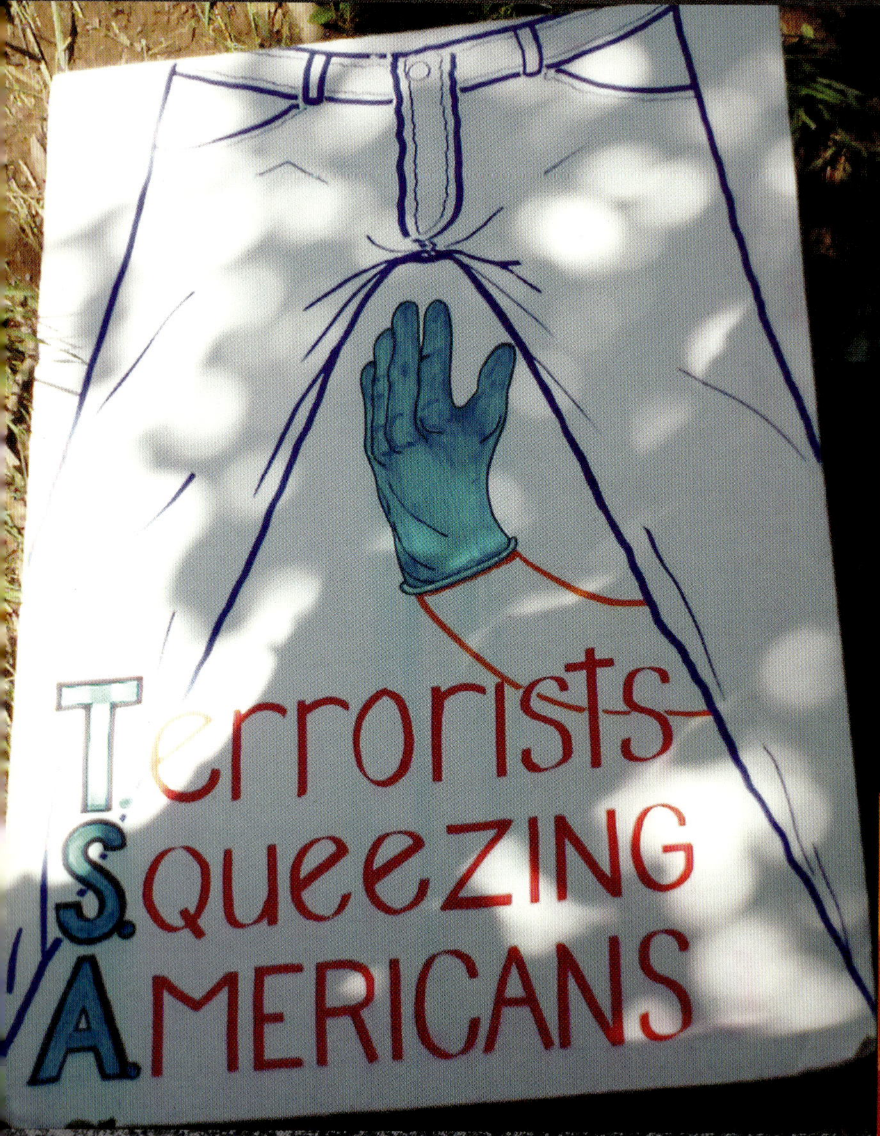

T. errorists
S. queezing
A. mericans

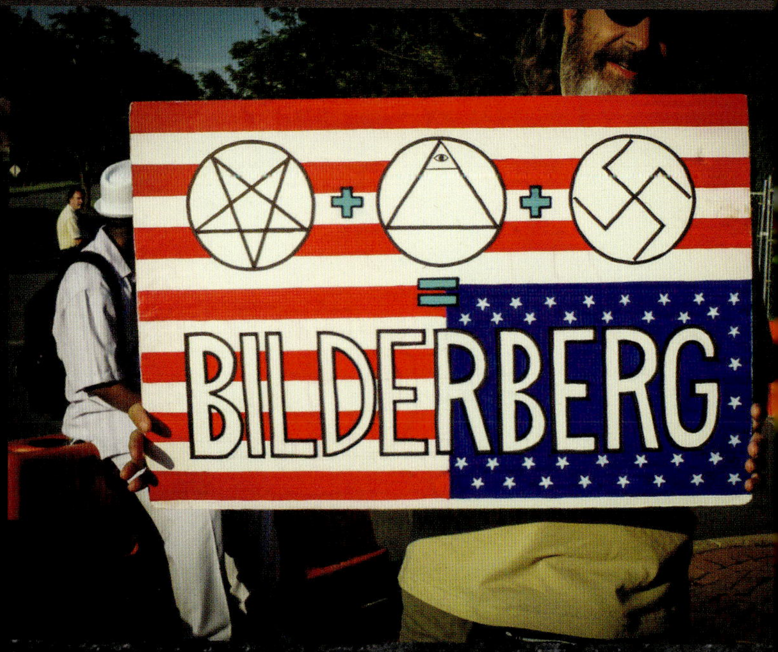

BILDERBERG

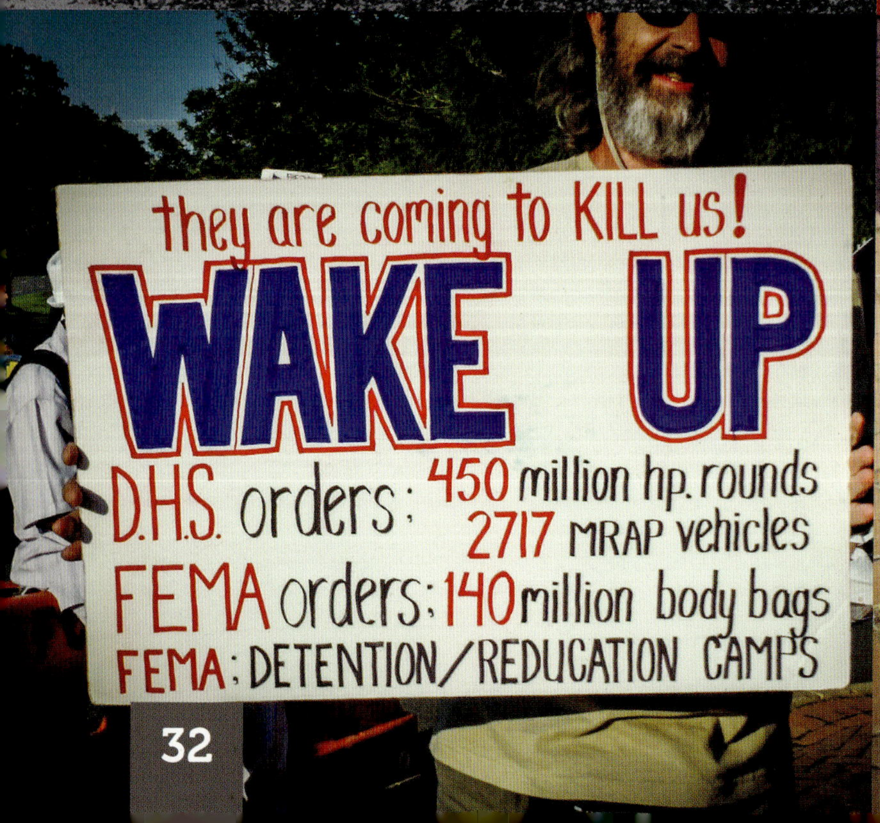

GOOGLE
BILDERBERG

they are coming to KILL us!
WAKE UP
D.H.S. orders: 450 million hp. rounds
2717 MRAP vehicles
FEMA orders: 140 million body bags
FEMA: DETENTION/REDUCATION CAMPS

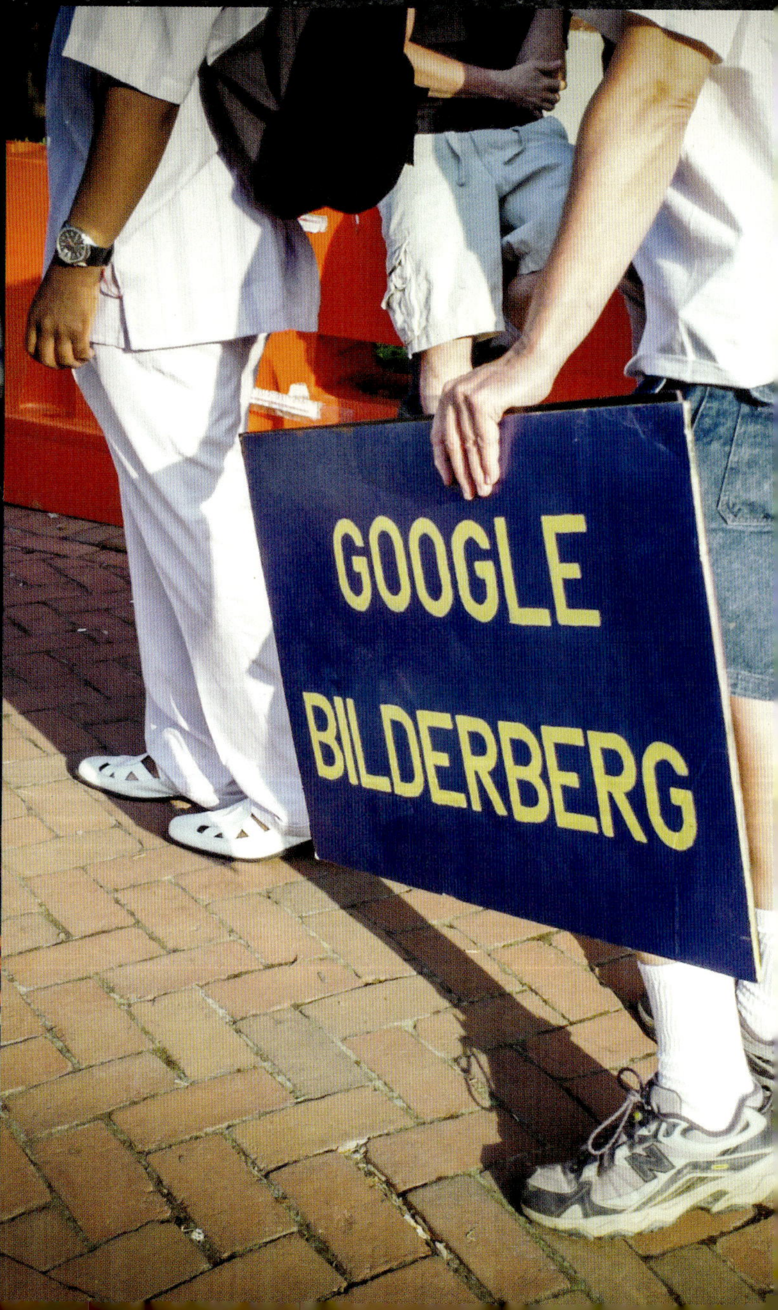

Pride Parade

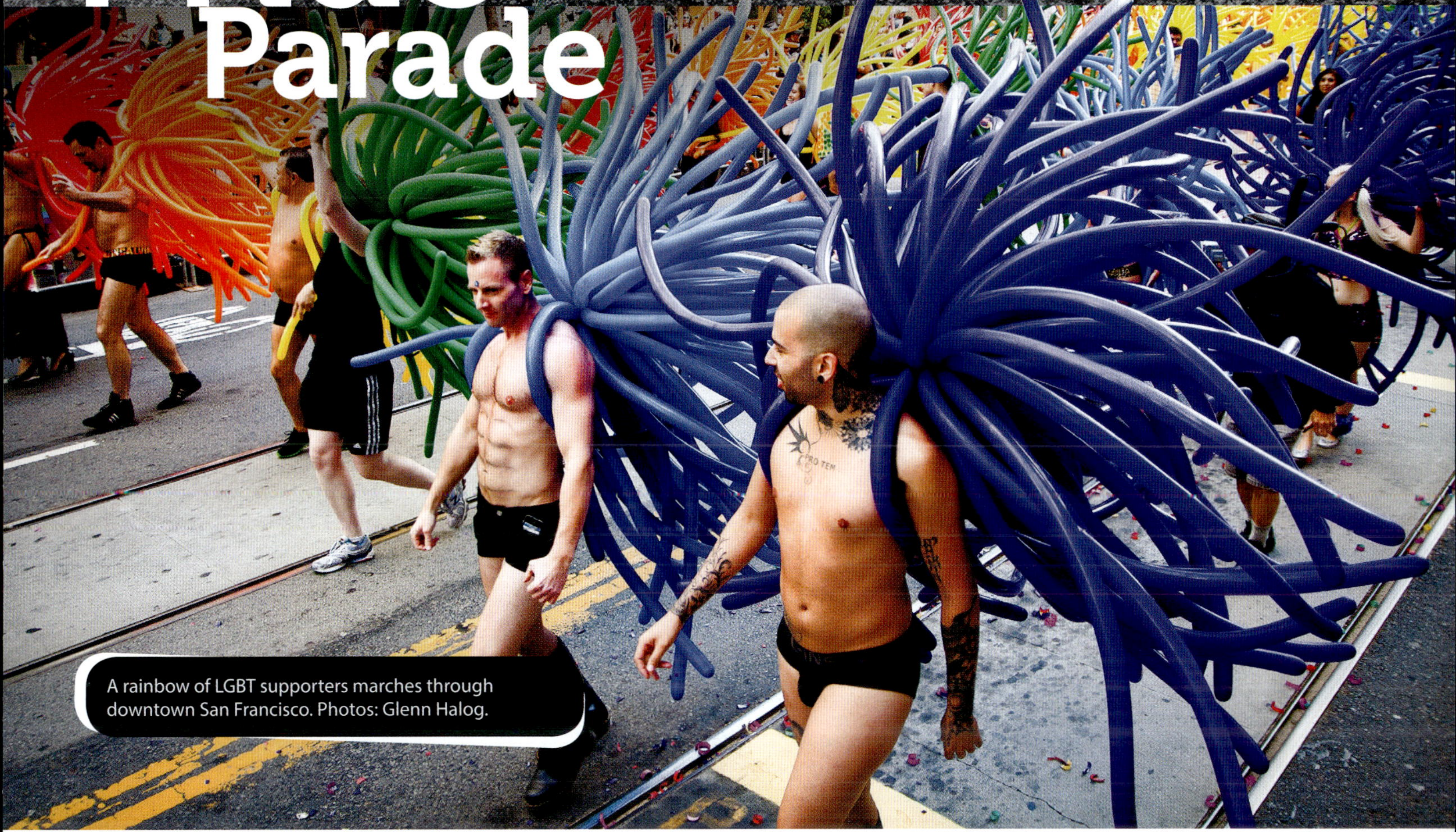

A rainbow of LGBT supporters marches through downtown San Francisco. Photos: Glenn Halog.

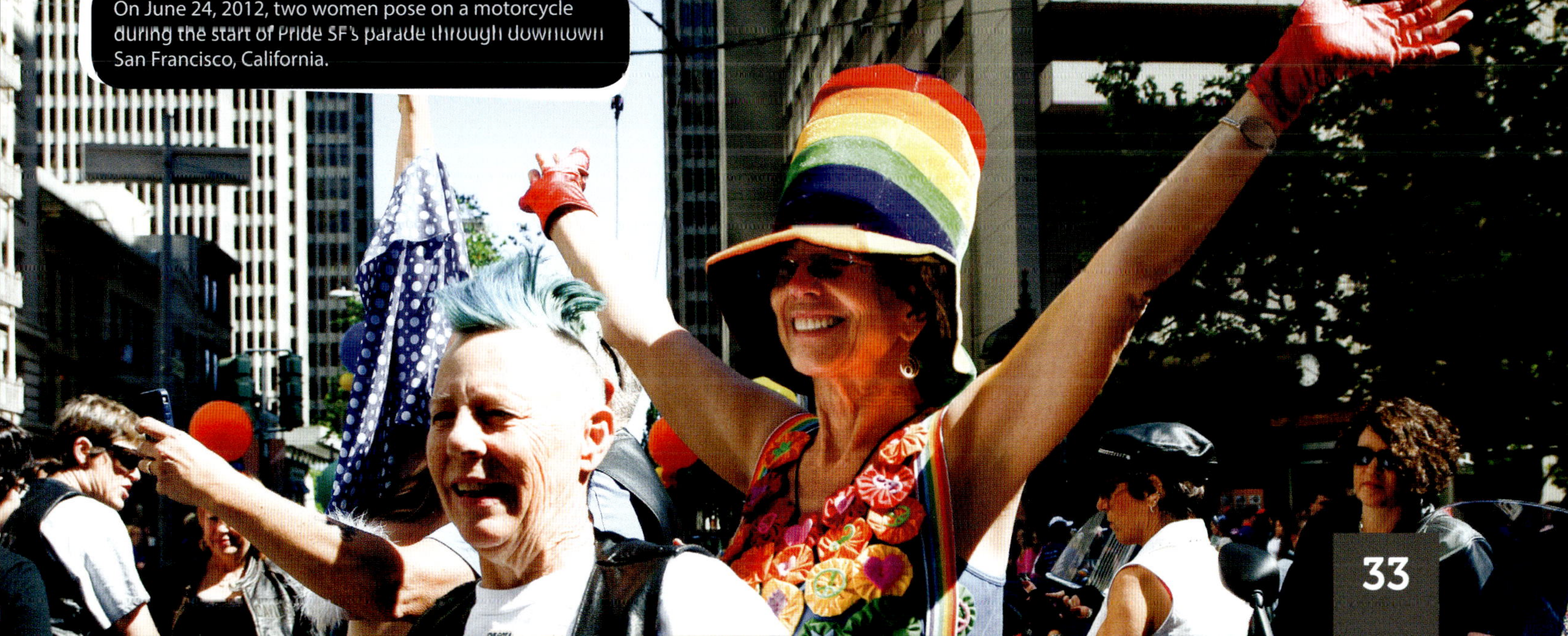

On June 24, 2012, two women pose on a motorcycle during the start of Pride SF's parade through downtown San Francisco, California.

Protesters in San Francisco try to drown out the message of the antigay protesters during the pride march.

A "pride dog" dresses up for the festivities.

This group of Church Ladies for Gay Rights attends Pride SF in support of gay marriage.

Tea Party Celebration

A layer of security guards manned the entrance to a Tea Party event hosted to celebrate America on July 4, 2012. Most Occupy activists and journalists asking to attend were denied entry. With a name inspired by the Boston Tea Party, the Tea Party is ostensibly a grassroots populist right-wing-to-Libertarian movement. It advocates less government, less taxes, and less federal spending. Staunchly patriotic, on its website the Tea Party boasts of "a strong belief in the foundational Judeo-Christian values" and was born out of the vacuum created by Ron Paul's failed 2008 presidential primary campaign. Detractors claim that the movement is more astroturf than grassroots, being backed by big-money political organizations such as the Koch Brothers–backed FreedomWorks and Americans for Prosperity.

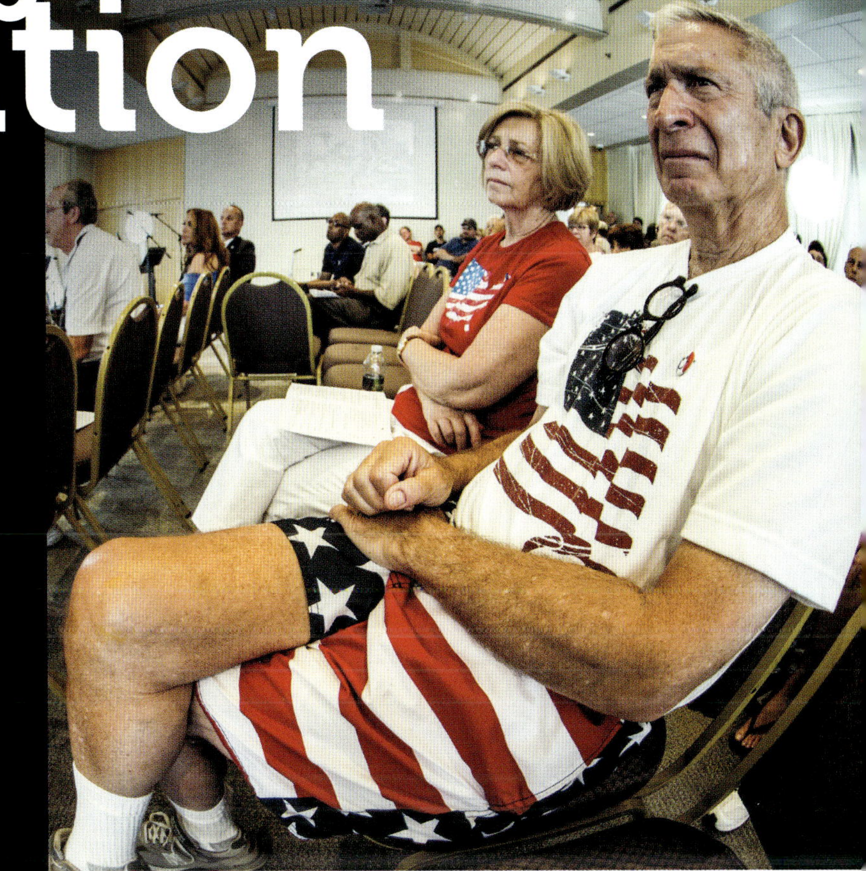

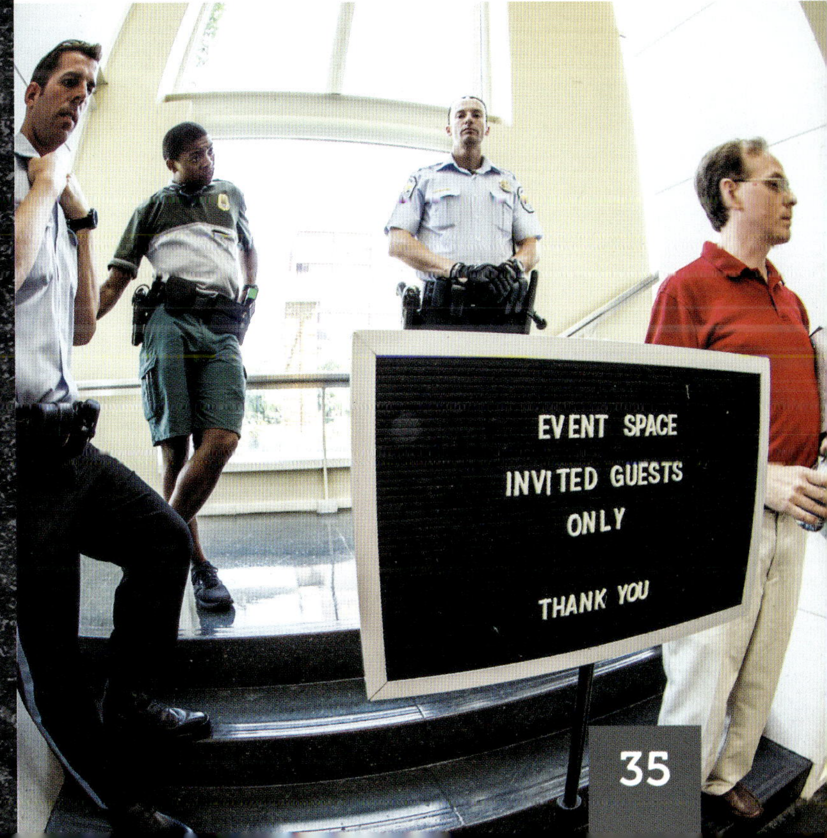

SlutWalk

On August 11, 2012, in Washington D.C., women dressed in "slutty" garb walk through the nation's capital for the annual "SlutWalk" for sex victims' rights. SlutWalk began in response to a comment made by a representative of the Toronto Police Service. While giving advice on rape prevention during a personal safety forum at York University on January 24, 2011, Constable Michael Sanguinetti said, "women should avoid dressing like sluts in order not to be victimized." Outraged by the insensitivity and inherent victim blaming exhibited by Sanguinetti's misguided statement, activists Sonya Barnett and Heather Jarvis co-founded SlutWalk and held their first march on April 3, 2011. The two chose to reclaim the word "slut" when naming their organization to challenge the judgment and double standards that surround its use. Since its inception, SlutWalk Toronto has inspired numerous sister groups and actions in 200 cities around the world. Photos: Andrew Bossi.

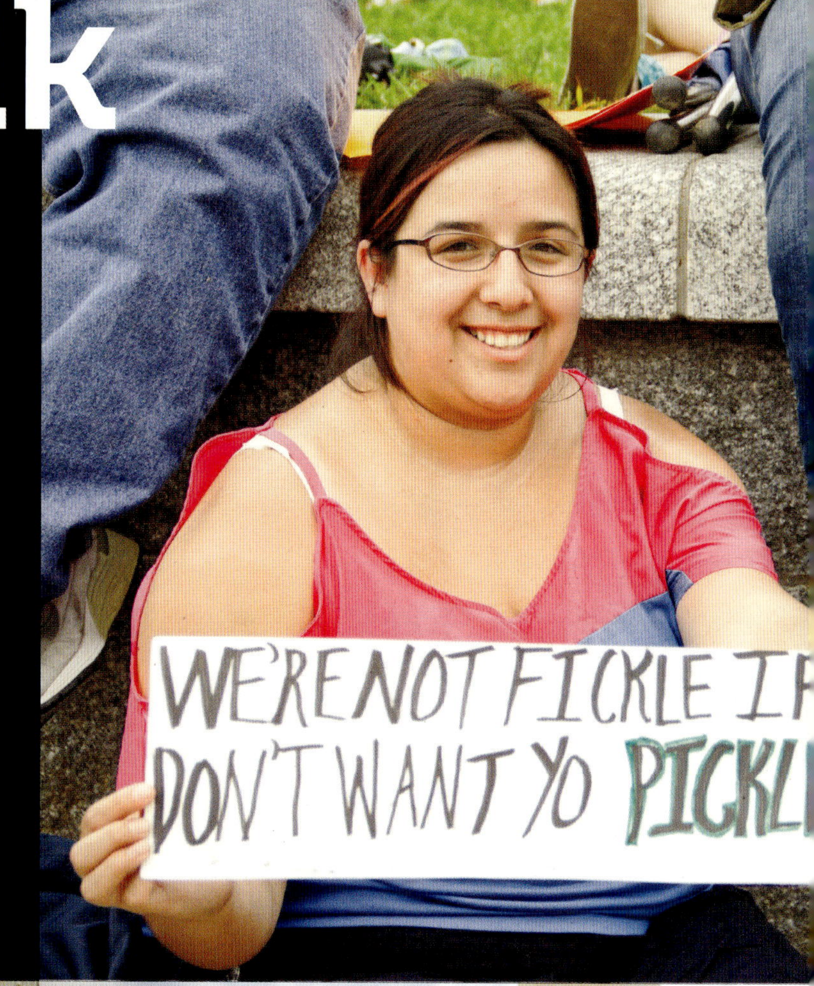

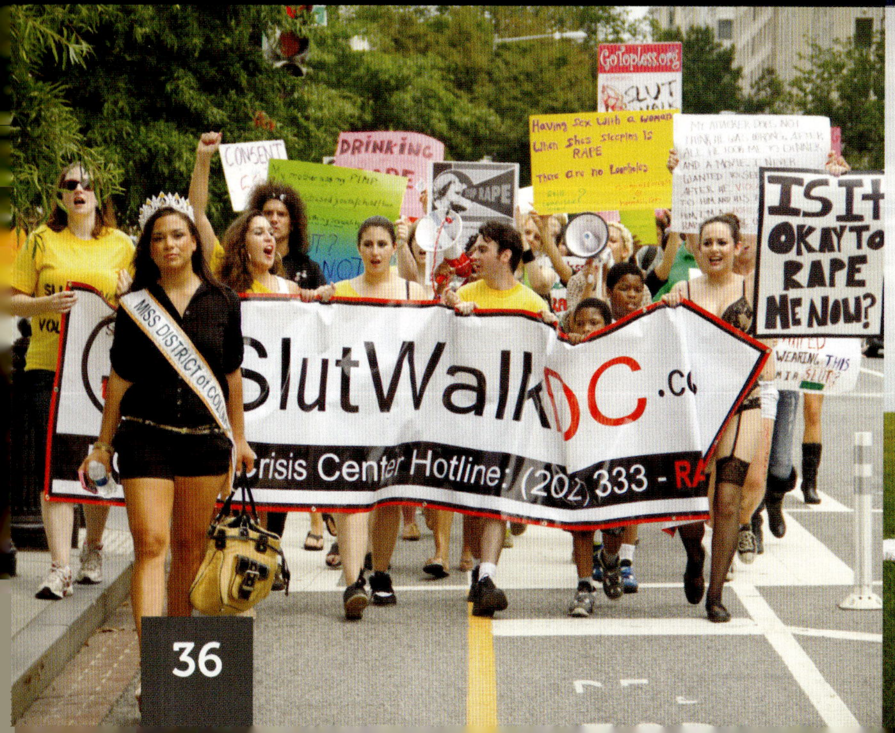

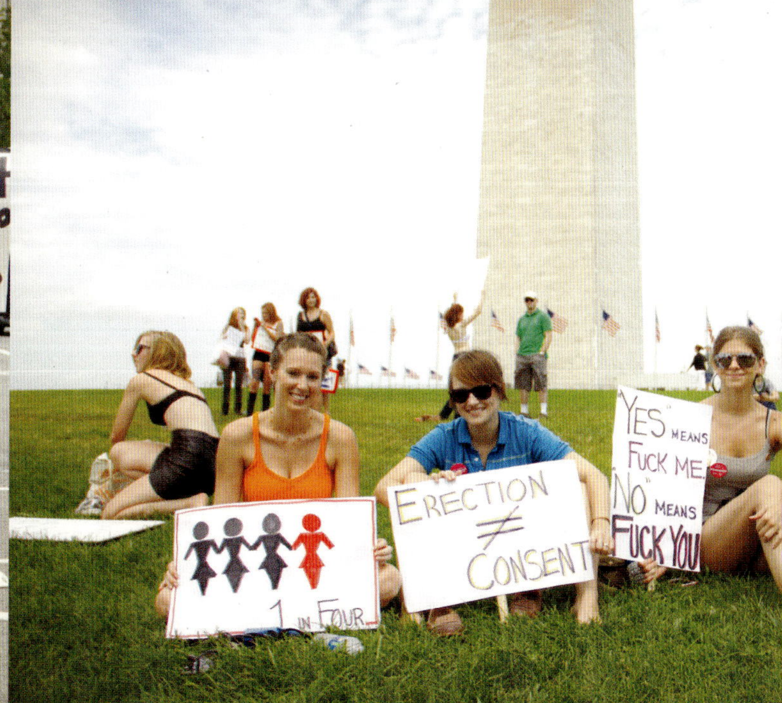

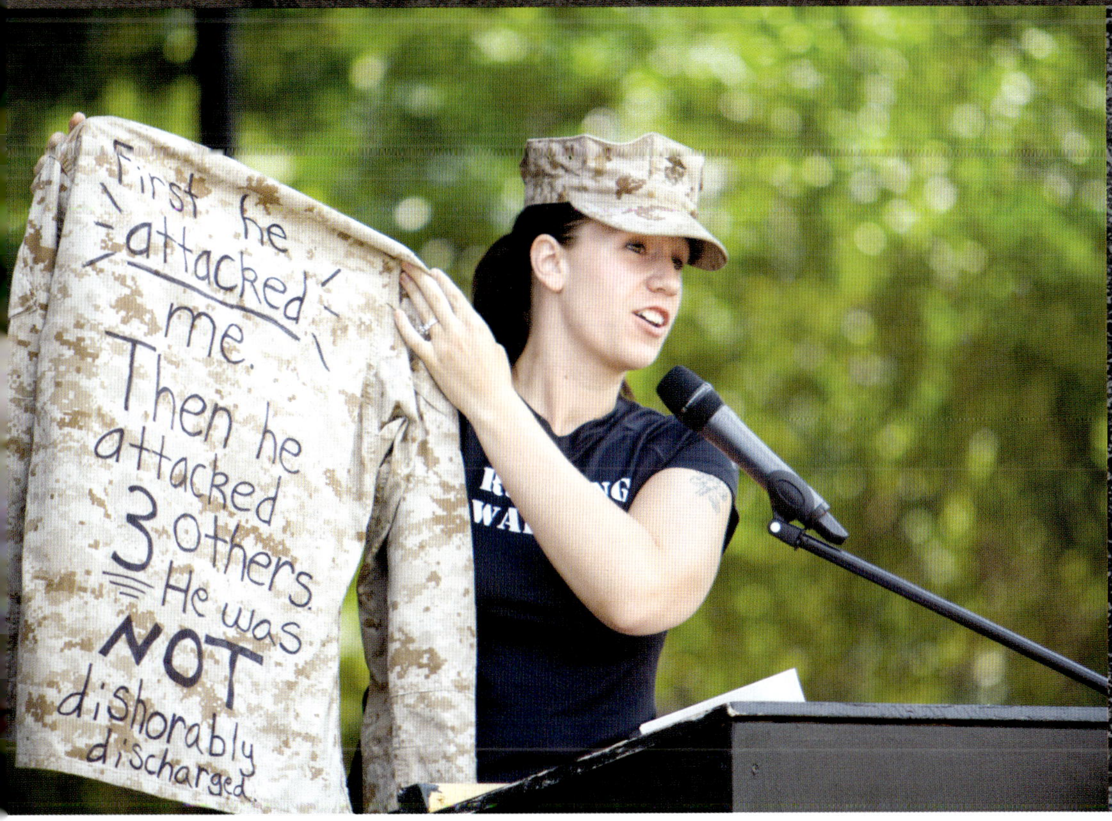

First he attacked me. Then he attacked 3 others. He was NOT dishonorably discharged.
Sluts unite 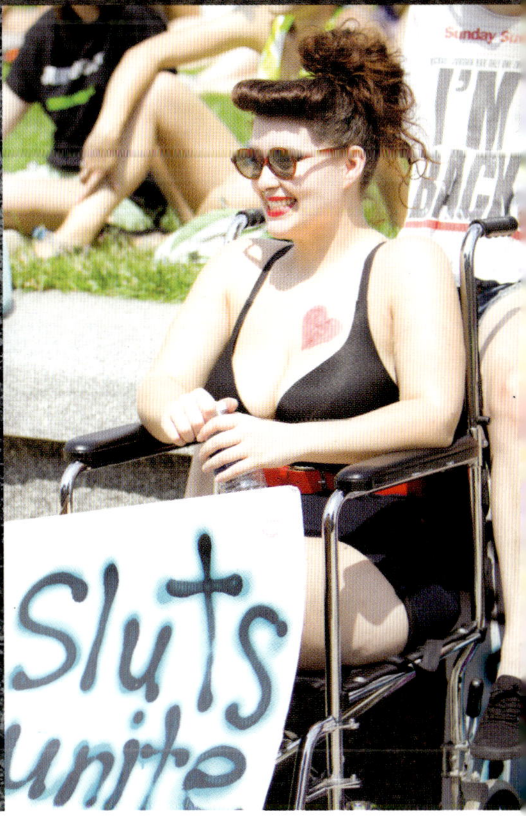 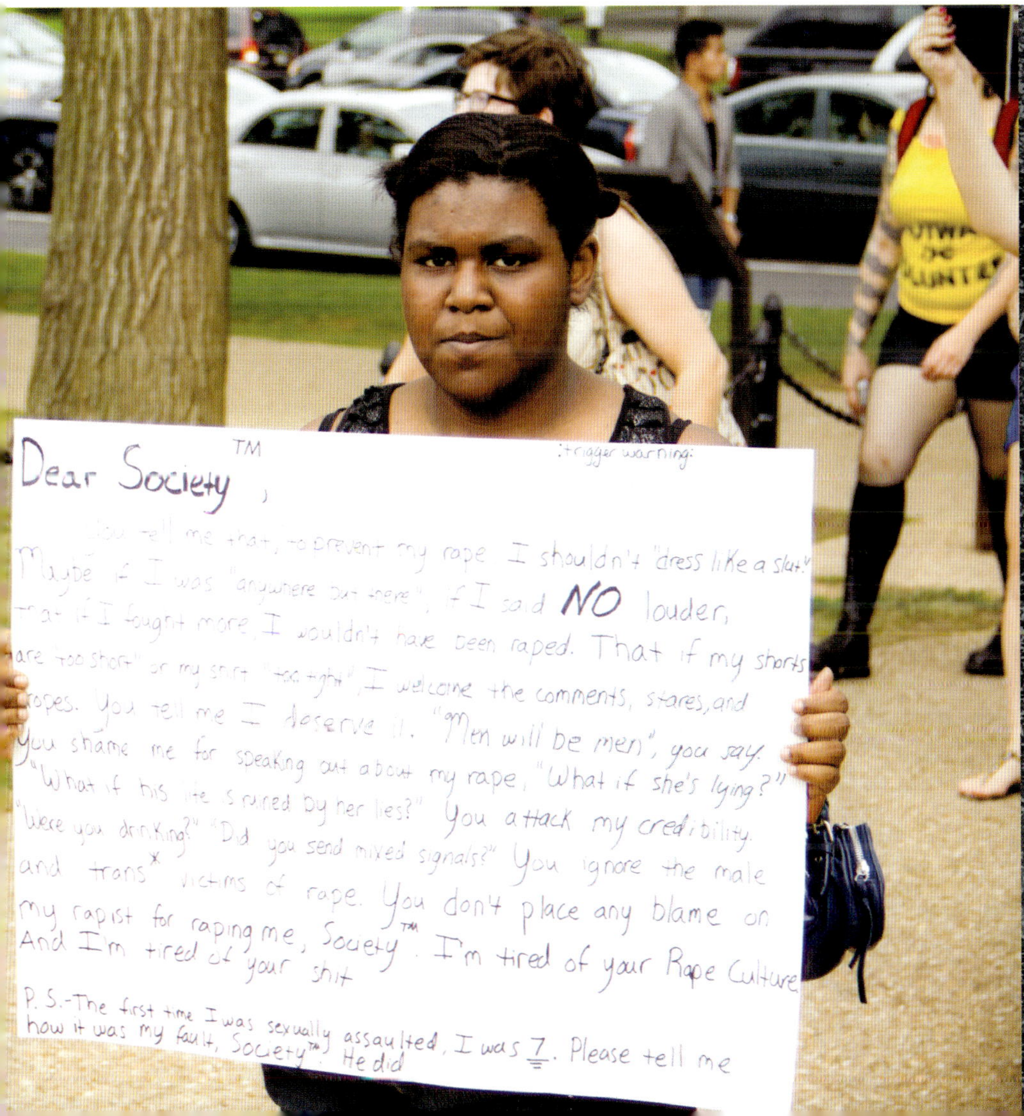
I WAS RAPED WEARING THIS AM I A SLUT?
Dear Society™,
:trigger warning:
You tell me that, to prevent my rape I shouldn't "dress like a slut." Maybe if I was "anywhere but there", if I said NO louder, that if I fought more, I wouldn't have been raped. That if my shorts are "too short" or my shirt "too tight", I welcome the comments, stares, and gropes. You tell me I deserve it. "Men will be men", you say. You shame me for speaking out about my rape, "What if she's lying?" "What if his life is ruined by her lies?" You attack my credibility. "Were you drinking?" "Did you send mixed signals?" You ignore the male and trans* victims of rape. You don't place any blame on my rapist for raping me, Society™. I'm tired of your Rape Culture. And I'm tired of your shit
P.S.-The first time I was sexually assaulted, I was 7. Please tell me how it was my fault, Society™. He did

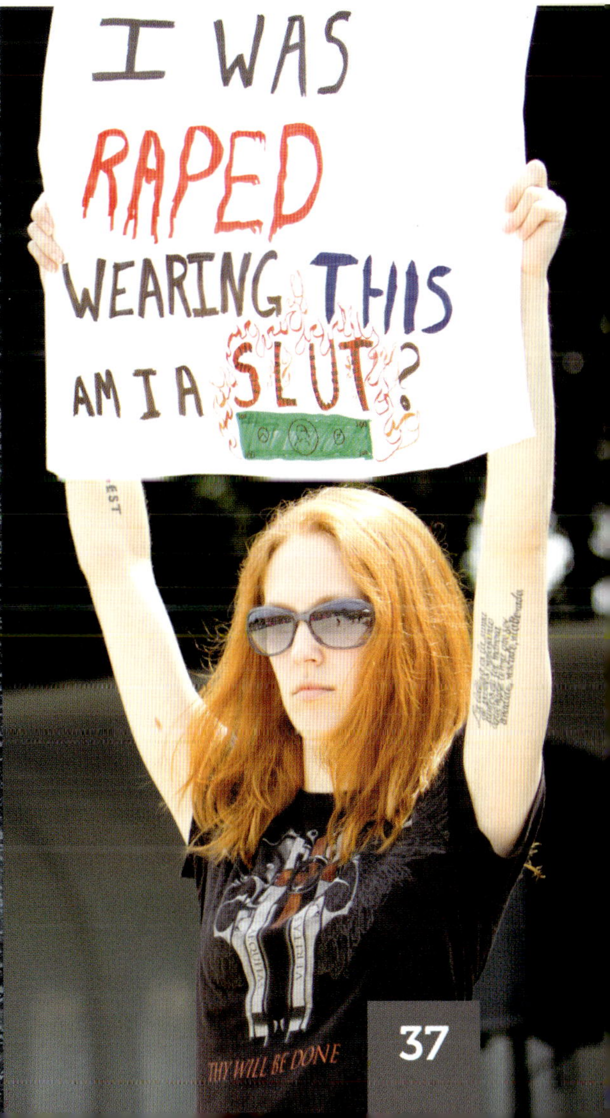

Occupy One-Year Anniversary

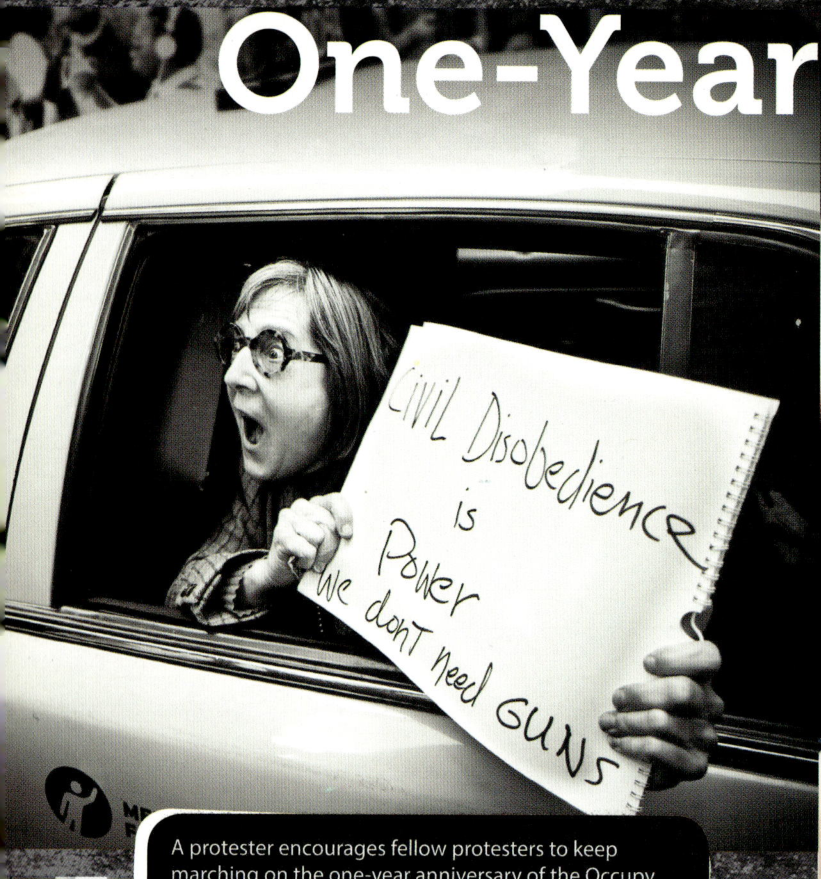

A protester encourages fellow protesters to keep marching on the one-year anniversary of the Occupy movement, September 17, 2012, in New York City.

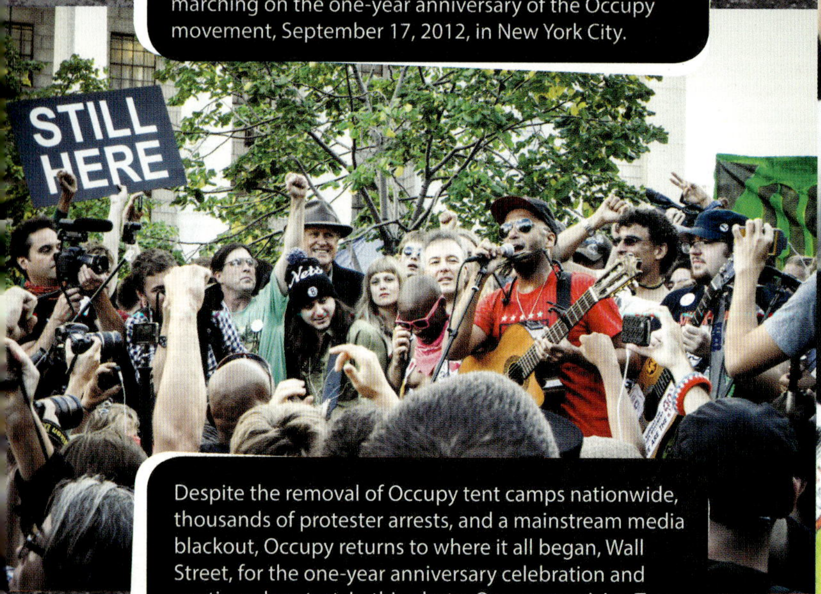

Despite the removal of Occupy tent camps nationwide, thousands of protester arrests, and a mainstream media blackout, Occupy returns to where it all began, Wall Street, for the one-year anniversary celebration and continued protest. In this photo, Occupy musician Tom Morello, a face of the movement, hosts a concert. Photo: Nicole Powers.

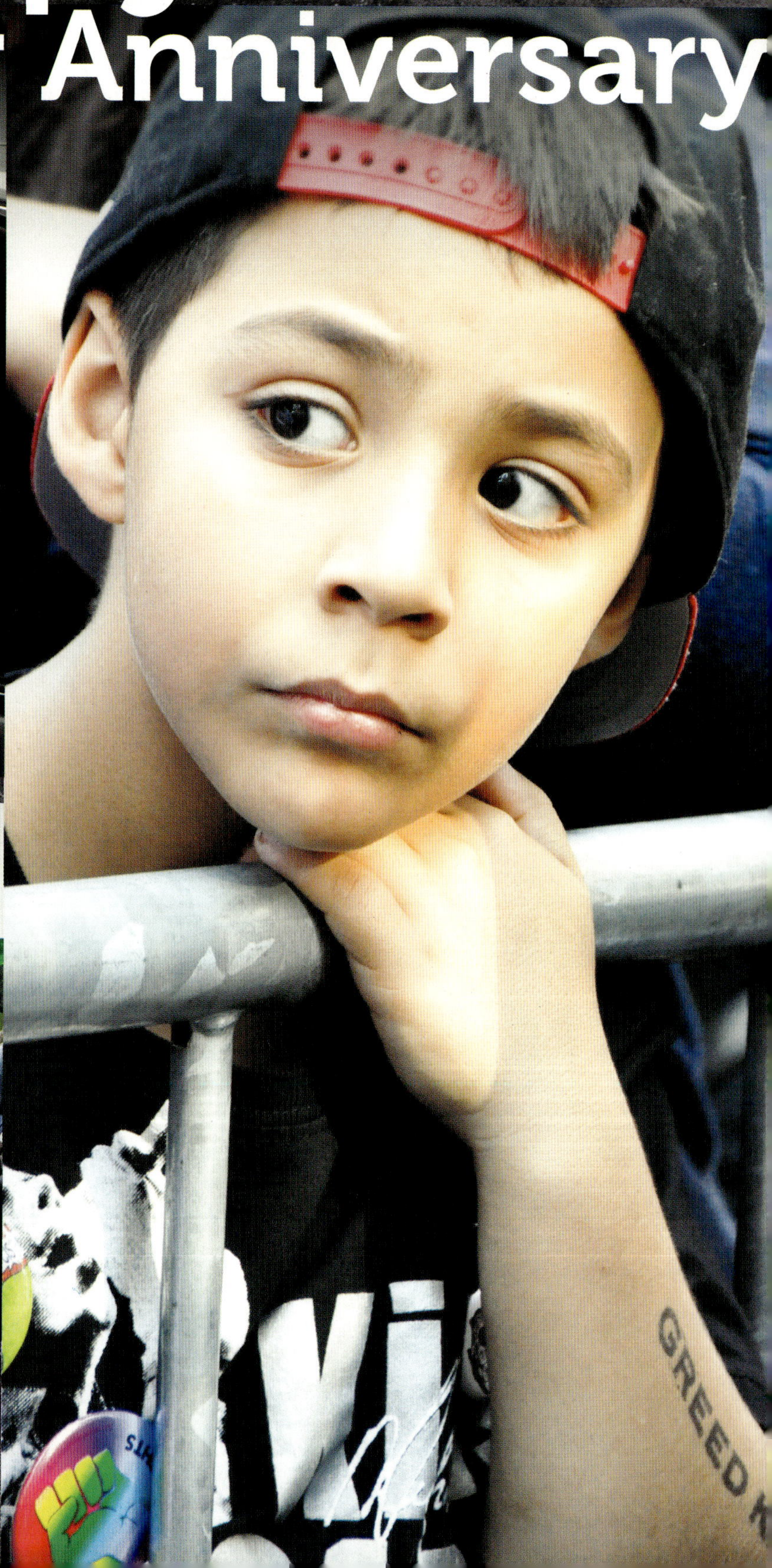

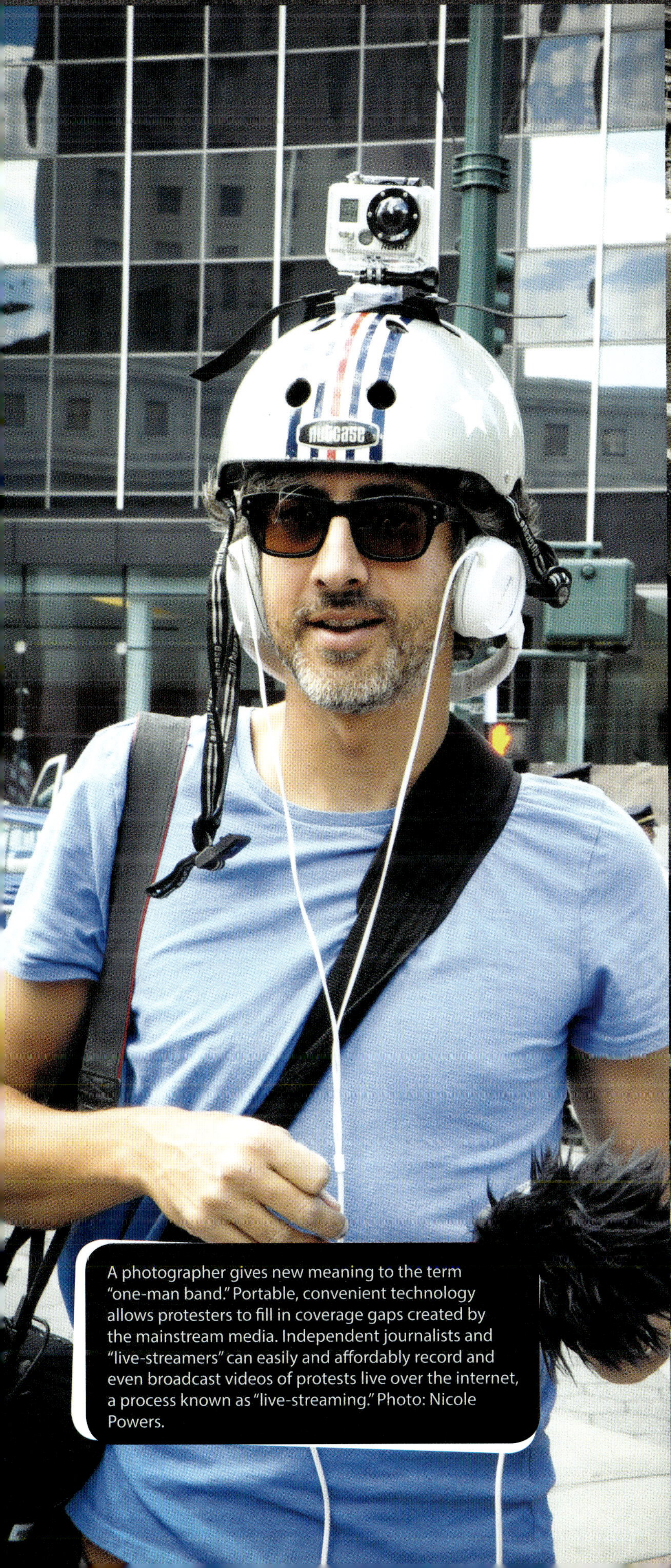

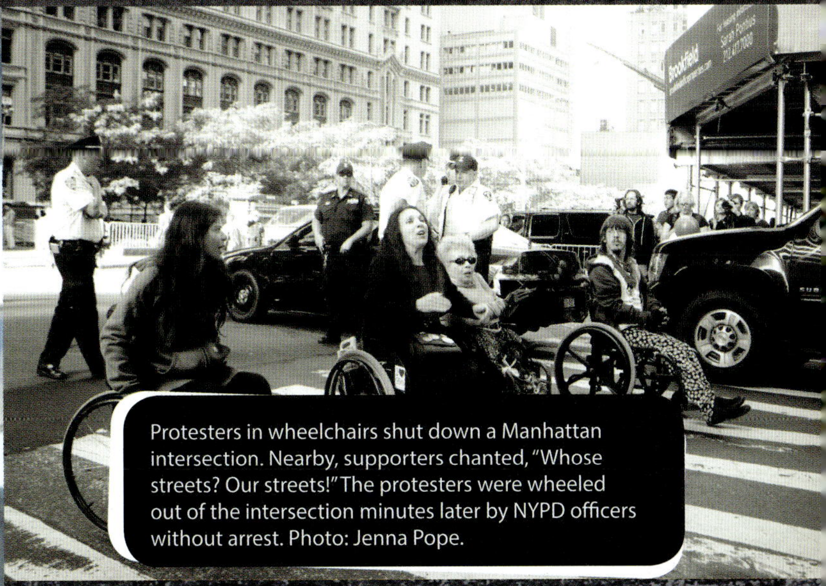

Protesters in wheelchairs shut down a Manhattan intersection. Nearby, supporters chanted, "Whose streets? Our streets!" The protesters were wheeled out of the intersection minutes later by NYPD officers without arrest. Photo: Jenna Pope.

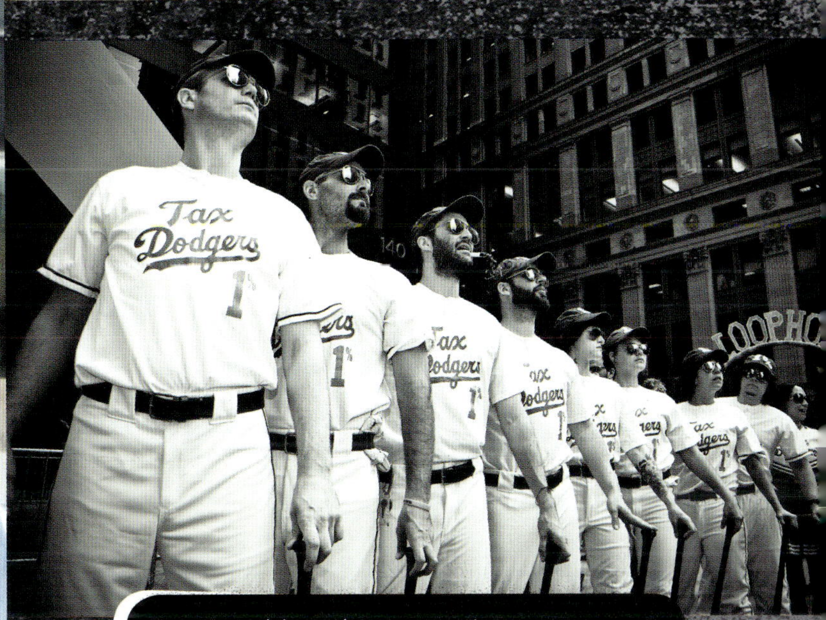

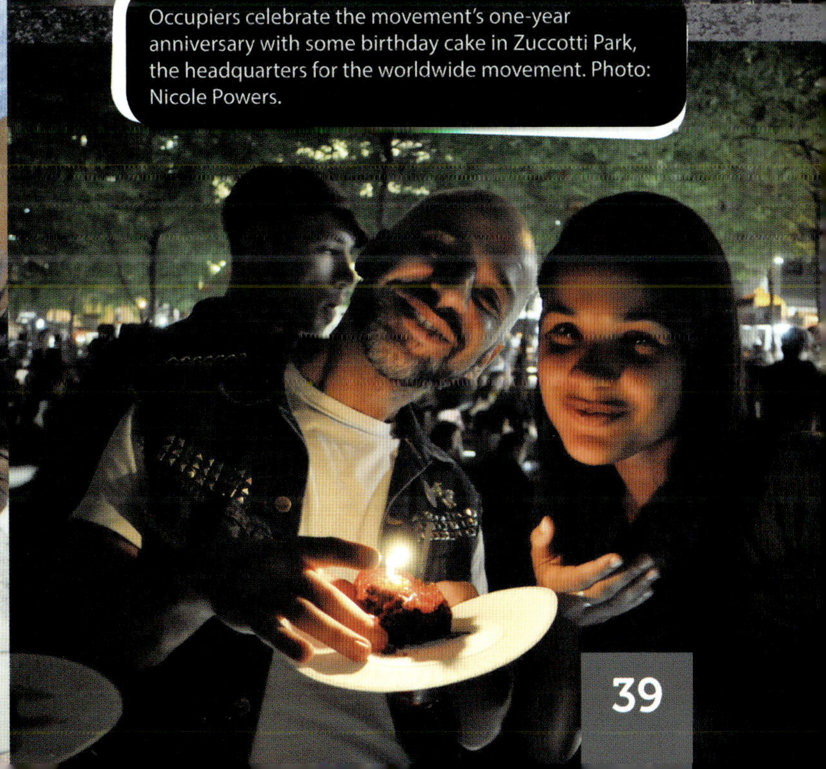

Occupiers celebrate the movement's one-year anniversary with some birthday cake in Zuccotti Park, the headquarters for the worldwide movement. Photo: Nicole Powers.

A photographer gives new meaning to the term "one-man band." Portable, convenient technology allows protesters to fill in coverage gaps created by the mainstream media. Independent journalists and "live-streamers" can easily and affordably record and even broadcast videos of protests live over the internet, a process known as "live-streaming." Photo: Nicole Powers.

Overpass Light Brigade

In Madison, Wisconsin, Overpass Light Brigade volunteers remind Wisconsin drivers that "corporations are not people." The bright idea of two University of Wisconsin–Milwaukee facility members, Lisa Moline and Lane Hall, the Overpass Light Brigade began as a creative endeavor to draw attention to the effort to recall union-busting Wisconsin governor Scott Walker. The duo's first artistic collaboration to protest Walker's election was a static sign that simply said, "Recall Walker." Unable to legally attach their LED creations to public property and wanting to make the project more collaborative, Moline and Hall graduated to using multiple single-letter signs and a team of volunteers dubbed "the holders of light" to spell out their messages. Displaying their illuminated slogans after dark in high-traffic areas for maximum impact, the Overpass Light Brigade preserve their work for posterity—and propagate it on the internet—through photographs and video. Photo: Jenna Pope.

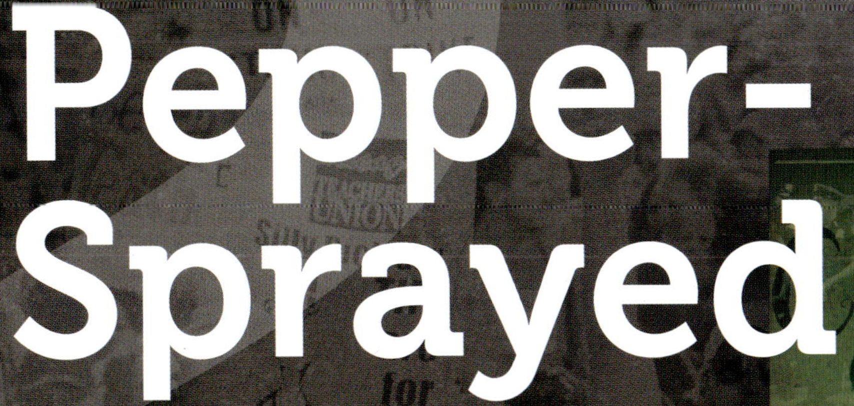

Pepper-Sprayed

Pepper spray is both friend and foe to protest movements nationwide. The more police use it, the angrier the public gets, and the more media attention is given to the protesters.

Pepper spray (also called OC spray after *oleoresin capsicum*, the active ingredient) is an inflammatory agent that causes tears, pain, and temporary blindness, literally forcing one's eyes to close. This chemical agent, albeit in a much less refined form, dates back to ancient China, when Chinese put ground cayenne chili pepper in rice paper and flung it at an opponent's eyes. It has since become much more sophisticated, potent, and controversial.

Although it is classed among the police weapons labeled "less than lethal," there has been some controversy around this classification due to a number of deaths caused by its application. People with heart or respiratory diseases are most prone to death.

The incident that perhaps propelled the Occupy protest movement into the public spotlight was the indiscriminate and senseless pepper-spraying of two women during a massive march in New York City on September 24, 2011. From that point forward, it could be argued that pepper spray has become symbolic of undeniably antidemocratic repression of American dissent, which is why we've devoted an entire chapter to its use on peaceful protesters.

One of the most outrageous instances of excessive use of force by police involving pepper spray use on peaceful protesters took place at the University of California, Davis campus in November 2011. Around a dozen students protesting tuition increases staged a peaceful sit-in on the quad, linking arms. When the students refused to disperse, UC Davis police officer Lt. John Pike walked up and down the line of seated protesters while shooting a thick stream of orange pepper spray into the their faces. A video of orange-faced students, screaming and crying in agony, went viral—creating international headlines and outrage. A photograph of Lt. Pike with a pepper-spray can in hand, nicknamed the "casual pepper-spraying cop," became an internet meme and was inserted into countless protest signs, famous artworks, and popular culture. Lt. Pike was later fired because of his behavior that day.

The sustained and highly visible political activism in American cities over the past couple of years has brought with it a brutal repression by increasingly militarized police departments intent on creating fear in the ranks of activists focused on bringing the status quo to a grinding halt.

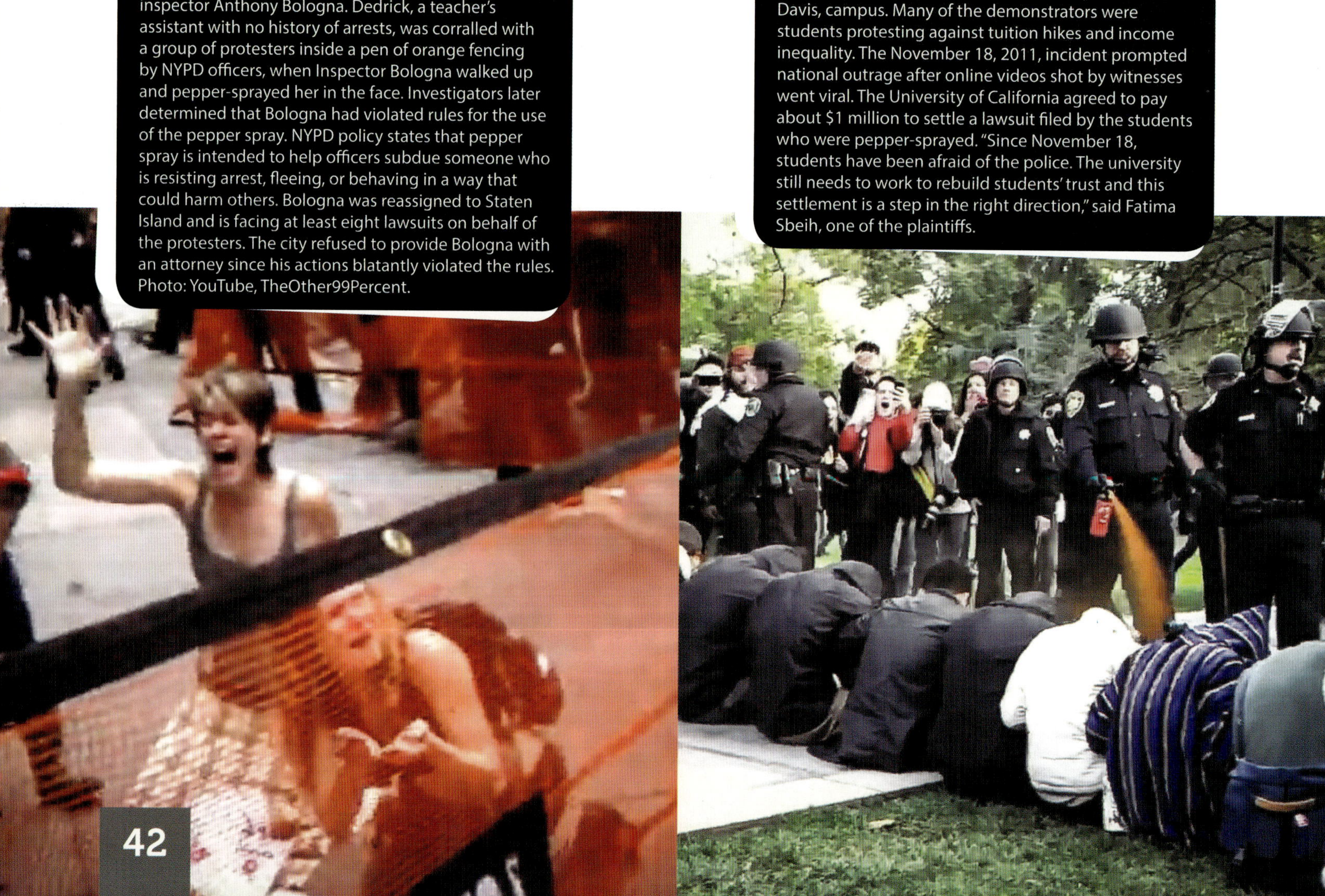

Kaylee Dedrick, 25, screams in pain after she is pepper-sprayed in the face by New York Police Department inspector Anthony Bologna. Dedrick, a teacher's assistant with no history of arrests, was corralled with a group of protesters inside a pen of orange fencing by NYPD officers, when Inspector Bologna walked up and pepper-sprayed her in the face. Investigators later determined that Bologna had violated rules for the use of the pepper spray. NYPD policy states that pepper spray is intended to help officers subdue someone who is resisting arrest, fleeing, or behaving in a way that could harm others. Bologna was reassigned to Staten Island and is facing at least eight lawsuits on behalf of the protesters. The city refused to provide Bologna with an attorney since his actions blatantly violated the rules. Photo: YouTube, TheOther99Percent.

An officer methodically sprays pepper spray in the faces of nonviolent protesters on the University of California, Davis, campus. Many of the demonstrators were students protesting against tuition hikes and income inequality. The November 18, 2011, incident prompted national outrage after online videos shot by witnesses went viral. The University of California agreed to pay about $1 million to settle a lawsuit filed by the students who were pepper-sprayed. "Since November 18, students have been afraid of the police. The university still needs to work to rebuild students' trust and this settlement is a step in the right direction," said Fatima Sbeih, one of the plaintiffs.

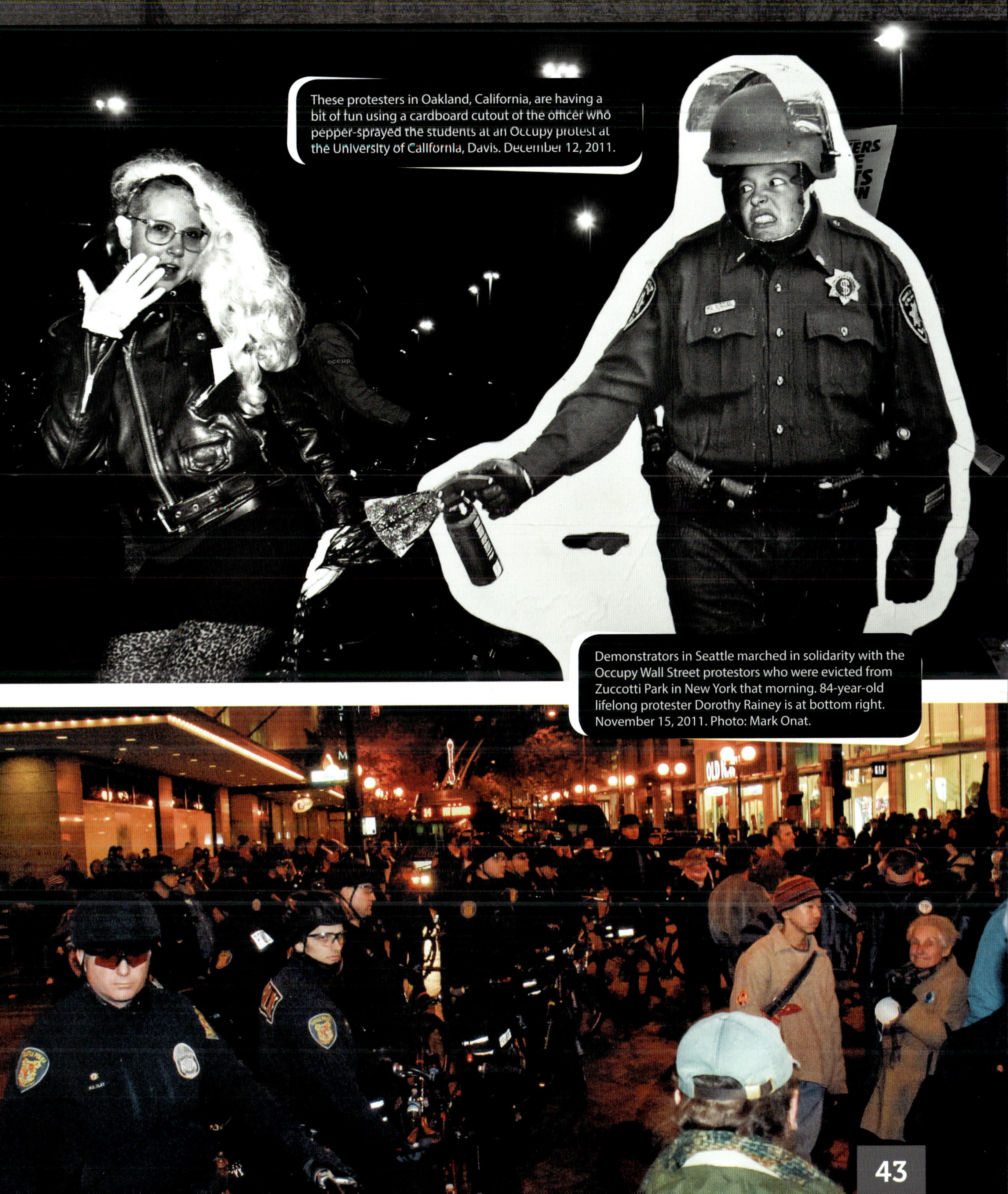

These protesters in Oakland, California, are having a bit of fun using a cardboard cutout of the officer who pepper-sprayed the students at an Occupy protest at the University of California, Davis. December 12, 2011.

Demonstrators in Seattle marched in solidarity with the Occupy Wall Street protestors who were evicted from Zuccotti Park in New York that morning. 84-year-old lifelong protester Dorothy Rainey is at bottom right. November 15, 2011. Photo: Mark Onat.

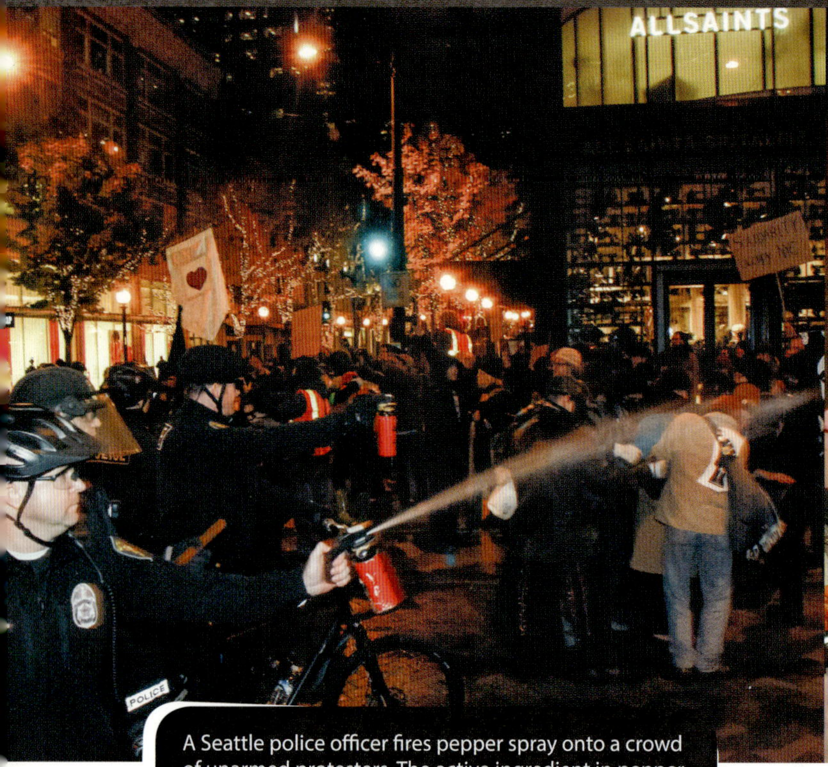

A Seattle police officer fires pepper spray onto a crowd of unarmed protesters. The active ingredient in pepper spray is capsaicin, which the active component in chili peppers. Capsaicin is an irritant that produces a burning sensation on any tissue it contacts. Photos on pages 44–47: Mark Onat.

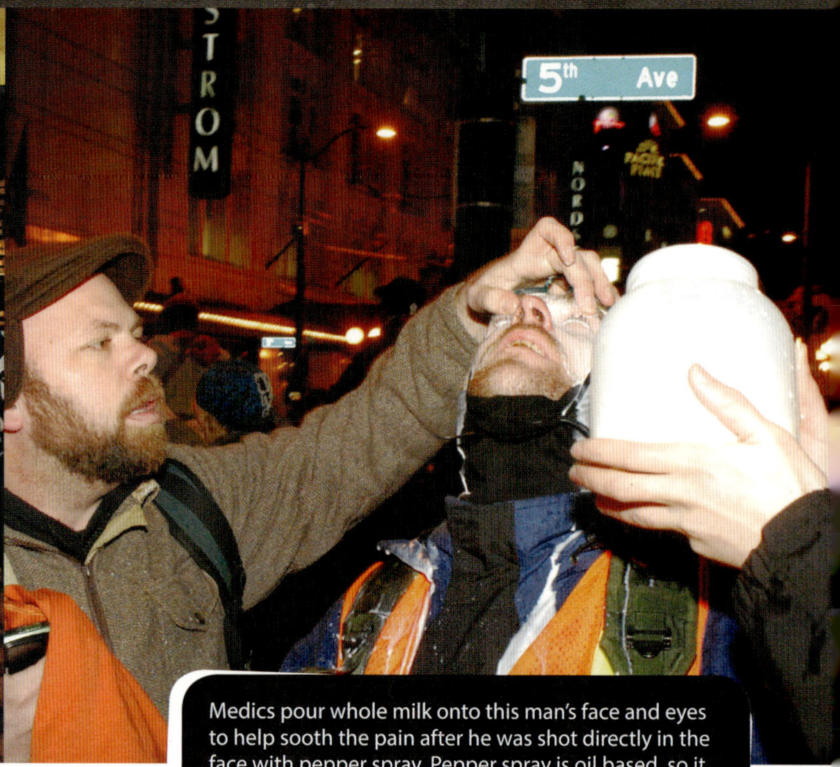

Medics pour whole milk onto this man's face and eyes to help sooth the pain after he was shot directly in the face with pepper spray. Pepper spray is oil based, so it won't wash away with water. The European Parliament Scientific and Technological Options Assessment (STOA) studied pepper spray versus tear gas and concluded, "The effects of pepper spray are far more severe than tear gas, including temporary blindness which lasts from 15" to 30 minutes, a burning sensation of the skin which lasts from 45 to 60 minutes, upper body spasms which force a person to bend forward, and uncontrollable coughing making it difficult to breathe or speak for between 3 to 15 minutes."

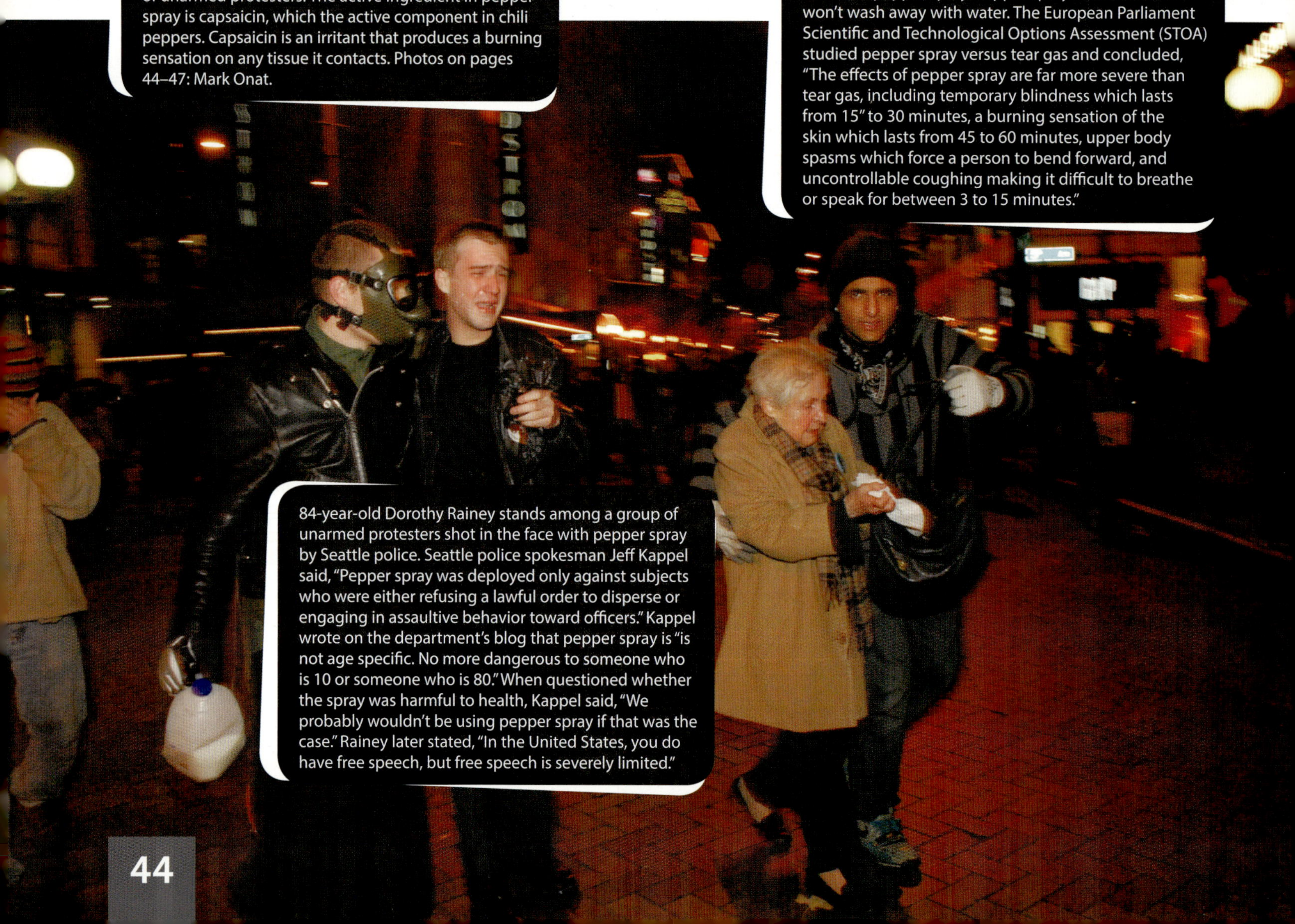

84-year-old Dorothy Rainey stands among a group of unarmed protesters shot in the face with pepper spray by Seattle police. Seattle police spokesman Jeff Kappel said, "Pepper spray was deployed only against subjects who were either refusing a lawful order to disperse or engaging in assaultive behavior toward officers." Kappel wrote on the department's blog that pepper spray is "is not age specific. No more dangerous to someone who is 10 or someone who is 80." When questioned whether the spray was harmful to health, Kappel said, "We probably wouldn't be using pepper spray if that was the case." Rainey later stated, "In the United States, you do have free speech, but free speech is severely limited."

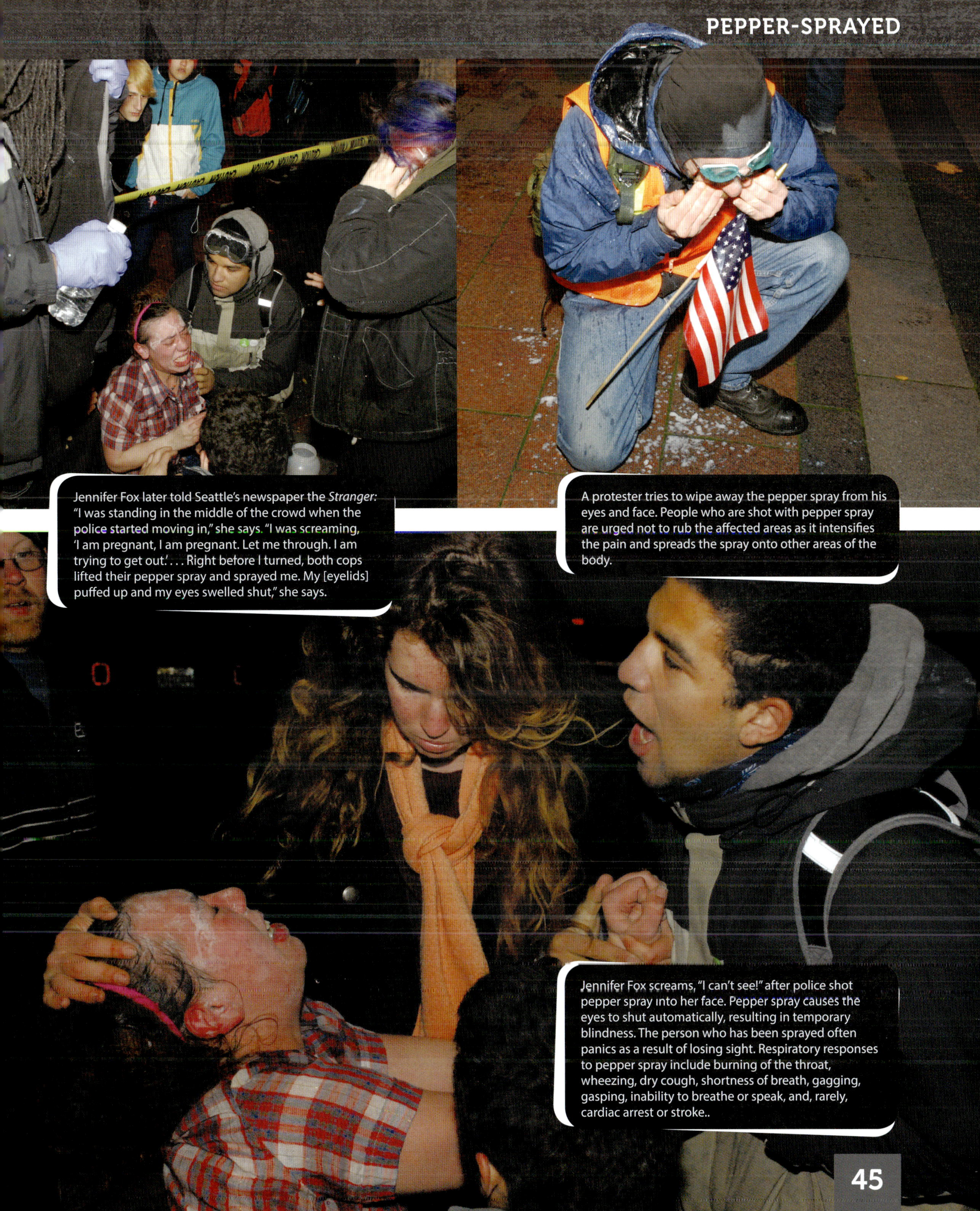

Jennifer Fox later told Seattle's newspaper the *Stranger:* "I was standing in the middle of the crowd when the police started moving in," she says. "I was screaming, 'I am pregnant, I am pregnant. Let me through. I am trying to get out.' . . . Right before I turned, both cops lifted their pepper spray and sprayed me. My [eyelids] puffed up and my eyes swelled shut," she says.

A protester tries to wipe away the pepper spray from his eyes and face. People who are shot with pepper spray are urged not to rub the affected areas as it intensifies the pain and spreads the spray onto other areas of the body.

Jennifer Fox screams, "I can't see!" after police shot pepper spray into her face. Pepper spray causes the eyes to shut automatically, resulting in temporary blindness. The person who has been sprayed often panics as a result of losing sight. Respiratory responses to pepper spray include burning of the throat, wheezing, dry cough, shortness of breath, gagging, gasping, inability to breathe or speak, and, rarely, cardiac arrest or stroke..

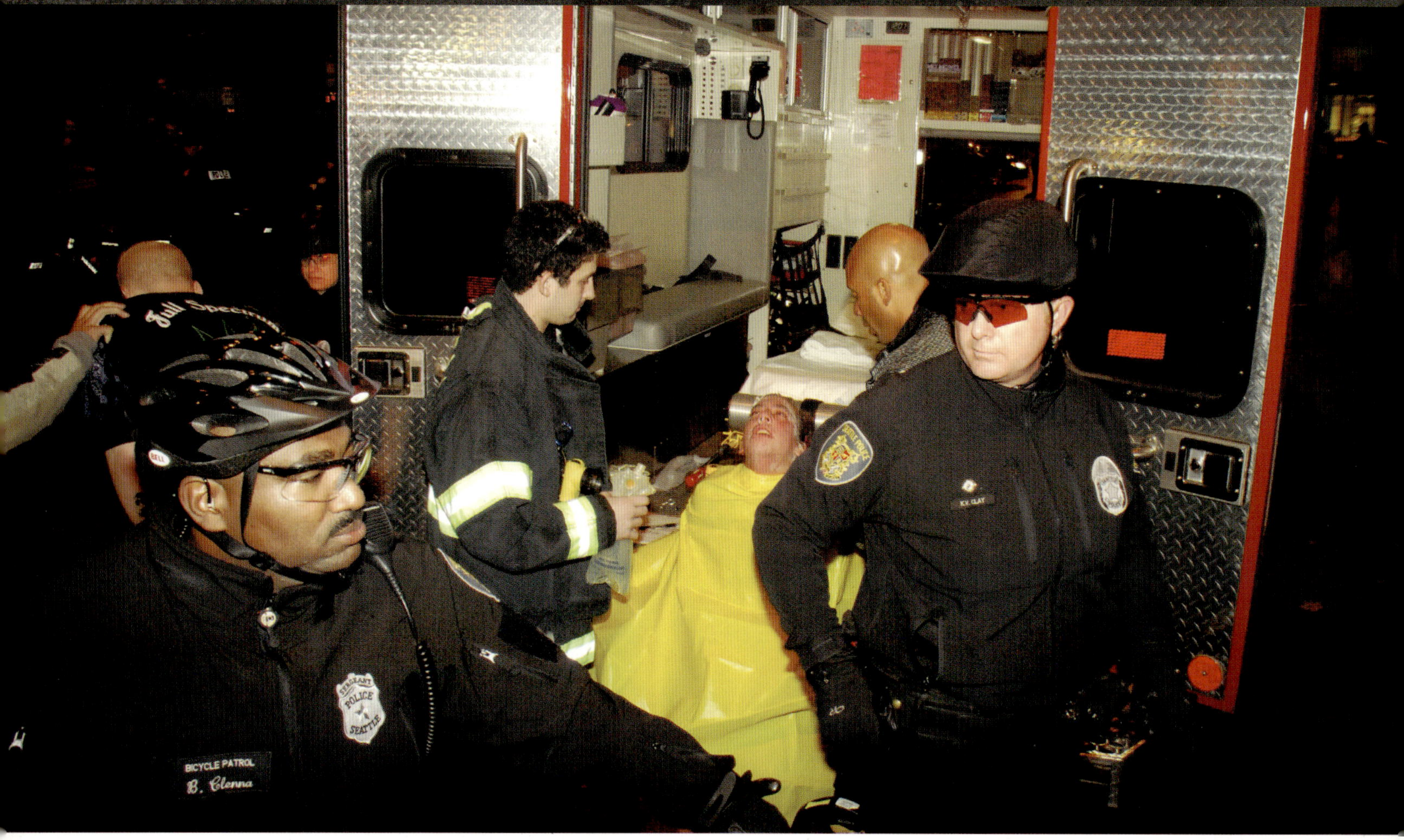

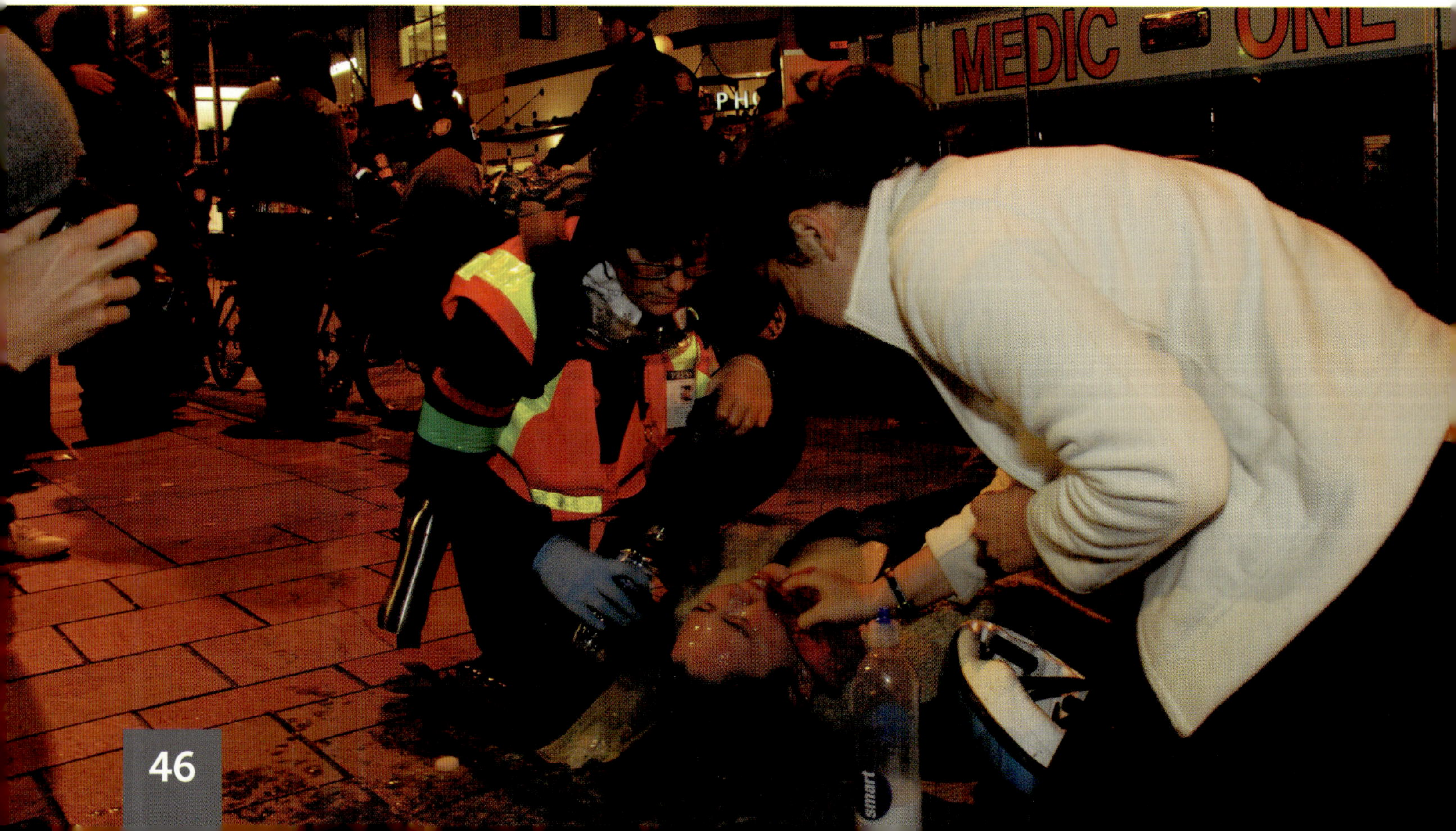

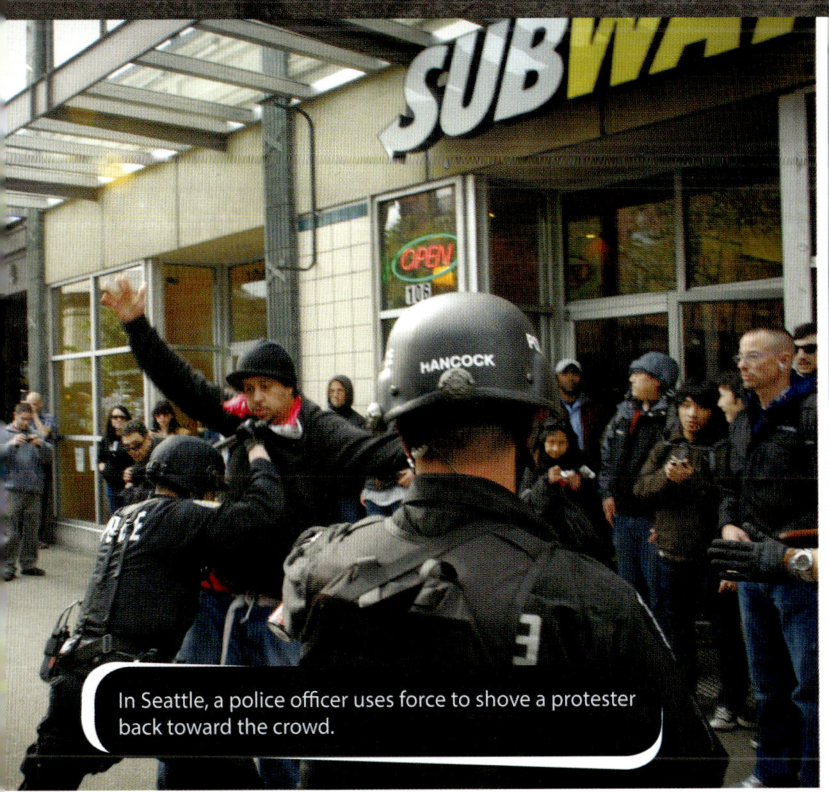

In Seattle, a police officer uses force to shove a protester back toward the crowd.

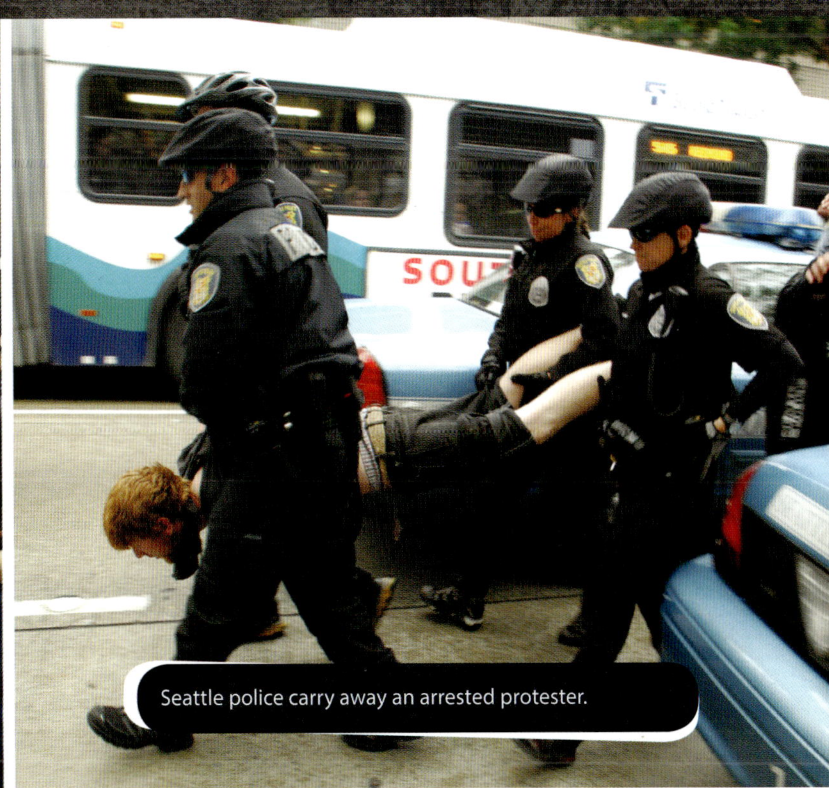

Seattle police carry away an arrested protester.

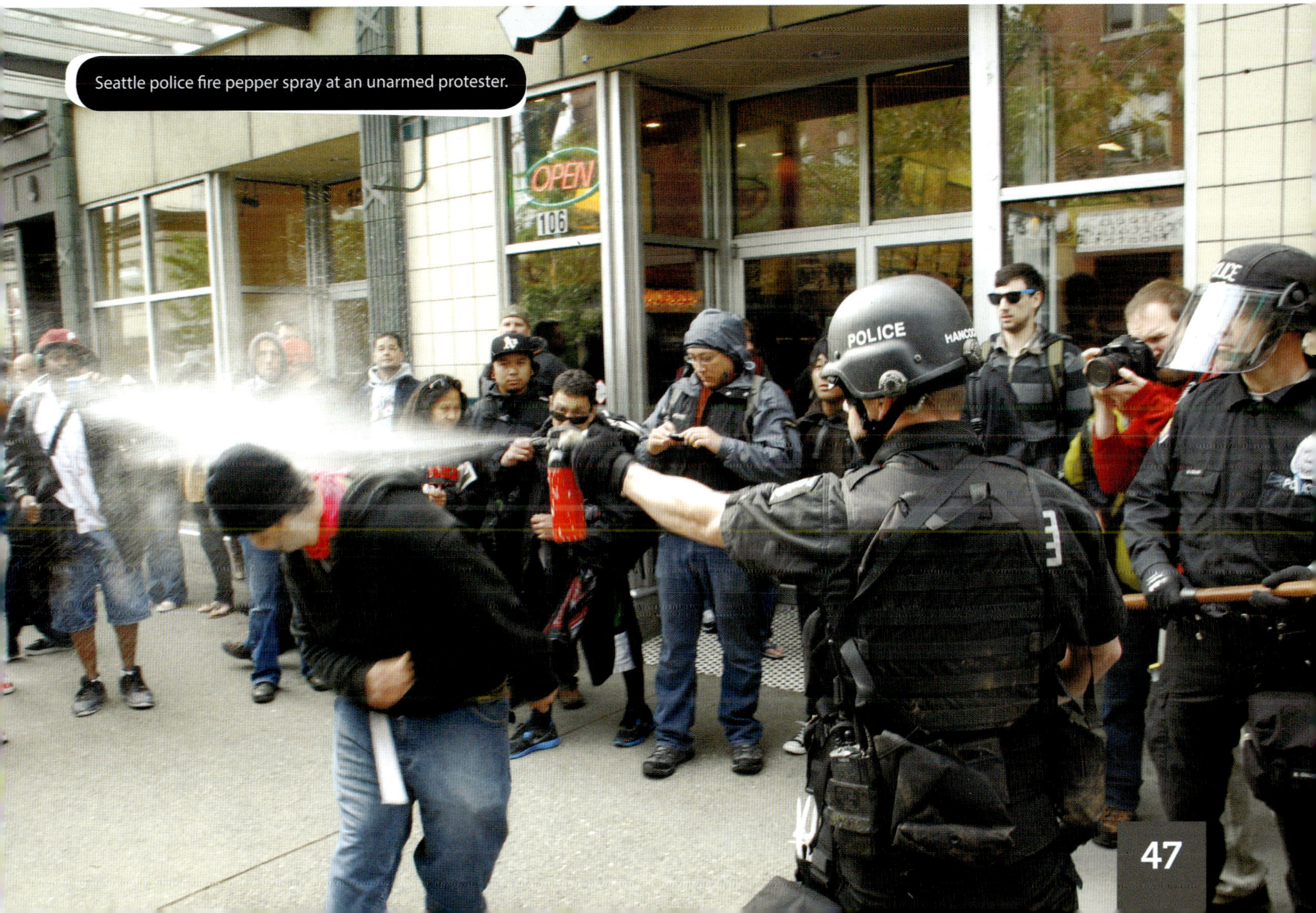

Seattle police fire pepper spray at an unarmed protester.

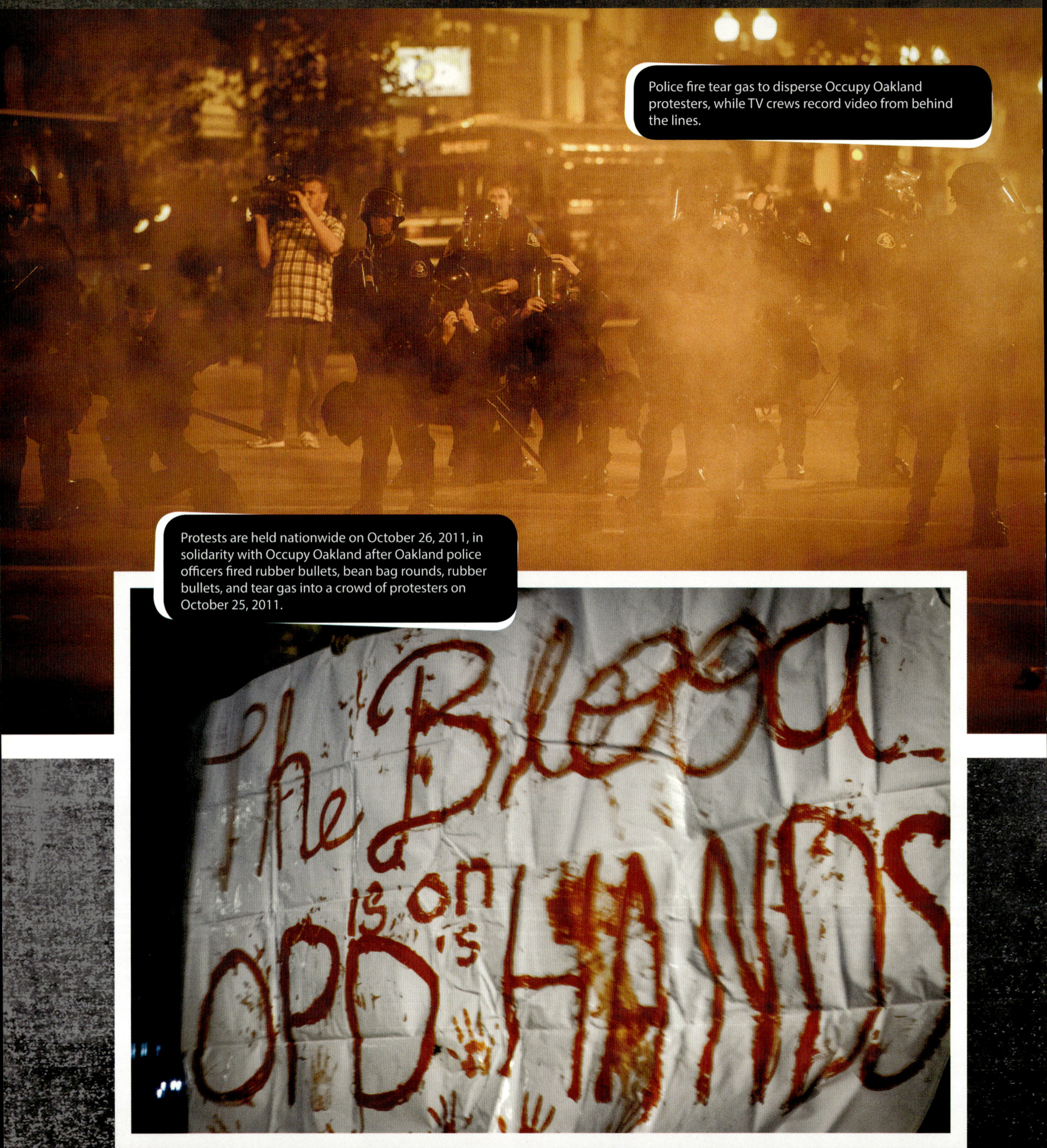

Police fire tear gas to disperse Occupy Oakland protesters, while TV crews record video from behind the lines.

Protests are held nationwide on October 26, 2011, in solidarity with Occupy Oakland after Oakland police officers fired rubber bullets, bean bag rounds, rubber bullets, and tear gas into a crowd of protesters on October 25, 2011.

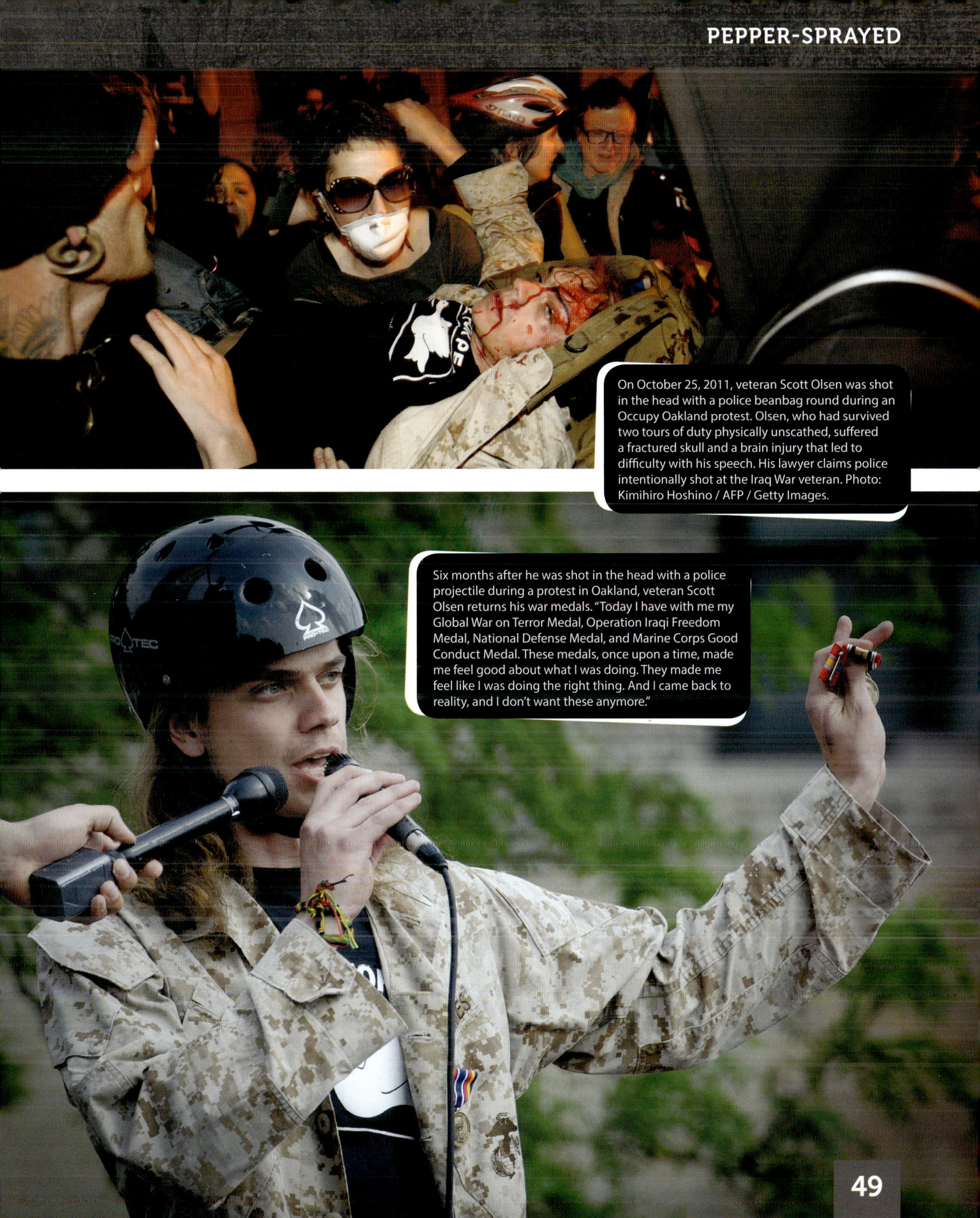

On October 25, 2011, veteran Scott Olsen was shot in the head with a police beanbag round during an Occupy Oakland protest. Olsen, who had survived two tours of duty physically unscathed, suffered a fractured skull and a brain injury that led to difficulty with his speech. His lawyer claims police intentionally shot at the Iraq War veteran. Photo: Kimihiro Hoshino / AFP / Getty Images.

Six months after he was shot in the head with a police projectile during a protest in Oakland, veteran Scott Olsen returns his war medals. "Today I have with me my Global War on Terror Medal, Operation Iraqi Freedom Medal, National Defense Medal, and Marine Corps Good Conduct Medal. These medals, once upon a time, made me feel good about what I was doing. They made me feel like I was doing the right thing. And I came back to reality, and I don't want these anymore."

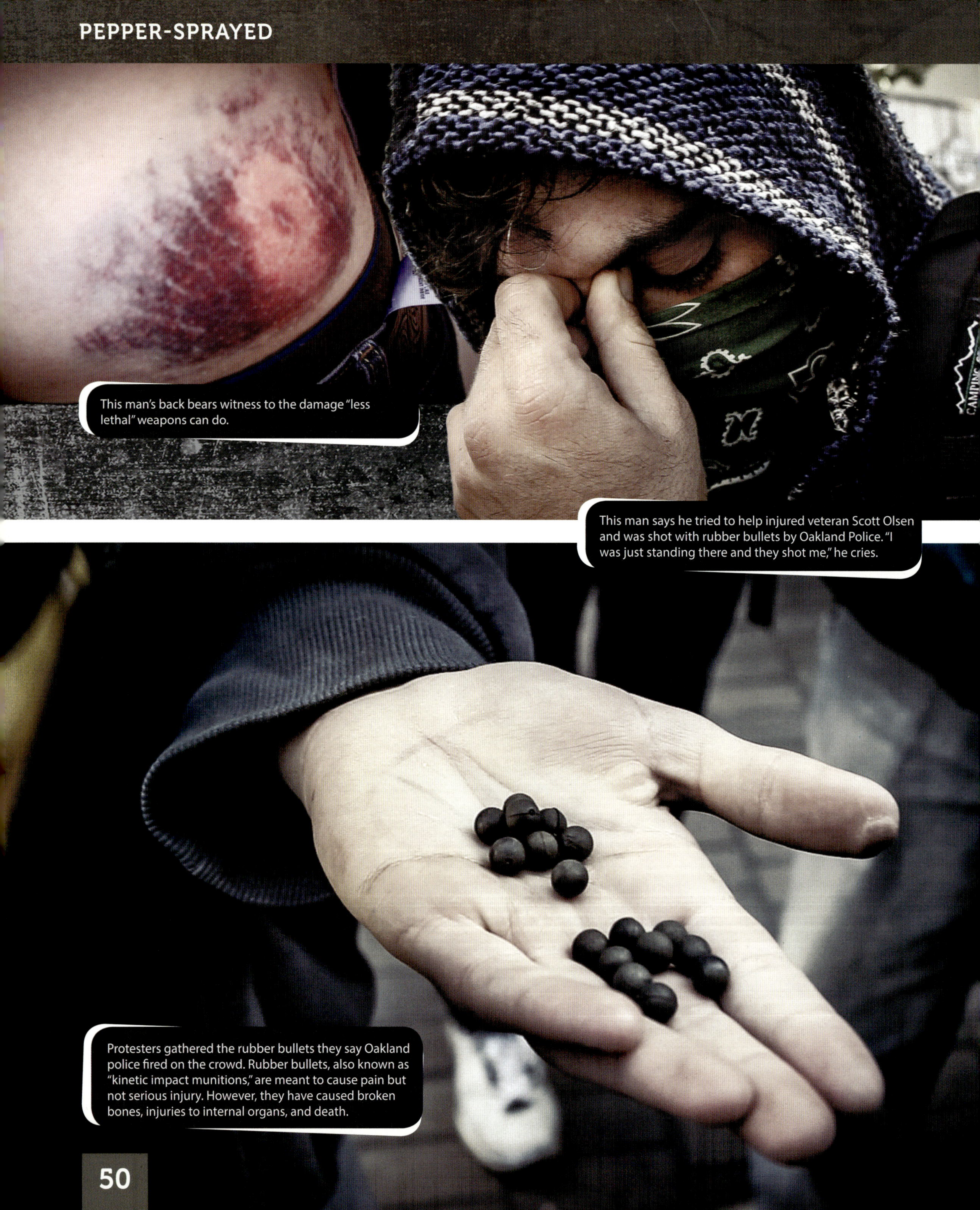

This man's back bears witness to the damage "less lethal" weapons can do.

This man says he tried to help injured veteran Scott Olsen and was shot with rubber bullets by Oakland Police. "I was just standing there and they shot me," he cries.

Protesters gathered the rubber bullets they say Oakland police fired on the crowd. Rubber bullets, also known as "kinetic impact munitions," are meant to cause pain but not serious injury. However, they have caused broken bones, injuries to internal organs, and death.

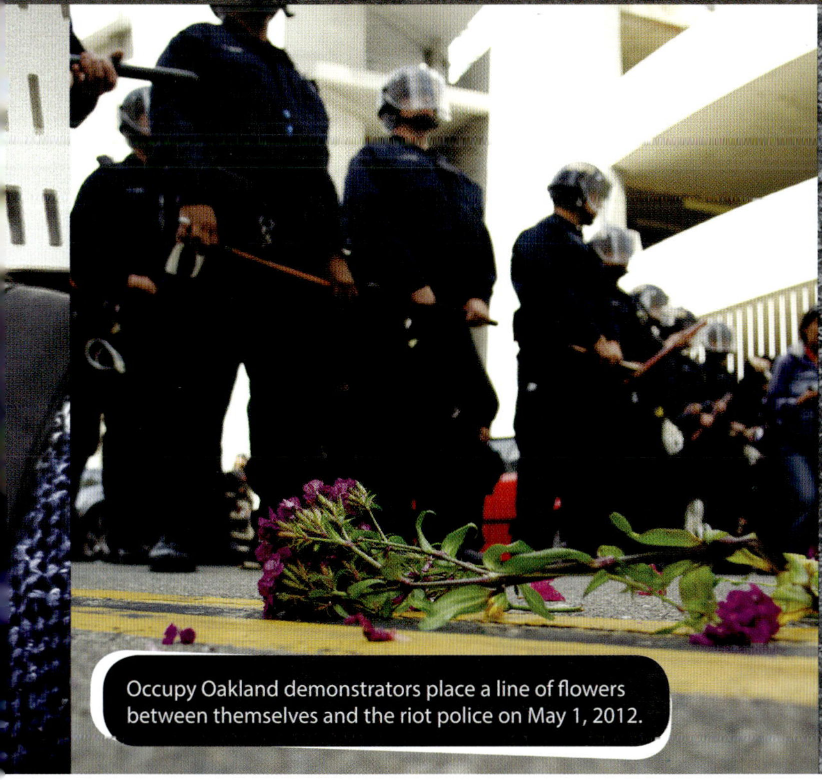

Occupy Oakland demonstrators place a line of flowers between themselves and the riot police on May 1, 2012.

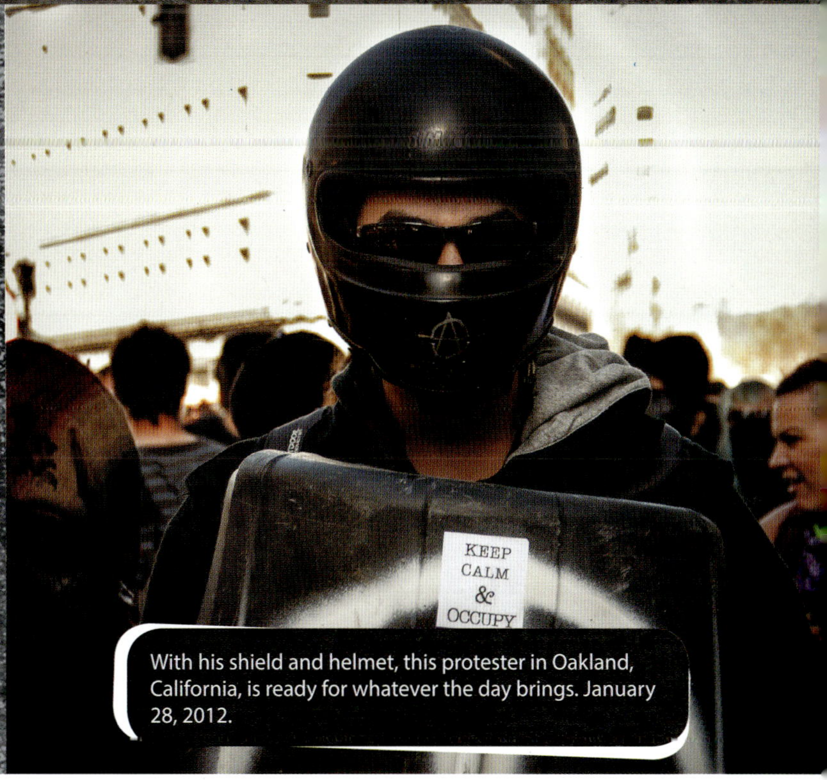

With his shield and helmet, this protester in Oakland, California, is ready for whatever the day brings. January 28, 2012.

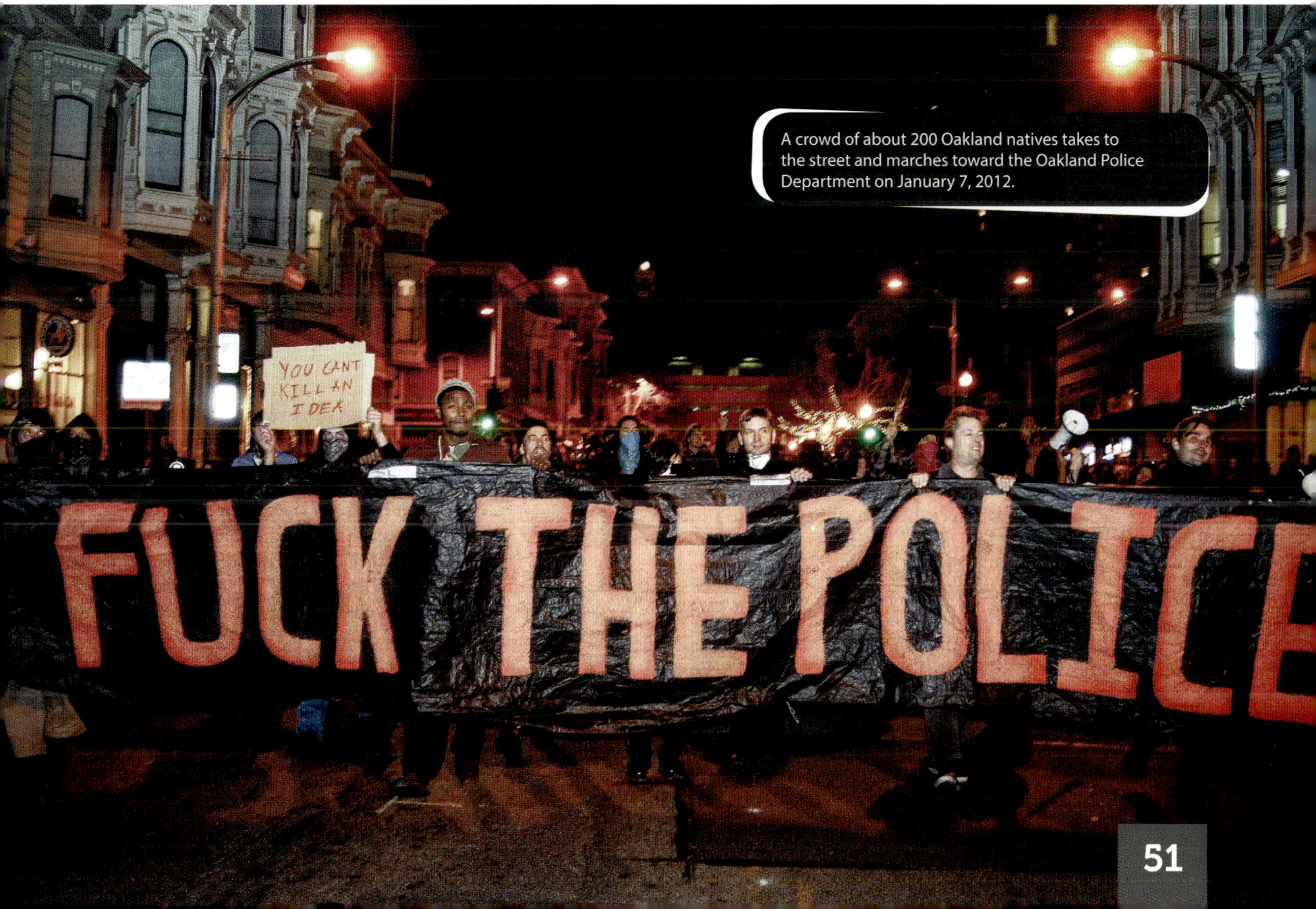

A crowd of about 200 Oakland natives takes to the street and marches toward the Oakland Police Department on January 7, 2012.

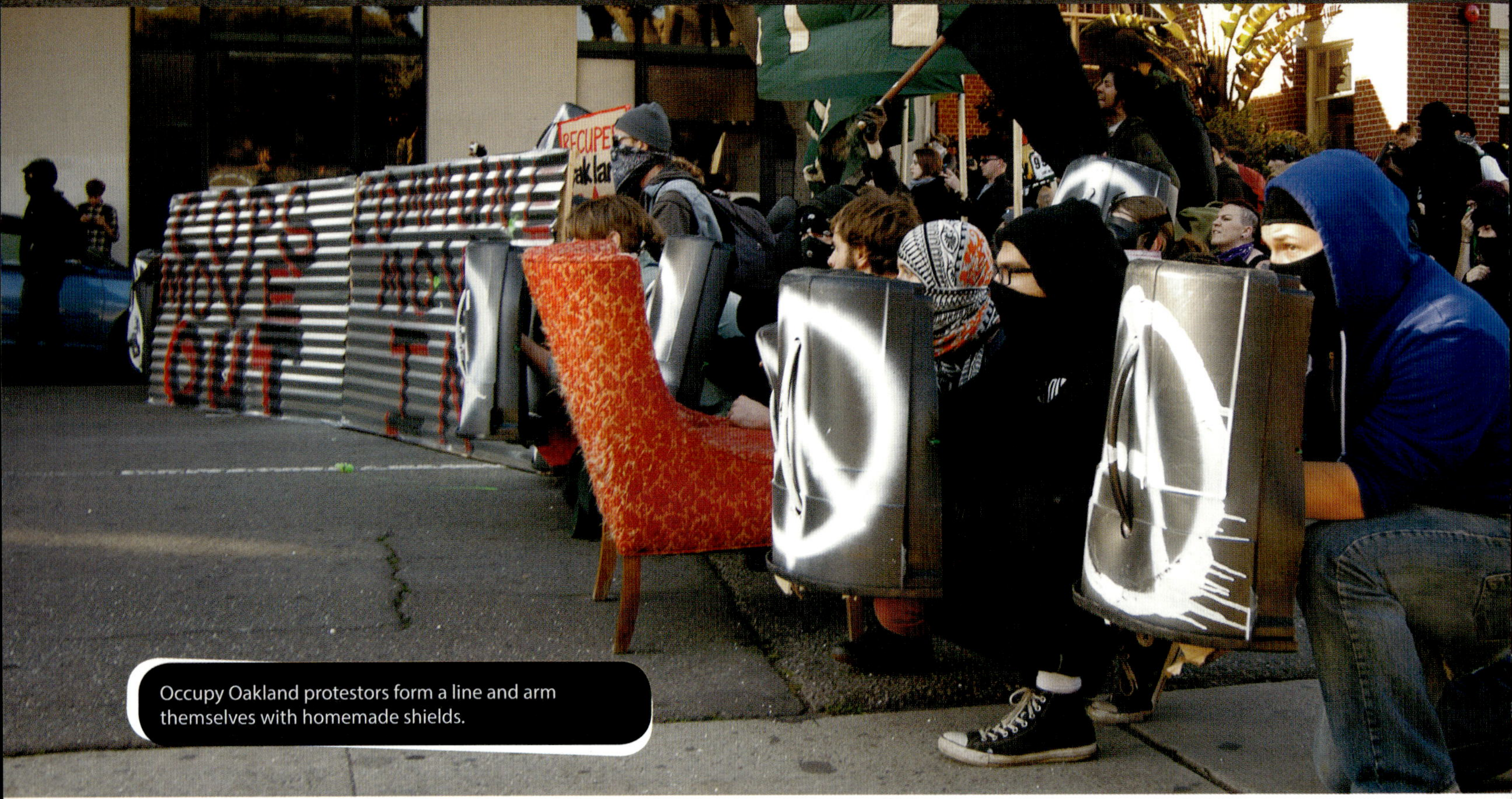

Occupy Oakland protestors form a line and arm themselves with homemade shields.

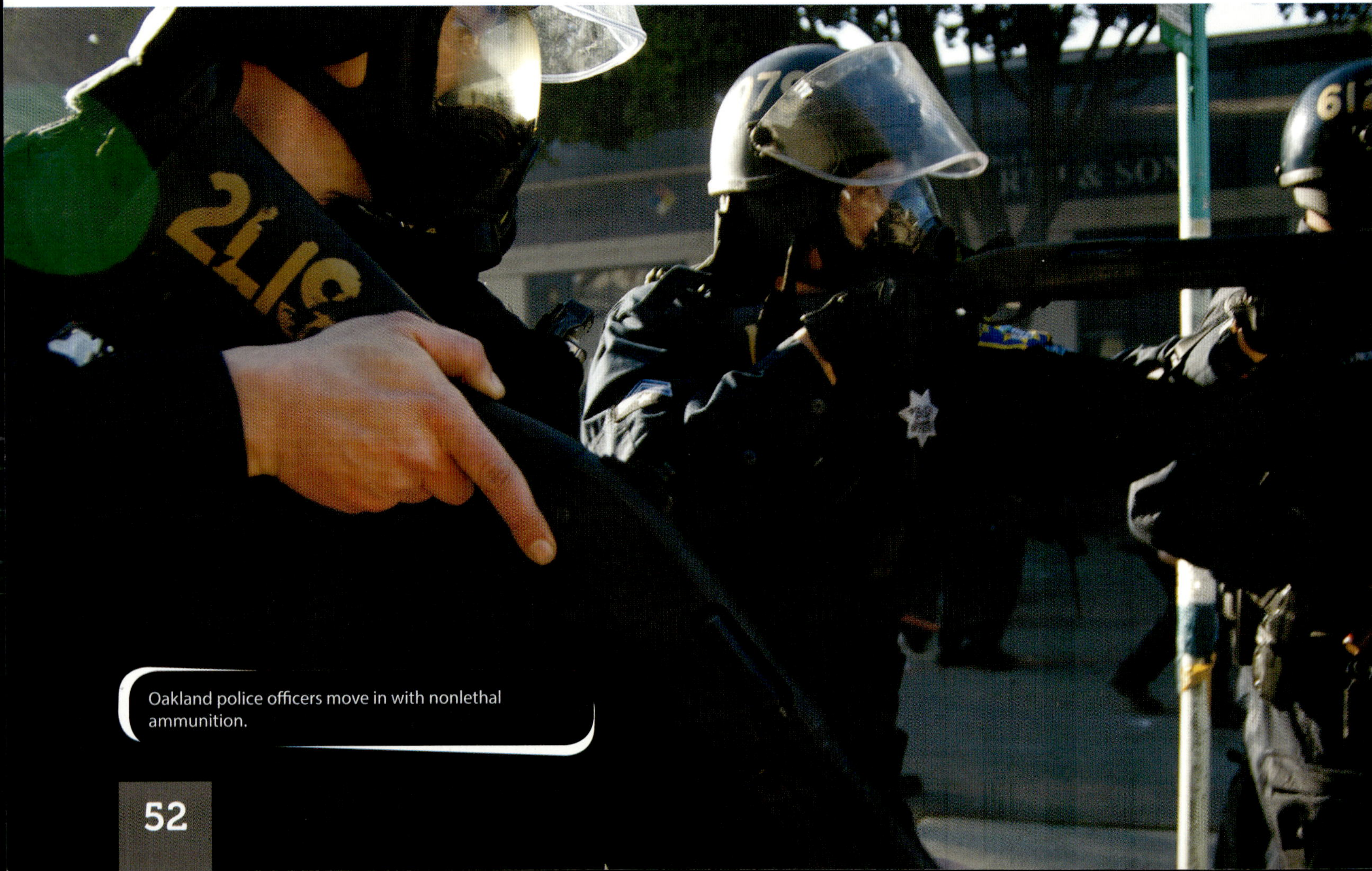

Oakland police officers move in with nonlethal ammunition.

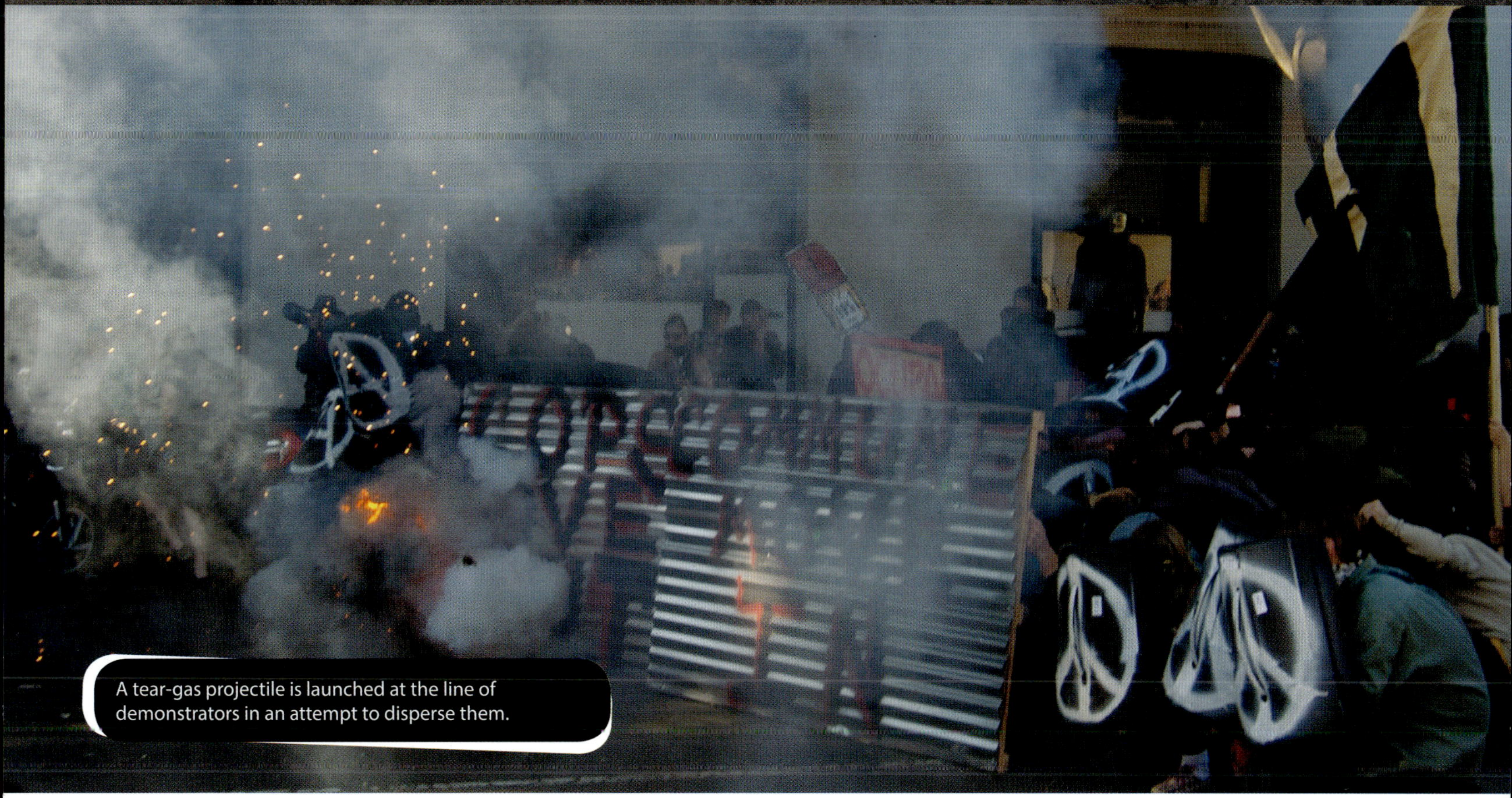

A tear-gas projectile is launched at the line of demonstrators in an attempt to disperse them.

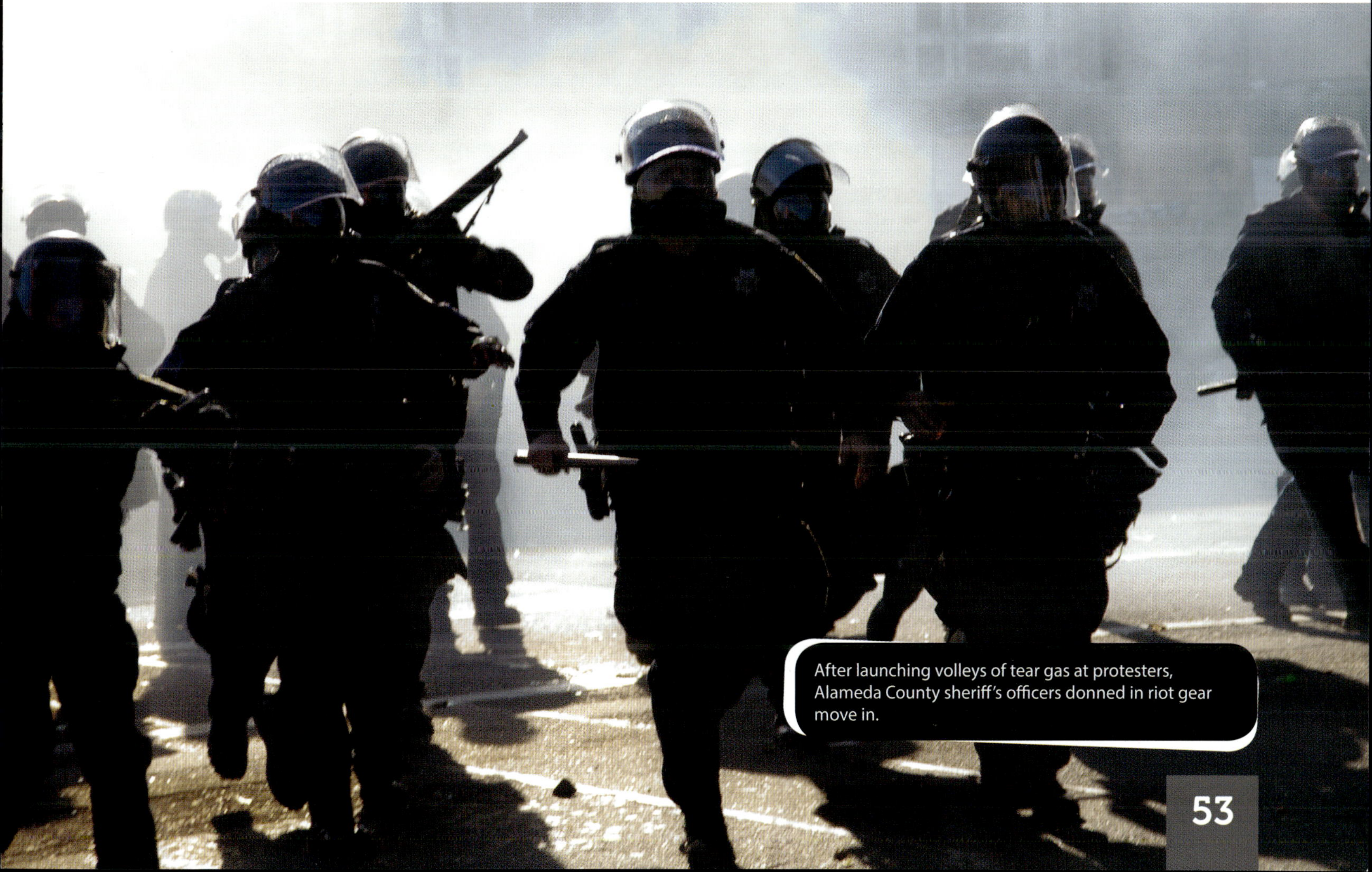

After launching volleys of tear gas at protesters, Alameda County sheriff's officers donned in riot gear move in.

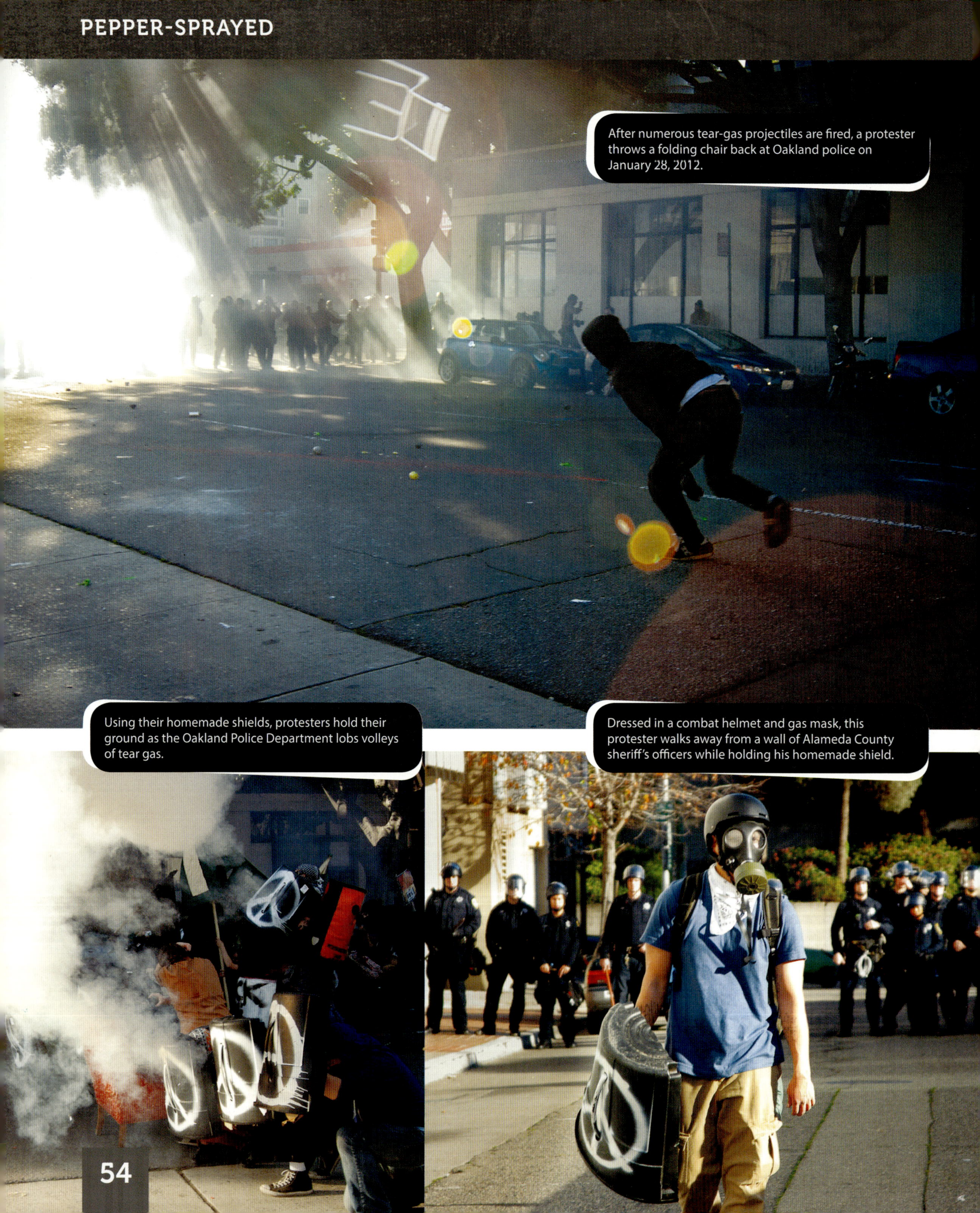

After numerous tear-gas projectiles are fired, a protester throws a folding chair back at Oakland police on January 28, 2012.

Using their homemade shields, protesters hold their ground as the Oakland Police Department lobs volleys of tear gas.

Dressed in a combat helmet and gas mask, this protester walks away from a wall of Alameda County sheriff's officers while holding his homemade shield.

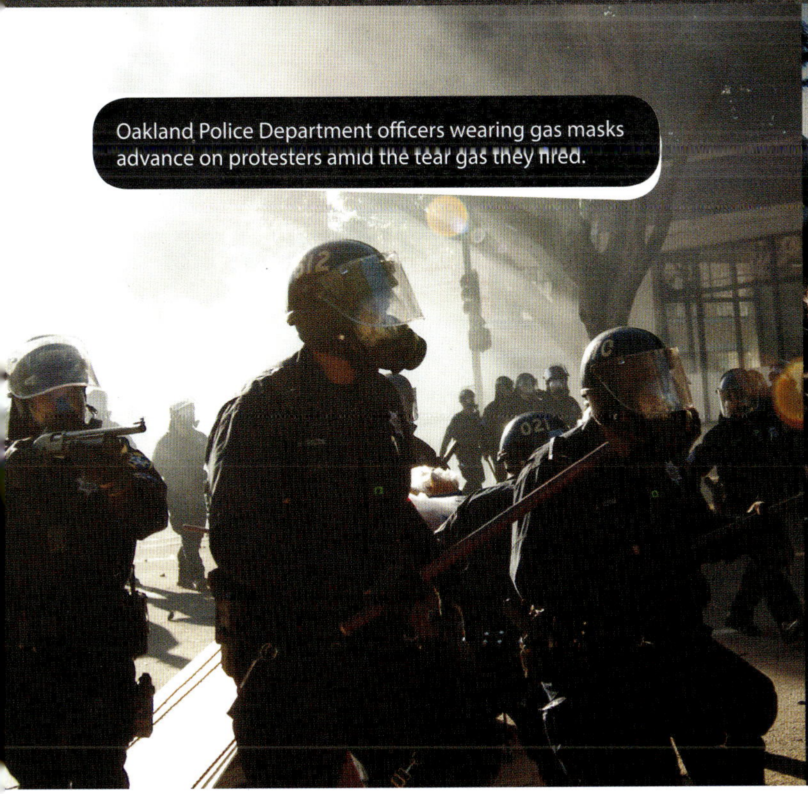

Oakland Police Department officers wearing gas masks advance on protesters amid the tear gas they fired.

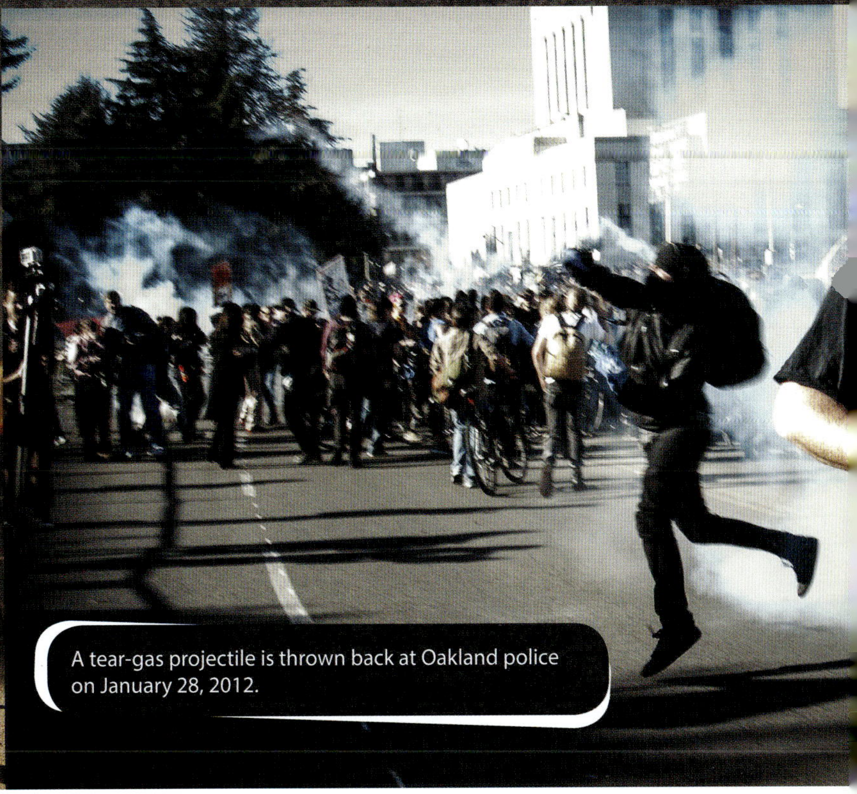

A tear-gas projectile is thrown back at Oakland police on January 28, 2012.

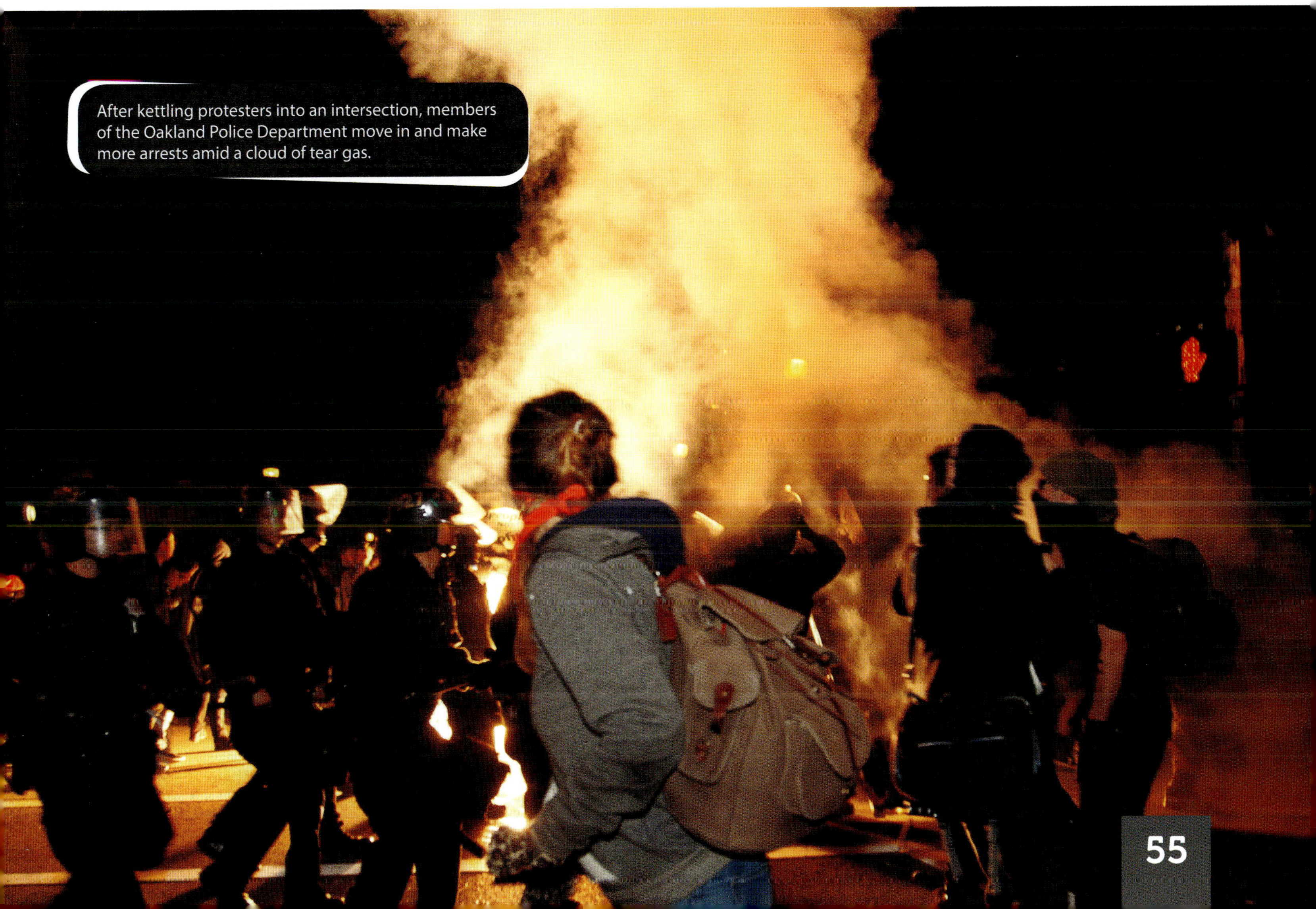

After kettling protesters into an intersection, members of the Oakland Police Department move in and make more arrests amid a cloud of tear gas.

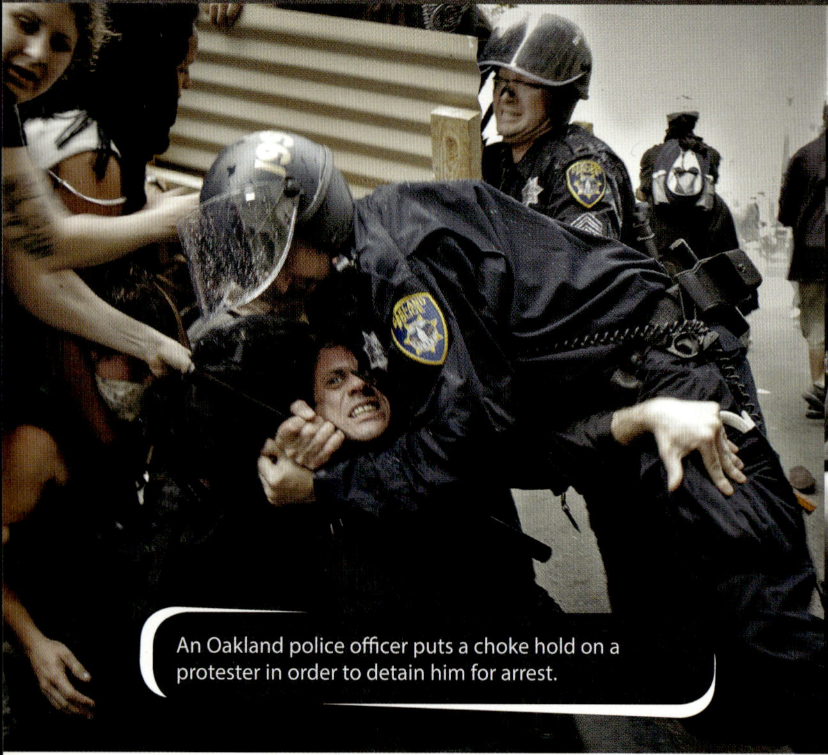

An Oakland police officer puts a choke hold on a protester in order to detain him for arrest.

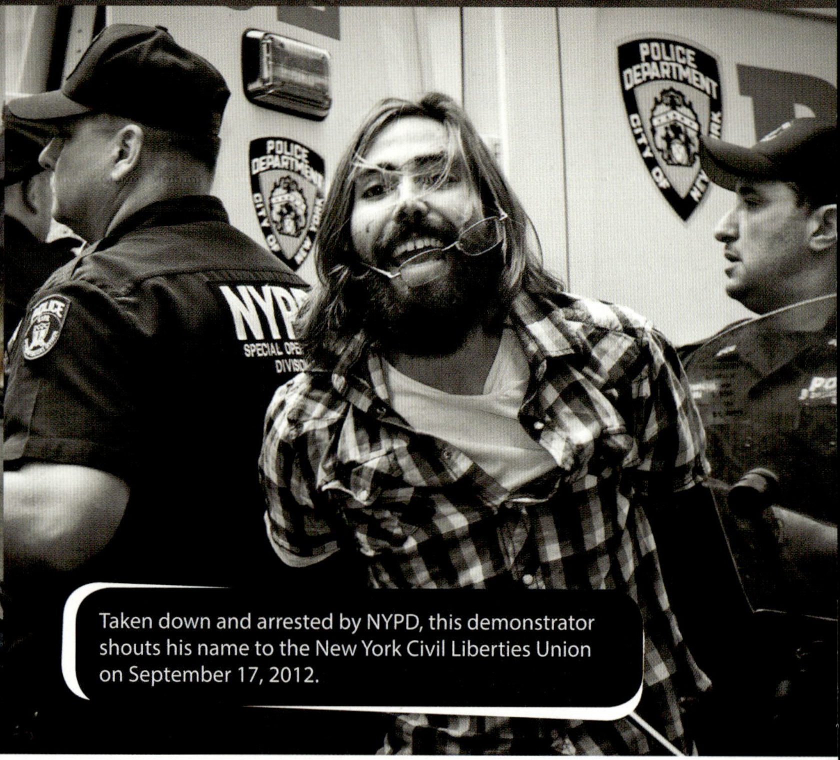

Taken down and arrested by NYPD, this demonstrator shouts his name to the New York Civil Liberties Union on September 17, 2012.

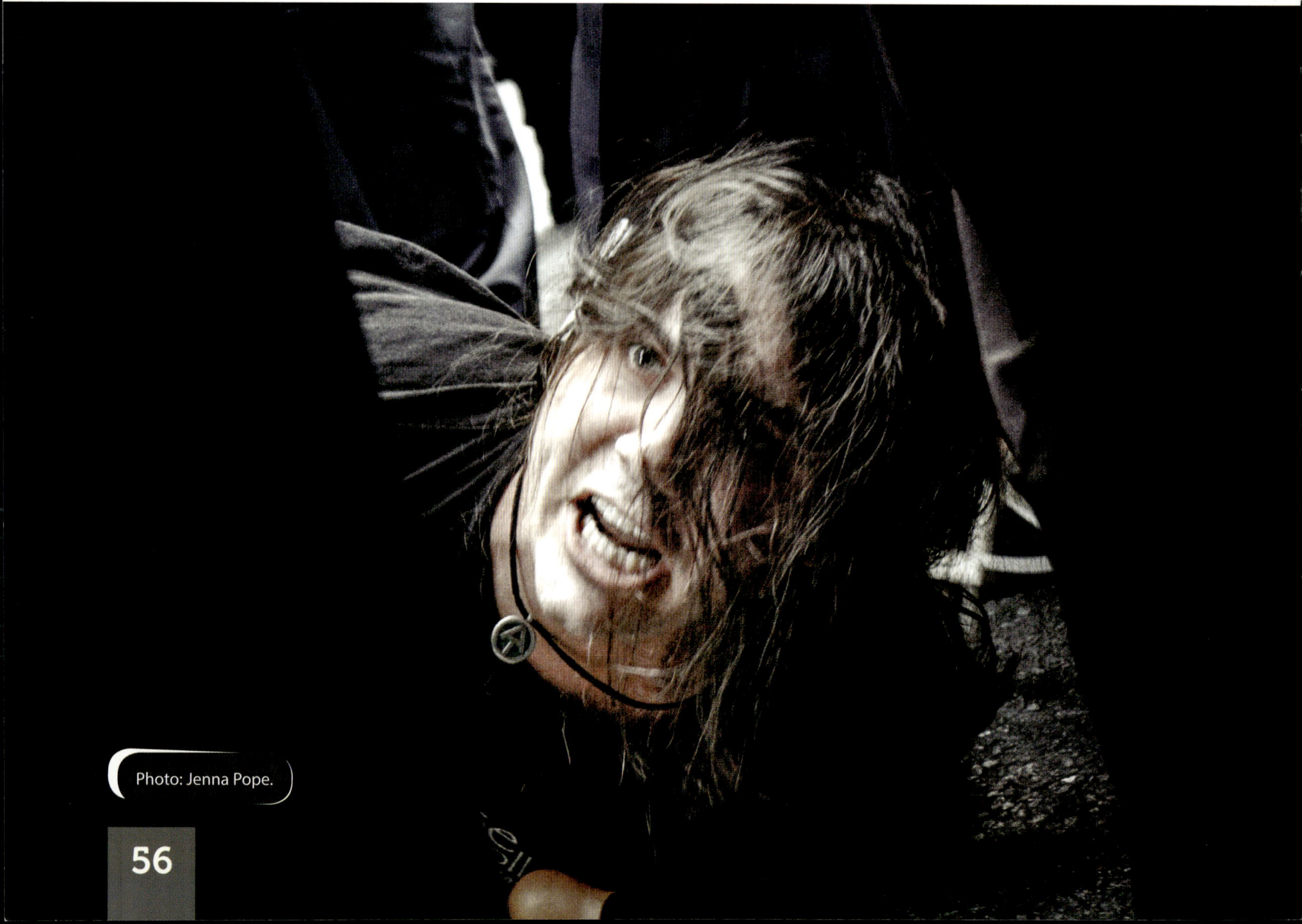

Photo: Jenna Pope.

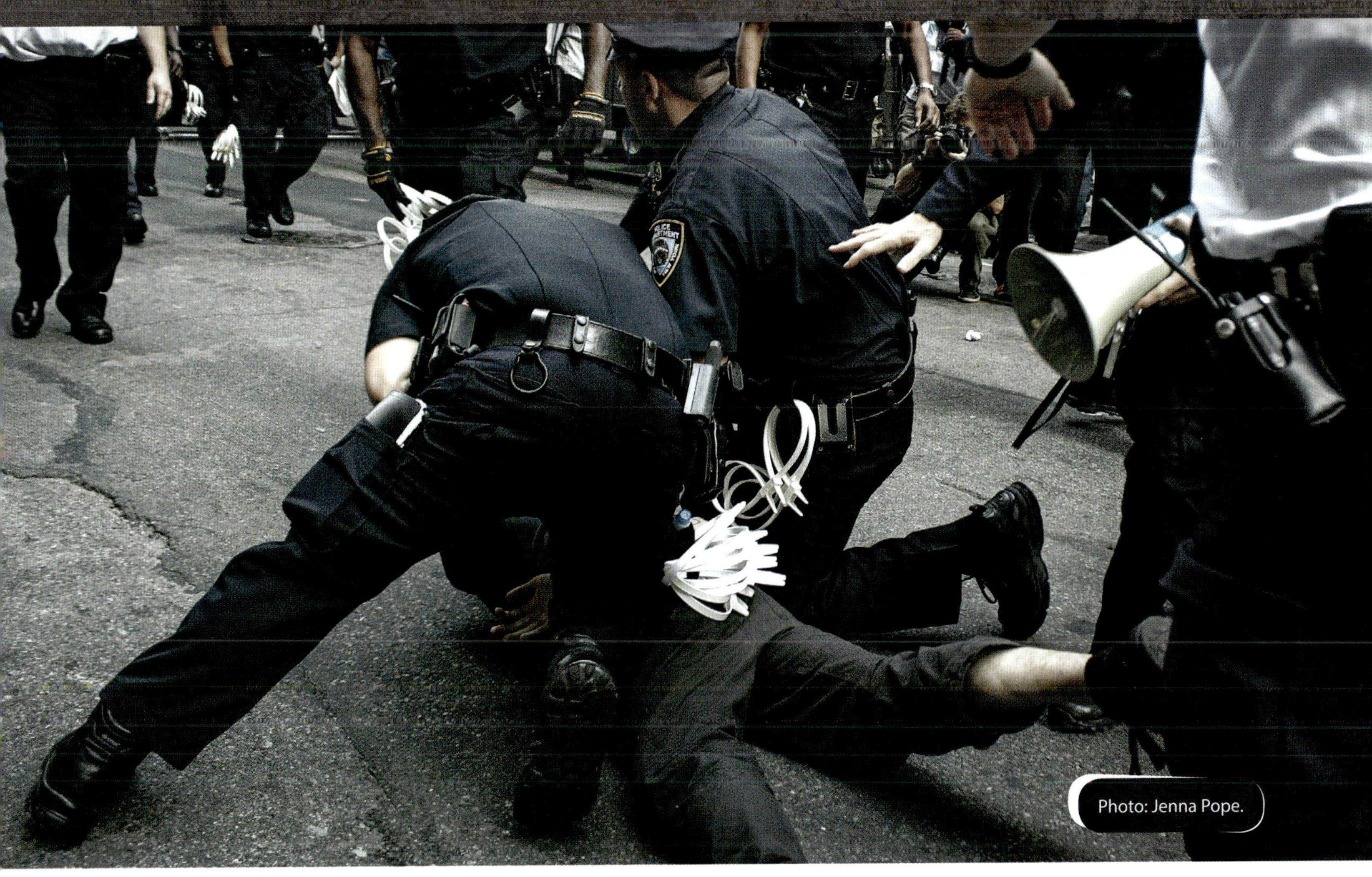

Photo: Jenna Pope.

NYPD stations are out in force at Liberty Square, New York City, on September 17, 2012.

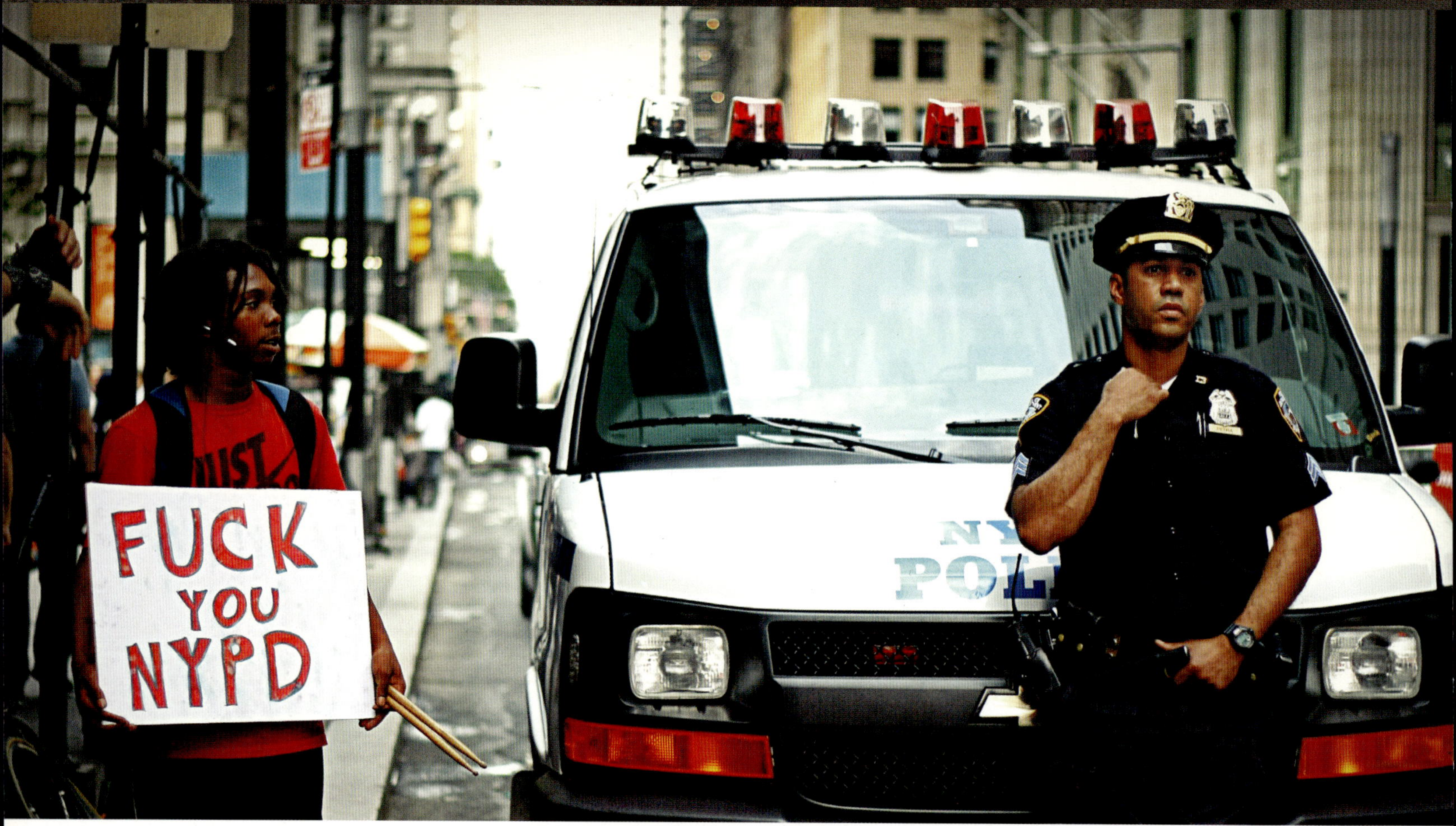

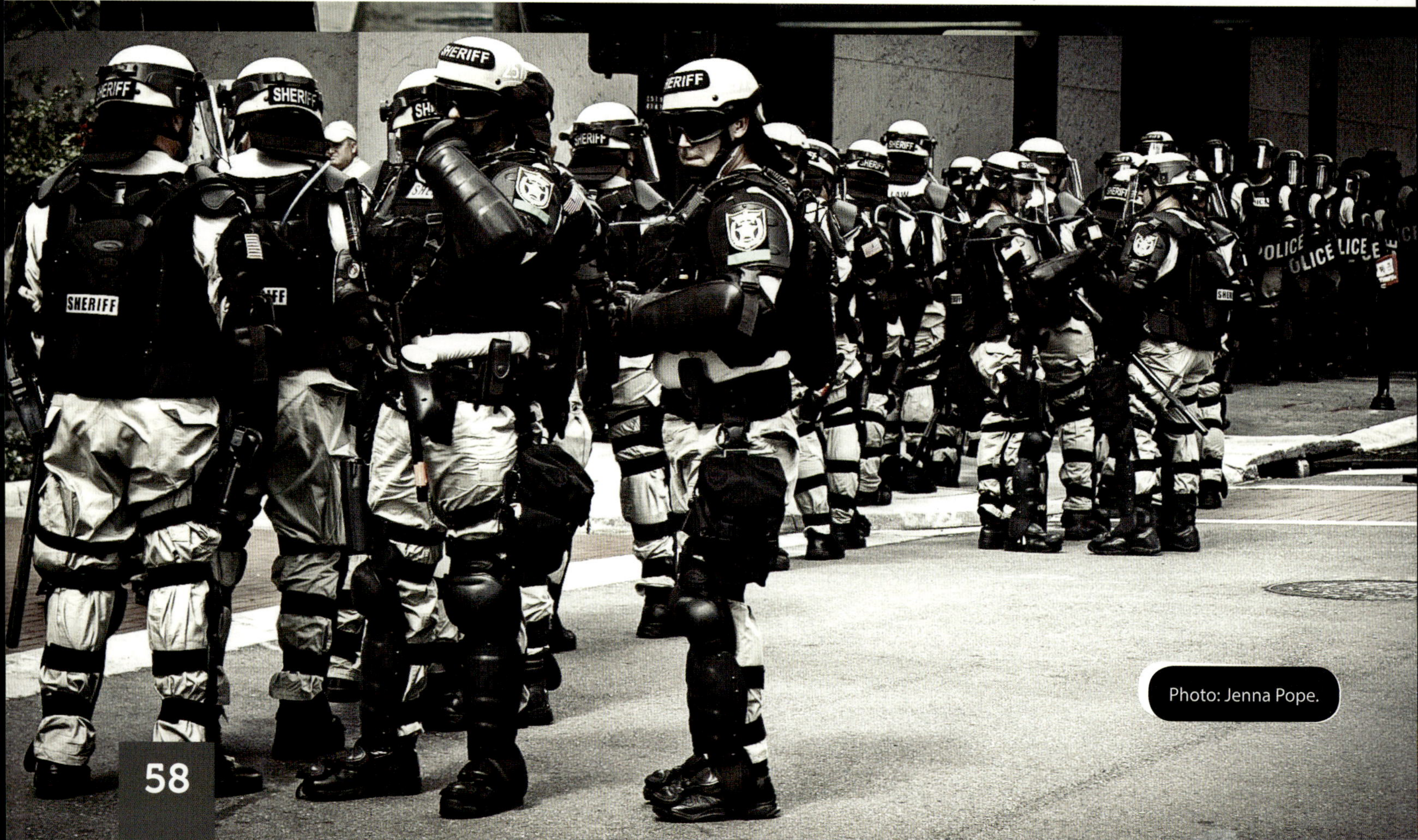

Photo: Jenna Pope.

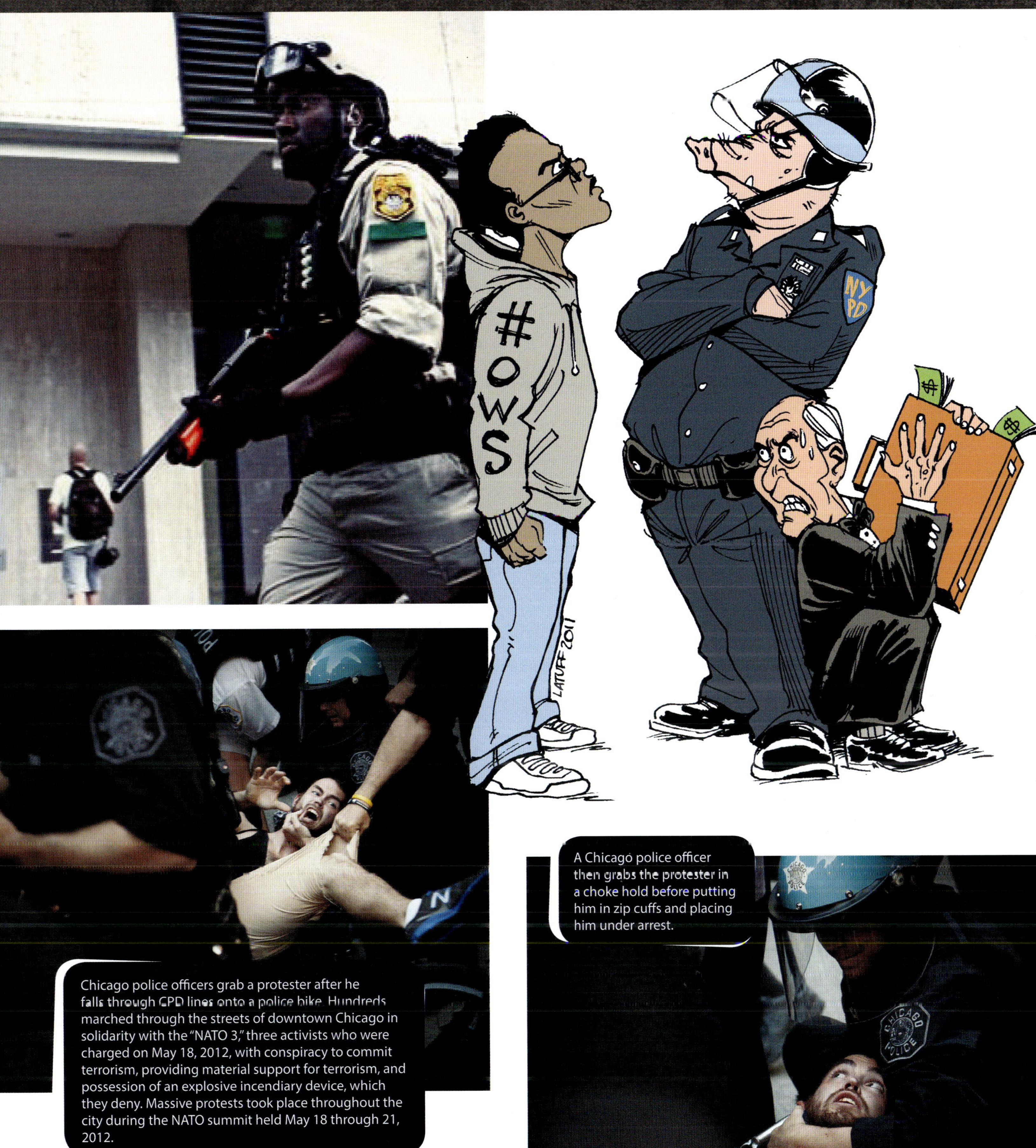

Chicago police officers grab a protester after he falls through CPD lines onto a police bike. Hundreds marched through the streets of downtown Chicago in solidarity with the "NATO 3," three activists who were charged on May 18, 2012, with conspiracy to commit terrorism, providing material support for terrorism, and possession of an explosive incendiary device, which they deny. Massive protests took place throughout the city during the NATO summit held May 18 through 21, 2012.

A Chicago police officer then grabs the protester in a choke hold before putting him in zip cuffs and placing him under arrest.

Afghanaheim

On Saturday, July 21, 2012, just a couple of miles away from the glitz of Disneyland in Anaheim, California, police officers approached 25-year-old Manuel Diaz. When Diaz took off running, the officers shot and killed him in broad daylight, in the middle of a neighborhood. As neighbors in the community gathered around Diaz's lifeless body lying in the grass and discovered he was unarmed, outrage and mistrust of the Anaheim Police Department grew.

That afternoon local men, women, and children gathered to voice their anger at the shooting. Police responded with a heavy hand, firing beanbags and pepper balls upon the crowd. Screams can be heard in a video of the incident that shows police advancing on the residents, guns drawn, as adults throw themselves over their children to shield them from the pepper balls and beanbags. A police dog lurches at the protesters, running after a mother and her one-year-old baby in a stroller before sinking his teeth into a man's arm. Anaheim police say the dog accidentally escaped from a patrol car.

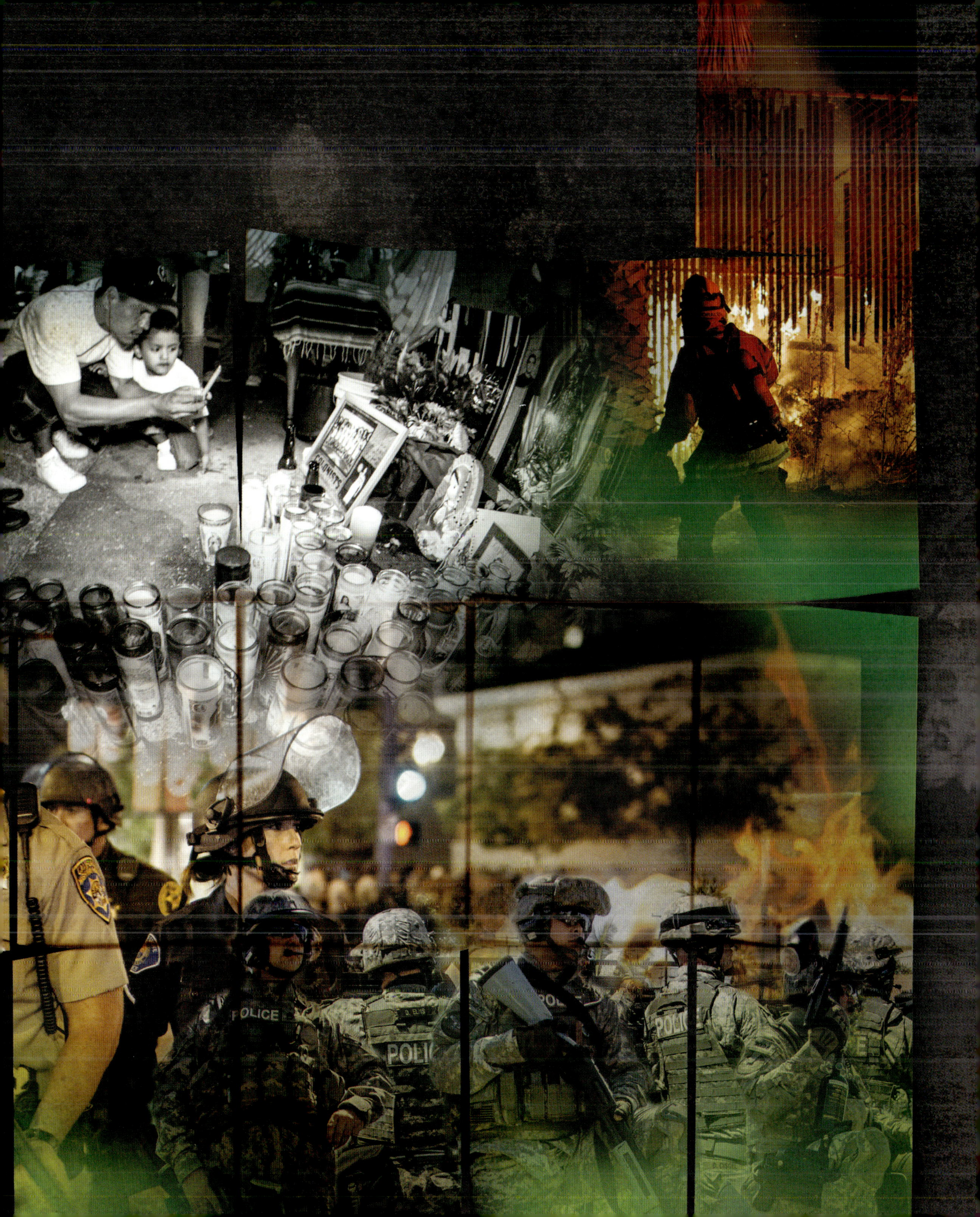
POLICE

Just one day after the Manuel Diaz killing, police gunned down 21-year-old Joel Mathew Acevedo, who was also unarmed.

The shootings, plus revelations that officers involved in the Diaz shooting attempted to buy cell phone footage of the incident to cover it up, brought tensions to a head, setting the stage for what happened next: a night of protests in the streets of Anaheim. Residents in this mostly Hispanic community felt threatened, disconnected from the majority-white Anaheim Police force.

After the group refused to disperse from outside City Hall and a bottle was thrown from the crowd toward the police, the police did something incredible: they began shooting indiscriminately into the crowds of protesters—including women and children—with rubber bullets, foam projectiles, and pepper balls. A woman limped down the street as blood flowed from two beanbag wounds on the back of her leg. Blood covered the head of a pedestrian who says he was struck in the head by a police projectile while walking home from work.

Journalists covering the event were also caught in the line of fire. The author of this book spent several minutes hidden between two U-Haul trucks to avoid being struck after she was shot at by a wall of officers. A local NBC news photographer was parking a car when a wall of police firing down the street approached him. The photographer ducked down in the driver's seat as a police projectile struck his windshield.

A week later, a group of protesters marched toward Disneyland. Although they didn't have concrete evidence, the protesters felt that the theme park had pressured Anaheim Police Department to heavily crack down on the nearby protests, as chaos is bad for business. The march was met by police dressed in militaristic camouflage uniforms and riding on the backs of trucks. Rows of dozens of similarly militarized officers blocked the intersection of the road leading to the amusement park. By some estimates, there were more armed, militarized officers on the streets of Anaheim that day than protesters.

The mainstream media failed in their watchdog role and instead assisted in covering up the events of Anaheim, whether they were ignoring attacks by police on their own reporters, not mentioning the outrageously militarized police uniforms, or calling the protests that consisted

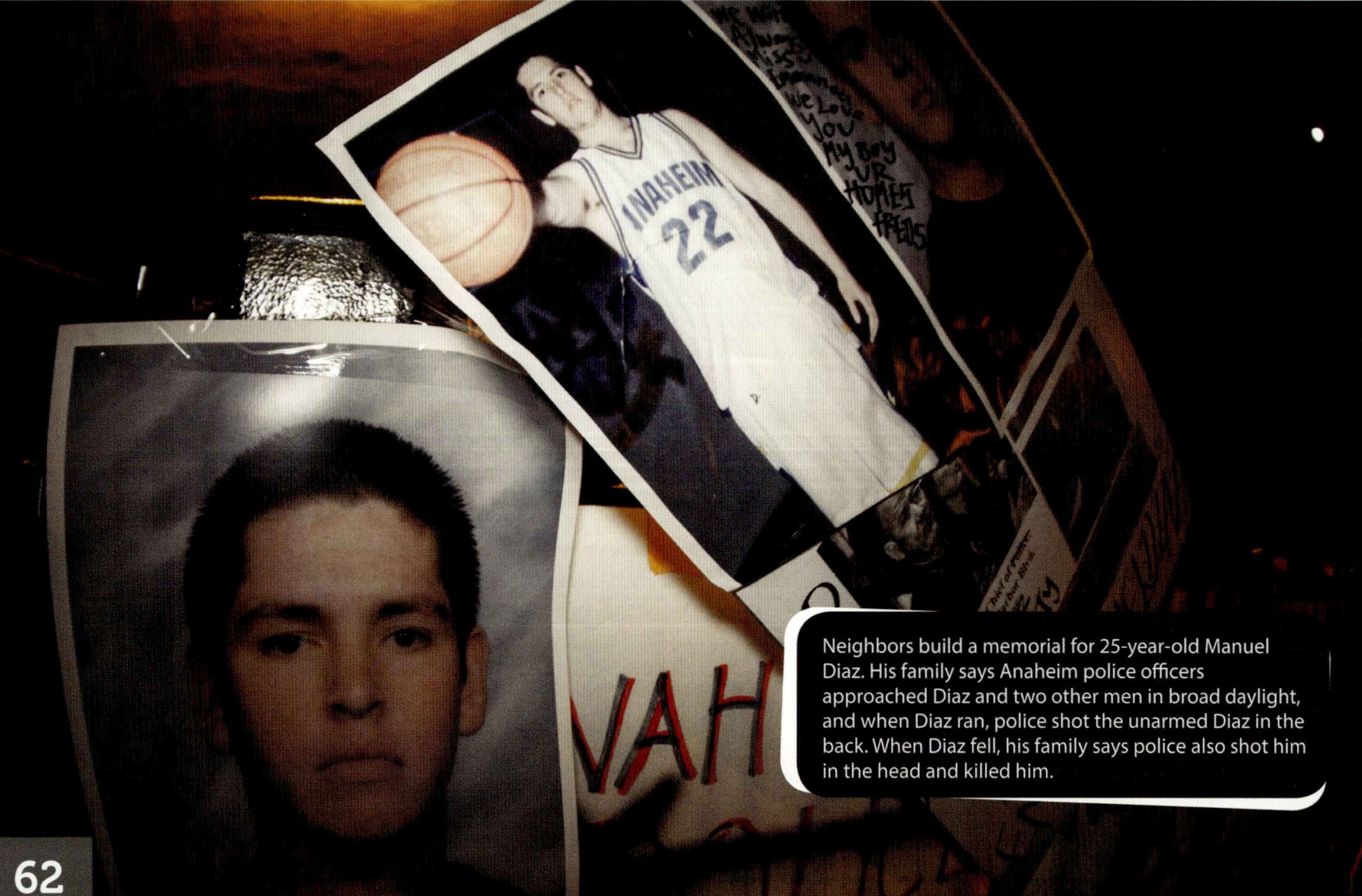

Neighbors build a memorial for 25-year-old Manuel Diaz. His family says Anaheim police officers approached Diaz and two other men in broad daylight, and when Diaz ran, police shot the unarmed Diaz in the back. When Diaz fell, his family says police also shot him in the head and killed him.

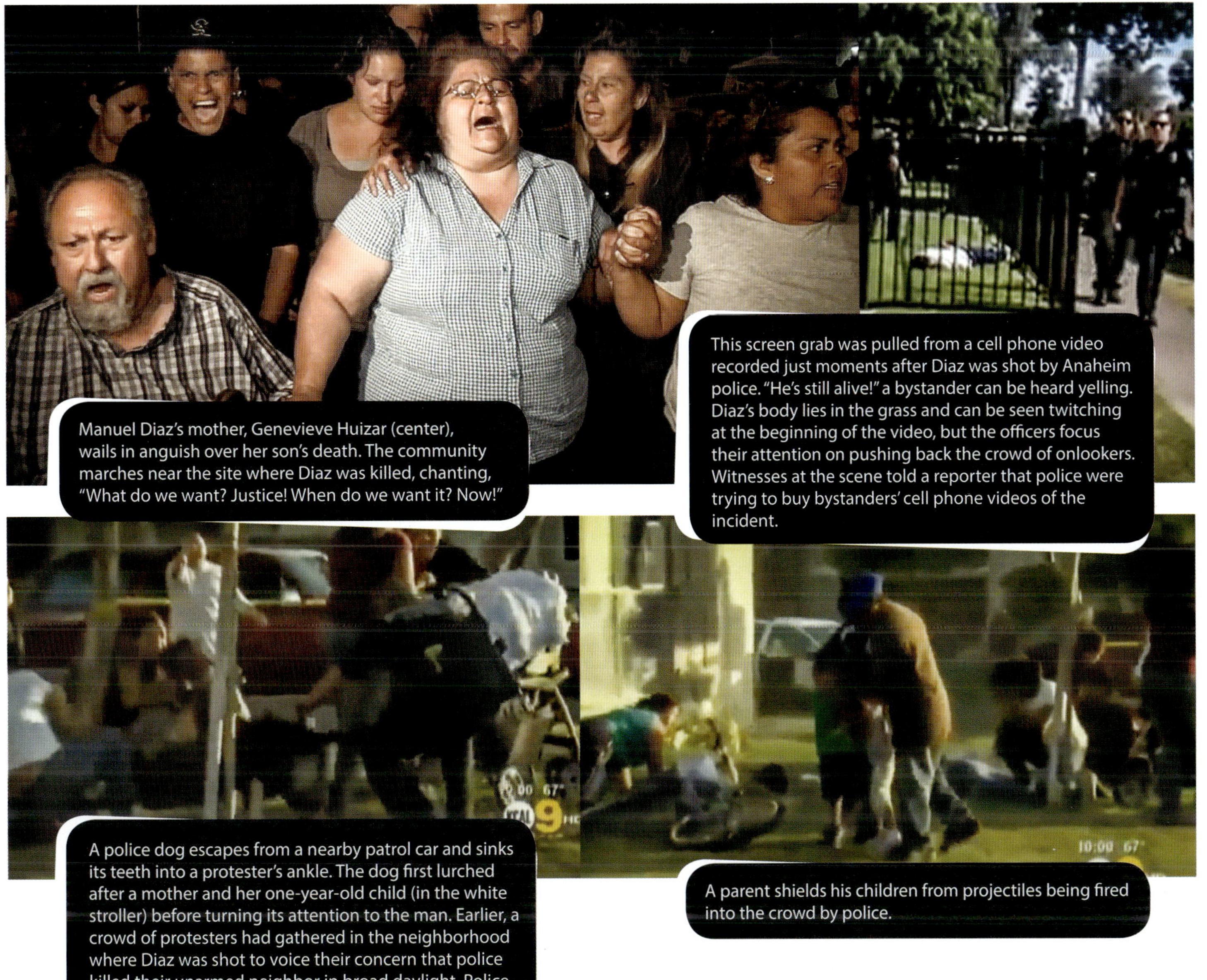

Manuel Diaz's mother, Genevieve Huizar (center), wails in anguish over her son's death. The community marches near the site where Diaz was killed, chanting, "What do we want? Justice! When do we want it? Now!"

This screen grab was pulled from a cell phone video recorded just moments after Diaz was shot by Anaheim police. "He's still alive!" a bystander can be heard yelling. Diaz's body lies in the grass and can be seen twitching at the beginning of the video, but the officers focus their attention on pushing back the crowd of onlookers. Witnesses at the scene told a reporter that police were trying to buy bystanders' cell phone videos of the incident.

A police dog escapes from a nearby patrol car and sinks its teeth into a protester's ankle. The dog first lurched after a mother and her one-year-old child (in the white stroller) before turning its attention to the man. Earlier, a crowd of protesters had gathered in the neighborhood where Diaz was shot to voice their concern that police killed their unarmed neighbor in broad daylight. Police responded by firing less lethal rounds into the crowd of unarmed neighbors, including children.

A parent shields his children from projectiles being fired into the crowd by police.

Friends carry away a boy injured after police stormed a neighborhood protest, firing less lethal rounds.

largely of women and children "riots." Without any independent investigation, some outlets immediately delegitimized Diaz by introducing him in their reports as a "suspected gang member" simply because that's what police told reporters.

Social media made the censorship slightly less relevant, as photos of Anaheim police dressed in military camo went viral, earning Anaheim the nickname "Afghanaheim." But even though the world had the evidence, an intense and galvanized outrage was not there. Because of the lack of national protest, the majority of the public appeared to accept the Anaheim Police Department's behavior, setting a national precedent for a new, militarized police state in America.

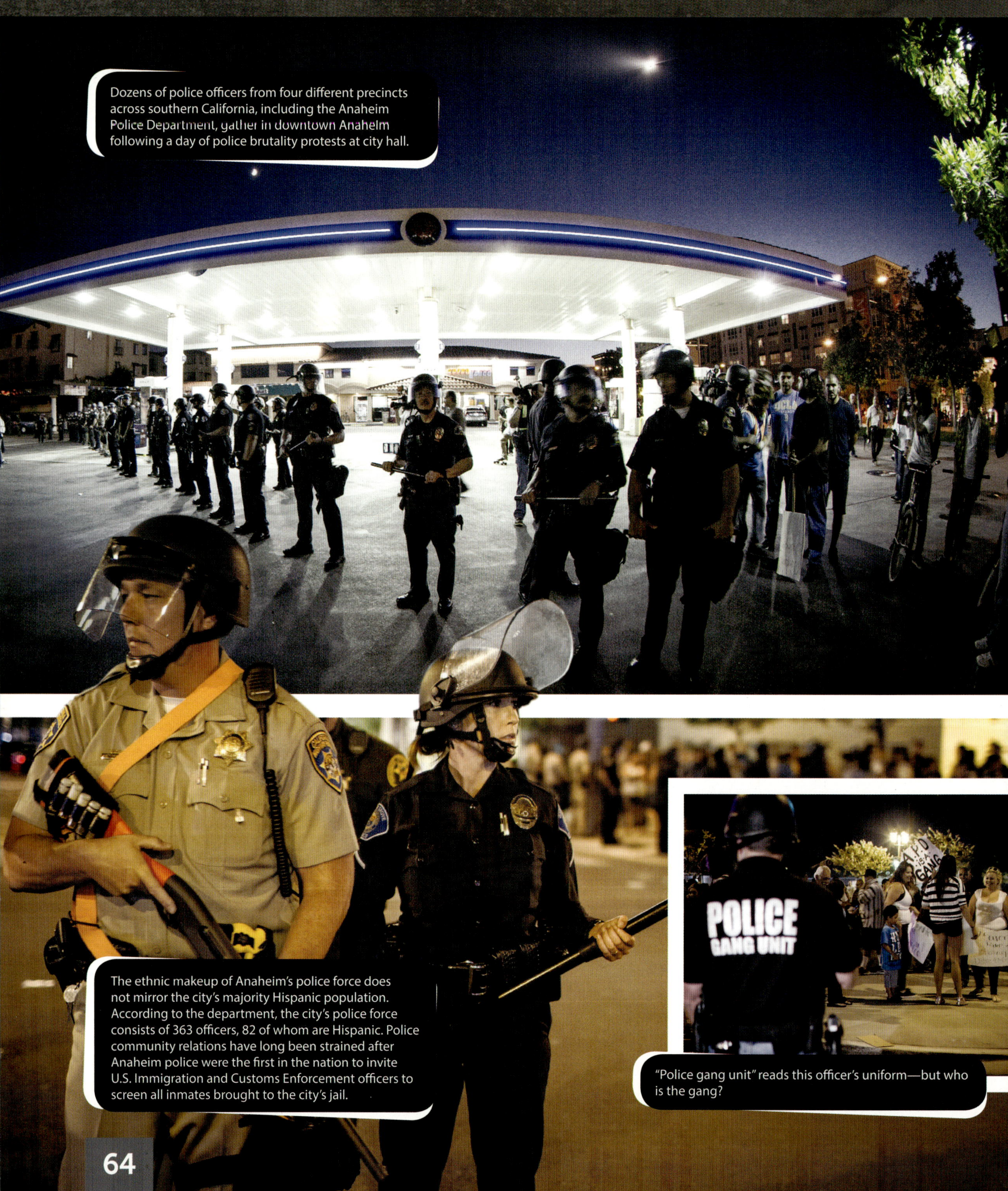

Dozens of police officers from four different precincts across southern California, including the Anaheim Police Department, gather in downtown Anaheim following a day of police brutality protests at city hall.

The ethnic makeup of Anaheim's police force does not mirror the city's majority Hispanic population. According to the department, the city's police force consists of 363 officers, 82 of whom are Hispanic. Police community relations have long been strained after Anaheim police were the first in the nation to invite U.S. Immigration and Customs Enforcement officers to screen all inmates brought to the city's jail.

"Police gang unit" reads this officer's uniform—but who is the gang?

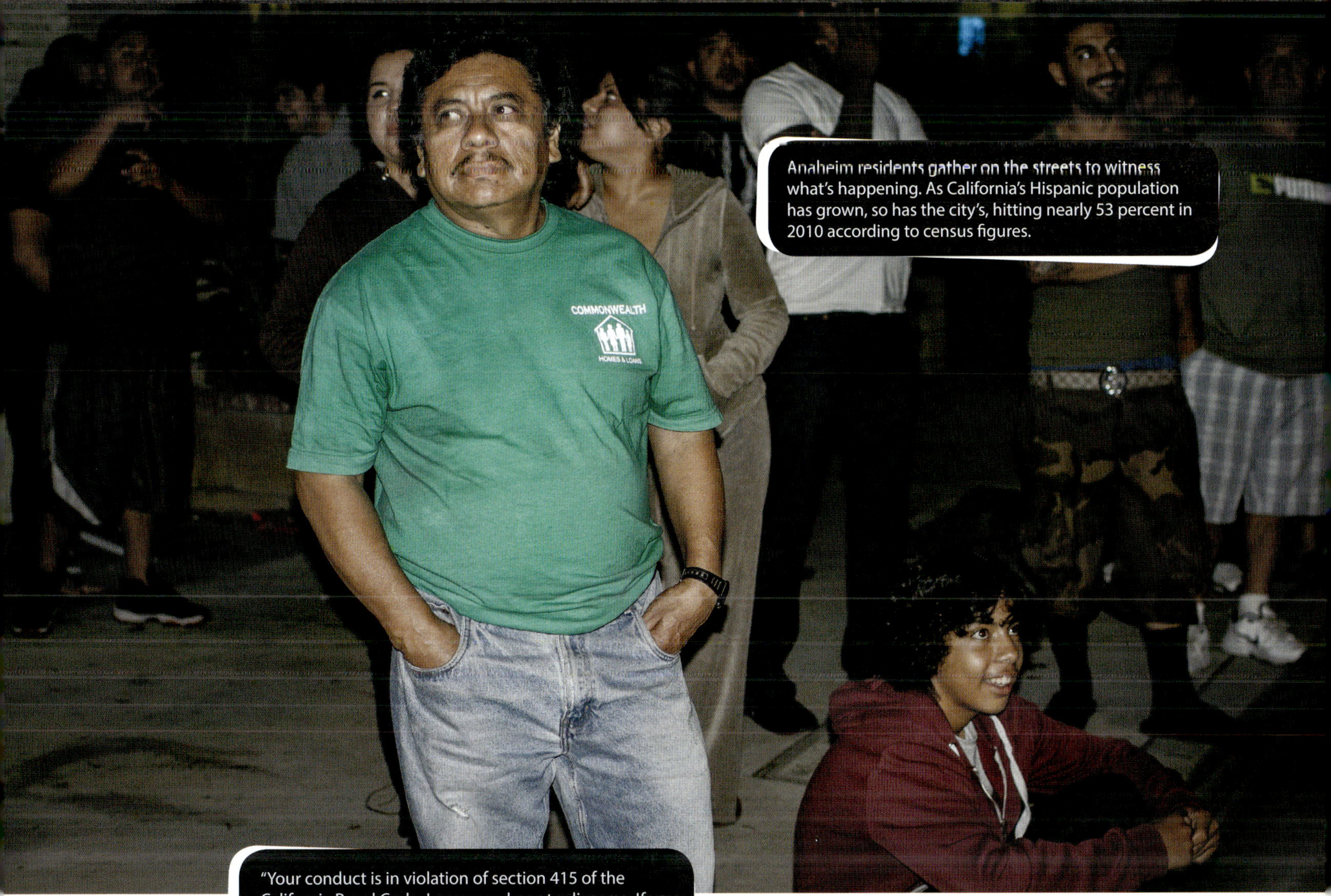

Anaheim residents gather on the streets to witness what's happening. As California's Hispanic population has grown, so has the city's, hitting nearly 53 percent in 2010 according to census figures.

"Your conduct is in violation of section 415 of the California Penal Code. I command you to disperse. If you do not you will be arrested for unlawful assembly." The officers order the protesters to disperse but do not issue a warning that less lethal rounds will be fired. A bottle and rocks are thrown from the crowd toward police. That provokes officers to then start to fire less lethal rounds indiscriminately into the crowd.

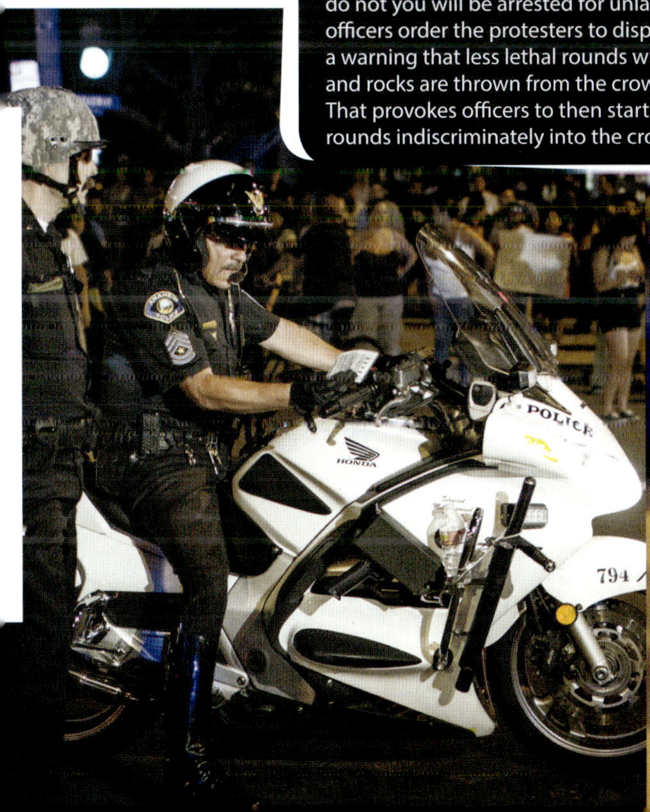

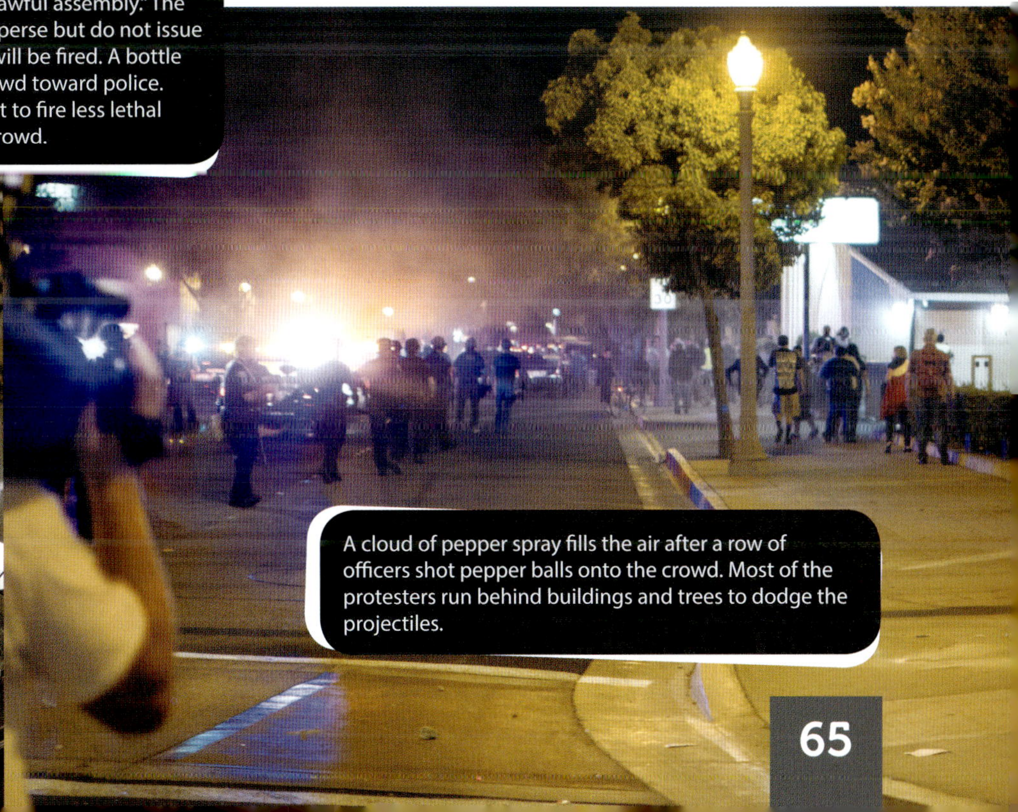

A cloud of pepper spray fills the air after a row of officers shot pepper balls onto the crowd. Most of the protesters run behind buildings and trees to dodge the projectiles.

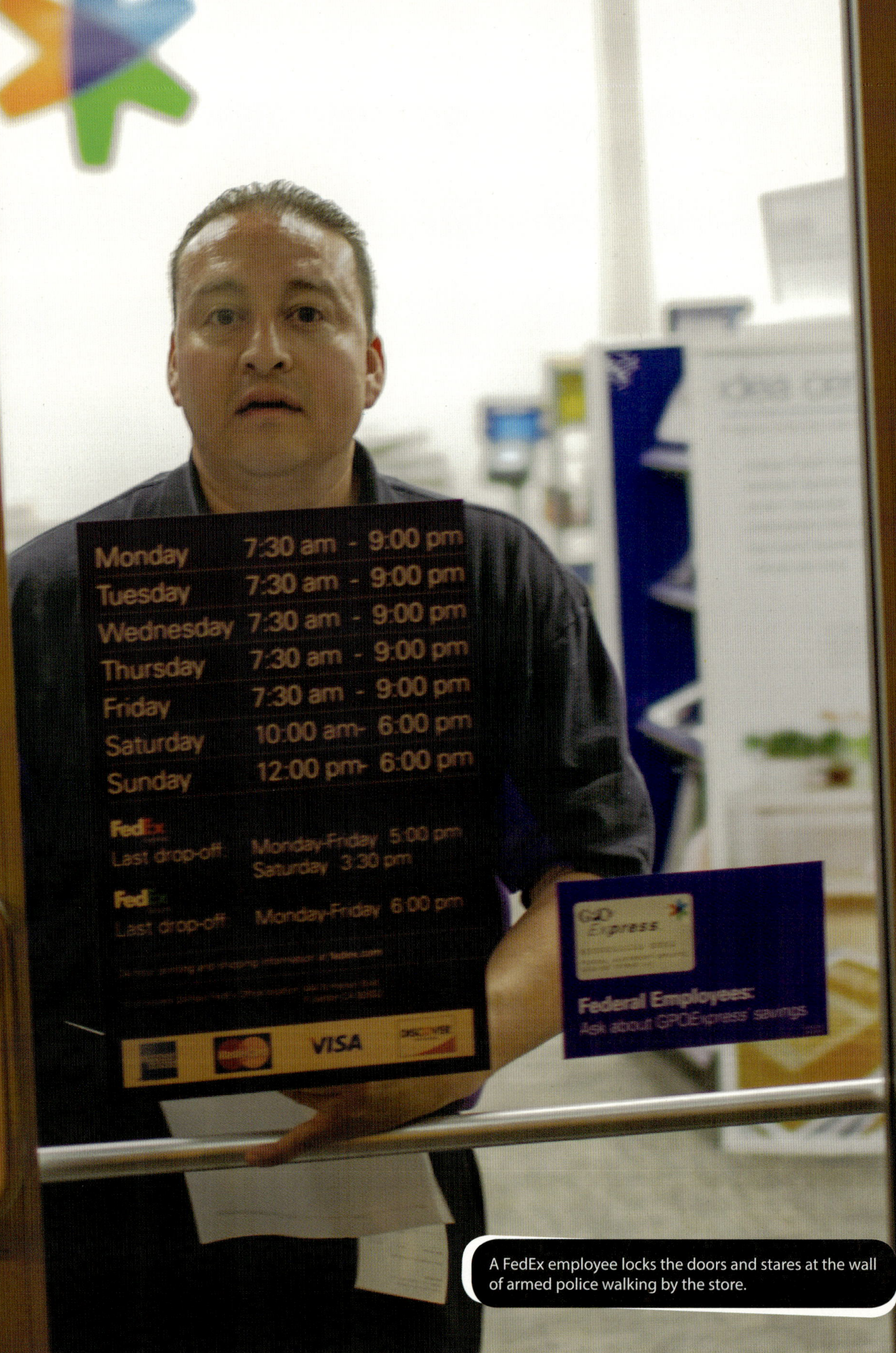

A FedEx employee locks the doors and stares at the wall of armed police walking by the store.

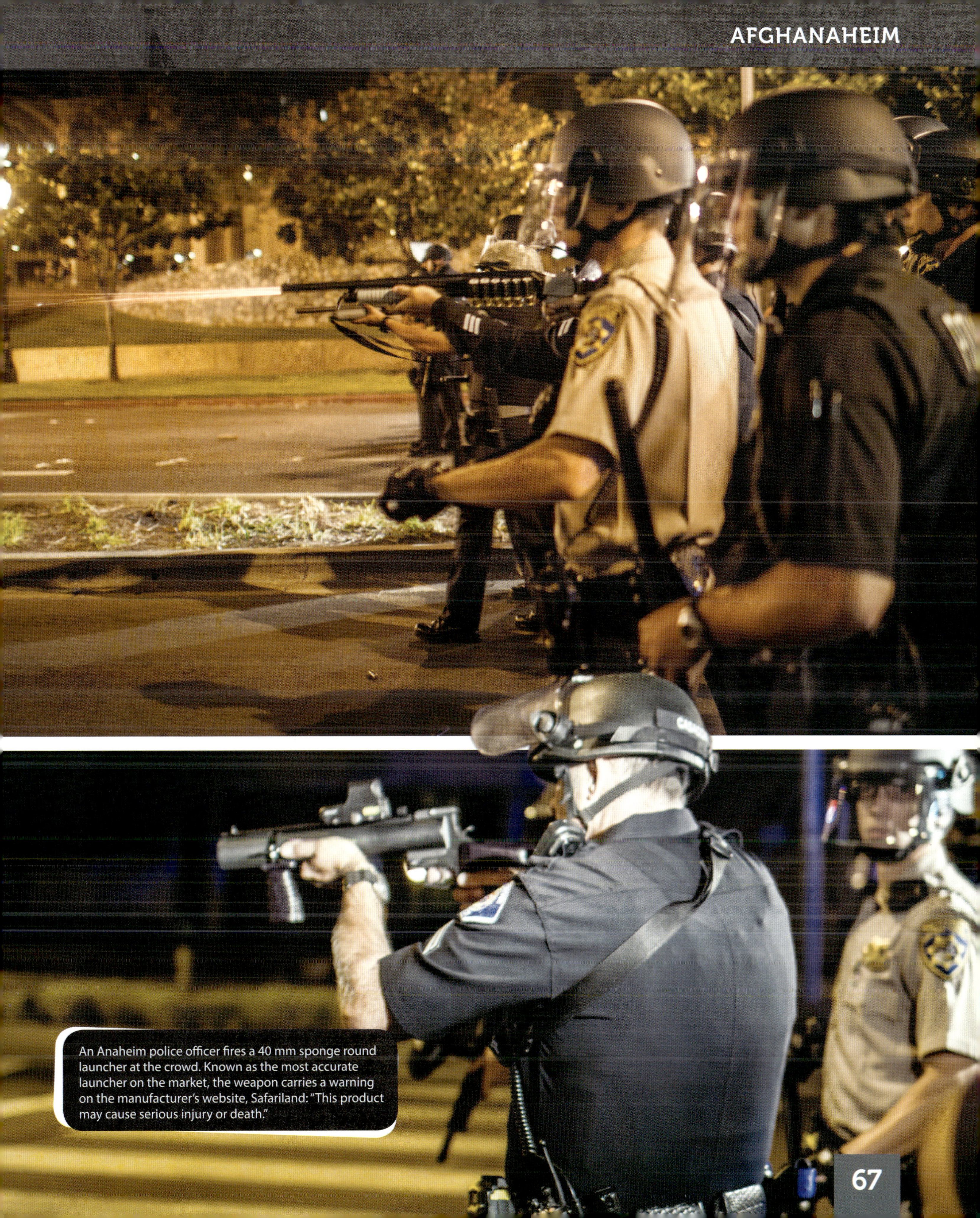

An Anaheim police officer fires a 40 mm sponge round launcher at the crowd. Known as the most accurate launcher on the market, the weapon carries a warning on the manufacturer's website, Safariland: "This product may cause serious injury or death."

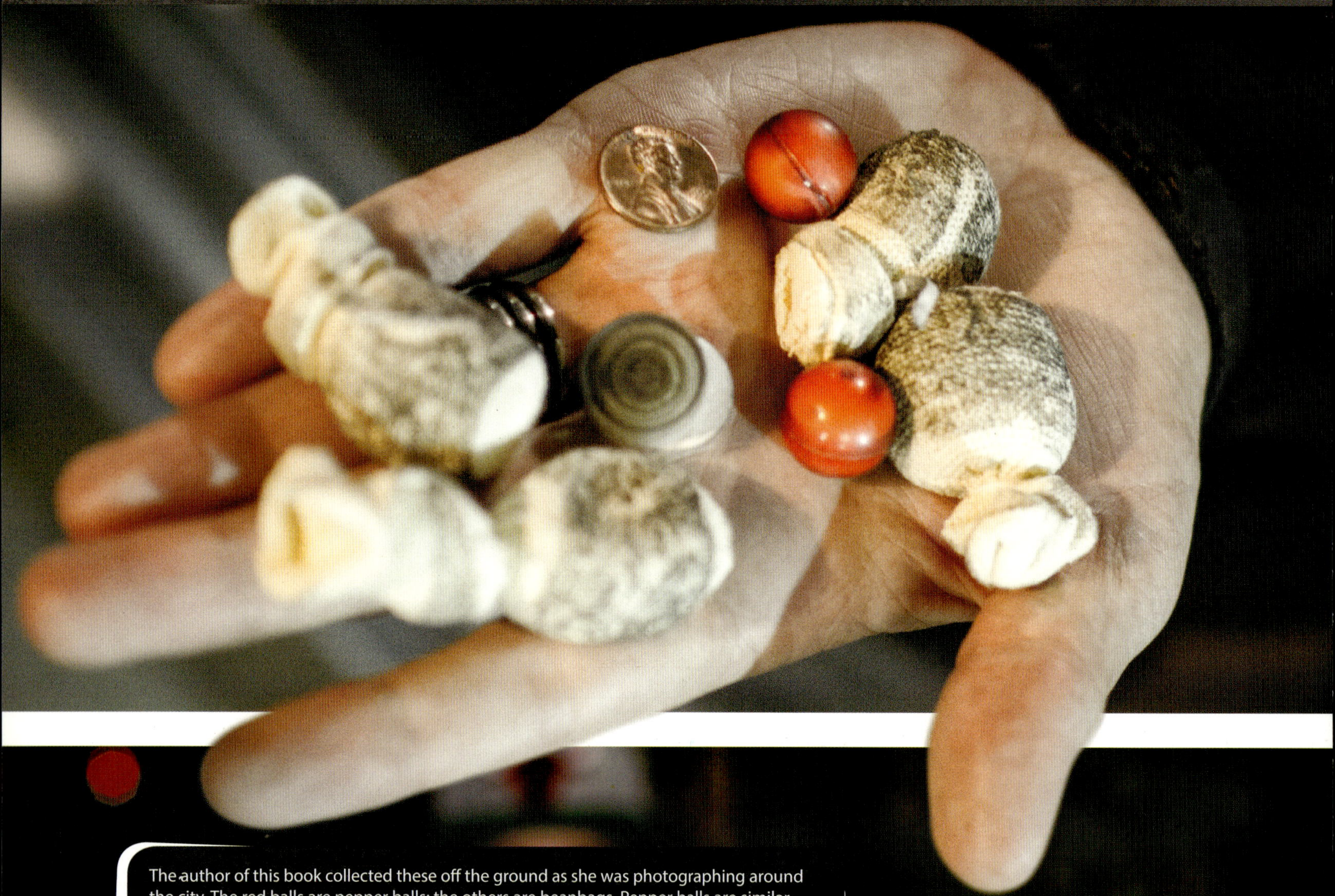

The author of this book collected these off the ground as she was photographing around the city. The red balls are pepper balls; the others are beanbags. Pepper balls are similar to paint balls. Upon impact, pepper-spray payload is released into the air. Deaths have occurred when the projectiles have been fired at inappropriate areas. In one well-publicized incident in 2004, the Boston Police Department killed a 21-year-old woman when they used a pepper-spray projectile weapon during a crowd control situation. The beanbag rounds contain a lead shot insulated by a fabric pillow. They are designed to deliver a hit that will not cause penetration but will result in a muscle spasm or other reaction. Like other weapons classed as "less lethal," they are intended to briefly render a suspect immobile without killing them. However, beanbags have proven to be lethal and can kill or severely injure. If someone is hit in the head, the round can break the neck or skull. If a round strikes a person in the chest, it can cause broken ribs and potentially drive them into the heart.

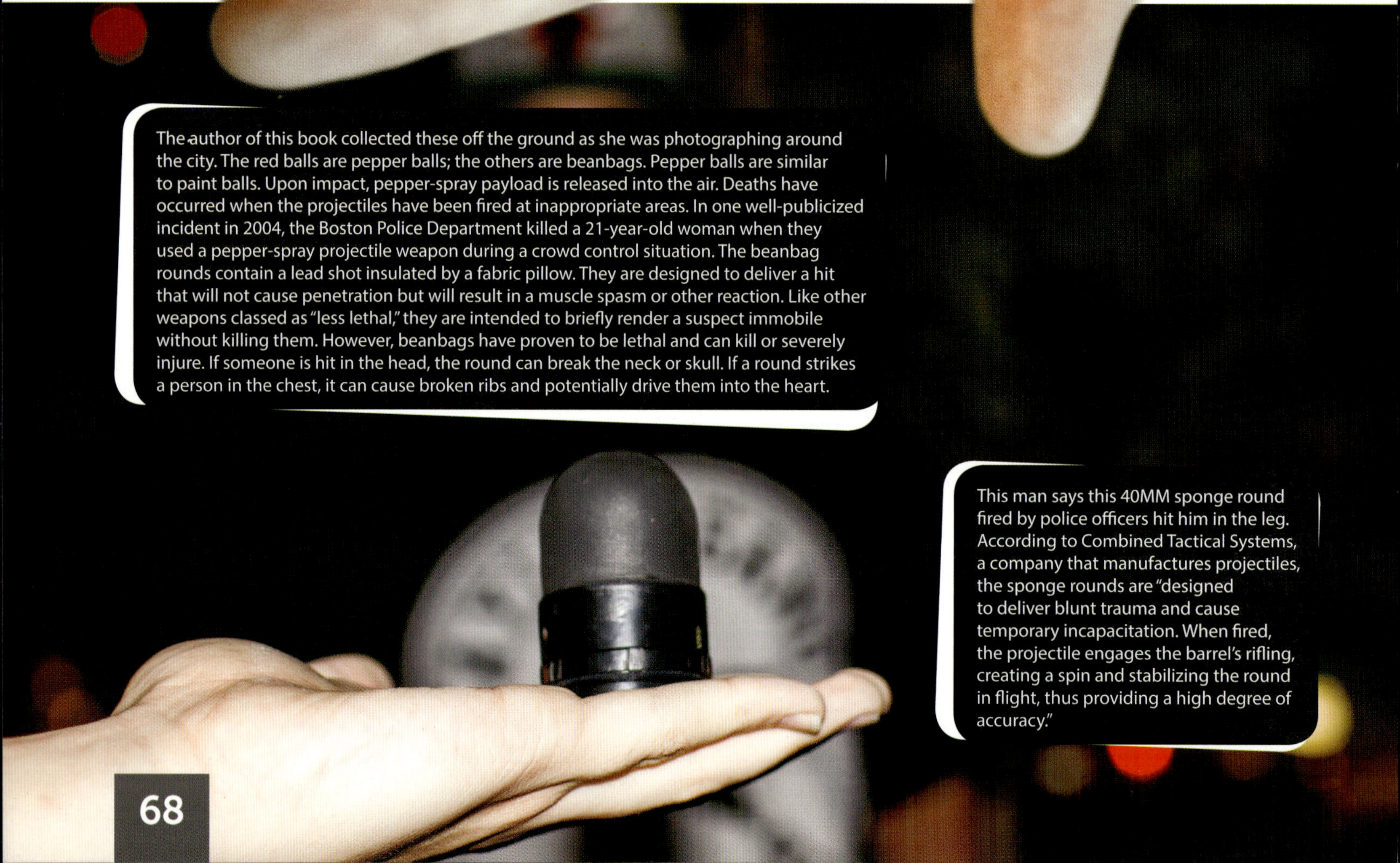

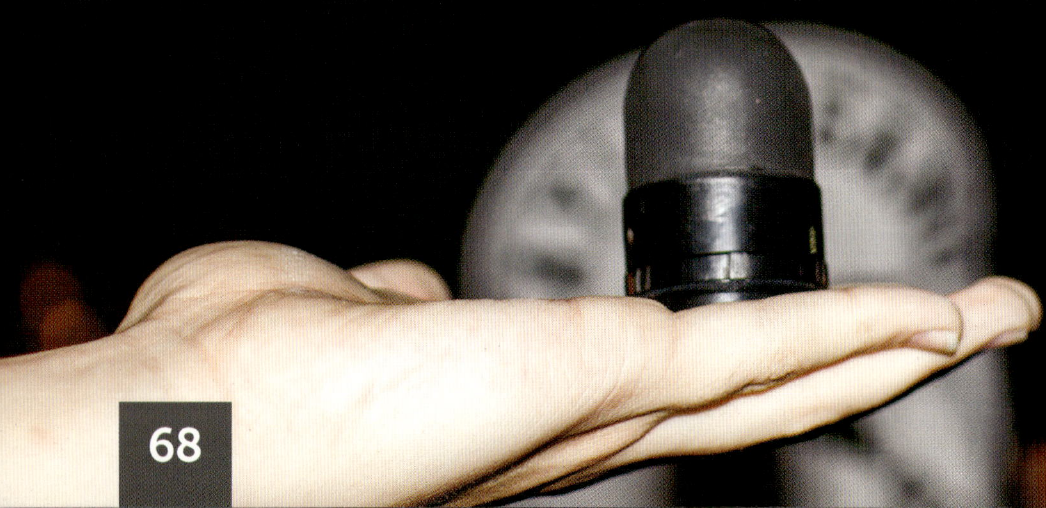

This man says this 40MM sponge round fired by police officers hit him in the leg. According to Combined Tactical Systems, a company that manufactures projectiles, the sponge rounds are "designed to deliver blunt trauma and cause temporary incapacitation. When fired, the projectile engages the barrel's rifling, creating a spin and stabilizing the round in flight, thus providing a high degree of accuracy."

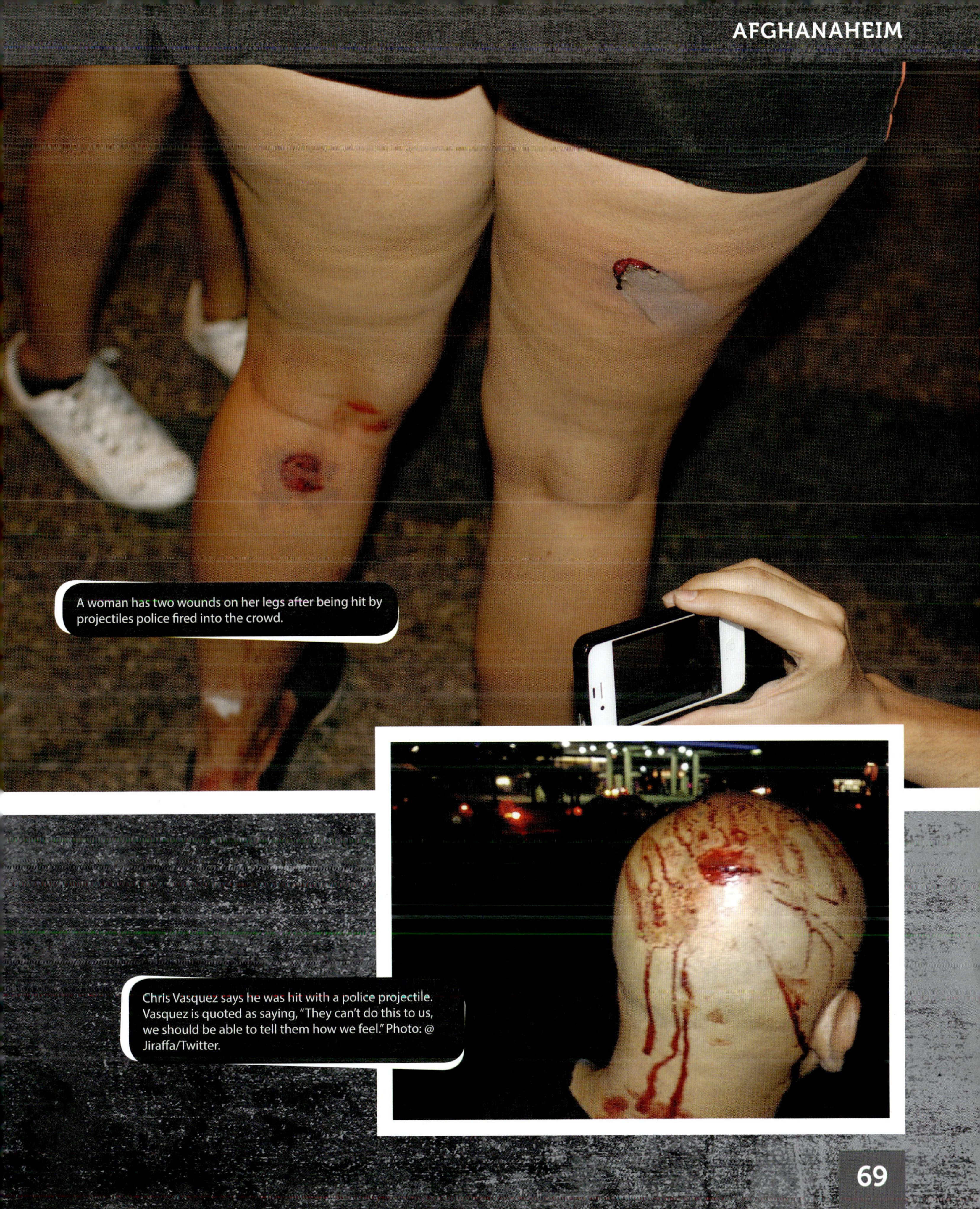

A woman has two wounds on her legs after being hit by projectiles police fired into the crowd.

Chris Vasquez says he was hit with a police projectile. Vasquez is quoted as saying, "They can't do this to us, we should be able to tell them how we feel." Photo: @ Jiraffa/Twitter.

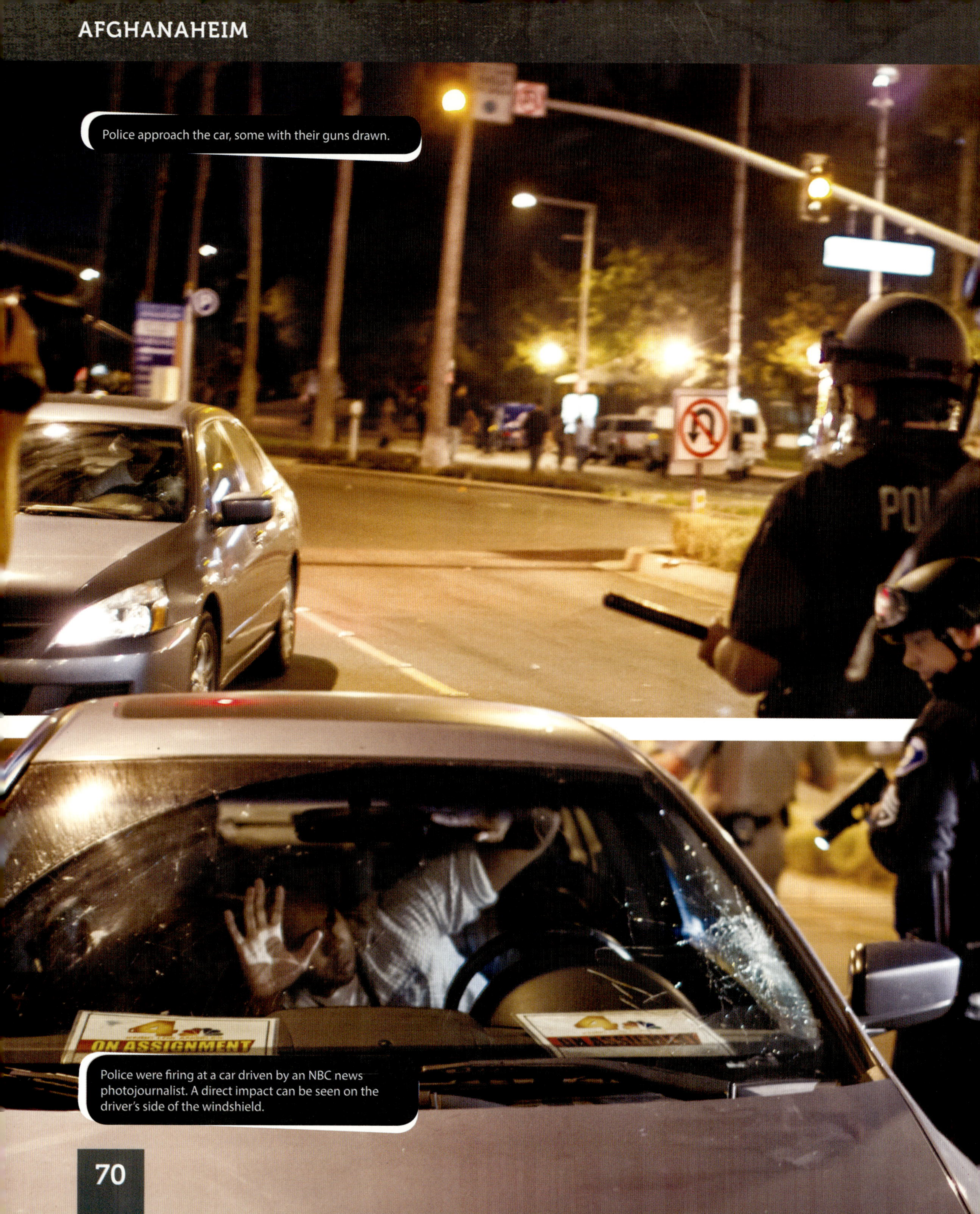

Police approach the car, some with their guns drawn.

Police were firing at a car driven by an NBC news photojournalist. A direct impact can be seen on the driver's side of the windshield.

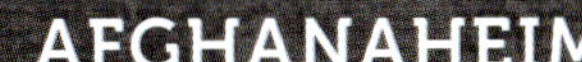

A dumpster is set on fire as a sign of protest.

The local Telemundo station hires security to protect journalists and equipment. But the most solid threat to journalists this night was police, not protesters. Three journalists were hit by impact rounds fired by the police.

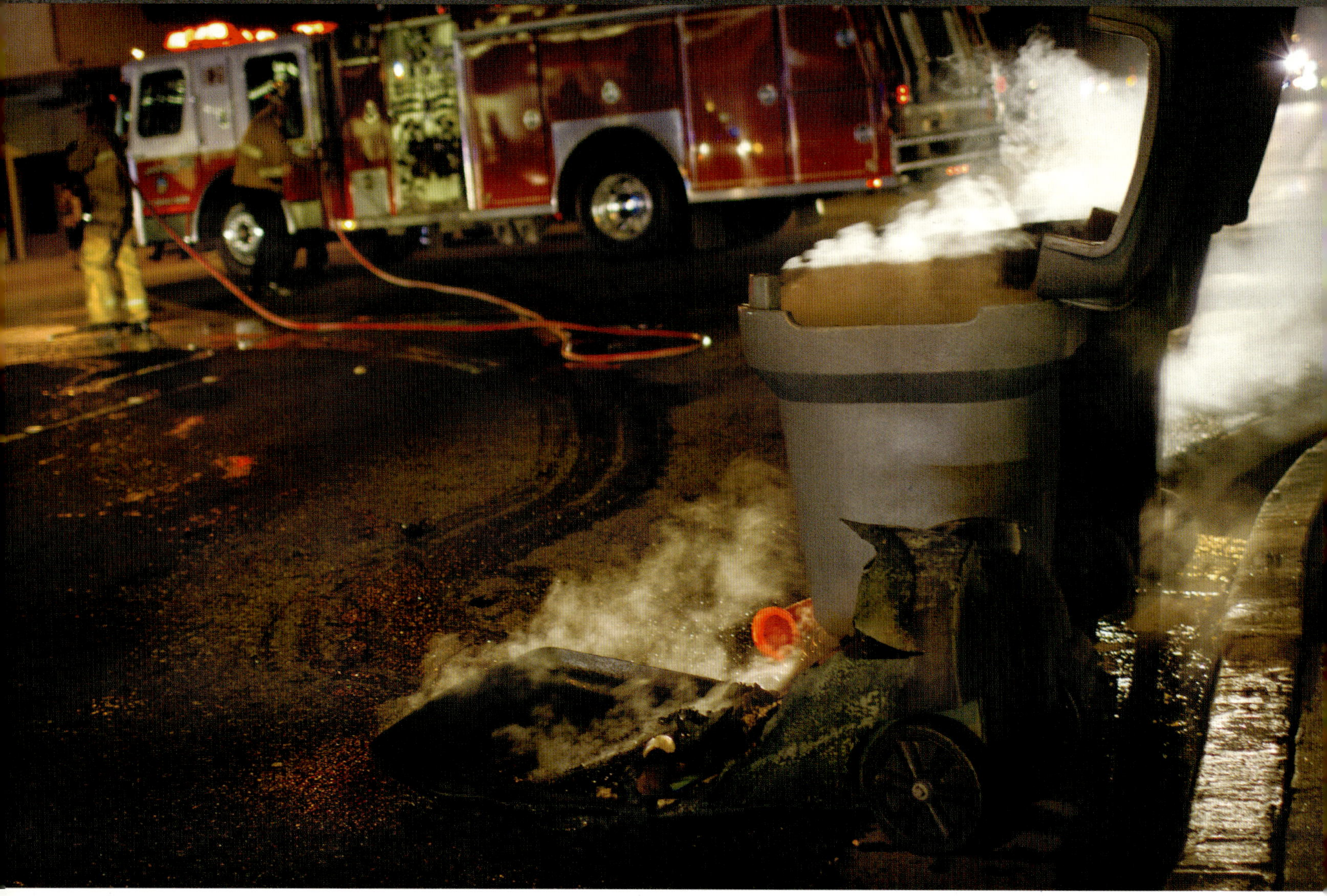

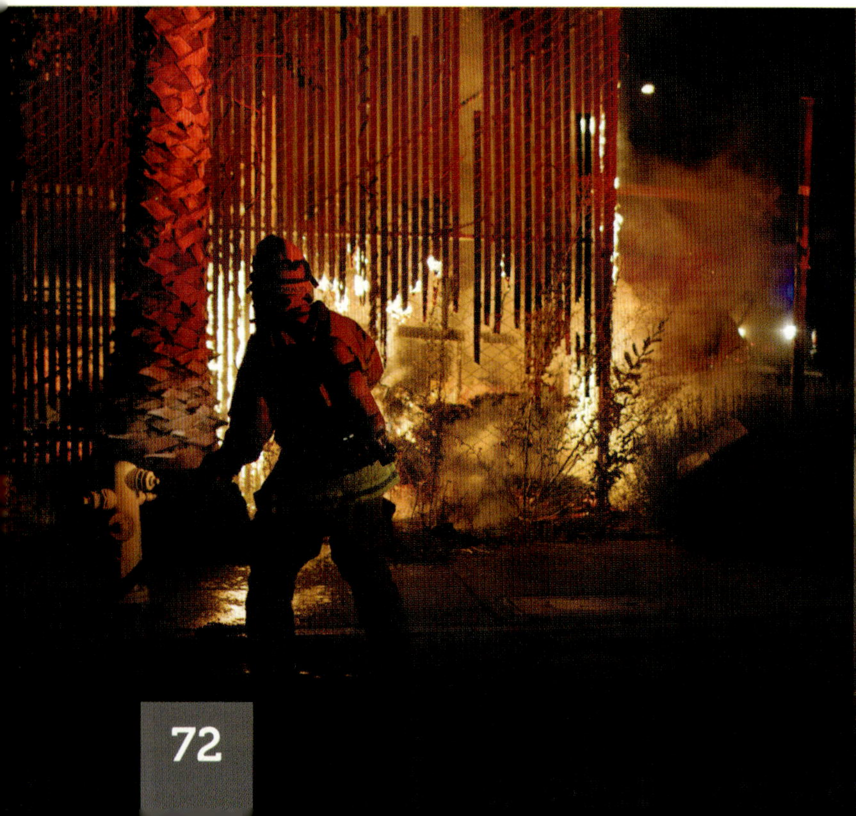

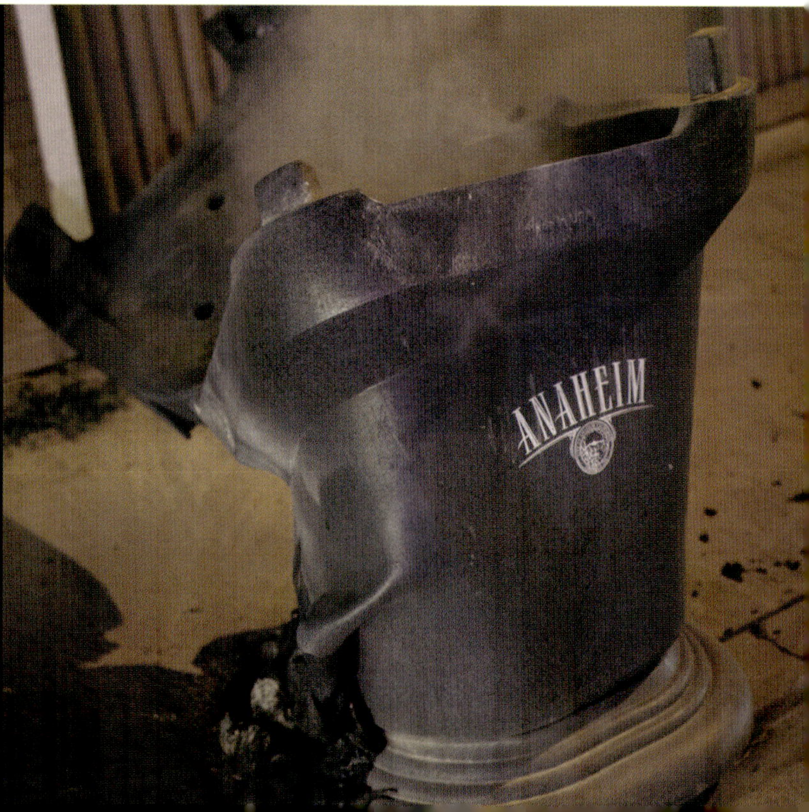

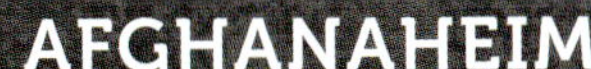

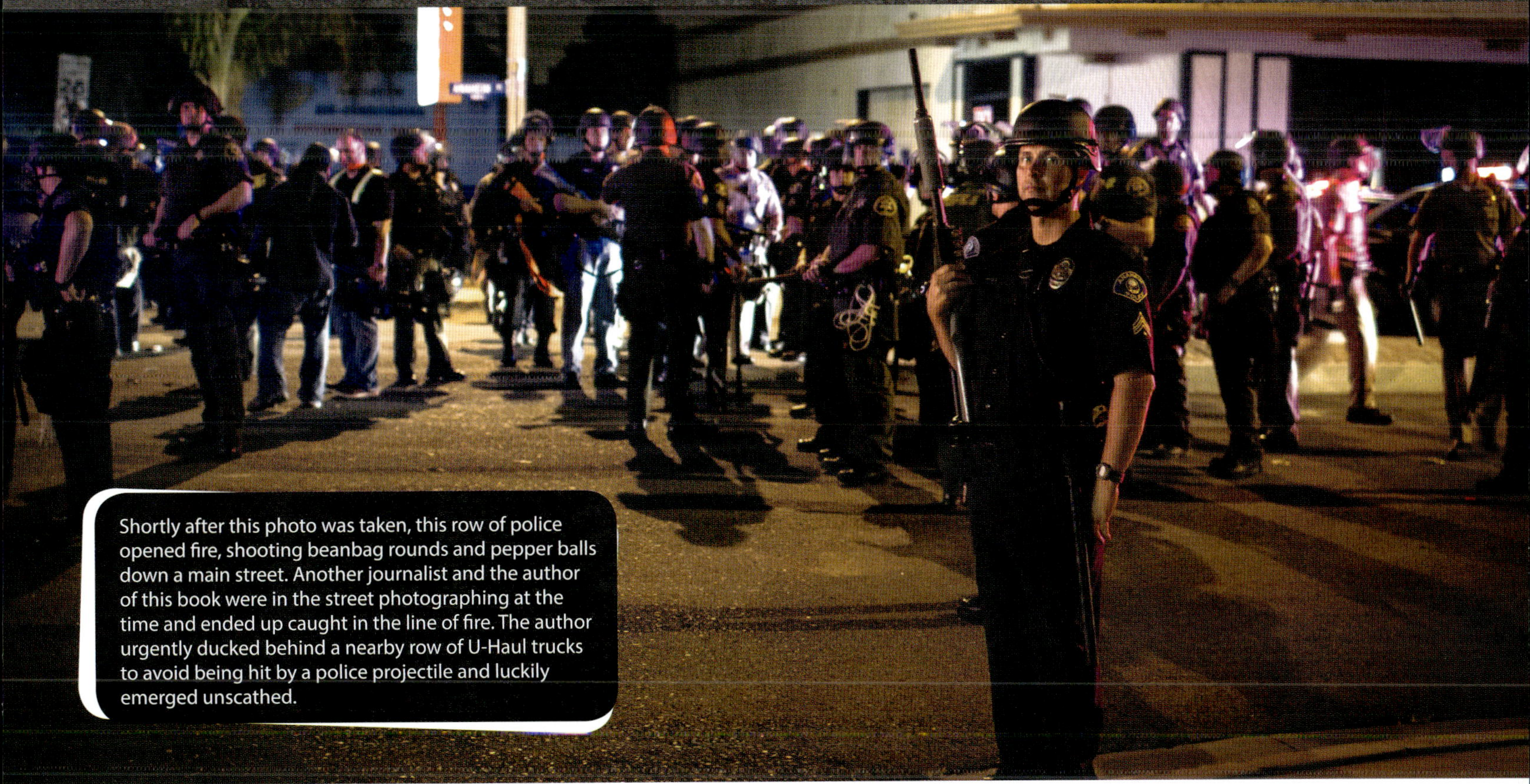

Shortly after this photo was taken, this row of police opened fire, shooting beanbag rounds and pepper balls down a main street. Another journalist and the author of this book were in the street photographing at the time and ended up caught in the line of fire. The author urgently ducked behind a nearby row of U-Haul trucks to avoid being hit by a police projectile and luckily emerged unscathed.

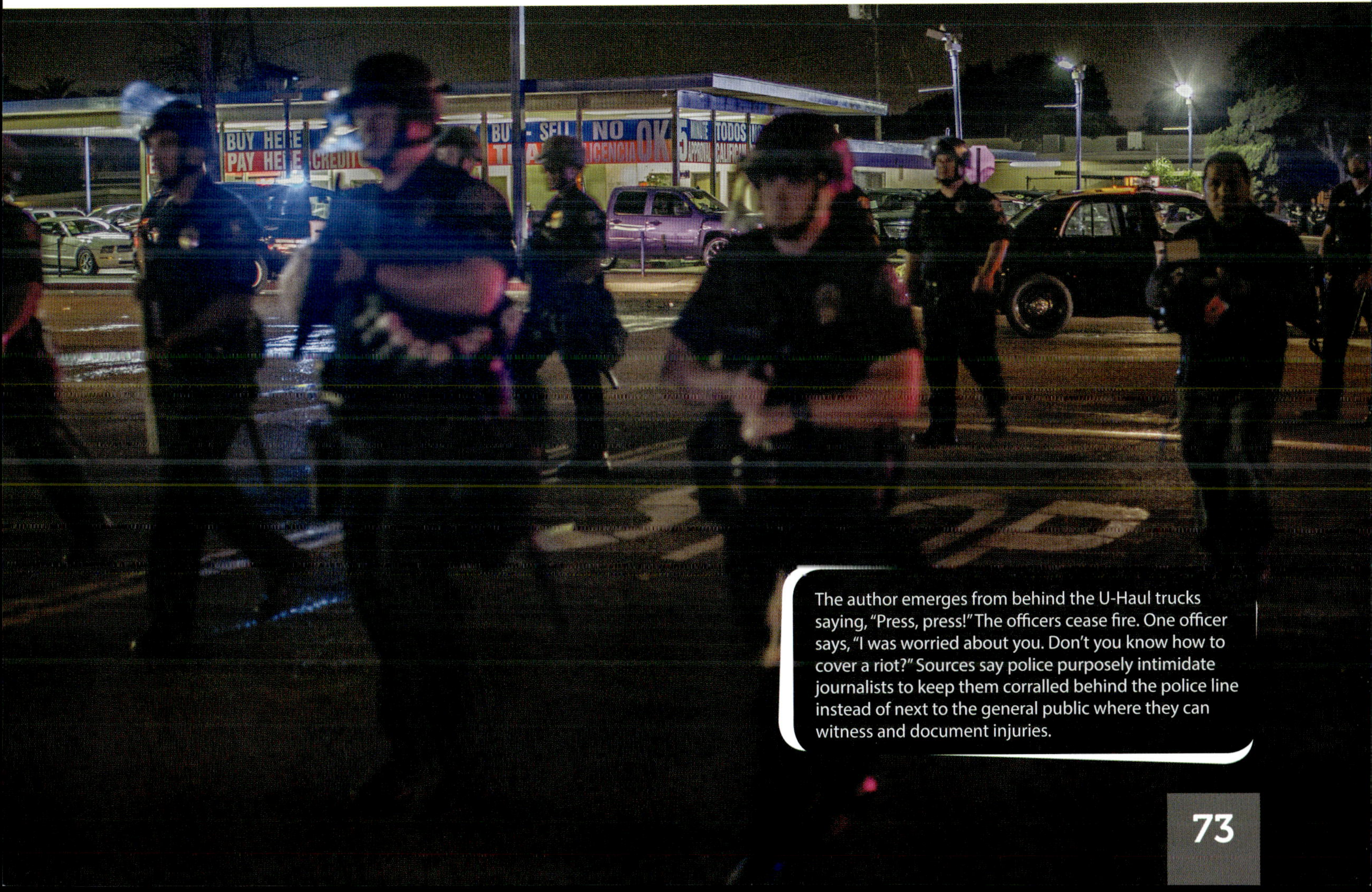

The author emerges from behind the U-Haul trucks saying, "Press, press!" The officers cease fire. One officer says, "I was worried about you. Don't you know how to cover a riot?" Sources say police purposely intimidate journalists to keep them corralled behind the police line instead of next to the general public where they can witness and document injuries.

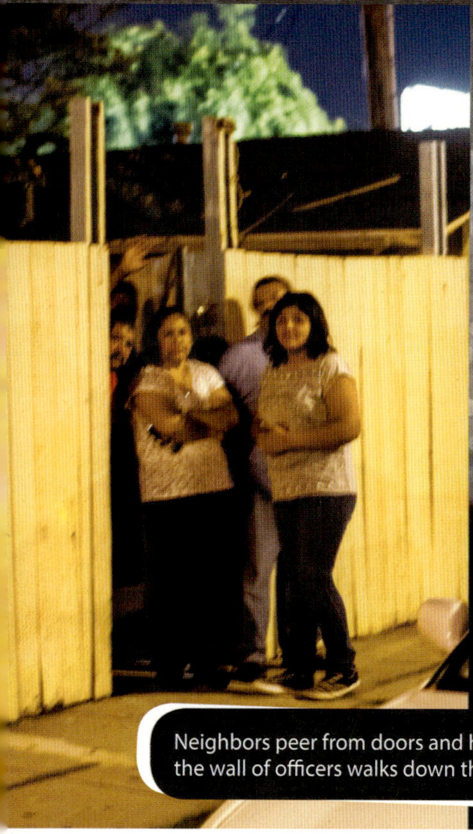

Neighbors peer from doors and hide in their homes as the wall of officers walks down the street.

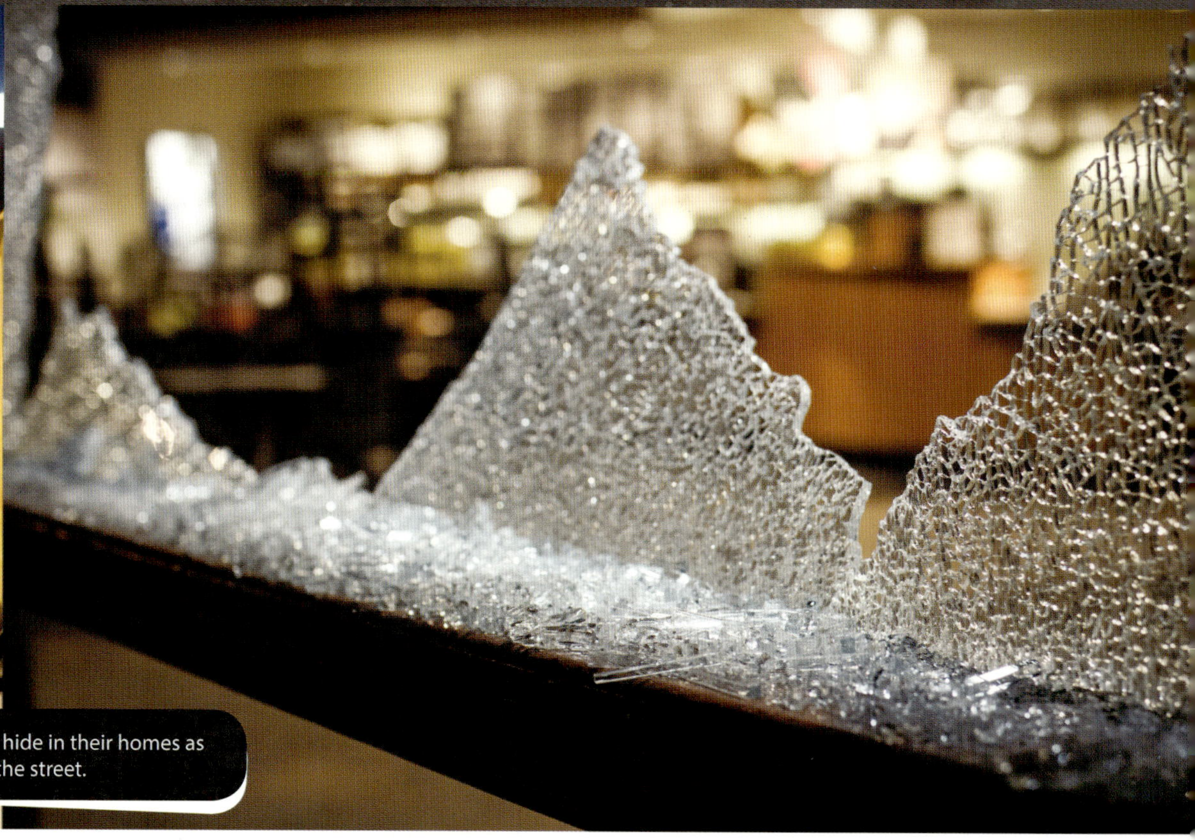

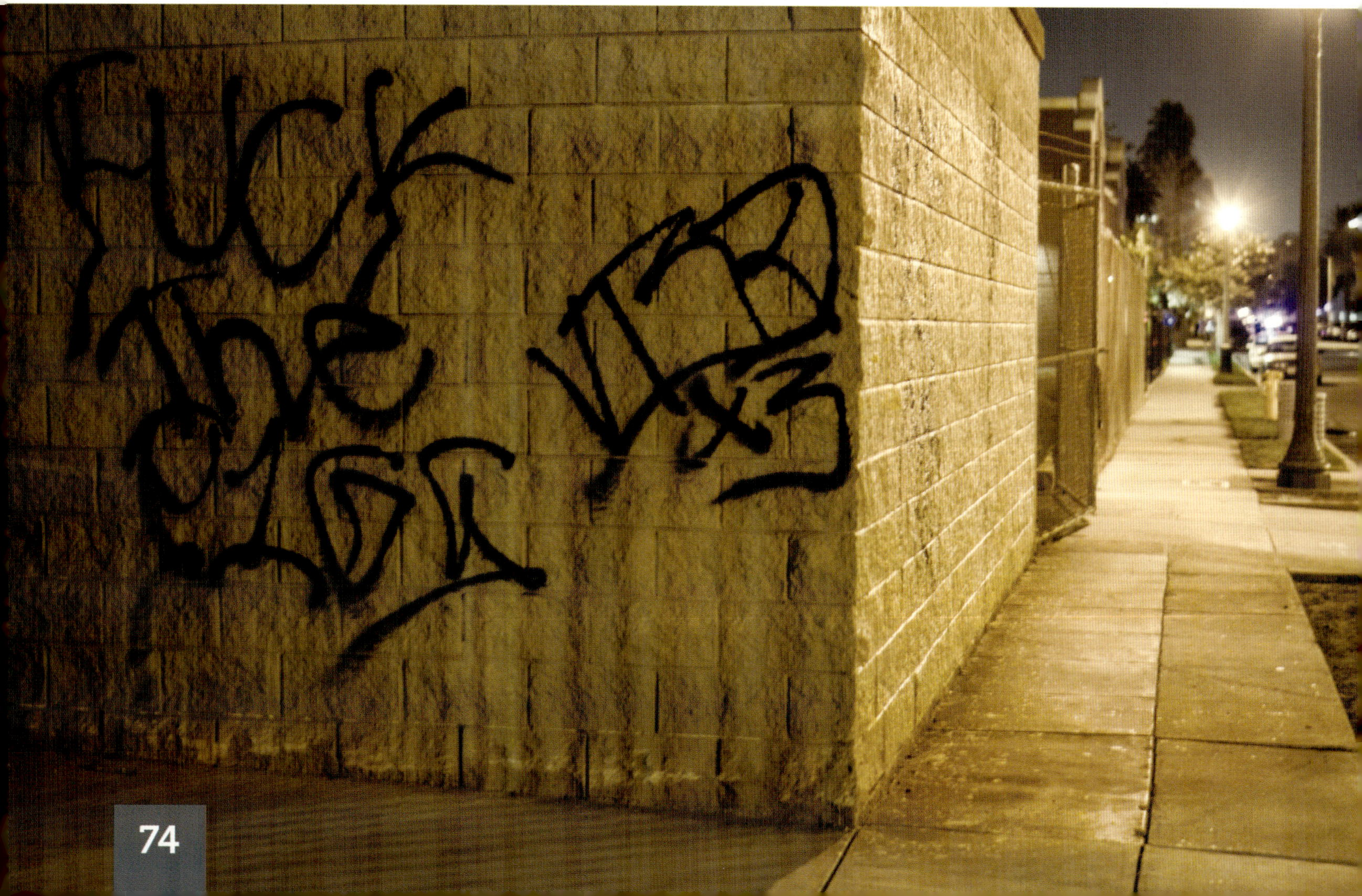

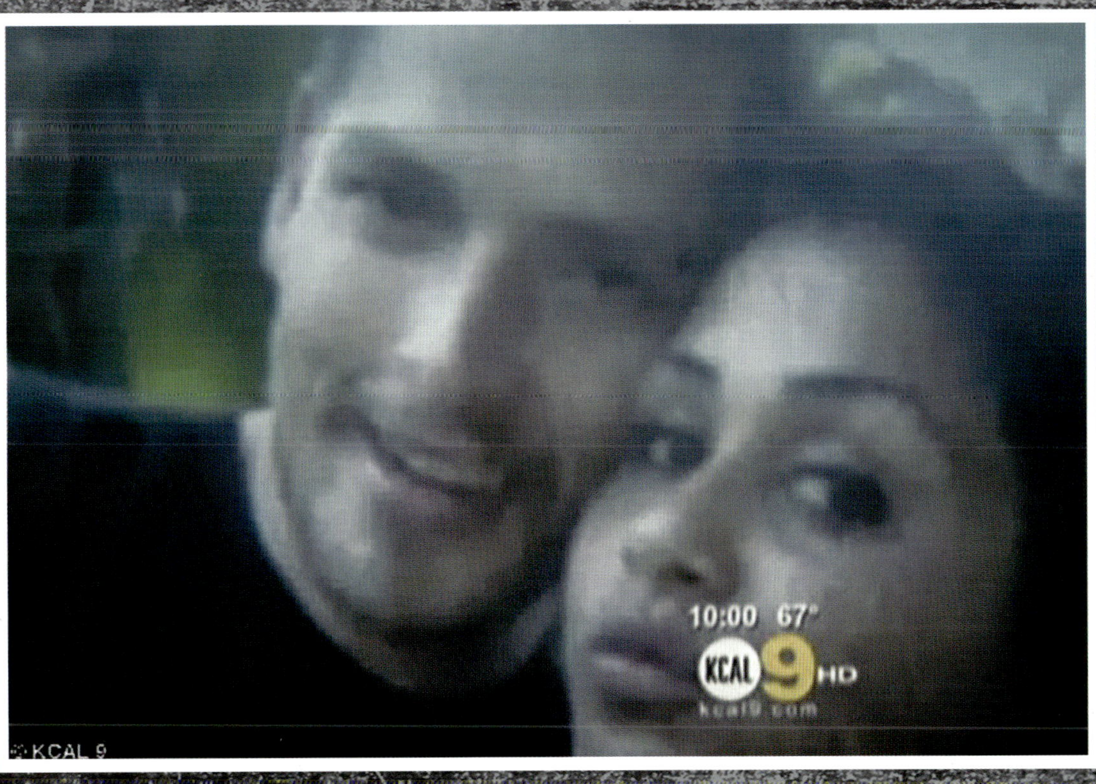

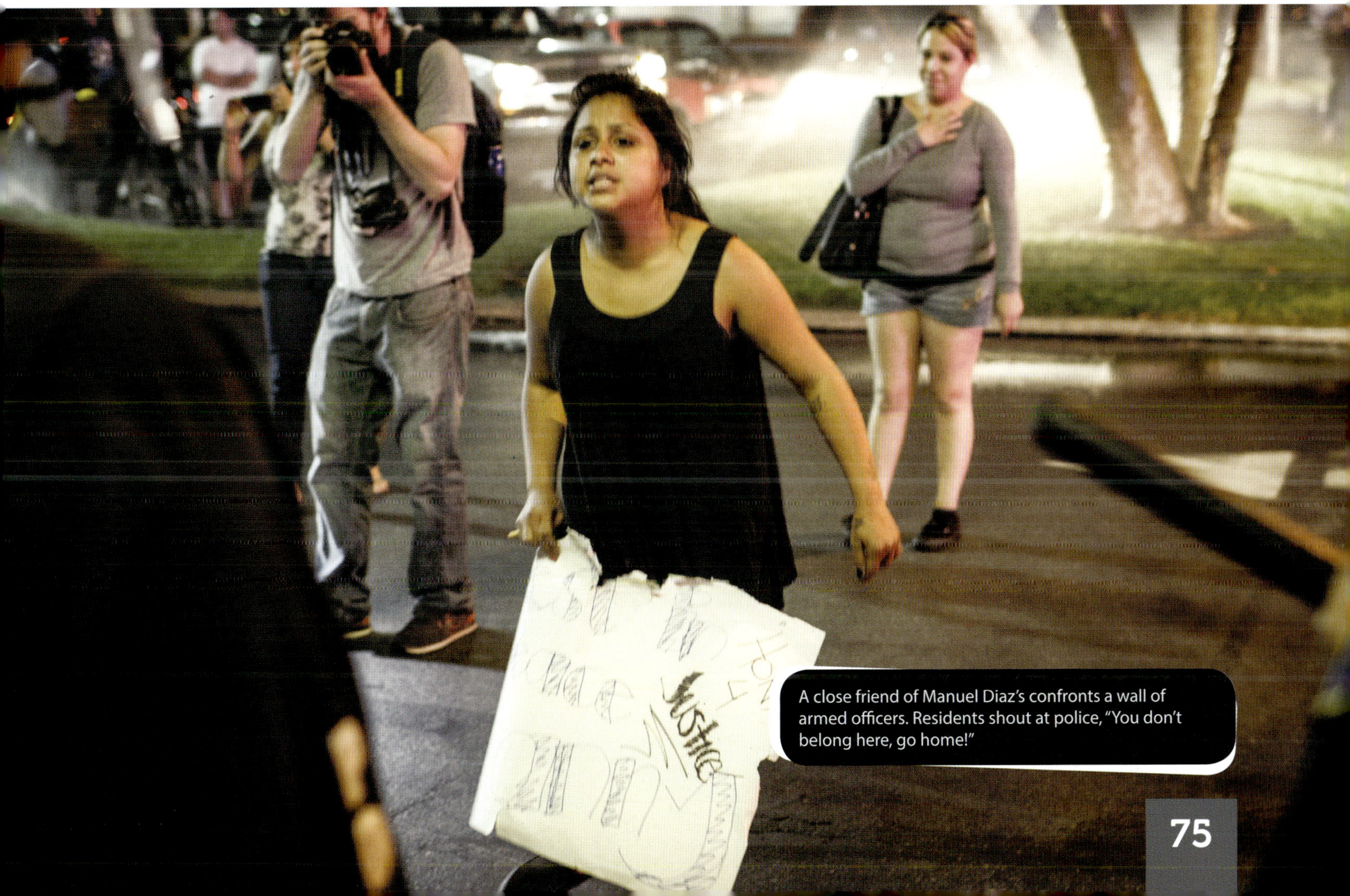

A close friend of Manuel Diaz's confronts a wall of armed officers. Residents shout at police, "You don't belong here, go home!"

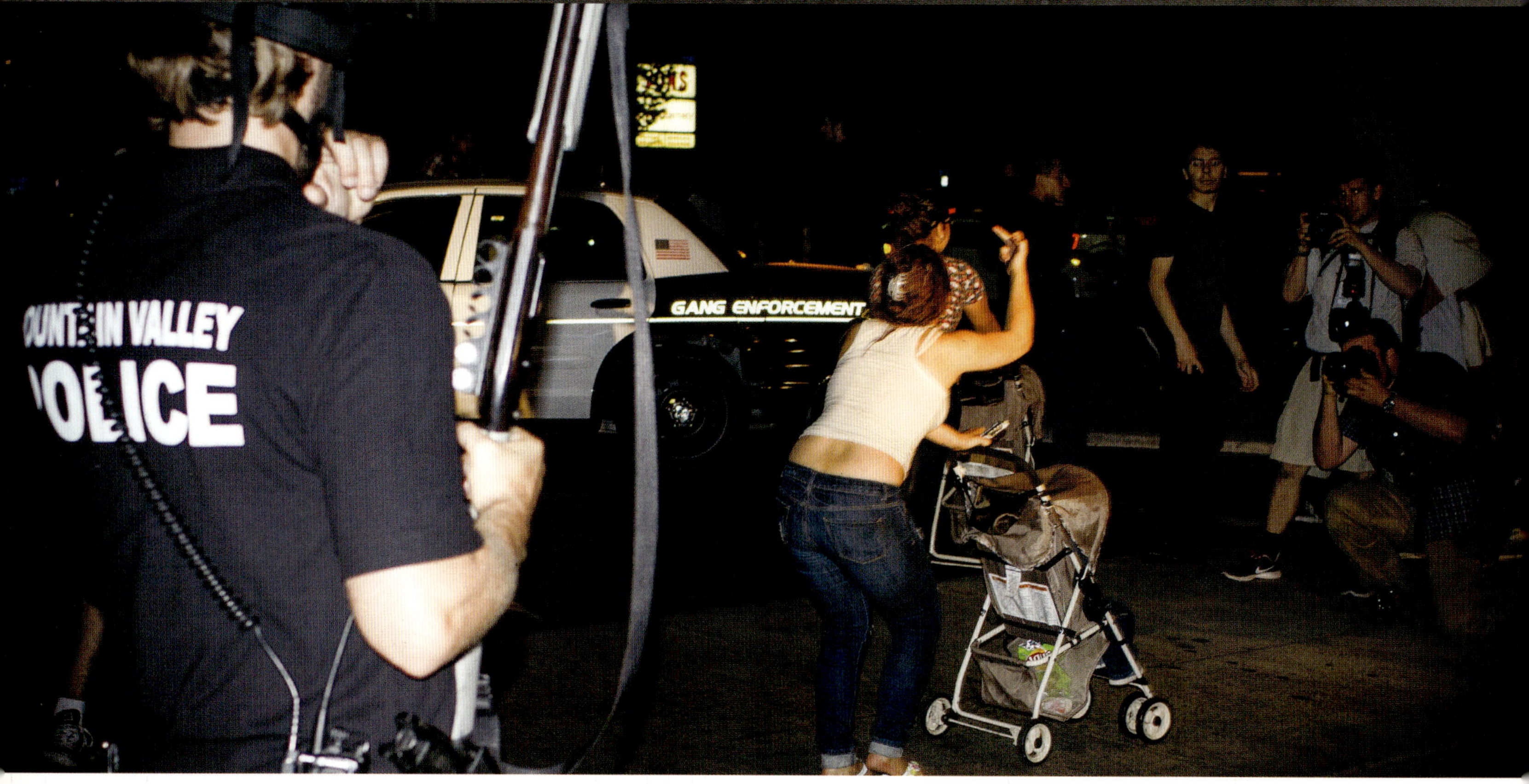

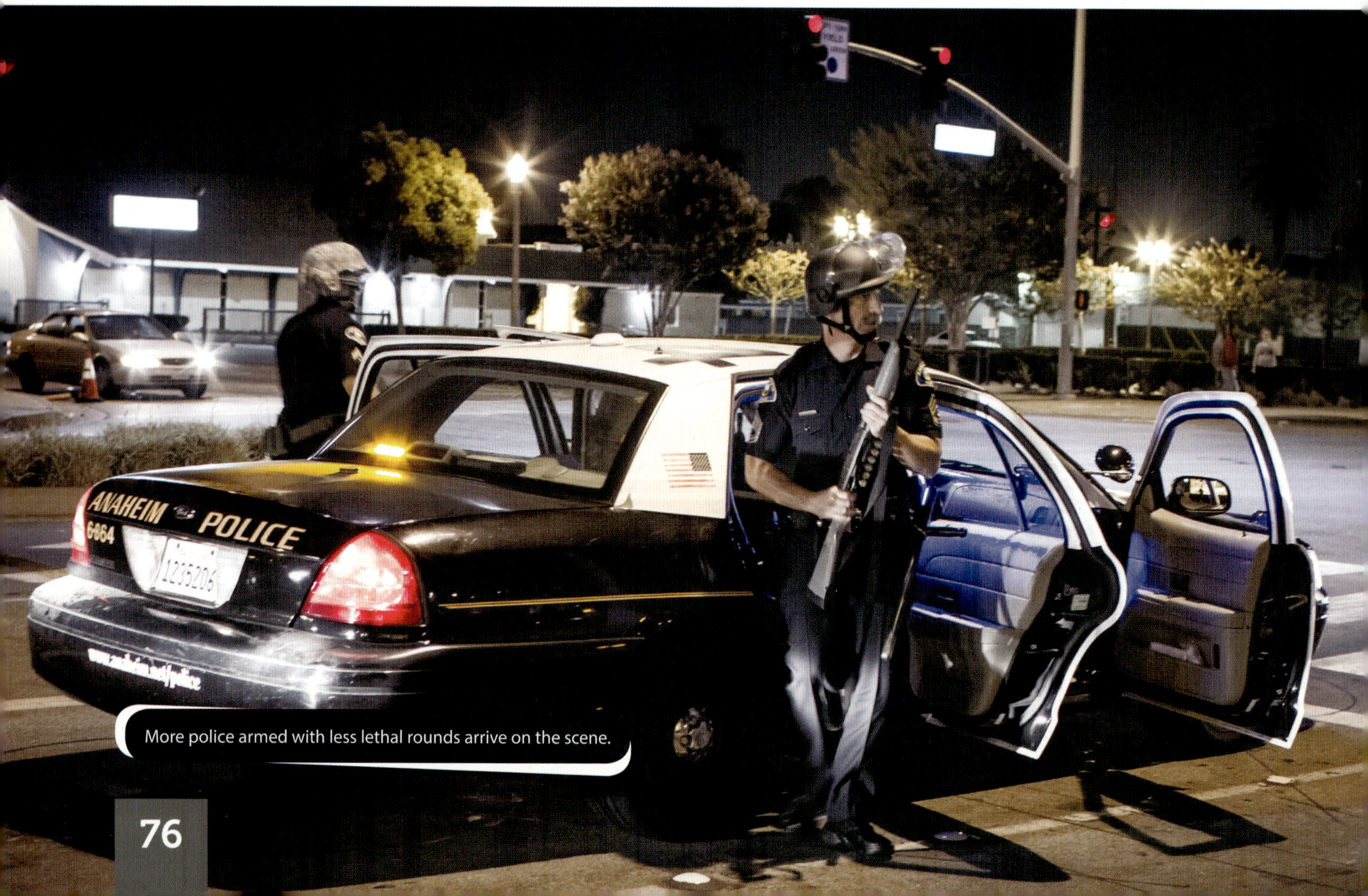

More police armed with less lethal rounds arrive on the scene.

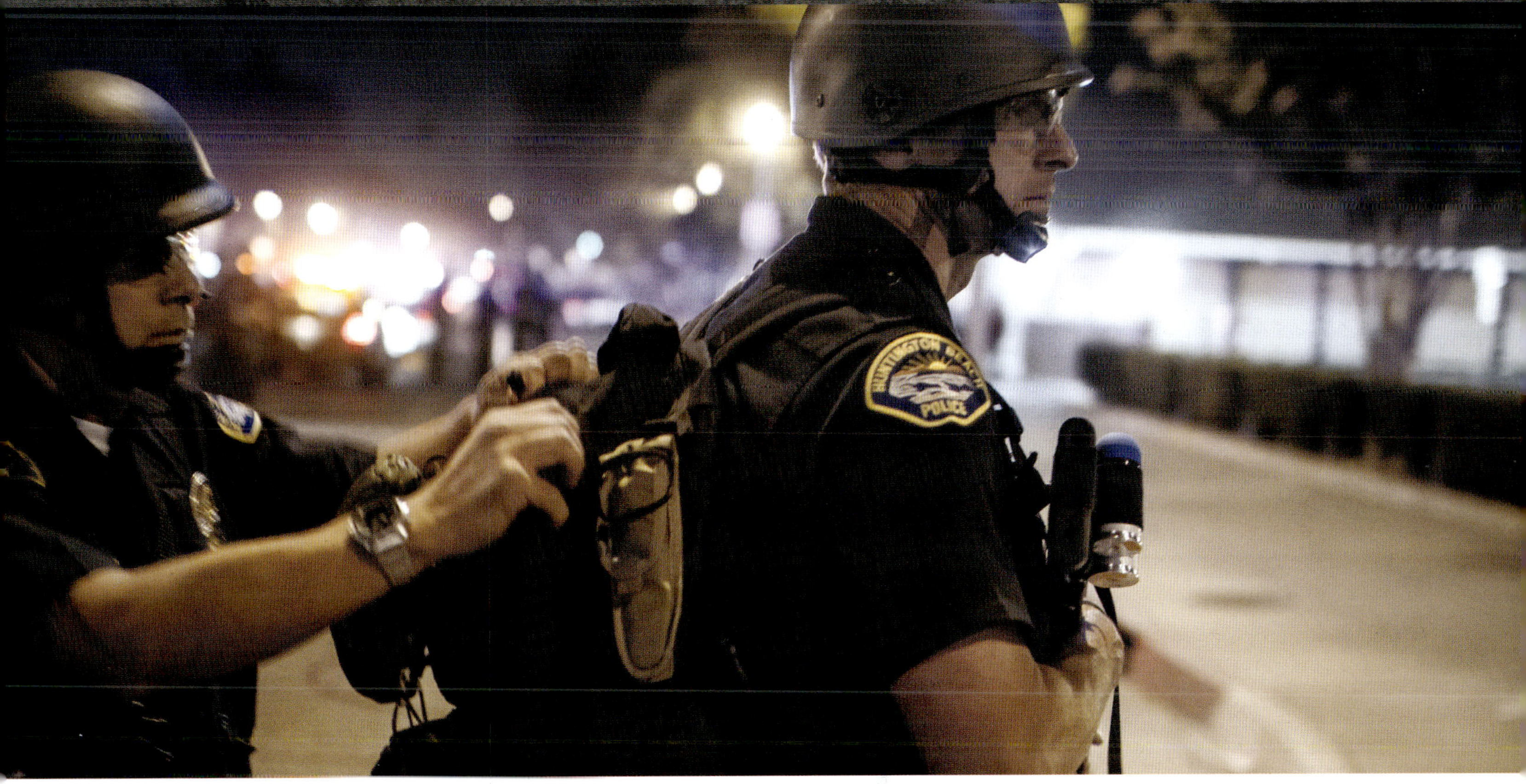

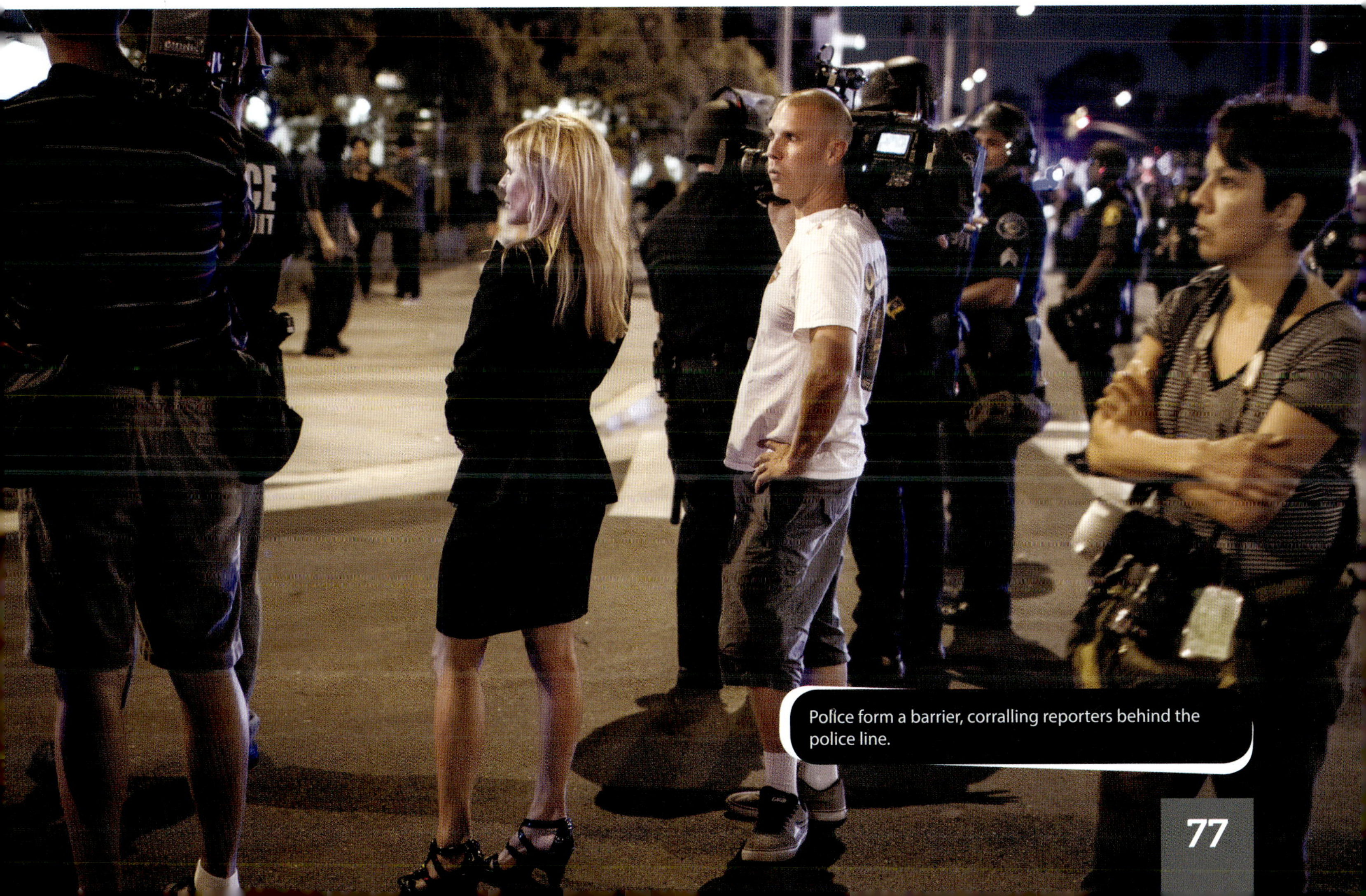

Police form a barrier, corralling reporters behind the police line.

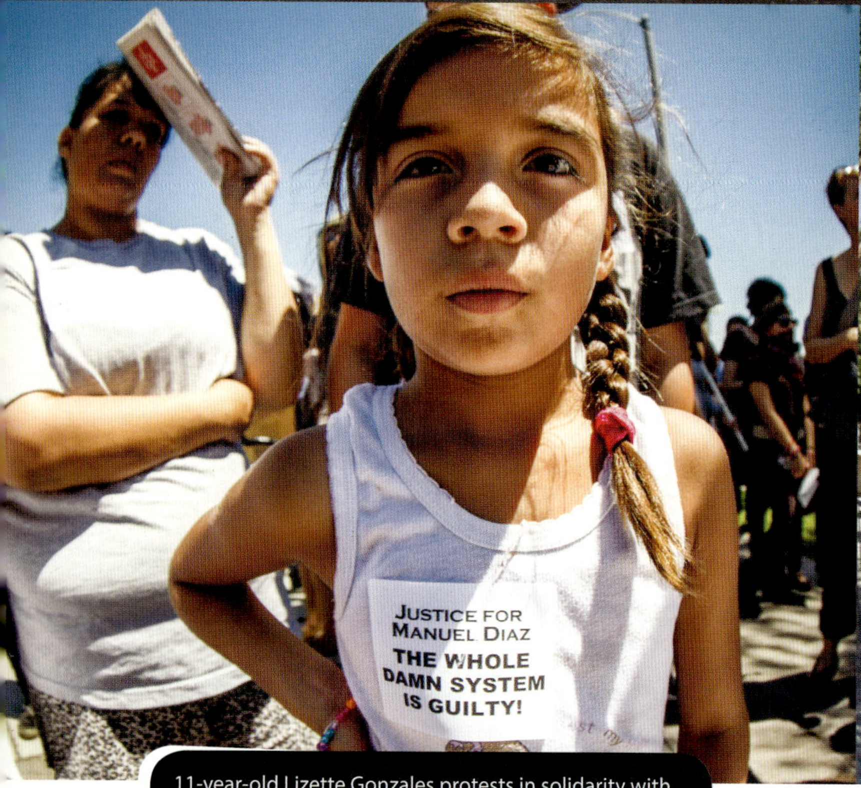

11-year-old Lizette Gonzales protests in solidarity with Manuel Diaz.

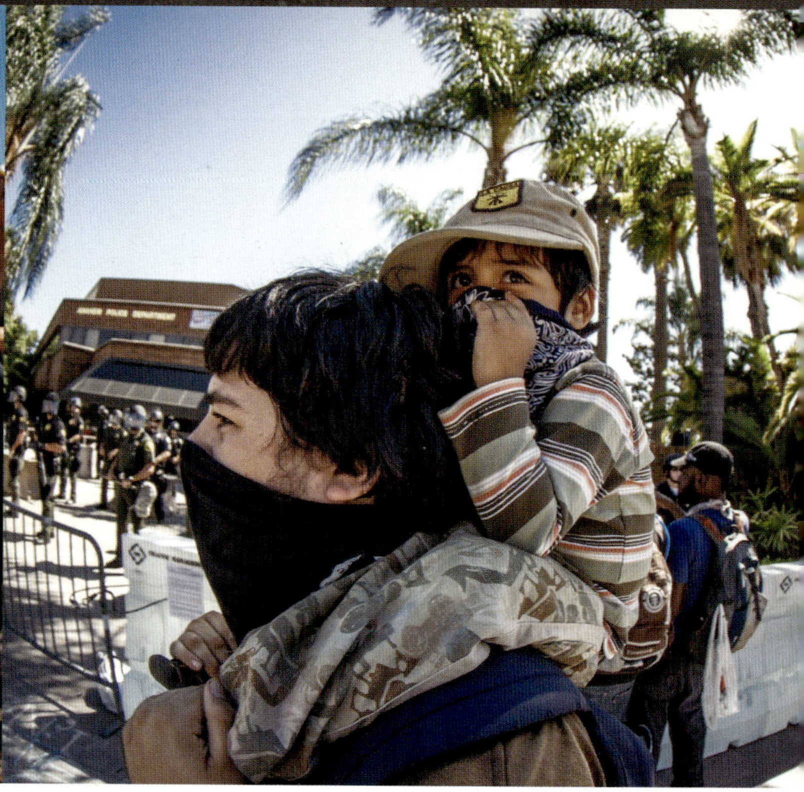

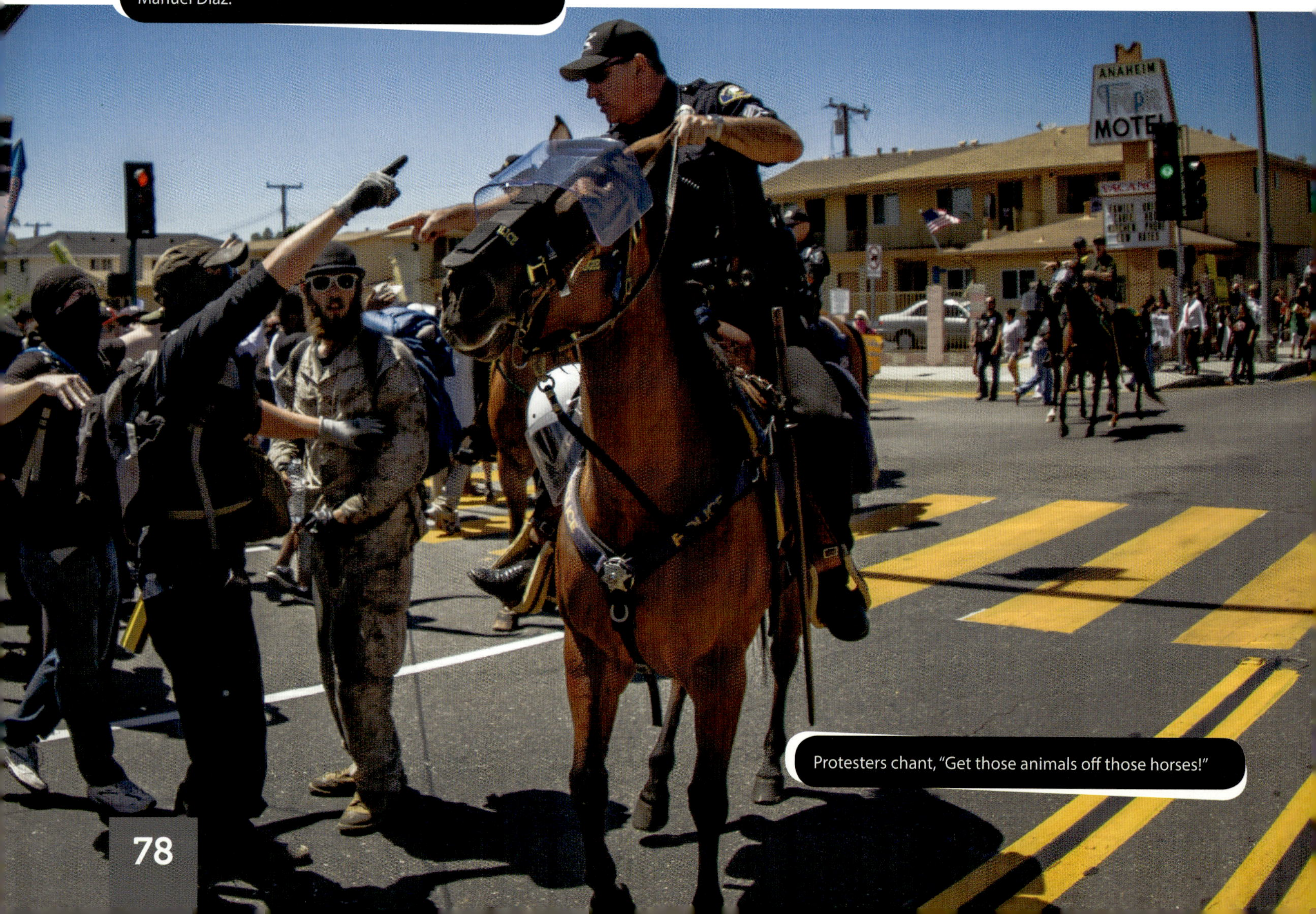

Protesters chant, "Get those animals off those horses!"

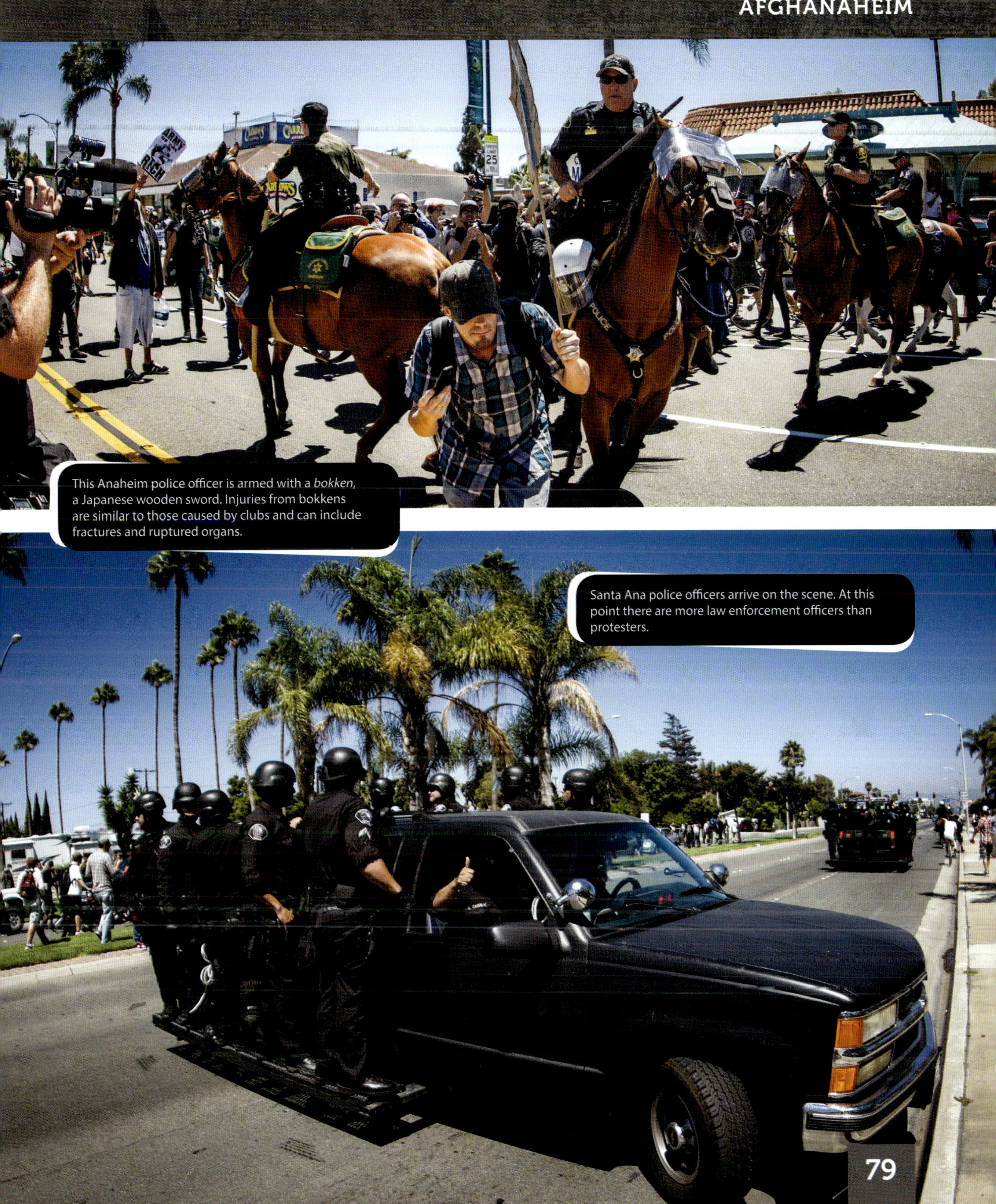

This Anaheim police officer is armed with a *bokken,* a Japanese wooden sword. Injuries from bokkens are similar to those caused by clubs and can include fractures and ruptured organs.

Santa Ana police officers arrive on the scene. At this point there are more law enforcement officers than protesters.

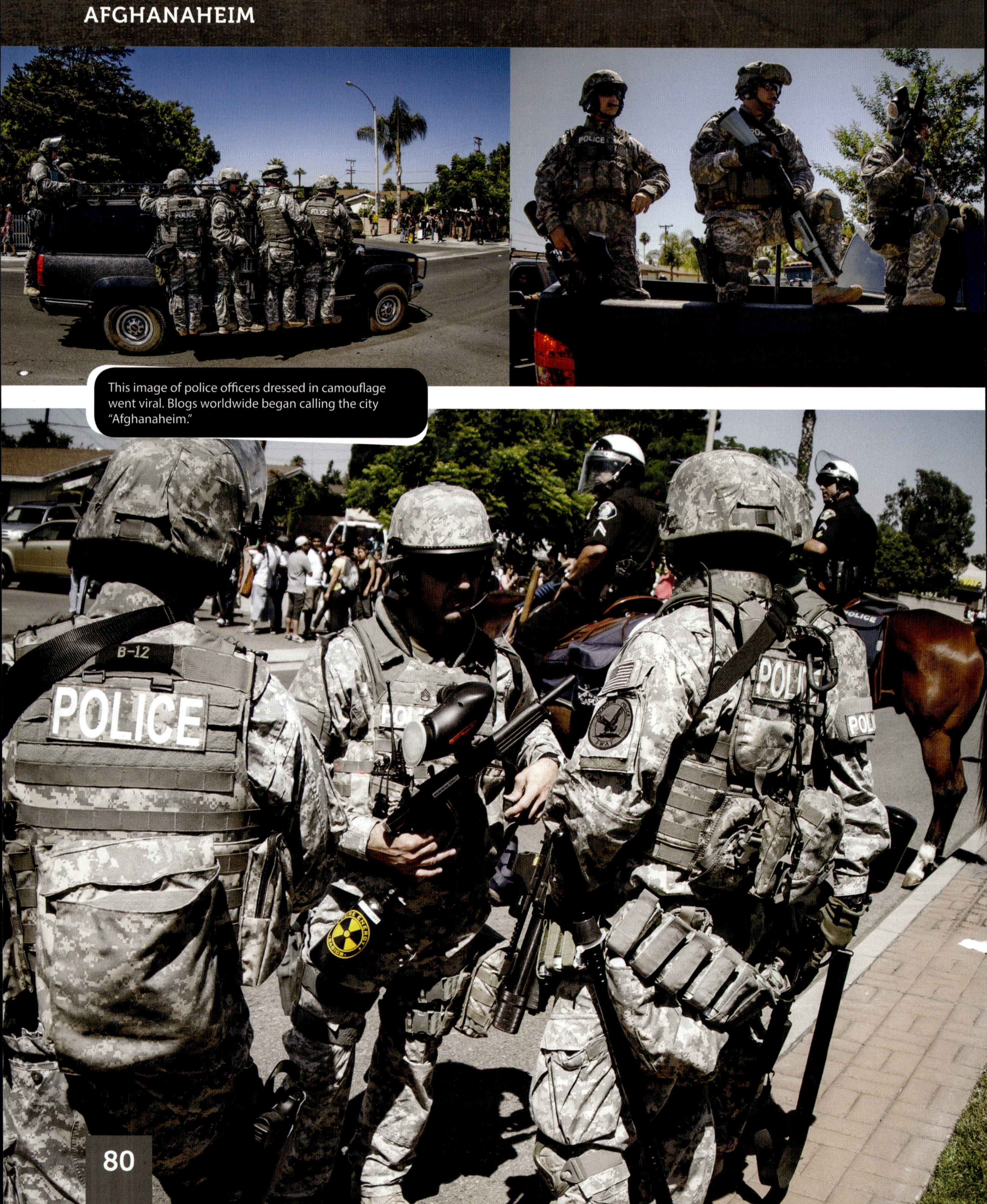

This image of police officers dressed in camouflage went viral. Blogs worldwide began calling the city "Afghanaheim."

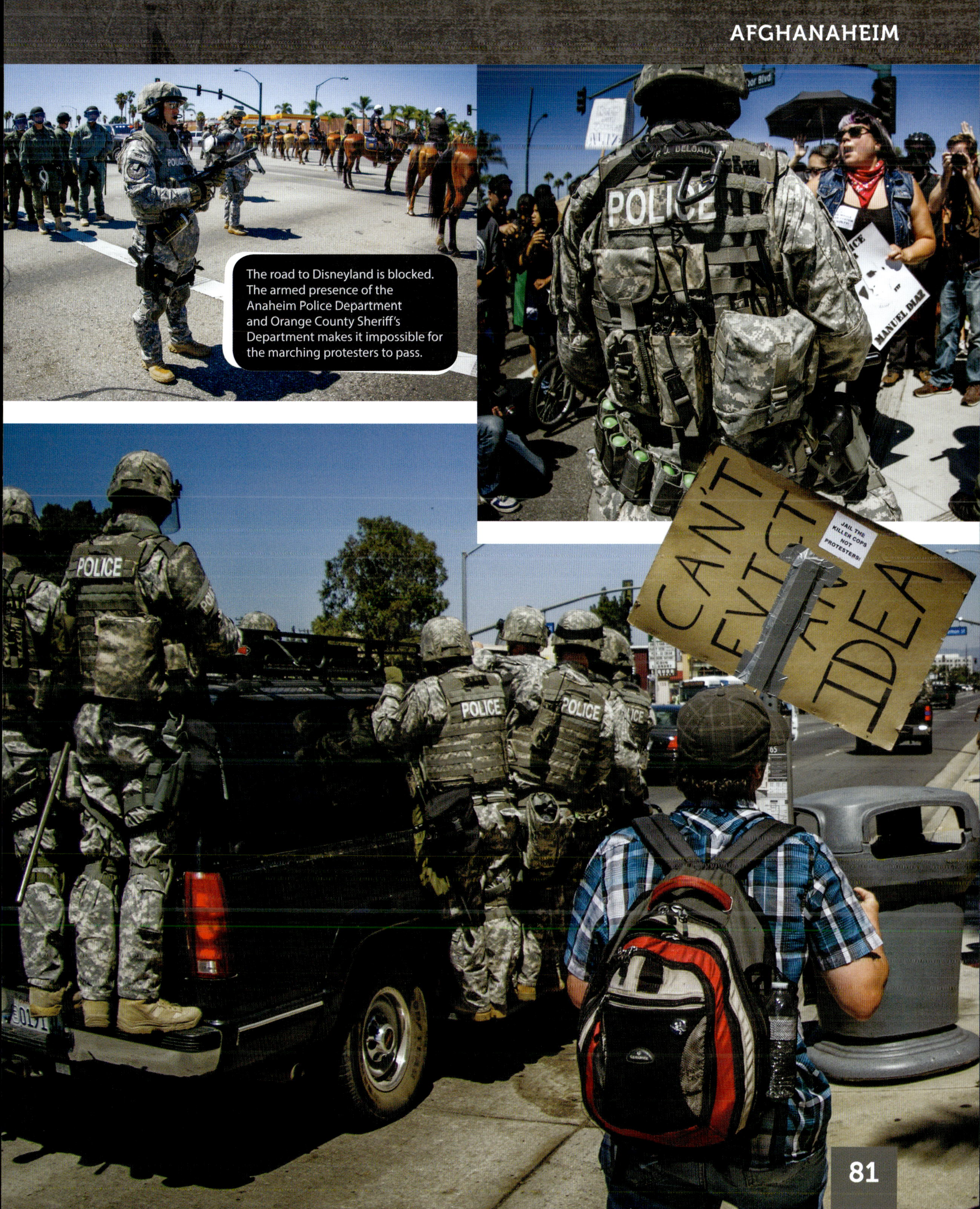

The road to Disneyland is blocked. The armed presence of the Anaheim Police Department and Orange County Sheriff's Department makes it impossible for the marching protesters to pass.

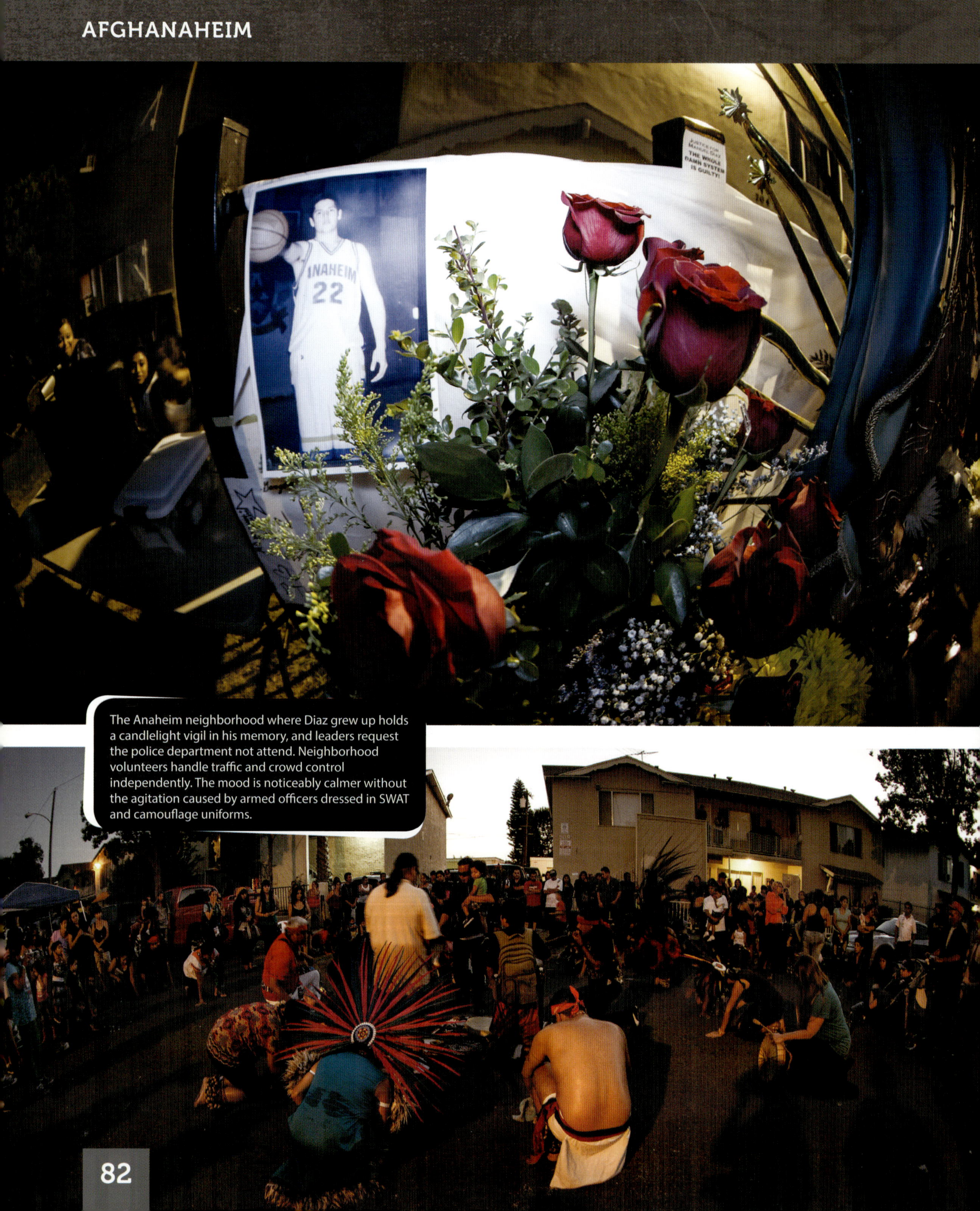

The Anaheim neighborhood where Diaz grew up holds a candlelight vigil in his memory, and leaders request the police department not attend. Neighborhood volunteers handle traffic and crowd control independently. The mood is noticeably calmer without the agitation caused by armed officers dressed in SWAT and camouflage uniforms.

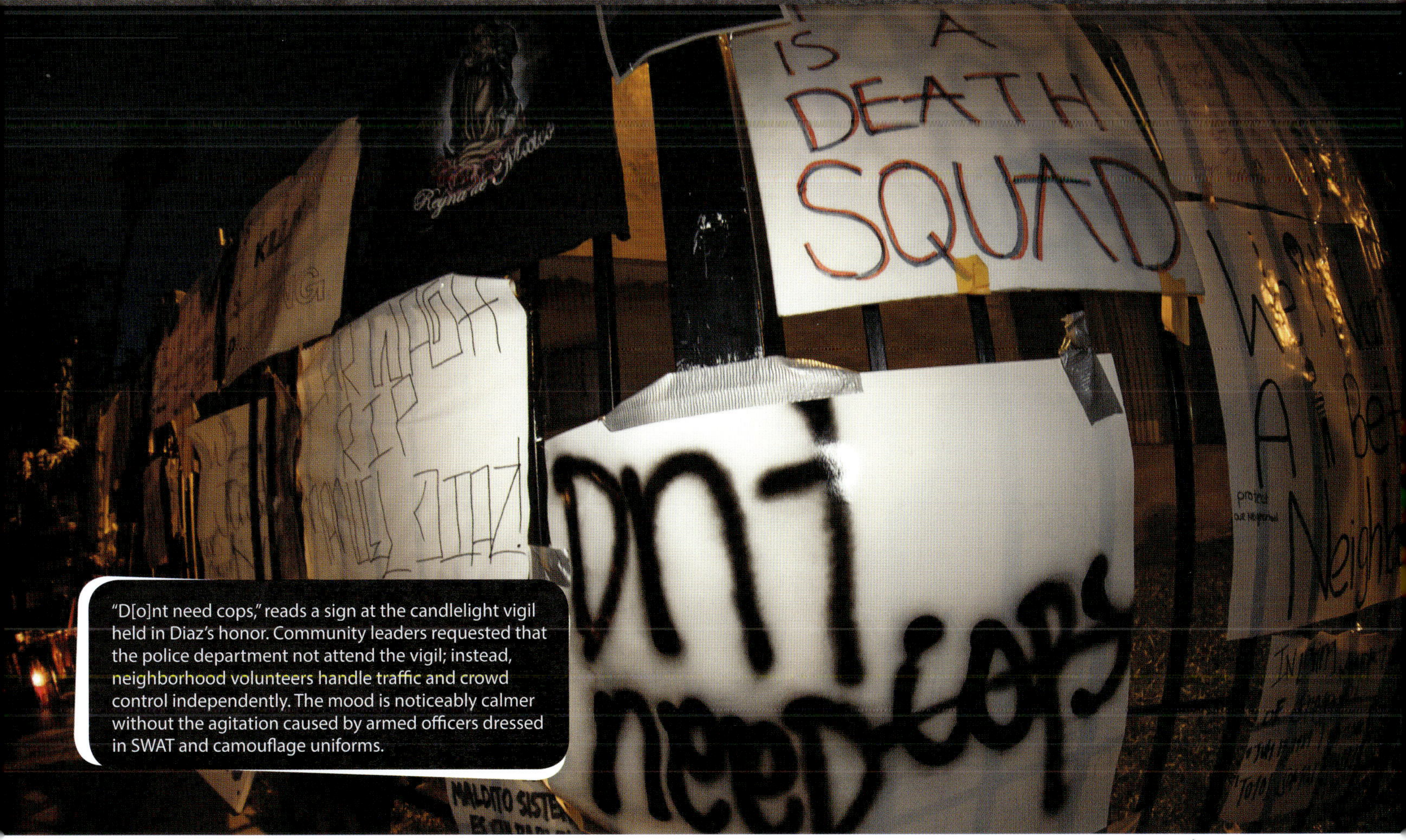

"D[o]nt need cops," reads a sign at the candlelight vigil held in Diaz's honor. Community leaders requested that the police department not attend the vigil; instead, neighborhood volunteers handle traffic and crowd control independently. The mood is noticeably calmer without the agitation caused by armed officers dressed in SWAT and camouflage uniforms.

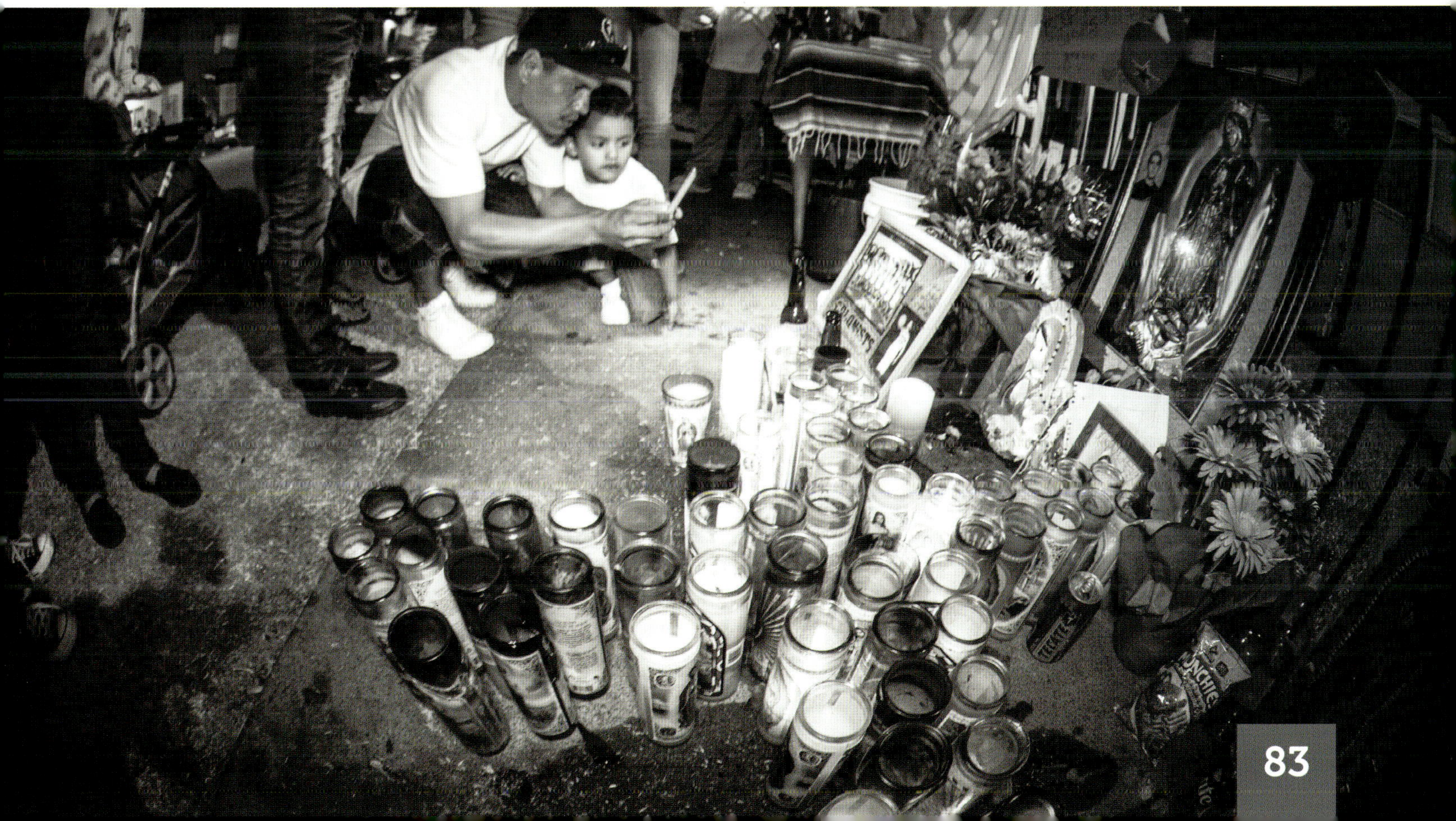

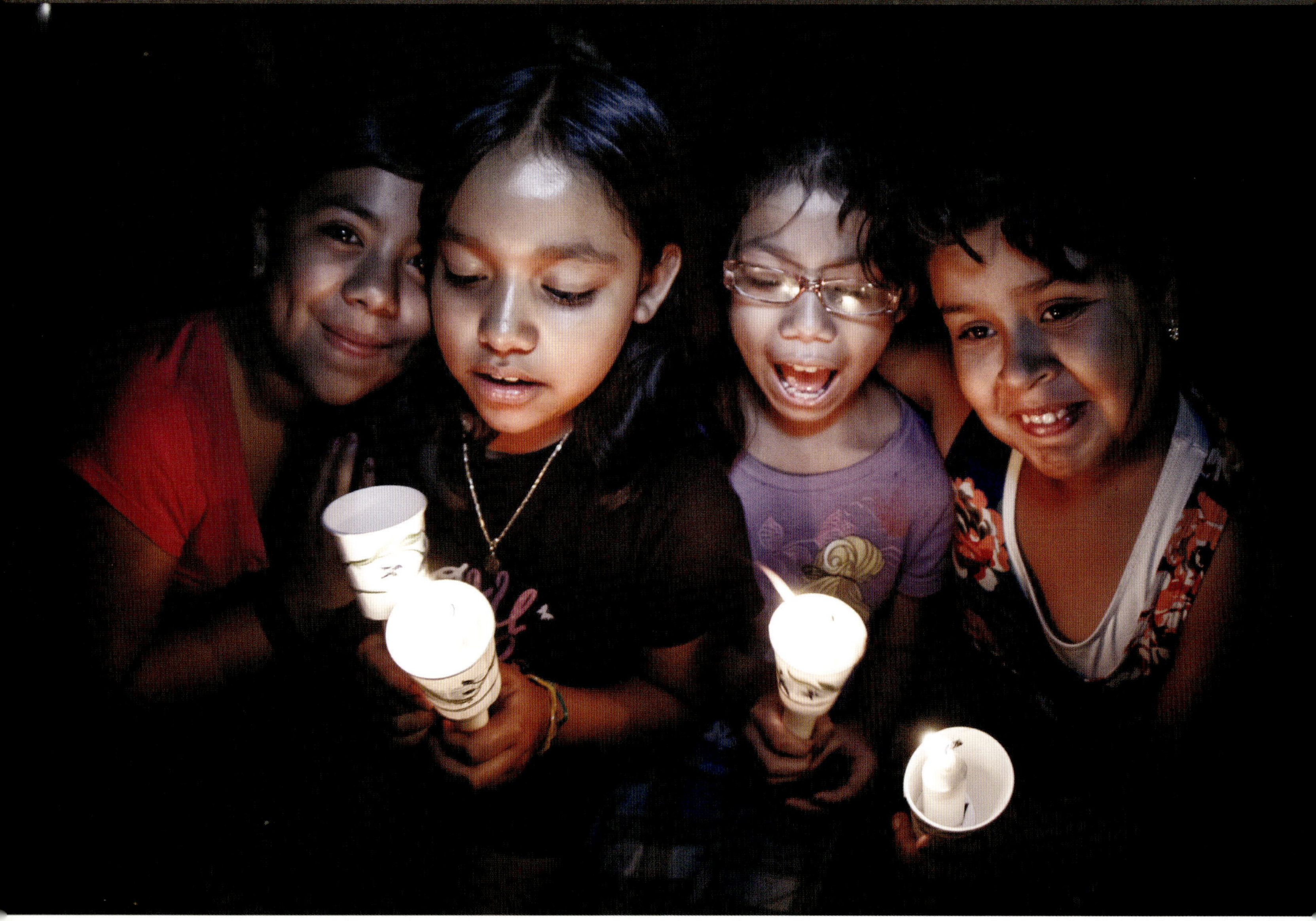

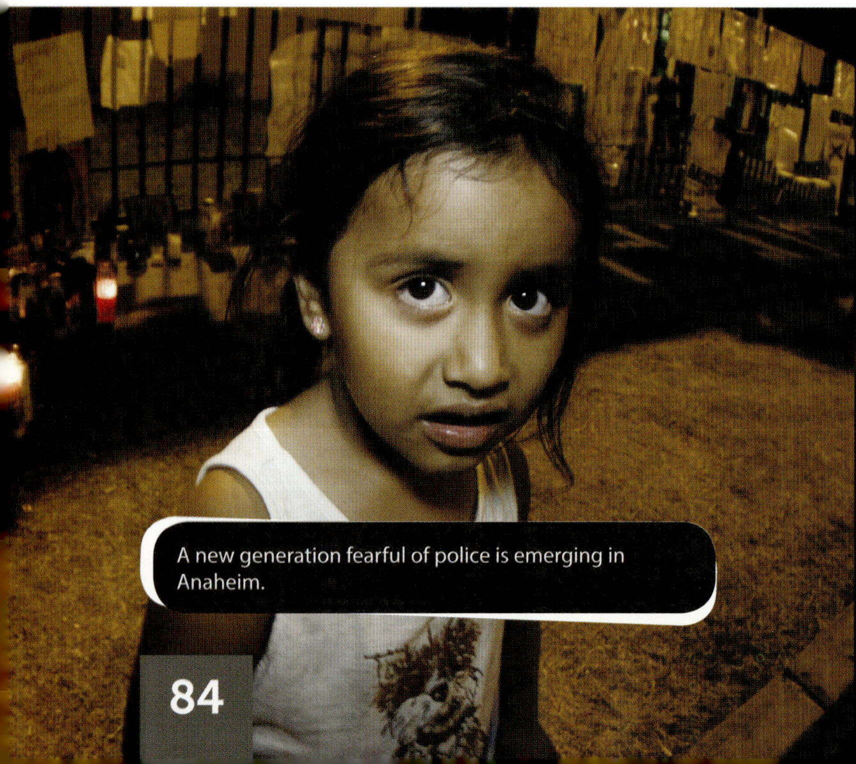

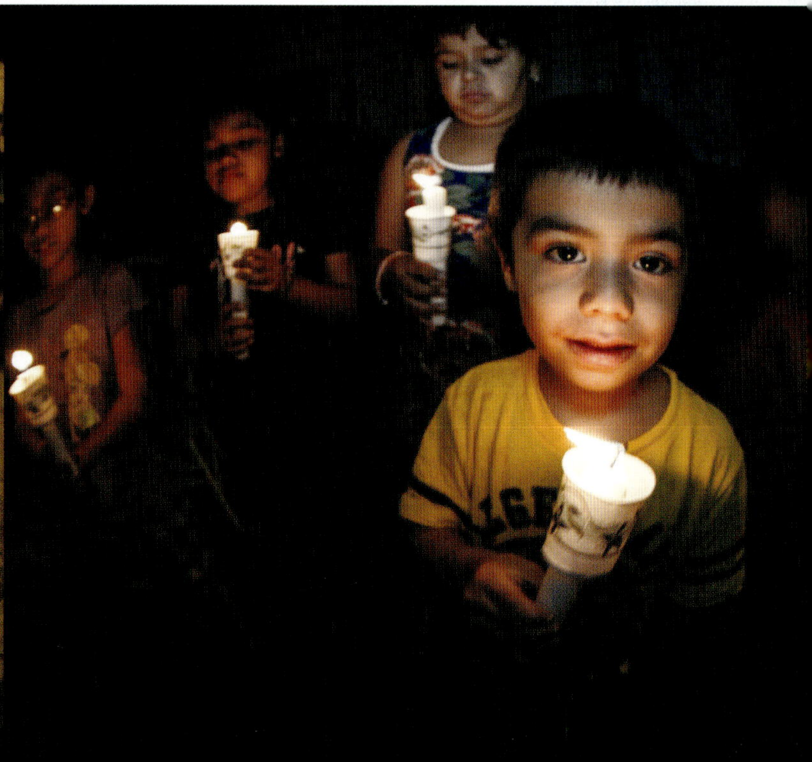

A new generation fearful of police is emerging in Anaheim.

Fort Hernandez

On August 21, 2012, the Hernandez family of nine received notice that they had five days to vacate their Van Nuys, California, home due to foreclosure. Instead of packing their bags, the family decided to fight back.

Upon receiving the eviction notice, the Hernandez family "fortified" the outside of their three-bedroom home with rows of couches, chairs, plywood, tents, and debris. Activists with Occupy San Fernando Valley constructed a large plywood barricade between the home and the street, and more than a dozen protesters camped out in tents in the front yard. On the roof, they wrote "Evict Banks" with Christmas lights. The property, home to four children, soon became known worldwide as "Fort Hernandez."

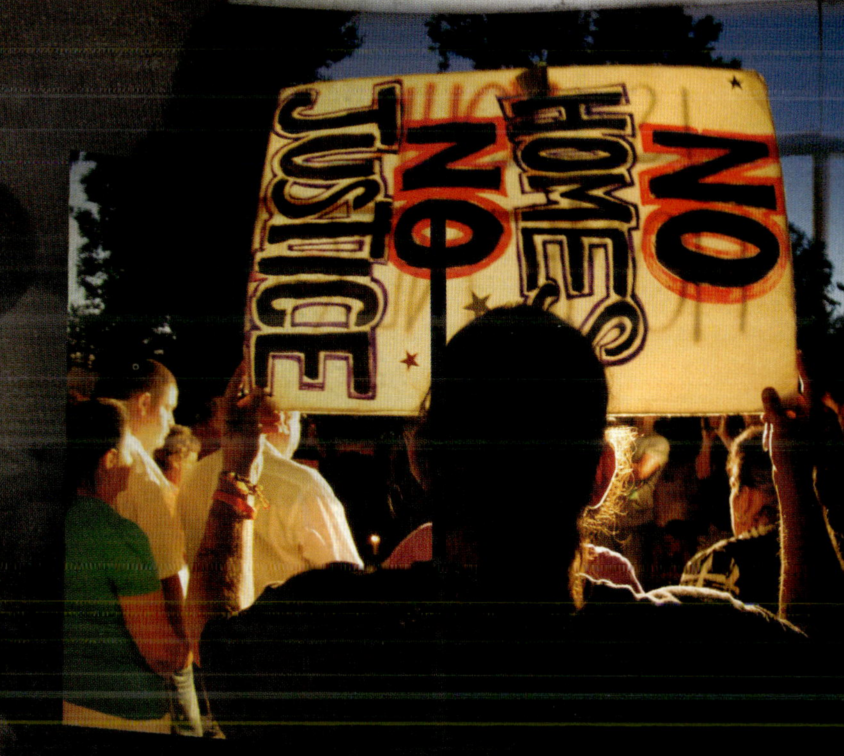

Javier Hernandez, who owned the home, said he had purchased the property in 2006 for $546,000. He signed a subprime mortgage with Countrywide requiring interest-only payments at first with an adjustable rate. "We didn't know exactly what we were getting ourselves into," Hernandez said.

When they received the eviction notice, the family said, they hadn't paid their mortgage in four and a half years—not since Bank of America, who acquired the loan from Countrywide, raised their monthly payments from $3,900 to $4,500. "Even with various members of our family contributing to the payments, the dramatic and sudden increase made it impossible to add into our budgets," Javier's brother Ulises Hernandez said.

When the housing bubble burst, the home lost over half its value. The past-due amount topped $250,000—more than the home's current value of $242,000.

The family said they weren't looking to stay in the house for free and that they had sought three loan modifications, all of which were denied. "What we were saying is, 'Come on, man, work with us,'" Ulises Hernandez said. On the third attempt, the family said, Bank of America sold the home at auction. A Bank of America spokeswoman said that Hernandez didn't submit the documentation requested during a 2011 modification review, giving the bank no choice but to go through with the foreclosure.

At the time of the protest, Occupy San Fernando Valley estimates, there were around 170 homes facing foreclosure in the Van Nuys 91405 zip code. Occupy San Fernando Valley says this form of direct-action foreclosure protest has been employed numerous times, always with some level of success.

The Fernandez family said they would not leave voluntarily and would resist nonviolently if authorities tried to evict them. "Civil disobedience at its finest," Ulises said. "My arrest is to draw attention to a national issue."

After spending four months successfully camped out in front of the house, Occupy LA activists were removed from the property on December 27, 2012, and the Fernandez family was evicted. According to Occupy San Fernando Valley, this was the most enduring foreclosure prevention protest in Southern California's history.

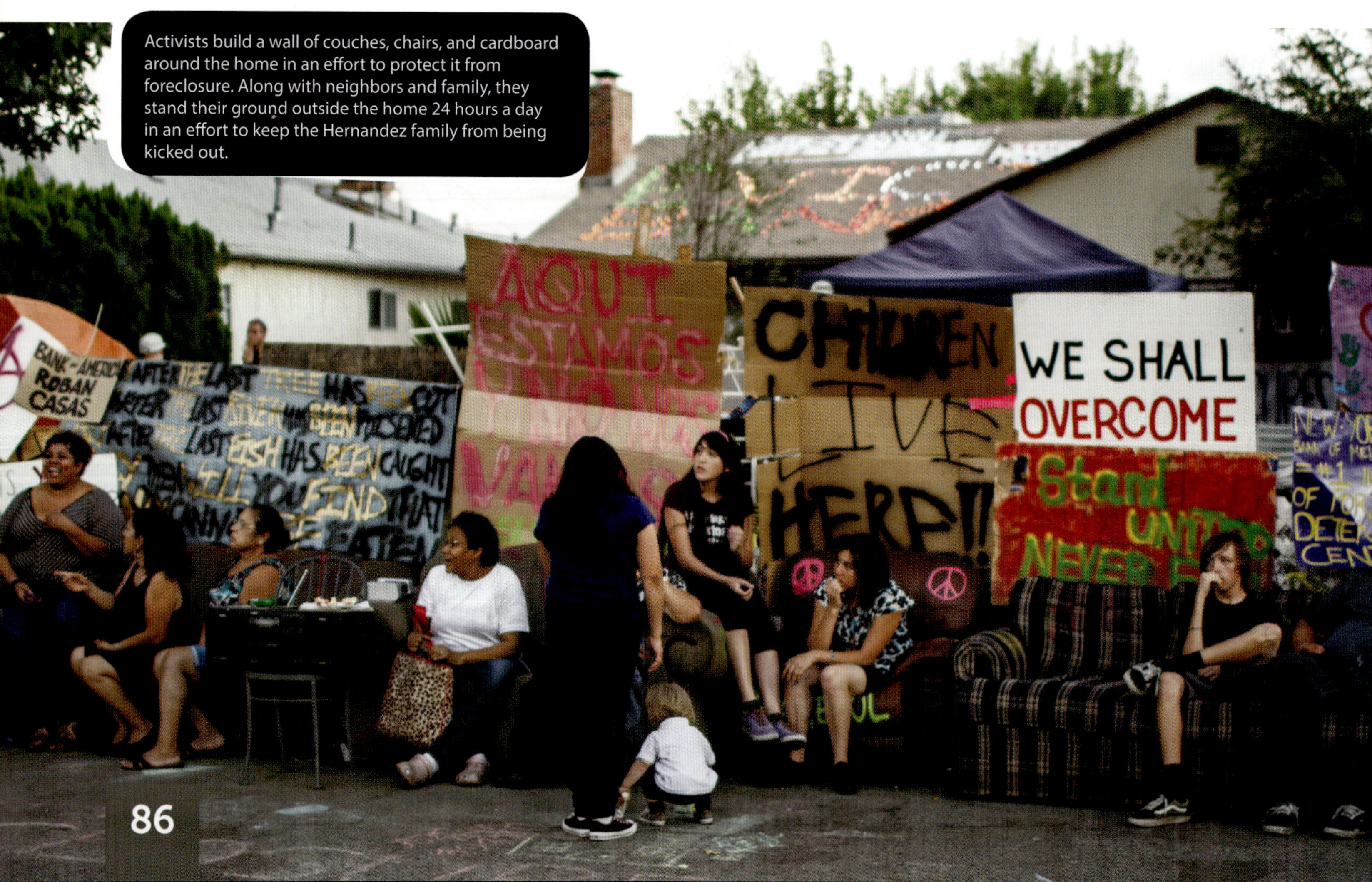

Activists build a wall of couches, chairs, and cardboard around the home in an effort to protect it from foreclosure. Along with neighbors and family, they stand their ground outside the home 24 hours a day in an effort to keep the Hernandez family from being kicked out.

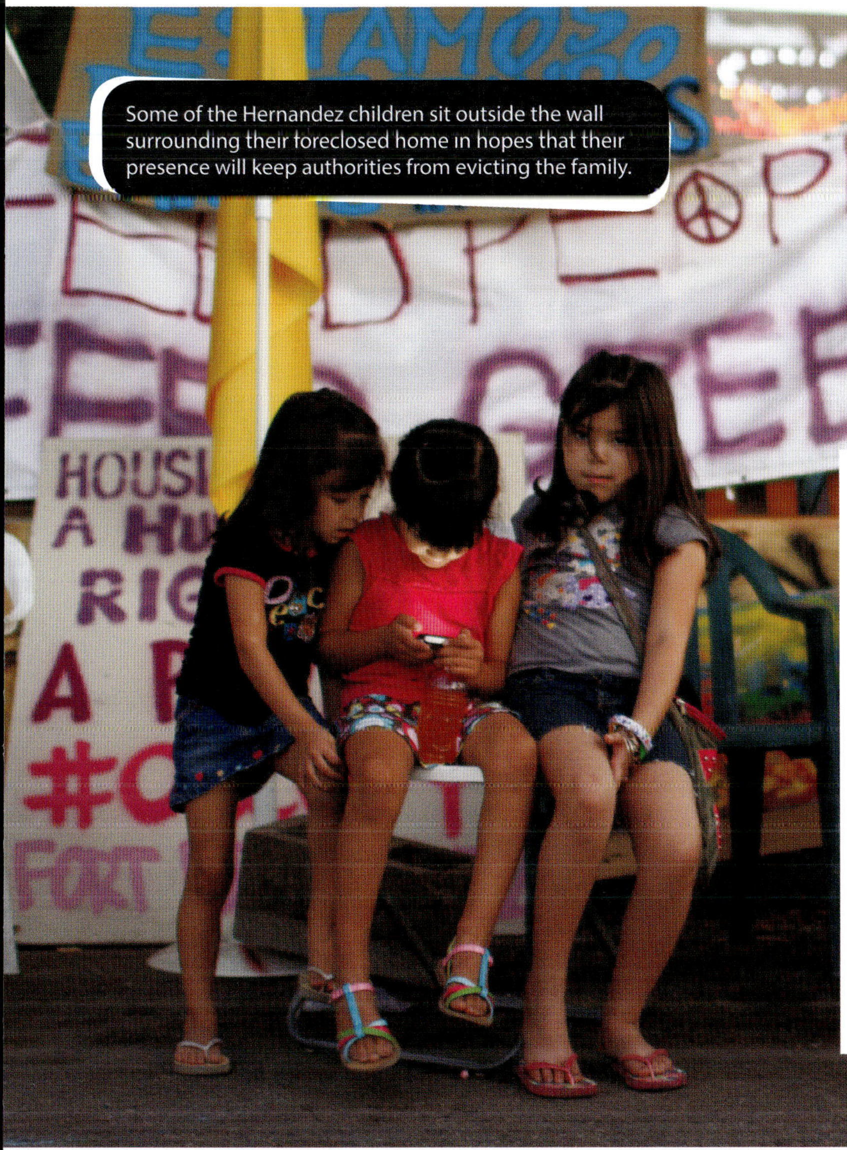

Some of the Hernandez children sit outside the wall surrounding their foreclosed home in hopes that their presence will keep authorities from evicting the family.

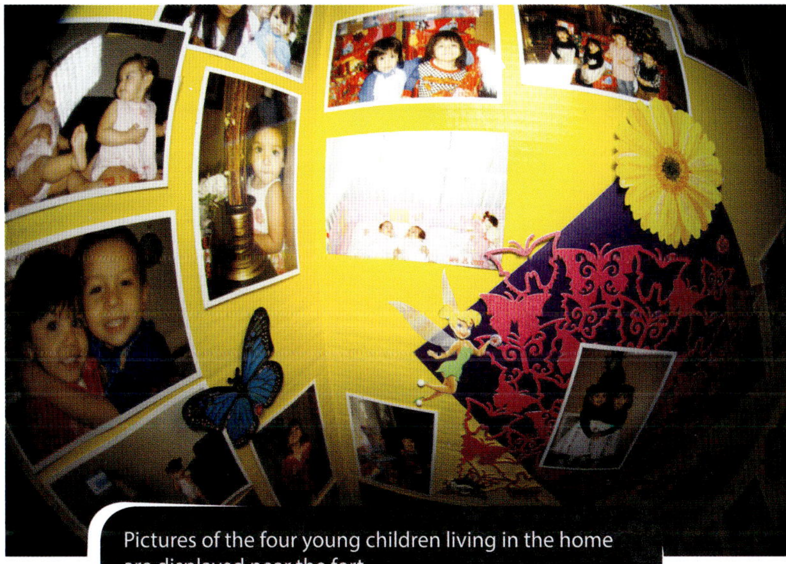

Pictures of the four young children living in the home are displayed near the fort.

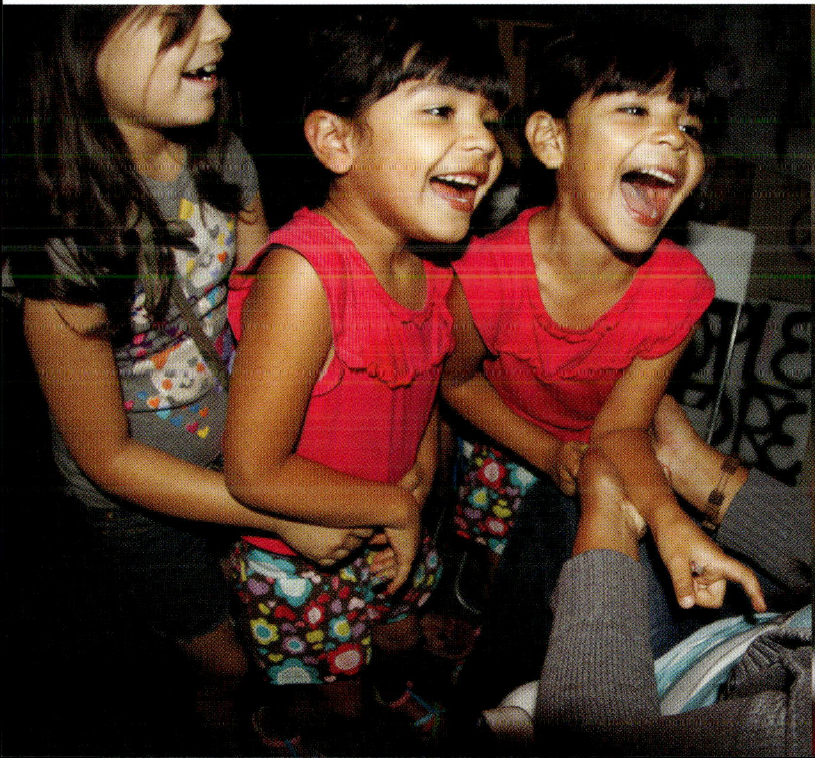

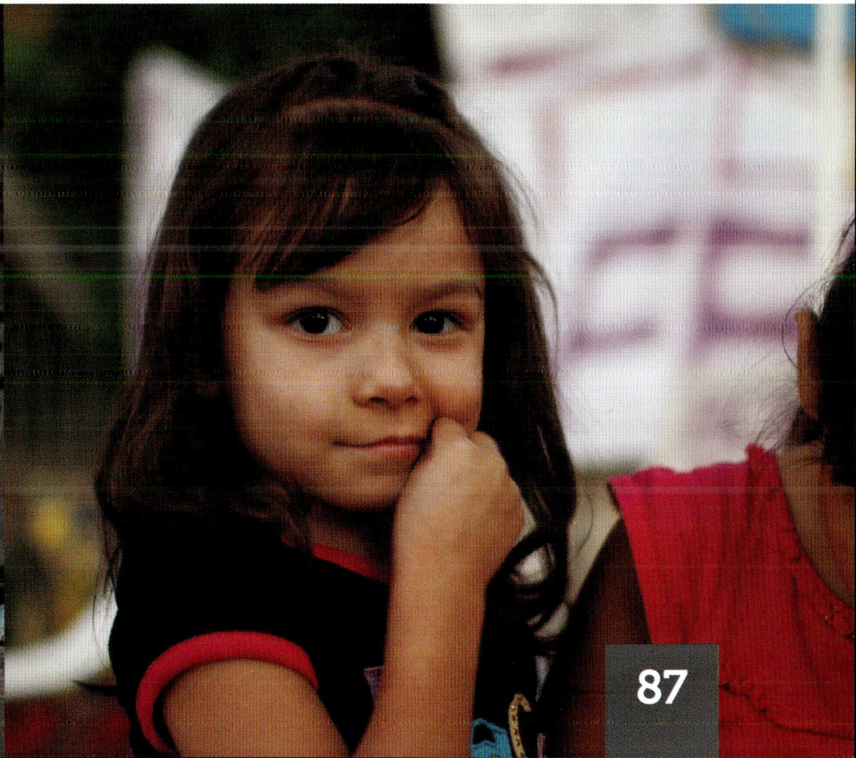

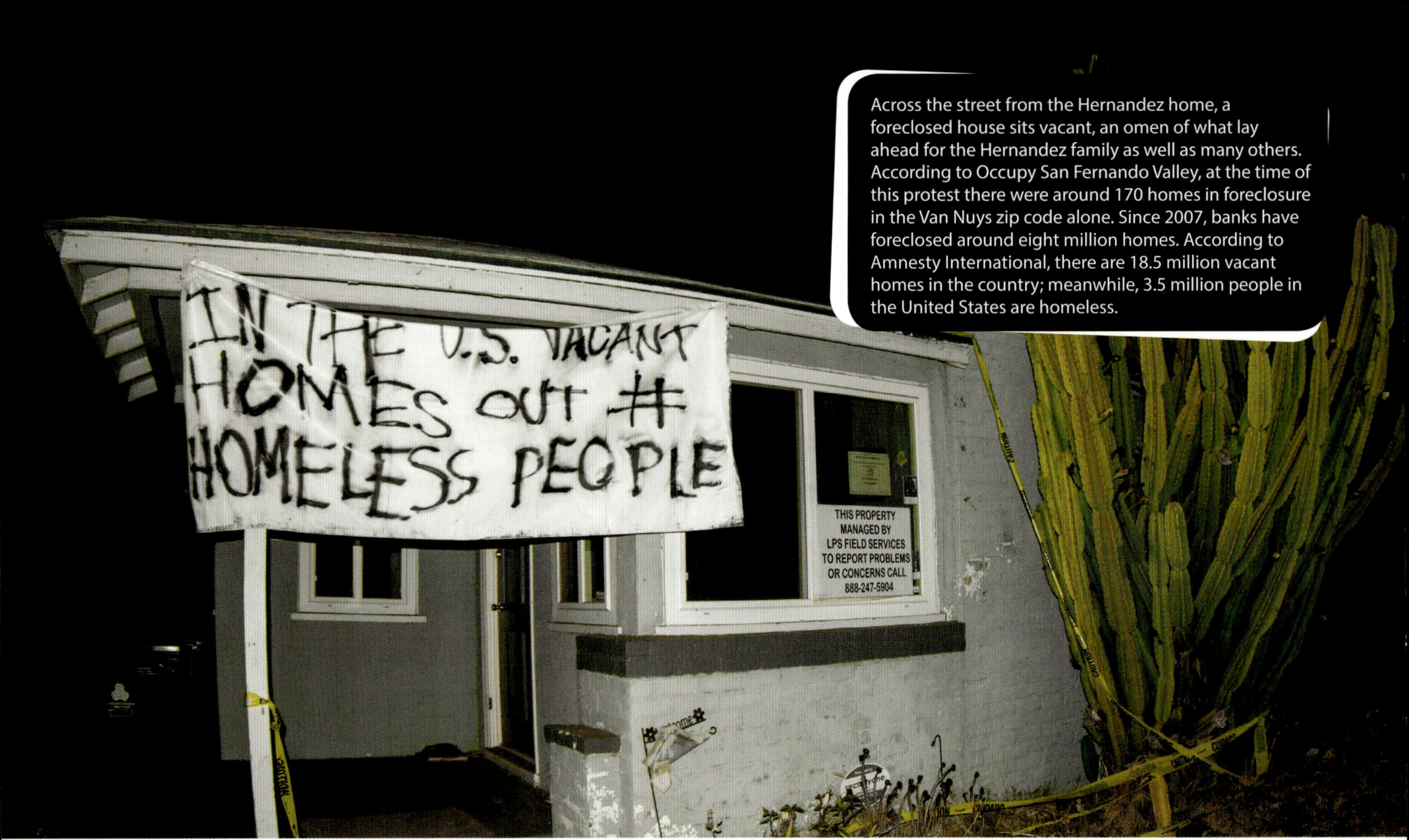

Across the street from the Hernandez home, a foreclosed house sits vacant, an omen of what lay ahead for the Hernandez family as well as many others. According to Occupy San Fernando Valley, at the time of this protest there were around 170 homes in foreclosure in the Van Nuys zip code alone. Since 2007, banks have foreclosed around eight million homes. According to Amnesty International, there are 18.5 million vacant homes in the country; meanwhile, 3.5 million people in the United States are homeless.

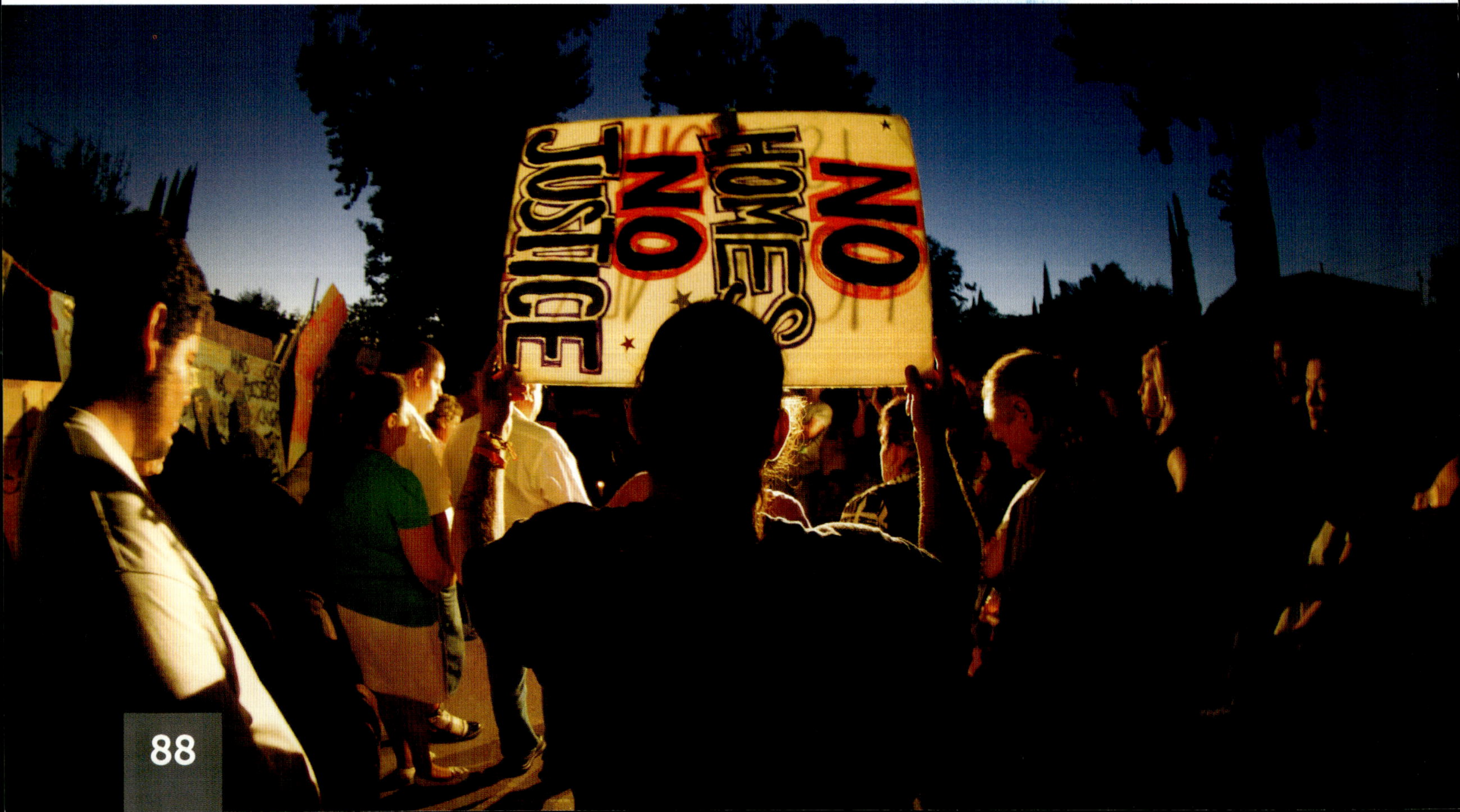

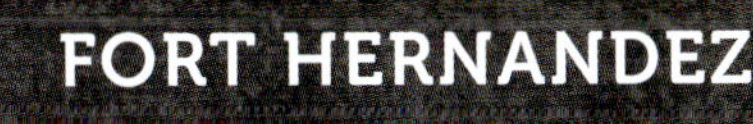

A protester equates rampant home foreclosures nationwide with the death of the American Dream.

The Hernandez children join the candlelight vigil to protect their home.

Protesters sleep in a tent barrier erected between the street and the entrance to the Hernandez home.

Activist Profile

Name: Ulises Hernandez
Age: 21
City: Van Nuys
Protesting since: November 2011
Affiliation: Occupy San Fernando Valley

What happened in your life that motivated you to attend your first protest? My first protest was the Million Man March for immigrant rights in 2006 at downtown LA.

How have you been protesting? I've been protesting by attending multiple actions, organizing actions with the community, and most recently refusing to leave my home, which is being fraudulently foreclosed upon.

Have you ever been pepper-sprayed, injured, or arrested while demonstrating? If so, what happened? On May first I was arrested for possession of vandalism tools. (It was a May First General Strike sticker on my backpack.) I was held for the night and released in the morning. There were no charges. I was released with a citation.

Have your efforts resulted in change? My efforts have resulted in change. More personal change than any other. Protesting and organizing have brought out the caring in me. I can no longer hear people's stories of injustice and just remain silent. I am here to do what I can to help anyone who has been oppressed by the system.

What's the most egregious mainstream misconception about protesters? That we are a bunch of dirty, homeless, jobless, uneducated bums who just sit around and complain.

When will you be satisfied, stop protesting? When pigs fly, or when we smash this capitalist, greedy, and corrupt government.

Favorite quote: *Todo para todos, nada para nosotros* (everything for everyone and nothing for ourselves).

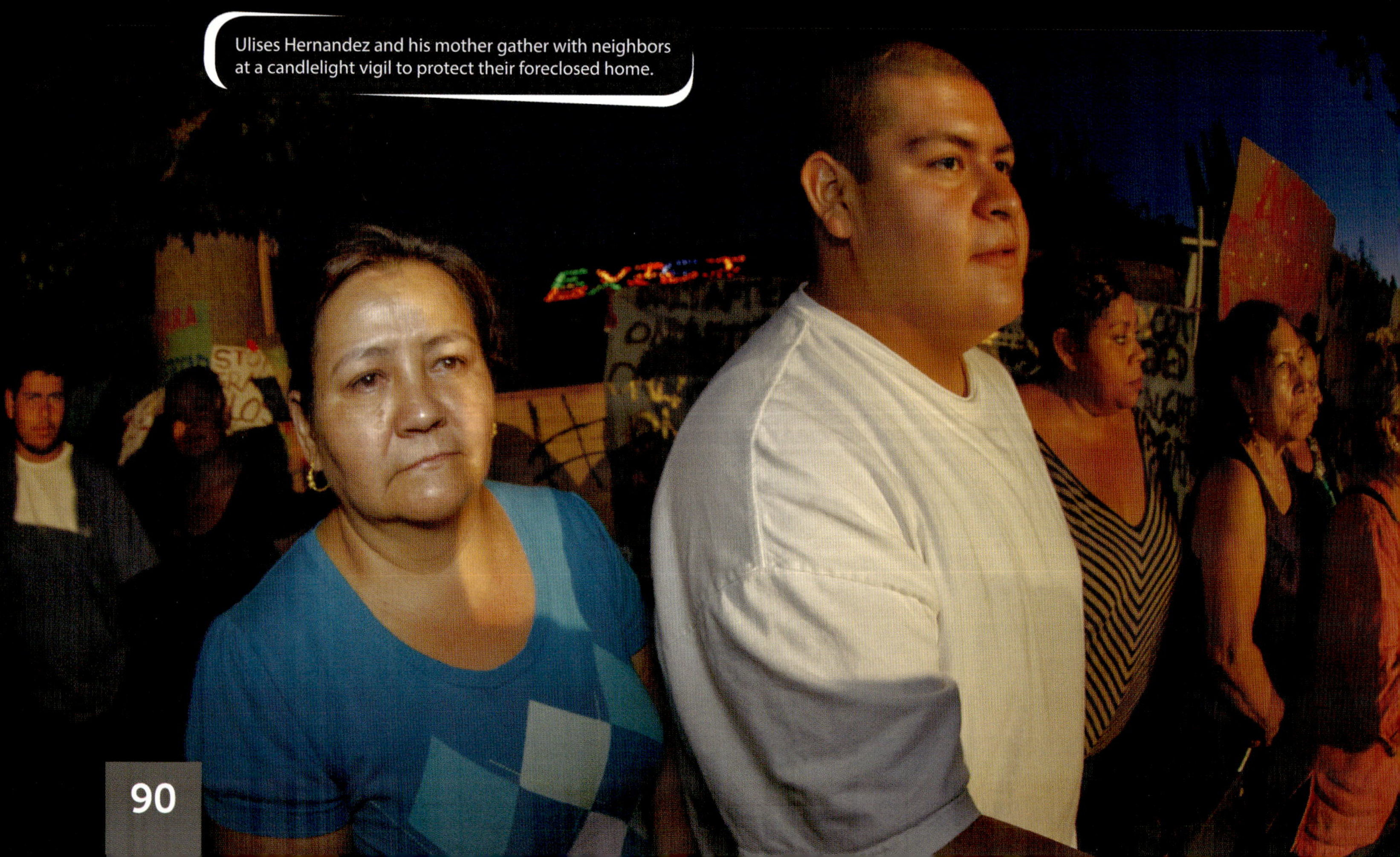

Ulises Hernandez and his mother gather with neighbors at a candlelight vigil to protect their foreclosed home.

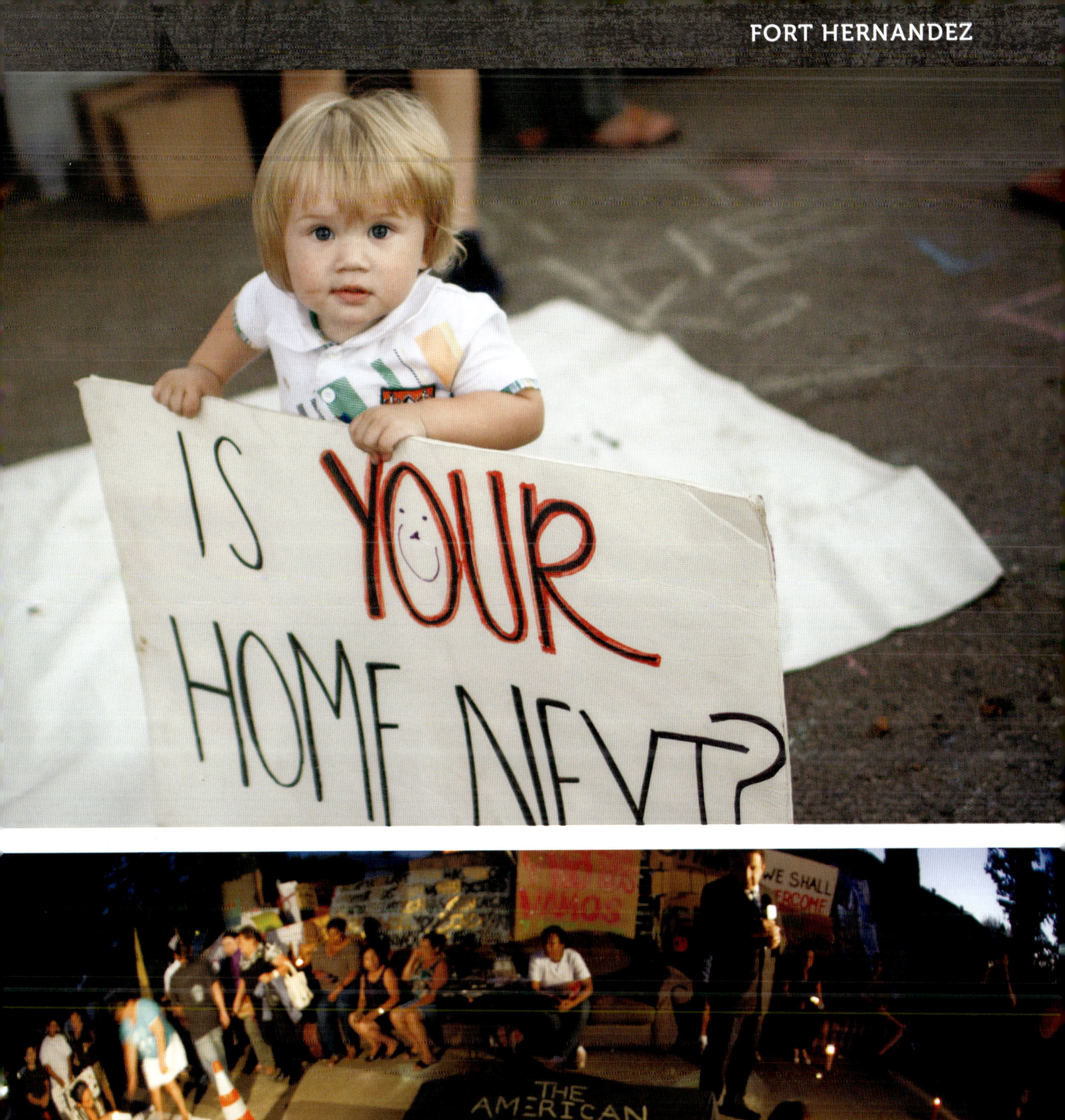

Neighbors and activists join the Hernandez family for a candlelight vigil in solidarity with families across the United States who have lost their homes to bank foreclosures.

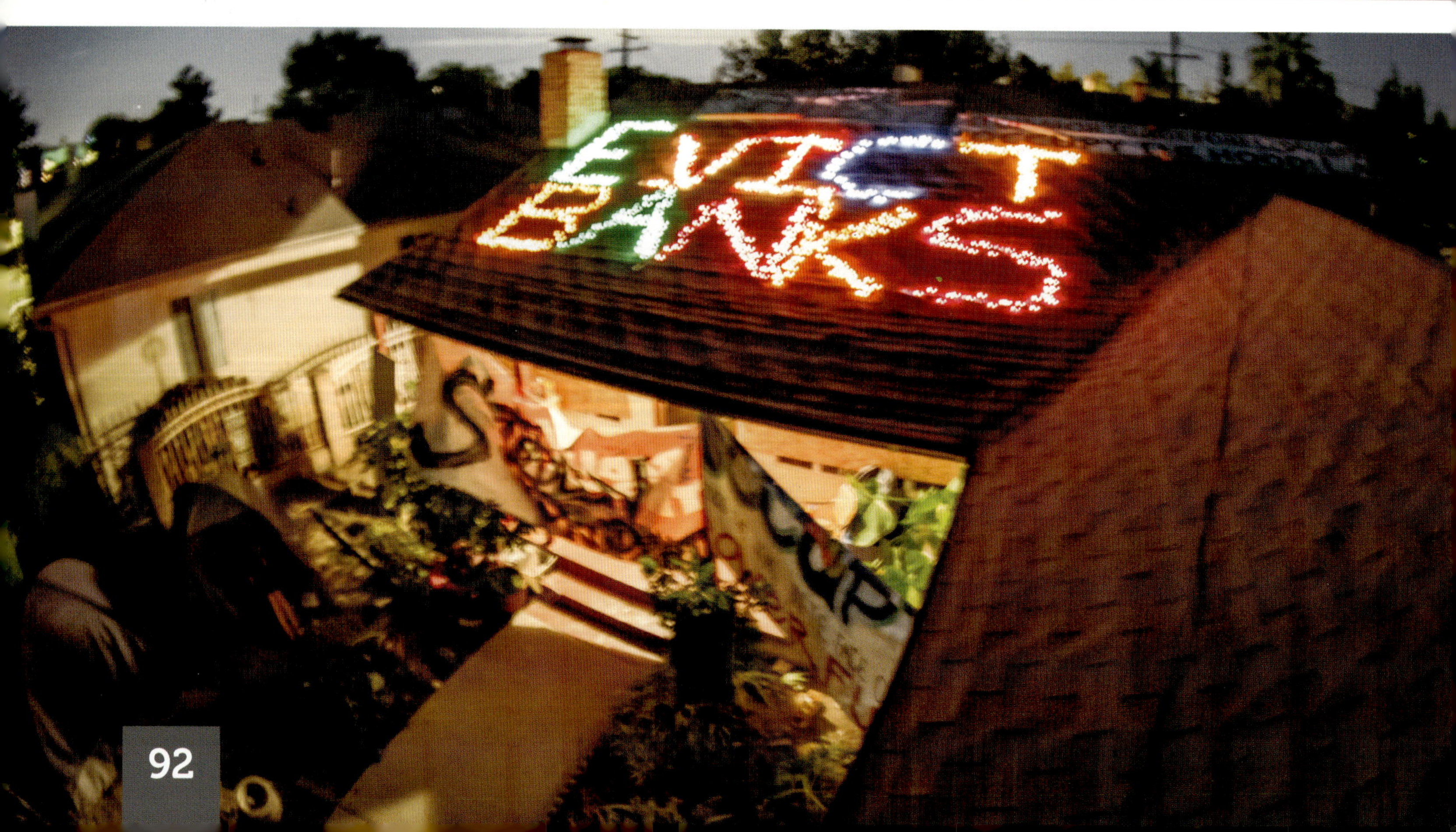
EVICT
BANKS

Go Topless

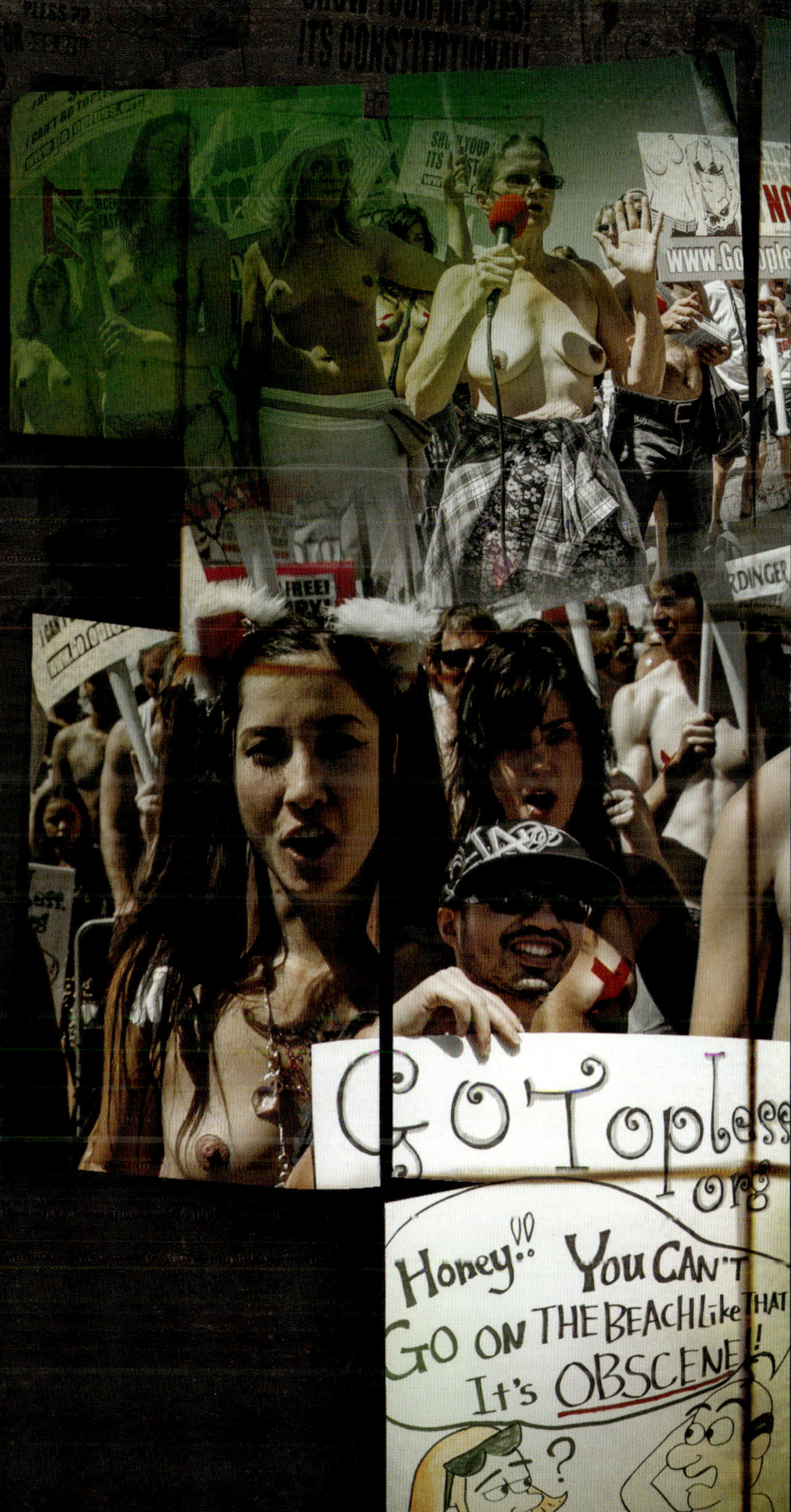

On a hot August afternoon in Venice Beach, California, onlookers gathered to photograph, record on video, and gawk at a crowd of women fighting for an often-overlooked right males take for granted—the right to go topless.

Currently, the only states that prohibit toplessness are Utah, Tennessee, and Indiana. There are 15 states in which the laws are ambiguous, and the majority of major U.S. cities (even within states where no prohibition exists) have passed ordinances banning toplessness.

Women who defy the law can be subject to arrest for disorderly conduct, although some, like Phoenix Feeley in New York City, sued the city after trial—and won.

The movement is spearheaded by GoTopless.org, and the activism has pointed out an undeniable double standard in American society and its legal system: why is it lawful for males to saunter shirtless when women cannot?

Activist Profile

Name: Lara H. Terstenjak
Age: 41
City: Los Angeles
Protesting since: 2008
Affiliation: www.gotopless.org
Twitter handle: @gotopless

What happened in your life that motivated you to attend your first protest? I have always been a supporter of women's causes and for equal rights. In 2007, the founder of the spiritual organization the Raëlian Movement, Raël, began the idea of doing an organization to support women's rights by demanding the same topless rights as men. The rule of equality: "all or none!" As I am Raëlian myself and believe very much in women's equality, it made complete sense to be involved with this new idea, and GoTopless.org was launched!

How have you been protesting? On the last Sunday of August or on Women's Equality Day around the U.S. I have done four of the five protests in Venice Beach, California, where it is still illegal to show a woman's nipple! So in Venice protests we have had to make latex fleshlike nipple pasties to cover our illegal nipples in our protest march down the Venice Beach boardwalk.

Have you ever been arrested? No, not yet. :)

Have your efforts resulted in change? Yes! First and foremost, MANY more women across the U.S. and around the world have come forth over the past five years and made topless marches in their cities on Go Topless Day. When GTDay first launched in 2008 it only covered four cities. It has now grown to 30 U.S. cities and 10 different countries around the world!

What's the most egregious mainstream misconception about protesters? In regard to topless protesters, the most common misconception is that people do not feel a concern with the imbalance of gender equality. They feel and see women's bodies as sex objects, and for centuries different areas of a woman's body has had to be covered by law—the ankles, knees, shoulders, belly, waist, etc. "With repression comes obsession." So if the "mainstream" can be educated that ALL humans are beautiful in how they were created and no part of the body is sinful, dirty, or dangerous, we can begin to change. And we have done so. Now it's time for the breast.

When will you be satisfied, stop protesting? When the U.S. Constitution's 14th Amendment is clearly respected by ALL U.S. states and all women can share the same topless rights as men.

Favorite quote: "Be the change you want to see." —Gandhi

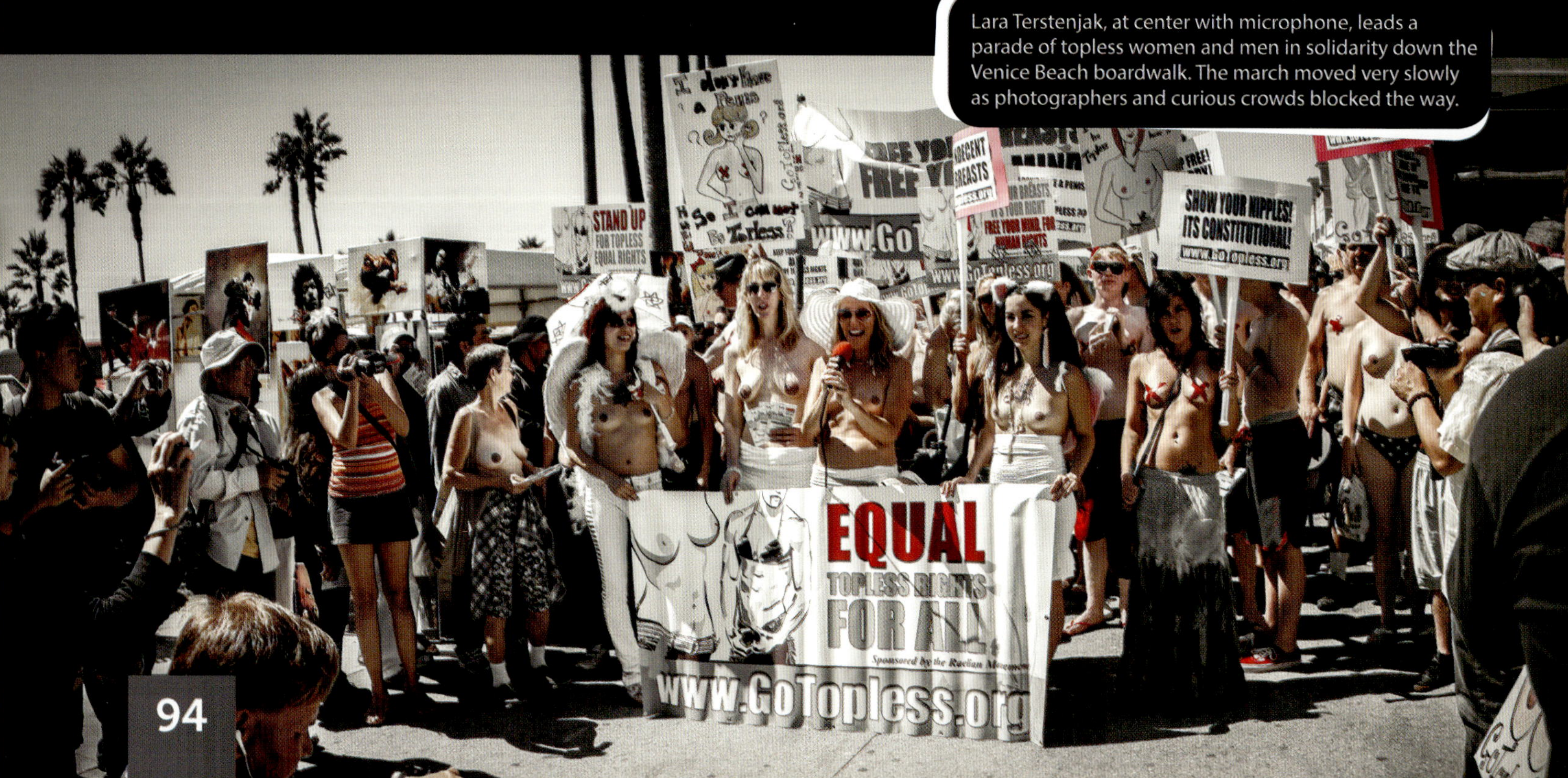

Lara Terstenjak, at center with microphone, leads a parade of topless women and men in solidarity down the Venice Beach boardwalk. The march moved very slowly as photographers and curious crowds blocked the way.

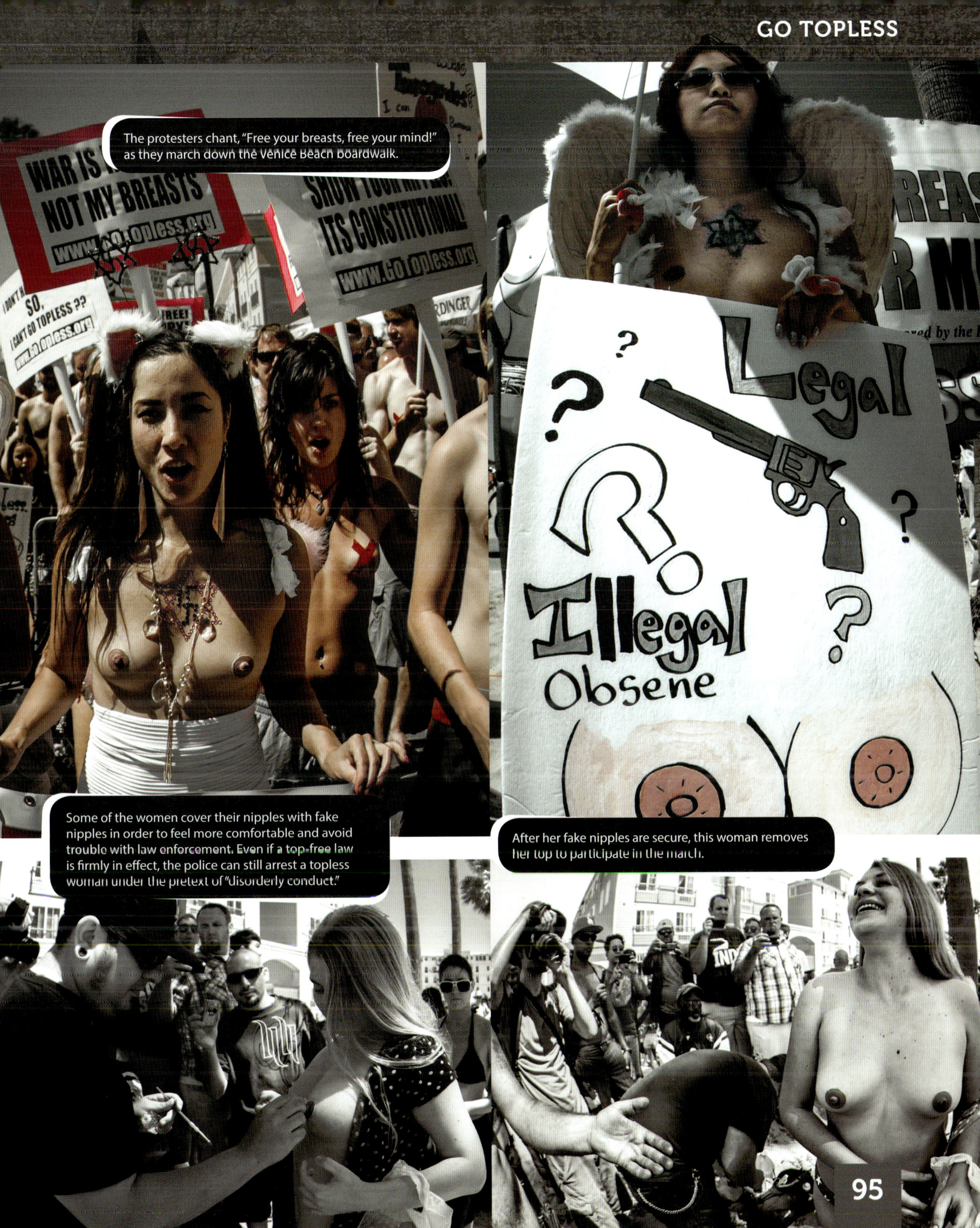

The protesters chant, "Free your breasts, free your mind!" as they march down the Venice Beach boardwalk.

Some of the women cover their nipples with fake nipples in order to feel more comfortable and avoid trouble with law enforcement. Even if a top-free law is firmly in effect, the police can still arrest a topless woman under the pretext of "disorderly conduct."

After her fake nipples are secure, this woman removes her top to participate in the march.

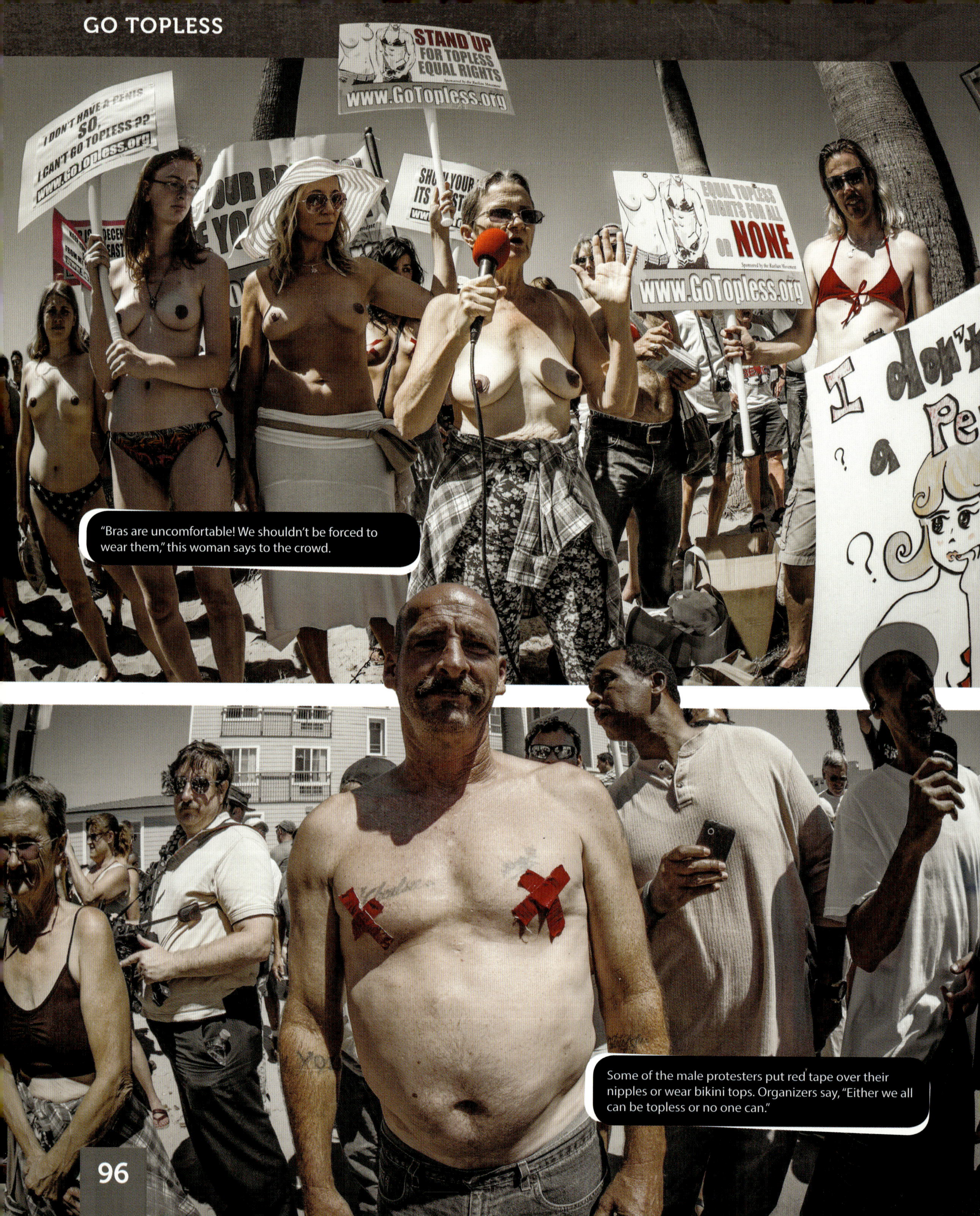

"Bras are uncomfortable! We shouldn't be forced to wear them," this woman says to the crowd.

Some of the male protesters put red tape over their nipples or wear bikini tops. Organizers say, "Either we all can be topless or no one can."

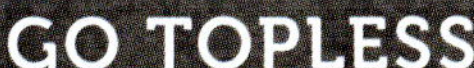

If men can venture into public with man boobs or "moobs," why can't a woman show her breasts? "What's the difference?" this man asks.

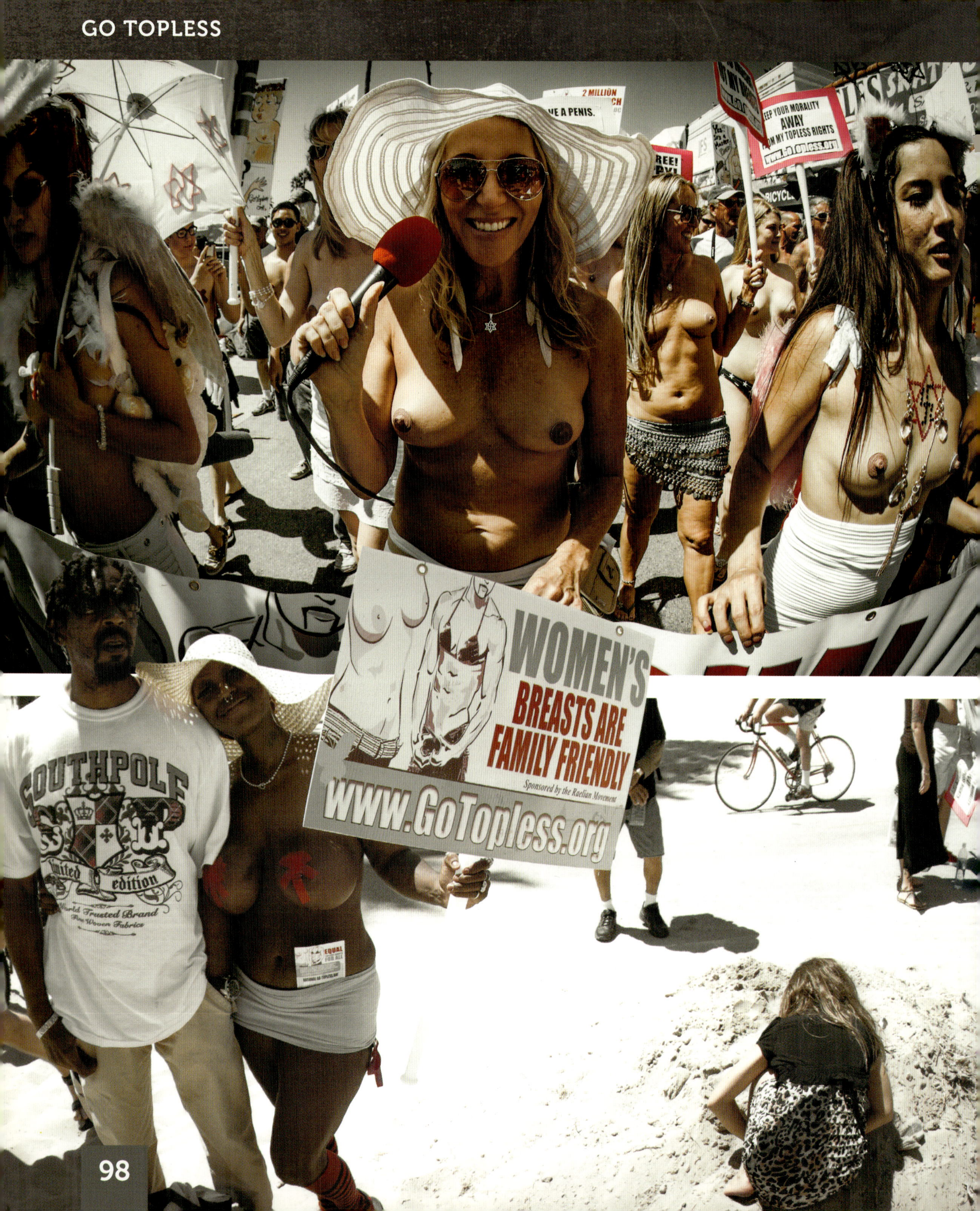

KEEP YOUR MORALITY AWAY FROM MY TOPLESS RIGHTS
www.gotopless.org
WOMEN'S
BREASTS ARE
FAMILY FRIENDLY
Sponsored by the Raelian Movement
www.GoTopless.org
SOUTHPOLE
Limited edition
World Trusted Brand
Fine Woven Fabrics

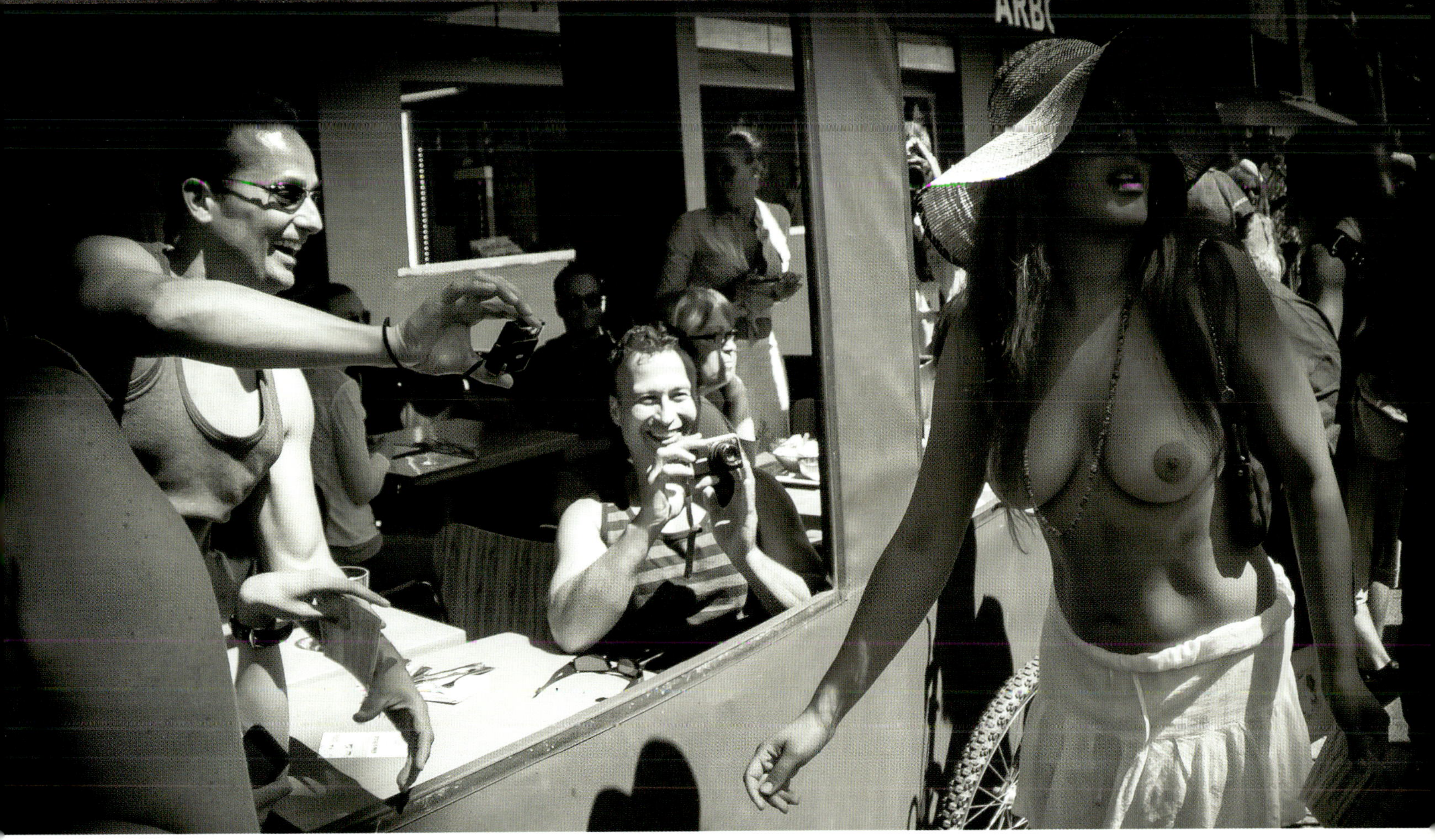

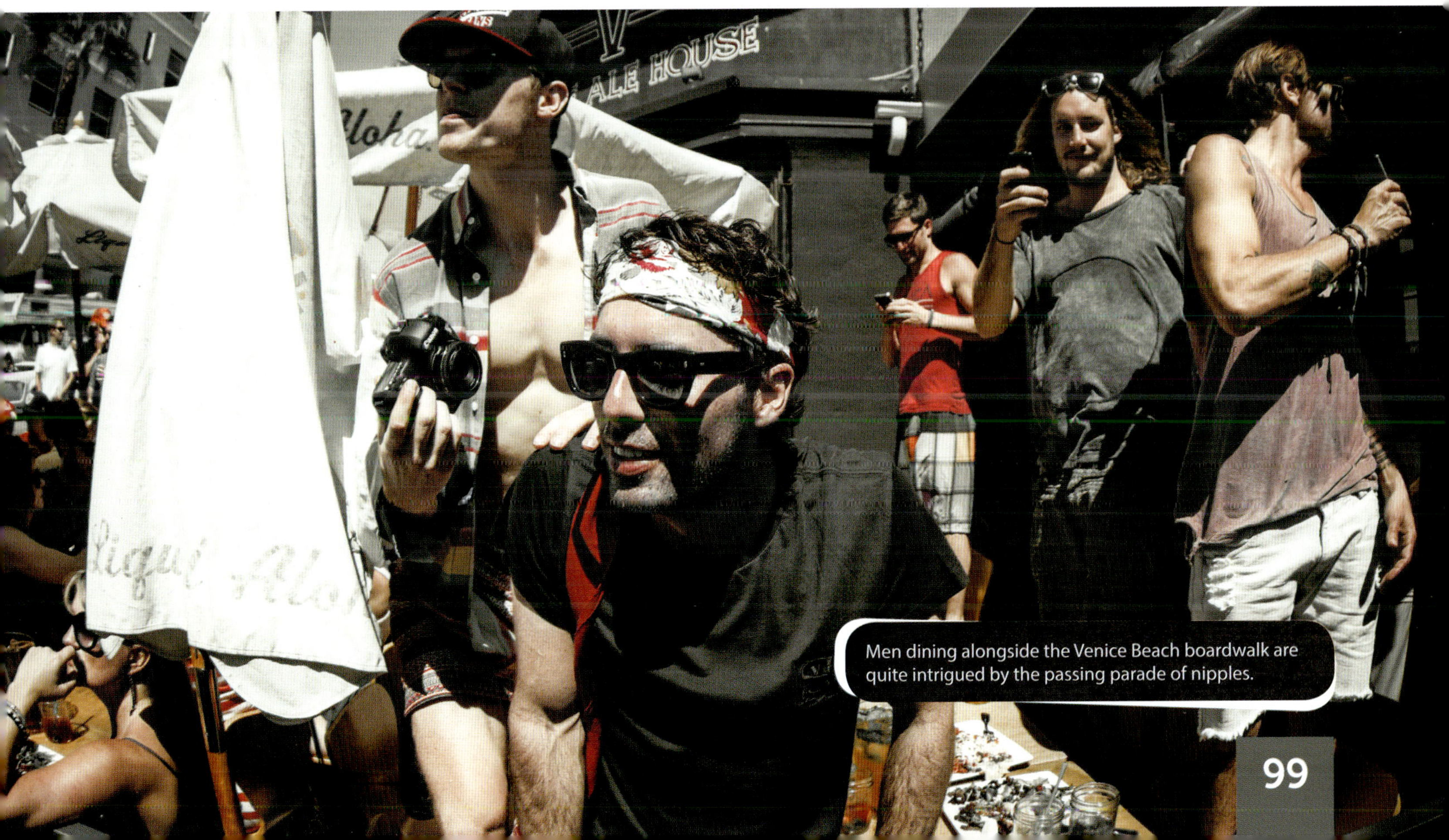

Men dining alongside the Venice Beach boardwalk are quite intrigued by the passing parade of nipples.

No NATO

On Sunday, May 20, 2012, protesters from across the country and the world descended on a heavily militarized Chicago—which boasted a thousands-strong police force in full body armor and mounted sound weapons called LRADs (used against pirates off the Somali coast, for example)—to protest the NATO military summit composed of over 60 nations.

The North American Treaty Organization (NATO) transformed from a primarily political organization to a military force after the attacks of September 11, 2001, when it moved military forces into Afghanistan, and solidified this function when it moved trainers

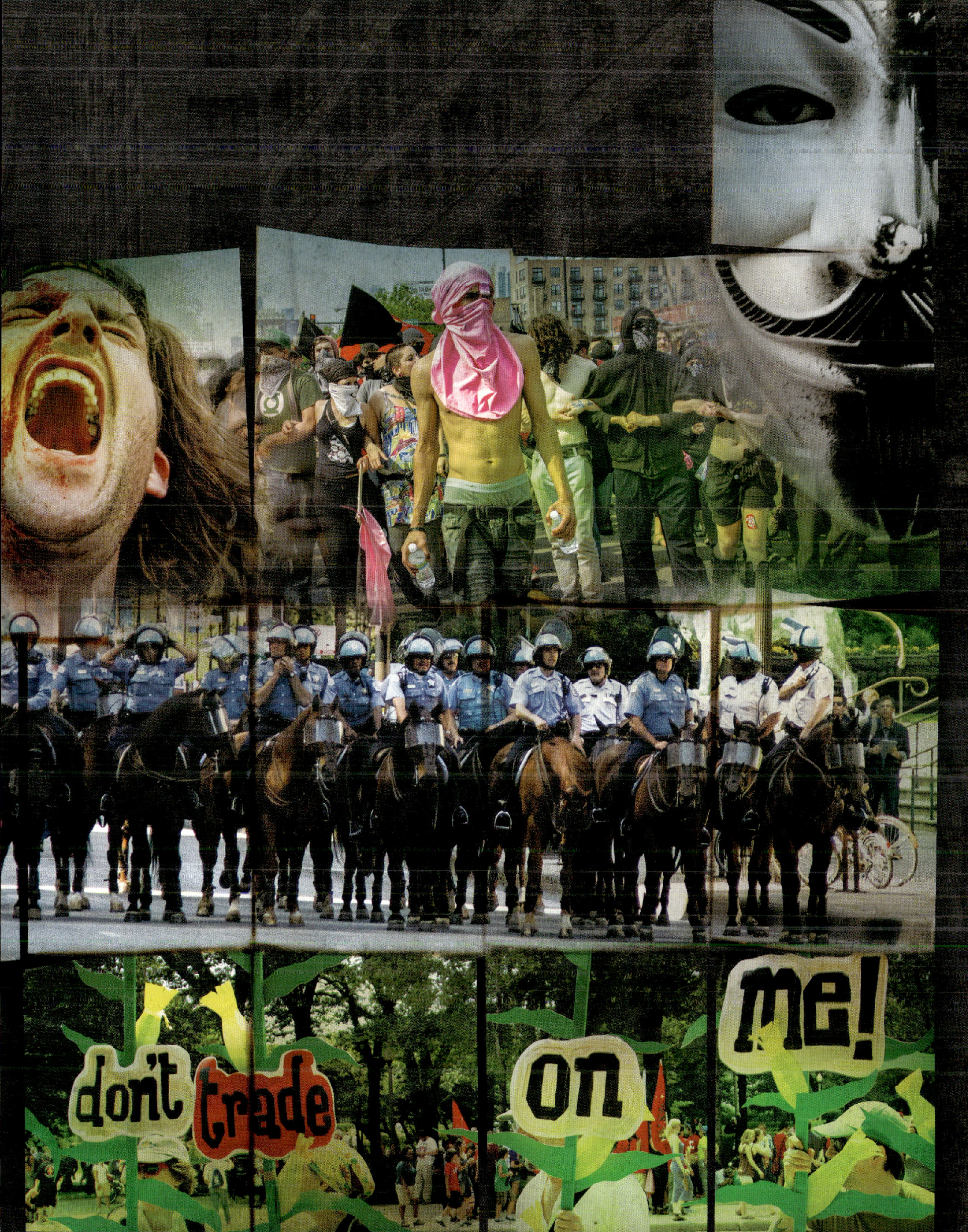

don't
trade
on
me!

The May 20, 2012, march was the culmination of a week of activism events leading up to NATO's arrival. The six days of demonstrations focused on Obama's former chief of staff—Rahm Emanuel, currently Chicago's mayor—and included Occupy Chicago, community groups advocating an end to the prison industrial complex, and activists staunchly opposed to Emanuel's plan to privatize Chicago's education system. Demonstrators even went so far as to protest outside the mayor's home, which was protected by a massive line of Chicago bicycle police. The theme of investing in communities instead of the military industrial complex dovetailed spectacularly with the opposition to NATO's presence the following Sunday.

The photos and accounts from those who attended the "no-NATO summit" will be forever remembered as snapshots from a moment in history when an incredibly broad spectrum of issues and people came together to protest militarism.

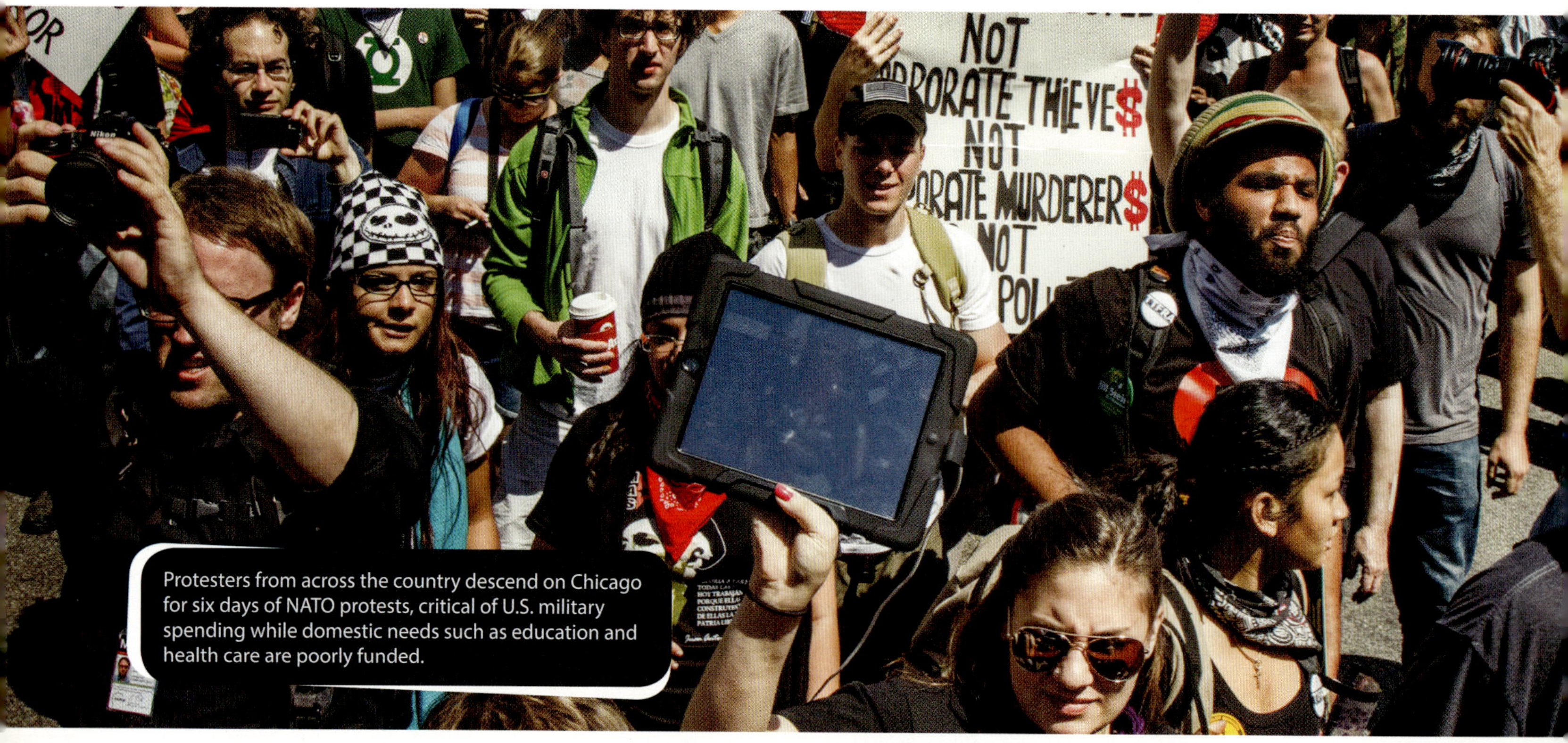

Protesters from across the country descend on Chicago for six days of NATO protests, critical of U.S. military spending while domestic needs such as education and health care are poorly funded.

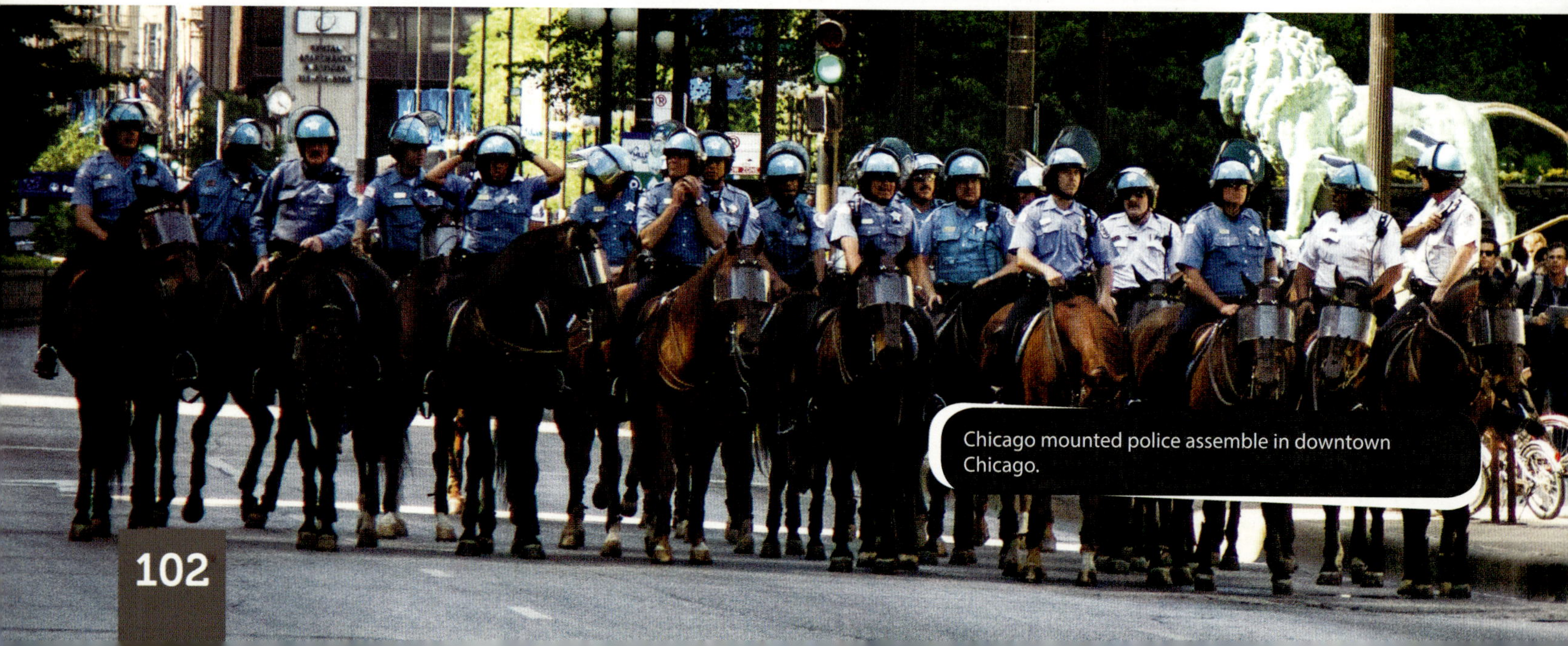

Chicago mounted police assemble in downtown Chicago.

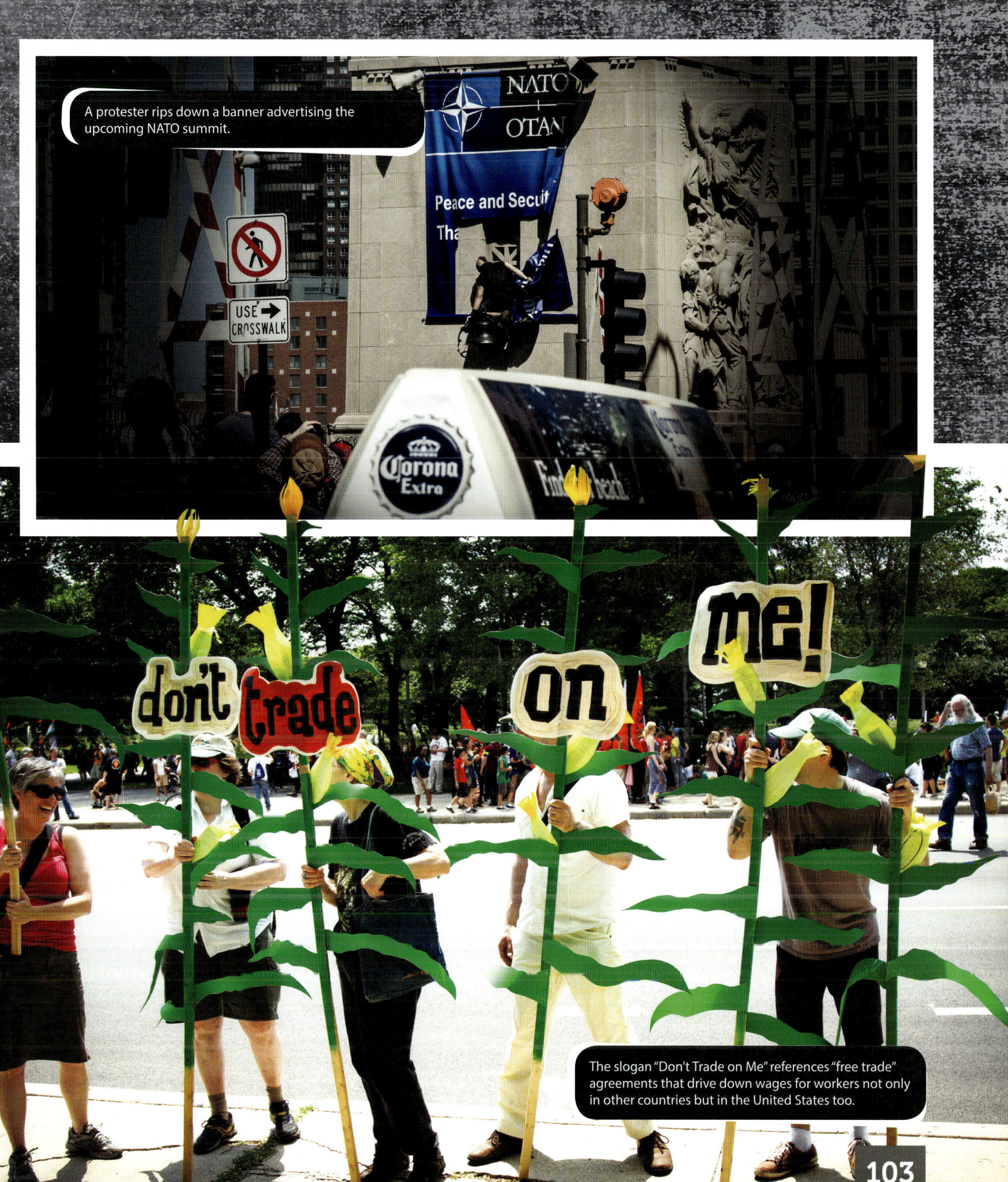

A protester rips down a banner advertising the upcoming NATO summit.

The slogan "Don't Trade on Me" references "free trade" agreements that drive down wages for workers not only in other countries but in the United States too.

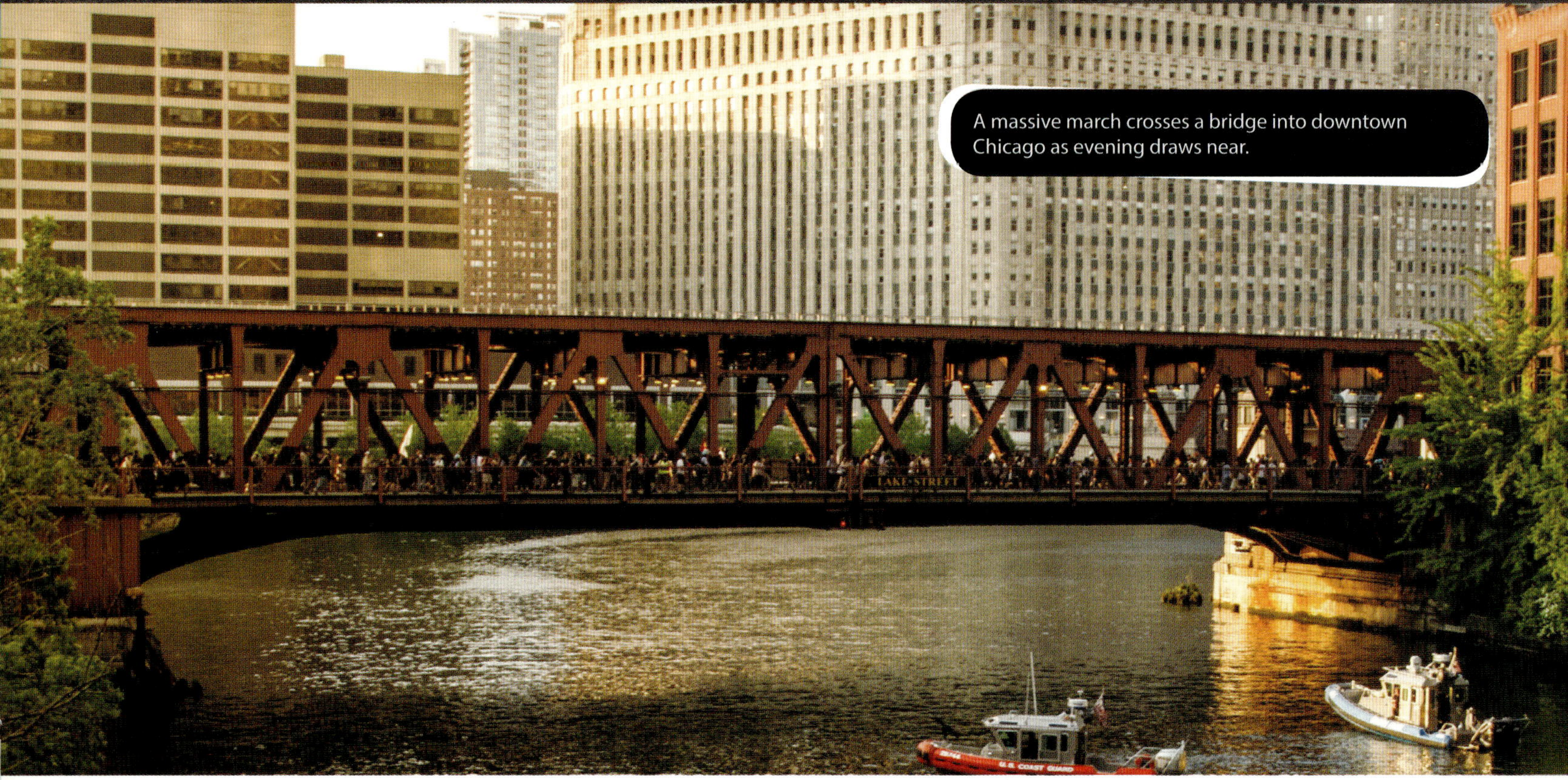

A massive march crosses a bridge into downtown Chicago as evening draws near.

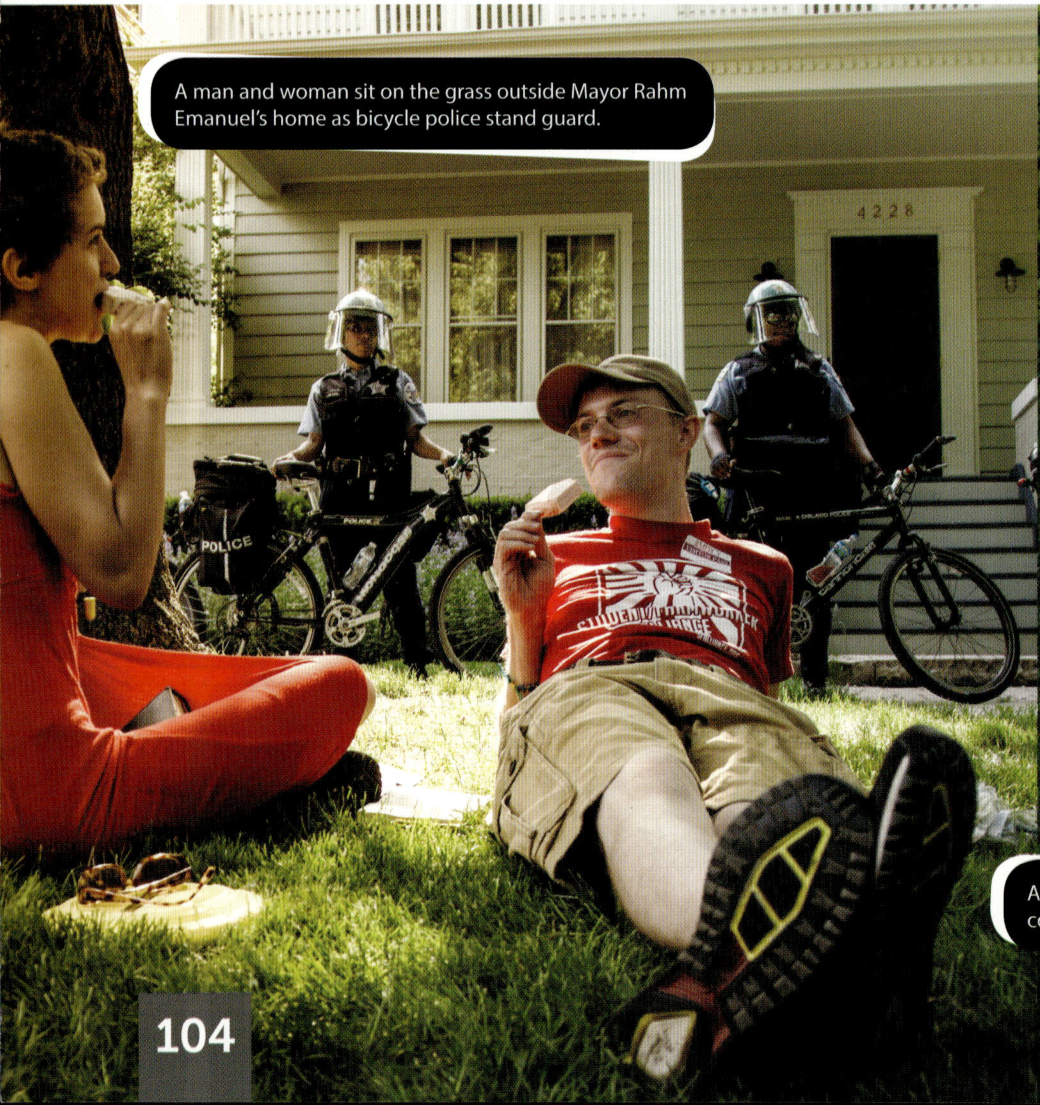

A man and woman sit on the grass outside Mayor Rahm Emanuel's home as bicycle police stand guard.

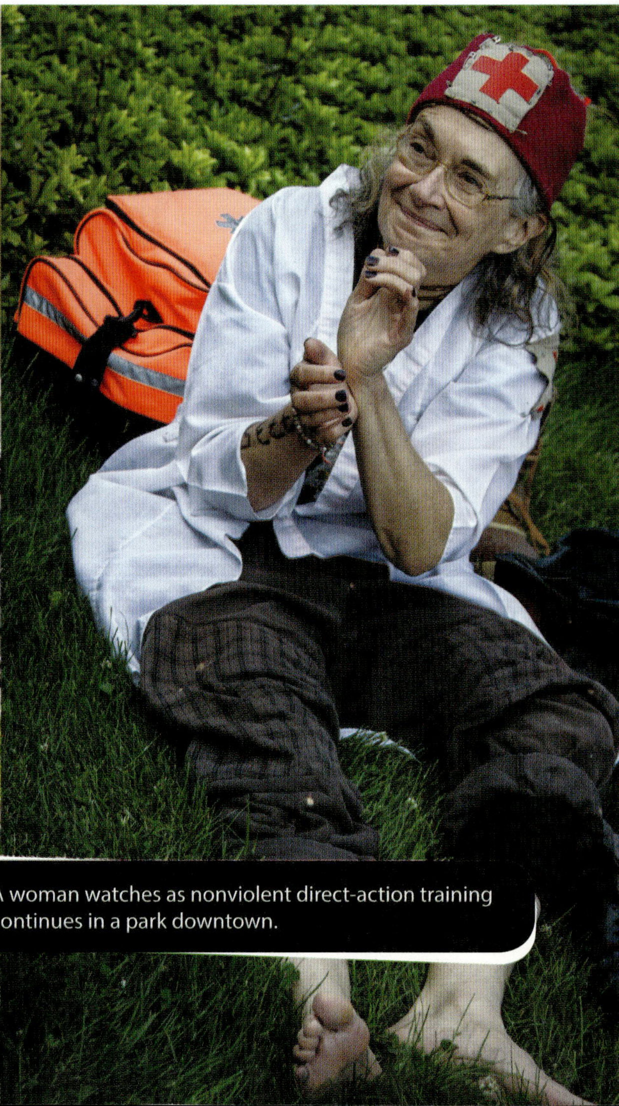

A woman watches as nonviolent direct-action training continues in a park downtown.

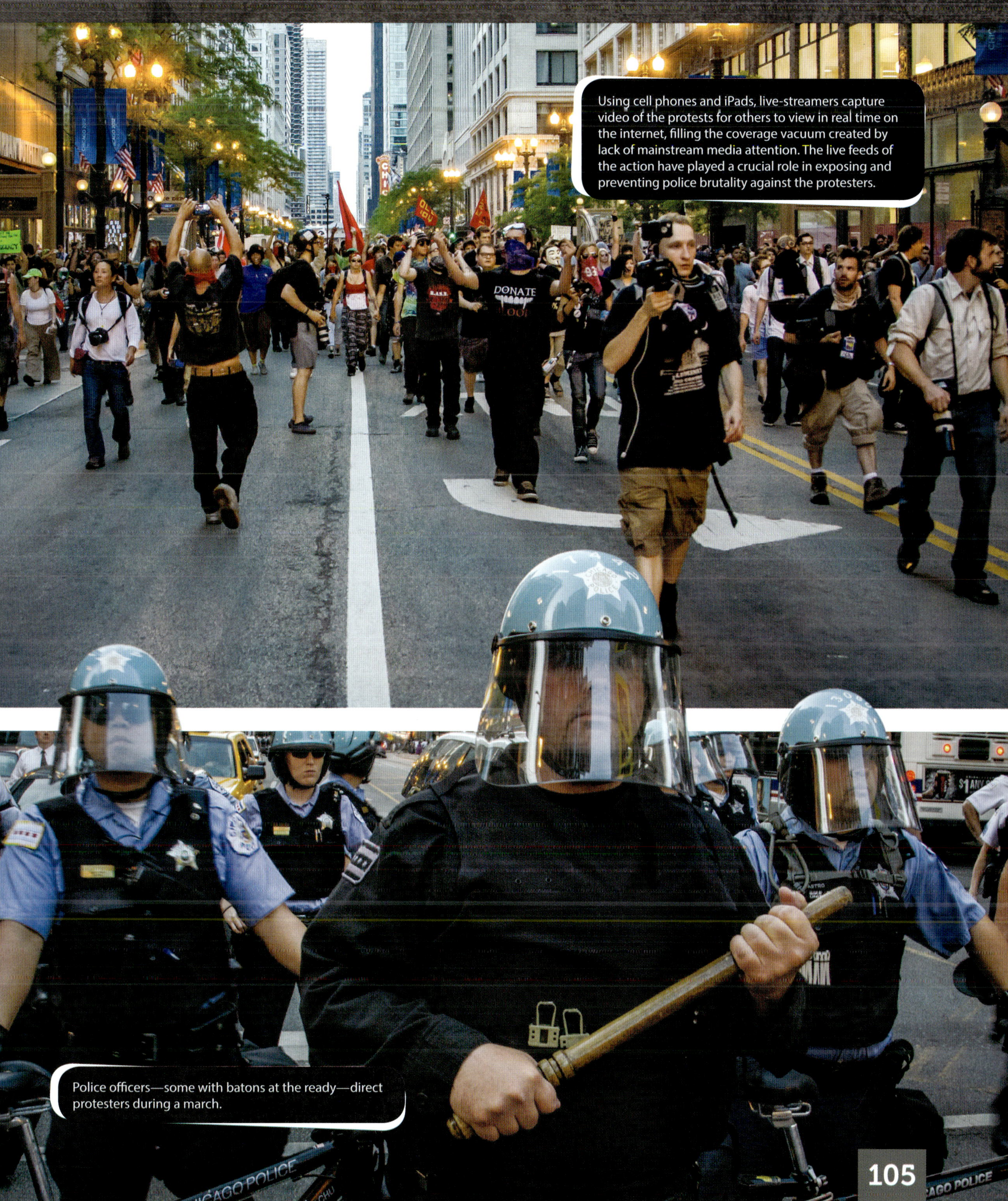

Using cell phones and iPads, live-streamers capture video of the protests for others to view in real time on the internet, filling the coverage vacuum created by lack of mainstream media attention. The live feeds of the action have played a crucial role in exposing and preventing police brutality against the protesters.

Police officers—some with batons at the ready—direct protesters during a march.

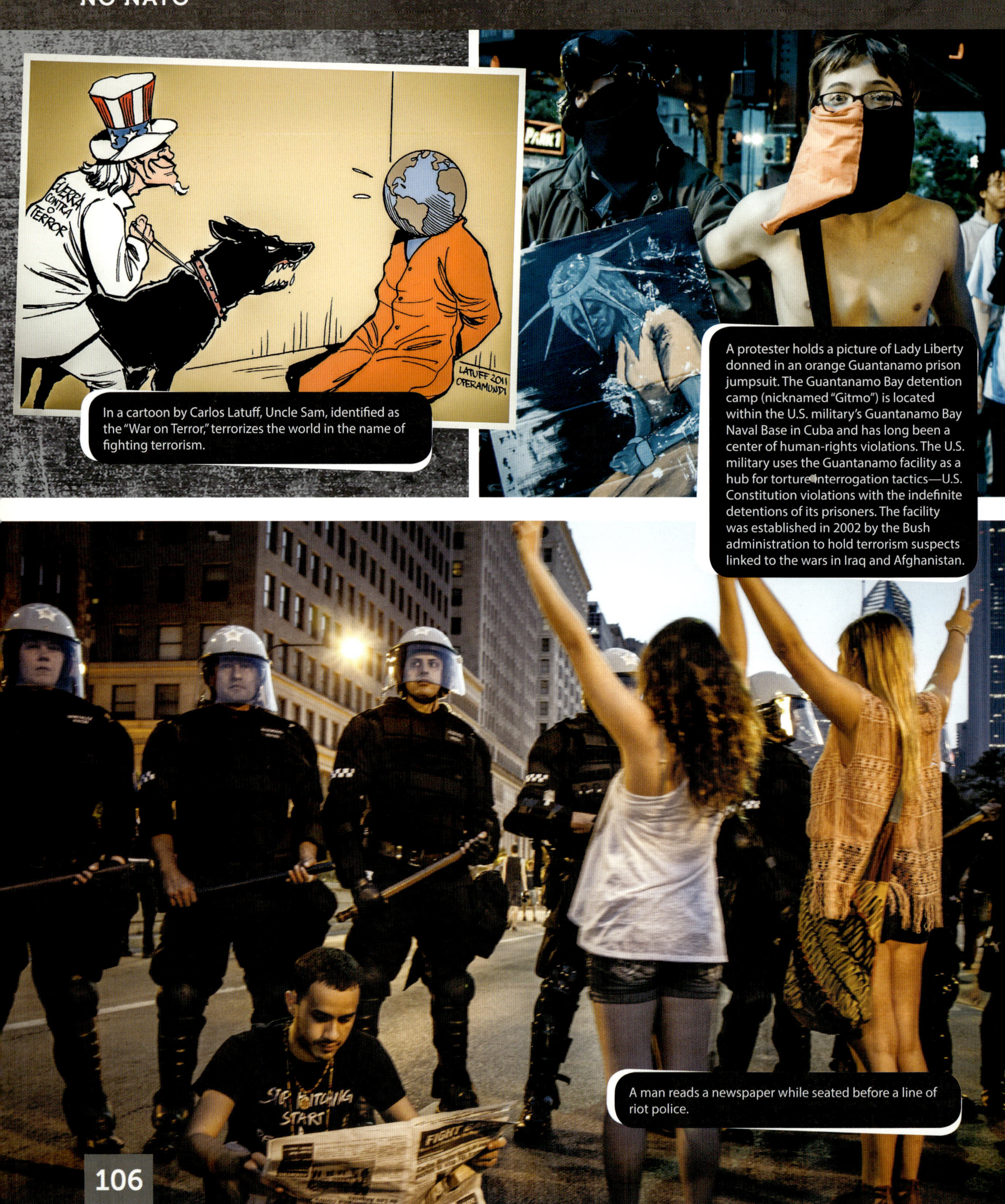

In a cartoon by Carlos Latuff, Uncle Sam, identified as the "War on Terror," terrorizes the world in the name of fighting terrorism.

A protester holds a picture of Lady Liberty donned in an orange Guantanamo prison jumpsuit. The Guantanamo Bay detention camp (nicknamed "Gitmo") is located within the U.S. military's Guantanamo Bay Naval Base in Cuba and has long been a center of human-rights violations. The U.S. military uses the Guantanamo facility as a hub for torture interrogation tactics—U.S. Constitution violations with the indefinite detentions of its prisoners. The facility was established in 2002 by the Bush administration to hold terrorism suspects linked to the wars in Iraq and Afghanistan.

A man reads a newspaper while seated before a line of riot police.

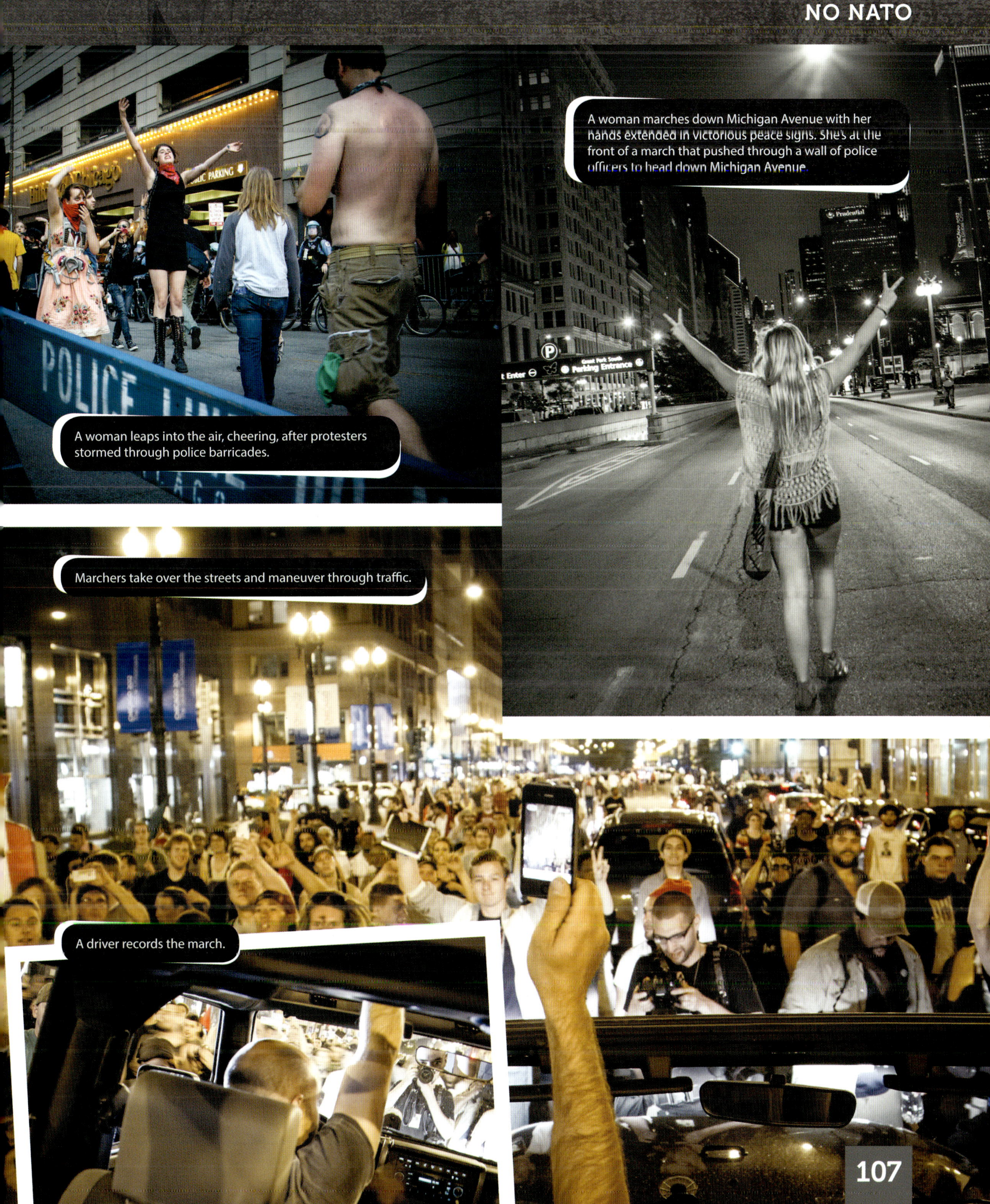

A woman leaps into the air, cheering, after protesters stormed through police barricades.

A woman marches down Michigan Avenue with her hands extended in victorious peace signs. She's at the front of a march that pushed through a wall of police officers to head down Michigan Avenue.

Marchers take over the streets and maneuver through traffic.

A driver records the march.

A protester dressed to participate in the "black bloc" method of protest. A black bloc is a tactic for protests and marches wherein individuals wear black clothing to conceal their identities and to allow the group to appear as one large unified mass. Methods of black-bloc protest have included vandalism but are mainly deployed as defensive moves to mislead the authorities, to unite a group of protesters to push through police blockades, and to treat protesters affected by riot-control weapons.

Masked protesters link arms, using black-bloc protest tactics.

A police patrol boat monitors unarmed protesters as they cross over the Chicago river. The police boats are armed with machine guns.

The black-bloc tactic is employed in front of a march to protect protesters from police.

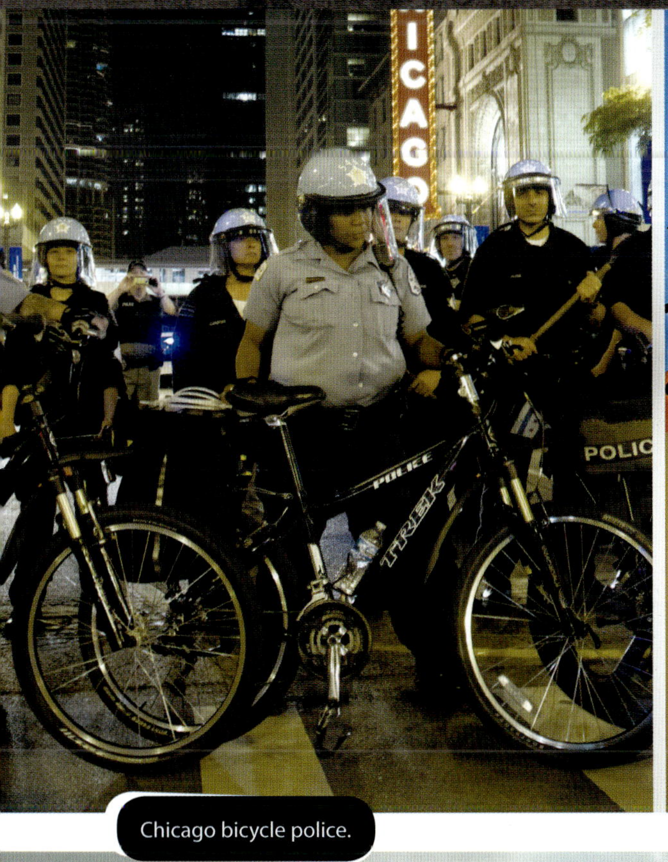

Chicago bicycle police.

In this cartoon by Carlos Latuff, President Barack Obama—in the form of a drone—obliterates a house in the Middle East, striking unarmed civilians. Obama justifies the use of drone devices as a way to fight terrorism, but residents say the drones are the real terrorists.

A protester holds aloft a drone replica during a march in Chicago. To date, more than 176 Pakistani children have been murdered as a result of U.S./NATO drone operations. Source: The Bureau of Investigative Journalism (thebureauinvestigates.com), "Drone Strikes in Pakistan 2004–2012," http://www.thebureauinvestigates.com/category/projects/drones/drones-pakistan/.

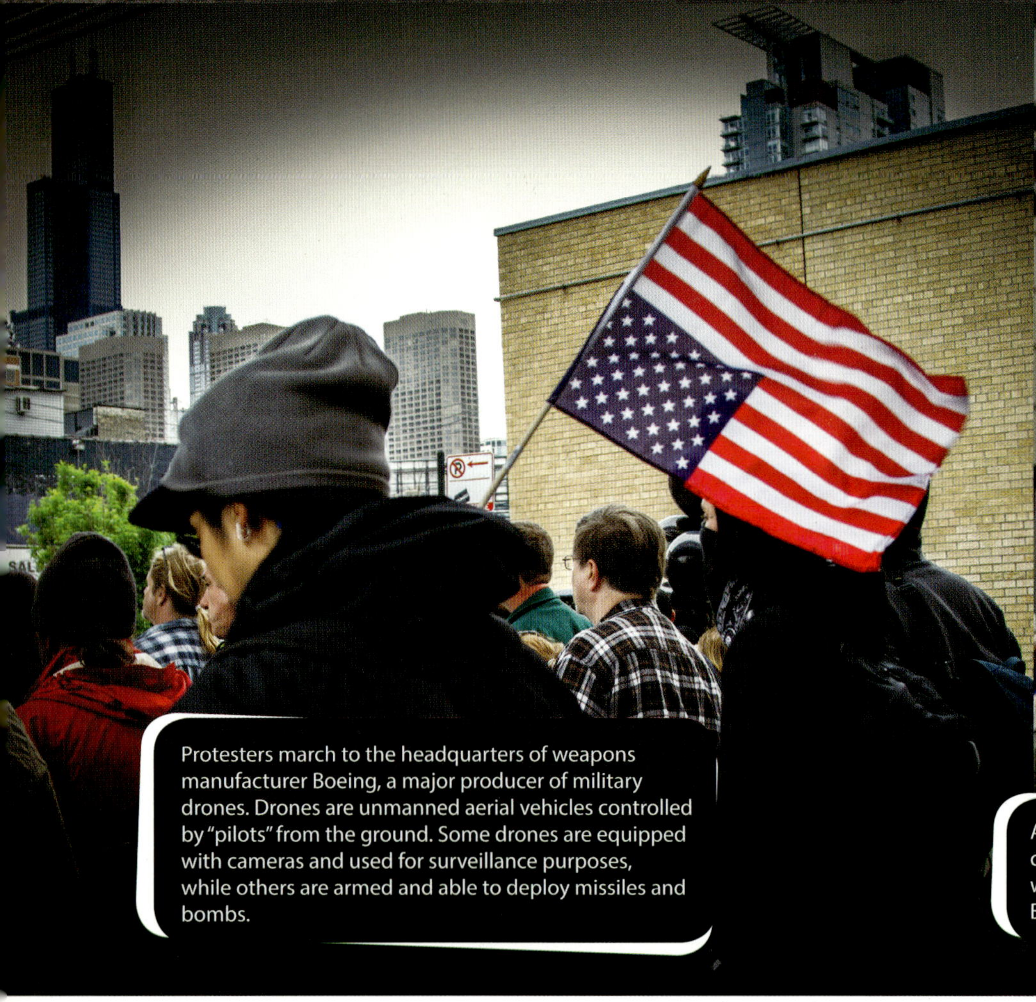

Protesters march to the headquarters of weapons manufacturer Boeing, a major producer of military drones. Drones are unmanned aerial vehicles controlled by "pilots" from the ground. Some drones are equipped with cameras and used for surveillance purposes, while others are armed and able to deploy missiles and bombs.

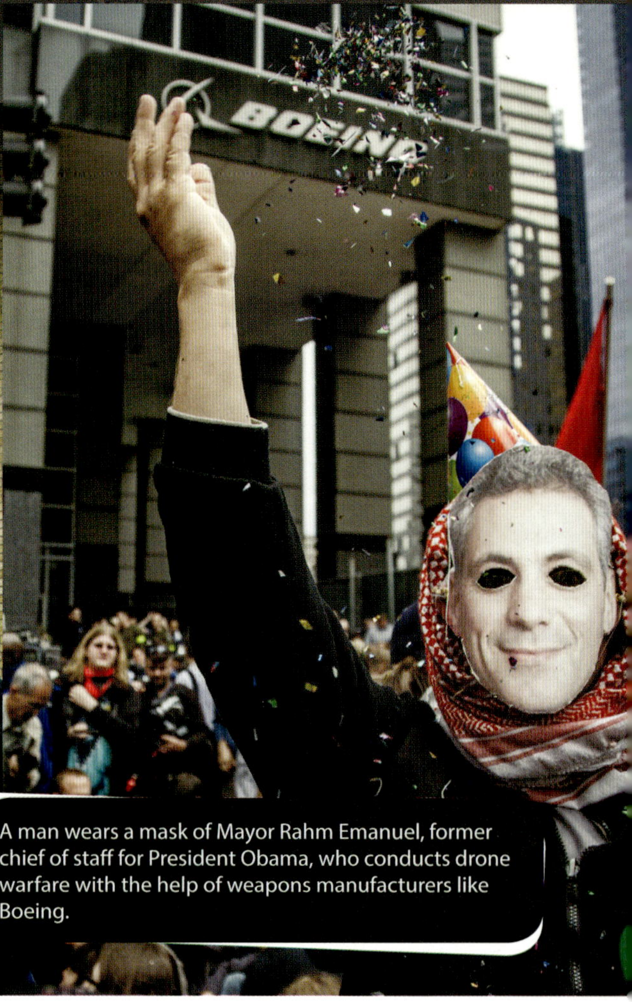

A man wears a mask of Mayor Rahm Emanuel, former chief of staff for President Obama, who conducts drone warfare with the help of weapons manufacturers like Boeing.

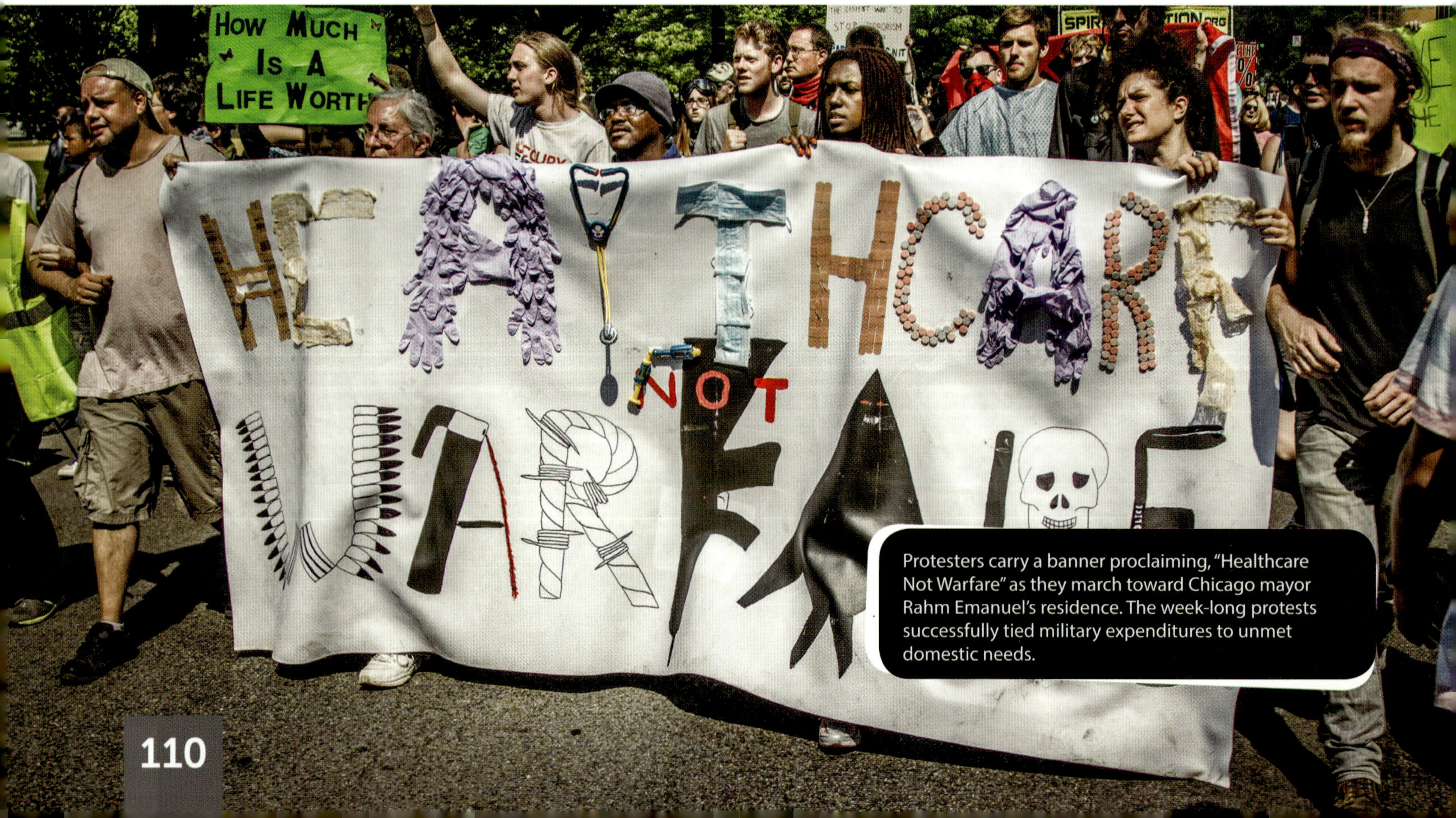

Protesters carry a banner proclaiming, "Healthcare Not Warfare" as they march toward Chicago mayor Rahm Emanuel's residence. The week-long protests successfully tied military expenditures to unmet domestic needs.

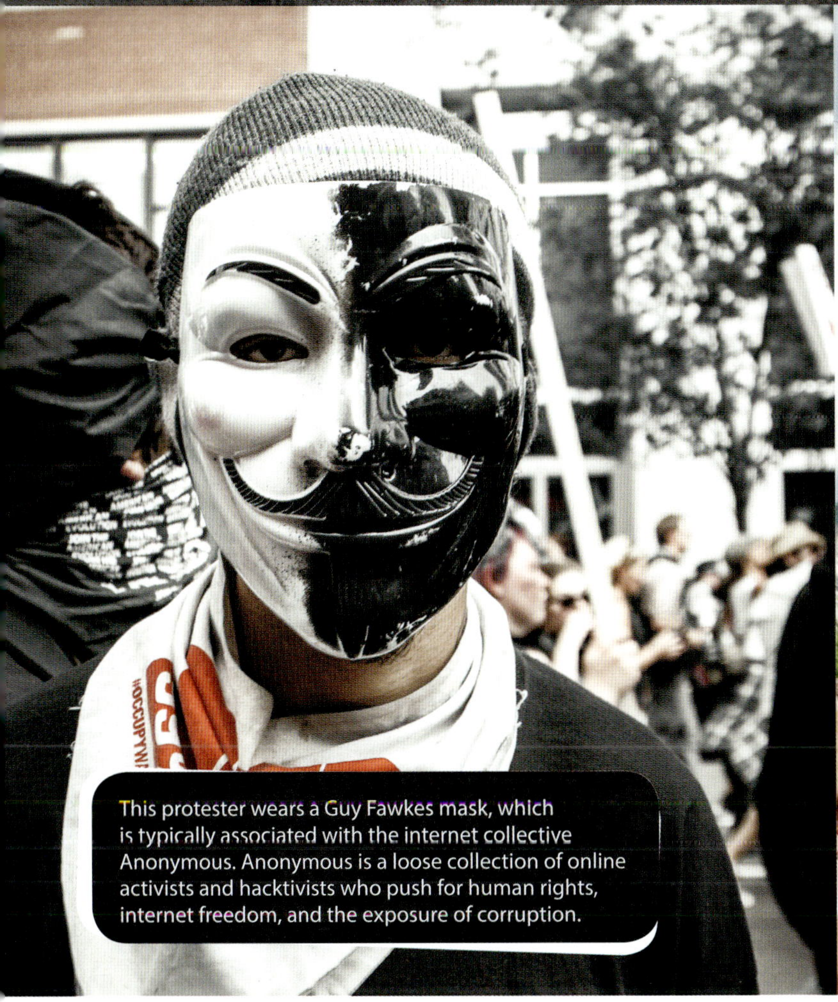

This protester wears a Guy Fawkes mask, which is typically associated with the internet collective Anonymous. Anonymous is a loose collection of online activists and hacktivists who push for human rights, internet freedom, and the exposure of corruption.

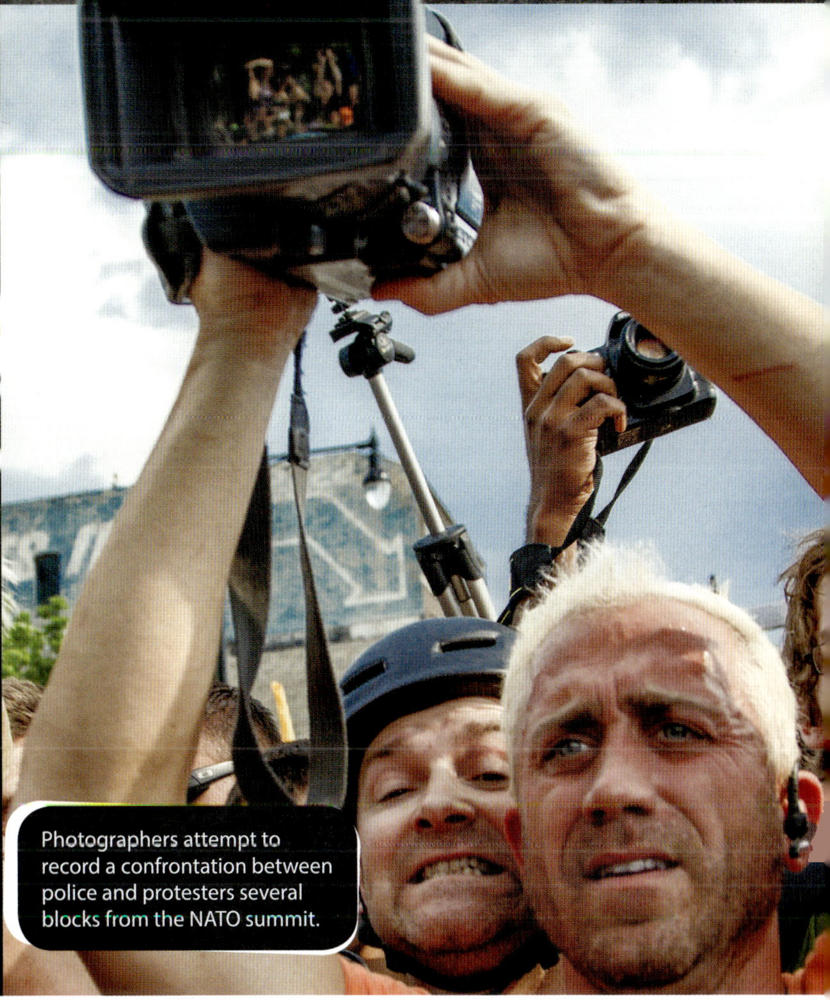

Photographers attempt to record a confrontation between police and protesters several blocks from the NATO summit.

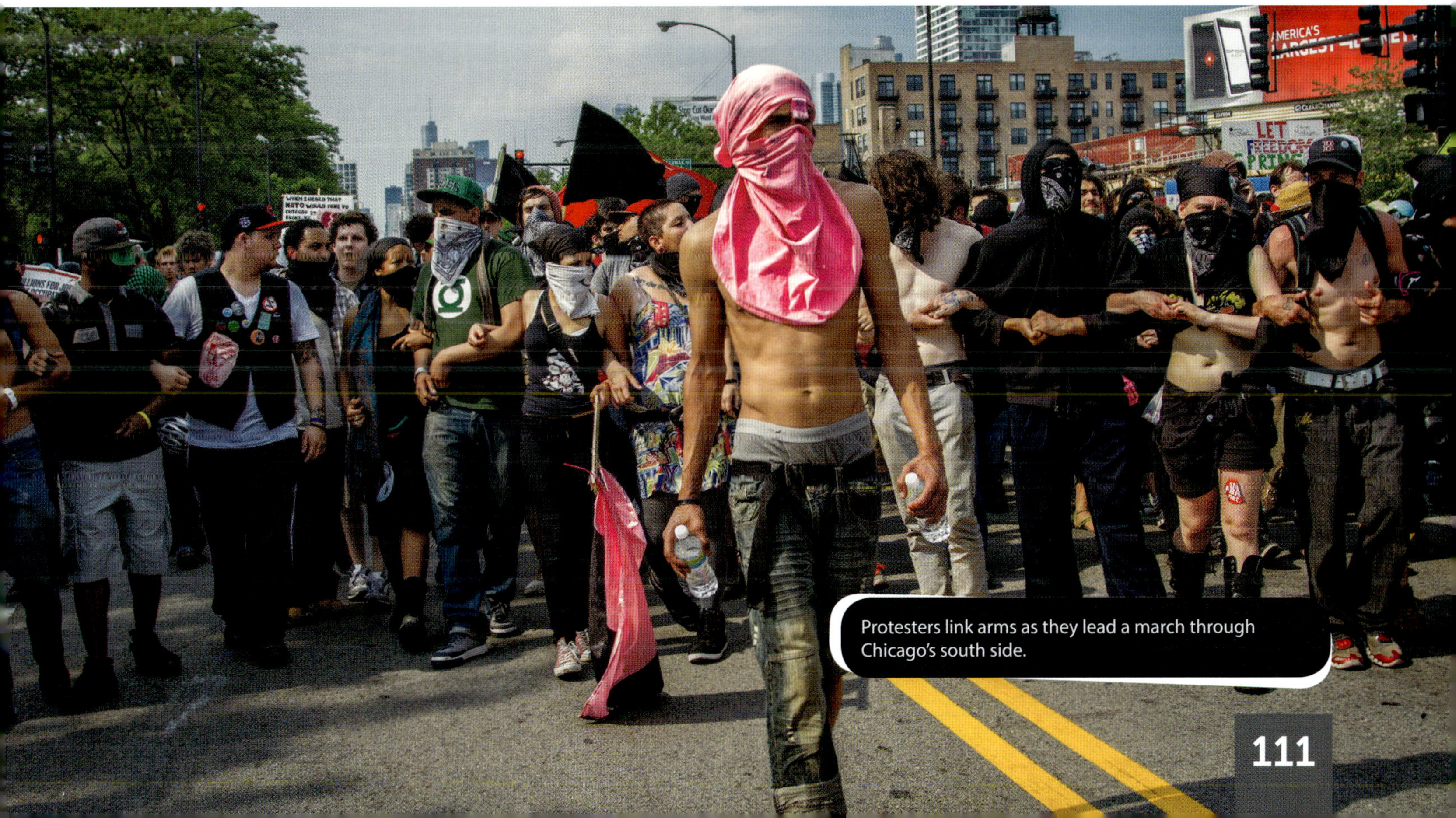

Protesters link arms as they lead a march through Chicago's south side.

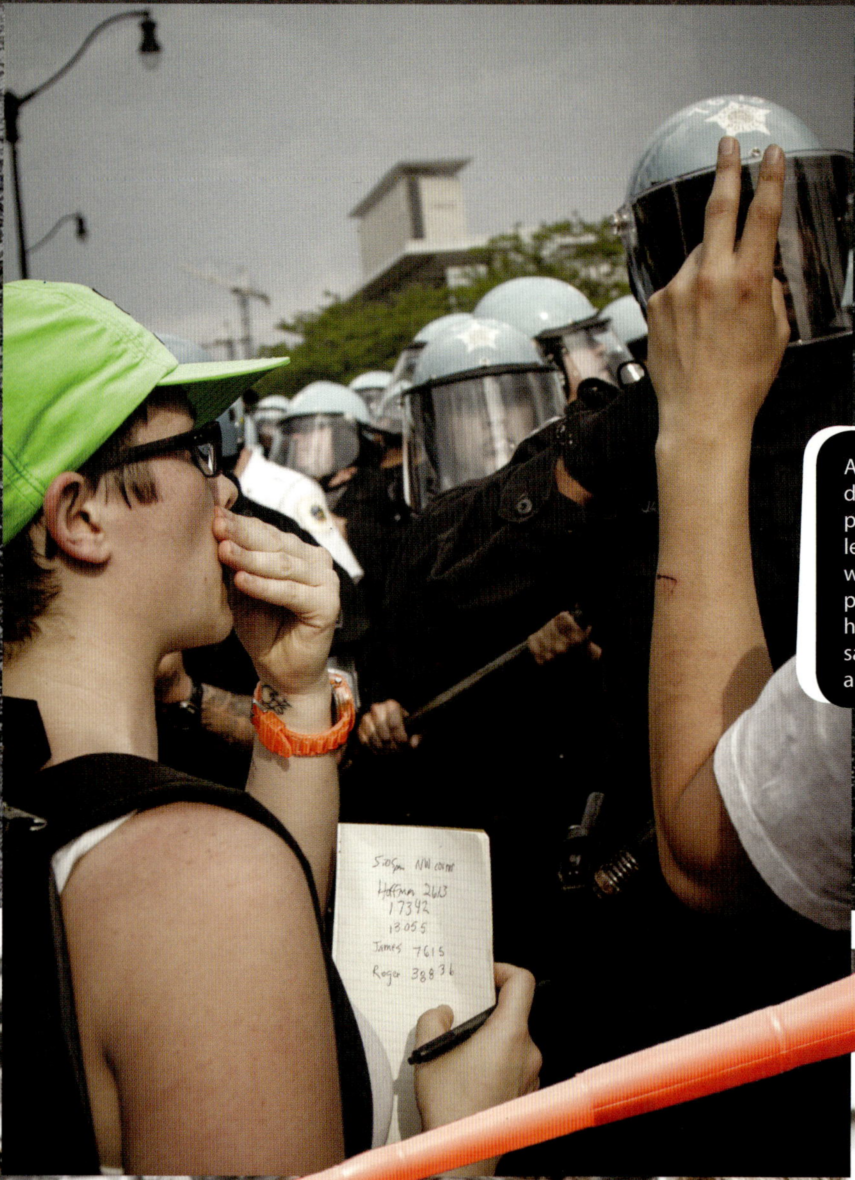

A National Lawyers Guild (NLG) legal observer writes down police badge numbers, taking notes on police and protester interaction. The NLG is a national nonprofit legal and political organization comprising legal workers, law students, and jailhouse lawyers. The NLG provides free legal representation to protesters who have been assaulted by police or unjustly arrested and says its mission is to use "the law to protect human rights above property interests and to attain social justice."

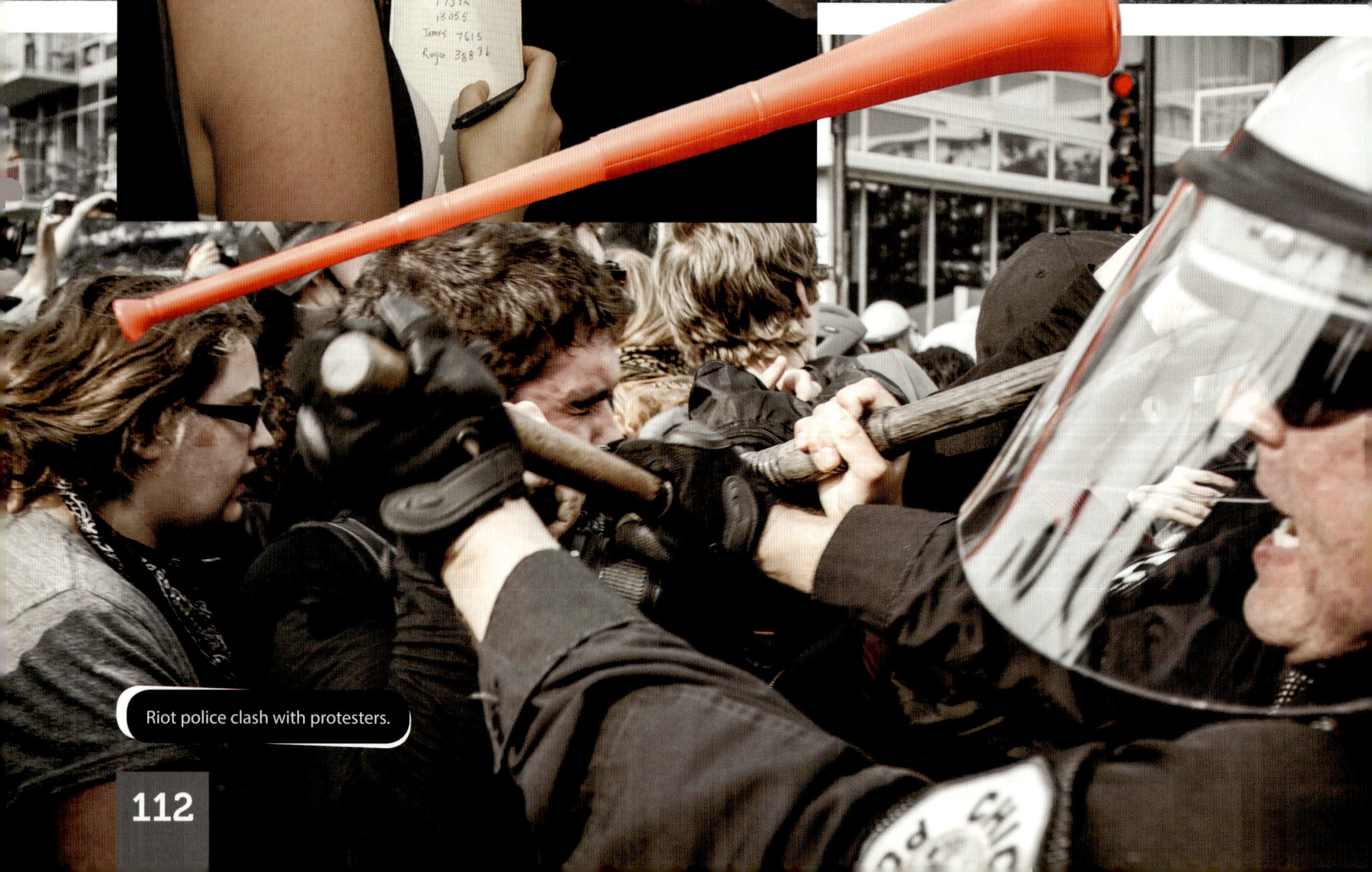

Riot police clash with protesters.

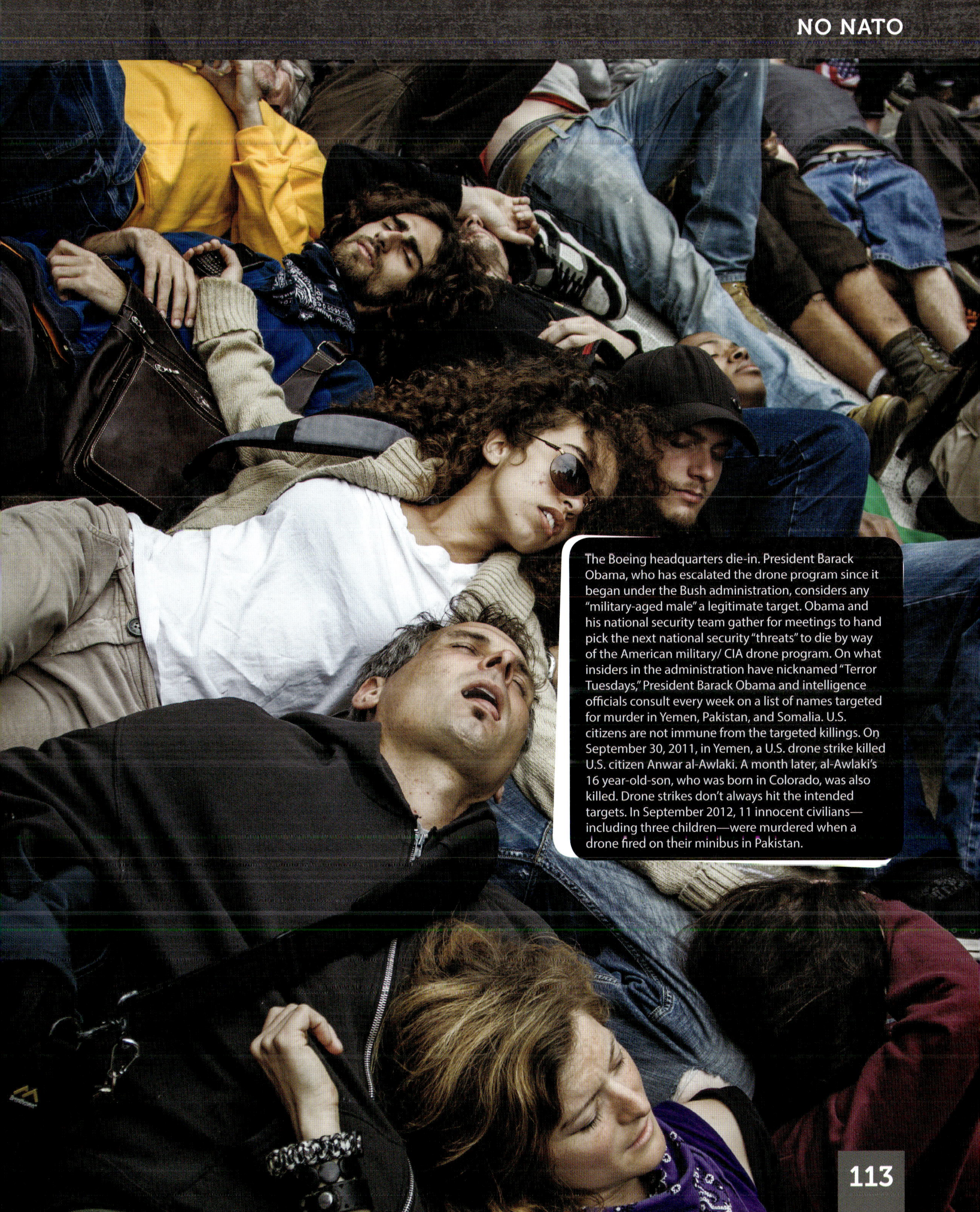

The Boeing headquarters die-in. President Barack Obama, who has escalated the drone program since it began under the Bush administration, considers any "military-aged male" a legitimate target. Obama and his national security team gather for meetings to hand pick the next national security "threats" to die by way of the American military/ CIA drone program. On what insiders in the administration have nicknamed "Terror Tuesdays," President Barack Obama and intelligence officials consult every week on a list of names targeted for murder in Yemen, Pakistan, and Somalia. U.S. citizens are not immune from the targeted killings. On September 30, 2011, in Yemen, a U.S. drone strike killed U.S. citizen Anwar al-Awlaki. A month later, al-Awlaki's 16 year-old-son, who was born in Colorado, was also killed. Drone strikes don't always hit the intended targets. In September 2012, 11 innocent civilians—including three children—were murdered when a drone fired on their minibus in Pakistan.

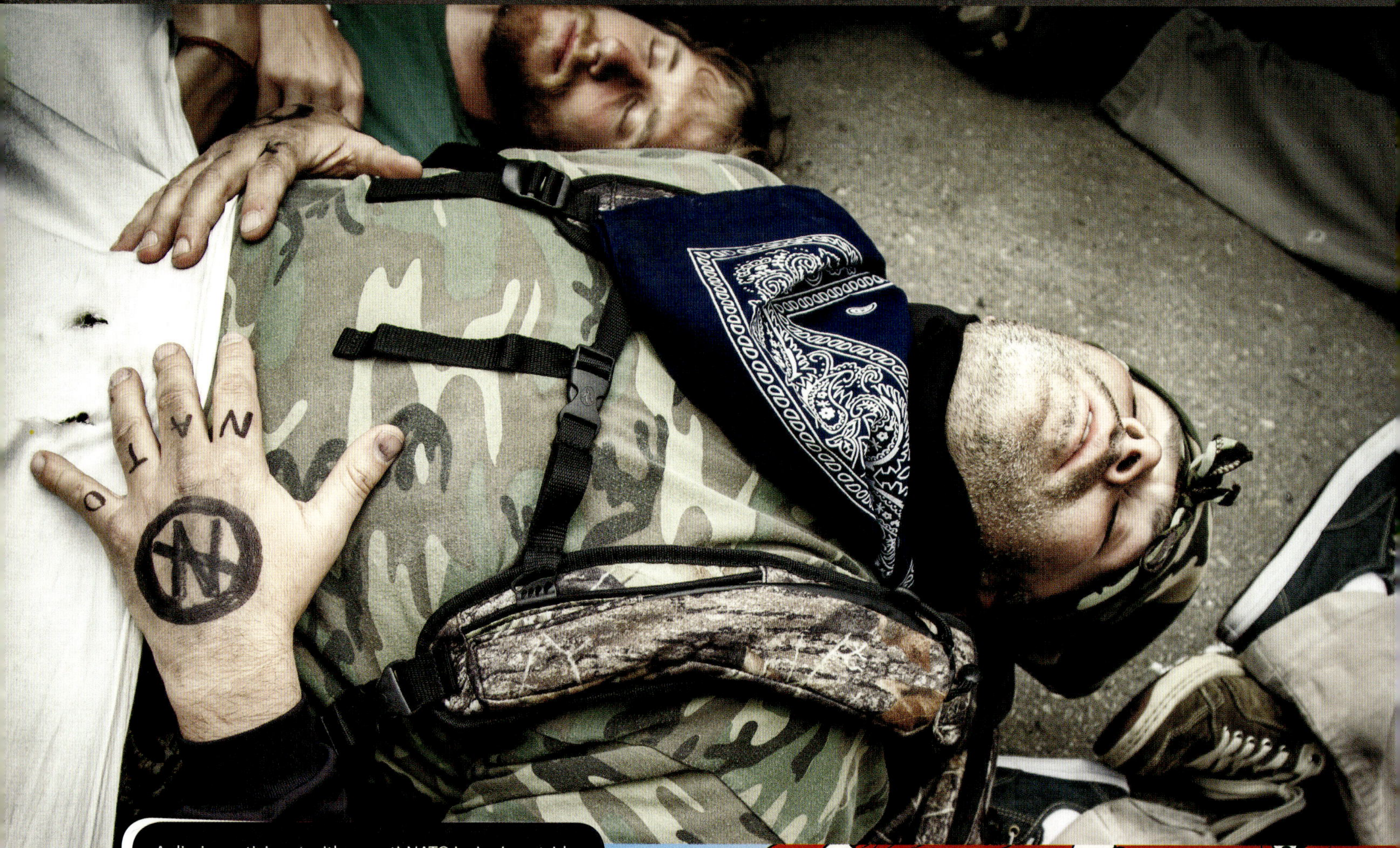

A die-in participant with an anti-NATO insignia outside of Boeing headquarters. President Obama justifies the use of drones to fight terrorism, but civilians in areas where U.S. drones are deployed say the drones are the real terrorists. A September 2012 report on the psychological effects of drones on residents noted major impacts on community life, including school attendance, sleep patterns, and post-traumatic stress disorder, as the community fears random strikes coming out of the sky.

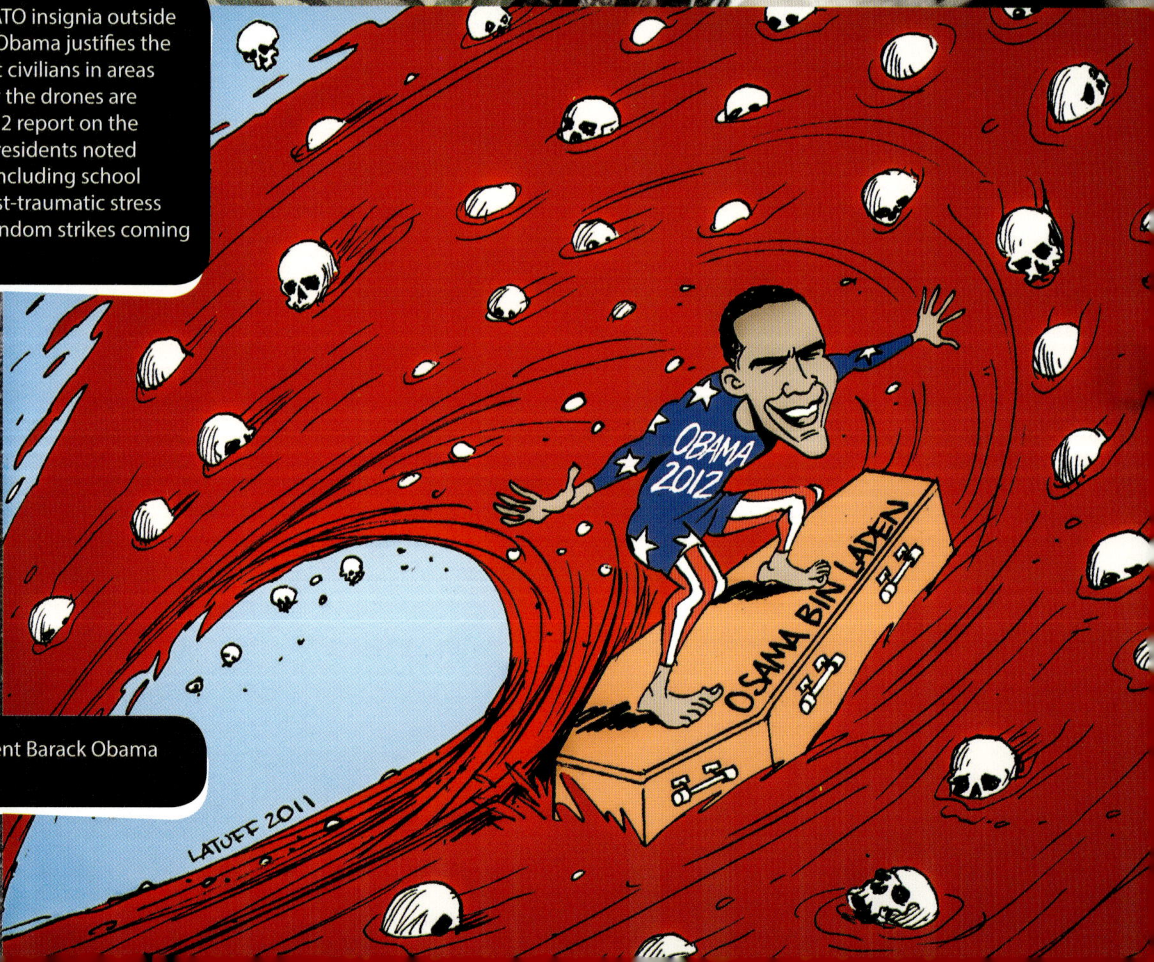

In a cartoon by Carlos Latuff, President Barack Obama rides a wave of death to reelection.

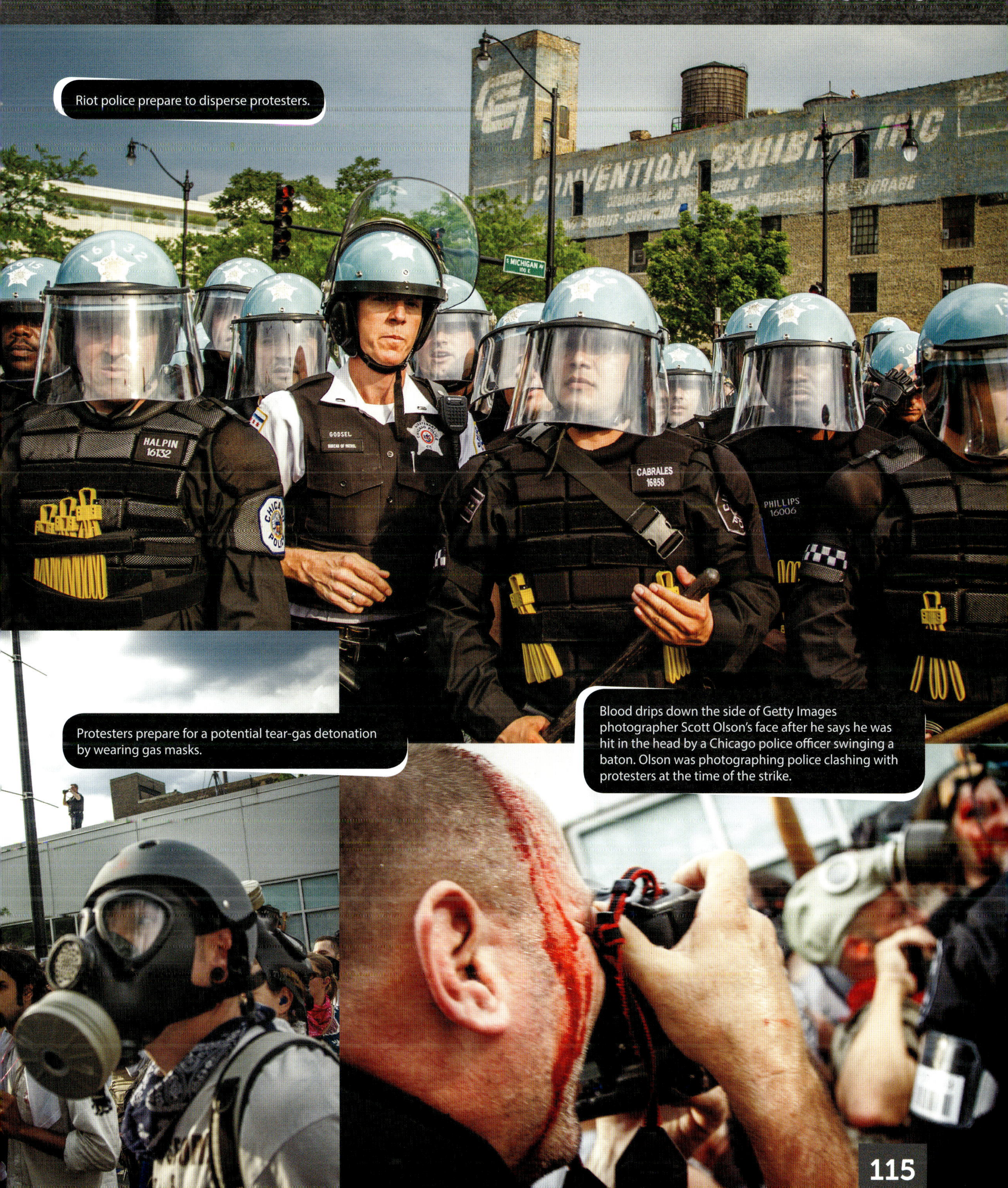

Riot police prepare to disperse protesters.

Protesters prepare for a potential tear-gas detonation by wearing gas masks.

Blood drips down the side of Getty Images photographer Scott Olson's face after he says he was hit in the head by a Chicago police officer swinging a baton. Olson was photographing police clashing with protesters at the time of the strike.

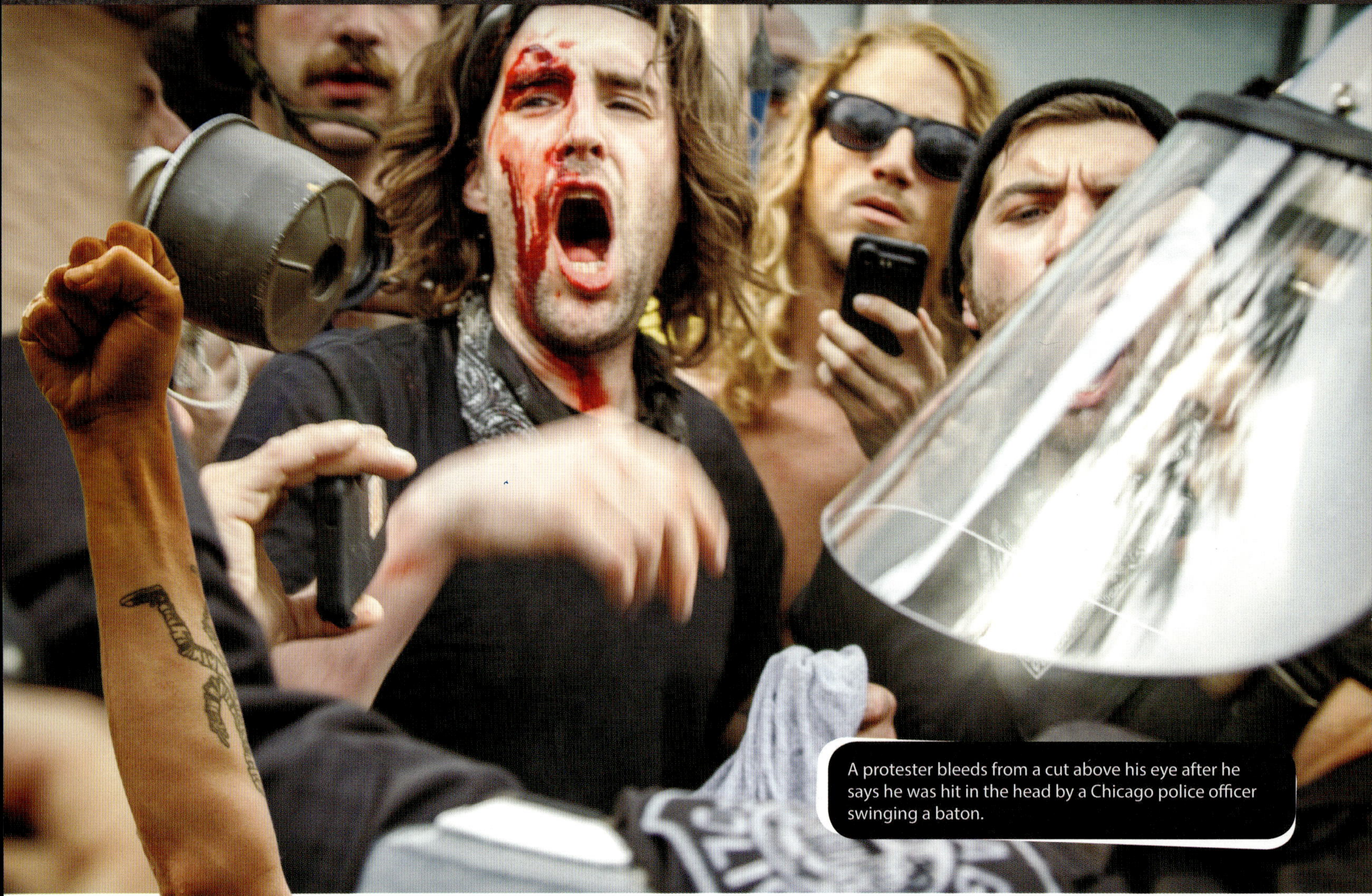

A protester bleeds from a cut above his eye after he says he was hit in the head by a Chicago police officer swinging a baton.

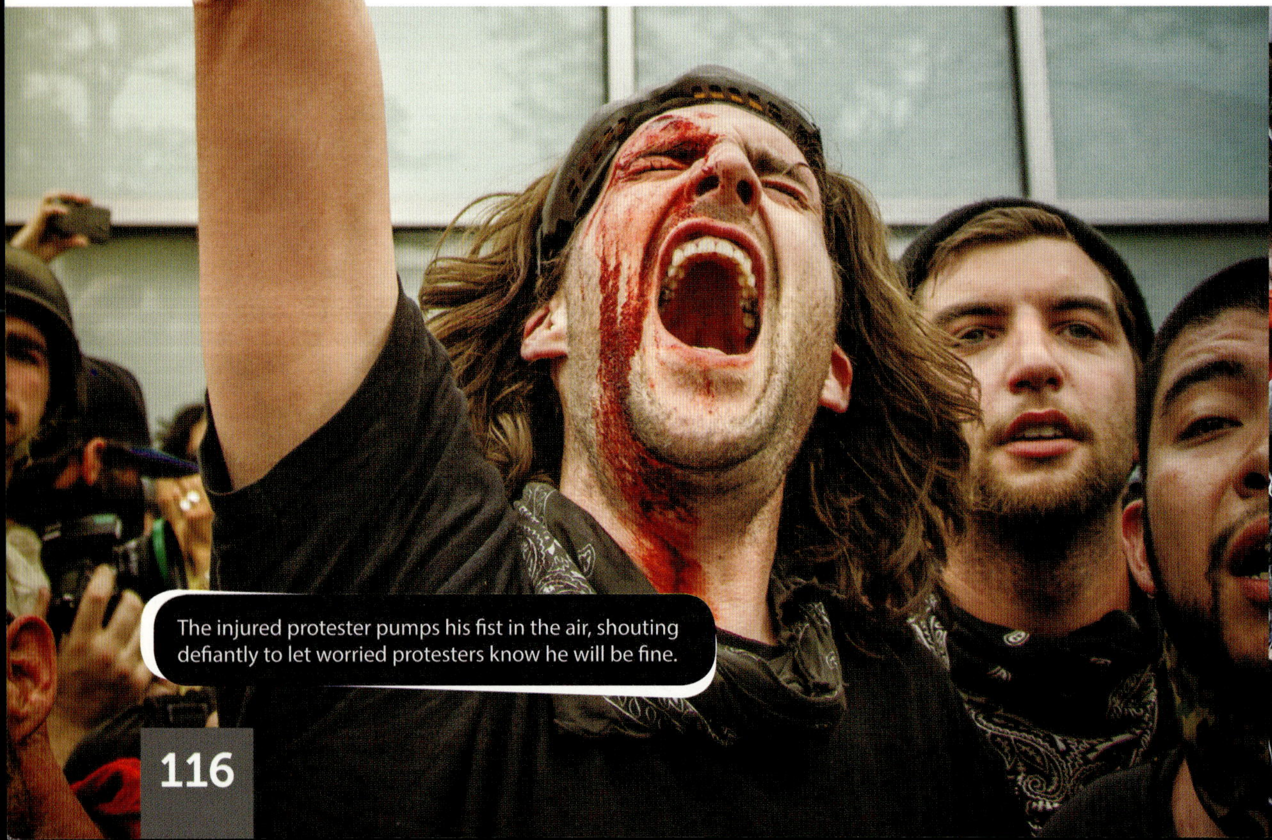

The injured protester pumps his fist in the air, shouting defiantly to let worried protesters know he will be fine.

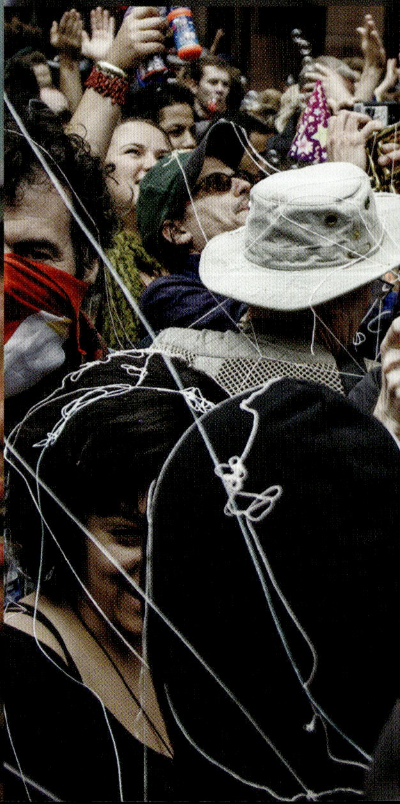

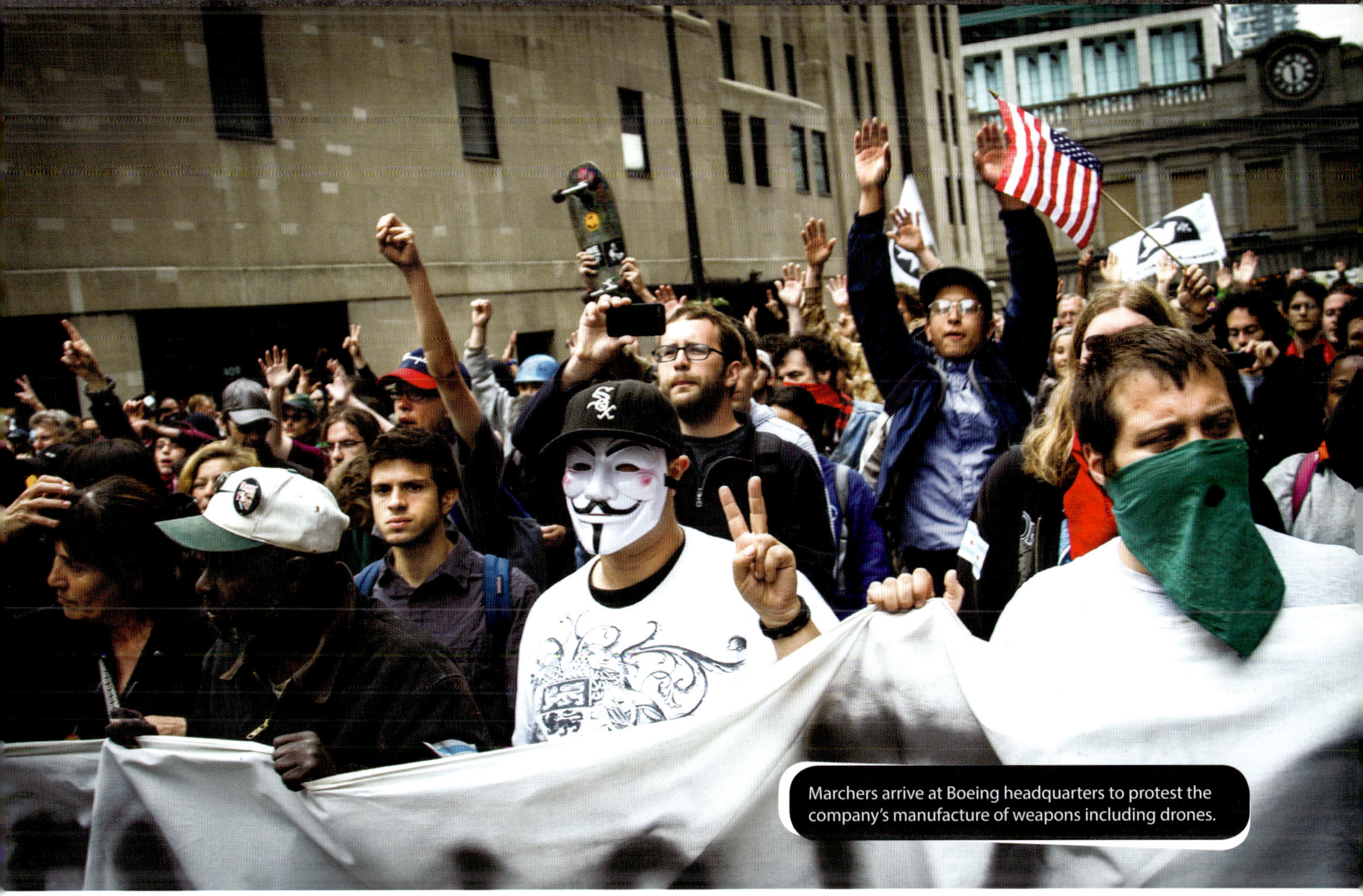

Marchers arrive at Boeing headquarters to protest the company's manufacture of weapons including drones.

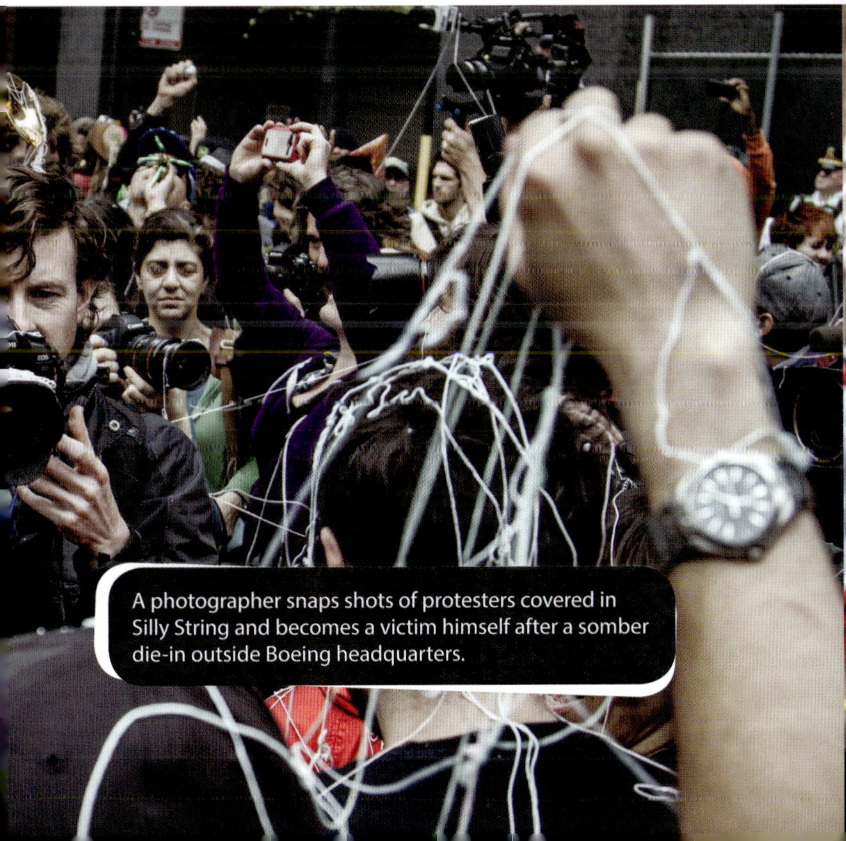

A photographer snaps shots of protesters covered in Silly String and becomes a victim himself after a somber die-in outside Boeing headquarters.

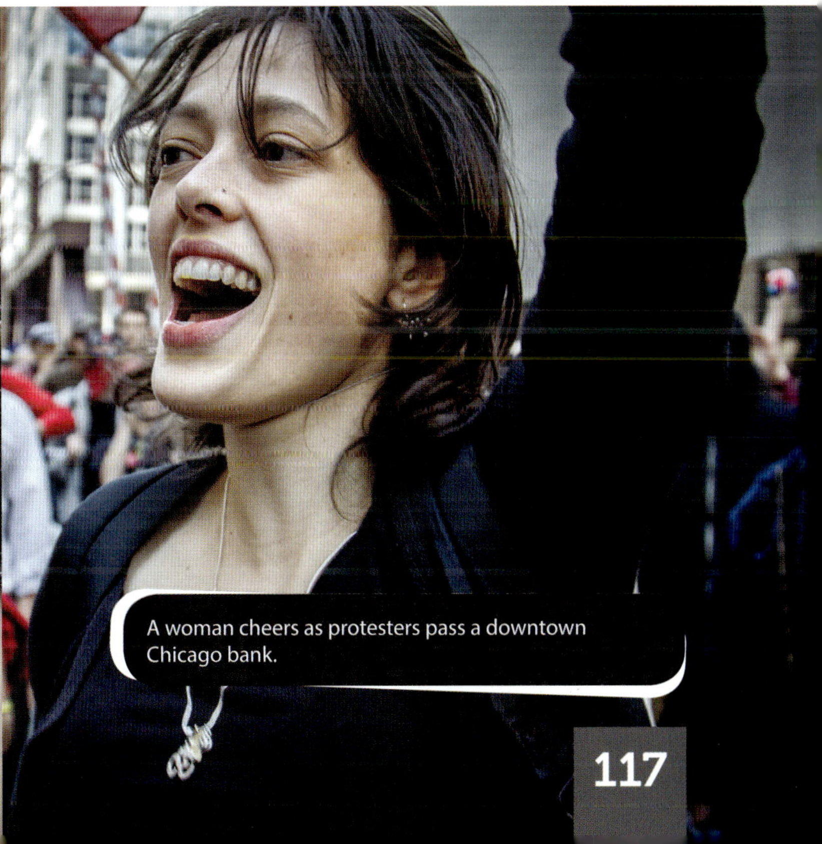

A woman cheers as protesters pass a downtown Chicago bank.

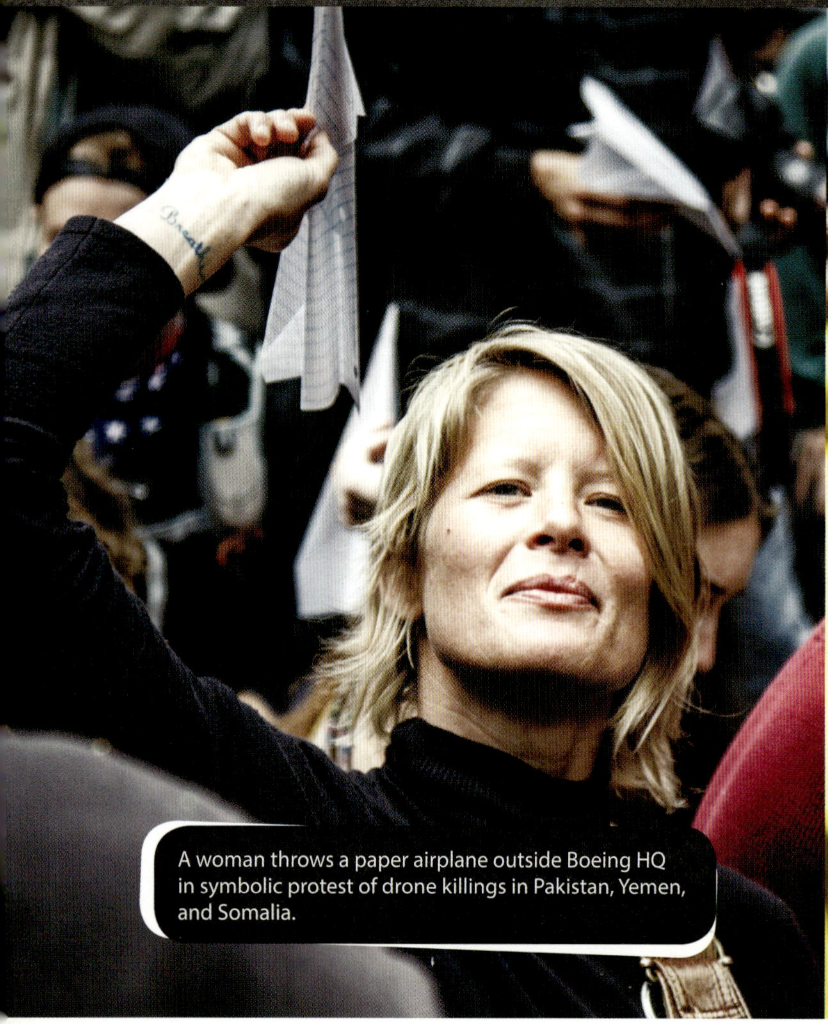

A woman throws a paper airplane outside Boeing HQ in symbolic protest of drone killings in Pakistan, Yemen, and Somalia.

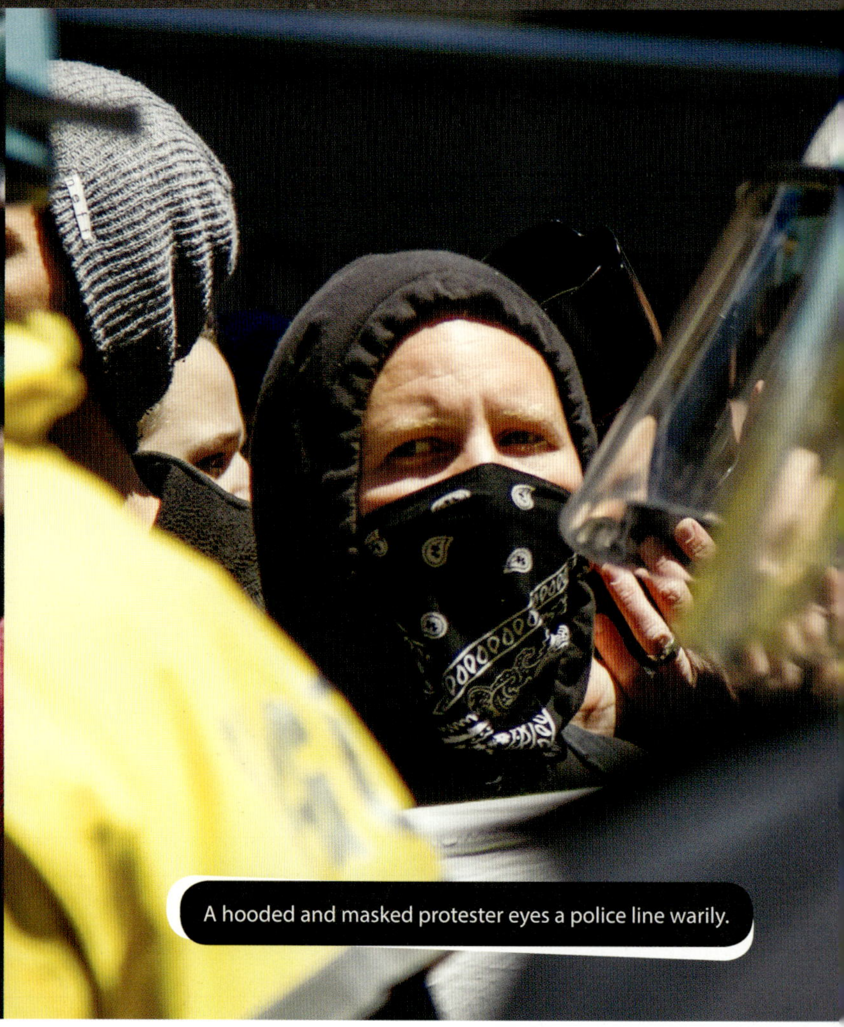

A hooded and masked protester eyes a police line warily.

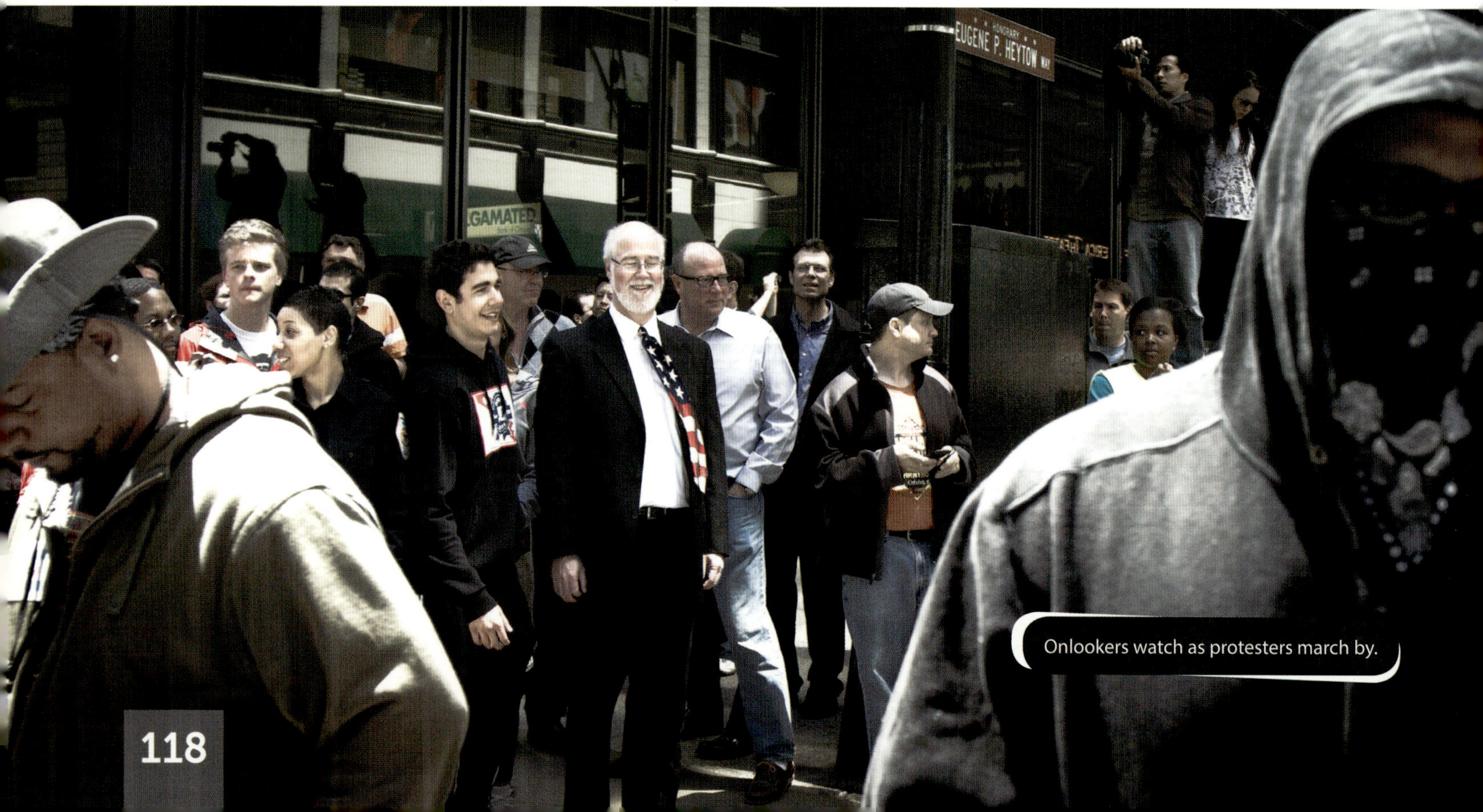

Onlookers watch as protesters march by.

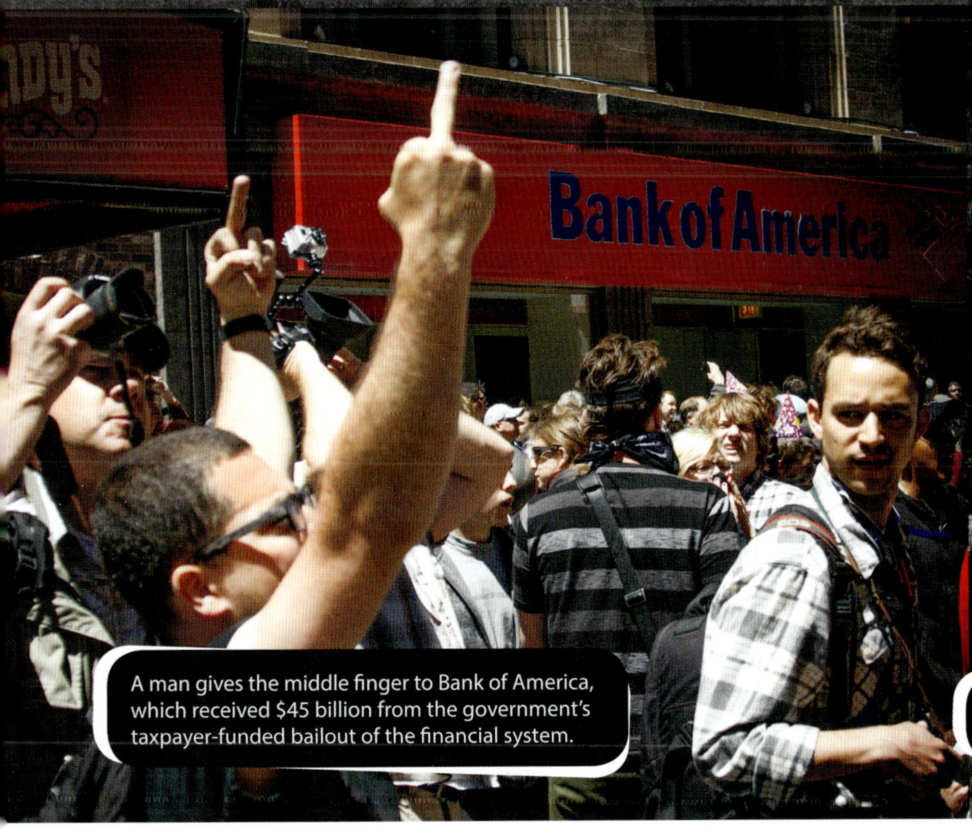

A man gives the middle finger to Bank of America, which received $45 billion from the government's taxpayer-funded bailout of the financial system.

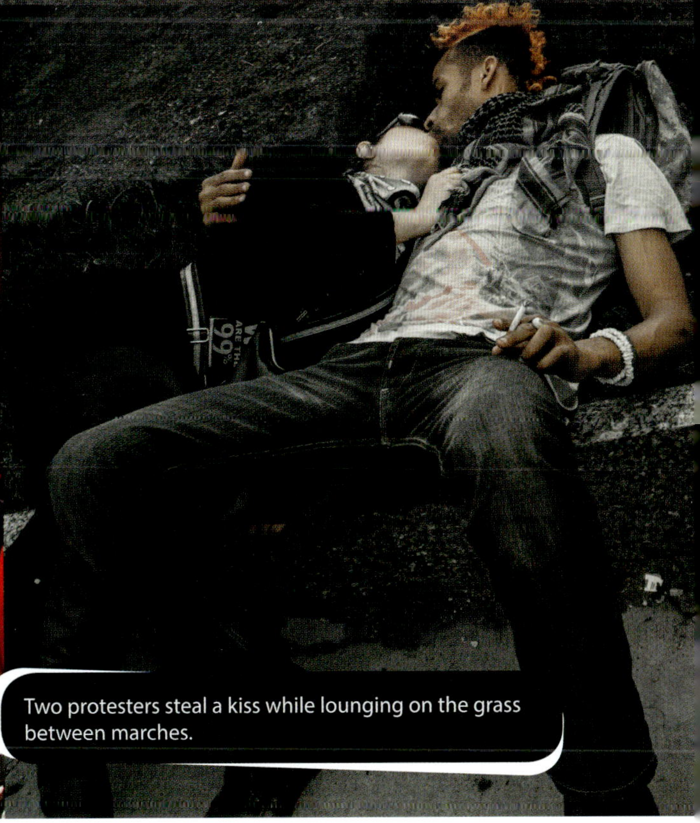

Two protesters steal a kiss while lounging on the grass between marches.

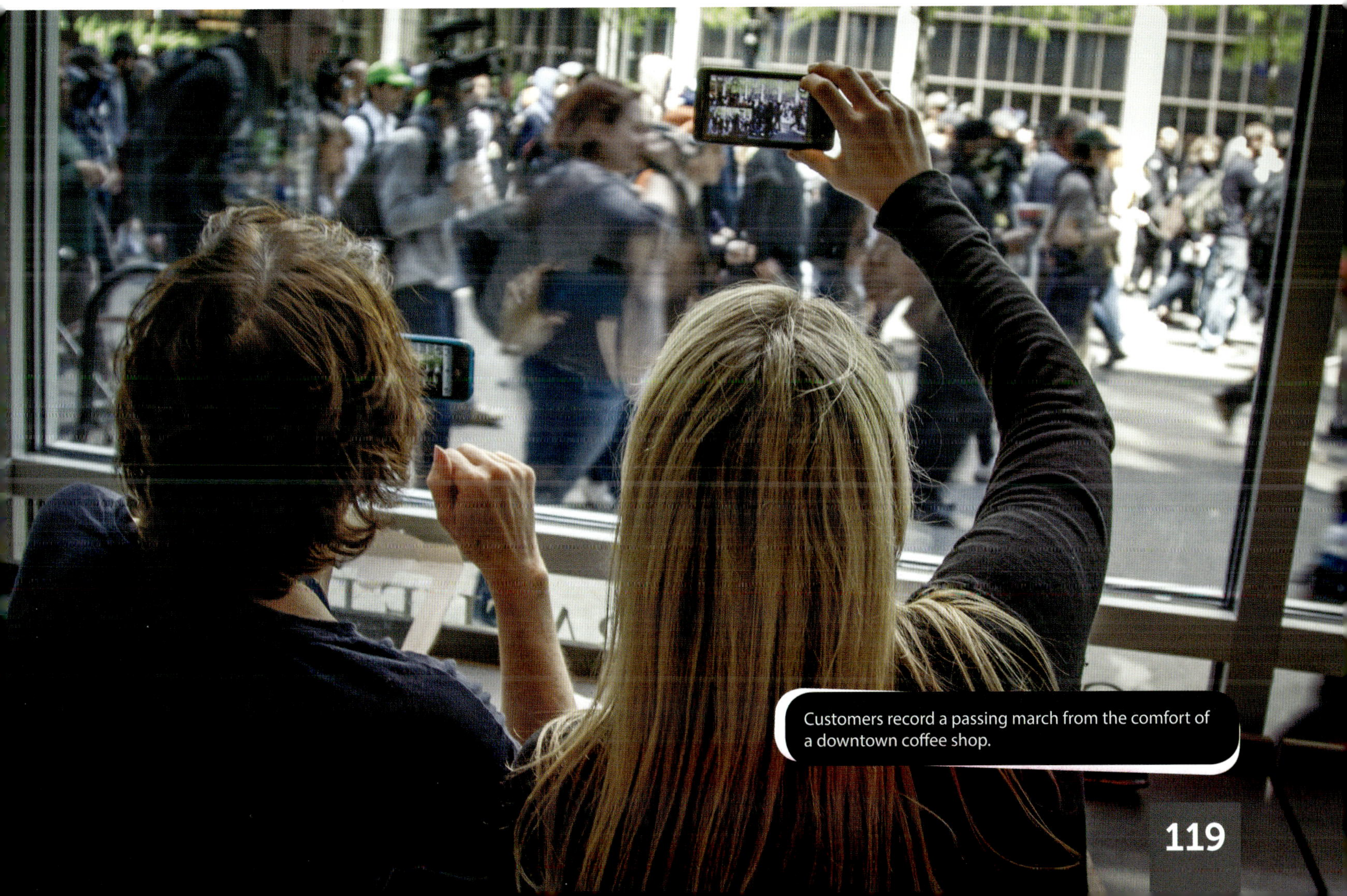

Customers record a passing march from the comfort of a downtown coffee shop.

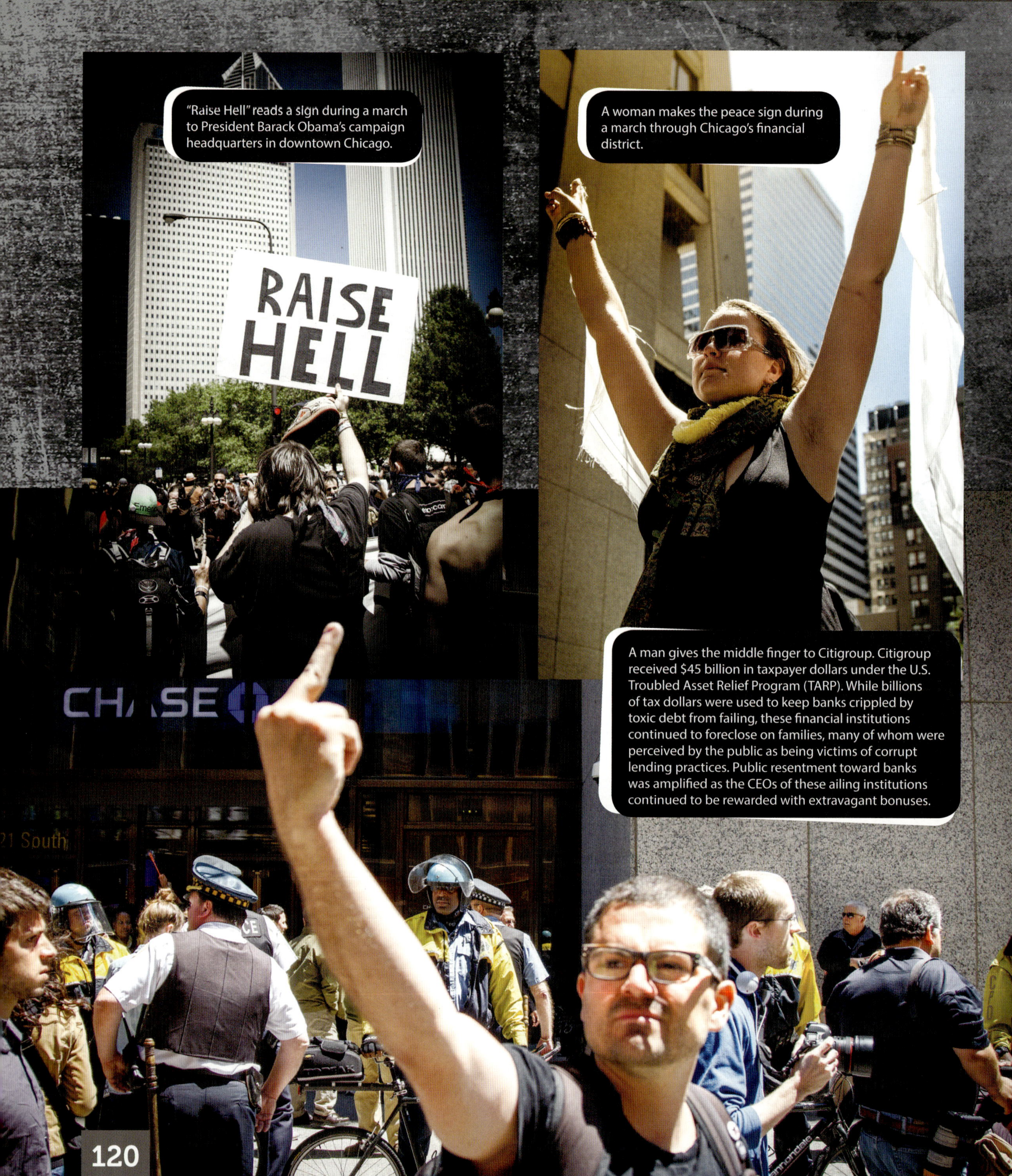

"Raise Hell" reads a sign during a march to President Barack Obama's campaign headquarters in downtown Chicago.

A woman makes the peace sign during a march through Chicago's financial district.

A man gives the middle finger to Citigroup. Citigroup received $45 billion in taxpayer dollars under the U.S. Troubled Asset Relief Program (TARP). While billions of tax dollars were used to keep banks crippled by toxic debt from failing, these financial institutions continued to foreclose on families, many of whom were perceived by the public as being victims of corrupt lending practices. Public resentment toward banks was amplified as the CEOs of these ailing institutions continued to be rewarded with extravagant bonuses.

A family watches a passing "No NATO" march from behind a line of riot police.

Office workers photograph the protest that is taking place outside.

Iraq and Afghanistan war veterans rally with thousands of protesters a few blocks away from the NATO summit to return their war medals and denounce the organization's war policies. Photo: Kevin Young.

A Chicago police officer performs surveillance on peaceful protesters outside President Obama's campaign headquarters.

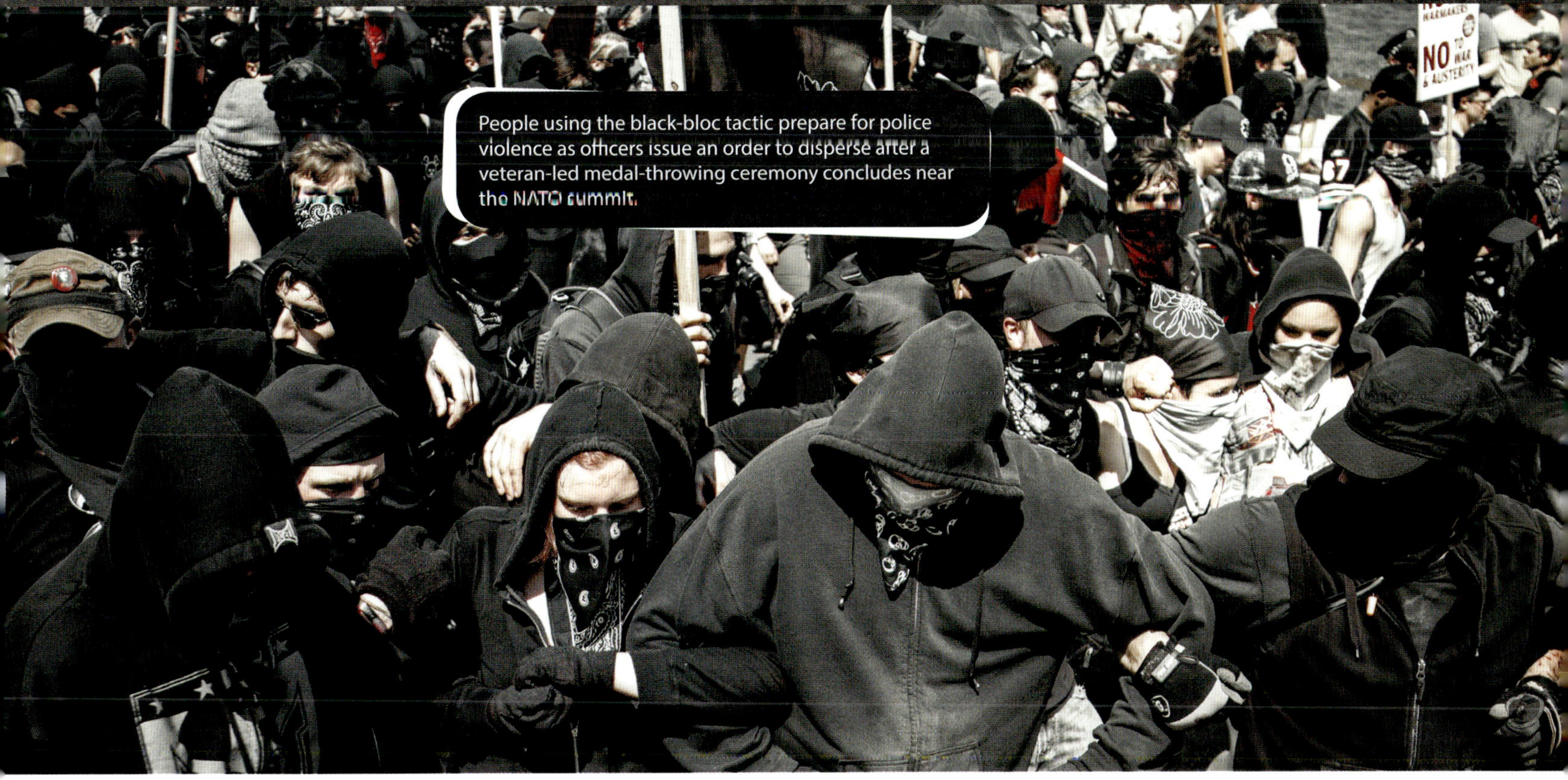

People using the black-bloc tactic prepare for police violence as officers issue an order to disperse after a veteran-led medal-throwing ceremony concludes near the NATO summit.

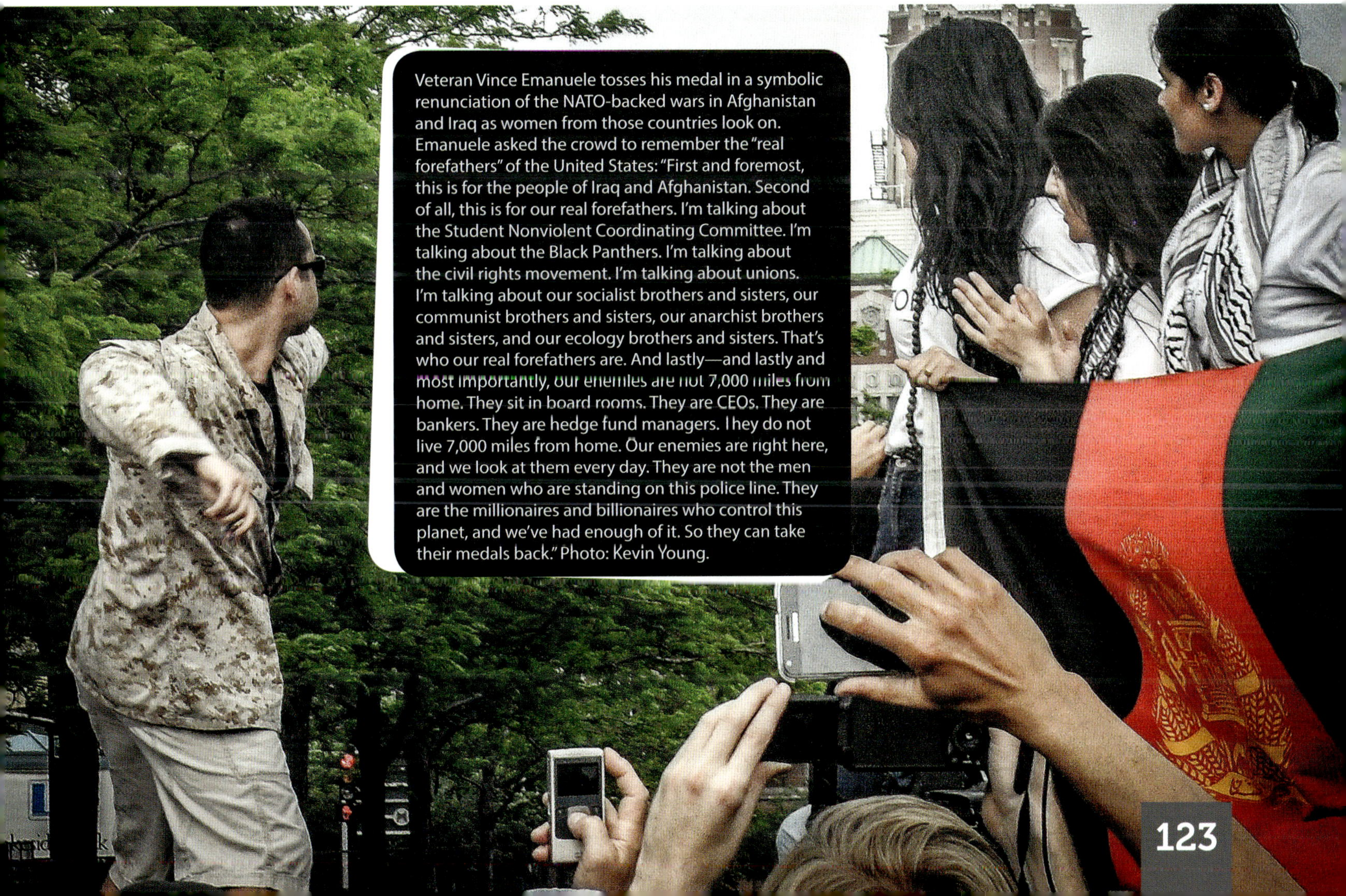

Veteran Vince Emanuele tosses his medal in a symbolic renunciation of the NATO-backed wars in Afghanistan and Iraq as women from those countries look on. Emanuele asked the crowd to remember the "real forefathers" of the United States: "First and foremost, this is for the people of Iraq and Afghanistan. Second of all, this is for our real forefathers. I'm talking about the Student Nonviolent Coordinating Committee. I'm talking about the Black Panthers. I'm talking about the civil rights movement. I'm talking about unions. I'm talking about our socialist brothers and sisters, our communist brothers and sisters, our anarchist brothers and sisters, and our ecology brothers and sisters. That's who our real forefathers are. And lastly—and lastly and most importantly, our enemies are not 7,000 miles from home. They sit in board rooms. They are CEOs. They are bankers. They are hedge fund managers. They do not live 7,000 miles from home. Our enemies are right here, and we look at them every day. They are not the men and women who are standing on this police line. They are the millionaires and billionaires who control this planet, and we've had enough of it. So they can take their medals back." Photo: Kevin Young.

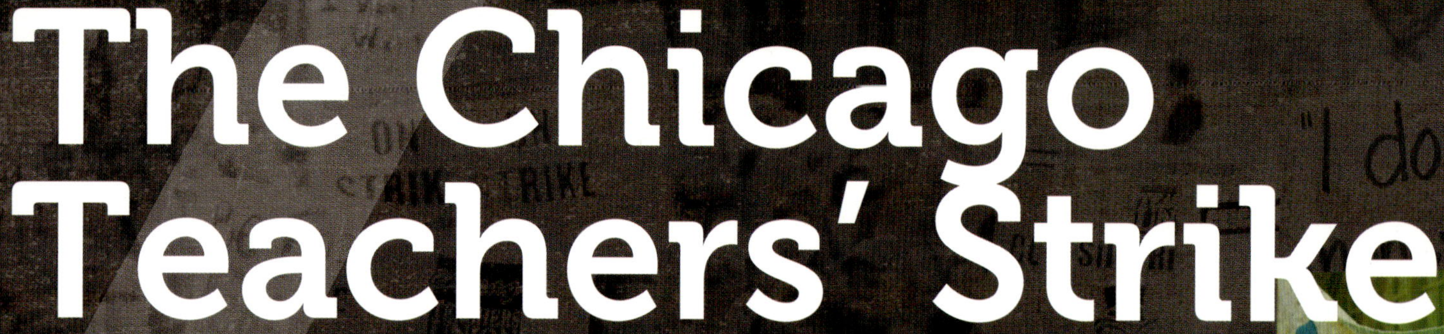

The Chicago Teachers' Strike

In the late hours of September 9, 2012, it was clear that negotiations between the Chicago Public School Board and the Chicago Teachers Union (CTU) were going nowhere. Concerned with contract issues, job security, new teacher evaluations tied to student performance, a longer school day, and a lack of support staff like counselors and psychologists, as well as infrastructure issues such as the lack of air conditioning in most of the aging school buildings, CTU President Karen Lewis said at a late-night press conference, "In the morning, no CTU members will be inside our schools."

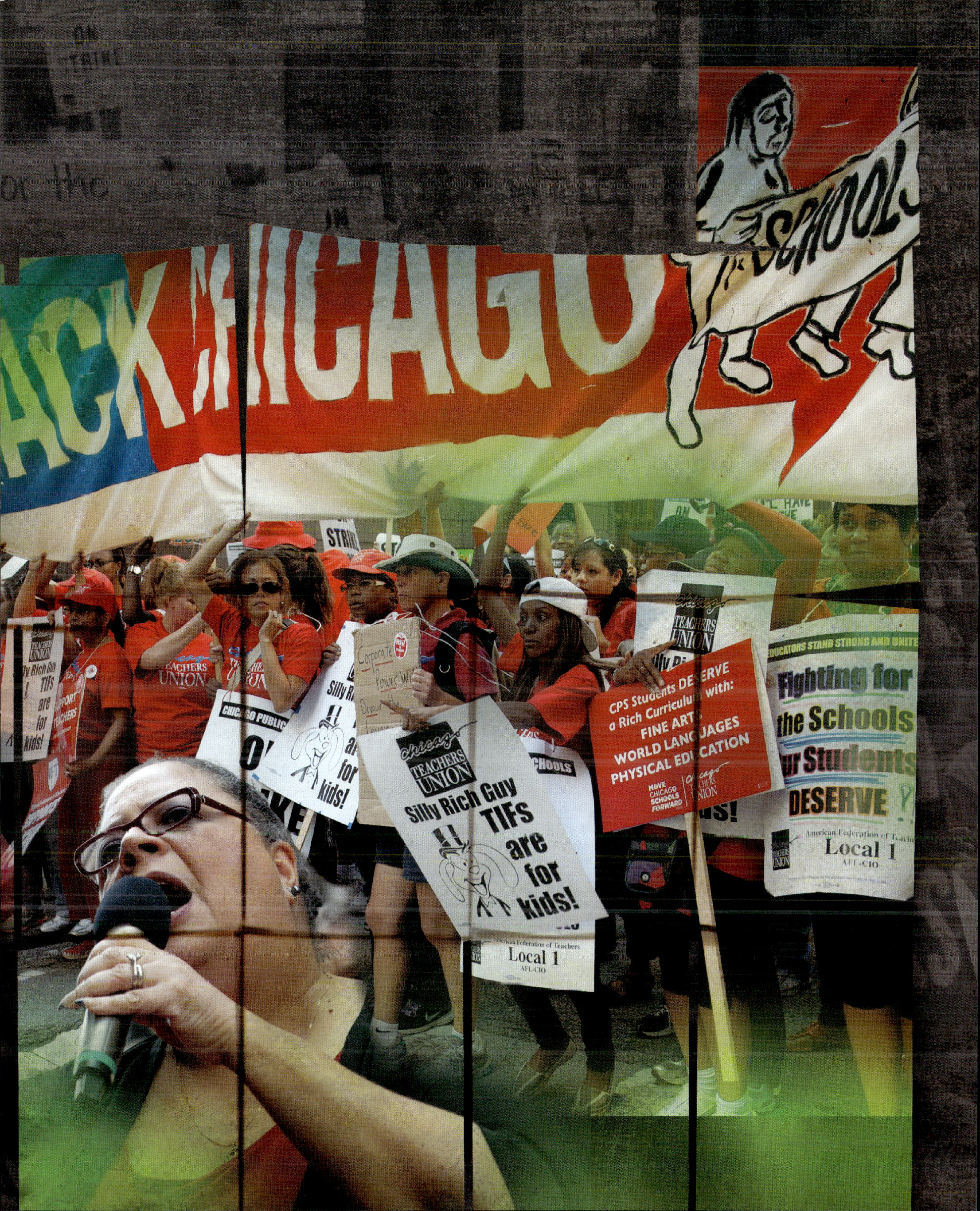
CHICAGO
SCHOOLS
Chicago Teachers Union
Silly Rich Guy
TIFs are for kids!
American Federation of Teachers
Local 1
AFL-CIO
CPS Students DESERVE a Rich Curriculum with:
FINE ARTS
WORLD LANGUAGES
PHYSICAL EDUCATION
MOVE CHICAGO SCHOOLS FORWARD
EDUCATORS STAND STRONG AND UNITE
Fighting for the Schools
DESERVE
American Federation of Teachers
Local 1
AFL-CIO

As the teachers walked the picket lines and the downtown streets on September 10, 2012, they had strong support among parents, students, and the community alike, many of whom turned out in large numbers to march and rally with thousands of CTU members each day throughout the week. Chicago, traditionally a strong Democratic and union town, found its Democratic mayor facing off against Karen Lewis—president of one of the largest teachers' unions in the country—on education reform. The city, under the leadership of mayor Rahm Emanuel, President Obama's former chief of staff, was also intent on closing dozens of failing schools in the years to come, planning to replace them with nonunionized public charter schools—reform that President Obama and his education secretary, Arne Duncan, former head of Chicago schools, had helped set up.

After the 350,000 students in the nation's third-largest school district had been out of their classrooms for more than a week, the city and the teachers' union managed to reach a tentative contract agreement on September 18, with the CTU voting to suspend the strike. The teachers' union characterized the strike as a victory based on a number of concessions, which included an increase in pay over what Chicago Public Schools was offering, the preservation of class size limit, a decreased focus on standardized testing, increased job creation for teachers, and no increases to the teachers' health care premiums. This proved a victory for the CTU as well as other unionists across the country. The strike was watched closely by teachers nationwide, giving them hope and the confidence to stand their ground and fight for the future of public education.

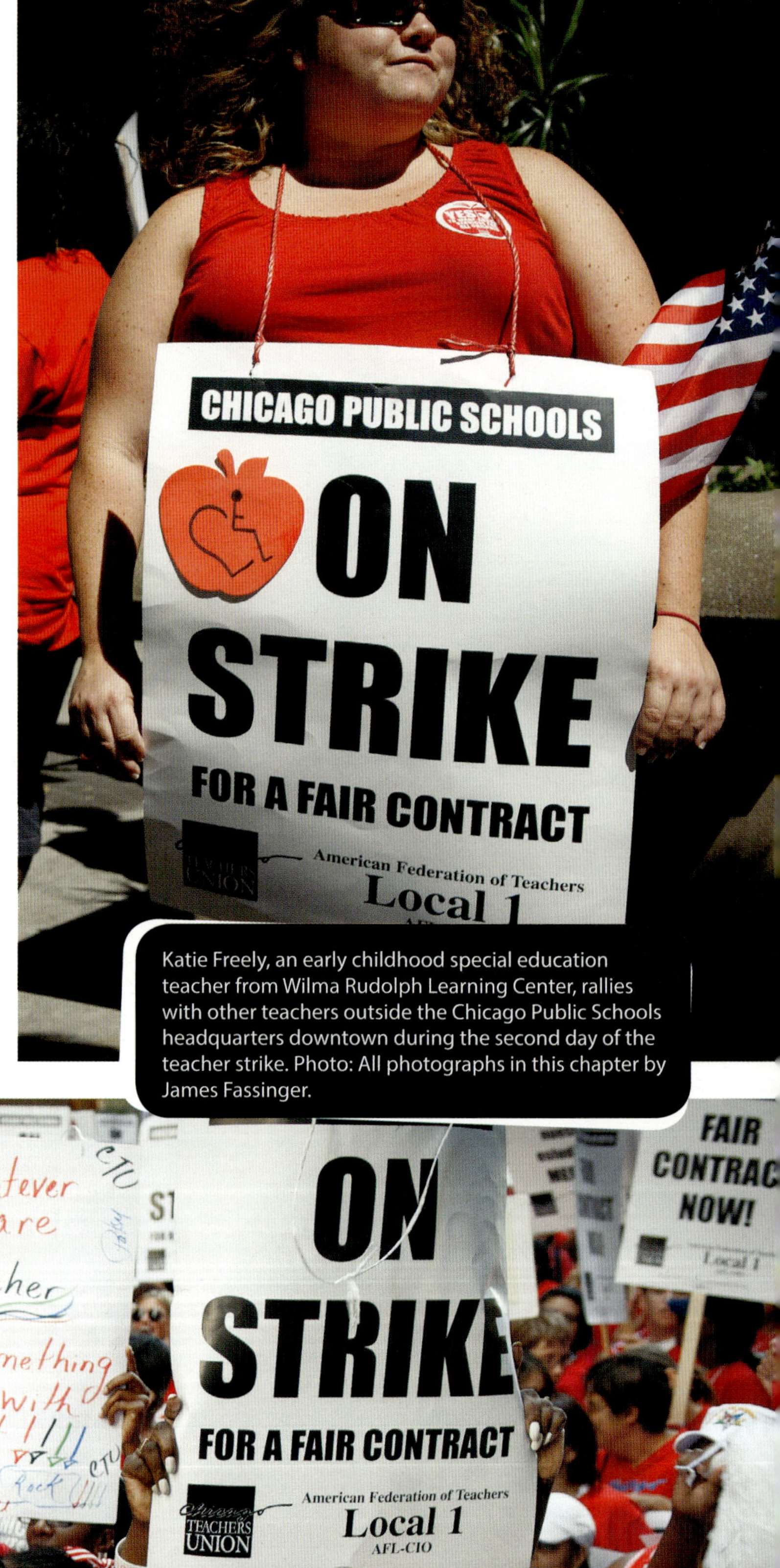

Katie Freely, an early childhood special education teacher from Wilma Rudolph Learning Center, rallies with other teachers outside the Chicago Public Schools headquarters downtown during the second day of the teacher strike. Photo: All photographs in this chapter by James Fassinger.

Chicago teachers rally in downtown Chicago during the second day of the strike after CTU leadership was unable to reach a contract agreement with the city's school board.

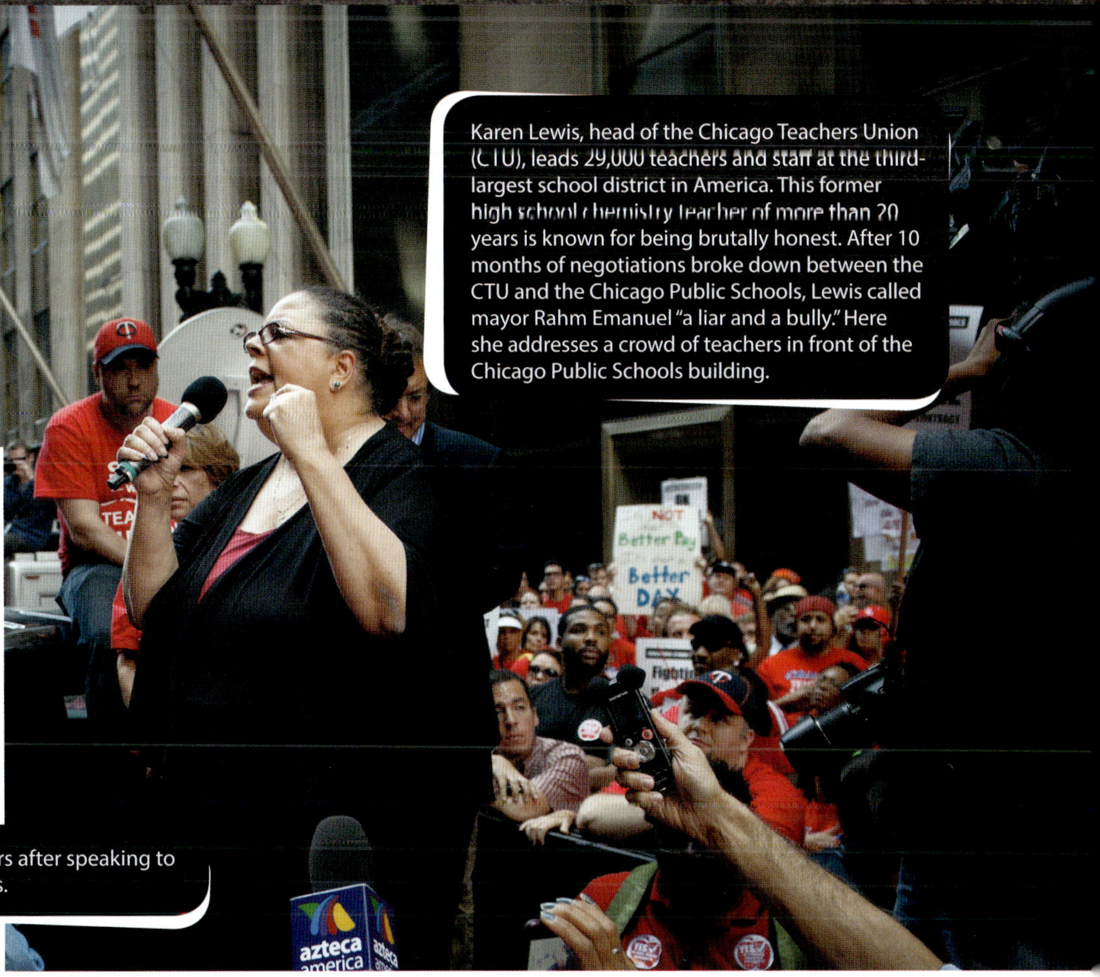

Karen Lewis, head of the Chicago Teachers Union (CTU), leads 29,000 teachers and staff at the third-largest school district in America. This former high school chemistry teacher of more than 20 years is known for being brutally honest. After 10 months of negotiations broke down between the CTU and the Chicago Public Schools, Lewis called mayor Rahm Emanuel "a liar and a bully." Here she addresses a crowd of teachers in front of the Chicago Public Schools building.

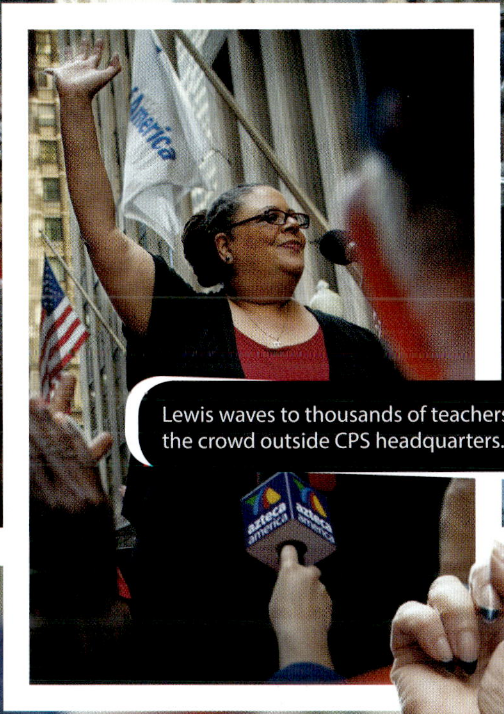

Lewis waves to thousands of teachers after speaking to the crowd outside CPS headquarters.

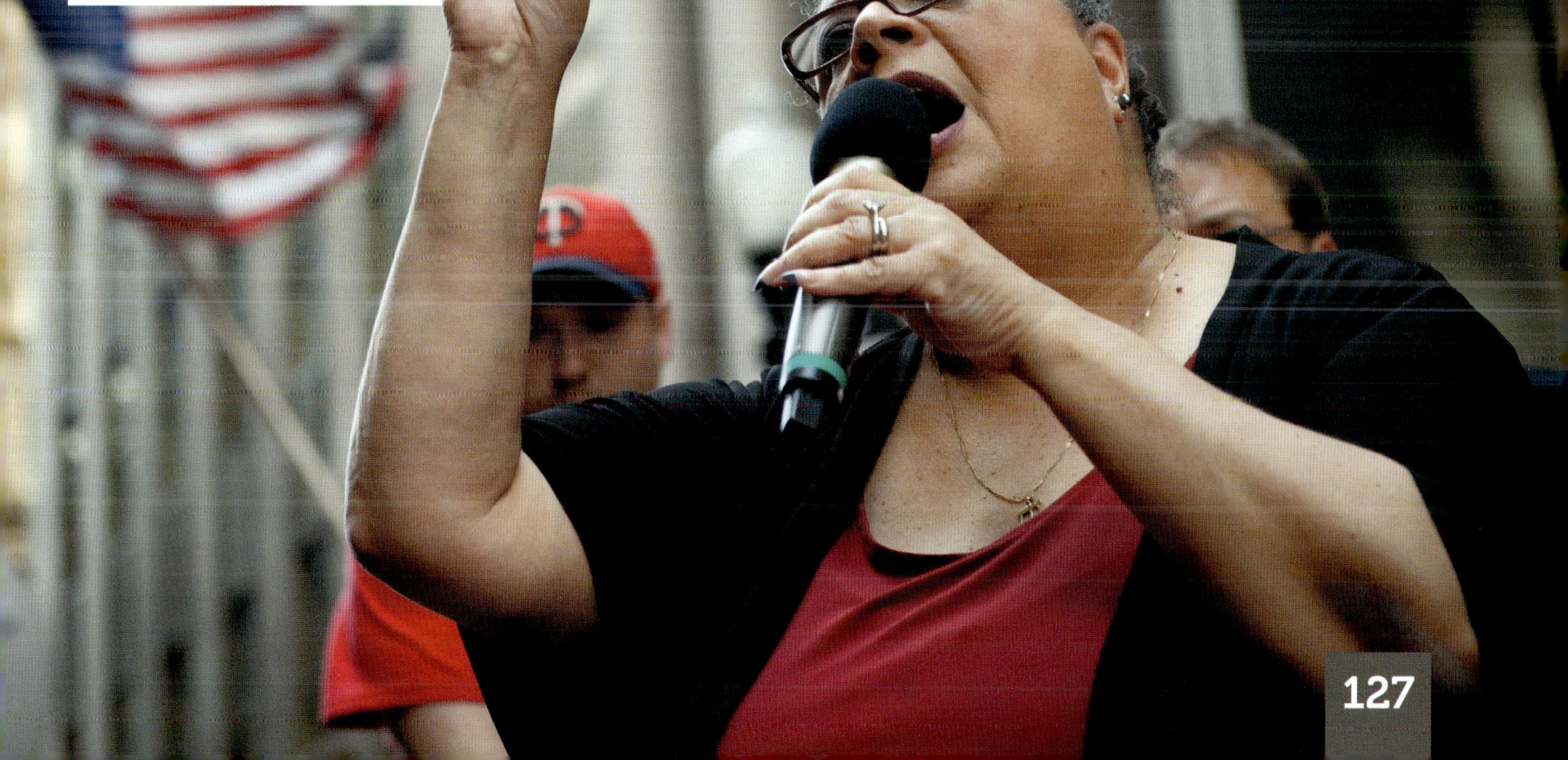

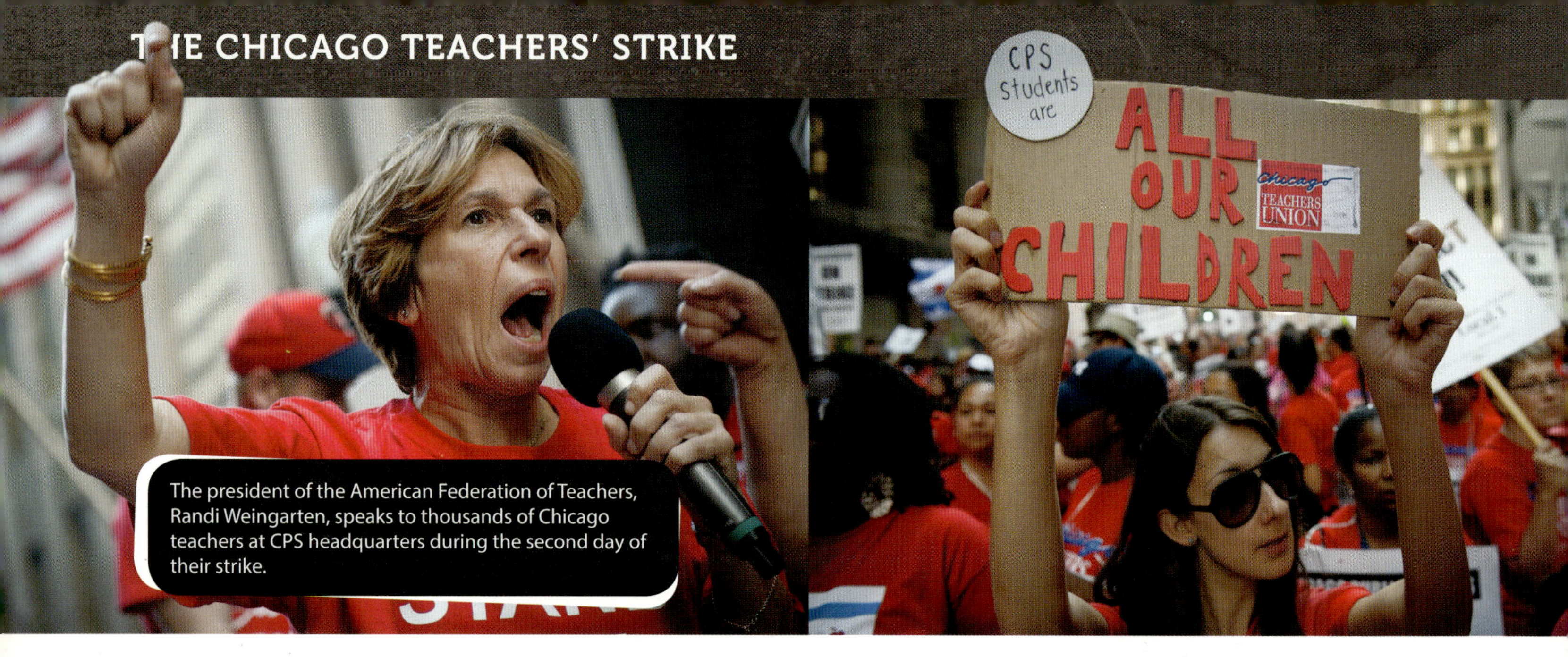

The president of the American Federation of Teachers, Randi Weingarten, speaks to thousands of Chicago teachers at CPS headquarters during the second day of their strike.

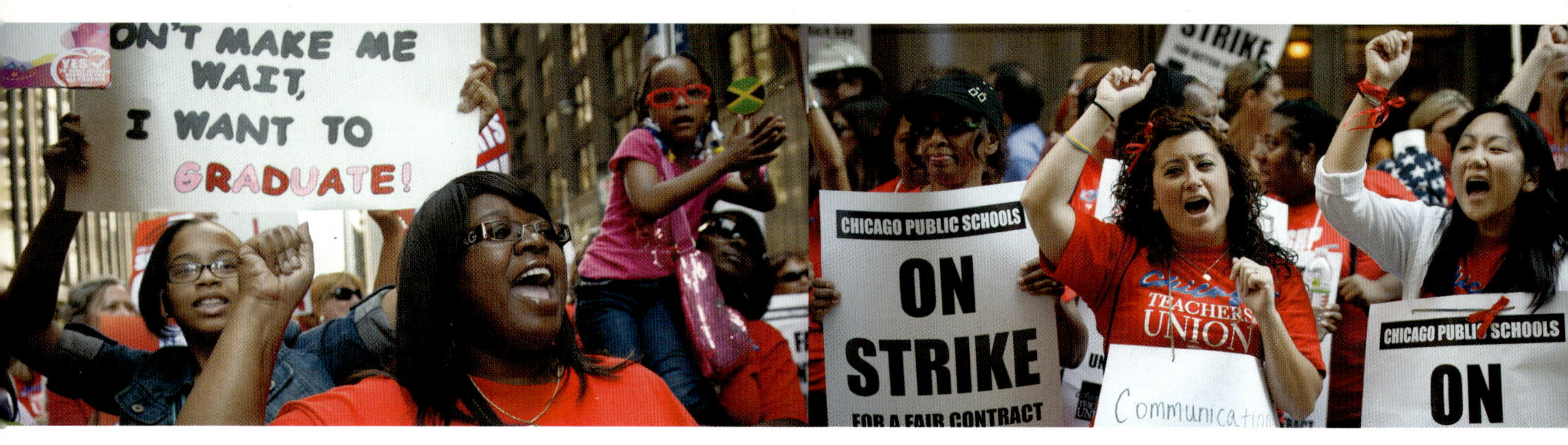

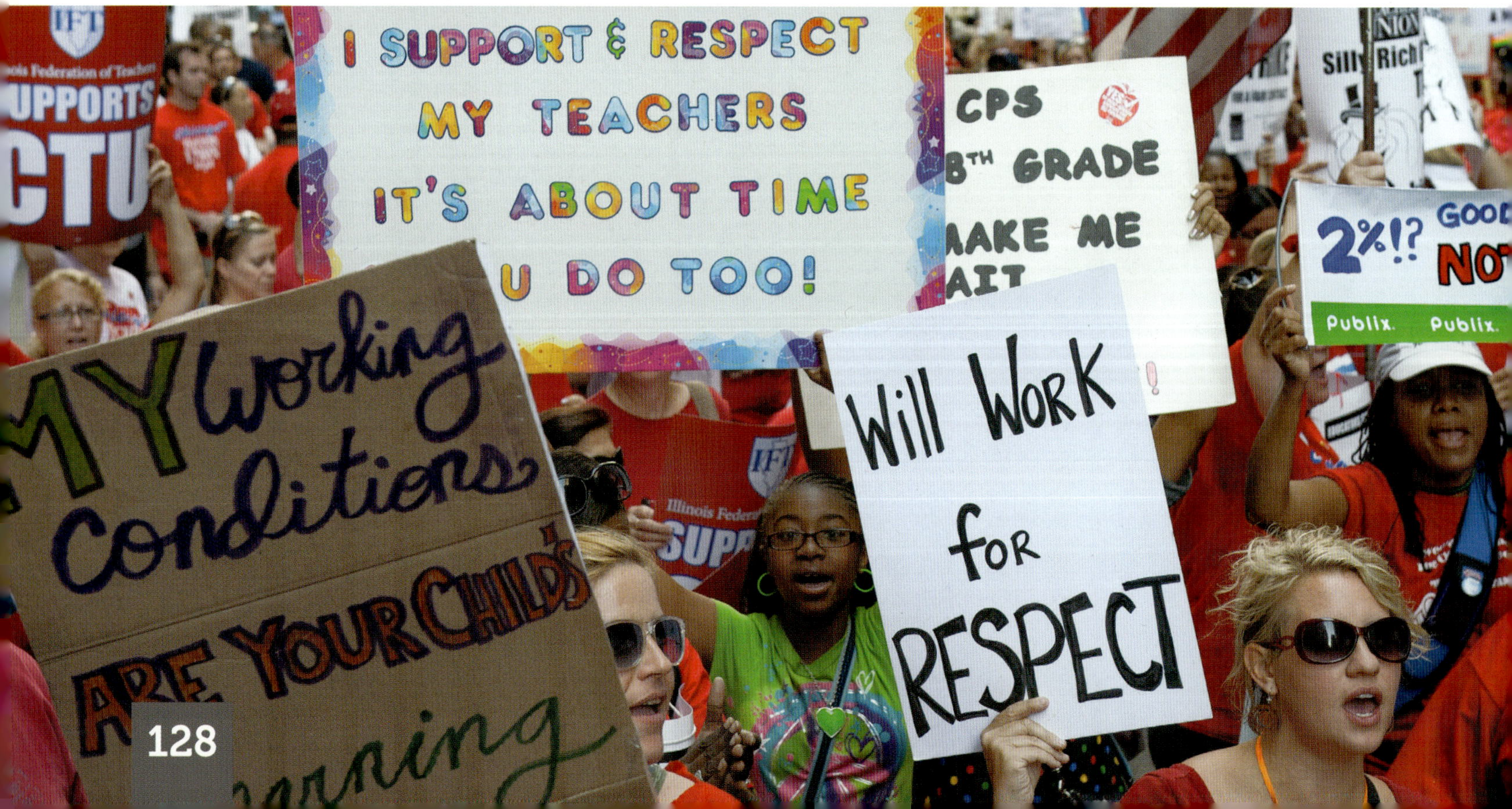

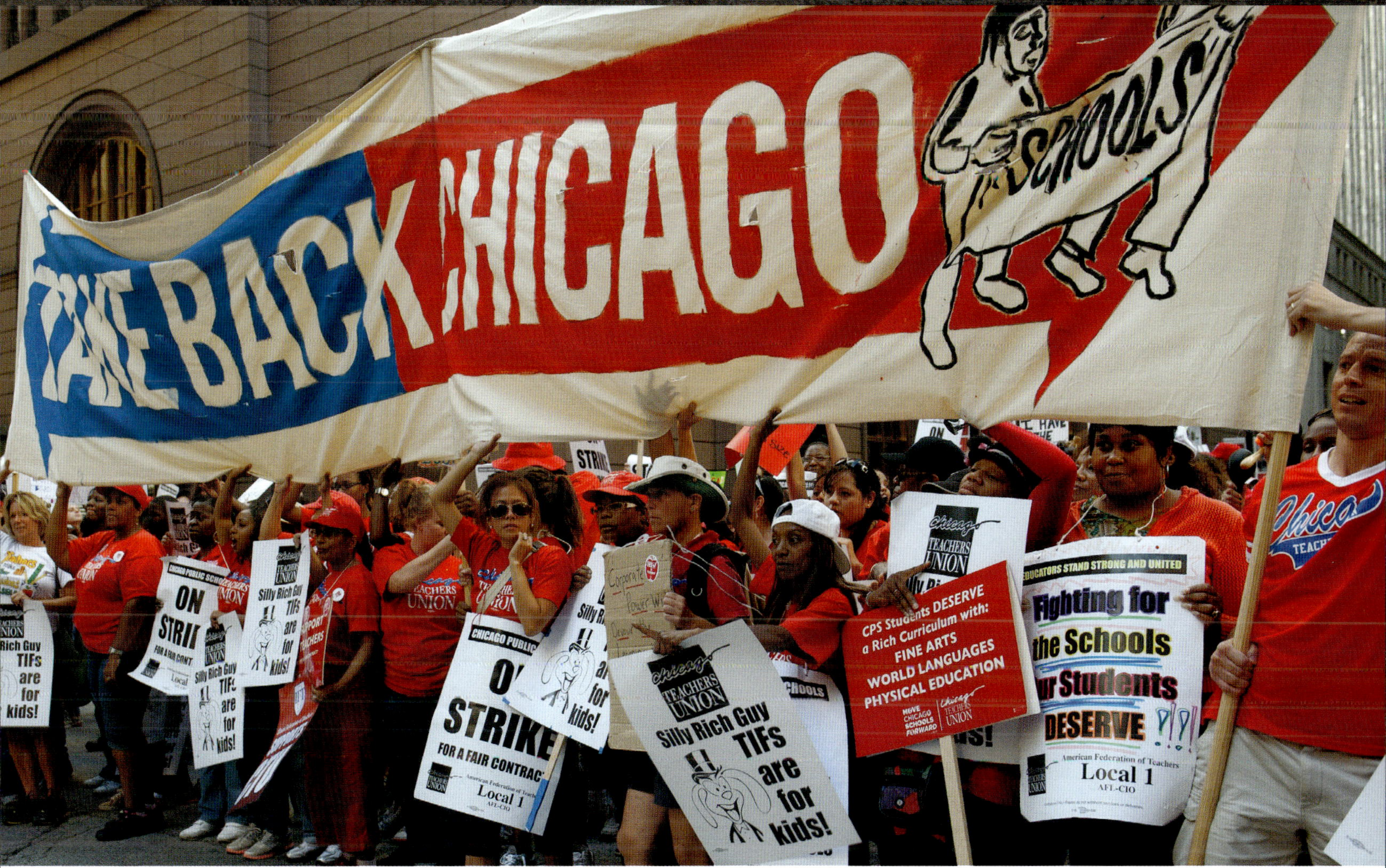

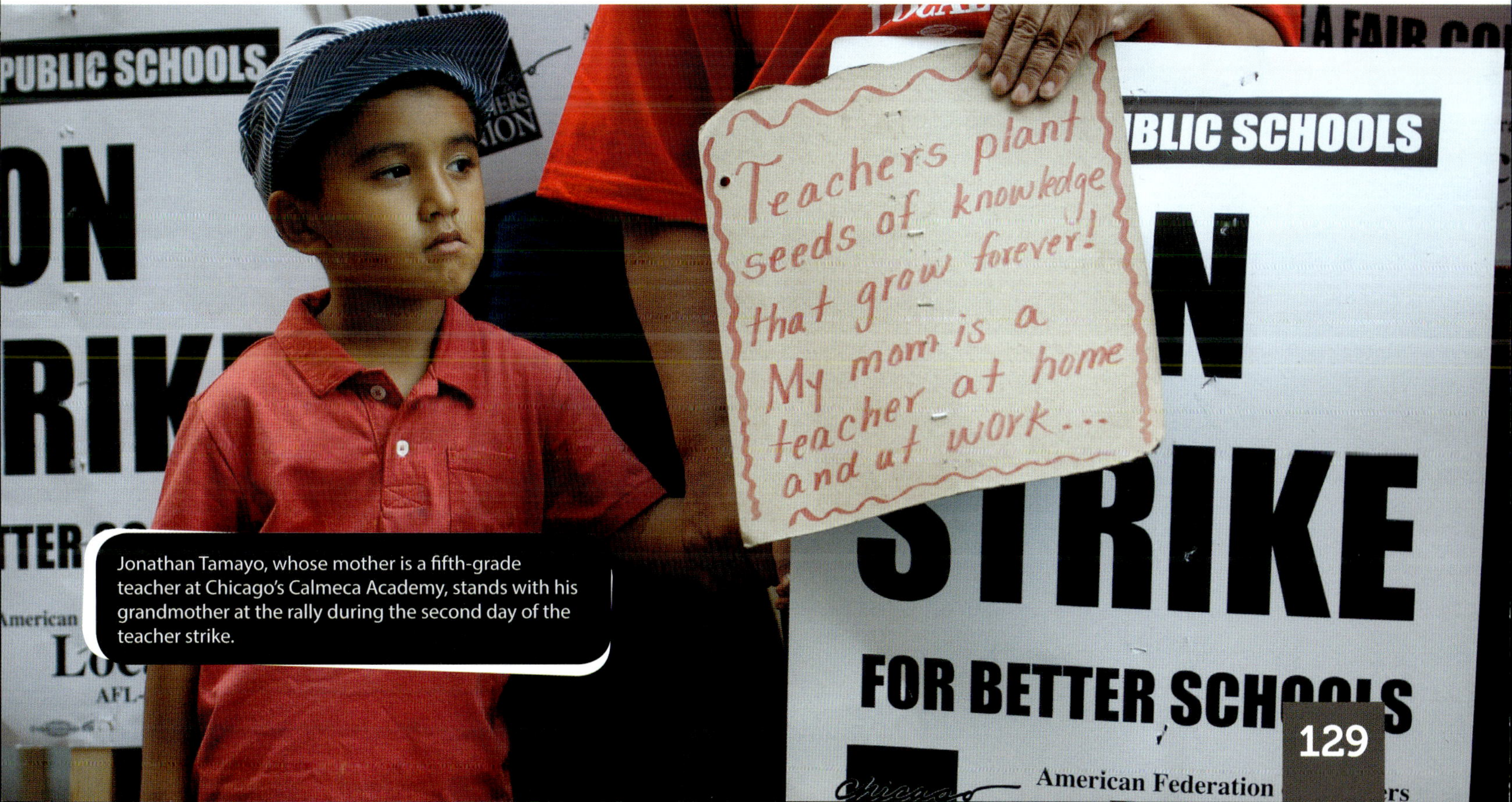

Jonathan Tamayo, whose mother is a fifth-grade teacher at Chicago's Calmeca Academy, stands with his grandmother at the rally during the second day of the teacher strike.

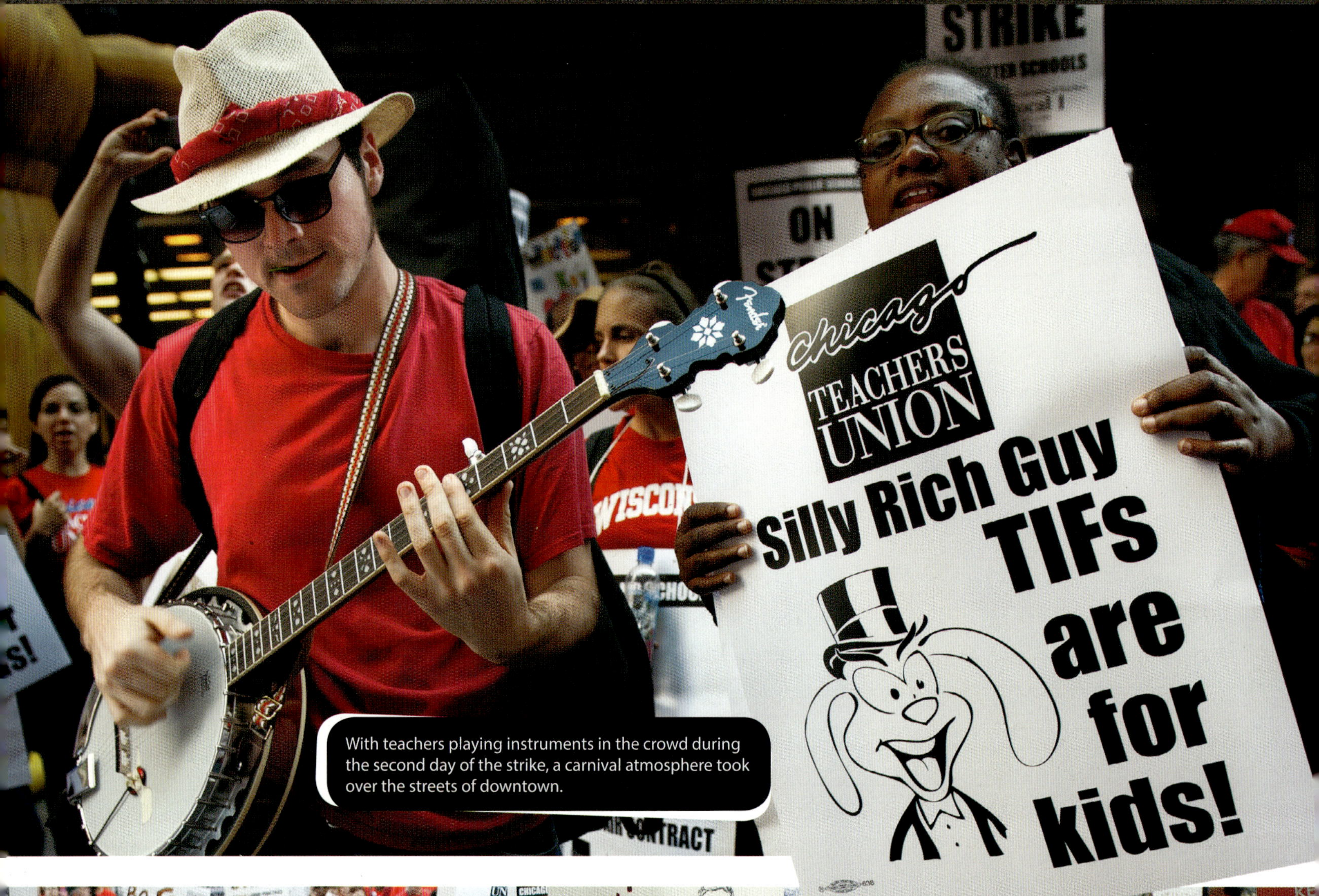

With teachers playing instruments in the crowd during the second day of the strike, a carnival atmosphere took over the streets of downtown.

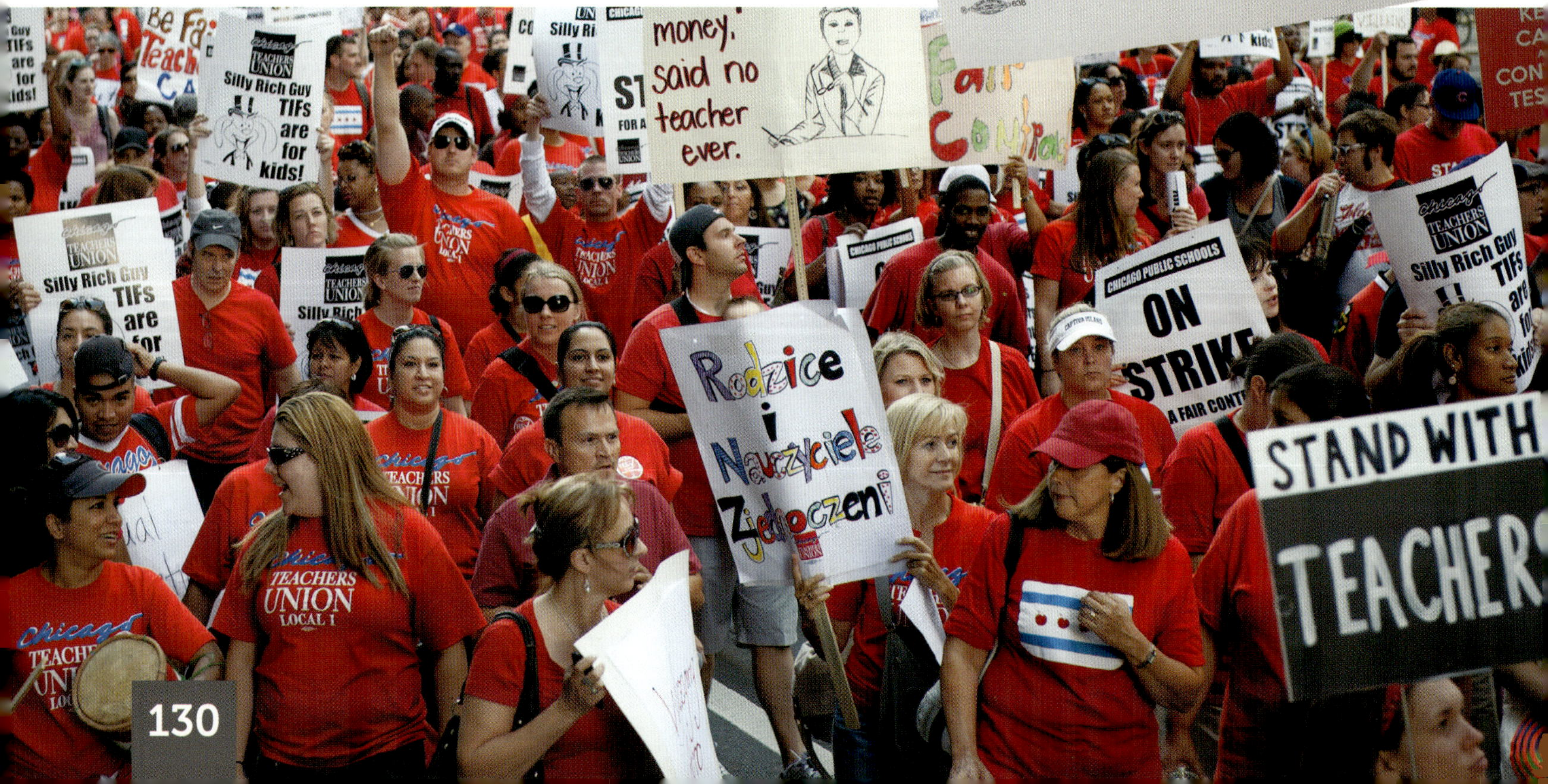

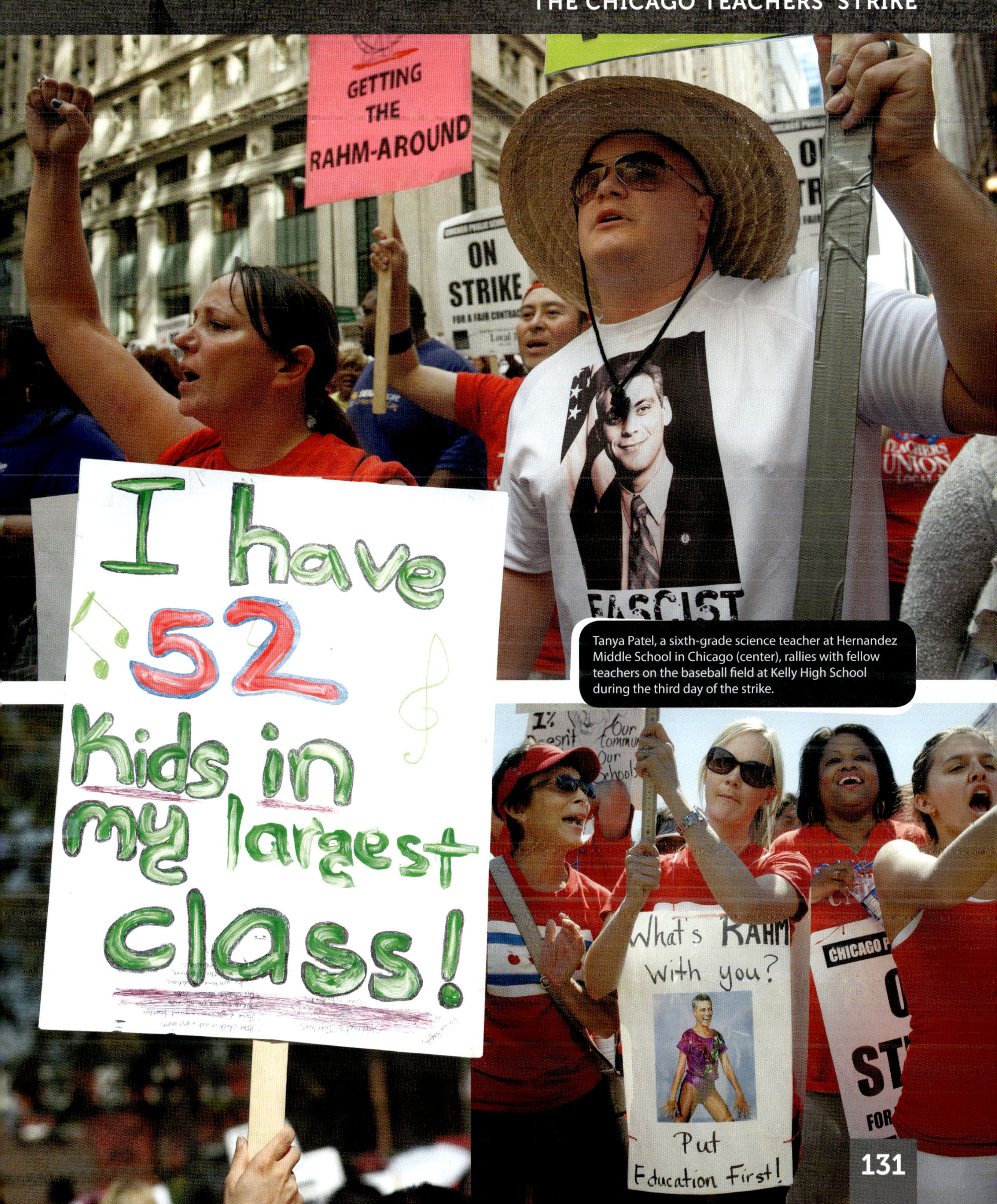

Tanya Patel, a sixth-grade science teacher at Hernandez Middle School in Chicago (center), rallies with fellow teachers on the baseball field at Kelly High School during the third day of the strike.

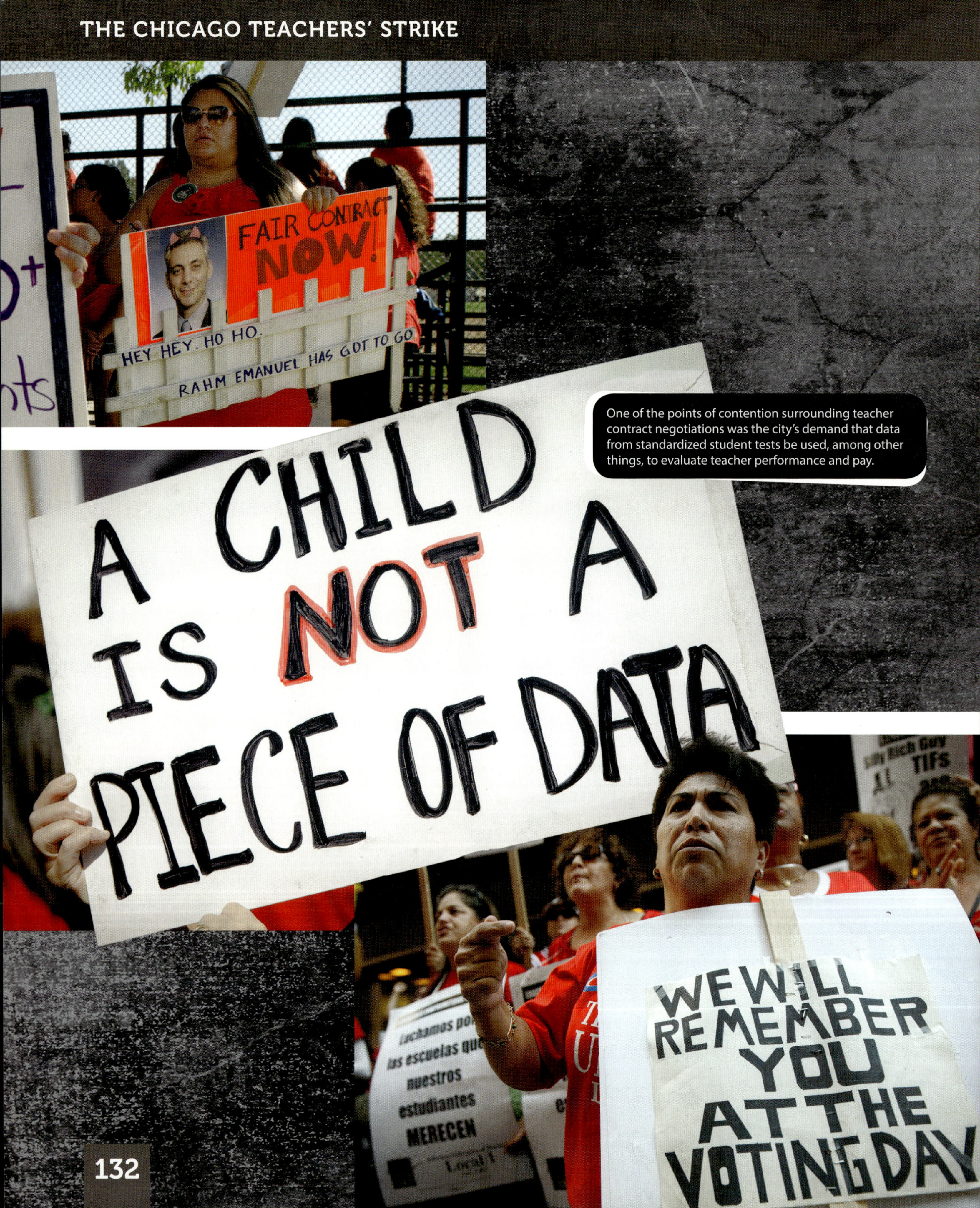

One of the points of contention surrounding teacher contract negotiations was the city's demand that data from standardized student tests be used, among other things, to evaluate teacher performance and pay.

Occupy Century Aluminum

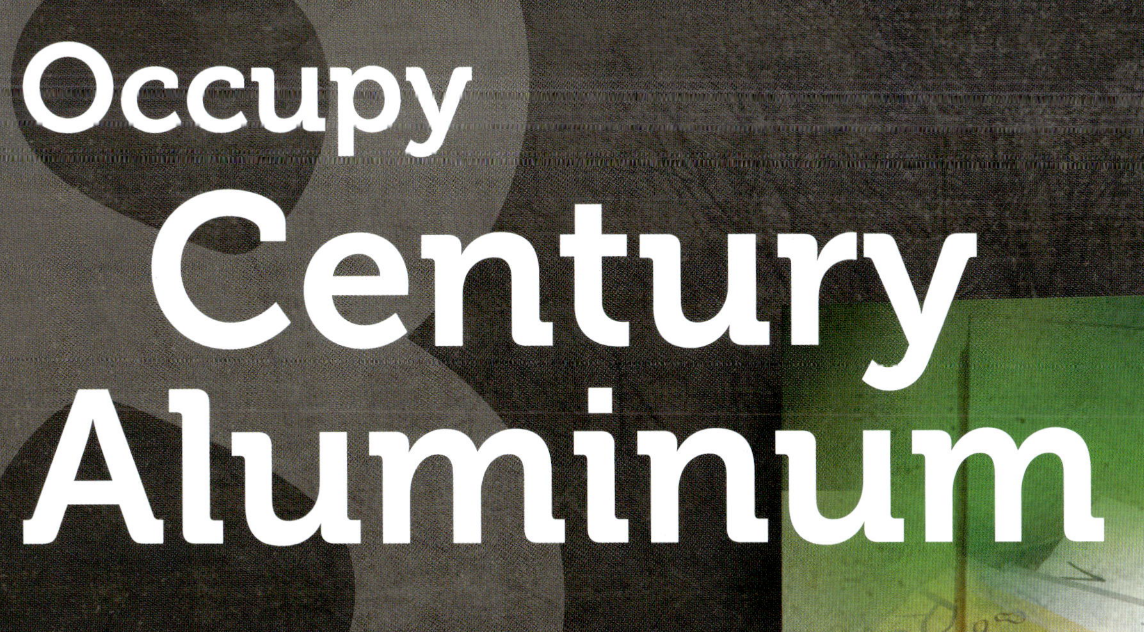

What happens when more than a dozen retirees in their 60s and 70s in Ravenswood, West Virginia, are betrayed by their longtime employer and lose health benefits promised to them for decades of dedicated service to their company?

One of the most inspiring—and ultimately successful—acts of resistance to stem from the Occupy movement.

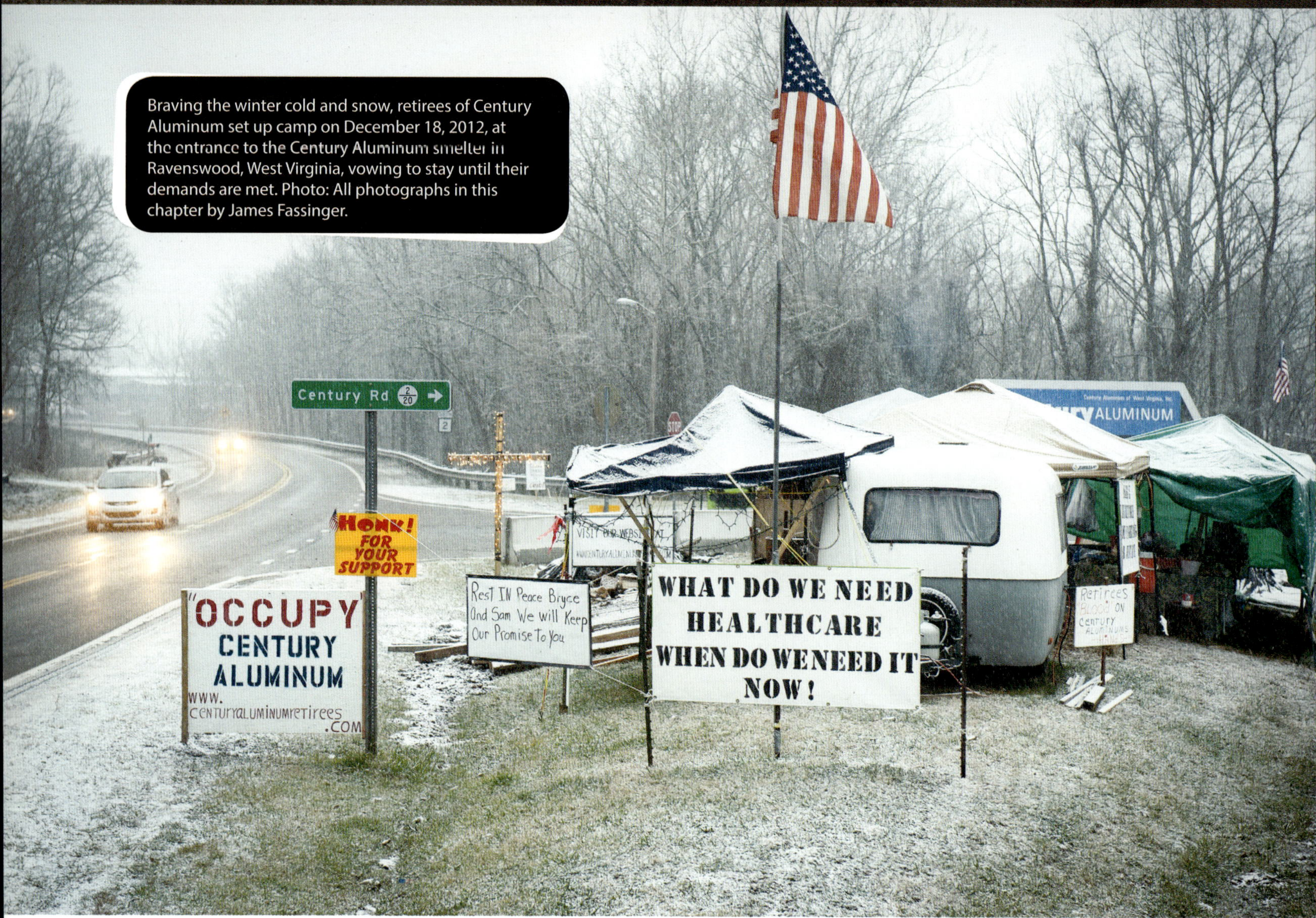

Braving the winter cold and snow, retirees of Century Aluminum set up camp on December 18, 2012, at the entrance to the Century Aluminum smelter in Ravenswood, West Virginia, vowing to stay until their demands are met. Photo: All photographs in this chapter by James Fassinger.

In tents and under cover of tarps, these seniors occupied a median strip in front of the now-shuttered Century Aluminum smelter, braving inclement mountain weather. Suffering from arthritis and hypertension—and even, in one protester's case, recovering from a stroke—they knew their goal was crystal clear and righteous: they wanted the health benefits promised—and then stolen—by Century Aluminum's "one-percenters."

After more than a year of struggling against this corporate Goliath, these retirees won back their health benefits, plus a settlement that included $44 million to be paid out over 10 years.

Said one organizer, "I'm elated that a bunch of little senior citizens can take on corporate giants in West Virginia." And win.

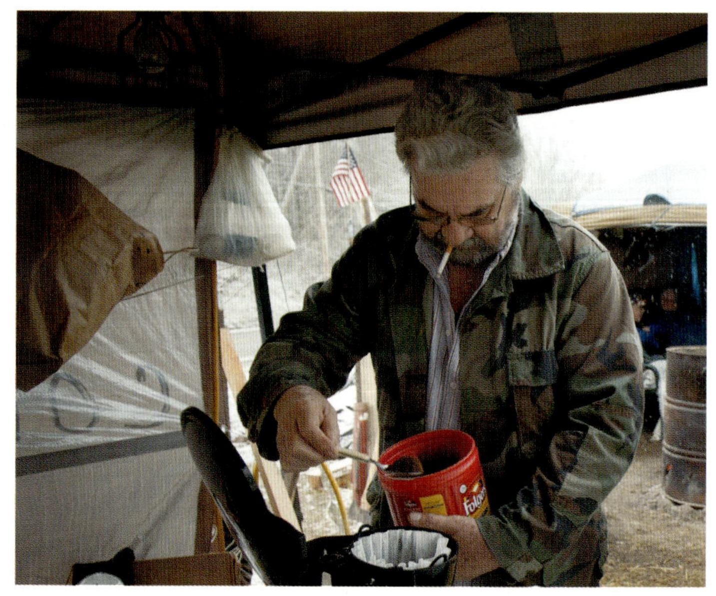

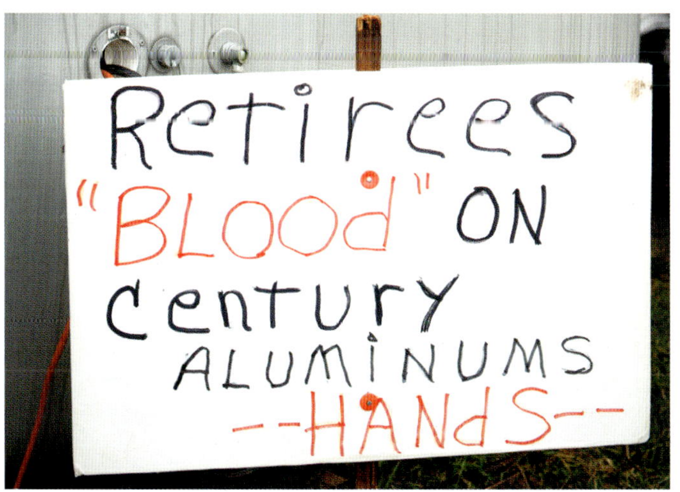

An Occupy Century Aluminum protest sign next to the group's camper, nicknamed "The White House."

A protester in an Obama mask waves to cars passing by the camp. Located on the median along State Route 2 and Century Rd., the camp is flanked by speeding auto traffic on one side and coal-hauling train traffic on the other. Just beyond the train tracks, barges haul West Virginia coal down the Ohio river.

Ron "Ripcord" Dixon from Evan, West Virginia, retired from Century in 2005 after 29 years as a millwright with the company. Dixon worked closely with Karen Gorrell, often traveling with her to Pittsburgh to meet with union lawyers representing them, as well as attending meetings at Century's headquarters in California to speak on the group's behalf.

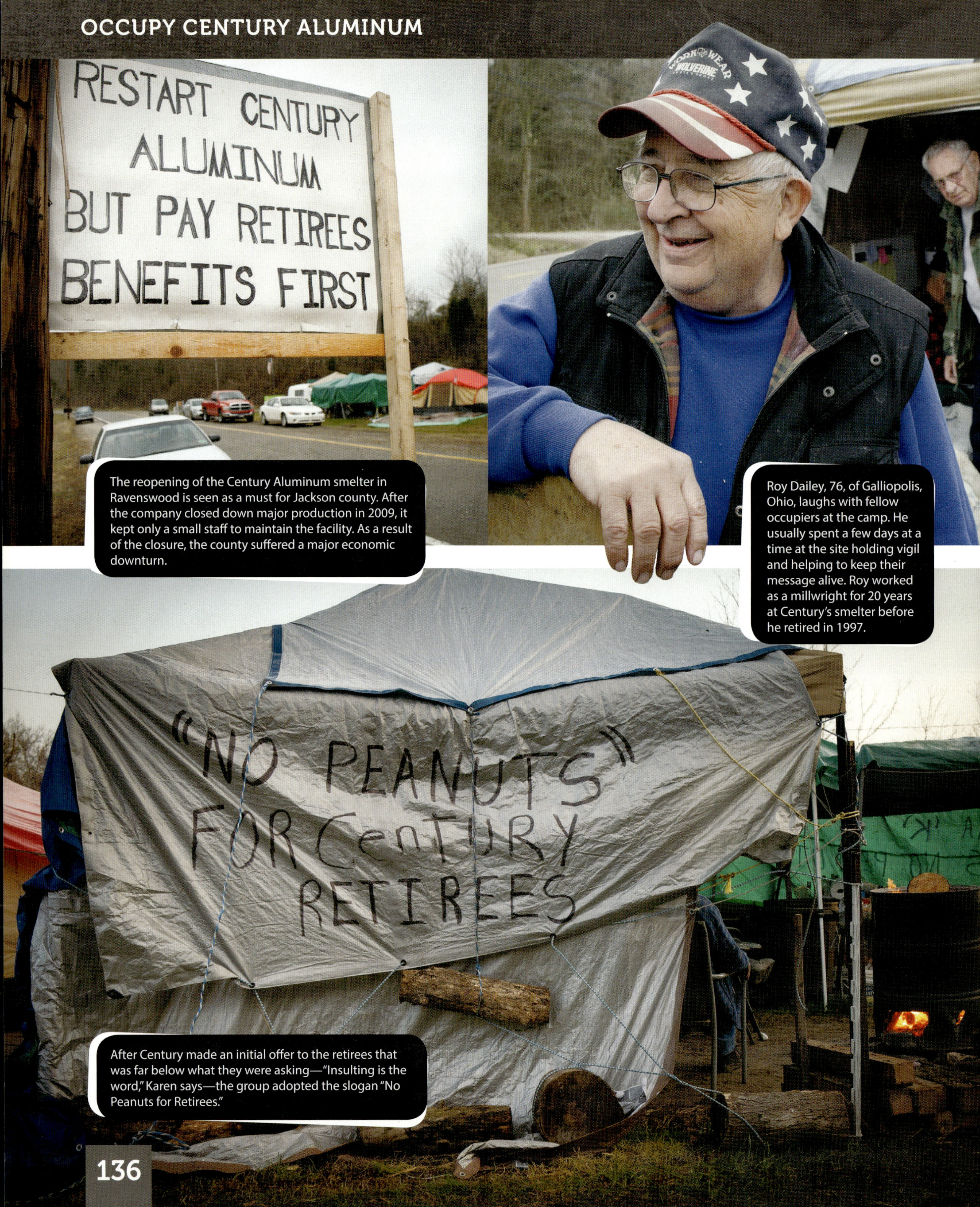

The reopening of the Century Aluminum smelter in Ravenswood is seen as a must for Jackson county. After the company closed down major production in 2009, it kept only a small staff to maintain the facility. As a result of the closure, the county suffered a major economic downturn.

Roy Dailey, 76, of Galliopolis, Ohio, laughs with fellow occupiers at the camp. He usually spent a few days at a time at the site holding vigil and helping to keep their message alive. Roy worked as a millwright for 20 years at Century's smelter before he retired in 1997.

After Century made an initial offer to the retirees that was far below what they were asking—"Insulting is the word," Karen says—the group adopted the slogan "No Peanuts for Retirees."

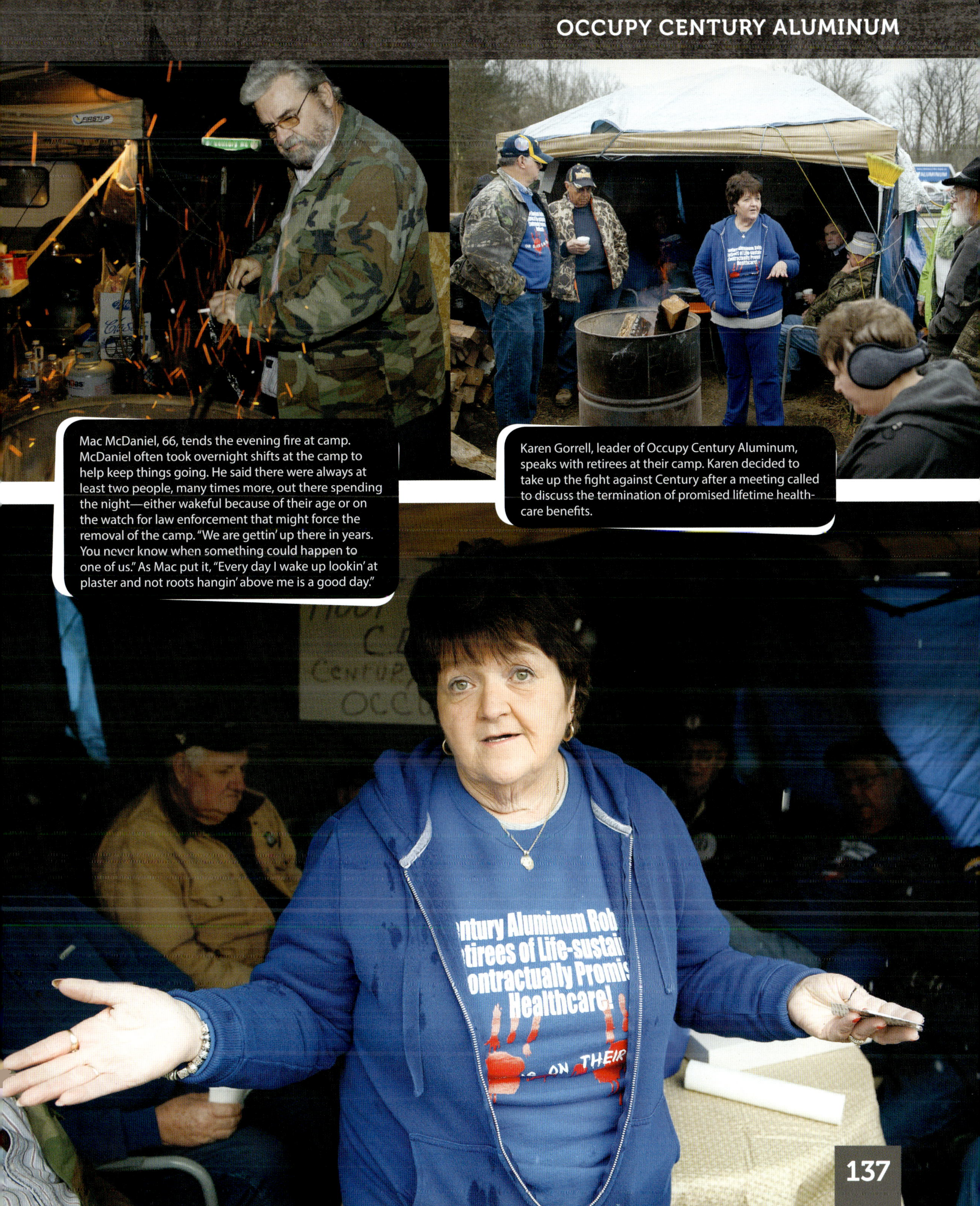

Mac McDaniel, 66, tends the evening fire at camp. McDaniel often took overnight shifts at the camp to help keep things going. He said there were always at least two people, many times more, out there spending the night—either wakeful because of their age or on the watch for law enforcement that might force the removal of the camp. "We are gettin' up there in years. You never know when something could happen to one of us." As Mac put it, "Every day I wake up lookin' at plaster and not roots hangin' above me is a good day."

Karen Gorrell, leader of Occupy Century Aluminum, speaks with retirees at their camp. Karen decided to take up the fight against Century after a meeting called to discuss the termination of promised lifetime health-care benefits.

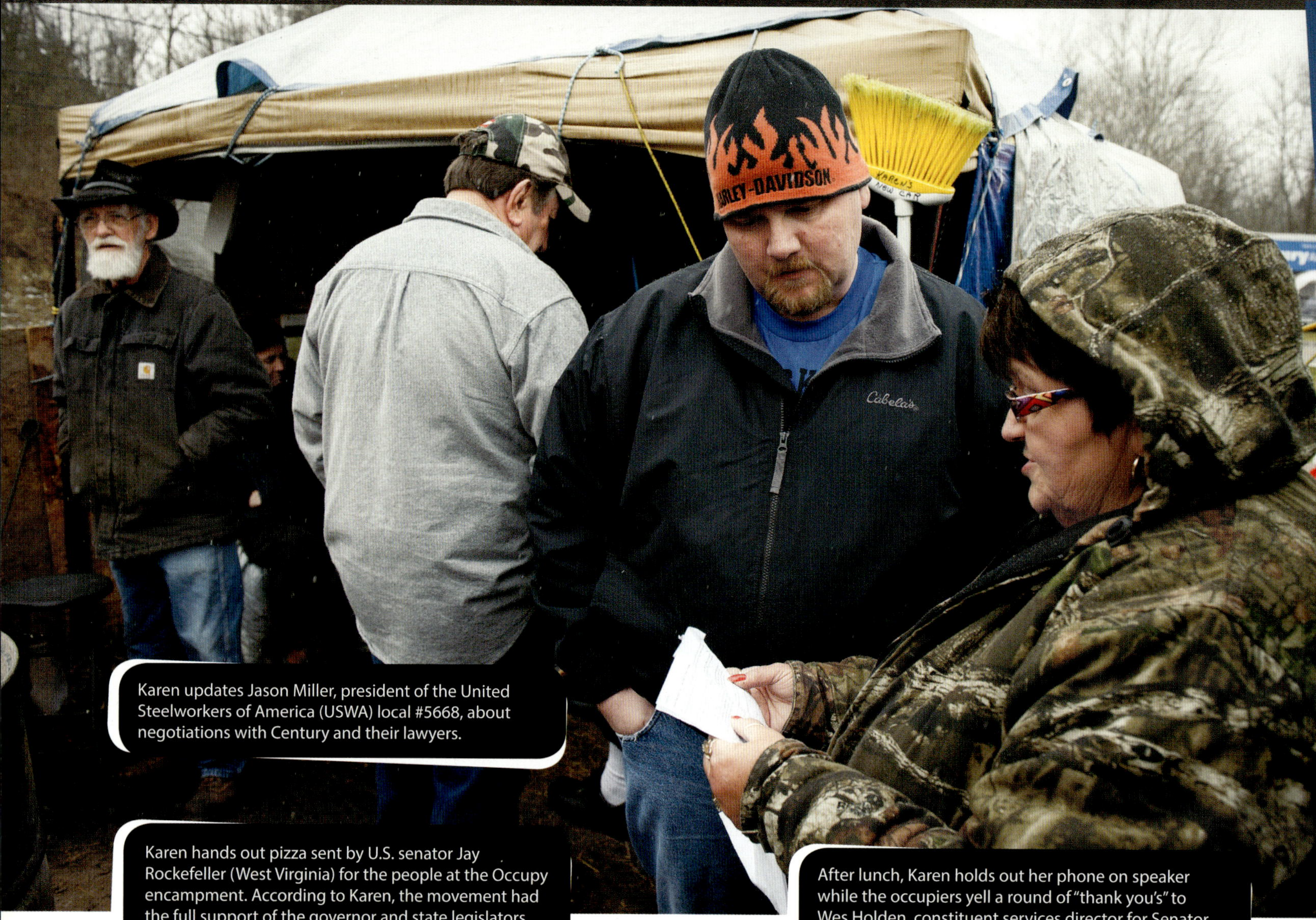

Karen updates Jason Miller, president of the United Steelworkers of America (USWA) local #5668, about negotiations with Century and their lawyers.

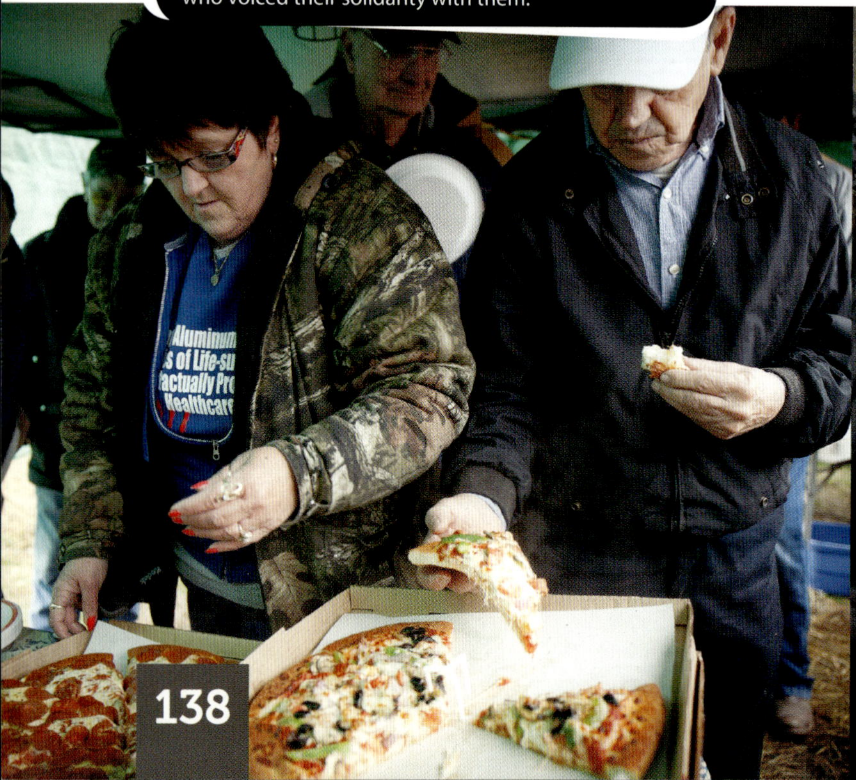

Karen hands out pizza sent by U.S. senator Jay Rockefeller (West Virginia) for the people at the Occupy encampment. According to Karen, the movement had the full support of the governor and state legislators, who voiced their solidarity with them.

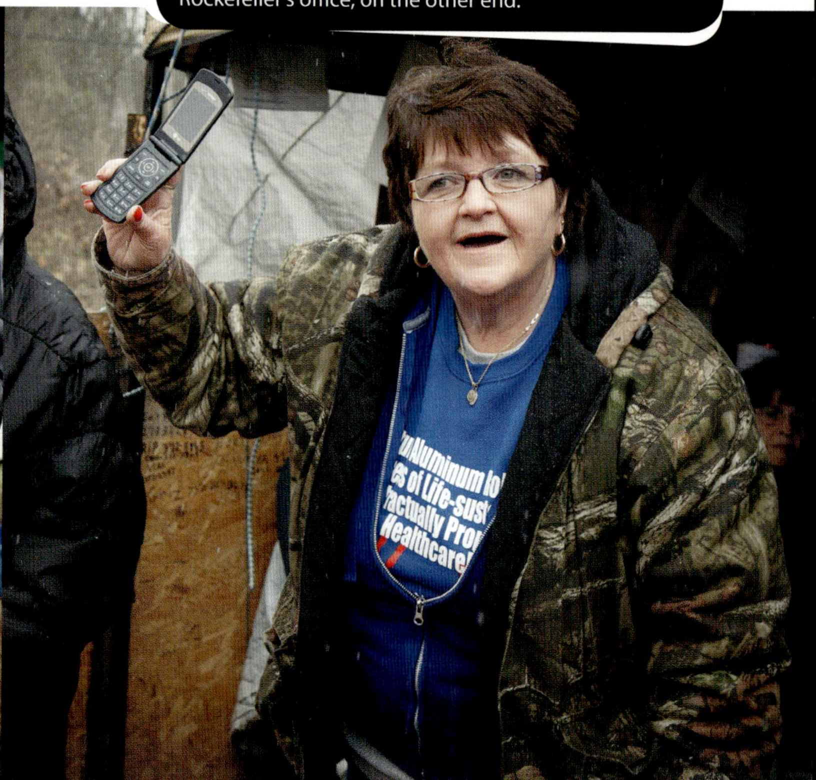

After lunch, Karen holds out her phone on speaker while the occupiers yell a round of "thank you's" to Wes Holden, constituent services director for Senator Rockefeller's office, on the other end.

A 75-Day WINTER OCCUPATION BY RETIREES ENDS IN VICTORY OVER CORPORATE GIANT

Occupy Century Aluminum was not your typical 99-percenter occupation. The average age of the occupiers was 70, and they had a clear message: "Give us our promised health care back!" On December 18, 2011, grandparents and great-grandparents who had worked most of their adult lives for Century Aluminum set up camp on the median of Route 2 near the entrance to the closed smelter in Ravenswood, West Virginia, to protest the loss of their benefits. The company had shuttered the smelter in 2009, axing 651 workers, but negotiated (and promised) to provide lifetime health-care benefits for its workers after they shut down the smelter. Although the company did not go bankrupt (it still operates other plants around the country), in June 2010 Century sent out letters informing retirees it was dropping their coverage. This even though decades before, in contract talks with the company, union workers had agreed to take an hourly pay cut as long as the difference was put into an account for lifetime health-care benefits. Century instead took all the money, more than $25 million, and then canceled their insurance. Many of these people and their families desperately needed the health care Century had promised. Gaining inspiration from Occupy encampments that had sprung up across America earlier in the year, the group decided to occupy the area in front of the smelter until Century Aluminum gave them their health-care benefits back.

The group's leader, Karen Gorrell, decided to take up the fight against Century after attending a meeting called to discuss the termination of their promised lifetime health-care benefits, which took place at the local #5668 United Steelworkers union hall. Outside the hall she met Bryce Turner, a retiree, and his wife. Turner told her he didn't know what he was going to do without health care, having just been diagnosed with leukemia. It was then, she says, that she realized she had to do something. With inspiration from the Occupy movement spreading across the country, she and other Century retirees decided to start their own occupation. Bryce Turner, the man who had inspired her to take up the fight, died before his benefits were returned, but Karen and the other protesters carried on the fight for their lives—in his honor.

On March 1, 2012, after 75 days of camping out in the freezing winter months, the retirees of Occupy Century Aluminum managed to beat the corporate giant Century. The company finally agreed to the return of $67 million in health-care benefits and back pay, with $40 million to be paid out in cash over the next 10 years and an additional $27 million tied to the price of aluminum on the London Metal Exchange (LME). This settlement would benefit 500 families in the community. After the tentative agreement, Karen Gorrell posted this on the group's Facebook page:

> Late this afternoon, with the help of the USWA's Tom Conway, the unending support of Governor Earl Ray Tomblin and Senator Jay Rockefeller, and many, many members of the West Virginia Legislature, the retirees were able to come to an agreement with Century Aluminum for restoration of benefits for the retirees. There are several other pieces of the puzzle that must come together before they will be effective, but we are confident that they will happen. The retirees are overwhelmed that the "little people" could dance with the big boys and win the justice we were seeking. It is an amazing story of how all can unite behind a common cause and if you TRULY believe, you really can make a difference. The good Lord was our leader and he showed us the way because we were on the right side of this fight. The lesson to be learned is this: "All things are possible if you only believe." Never, ever give up, no matter how long the journey.

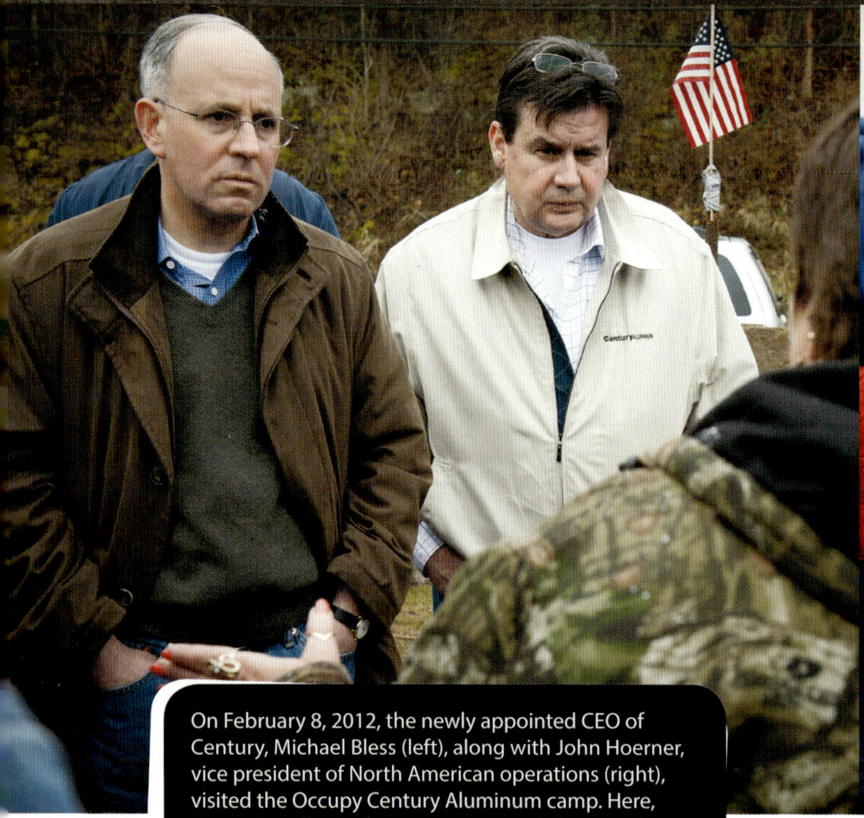

On February 8, 2012, the newly appointed CEO of Century, Michael Bless (left), along with John Hoerner, vice president of North American operations (right), visited the Occupy Century Aluminum camp. Here, Karen Gorrell tells the executives the difficulties that the Century retirees are going through without the health-care benefits they were promised—and paid for with decades of loyalty to the company.

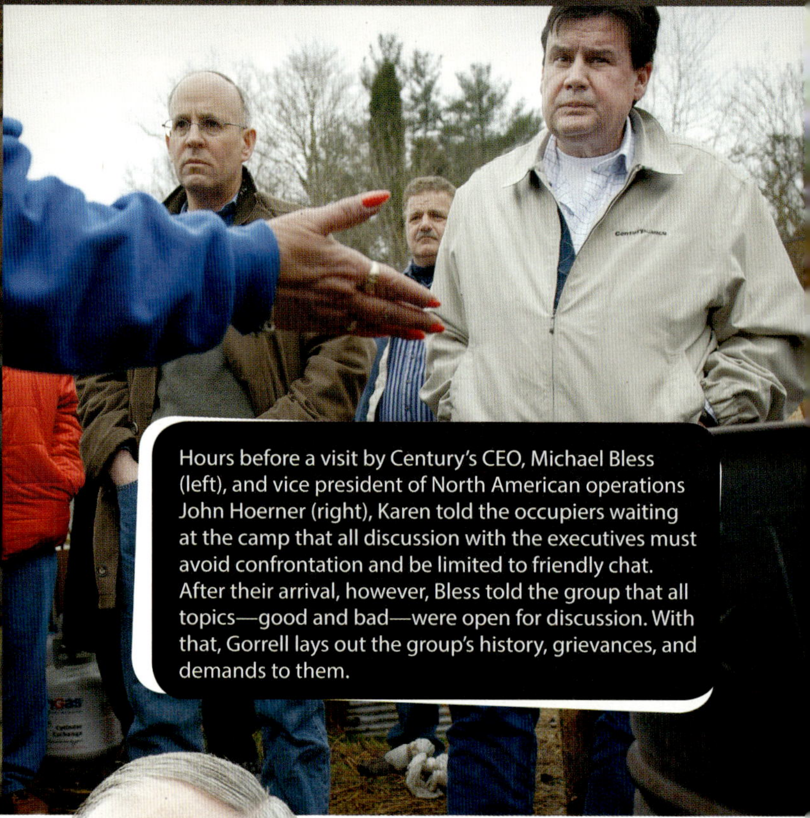

Hours before a visit by Century's CEO, Michael Bless (left), and vice president of North American operations John Hoerner (right), Karen told the occupiers waiting at the camp that all discussion with the executives must avoid confrontation and be limited to friendly chat. After their arrival, however, Bless told the group that all topics—good and bad—were open for discussion. With that, Gorrell lays out the group's history, grievances, and demands to them.

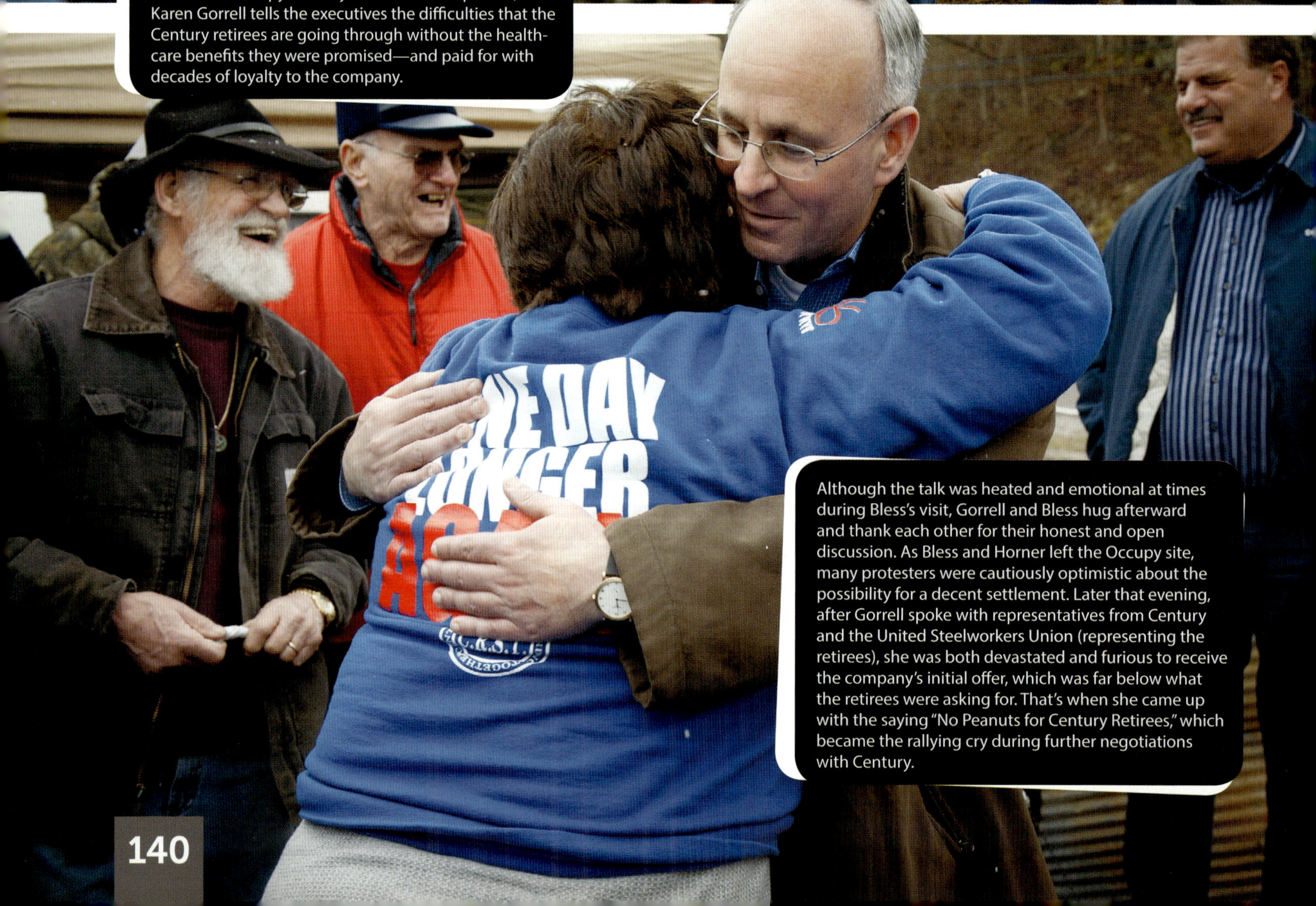

Although the talk was heated and emotional at times during Bless's visit, Gorrell and Bless hug afterward and thank each other for their honest and open discussion. As Bless and Horner left the Occupy site, many protesters were cautiously optimistic about the possibility for a decent settlement. Later that evening, after Gorrell spoke with representatives from Century and the United Steelworkers Union (representing the retirees), she was both devastated and furious to receive the company's initial offer, which was far below what the retirees were asking for. That's when she came up with the saying "No Peanuts for Century Retirees," which became the rallying cry during further negotiations with Century.

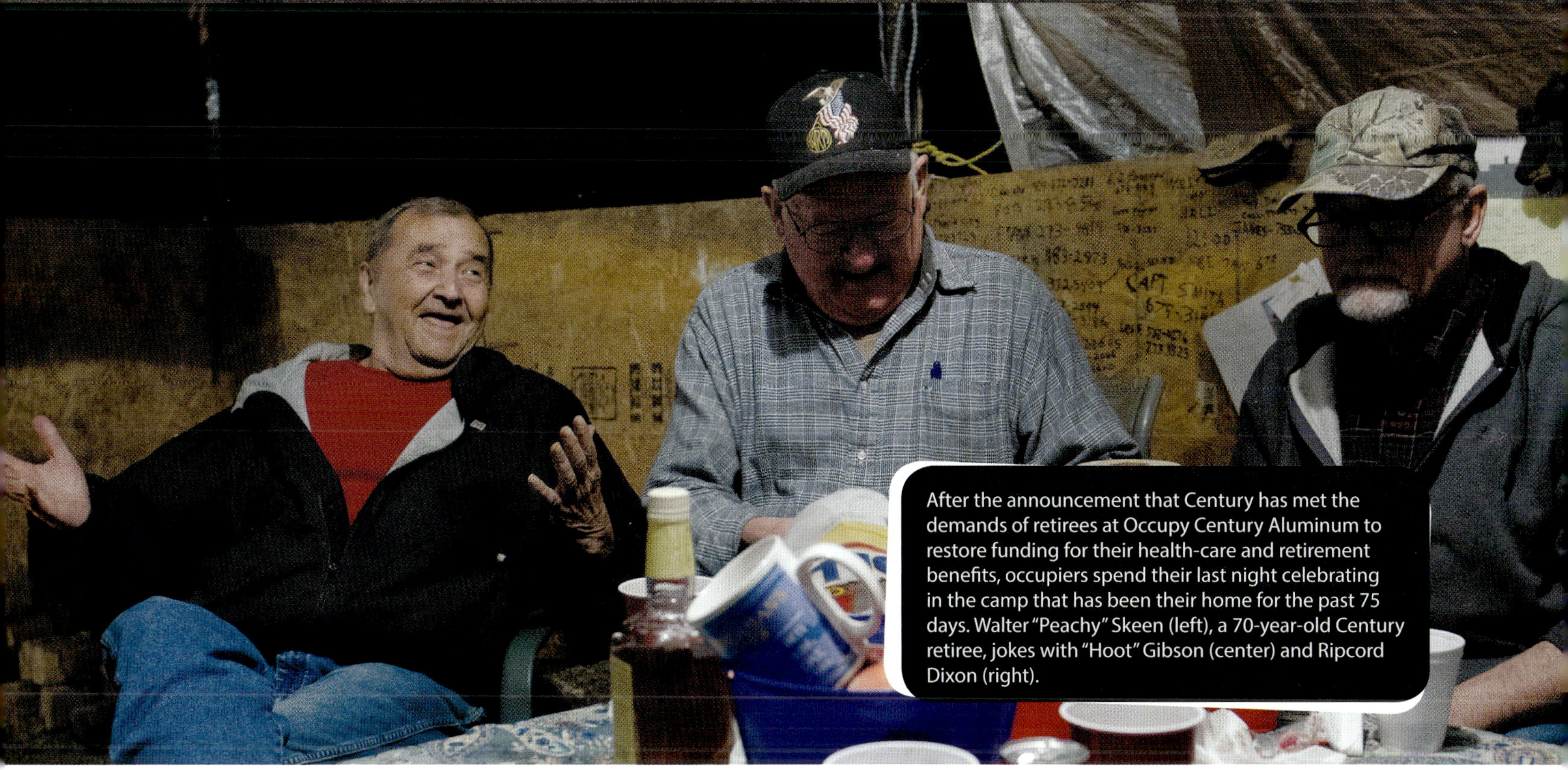

After the announcement that Century has met the demands of retirees at Occupy Century Aluminum to restore funding for their health-care and retirement benefits, occupiers spend their last night celebrating in the camp that has been their home for the past 75 days. Walter "Peachy" Skeen (left), a 70-year-old Century retiree, jokes with "Hoot" Gibson (center) and Ripcord Dixon (right).

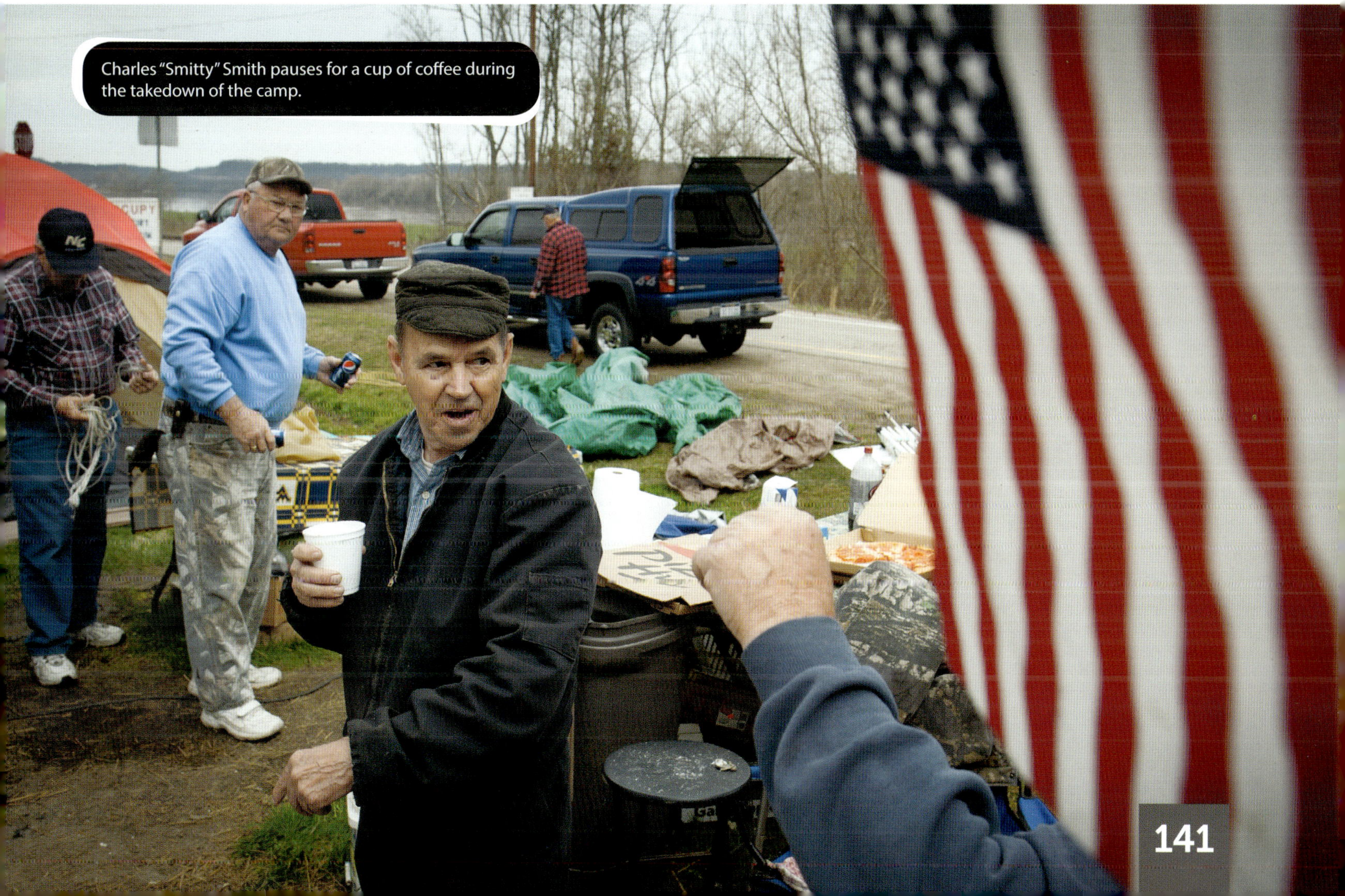

Charles "Smitty" Smith pauses for a cup of coffee during the takedown of the camp.

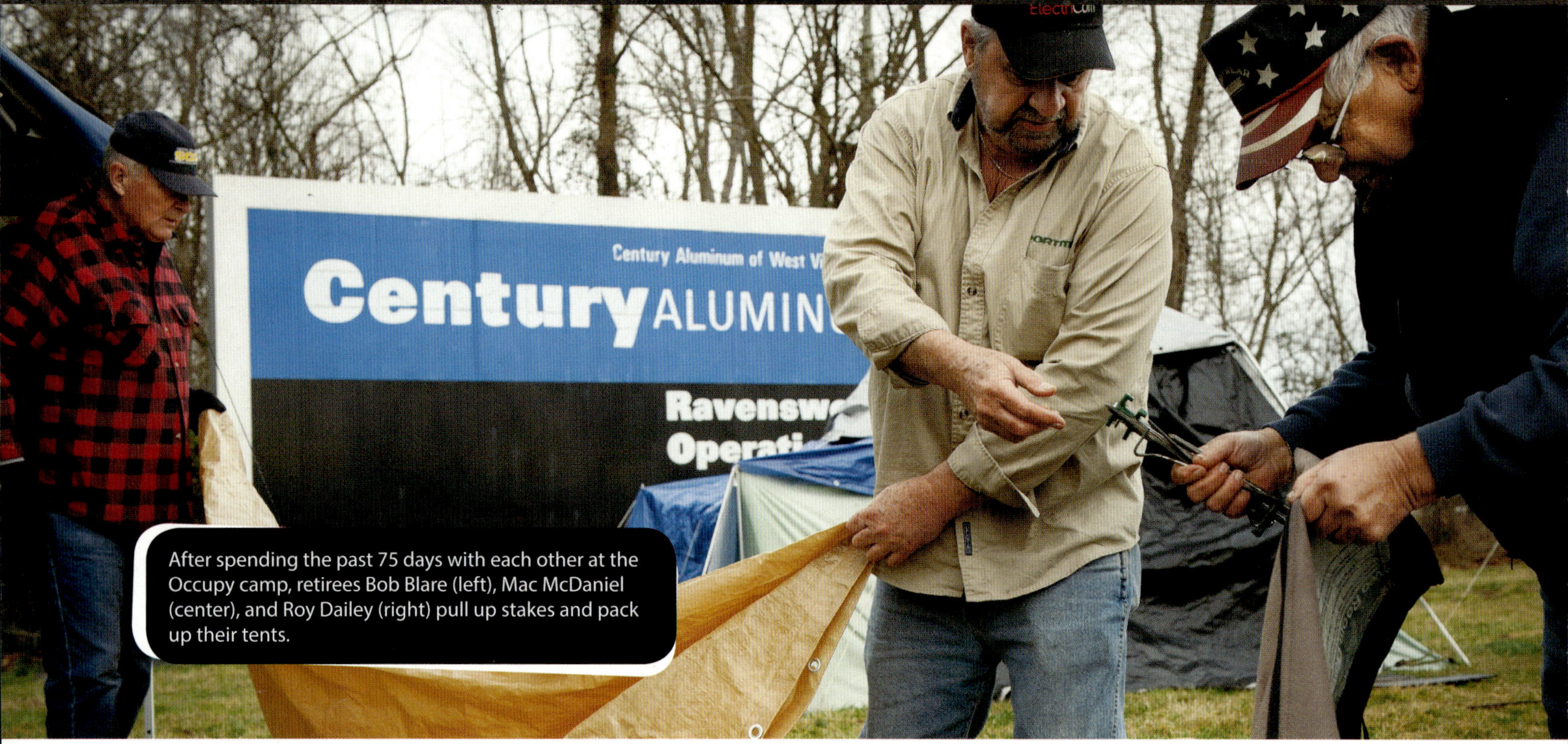

After spending the past 75 days with each other at the Occupy camp, retirees Bob Blare (left), Mac McDaniel (center), and Roy Dailey (right) pull up stakes and pack up their tents.

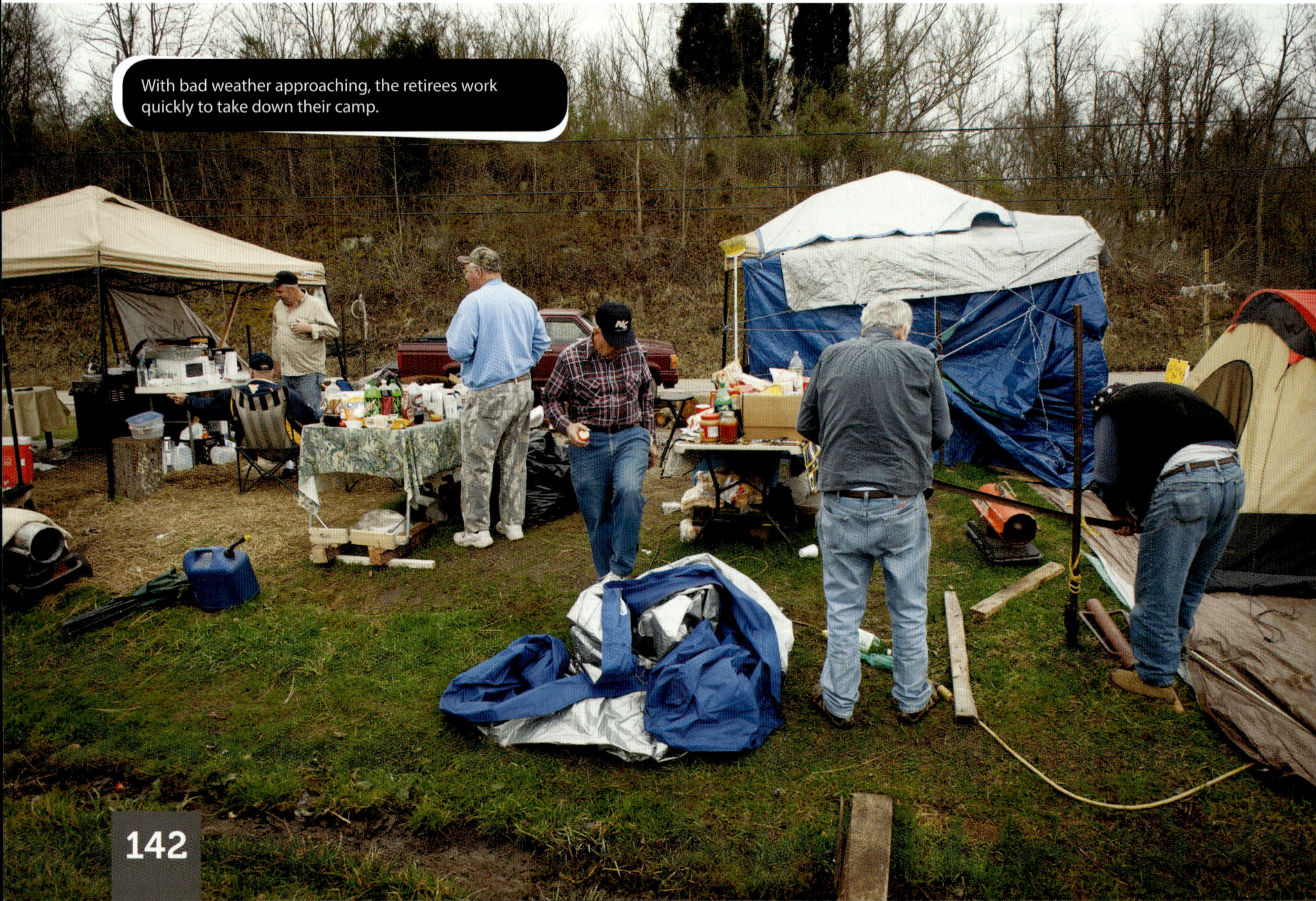

With bad weather approaching, the retirees work quickly to take down their camp.

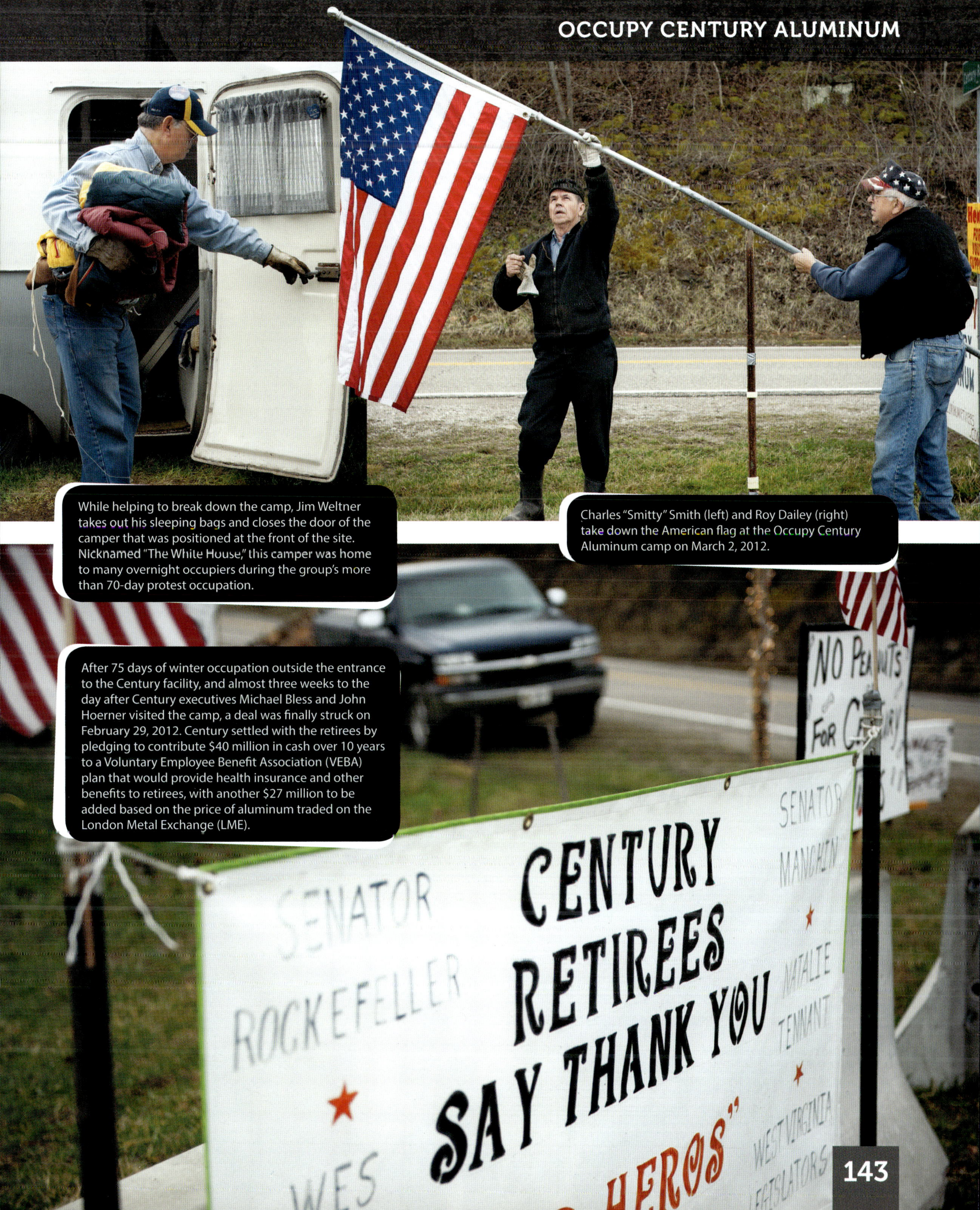

While helping to break down the camp, Jim Weltner takes out his sleeping bags and closes the door of the camper that was positioned at the front of the site. Nicknamed "The White House," this camper was home to many overnight occupiers during the group's more than 70-day protest occupation.

Charles "Smitty" Smith (left) and Roy Dailey (right) take down the American flag at the Occupy Century Aluminum camp on March 2, 2012.

After 75 days of winter occupation outside the entrance to the Century facility, and almost three weeks to the day after Century executives Michael Bless and John Hoerner visited the camp, a deal was finally struck on February 29, 2012. Century settled with the retirees by pledging to contribute $40 million in cash over 10 years to a Voluntary Employee Benefit Association (VEBA) plan that would provide health insurance and other benefits to retirees, with another $27 million to be added based on the price of aluminum traded on the London Metal Exchange (LME).

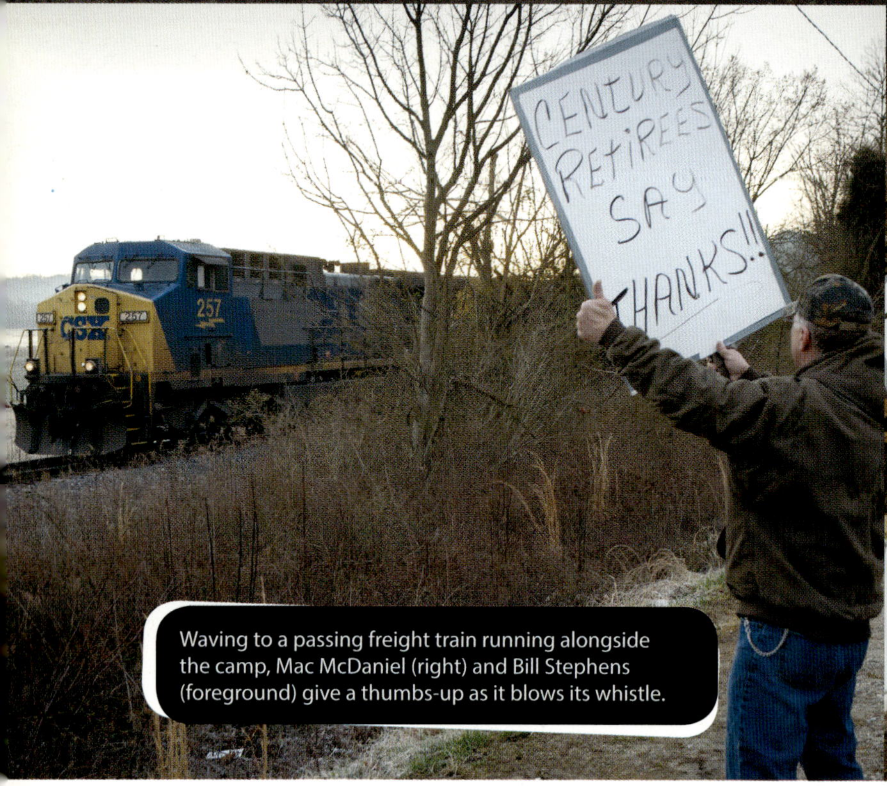

Waving to a passing freight train running alongside the camp, Mac McDaniel (right) and Bill Stephens (foreground) give a thumbs-up as it blows its whistle.

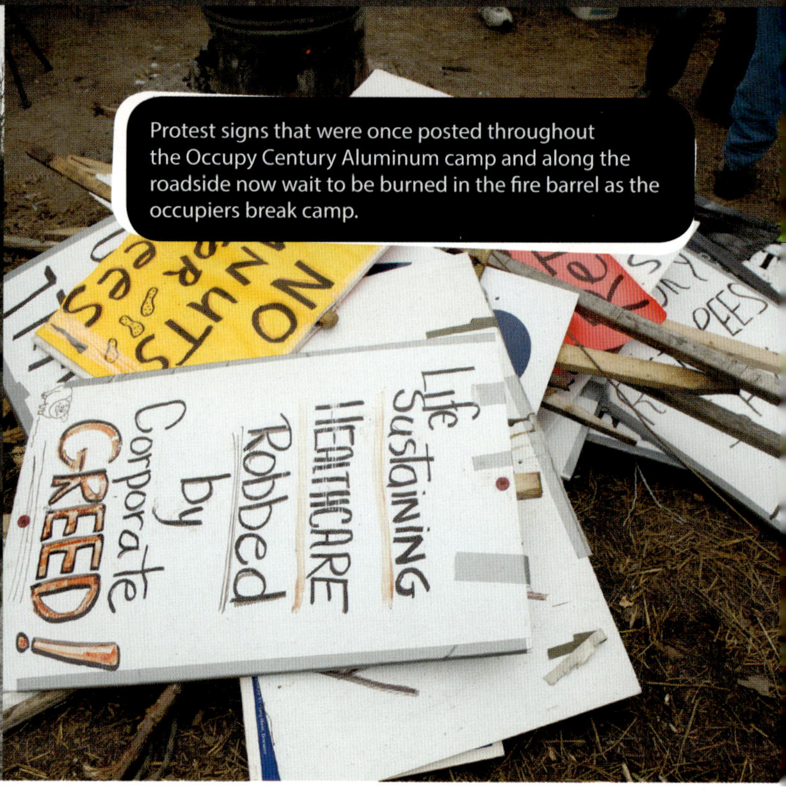

Protest signs that were once posted throughout the Occupy Century Aluminum camp and along the roadside now wait to be burned in the fire barrel as the occupiers break camp.

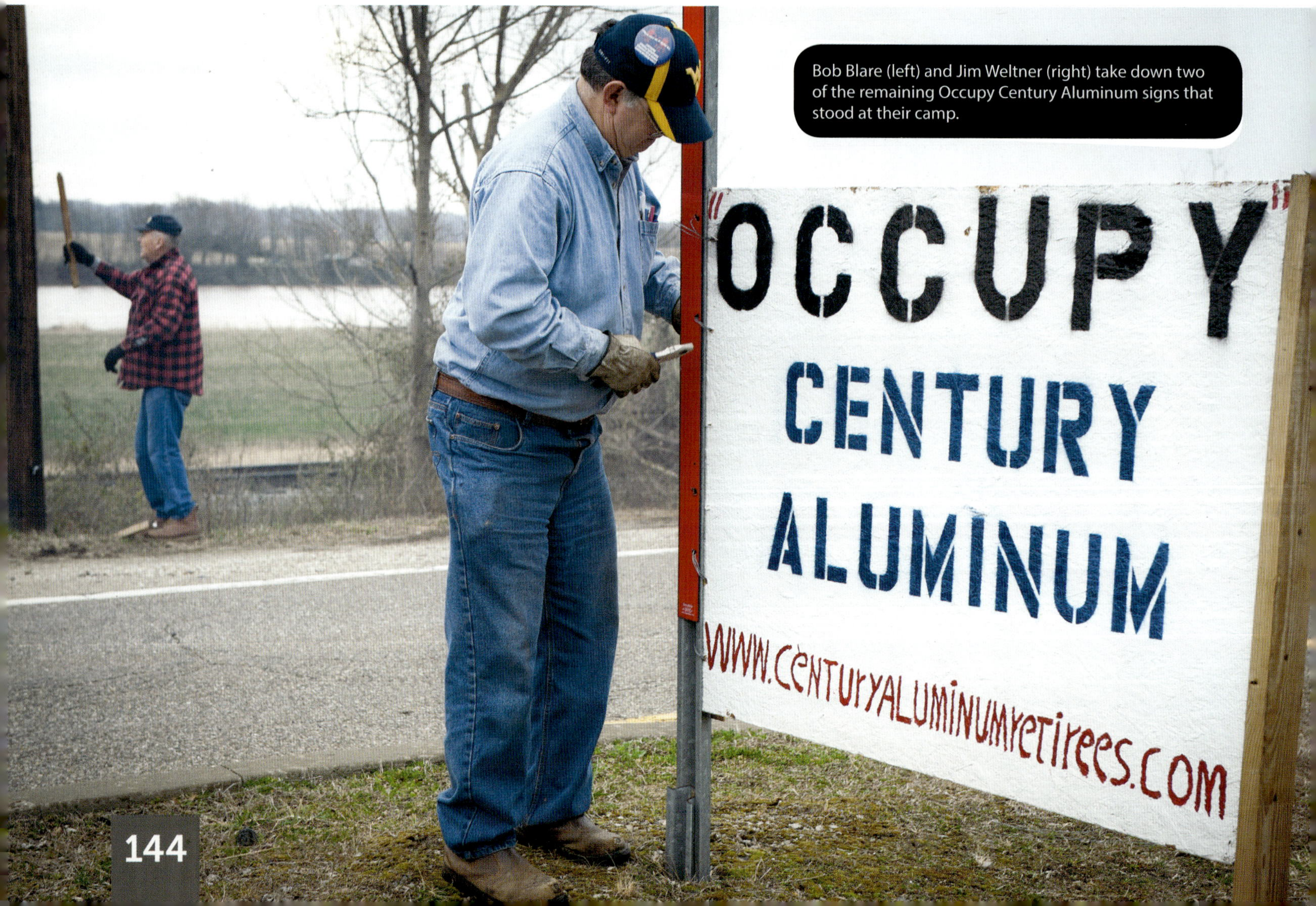

Bob Blare (left) and Jim Weltner (right) take down two of the remaining Occupy Century Aluminum signs that stood at their camp.

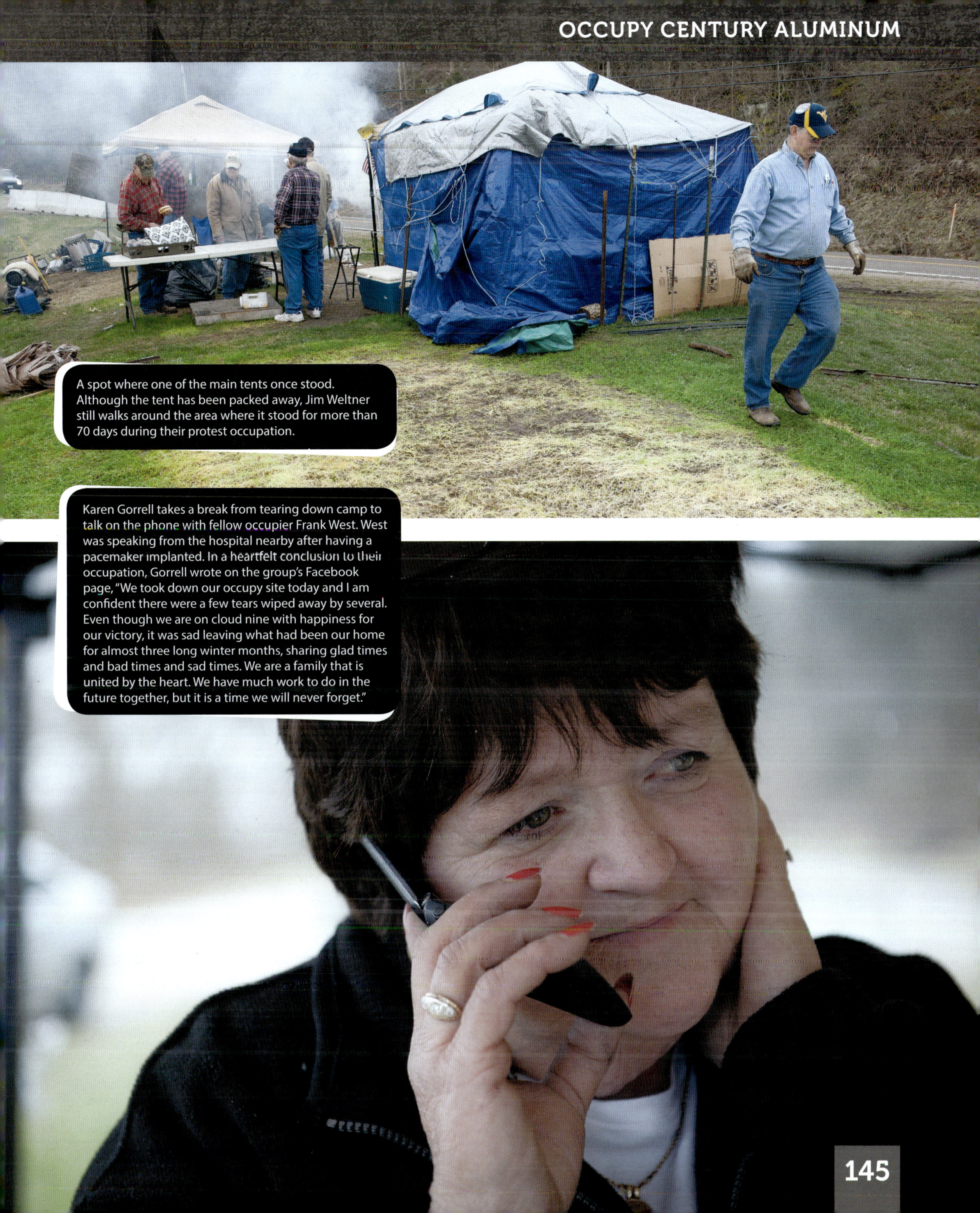

A spot where one of the main tents once stood. Although the tent has been packed away, Jim Weltner still walks around the area where it stood for more than 70 days during their protest occupation.

Karen Gorrell takes a break from tearing down camp to talk on the phone with fellow occupier Frank West. West was speaking from the hospital nearby after having a pacemaker implanted. In a heartfelt conclusion to their occupation, Gorrell wrote on the group's Facebook page, "We took down our occupy site today and I am confident there were a few tears wiped away by several. Even though we are on cloud nine with happiness for our victory, it was sad leaving what had been our home for almost three long winter months, sharing glad times and bad times and sad times. We are a family that is united by the heart. We have much work to do in the future together, but it is a time we will never forget."

Occupy National Gathering

The Occupy National Gathering kicked off on June 30, 2012, and included what organizers called "five days of movement building, camaraderie, and direct action." The gathering was the first of its kind, with Occupy activists from across the country—and even from Canada and Spain—converging on Philadelphia to participate in collectively building a "vision for a new democratic future."

Eschewing the traditional consensus-building process, groups of five or so attendees met to discuss and record what they would like the movement to address—including goals ranging from ending corporate personhood and the prison industrial complex to vaguer goals such as closing the wealth gap between rich and poor. At the end of the five days, the "best" ideas rose to the top—meaning the most oft-cited objectives or visions. A document was then drafted and taken up to New York City's Zuccotti Park, the birthplace of the Occupy movement, via the Occupy Guitarmy's 99-mile march from Philadelphia to Lower Manhattan.

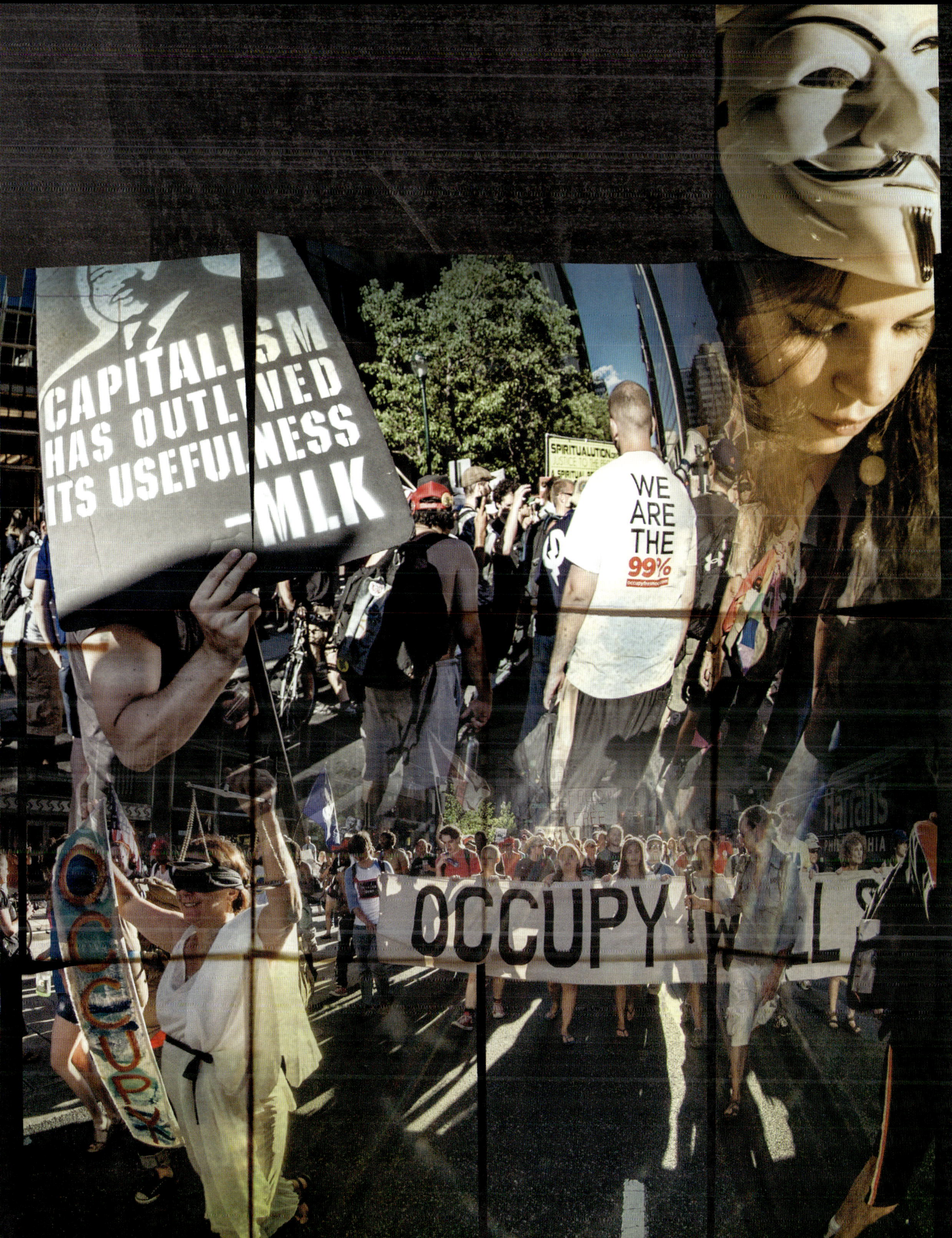
CAPITALISM
HAS OUTLIVED
ITS USEFULNESS
—MLK
WE
ARE
THE
99%
OCCUPY
OCCUPY

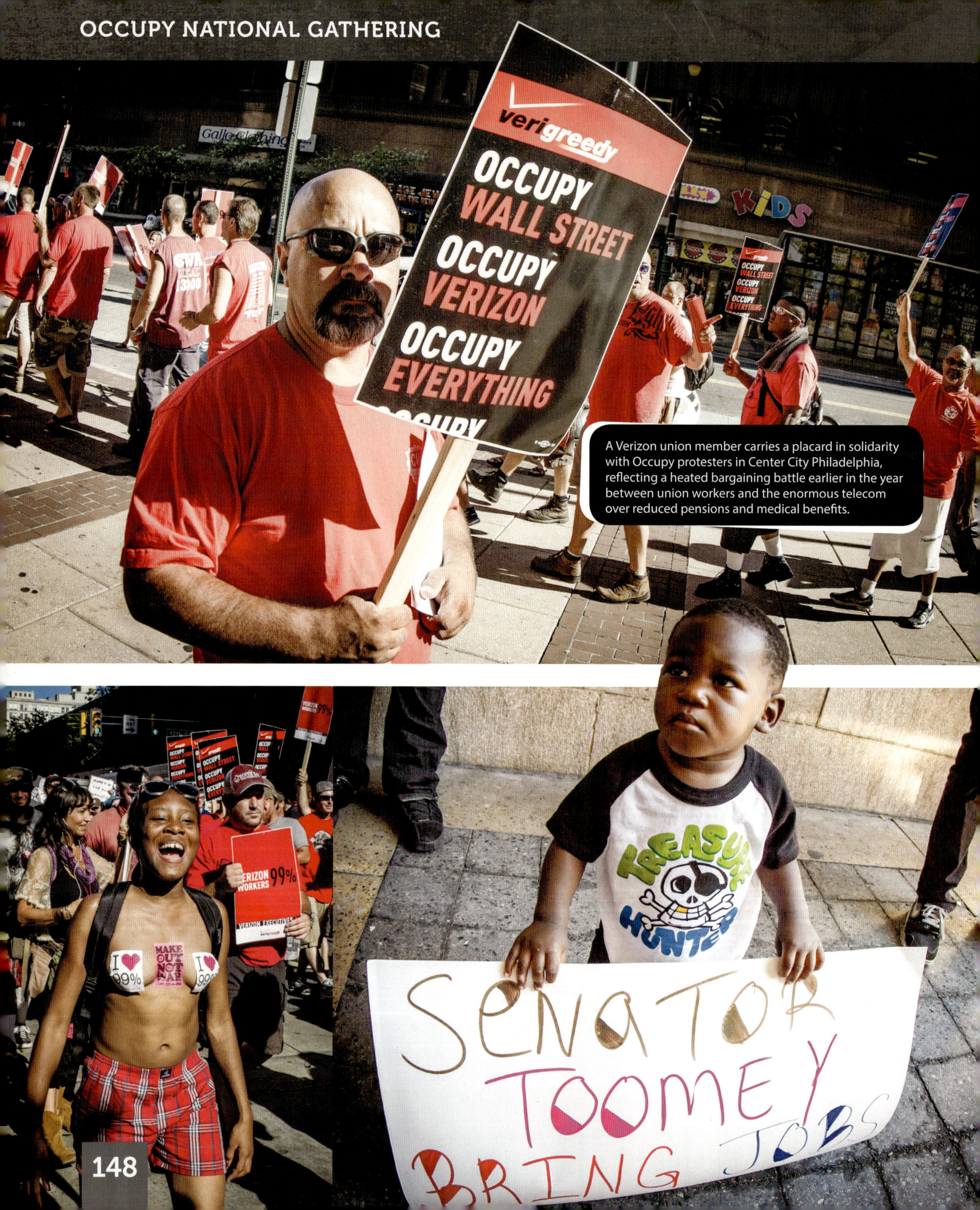

A Verizon union member carries a placard in solidarity with Occupy protesters in Center City Philadelphia, reflecting a heated bargaining battle earlier in the year between union workers and the enormous telecom over reduced pensions and medical benefits.

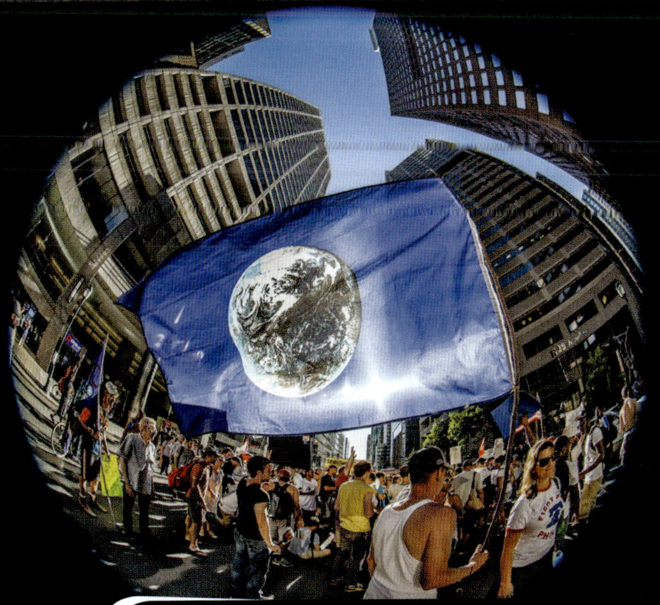

Protesters rally in front of a bank in Center City Philadelphia, decrying the lack of Wall Street accountability.

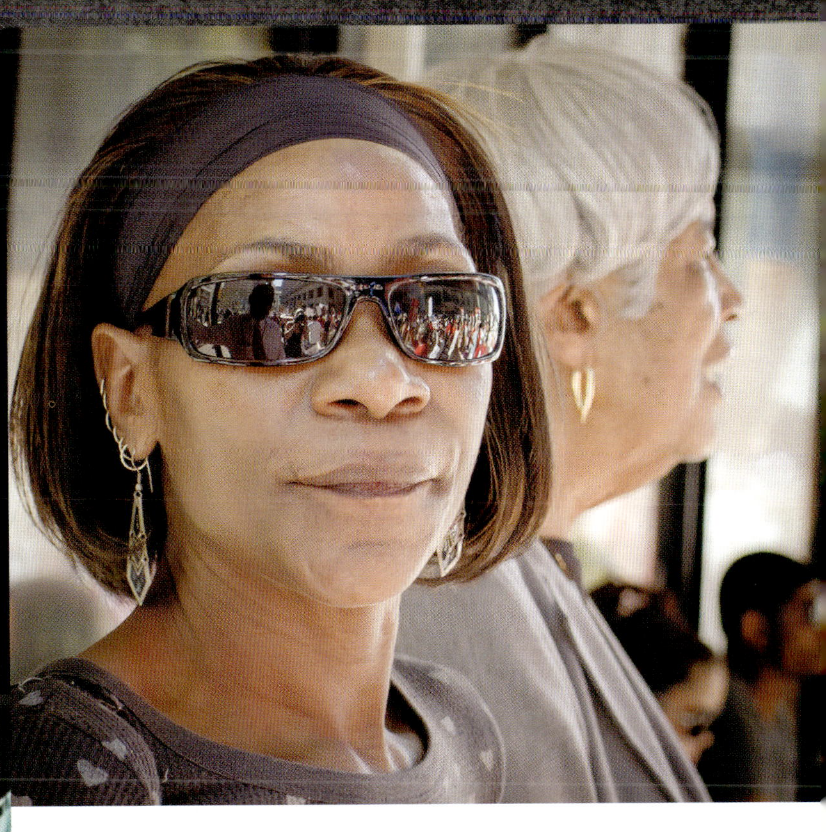

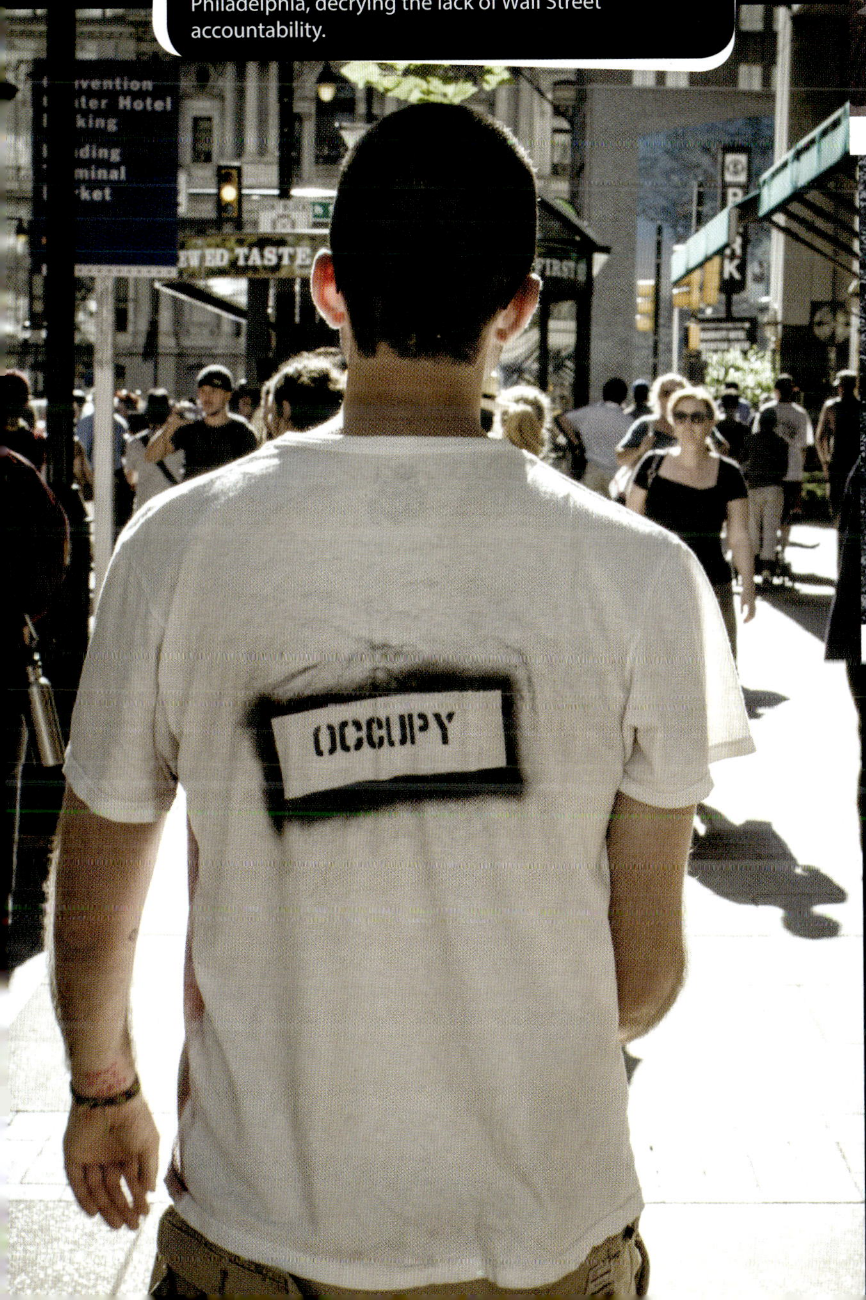

A massive march through Center City, Philadelphia, kicks off the first Occupy National Gathering.

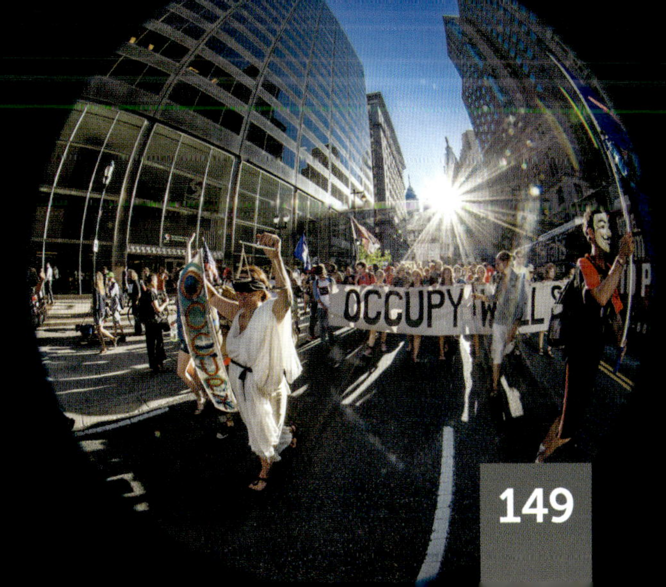

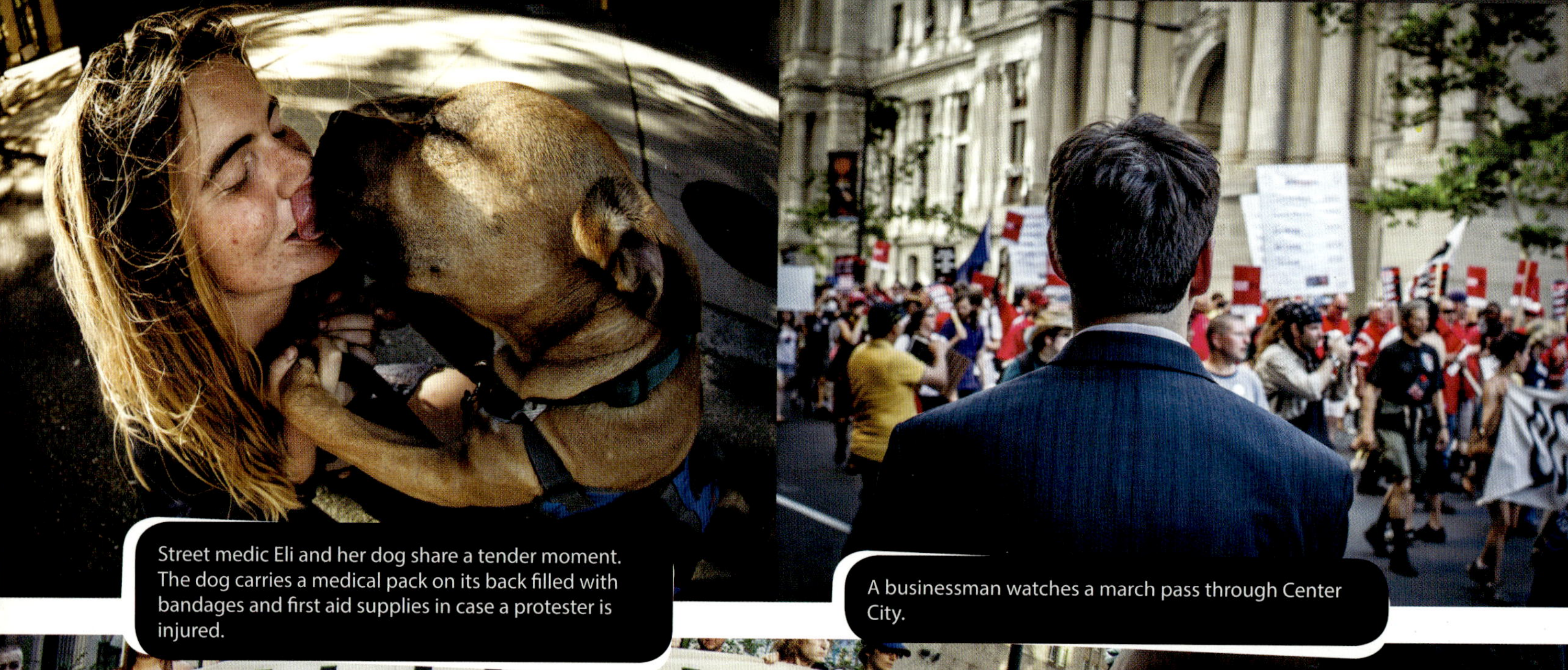

Street medic Eli and her dog share a tender moment. The dog carries a medical pack on its back filled with bandages and first aid supplies in case a protester is injured.

A businessman watches a march pass through Center City.

CUPY WALL ST

Eli walks her dog in the opening march for the Occupy National Gathering. She would later make the trek with more than 100 other protesters on the 99-mile march from Philadelphia to New York City at the gathering's conclusion.

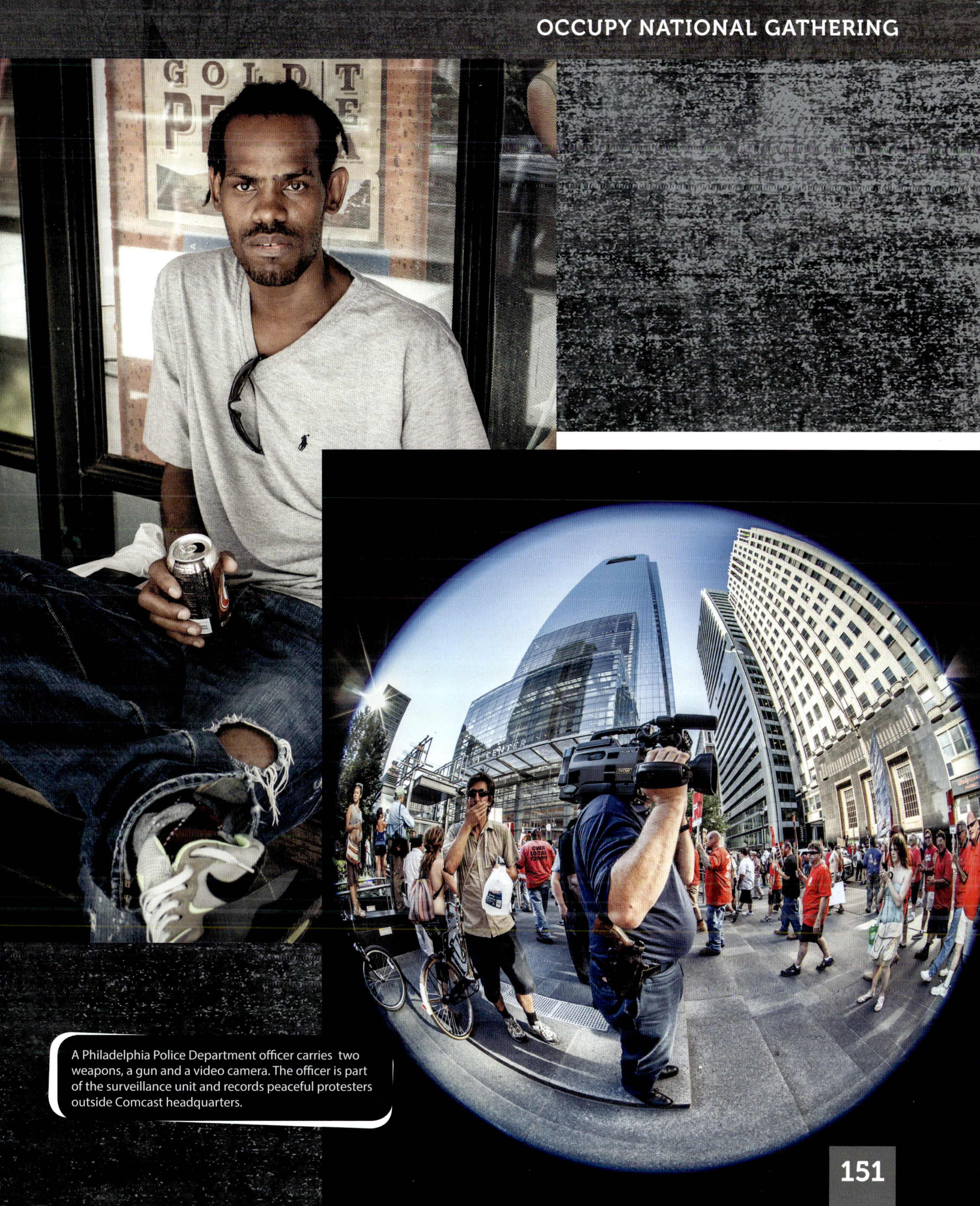

A Philadelphia Police Department officer carries two weapons, a gun and a video camera. The officer is part of the surveillance unit and records peaceful protesters outside Comcast headquarters.

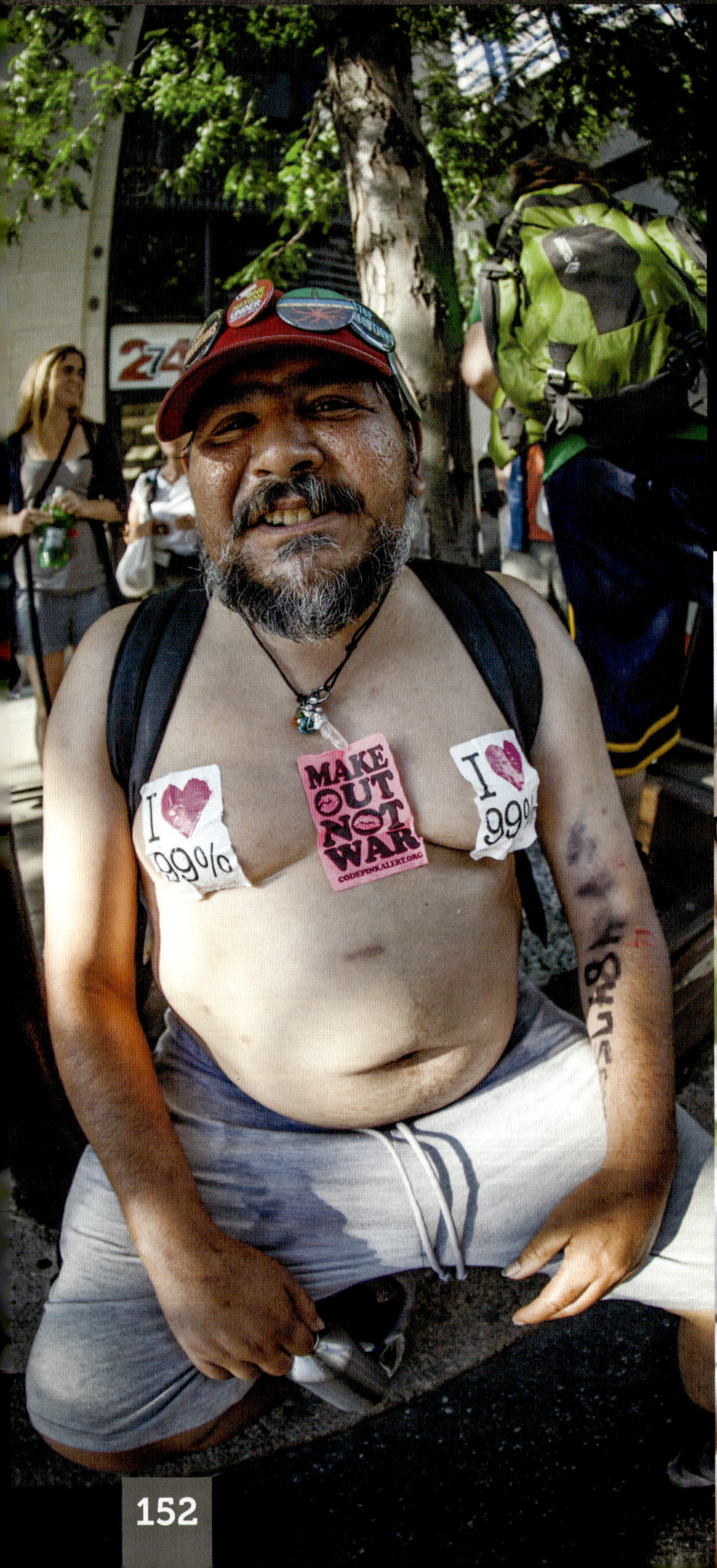
I ♥ 99%
MAKE OUT NOT WAR
CODEPINKALERT.ORG
I ♥ 99%

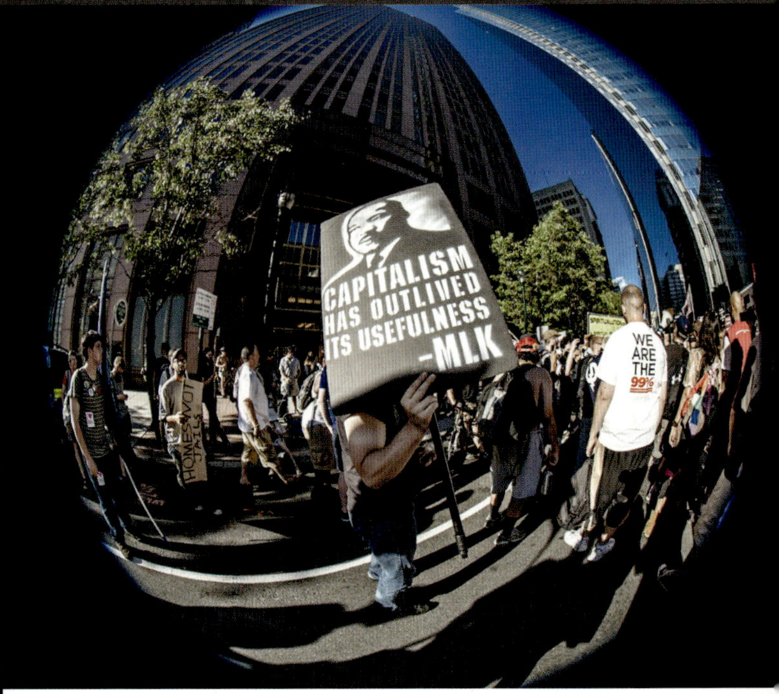
CAPITALISM HAS OUTLIVED ITS USEFULNESS -MLK
WE ARE THE 99%

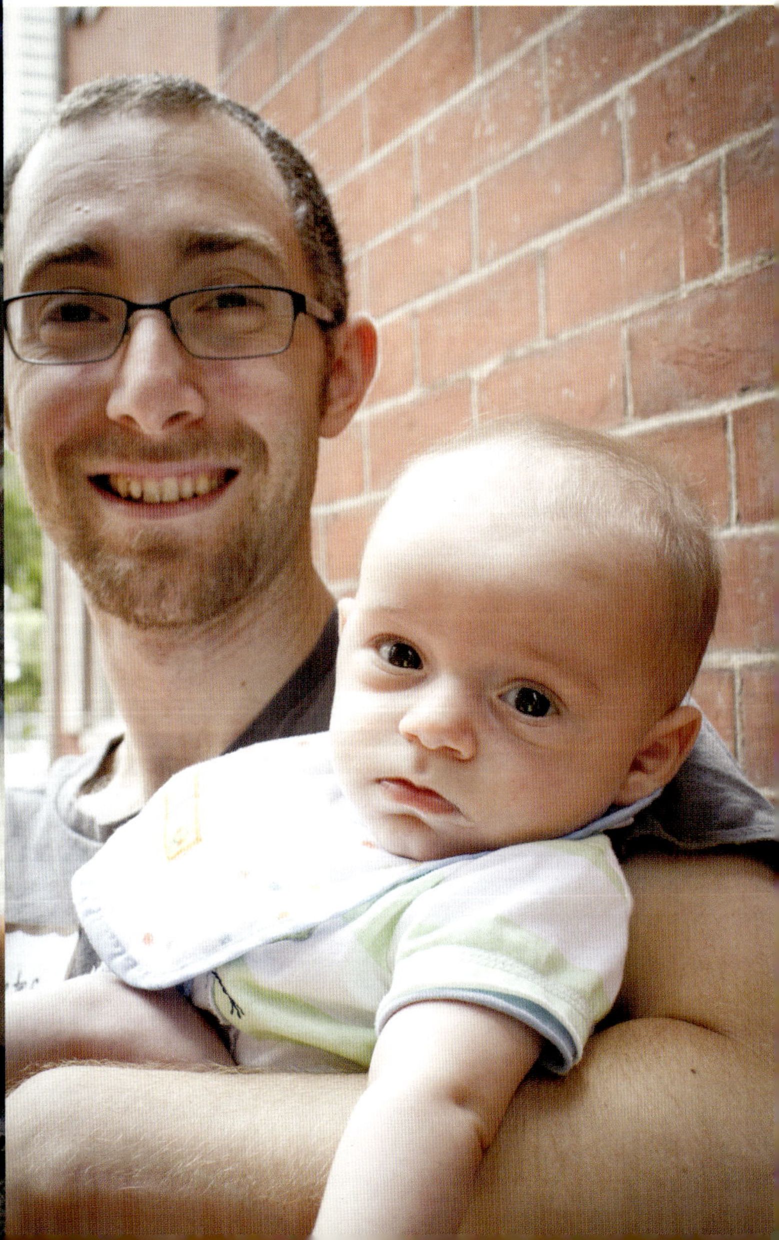

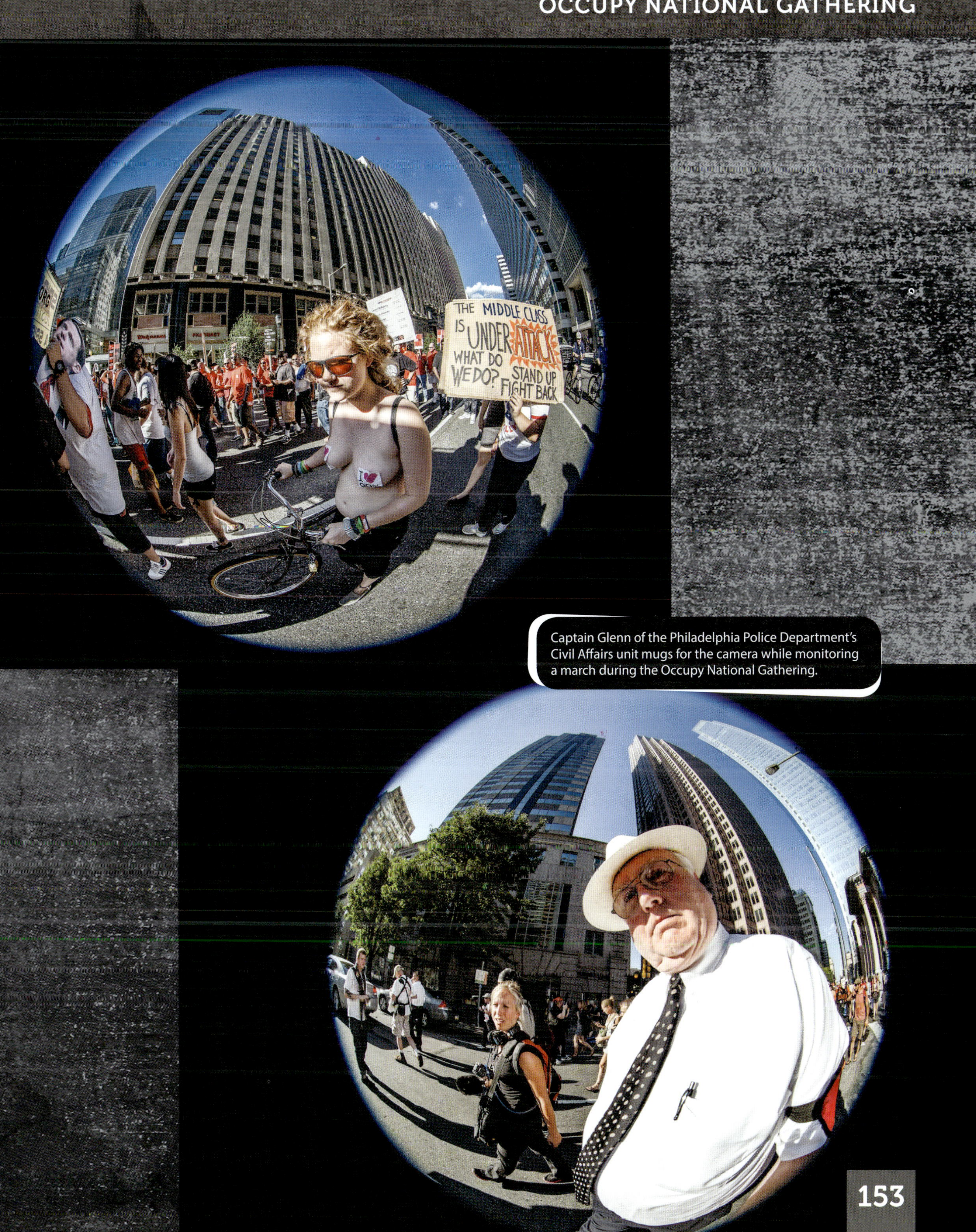

Captain Glenn of the Philadelphia Police Department's Civil Affairs unit mugs for the camera while monitoring a march during the Occupy National Gathering.

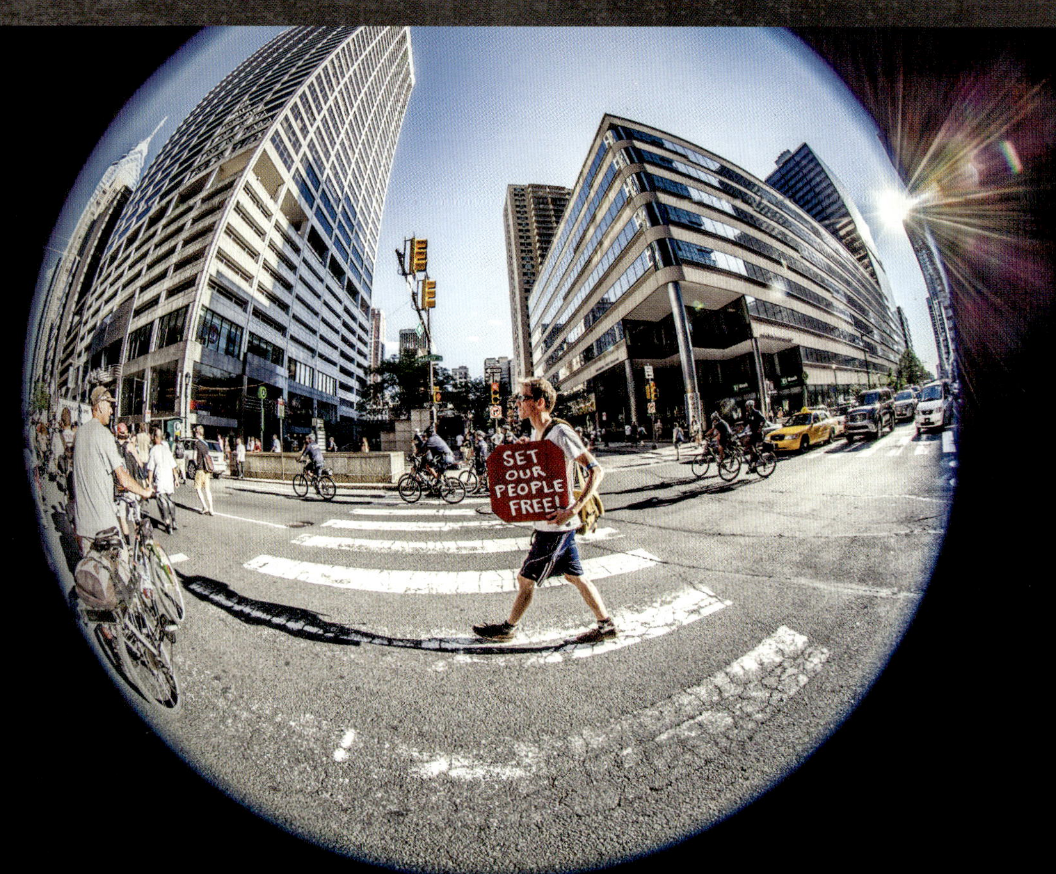
SET
OUR
PEOPLE
FREE!

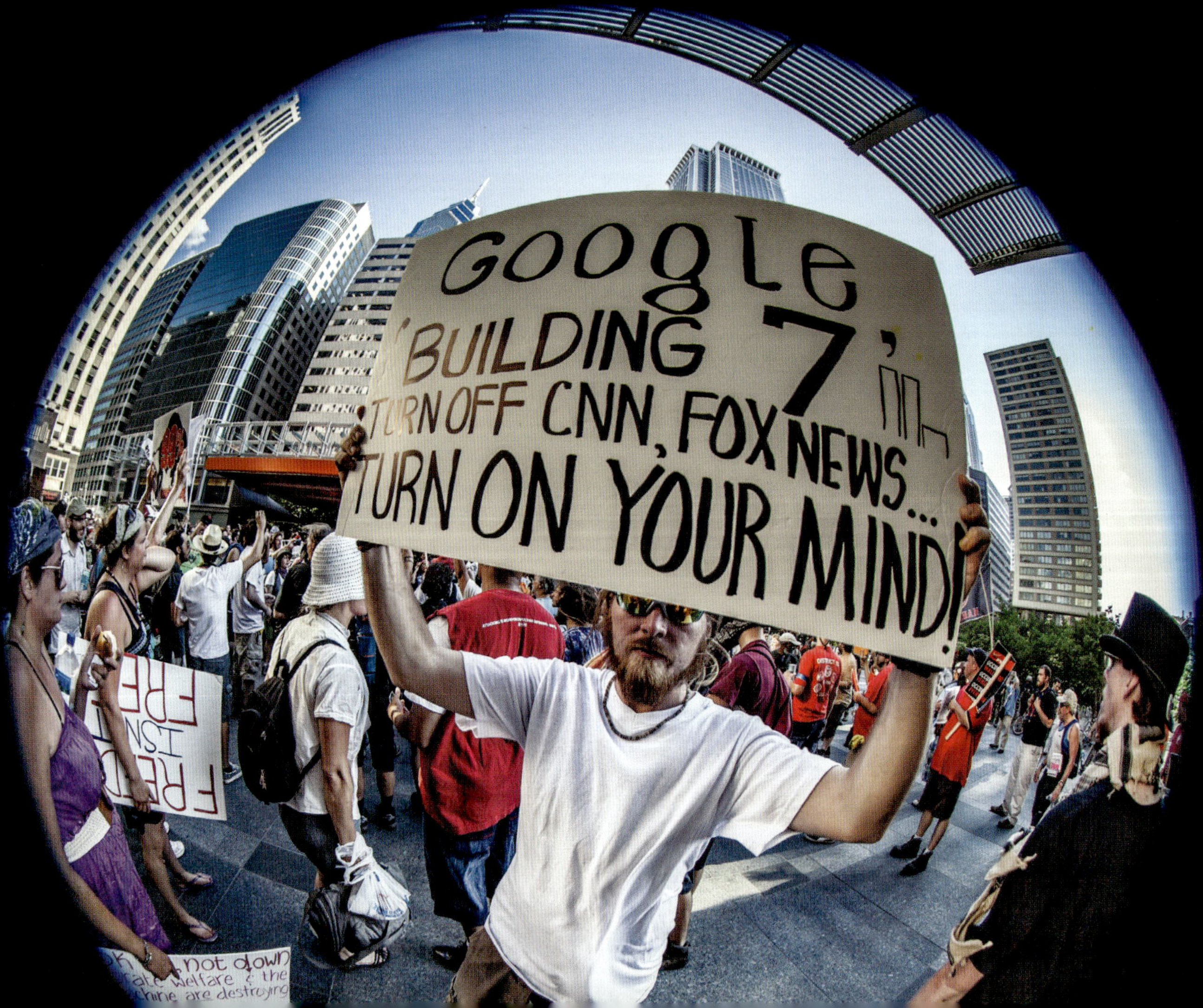

Google
'BUILDING 7'
TURN OFF CNN, FOX NEWS...
TURN ON YOUR MIND!
FREEDOM
ISN'T
FREE

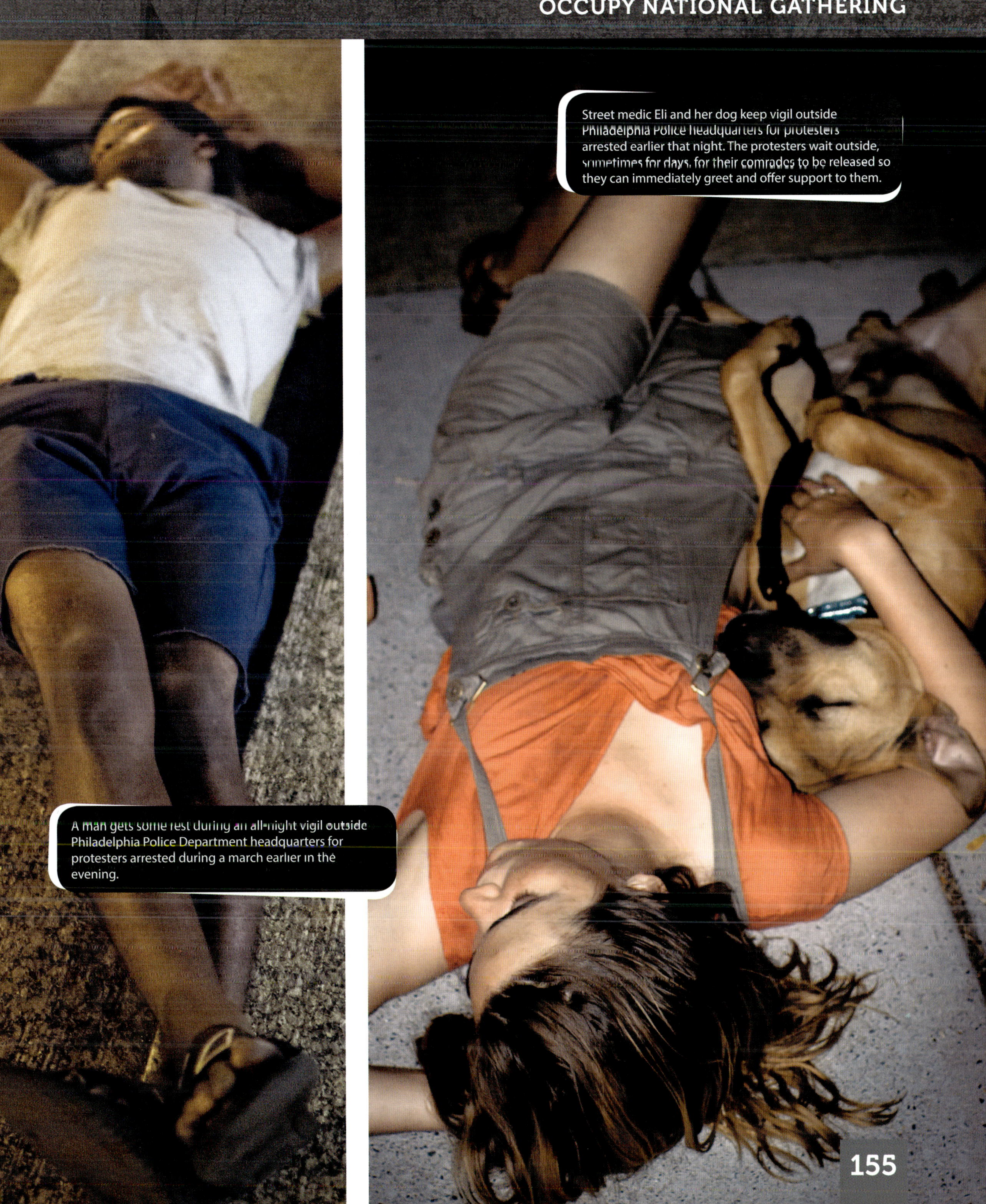

Street medic Eli and her dog keep vigil outside Philadelphia Police headquarters for protesters arrested earlier that night. The protesters wait outside, sometimes for days, for their comrades to be released so they can immediately greet and offer support to them.

A man gets some rest during an all-night vigil outside Philadelphia Police Department headquarters for protesters arrested during a march earlier in the evening.

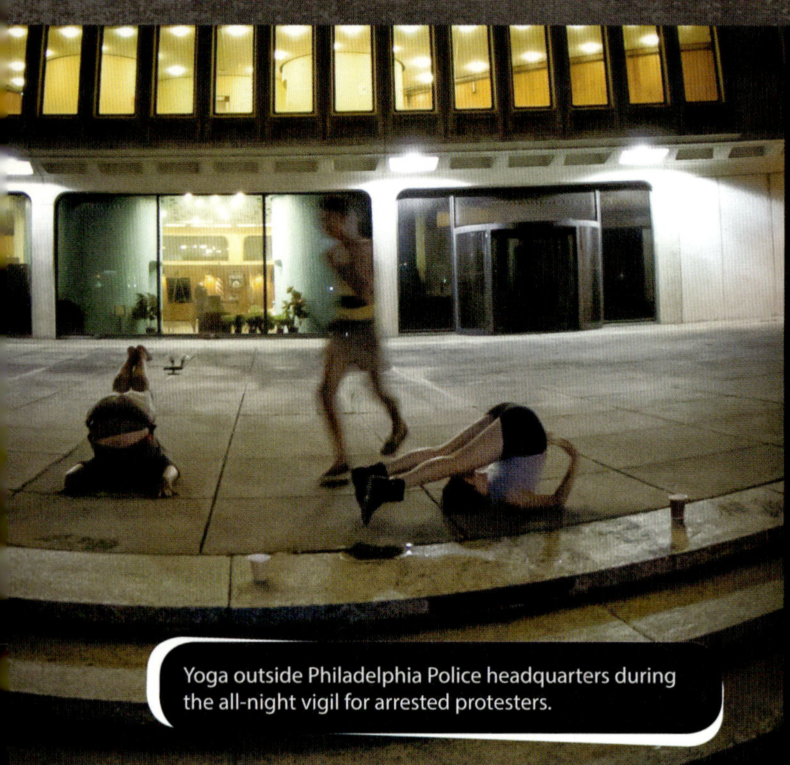

Yoga outside Philadelphia Police headquarters during the all-night vigil for arrested protesters.

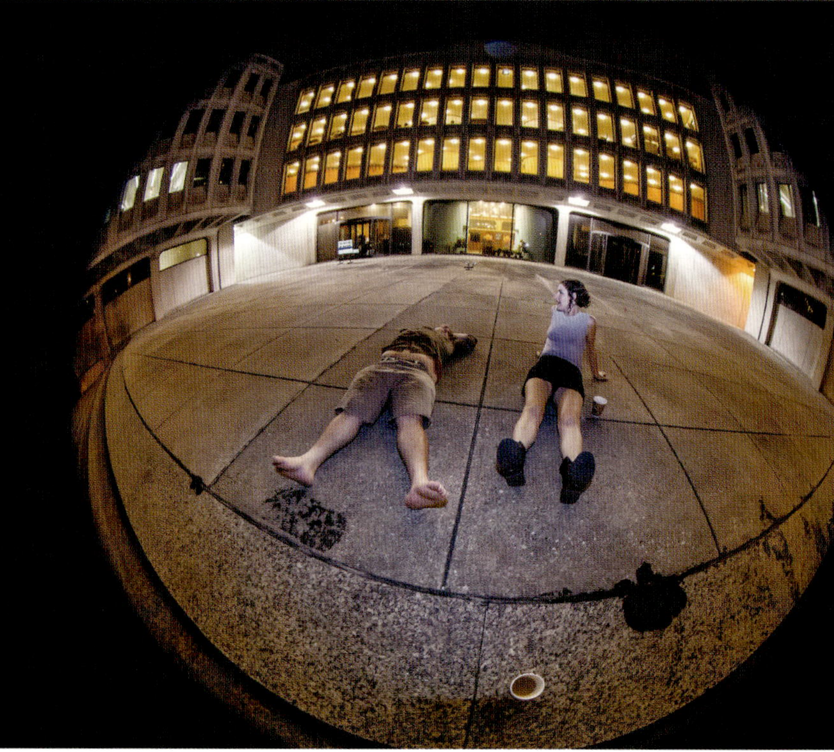

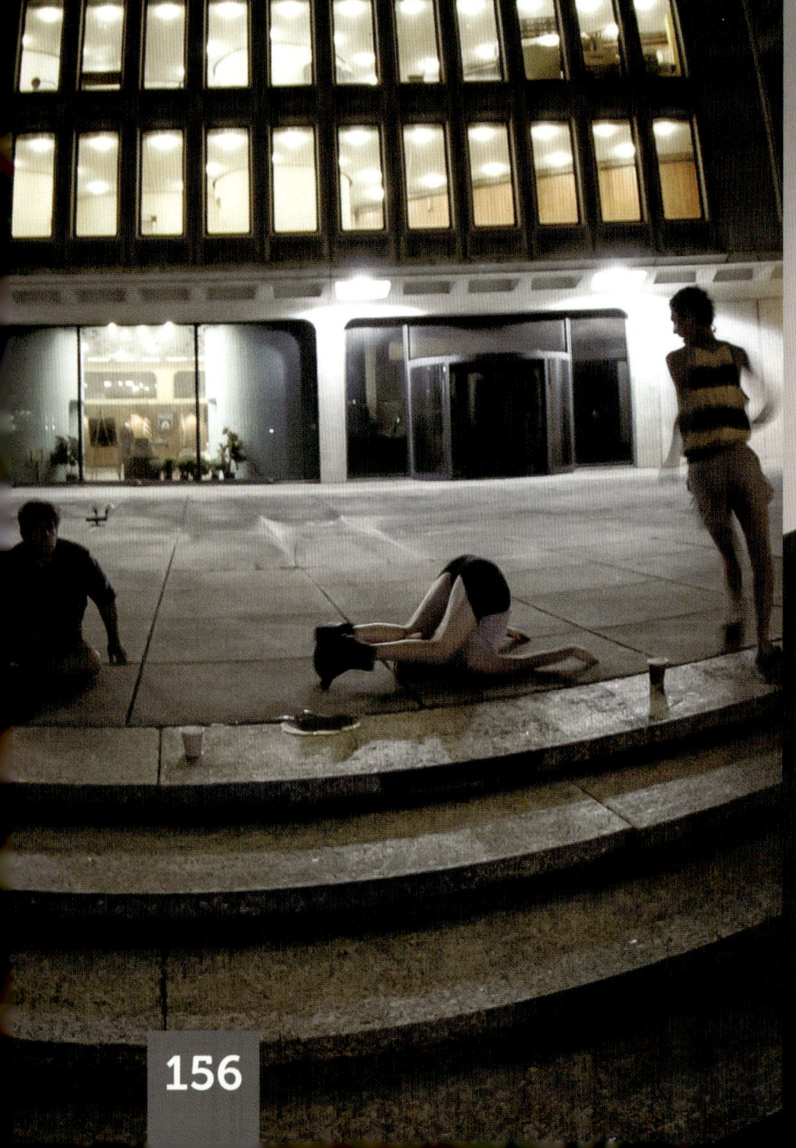

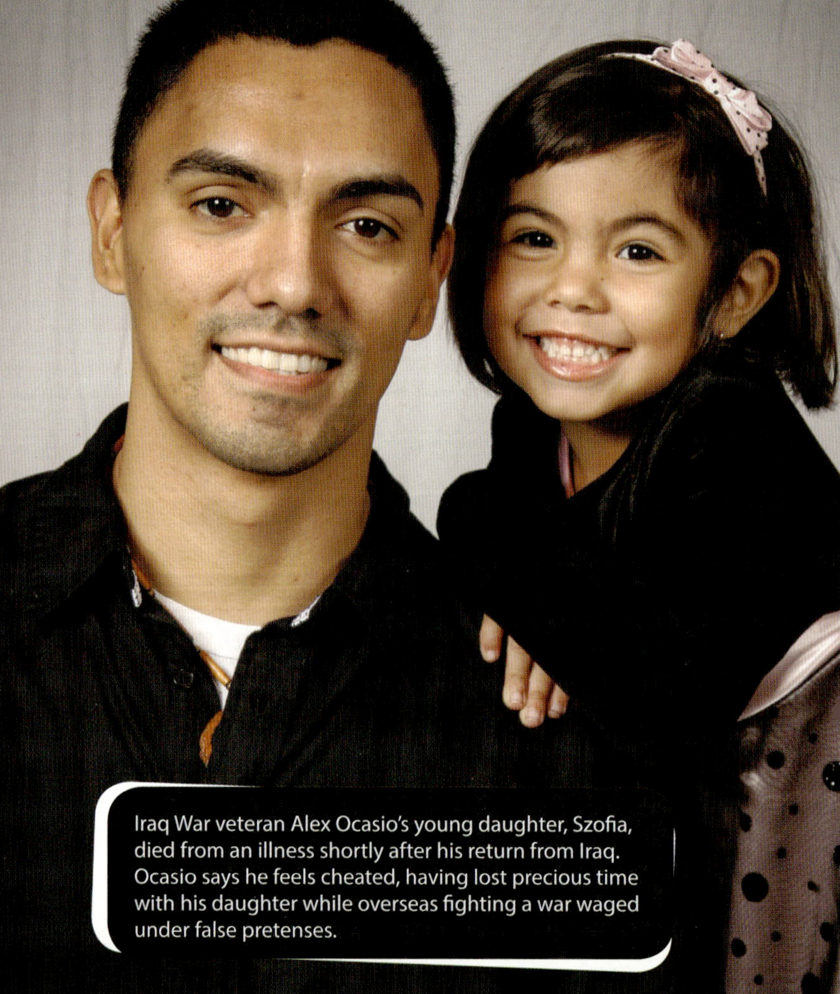

Iraq War veteran Alex Ocasio's young daughter, Szofia, died from an illness shortly after his return from Iraq. Ocasio says he feels cheated, having lost precious time with his daughter while overseas fighting a war waged under false pretenses.

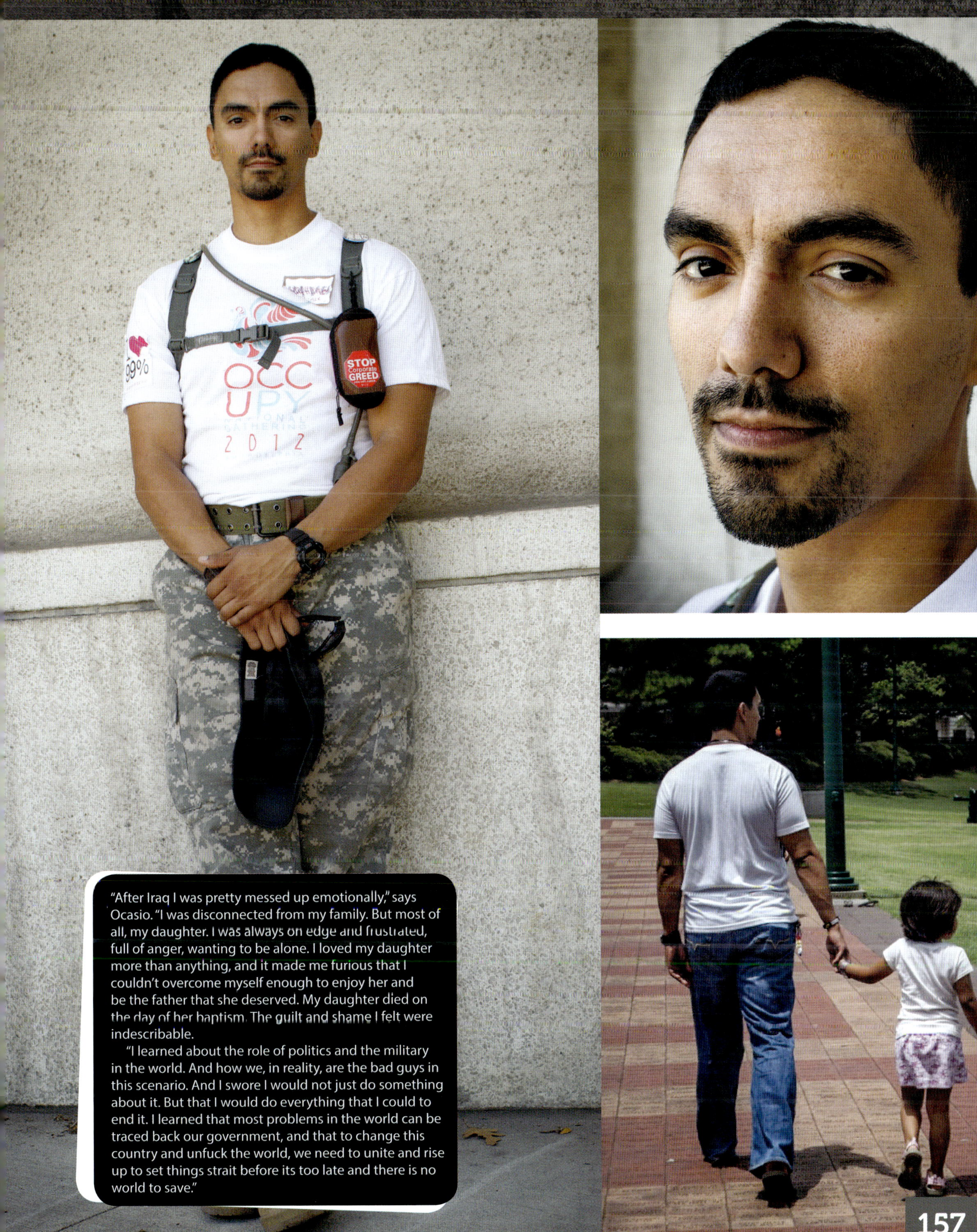

"After Iraq I was pretty messed up emotionally," says Ocasio. "I was disconnected from my family. But most of all, my daughter. I was always on edge and frustrated, full of anger, wanting to be alone. I loved my daughter more than anything, and it made me furious that I couldn't overcome myself enough to enjoy her and be the father that she deserved. My daughter died on the day of her baptism. The guilt and shame I felt were indescribable.

"I learned about the role of politics and the military in the world. And how we, in reality, are the bad guys in this scenario. And I swore I would not just do something about it. But that I would do everything that I could to end it. I learned that most problems in the world can be traced back our government, and that to change this country and unfuck the world, we need to unite and rise up to set things strait before its too late and there is no world to save."

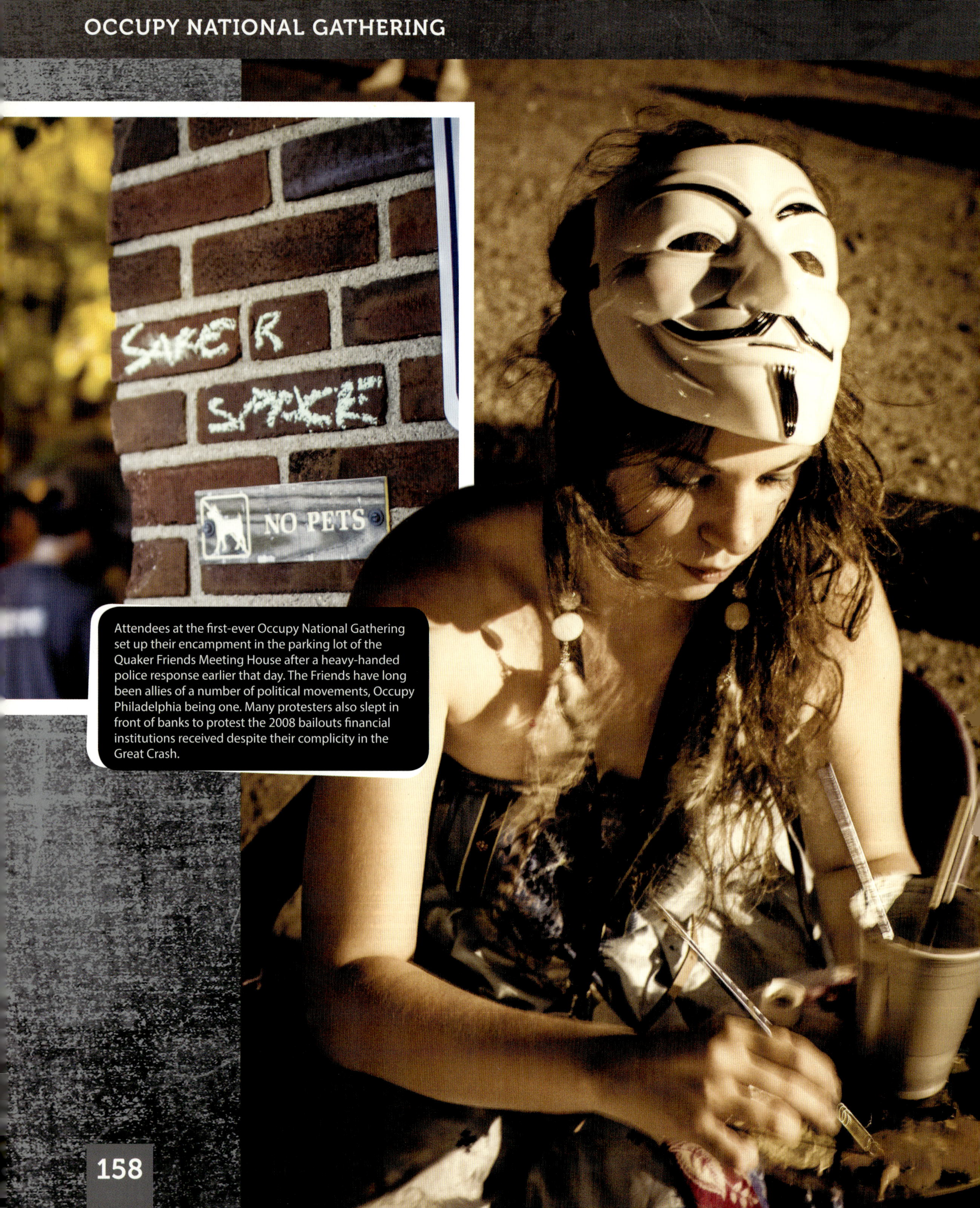

Attendees at the first-ever Occupy National Gathering set up their encampment in the parking lot of the Quaker Friends Meeting House after a heavy-handed police response earlier that day. The Friends have long been allies of a number of political movements, Occupy Philadelphia being one. Many protesters also slept in front of banks to protest the 2008 bailouts financial institutions received despite their complicity in the Great Crash.

A woman paints a picture of the Internet collective known as Anonymous.

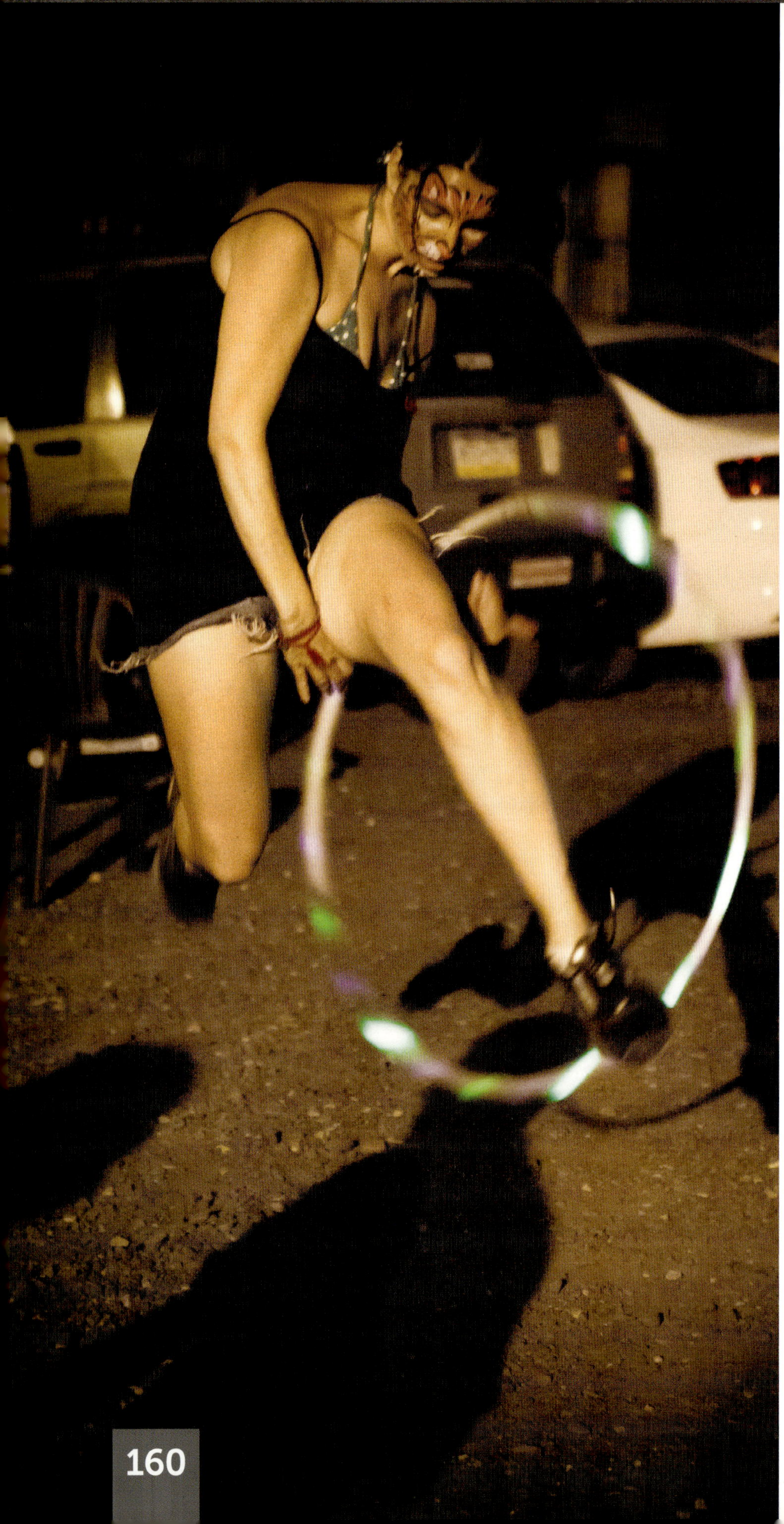

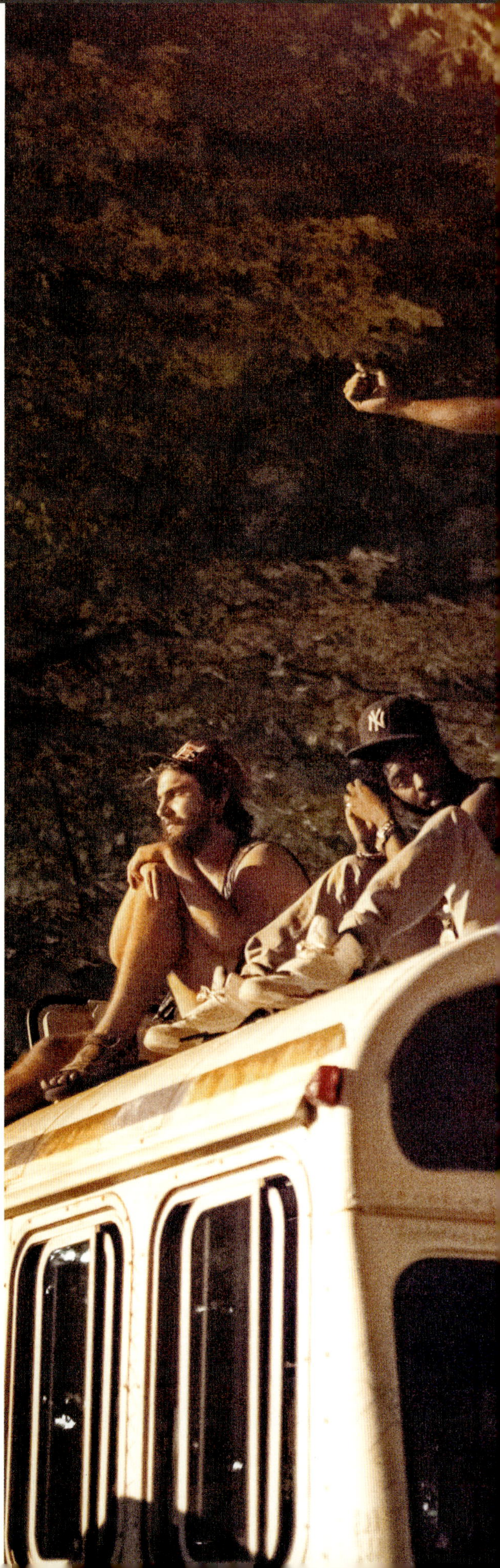

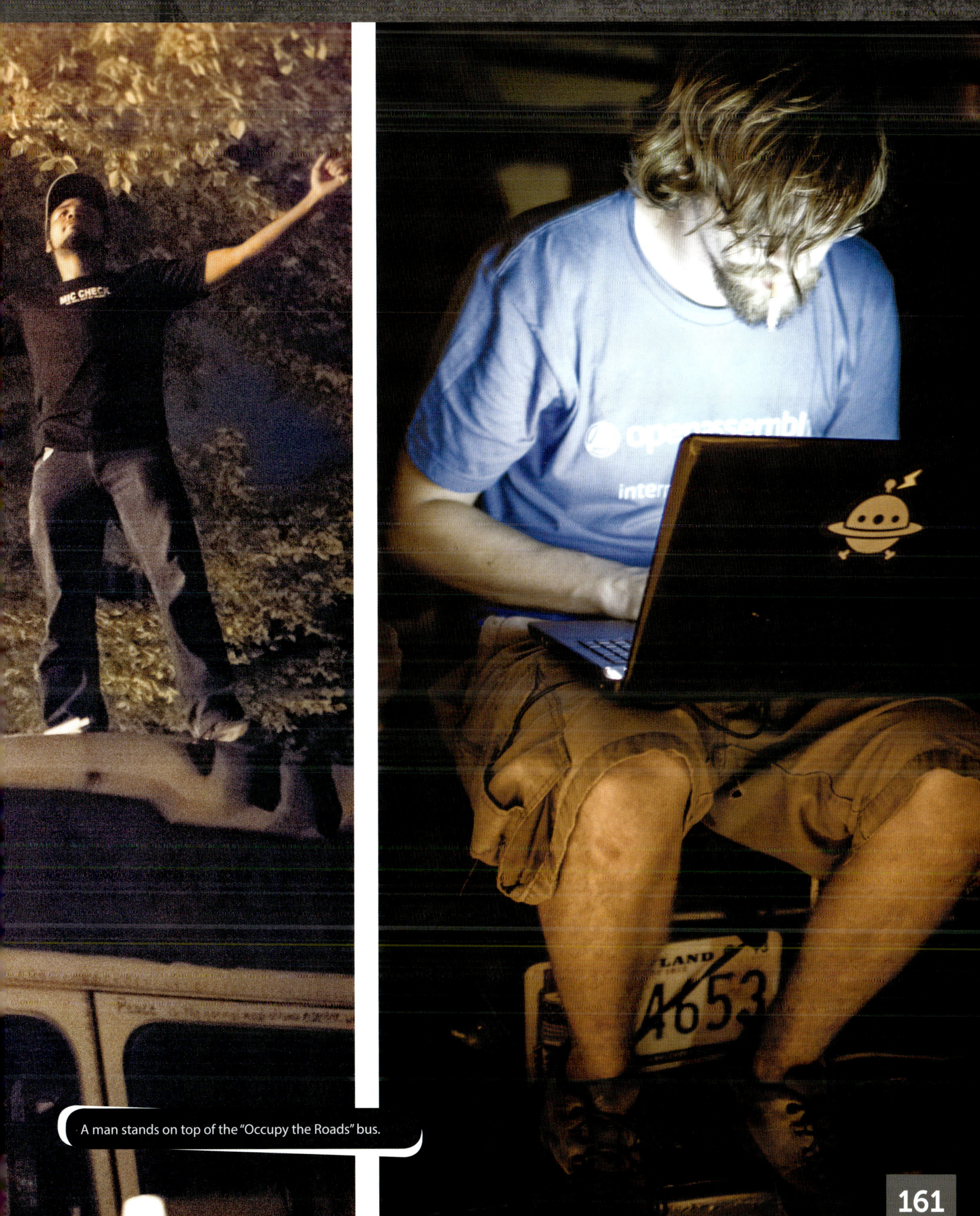

A man stands on top of the "Occupy the Roads" bus.

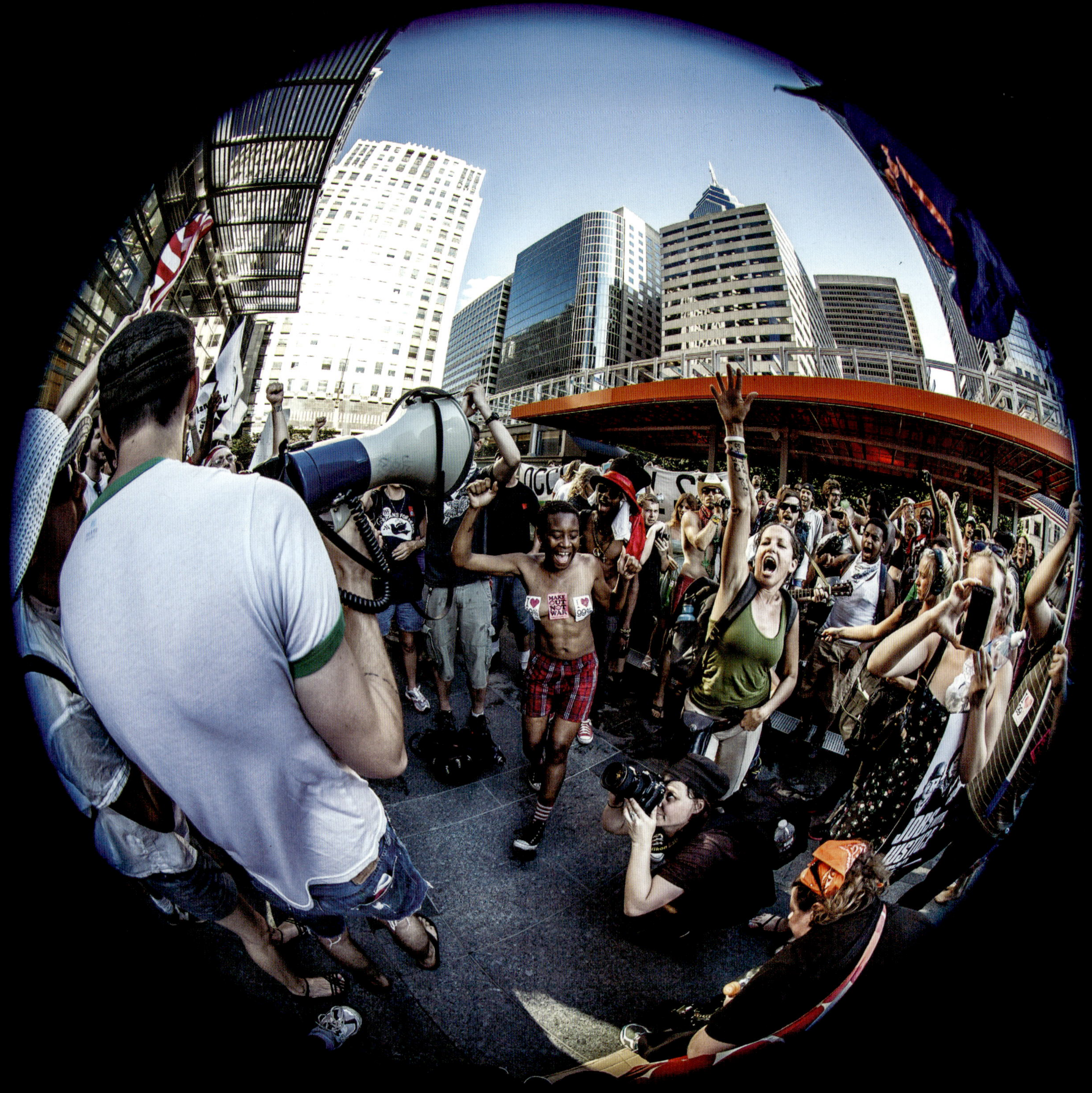

A man with a bullhorn rallies protesters outside of Comcast's corporate headquarters in downtown Philadelphia to cry foul on the corporation's history of avoiding corporate taxes.

The Keystone Pipeline Protest

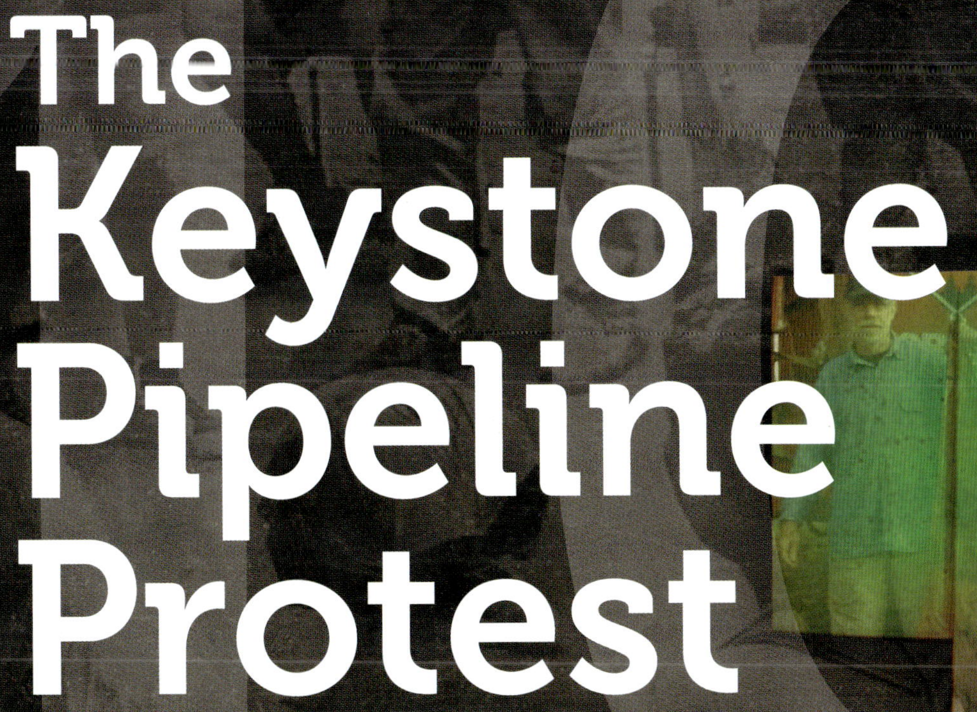

Protesters in East Texas are using direct-action tactics and putting their bodies in harm's way in a dramatic last-ditch effort to slow down or halt construction of the Keystone Pipeline. The activists and residents fear the pipeline will pollute their groundwater or lead to a devastating oil spill, so they're building tree forts to stop ground-clearing efforts, while others are chaining themselves to equipment to stop the onslaught of heavy machinery.

Beginning in 2011, opposition against the expansion of the Keystone Pipeline System began in the form of petitions and protests throughout the United States by various landowners and environmental groups. The Keystone Pipeline System currently transports synthetic crude oil from Hardisty, Alberta, Canada, to refineries and oil hubs throughout the United States.

The expansion project, proposed by Keystone Pipeline owner TransCanada Corporation, includes constructing additional branches of the pipeline. The Cushing MarketLink addition would mean expanding the pipeline from Cushing, Oklahoma, to gulf ports near Port Arthur, Texas. The other expansion, much larger in scale, would begin at the pipeline's current starting point in Alberta, Canada, and end in Steele City, Nebraska.

Opponents of the pipeline additions include various environmental groups, such as the Sierra Club, the National Wildlife Federation, and Greenpeace. The pipeline's original proposal included a portion that would cross a large portion of the Ogallala Aquifer, one of the world's largest reserves of freshwater. The Ogallala spans 174,000 square miles, supplies 30 percent of the United States' total irrigation water, and provides up to 82 percent of the drinking water for 2.3 million Americans. Additional portions of the pipeline involve construction in the Sandhills of Nebraska, the largest wetland ecosystem in the United States. Accord-

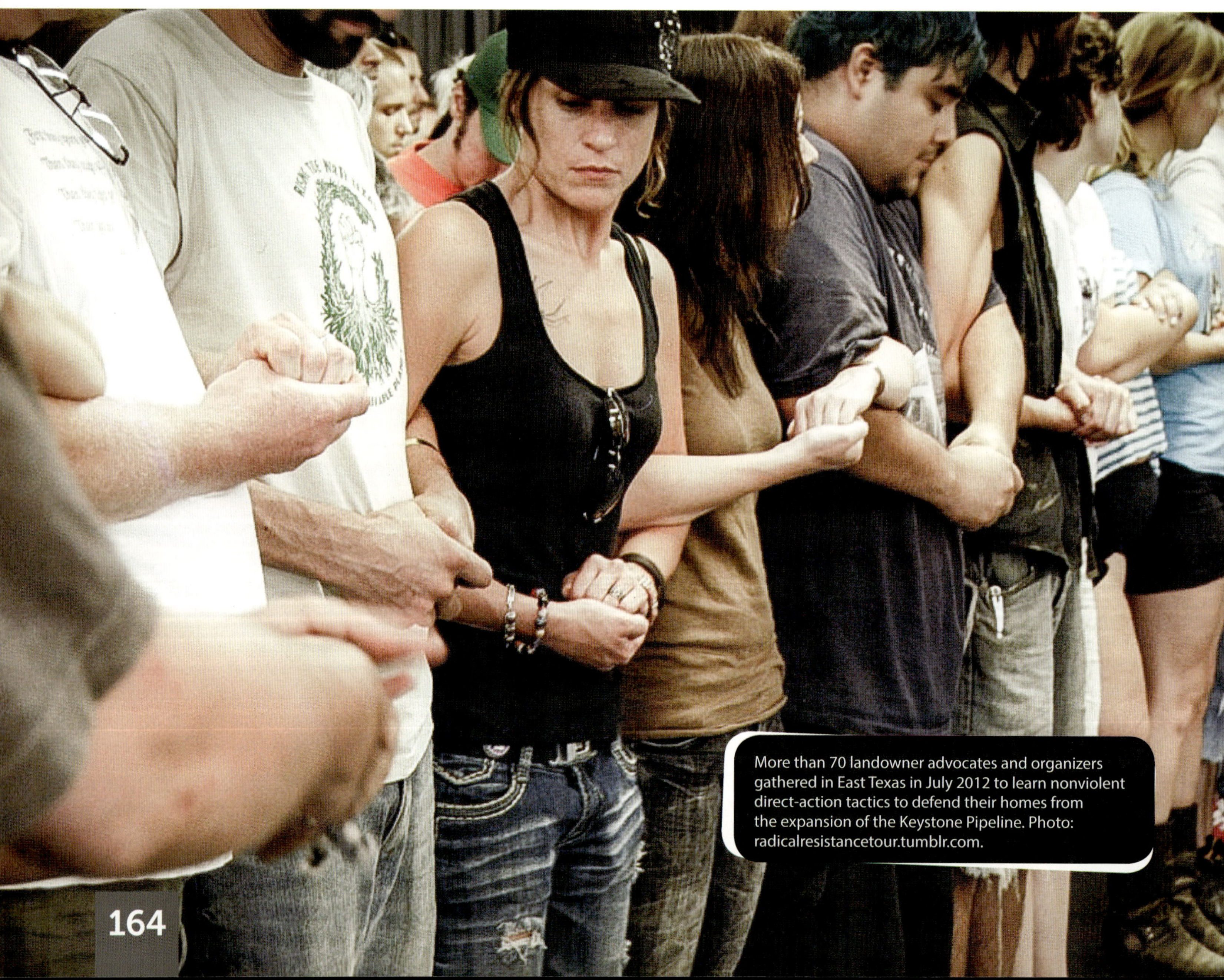

More than 70 landowner advocates and organizers gathered in East Texas in July 2012 to learn nonviolent direct-action tactics to defend their homes from the expansion of the Keystone Pipeline. Photo: radicalresistancetour.tumblr.com.

ing to the World Wildlife Fund, as much as 85% of the Sandhills is an intact natural ecoregion.

Direct-action protests have also occurred throughout the state of Texas, where landowners have been faced with eminent-domain lawsuits by TransCanada Corporation. Residents have claimed the corporation has used harassment and aggressive tactics to obtain their property for the use of pipeline construction. Activists from throughout the United States have converged in Texas, building camps and holding civil-disobedience training in hopes of stopping or delaying pipeline construction.

In October of 2012, protesters from a range of ages and socioeconomic status built temporary "forts" in the tops of trees in Winnsboro, Texas, that had been designated to be cleared for the pipeline. Texas residents claim that lawsuits seeking eminent domain of their property are illegal because construction of the Keystone XL pipeline in that region hadn't yet received federal approval. On October 11, *New York Times* reporter Dan Frosch and freelance photographer Brandon Thibodeaux were also threatened with arrest by police and TransCanada Corporation security while attempting to cover the event. Photos by TarSandsBlockade.org unless othrwise noted.

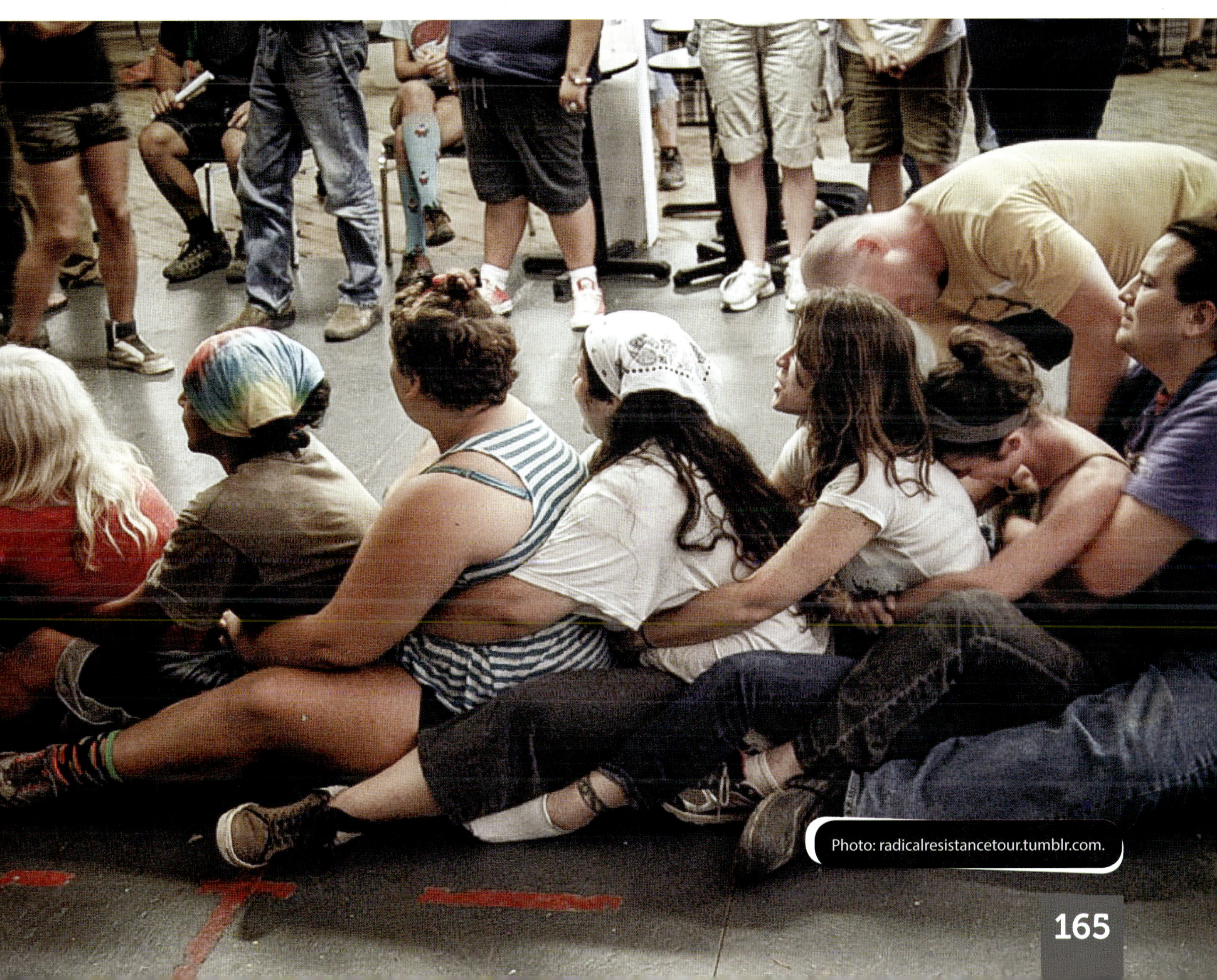

Photo: radicalresistancetour.tumblr.com.

A human blockade position known as the "turtle." Activists say the locking of arms makes it more difficult for authorities to clear the protesters and make arrests.

Protesters are practicing a method of body blockade called "the octopus."

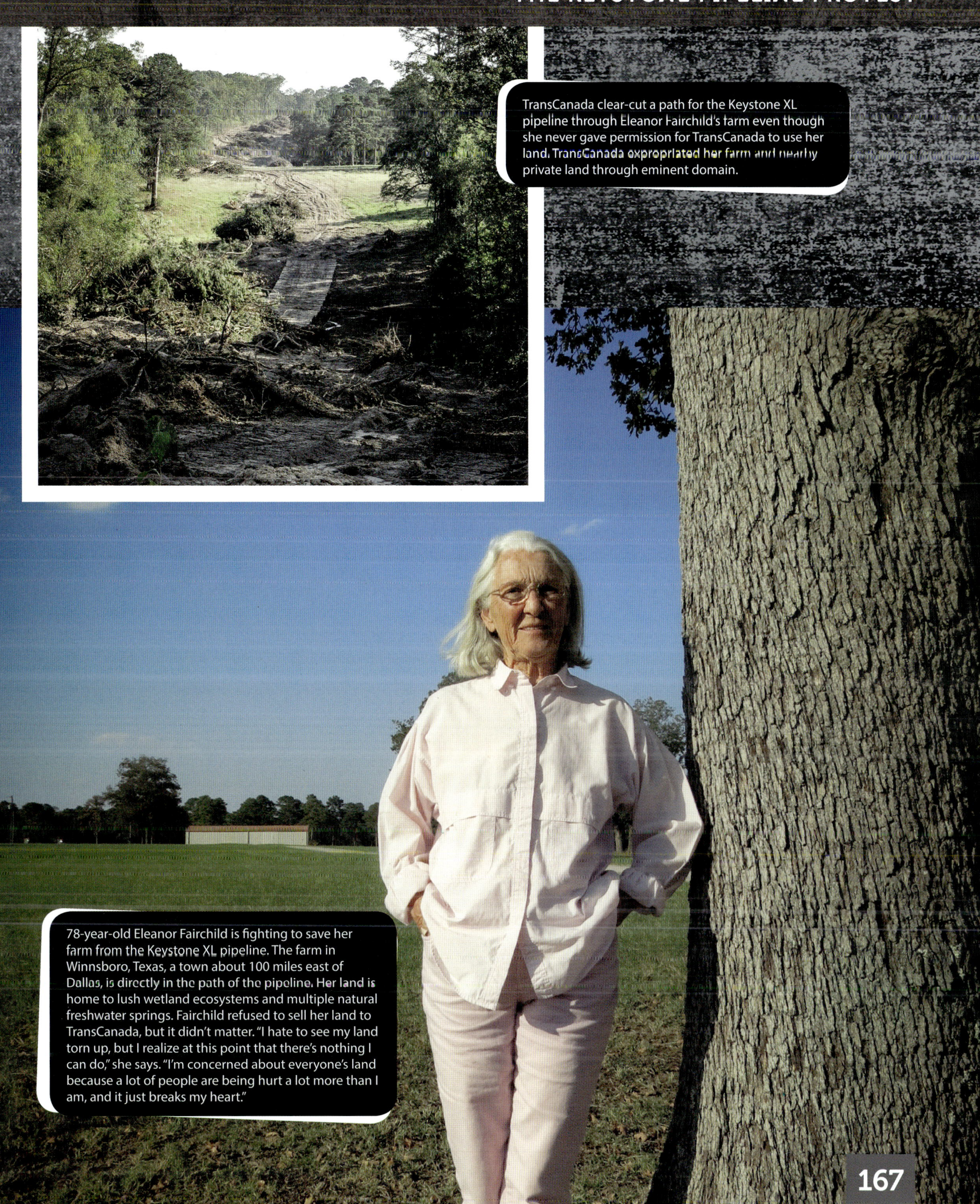

TransCanada clear-cut a path for the Keystone XL pipeline through Eleanor Fairchild's farm even though she never gave permission for TransCanada to use her land. TransCanada expropriated her farm and nearby private land through eminent domain.

78-year-old Eleanor Fairchild is fighting to save her farm from the Keystone XL pipeline. The farm in Winnsboro, Texas, a town about 100 miles east of Dallas, is directly in the path of the pipeline. Her land is home to lush wetland ecosystems and multiple natural freshwater springs. Fairchild refused to sell her land to TransCanada, but it didn't matter. "I hate to see my land torn up, but I realize at this point that there's nothing I can do," she says. "I'm concerned about everyone's land because a lot of people are being hurt a lot more than I am, and it just breaks my heart."

No contact Cutting Trees 9-29-12

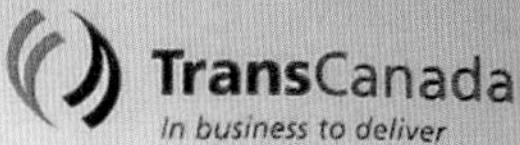

Gulf Coast Project
2700 Post Oak Blvd., Ste 400
Houston, TX 77056
1.866.585.7063
GulfCoastProject@TransCanada.com

August 17, 2012

Dear Landowner:

On July 16th, 2012 the U.S. Army Corps of Engineers issued the third and final permit needed to start construction of TransCanada's Gulf Coast Project. We are writing to provide you with more information on this development and to confirm that construction of the 485-mile pipeline project will begin in the coming weeks.

Building the Gulf Coast Project will follow a phased approach, with thousands of workers involved in construction of the pipeline mobilizing to multiple locations over the next several months. In many ways, construction of the Gulf Coast Project will be like an assembly line in which one crew follows another down the right of way to build a pipeline utilizing the latest materials and technologies to meet or exceed all safety standards and regulations.

Before work begins on your property, we will contact you to make you aware that work is approaching, provide more details, and answer any questions you might have. Of course, you are always welcome to contact us at the following regional offices:

Holdenville Office Spread 1
Jeremy Capuccio - Supervisor
225 Kingberry Road
Holdenville, OK 74848
405-379-9350

Tyler Office Spread 2
Don Davis – Supervisor
3200 Troup Hwy.
Suite 336
Tyler, TX 75701
903-533-0201

Sour Lake Spread 3
Lisa Chavers – Supervisor
420 Hwy. 105 East
Sour Lake, TX 77659
409-287-4400

The Gulf Coast Project Team looks forward to working with you during the construction of this important energy infrastructure project and invites you to contact us anytime if you have questions or concerns.

Sincerely,

Randy Hutson
An independent contractor to TransCanada,
Land Manager, Gulf Coast Project
rhutson@ufsrw.com

A letter TransCanada sent to Eleanor Fairchild to inform her that, regardless of whether they had her permission, they would begin tearing up her land. Fearing risks to her land and her health, Fairchild had refused to sell her land to TransCanada. The letter, dated August 17, 2012, states, "Before work begins on your property, we will contact you to make you aware that work is approaching, provide more details, and answer any questions you might have." But Fairchild says on August 29, 2012, TransCanada's heavy equipment arrived without warning and began tearing up her farm.

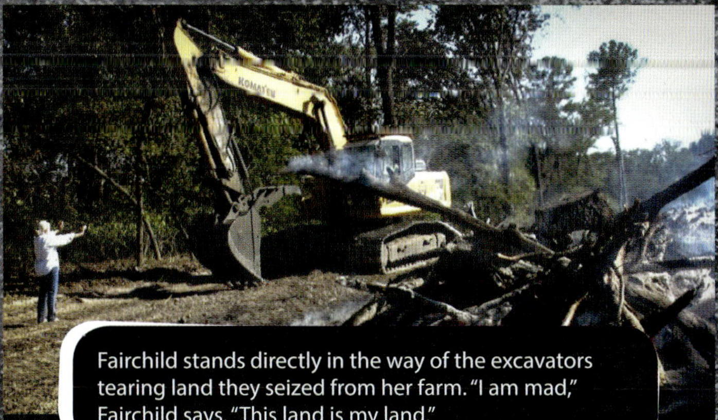

Fairchild stands directly in the way of the excavators tearing land they seized from her farm. "I am mad," Fairchild says. "This land is my land."

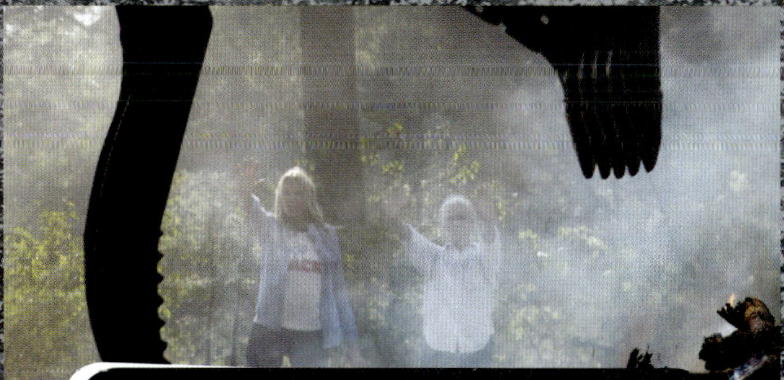

Activist and actress Darryl Hannah joins Eleanor Fairchild. The two stand in the way of the machinery to attempt to prevent it from moving forward and clear-cutting more land.

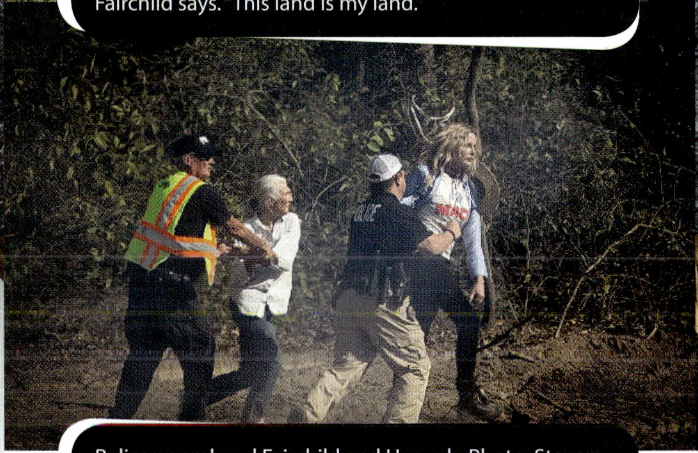

Police apprehend Fairchild and Hannah. Photo: Steven DaSilva.

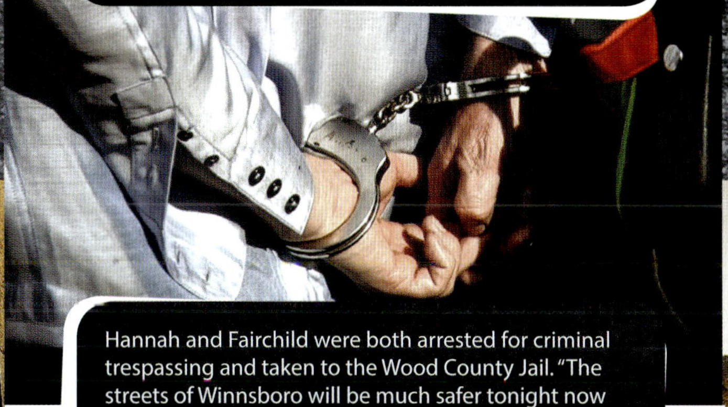

Hannah and Fairchild were both arrested for criminal trespassing and taken to the Wood County Jail. "The streets of Winnsboro will be much safer tonight now that they've gotten that 78-year-old great-grandmother off the streets," Hannah's manager, Paul Bassis, said.

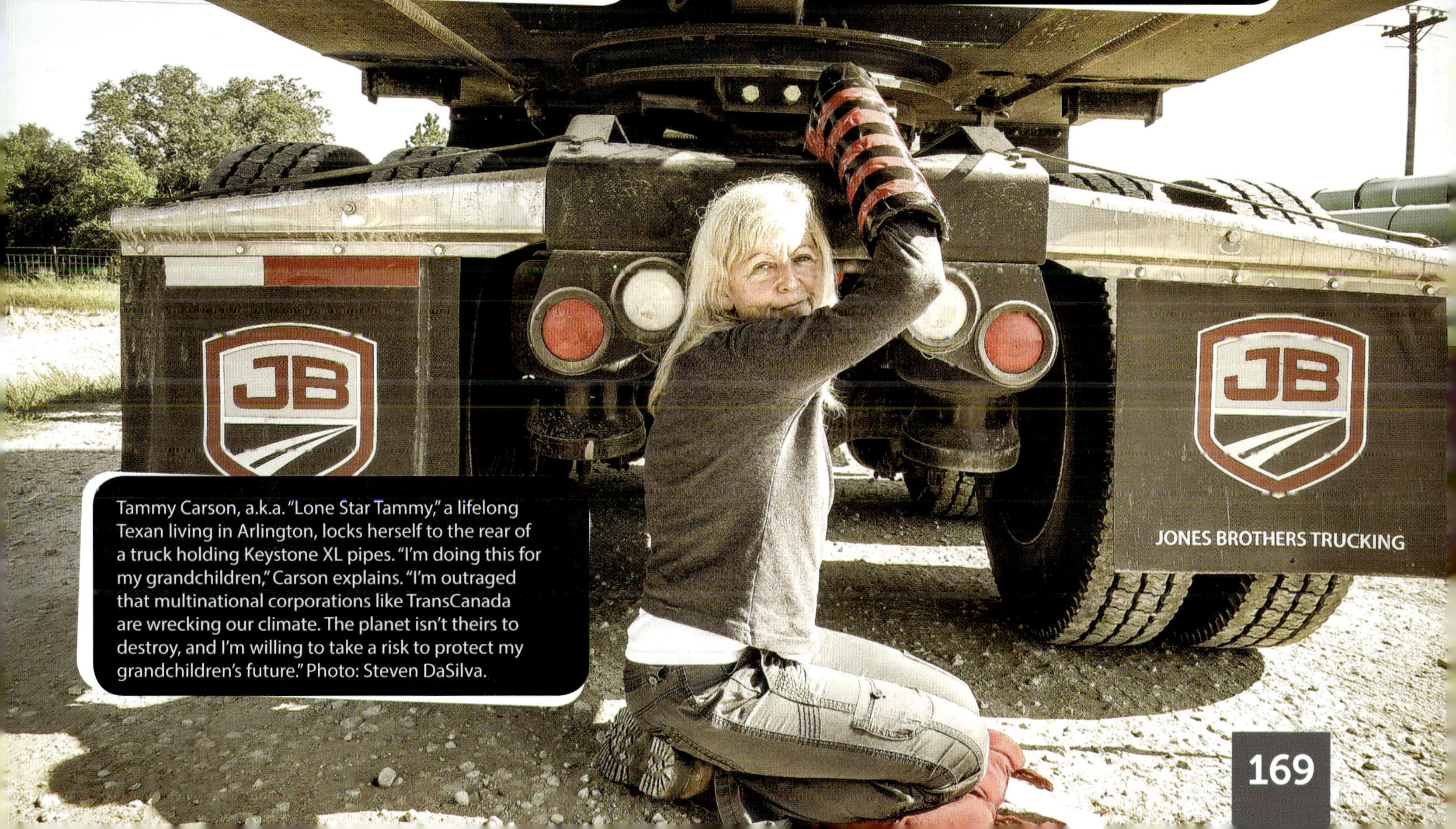

JB

JONES BROTHERS TRUCKING

Tammy Carson, a.k.a. "Lone Star Tammy," a lifelong Texan living in Arlington, locks herself to the rear of a truck holding Keystone XL pipes. "I'm doing this for my grandchildren," Carson explains. "I'm outraged that multinational corporations like TransCanada are wrecking our climate. The planet isn't theirs to destroy, and I'm willing to take a risk to protect my grandchildren's future." Photo: Steven DaSilva.

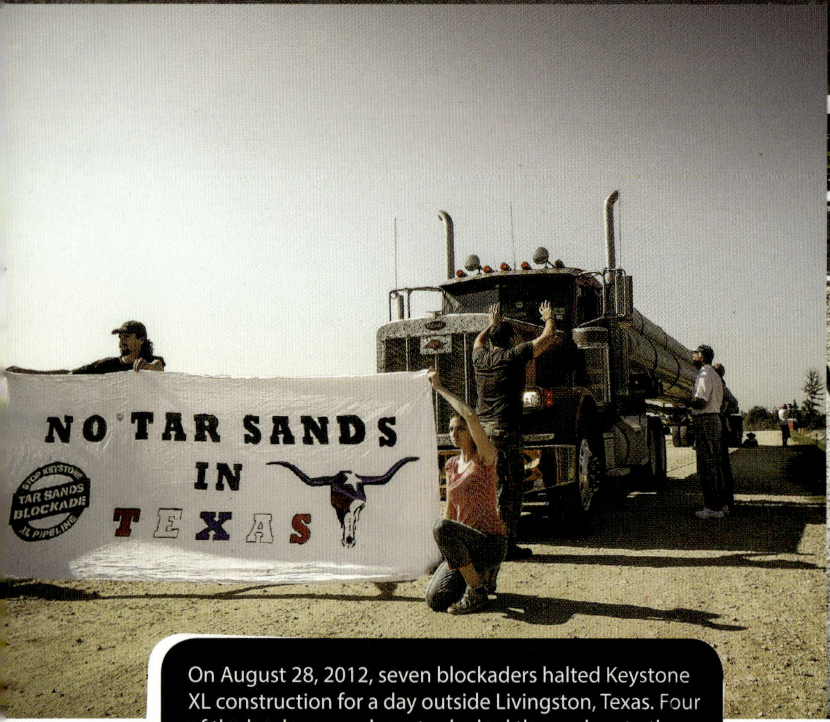

On August 28, 2012, seven blockaders halted Keystone XL construction for a day outside Livingston, Texas. Four of the landowner advocates locked themselves to the underside of a massive truck carrying 36" pipe intended for Keystone XL construction. They also successfully blocked the entrance of the pipeyard and rendered construction activity impossible until authorities were able to make arrests. Photo: Steven DaSilva.

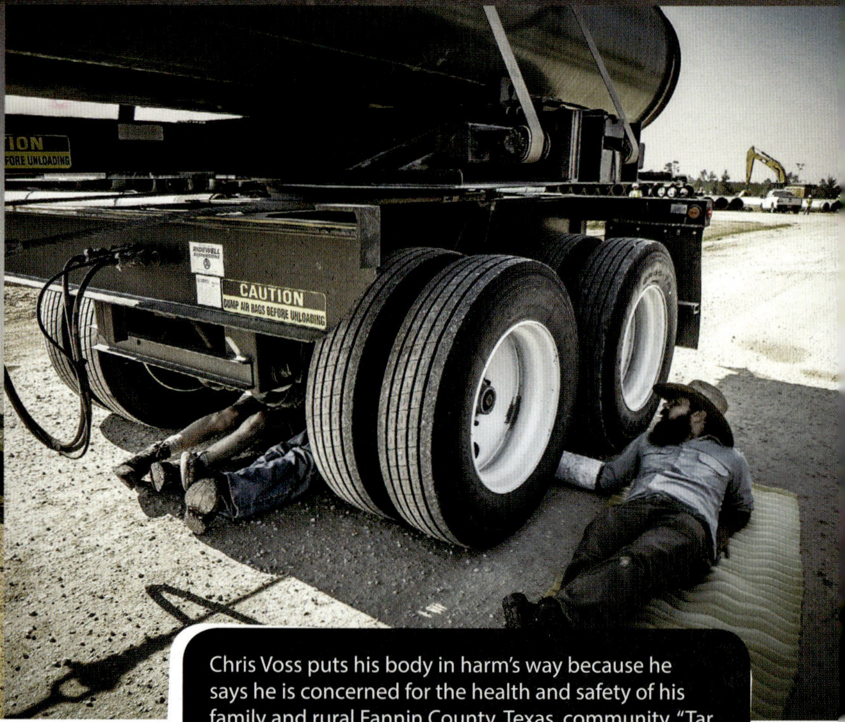

Chris Voss puts his body in harm's way because he says he is concerned for the health and safety of his family and rural Fannin County, Texas, community. "Tar sands pipelines have a terrifying history of leaks," Voss explains. "Keystone XL threatens our water, which is part of the commons. I can't just stand aside while our collective commons are being taken, controlled, and polluted." Photo: Steven DaSilva.

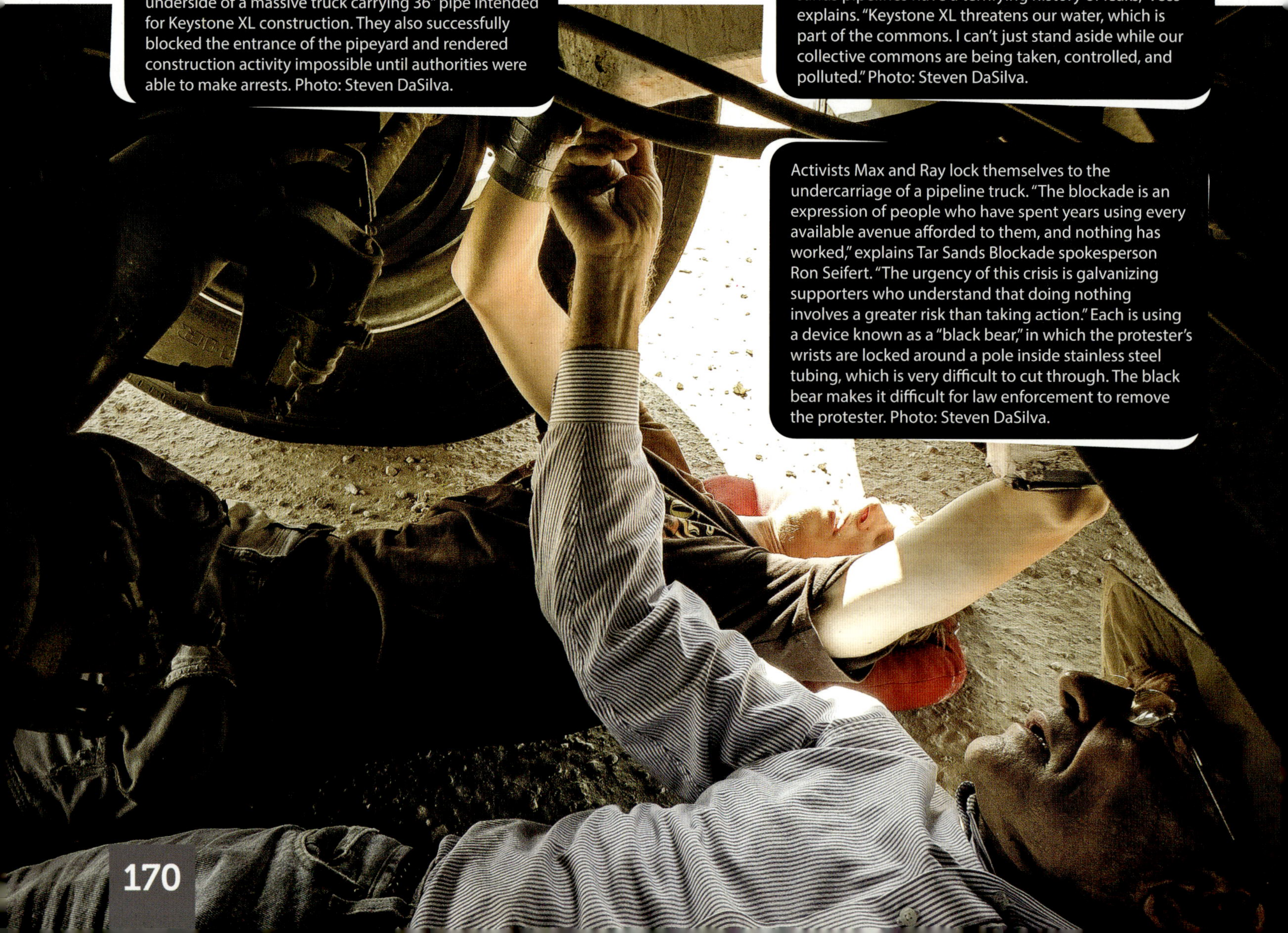

Activists Max and Ray lock themselves to the undercarriage of a pipeline truck. "The blockade is an expression of people who have spent years using every available avenue afforded to them, and nothing has worked," explains Tar Sands Blockade spokesperson Ron Seifert. "The urgency of this crisis is galvanizing supporters who understand that doing nothing involves a greater risk than taking action." Each is using a device known as a "black bear," in which the protester's wrists are locked around a pole inside stainless steel tubing, which is very difficult to cut through. The black bear makes it difficult for law enforcement to remove the protester. Photo: Steven DaSilva.

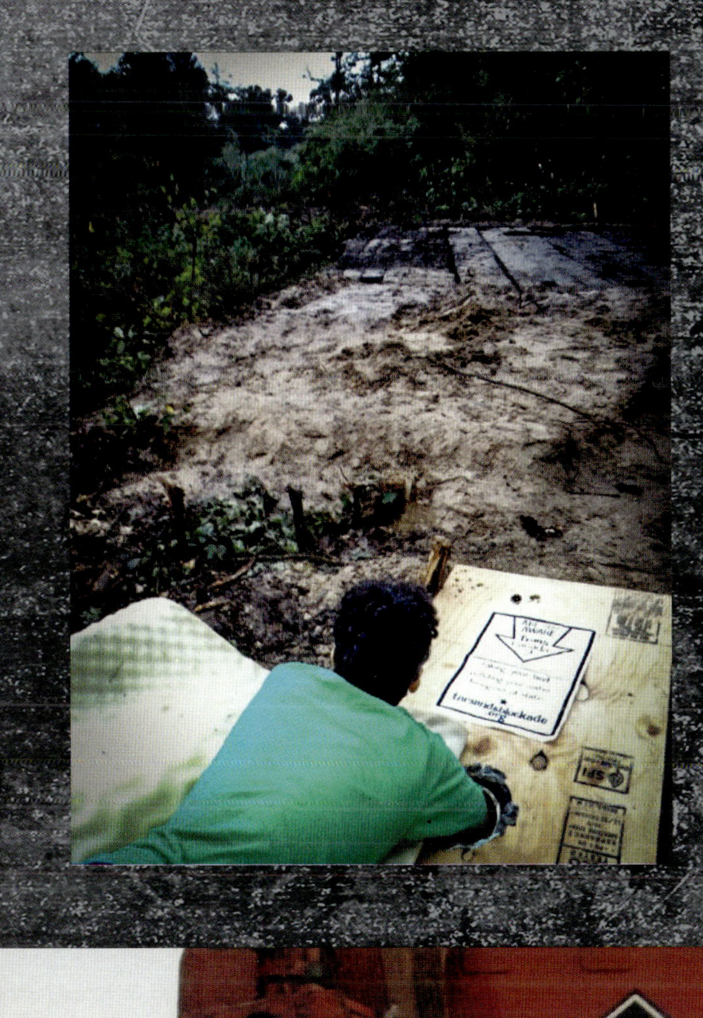

Houston resident Alejandro de la Torre locks his body to an underground capsule in the path of Keystone XL to protect a family farm from destruction. "I was raised in New Orleans, so I've seen how local communities suffer at the hands of multinational corporations," says de la Torre. "I'm willing to risk arrest today to stop this Tar Sands pipeline because I have the privilege to help protect the safety of those most affected. Keystone XL endangers the health and safety of everyone from the landowners and their families now threatened by cancer-causing leaks, to the refinery communities in Houston that have to breathe the dirty air, as well as people of color around the world who are disproportionately affected by climate change."

On September 19, 2012, in Winnsboro, Texas, three landowner advocates and climate justice organizers locked themselves to pieces of machinery critical for clear-cutting trees for construction of the Keystone XL pipeline. Their actions shut down construction for the morning.

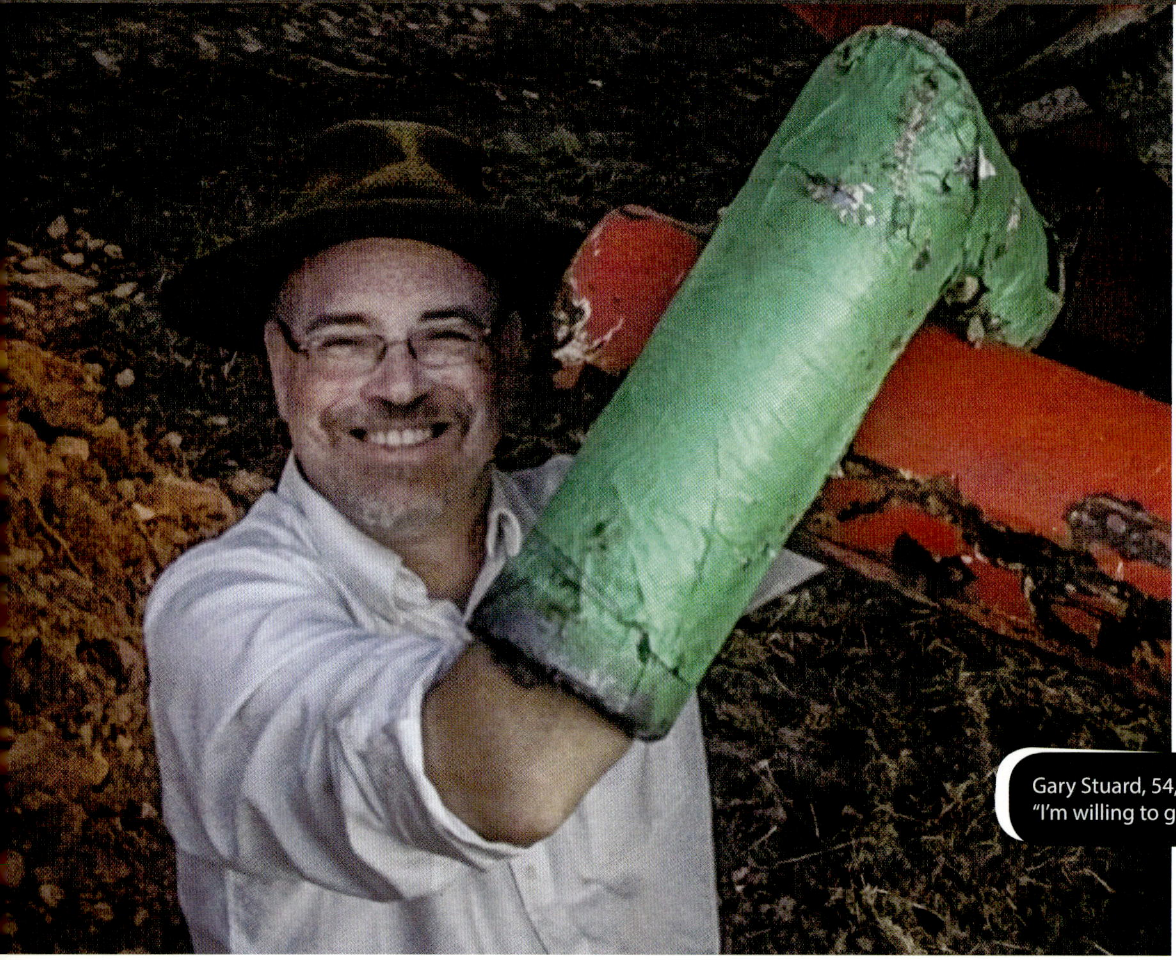

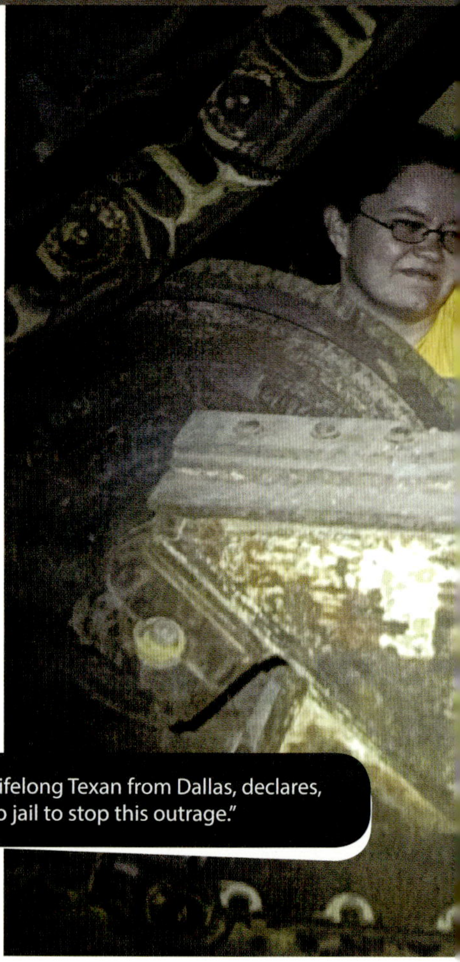

Gary Stuard, 54, a lifelong Texan from Dallas, declares, "I'm willing to go to jail to stop this outrage."

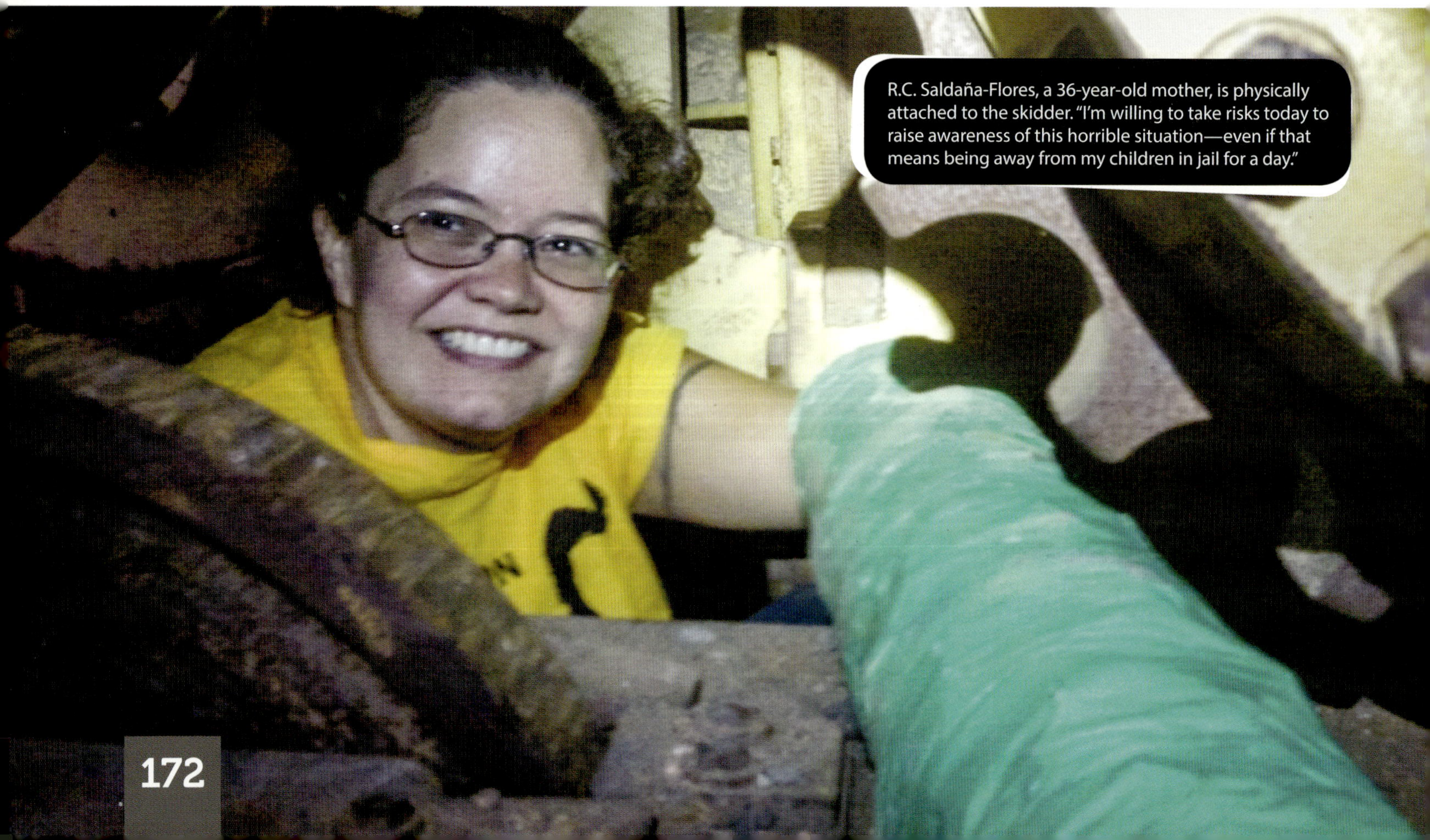

R.C. Saldaña-Flores, a 36-year-old mother, is physically attached to the skidder. "I'm willing to take risks today to raise awareness of this horrible situation—even if that means being away from my children in jail for a day."

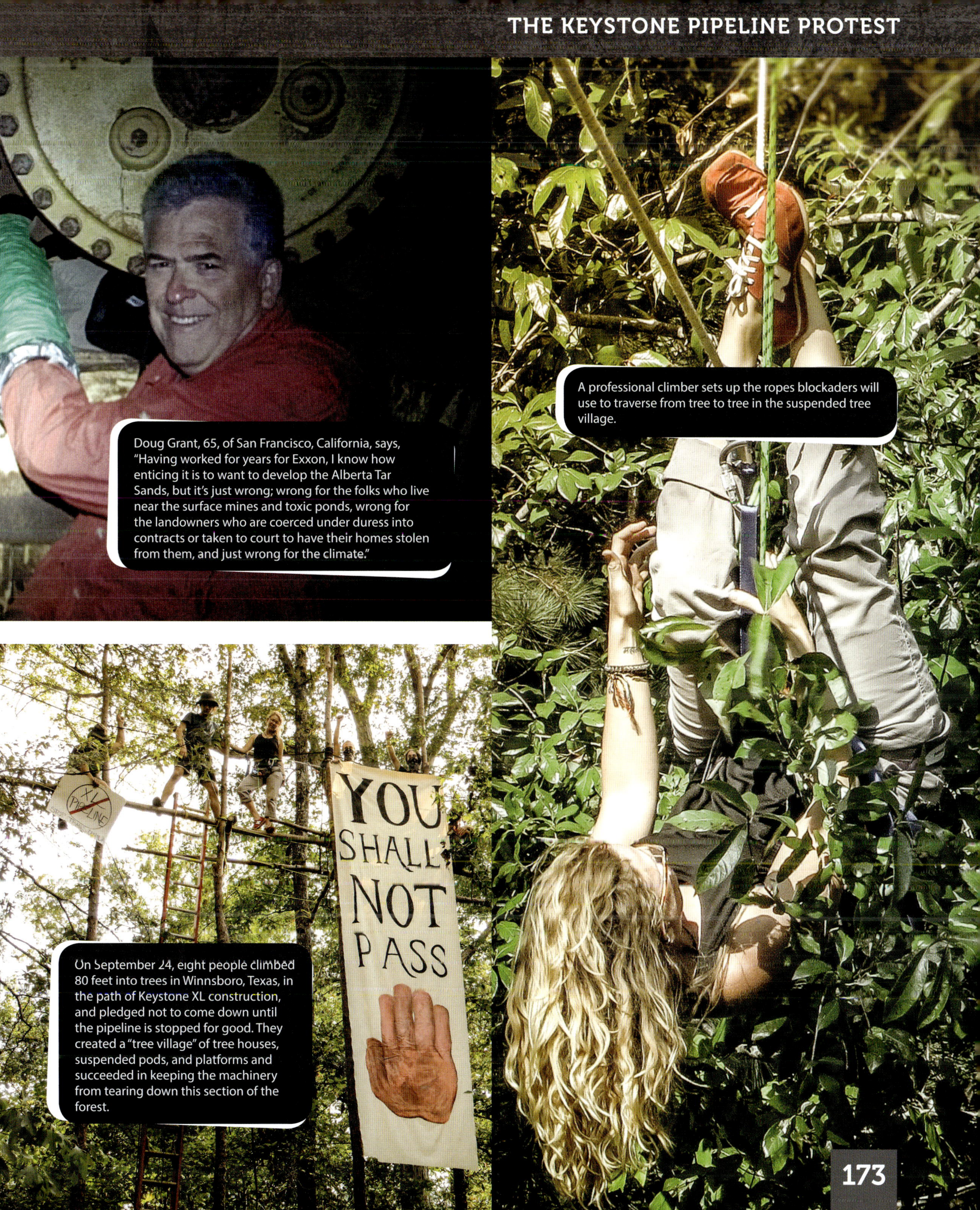

Doug Grant, 65, of San Francisco, California, says, “Having worked for years for Exxon, I know how enticing it is to want to develop the Alberta Tar Sands, but it’s just wrong; wrong for the folks who live near the surface mines and toxic ponds, wrong for the landowners who are coerced under duress into contracts or taken to court to have their homes stolen from them, and just wrong for the climate.”

A professional climber sets up the ropes blockaders will use to traverse from tree to tree in the suspended tree village.

On September 24, eight people climbed 80 feet into trees in Winnsboro, Texas, in the path of Keystone XL construction, and pledged not to come down until the pipeline is stopped for good. They created a “tree village” of tree houses, suspended pods, and platforms and succeeded in keeping the machinery from tearing down this section of the forest.

TransCanada clear-cuts the forest leading up to the doorstep of Tar Sands Blockade's tree village.

A tree sitter. Photo: Laura Borealis.

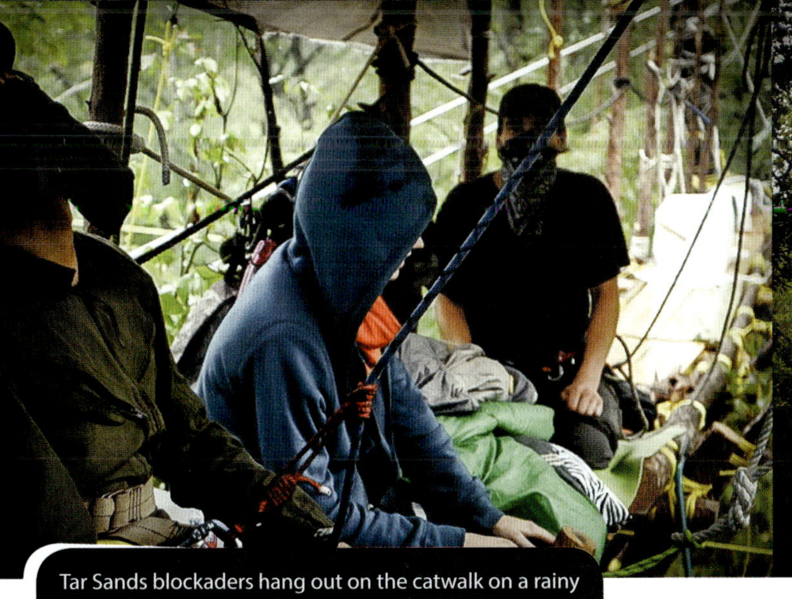

Tar Sands blockaders hang out on the catwalk on a rainy day. Photo: Laura Borealis.

The tree village consists of suspended pods and tree houses. This protester covers himself in a tarp in an attempt to stay dry during a rain shower.

"No jobs on a dead planet," warns this banner raised by the tree sitters.

A tree sitter rappels down the side of a tree to gather more supplies. Eventually, law enforcement surrounded the tree village and arrested the blockaders when they descended. Photo: Laura Borealis.

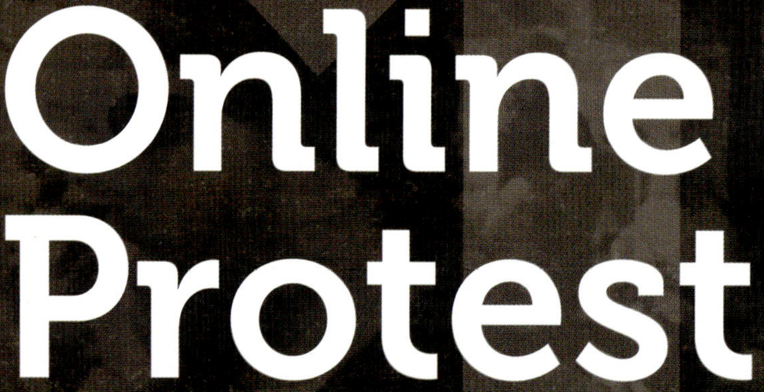

Online Protest

Protest has moved off of the streets and onto the web, and the incredible potential for online protest to galvanize and evoke swift change is frightening to the corrupt.

Online protest has come into its own, with platforms like Facebook and Twitter playing no small part in social movements ranging from Occupy Wall Street to the Arab Spring. While these movements use the Web to inspire individuals to participate as well as to disseminate information, the group that has truly spearheaded online activism is the "hacktivist" (from "hack," as in computer hacking, plus "activist") collective known as Anonymous.

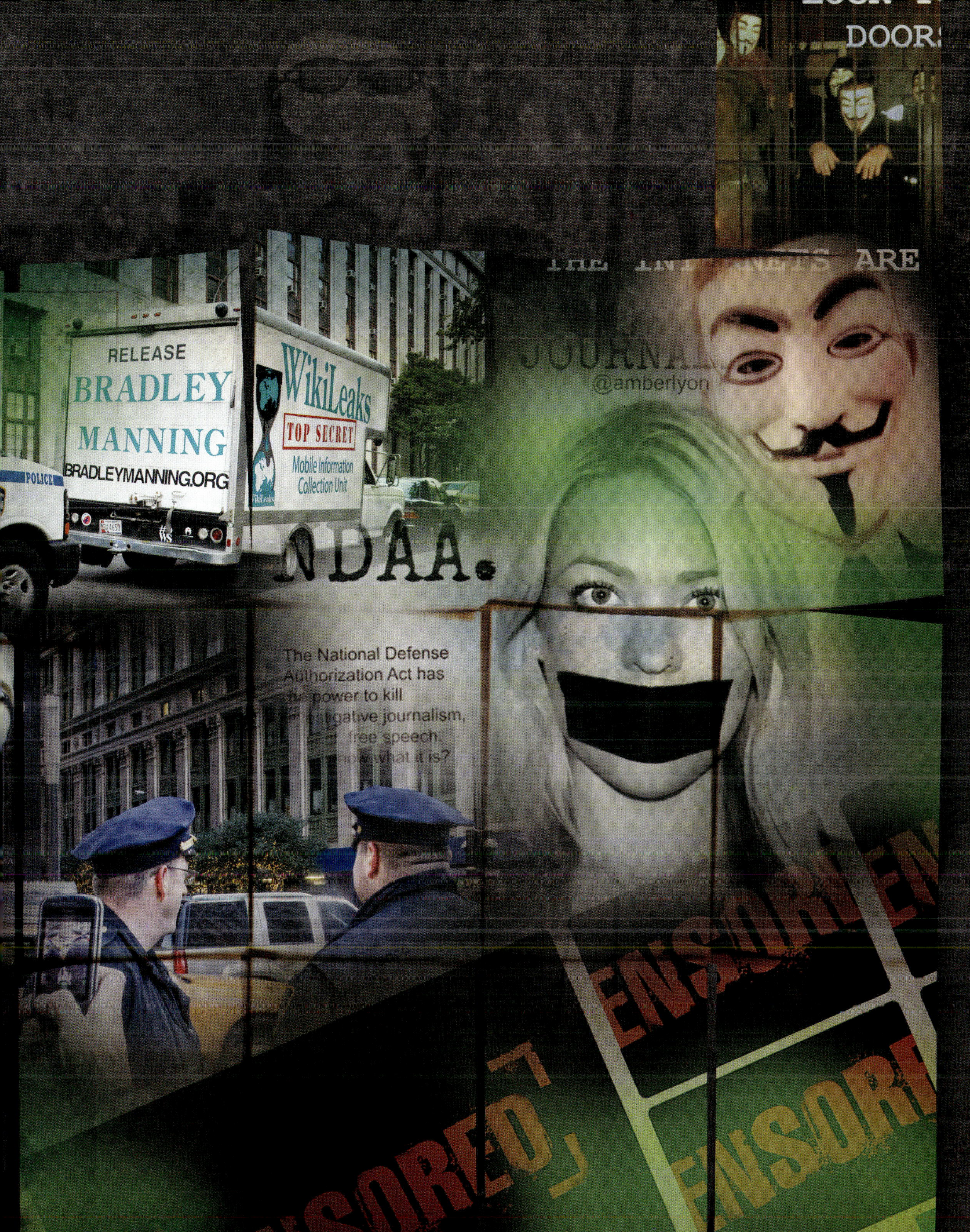
DOORS
ARE
RELEASE
BRADLEY
MANNING
BRADLEYMANNING.ORG
WikiLeaks
TOP SECRET
Mobile Information
Collection Unit
POLICE
NDAA.
@amberlyon
The National Defense
Authorization Act has
power to kill
free speech.
what it is?

Anonymous uses "ops" (short for "operations")—the equivalent of issue campaigns—to raise awareness of issues ranging from abuse of Church of Scientology adherents and police brutality in minority communities to support in Arab Spring protests and the Occupy Wall Street movement.

Protests can often take the form of distributed denial-of-service (DDoS) attacks, which essentially target websites and crash them by overloading a server. DDoS attacks are mainly harmless, rarely if ever causing damage to actual hardware, and because of this, supporters liken DDoS to digital sit-ins. They operate much as traditional, real-world sit-ins have disrupted business as usual in settings ranging from lunch counters during the civil rights movement to banks during Occupy protests. Naturally, authorities seek to clamp down on this activity. A prime example of authoritarian crackdown on this form of civil disobedience is the arrest of the protesters known as the PayPal 14, who temporarily brought down the high-profile online payment site after the company cut off WikiLeaks fundraising.

Another powerful form of online protest is recording, uploading, and disseminating evidence of police brutality during protests. The Occupy Wall Street movement might not have exploded in the manner it did were it not for video footage of women being indiscriminately pepper-sprayed by the New York Police Department. The infamous video went viral, subsequently focusing attention on the movement's efforts in a way not seen before.

An examination of how online protest has changed political and social culture would be incomplete without mentioning WikiLeaks, the online, nonprofit news and document leak site. In 2007, WikiLeaks—and online political activism—exploded into public consciousness and mainstream media with the release of a highly controversial video leak of a U.S. war crime in Iraq. The video, which revealed U.S. troops shooting and killing a Reuters journalist, adult civilians, and a family who came to the others' rescue, was leaked via the WikiLeaks website. The video went viral and forever changed the perception of online activism, as well as opening up heated debate about the issue of state secrets, classification, and the definition and role of journalism. Some also claim that WikiLeaks stirred the debate about U.S. military involvement in Iraq, pulling back the curtain on the dehumanizing effect war has on the human psyche and how that impacts the lives of civilians in the grip of U.S. empire.

Another online protest phenomenon that has played a very important role in changing activism and its messaging

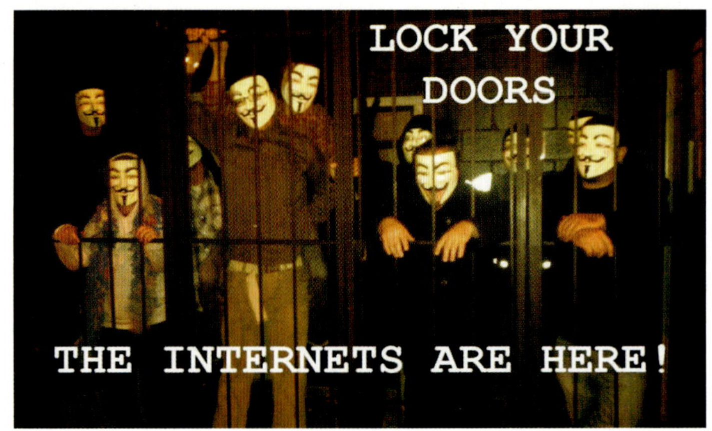

is the "meme." Wikipedia defines a meme as "an idea, behavior or style that spreads from person to person within a culture." It has had a profound impact as a vehicle for conveying a cultural or political idea in a concise picture-text combination, often instantly understandable. A lighthearted example of meme culture can be found in the "lolcat" series, which consists of photos of cats with funny captions. (The name is derived from the common text abbreviation LOL for "laugh out loud.") An example of a more political variation on the lolcat meme would be a photo of a stern cat staring at the viewer with the caption "Big Brother Kitty . . . Watches You On The Internet."

A powerful example of how online protest has effected real-world change is, without question, the prevention of the Stop Online Piracy Act, or SOPA, from becoming law in Congress. Through a social media campaign that spilled into real-world protests in cities across America—and the world—as well as the first ever online "strike," when Wikipedia and other websites shut down in opposition to the proposed legislation, SOPA was not passed because Congress bowed to public pressure.

Online protest makes authorities fearful, because it changes the playing field. After all, it is easier to crack down on protesters in the street with brute force than it is to stifle dissent on the Web—for now, at least.

WIKILEAKS

WikiLeaks is a nonprofit organization working to promote government and corporate transparency around the globe. It's responsible for publishing classified documents and private emails that it considers are in the public interest. The whistleblower group was founded by Australian internet activist Julian Assange in 2006. WikiLeaks is responsible for releasing the Iraq War Logs, the Afghan War Diary, and a trove of over 250,000 State Department diplomatic cables. The latter event, dubbed Cablegate, was the largest release of classified material in U.S. history (see also Bradley Manning). Various human rights organizations including Amnesty International have criticized WikiLeaks for not doing a better job of redacting names from thousands of war documents it published, jeopardizing the safety of Afghans who had aided the U.S. military.

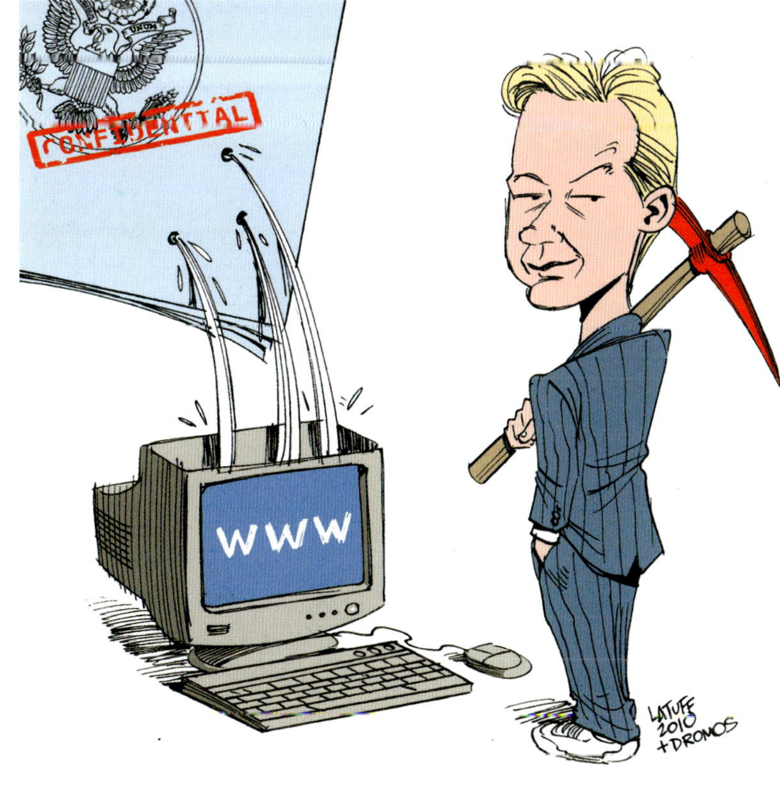

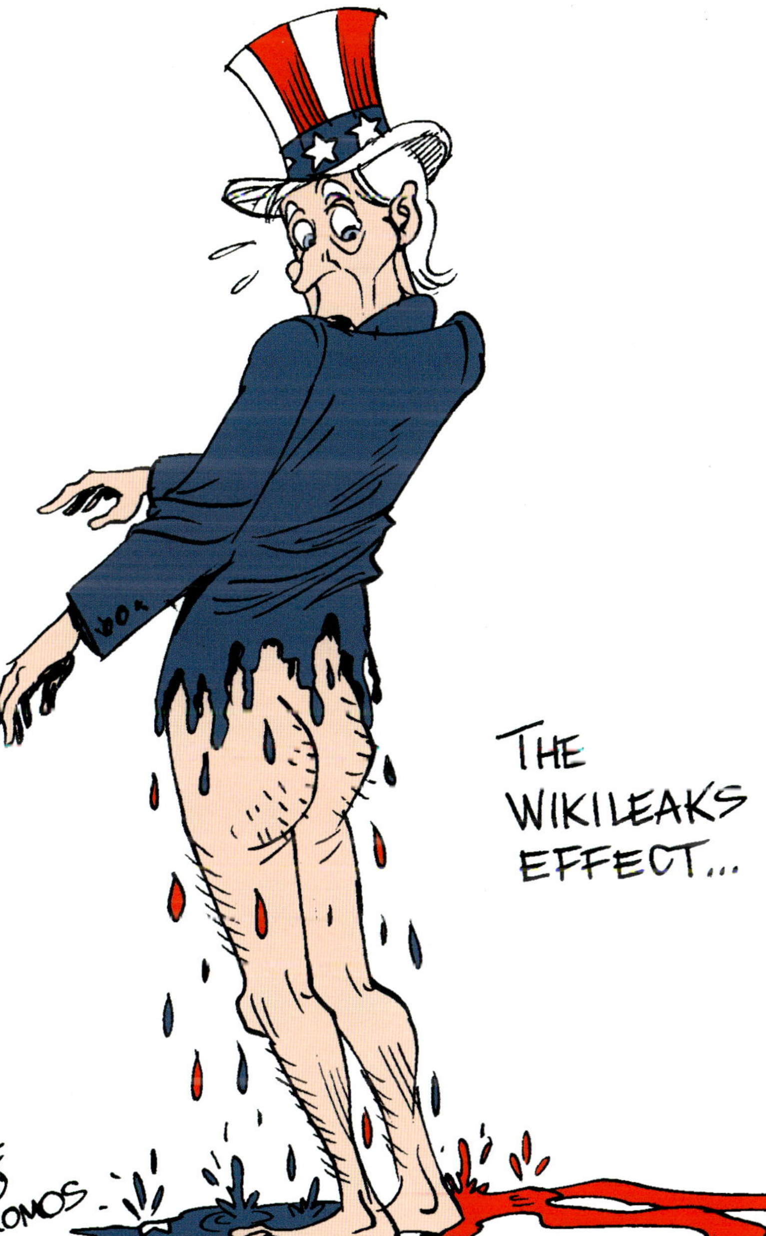

WikiLeaks has received praise from millions worldwide for revealing classified aspects of the wars, including thousands of previously unreported civilian deaths, unknown incidences of friendly fire, and links between a Pakistani intelligence agency and the Taliban. WikiLeaks received massive media attention in 2010 for releasing footage of a U.S. Apache helicopter firing upon—and killing—Iraqi civilians and two Reuters journalists. The "collateral murder" video clearly depicted the soldiers violating the U.S. military rules of engagement by intentionally firing on a wounded civilian crawling along the ground.

In February 2012, WikiLeaks released 5 million emails captured from the server of Stratfor, a private Texas-based security firm. The release, which was passed to WikiLeaks by the Anonymous hacktivist collective, revealed detailed plans to implement a secret public surveillance system called TrapWire that would use cutting-edge facial-recognition technology to monitor American citizens.

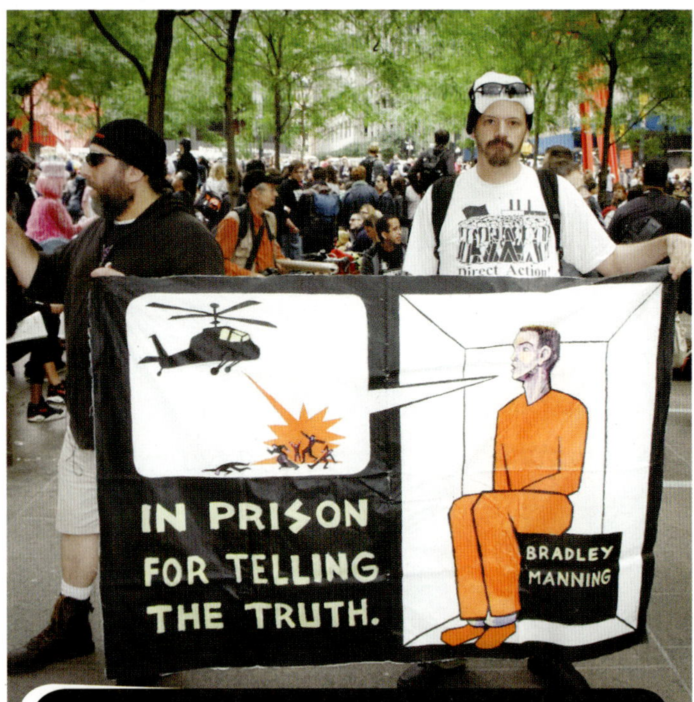

Two men protest the detainment of U.S. Army Private Bradley Manning, who was found guilty of leaking classified U.S. military documents to WikiLeaks. Data culled from the release included information on thousands of previously unreported civilian deaths in the Middle East and secret transmissions between diplomats and the U.S. State Department from 274 embassies around the globe. It was the largest known leak of classified documents in U.S. history. Due to the nature of the leaked material, which included evidence of numerous war crimes committed by the U.S. military, Manning has been characterized by supporters as a patriot. On July 30, 2013, a military judge convicted him of multiple counts of espionage, theft, and other charges. Photo: Jenna Pope.

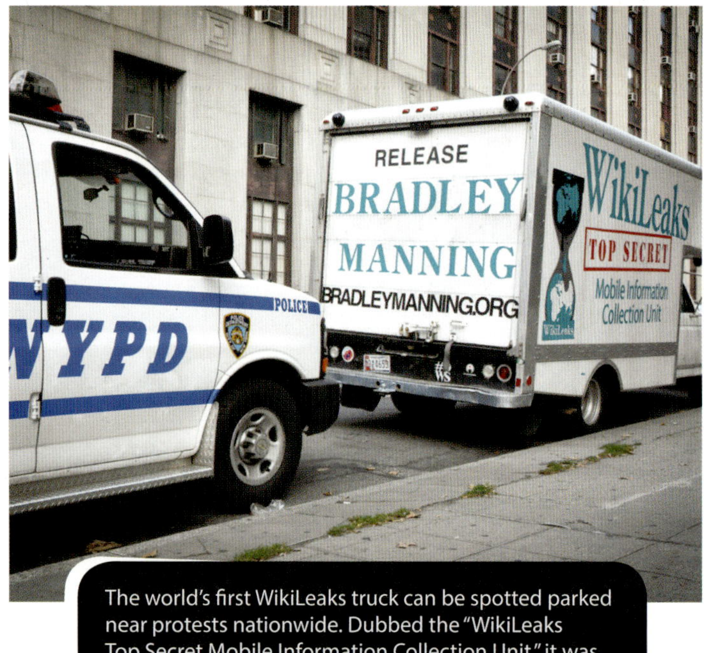

The world's first WikiLeaks truck can be spotted parked near protests nationwide. Dubbed the "WikiLeaks Top Secret Mobile Information Collection Unit," it was created when founder Clark Stoeckley transformed an old U-Haul truck into a creative vehicle for political activism.

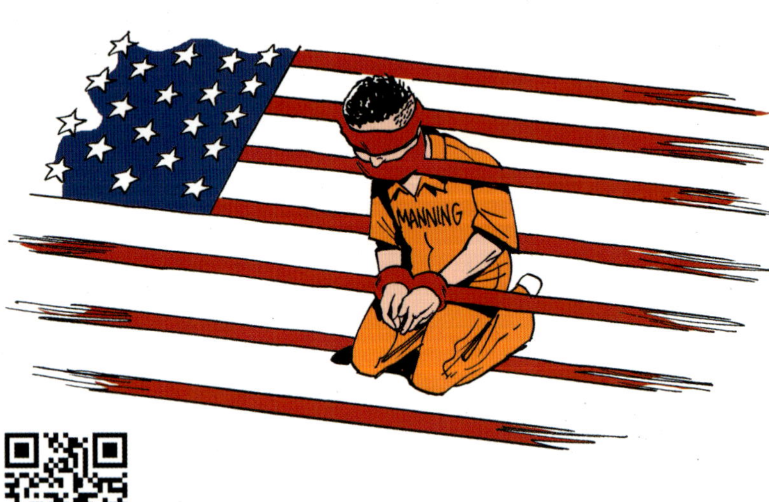

LATUFF 2012 WWW.BRADLEYMANNING.ORG

ANONYMOUS

Anonymous is a worldwide collective of individuals who are involved in various acts of activism in both the virtual and real worlds. Most individuals (known as "Anons") associated with Anonymous refuse to identify themselves as members because they claim it is not a tangible organization. Instead, Anons prefer to classify Anonymous as an idea, the logic being that "you can't arrest an idea." The number of individuals who claim they are in allegiance with the Anonymous ideology has been estimated to be between 50,000 and more than 1 million worldwide.

Anonymous was spawned on 4chan, an anything-goes discussion forum that allowed users to post text and images anonymously—hence the name. Because memes and sometime elaborate pranks were the capital whereby users gained status, the initial focus of Anons was to provoke the "lulz" (a bastardized pluralization of the acronym for "laugh out loud"). The first major Anonymous endeavor of a more serious nature was aimed at the Church of Scientology. Project Chanology, as it was known, was undertaken in retaliation for attempts by the church to censor the media after Anons popularized a particularly lulzy church motivational video featuring its most famous member, Tom Cruise. Following the success of that operation, and prompted by attacks on internet freedoms, Anonymous began a series of operations to combat censorship.

Anonymous has been popularized in modern culture for their acts of hacktivism, the most common form of which is distributed denial-of-service (DDoS) attacks. A DDoS attack is a digital "sit-in," similar in effect to a group of people sitting down and blocking the entrance to a building. In a DDoS, a website is flooded with so much traffic that it temporarily shuts down. Once the people stand up and leave, or online when the traffic stops, the building is now accessible, and online the site is back up and running. DDoS attacks are relatively harmless since they are nondestructive and merely temporarily prevent users from reaching a website by overwhelming servers with manufactured traffic. DDoS attacks are usually performed as an act of protest, the

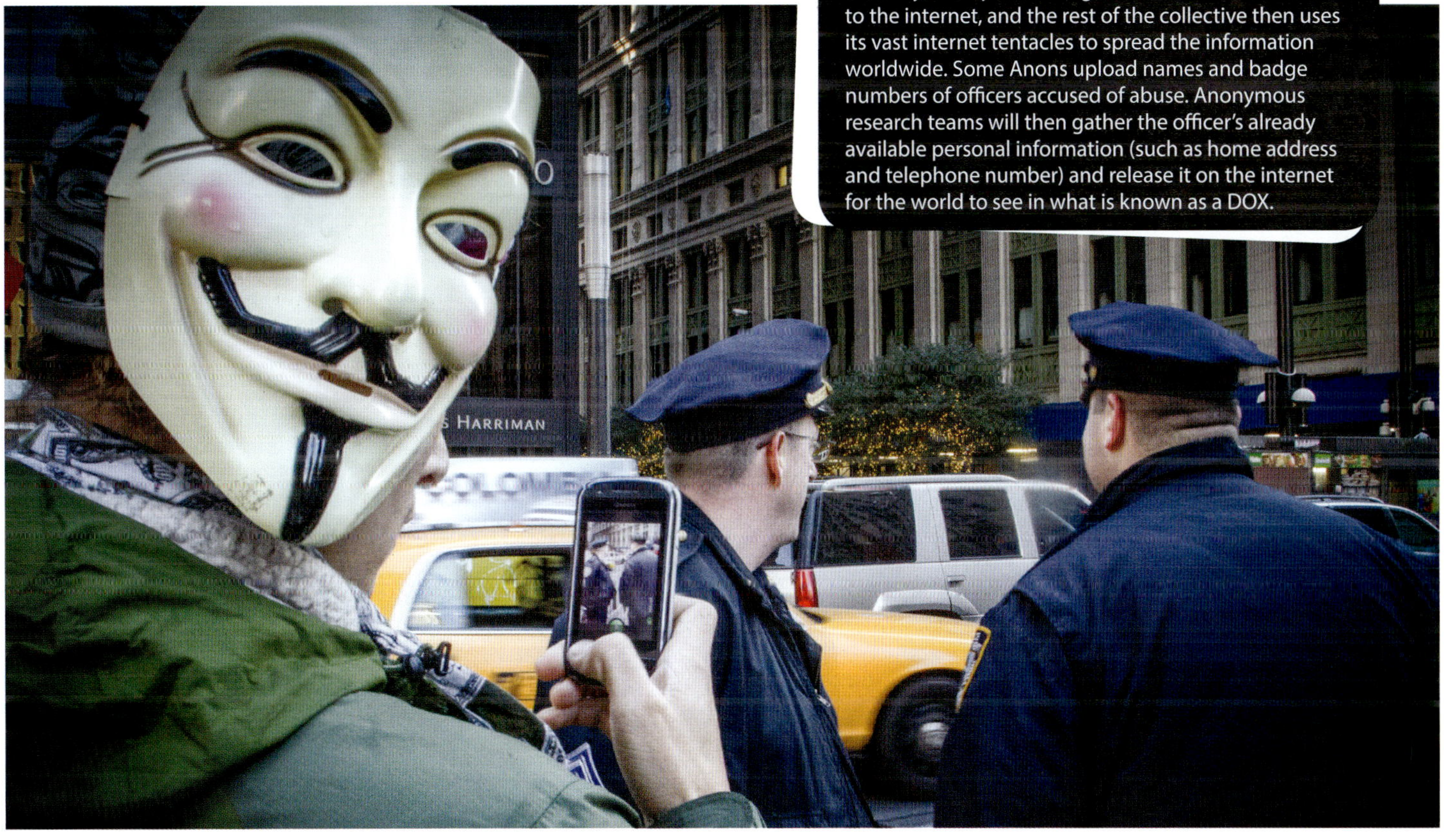

A supporter of the internet collective Anonymous keeps watch on two New York Police Department officers near Zuccotti Park. Anonymous has an army of supporters on the ground, known as "Anons," who use cell phone cameras to photo-document police brutality against the protesters, filling in gaps created by a deficiency in mainstream media coverage of the protests.

Once an Anon documents suspected police brutality, she uploads images and videos of the incident to the internet, and the rest of the collective then uses its vast internet tentacles to spread the information worldwide. Some Anons upload names and badge numbers of officers accused of abuse. Anonymous research teams will then gather the officer's already available personal information (such as home address and telephone number) and release it on the internet for the world to see in what is known as a DOX.

primary targets being government and corporate websites that engage in activities Anonymous deems unethical. The attack requires the consensus and cooperation of dozens, if not hundreds, of individuals in order to be effective, and is why many view Anonymous as a "hive mind."

In addition to DDoS attacks, Anonymous has been responsible for acts of cyber-vigilantism. Servers that host child pornography have frequently been hacked and the personal information of users released to the public, leading to arrests. The servers of a private intelligence firm called Stratfor were penetrated by Anonymous, and 200 gigabytes of information was downloaded and given to the whistle-blower website WikiLeaks. The files included information about TrapWire, a secret nationwide program that utilized public surveillance cameras to collect facial-recognition data. Anonymous is also widely recognized as having played an important support role in the Arab Spring, helping activists in Egypt gain access to the internet after President Hosni Mubarak effectively shut it off.

As well as providing tactical and technological support, Anonymous was also heavily present on the streets during the Occupy Wall Street protests. They usually distinguished themselves in public through the use of Guy Fawkes masks, as popularized by the graphic novel (and, later, the movie) *V for Vendetta*. Due to the frequency of incidents involving police brutality, the group widely disseminated literature that taught protesters how to treat wounds caused by less-lethal police weaponry and teargas. In some occupations, Anonymous Medics were present to provide first-hand emergency medical care to protesters with minor injuries.

While Anonymous has sometimes been demonized by the media, and various governments have claimed the group is a terrorist organization, the actions of Anons are generally far from malevolent. Anonymous has consistently declared that its primary goal is to protect freedom of expression and promote justice and equality.

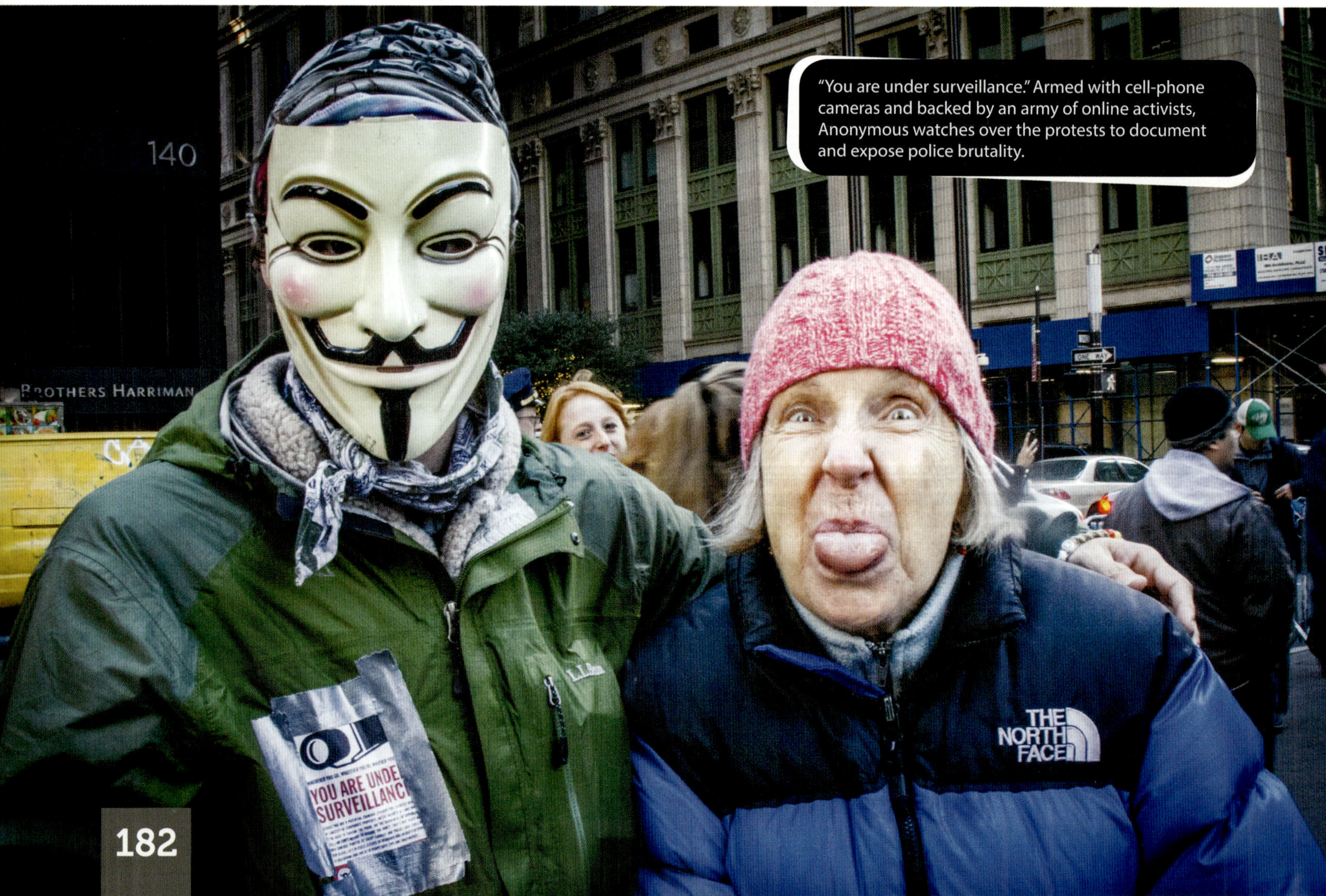

"You are under surveillance." Armed with cell-phone cameras and backed by an army of online activists, Anonymous watches over the protests to document and expose police brutality.

Activist Profile

Name: We are Anonymous.
Age: Late 20s
City: Dallas, Texas
Protesting since: Operation Payback, 2010
Affiliation: Anonymous

What happened in your life that motivated you to attend your first protest? I thought Chanology was great for lulz, but it wasn't until members of Anonymous began attacking targets that were propagating online censorship that I truly saw the value in it. Attacks on the MPAA in particular piqued my interest. The MPAA is a lobbying machine that would rather attack technological innovation than change their own business model to profit from advancements in the way data is shared. These are the people that fought the introduction of VHS tapes, for God's sake. I felt like they were trying to prevent advancements in information sharing to maintain their profits and they were using our political system to do it. Chris Dodd, the CEO of the MPAA, is a former U.S. senator. He epitomizes everything that is wrong with this revolving-door system our elected officials enjoy. Politicians take campaign contributions from corporations, get elected into office, and support legislation that benefits those companies, and then go to work for them after they leave office. It's disgusting, and while everyday Americans have little recourse, as Anonymous I was given a voice.

How have you been protesting? Anonymous has been involved in numerous operations that have subverted the fascist policies of governments and abuse of power by corporations worldwide. Perhaps the most famous was the operation to avenge Julian Assange on behalf of WikiLeaks. After the release of classified U.S. documents, companies including PayPal, Amazon, and MasterCard began freezing donations, cutting WikiLeaks off from their supporters. In response, Anonymous began shutting down their websites through the use of coordinated DDoS attacks. And PayPal released the remaining funds in the account. Let's be clear:

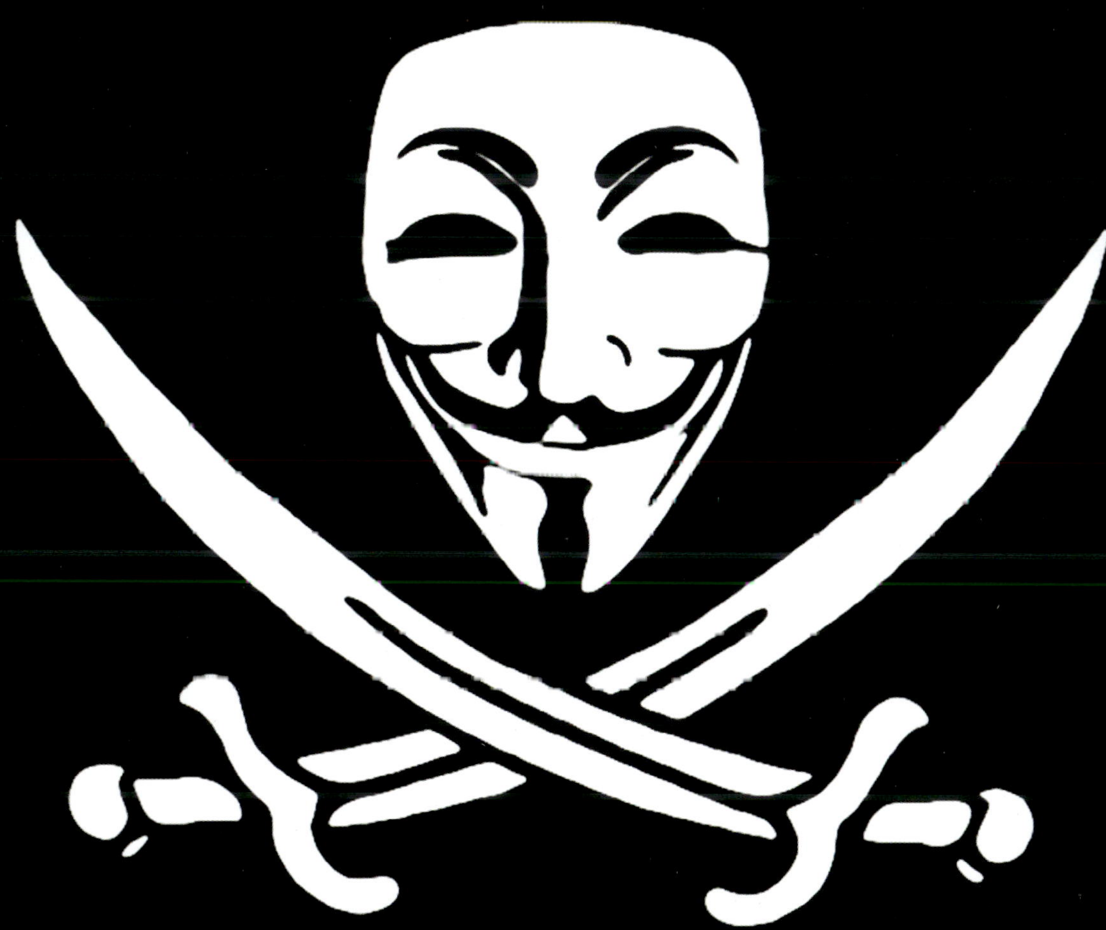

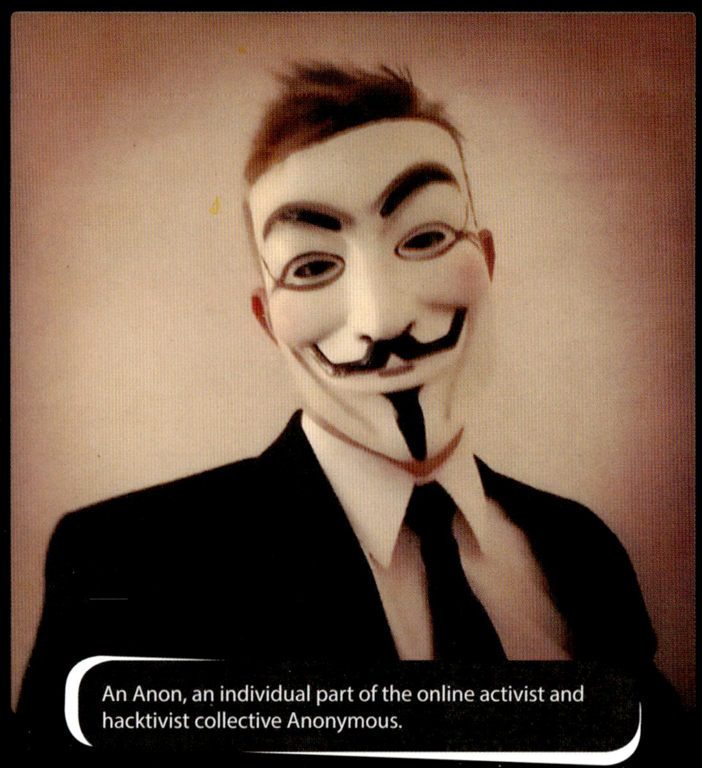

An Anon, an individual part of the online activist and hacktivist collective Anonymous.

DDoS is the online equivalent of blocking the entrance to a building, something activists have been doing for decades. The fact that arrested members of Anonymous are being charged with felonies, facing upwards of 10 years in prison, is a travesty of the American justice system. Anonymous has also used their hacking expertise to reveal the identities of countless child pornographers (you're welcome, FBI).

Once upon a time, the Egyptian people took to the streets to tell their fascist, CIA-backed asshole dictator, "Go fuck yourself." Dictator Mubarak responded by ordering his army of creepy armor-clad police to publicly execute protesters. In the worst case of fail ever, Mubarak failed to calculate the blowback from shutting down almost all of Egypt's internet service. For great justice, Anonymous shut down all of Mubarak's websites and began training individuals on the streets how to access the internet through other means so they could continue coordinating their protests online. It was a signal to all governments that if you try to censor the internet to oppress peaceful protests, you can Expect Us. Mubarak is now enjoying a quiet life retirement in Tora Prison, Cairo, lulz.

Have you ever been arrested? Several times by the Dallas Police department in acts of what I consider to be a gross abuse of authority. I was pepper-sprayed once by police officers while sitting handcuffed quietly on the curb. They called me a number of homophobic slurs before taking me to jail. This was not during an act of protest with Occupy. However, I think the most amazing thing I witnessed during Occupy Dallas was a march to a police station. It was led by over 20 members of Occupy that had been arrested two days before during an act of civil disobedience, which included a few acts of brutality. Once released, they organized a march to protest attacks against police pensions. It was a truly selfless act.

Have your efforts resulted in change? They have changed me. I'm a better-informed, more compassionate human being because of my work with Anonymous and Occupy. Basically, I'm an enlightened citizen. If you want to know if our efforts have changed anything, ask the community bankers in my area about the thousands of accounts they've opened for people fleeing multinational financial institutions. As an individual, I think my biggest contribution has been knowledge. If I can inform even one person a day about the level of corruption in our government, and they are willing to stand up against it, I know I'm having an impact.

What's the most egregious mainstream misconception about protesters? A lot of people complained about targeted interviews during Occupy protests. The media would walk through a group of protesters and seek out individuals that they thought would perform poorly during an interview. The misconception, I thought, was that these people didn't deserve to be there just because they were ill-informed. Do you honestly think that just because someone can't eloquently describe the levels of corruption and inequality in our financial and political systems they don't deserve to have a voice? You don't need a master's degree in economics these days to know how badly you're getting fucked.

When will you be satisfied, stop protesting? Never. Even if I saw a sweeping change in the way political campaigns are financed, if our government began to respond to the will of the people and not just the agendas of the 1%, if war was outlawed, bankers were put on trial for crashing our economy and true equality was realized, we couldn't let up. As soon as we became docile, some greedy fuck would try to screw us over to make a buck. It's just the way it is.

Favorite quote: "The war is not meant to be won, it is meant to be continuous." —George Orwell (1903–1950)

ACTA

ACTA (Anti Counterfeiting Trade Agreement) is a treaty proposed by the World Trade Organization drafted first by the United States. It was feared that the treaty would give governments the authority to shut down any website that they felt infringed upon international copyright laws. The treaty was negotiated in secret because, according to both the Bush and Obama administrations, revealing any aspects of it would have "threatened national security." In October 2011, President Obama signed the treaty despite an open letter by over 75 constitutional law professors urging him not to do so. ACTA resulted in worldwide protests, including Anonymous DDoS attacks against the Motion Picture Association of America (MPAA) and the Recording Industry Association of America (RIAA), who had lobbied for the trade agreement.

SOPA

The Stop Online Piracy Act (SOPA), also known as HR 3261, was a bill introduced by Congressman Lamar S. Smith (R-TX) on October 26, 2011. If passed, it would have granted government agencies the right to shut down any website they claimed was hosting content that infringed upon international copyright laws. The language of the bill

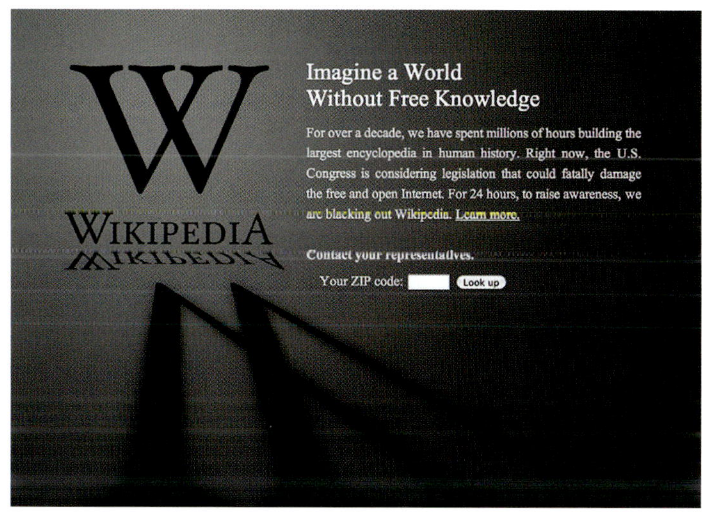

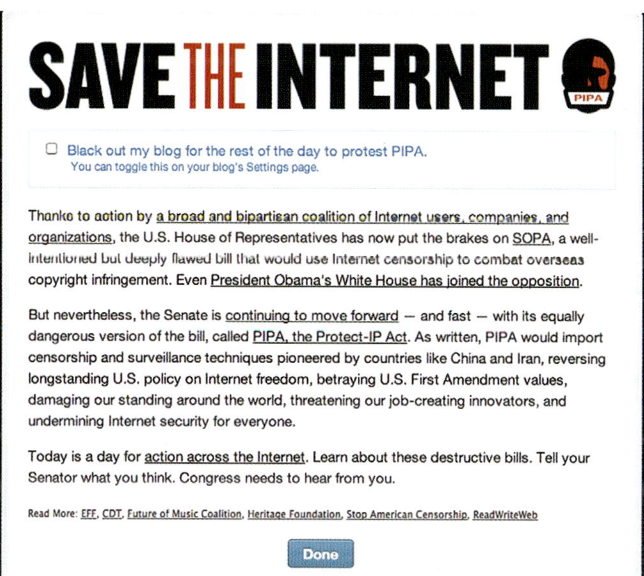

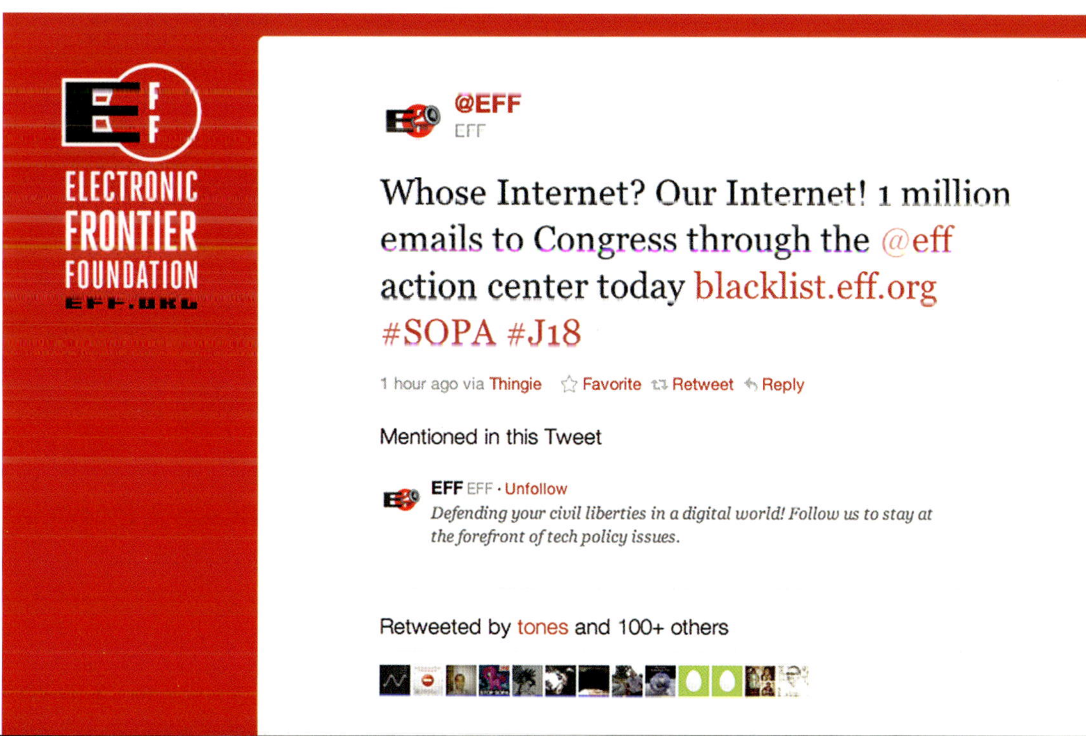

was criticized as being poorly defined, and it was feared users themselves could potentially be held criminally liable for uploading copyrighted material. The Electronic Frontier Foundation, a nonprofit digital-rights advocacy group, claimed that enforcement of SOPA could have disastrous effects on e-commerce and everyday internet usage. On January 18, 2012, Wikipedia, Reddit, and an estimated 7,000 other websites participated in a coordinated online protest against SOPA by blacking out all of their content. Anonymous joined the online protest, crashing the websites of SOPA supporters such as the MPAA and government agencies such as the Justice Department and FBI. As of January 19, more than 4.5 million people had signed an anticensorship petition promoted on Google's home page. On January 20, the House Judiciary Committee postponed plans to draft the bill indefinitely.

PIPA

The PROTECT IP Act (PIPA), also known as the Preventing Real Online Threats to Economic Creativity and Theft of Intellectual Property Act or Senate Bill 968, was introduced by Patrick Leahy (D-VT), head of the Senate Judiciary Committee, on May 12, 2011. If passed, PROTECT IP would have given the Department of Justice authority to issue court orders to halt all financial transactions to and from any website it deemed in violation of international copyright law. Critics of the bill claimed that PROTECT IP was authored by entertainment industry lobbyists who had contributed more than $900,000 to Judiciary Committee

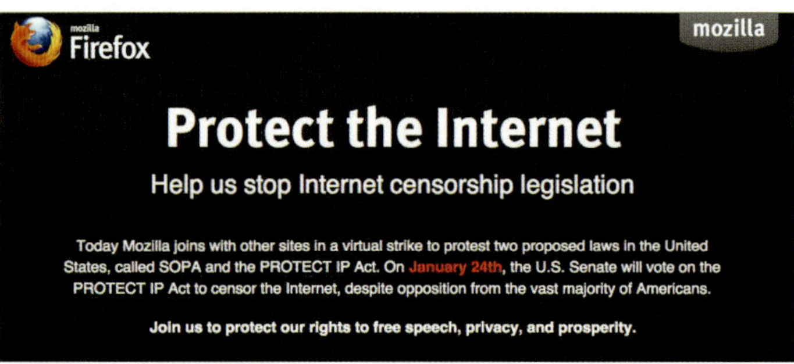

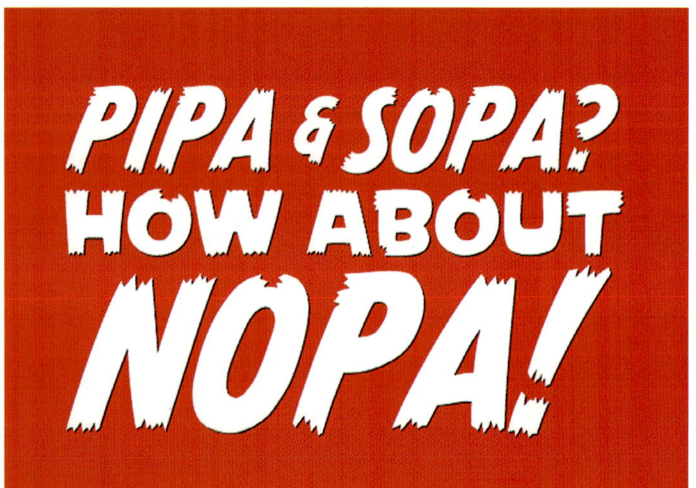

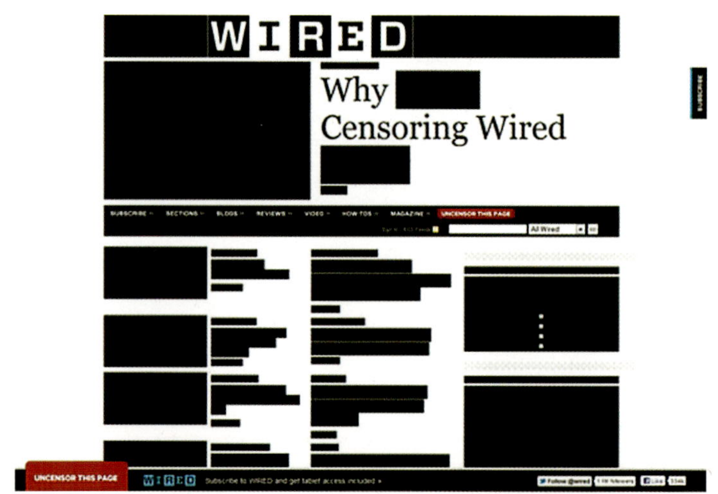

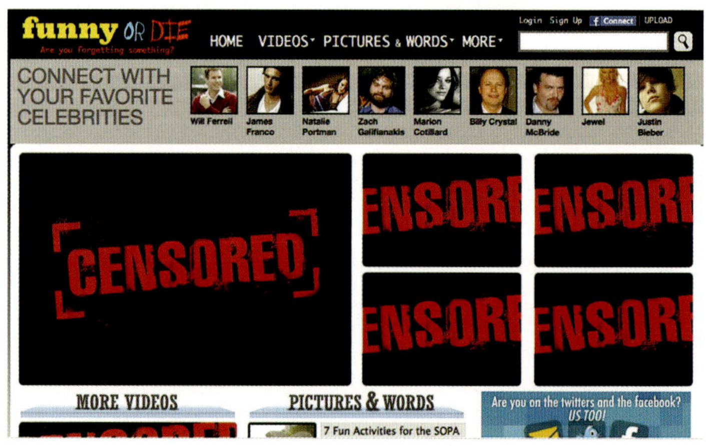

members and was designed to give entertainment trade associations the authority to censor the internet for financial gain. Chris Dodd, head of the MPAA, publicly threatened to pull all financial support for the Obama campaign on Fox News after the White House chose not to support the bill. Considered the sister act to SOPA, PIPA was also targeted by the mass January 18, 2012, online protests. Like SOPA, PIPA was subsequently shelved indefinitely.

INTERNET MEMES

On the ground, protesters strive to create alluring protest signs to make their message stand out from the rest. Online, those protest signs have evolved into memes. Internet memes are concepts that spread rapidly from person to person on the internet through social media, email, blogs, and forums. Online protesters create meme photos to rapidly spread awareness and to expose corruption. A catchy meme sprinkled with some humor has the potential to go viral and be viewed by millions in a matter of hours, making memes a free and convenient form of online protest.

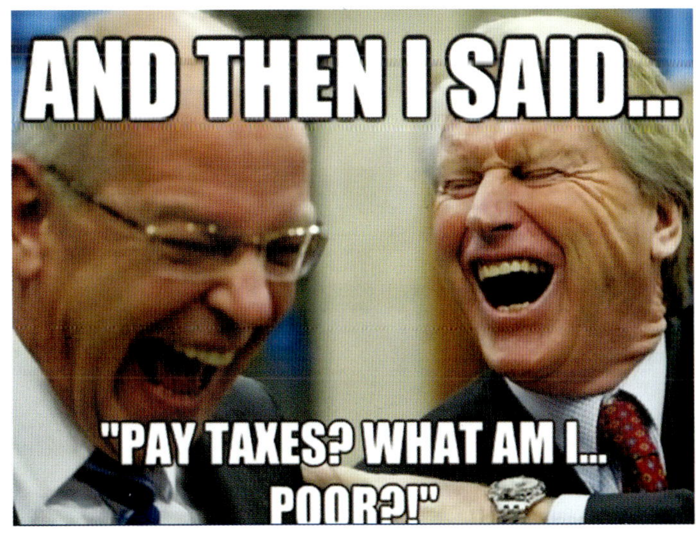

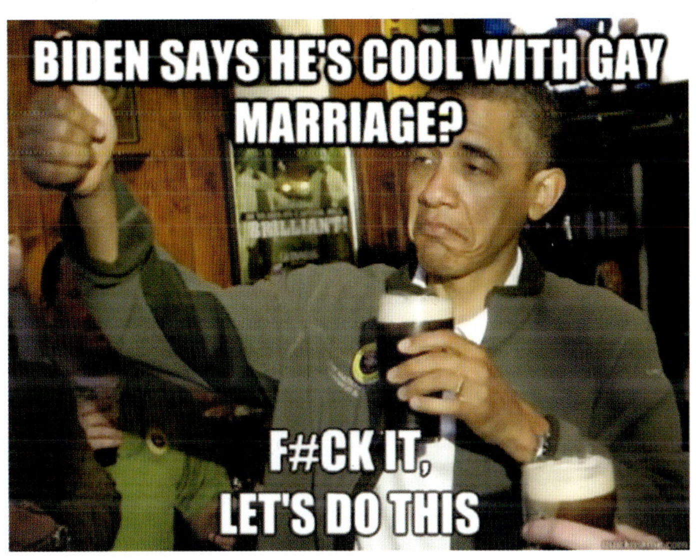

On January 18, 2012, more than 7,000 websites went black in protest of anti-piracy legislation (including the Stop Online Piracy Act, or SOPA) or posted information to educate visitors about the bills.

Critics of the legislation argue that, should SOPA be passed into law, it would create a dangerous atmosphere where government would be able to stifle online free speech and innovation by allowing law enforcement agencies to shut down entire web domains because of infringing content on blog posts or a single web page.

What Congress did not anticipate was the unprecedented push-back this proposed legislation would receive from freedom-of-information advocates such as the online activist collective known as Anonymous as well as entities like Google, Reddit, and Wikipedia. This opposition came in the form of internet blackouts initiated by Wikipedia, Reddit, and a host of other websites—the first "internet strike" in history—as well as Anonymous hackivists launching widespread distributed denial-of-service attacks (DDoS) to disrupt access to a number of pro-SOPA company websites, ranging from CBS.com to the Recording Industry Association of America (RIAA).

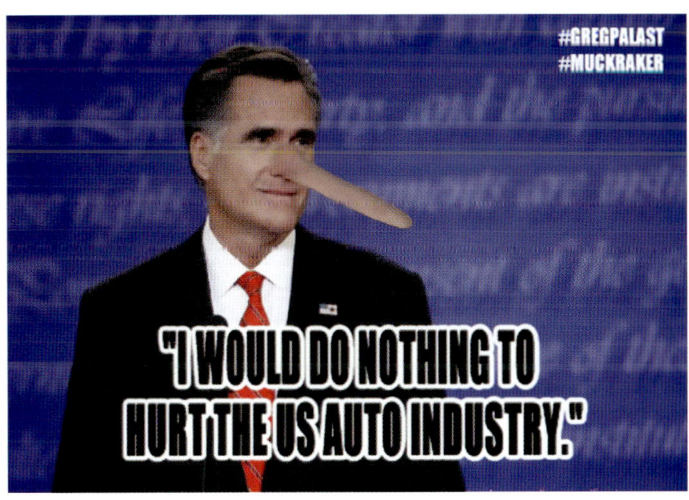

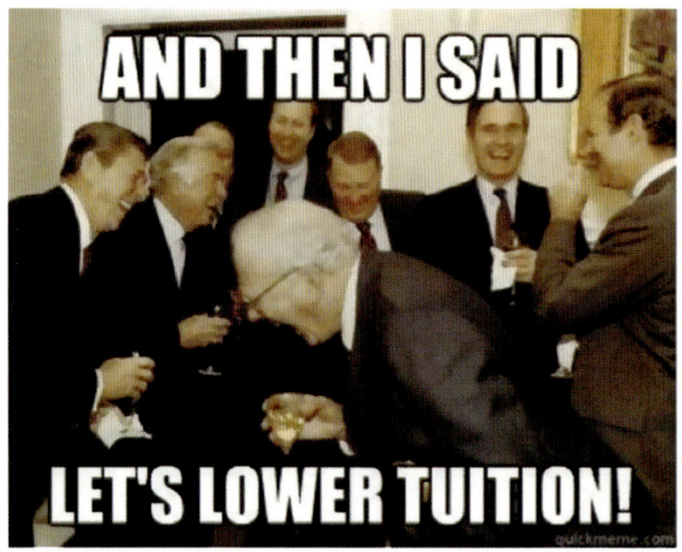
AND THEN I SAID
LET'S LOWER TUITION!
quickmeme.com

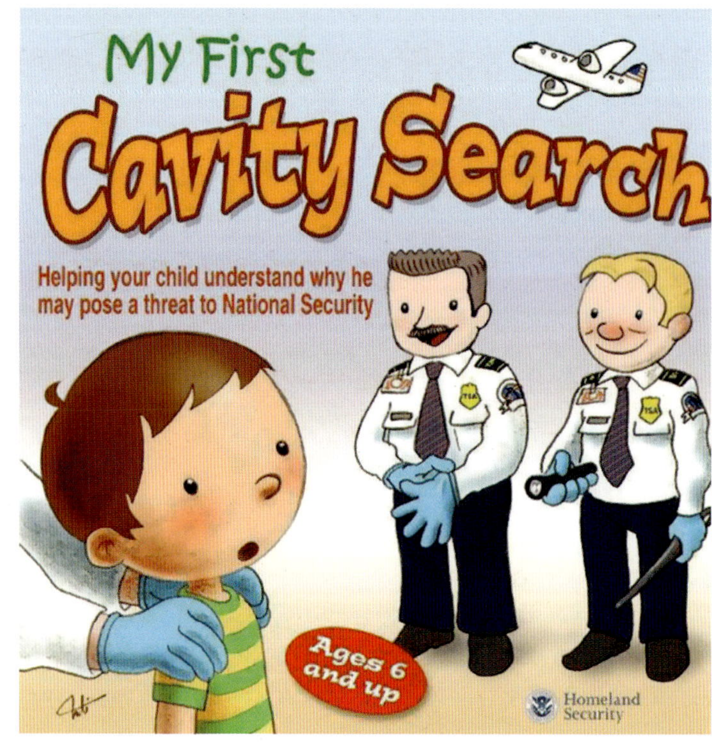
My First
Cavity Search
Helping your child understand why he may pose a threat to National Security
Ages 6 and up
Homeland Security

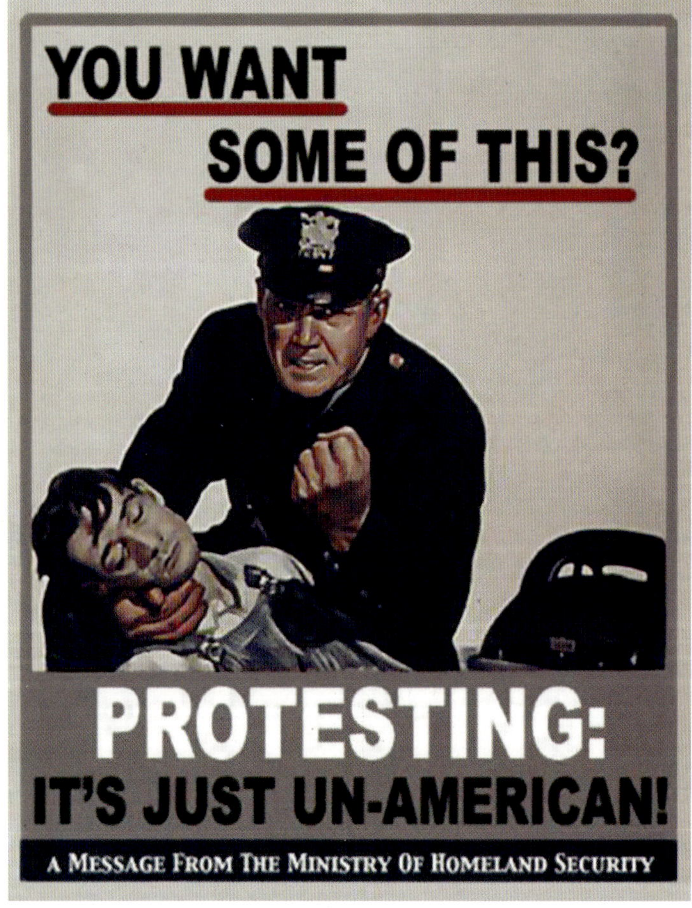
YOU WANT
SOME OF THIS?
PROTESTING:
IT'S JUST UN-AMERICAN!
A MESSAGE FROM THE MINISTRY OF HOMELAND SECURITY

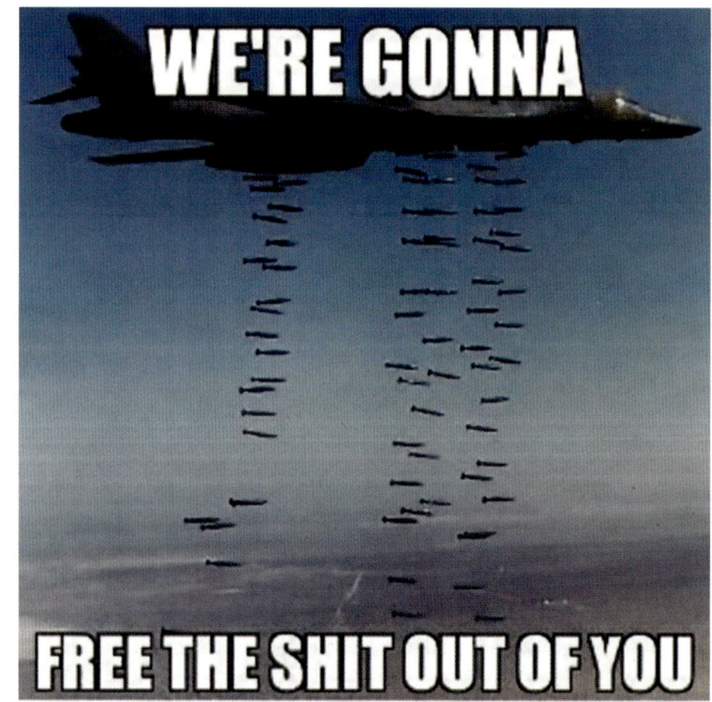
WE'RE GONNA
FREE THE SHIT OUT OF YOU

THE Ethics OF DIGITAL Direct Action

By Gabriella Coleman

The political movement known as Anonymous has managed to capture the attention of the media, the hearts of many supporters, and the ire of many spectators after an eight-month spree of political interventions, stretching from distributed denial-of-service (DDoS) campaigns to human rights technical assistance in Tunisia to a more recent spate of hacks under the guise of Operation AntiSec.

The state has now fully entered the fray with its own flurry of activity. In the past month, 22 alleged participants in the United States and the United Kingdom have been arrested, the bulk of them (14) in connection with a single operation: the spectacular wave of DDoS attacks aimed directly at protesting actions taken by MasterCard and PayPal in December 2010. These were launched after these companies refused to accept donations for WikiLeaks front man Julian Assange, soon after the activist organization released a trove of diplomatic cables. Hackers and activists supporting the DDoS campaign (and certainly not all do support the campaign) regard this act as legitimate protest activity, akin to a blockade or "digital sit-in." Yet, if convicted, the participants of Anonymous could be charged with felonies and land in prison with excessive punishments.

On July 20, 2011, a day after the U.S.-based arrests, FBI officials offered a rare glimpse into its justification for the crackdown, citing a need to nip "chaos" in the bud: "We want to send a message that chaos on the internet is unacceptable," said Steven Chabinsky, deputy assistant FBI director. Although most of the arrests were for the DDoS campaign, the FBI official never differentiated between hacking and DDoSing. The former is defined by computer break-ins or trespassing, while the latter refers to gumming up a server by bombarding it with too many requests. Curiously, this official also never went so far as to label the alleged participants criminals, terrorists, or vigilantes.

By complaining about Anonymous's tactics in the absence of any stated criminal offense, the FBI appears to acknowledge, if in a somewhat oblique fashion, that the hunt for some Anons is politically motivated. The FBI also appears to acknowledge that, in contrast to terrorists and criminals, whom the state is justified in prosecuting since they have violated the contract that ostensibly undergirds social norms in modern civil society, members of Anonymous (hereafter Anons) are in fact exercising their rights as citizens to demonstrate on behalf of "causes" they believe in: "[Even if] hackers can be believed to have social causes, it's entirely unacceptable to break into websites and commit unlawful acts. There has not been a large-scale trend toward using hacking to actually destroy websites, [but] that could be appealing to both criminals or terrorists. That's where the 'hacktivism,' even if currently viewed by some as a nuisance, shows the potential to be destabilizing," insisted Chabinsky, in language that mirrors critiques of 1960s-era social movements.

Of course these brief statements should not be taken as the state's sole, much less its final, words on Anonymous. They are interesting insofar as they gesture toward a social fact concerning Anonymous's increasingly prominent role in social protest movements: Many of their actions are politically motivated and conscientious, and the December 2010 DDoS campaign, Operation Avenge Assange, was no exception.

DDoS Campaigns Can Be Legitimate Tactics

Whether or not one agrees with all of Anonymous's many tactics—some of them being illegal and disruptive, others falling into the province of peaceful and legal human rights assistance, and still others existing in a gray moral and legal zone—under certain circumstances, the DDoS can be considered nonviolent protest in line with well-recognized protocols for public assembly, the difference being the medium.

Of course, as with any form of public assembly, some Anons are merely along for the ride. Others might in fact exhibit reckless behavior.

But this is an inevitable feature of Anonymous's platform, open to seasoned activists and newcomers alike: some novice participants cut their teeth on politics for the first time with their Anonymous brethren, forming, no doubt, an individual political consciousness, which has fed into a more robust sense of democracy in action, especially after Anons held campaigns in support of the uprisings in the Middle East and Africa that have helped to displace authoritarian regimes that had managed to exploit their constituencies for decades on end.

Even if the FBI is ambivalent about explicitly denouncing Anonymous as a criminal threat, its tactics of arrest and intimidation and its criminalization of all tactics used by Anons, such as DDoS, constitute an approach to security and surveillance that deserves critical attention, especially if any of these arrests move to trials.

There are many ways to think of the DDoS campaign against PayPal and MasterCard, but one way we might think of it is as digital direct action. Emerging organically, this movement did not wait for a judge, politician, nor a journalist to declare a legal or moral judgment. Citizens took matters into their own hands. In less than 24 hours, a large assembly of citizens took not to the streets where protest activity traditionally unfolds, but to the digital agora to act on their own accord, to loudly assert their opinion on a matter, and to act directly against those actors they felt were acting unjustly. If they happened to break laws, these laws were viewed, with good reason, to be unjust.

Like all traditions, direct action is diverse in its make-up, tactics, history, and purpose. At times, activists seek to block access in order to protect a resource, as with tree sit-ins in the Pacific Northwest or blocking Japanese whaling ships in the Southern Ocean as carried out by Sea Shepherd. In the long tradition of Plowshares actions, the intent is to get arrested in order to publicize an issue. Anonymous rendered MasterCard and PayPal's web pages defunct for a number of days by flooding their servers with too many requests and did so to garner media attention, to make their platform visible, and to demand that Assange be given due process. In this sense, they were successful, no matter what the outcome of the case made against them.

What made the events of December 2010 unusual—and extraordinary—as a moment of direct action poses a challenge for prevailing theories of civil disobedience. Many of the most notable acts of civil disobedience, even virtual sit-ins, have been organized by small affinity groups in which participants are public and typically well aware of the legal consequences of their actions. Some participants in these actions even have their lawyer's phone number written on their arm in permanent marker.

Anonymous, which prides itself on *not* having a readily identifiable, corporate form, was powerless to defend itself using these methods. Thus, as the December events unfolded, I was glued to the computer watching how Anons would or even could minimize the risk and chaos that to some degree characterized these interactions. Remarkably, "the hive mind," as they refer to themselves, never spun out of control. They stayed on target and conjoined their disruptions with manifestos and videos explaining their rationales.

But at the time, one thing was clear and has been repeated by sympathetic and unsympathetic observers alike: Many participants were likely unaware of the legal risk they were taking, and did not have lawyers to contact in the face of a future arrest. The spectacular events of December, combined with the recent arrests, have of course changed all of this; many of us have now been educated as to the risks at hand.

The legal risks and the philosophical subtleties of DDoS as a disruptive direct action tactic no longer reside within the sole province of a smaller circle of activists who have practiced and theorized this tradition for over a decade. A much larger swath of citizens have subsequently entered the fray. In light of these arrests, whether or not DDoS campaigns are always an effective political sword to wield (and they are strong arguments to be made on both sides) is not the primary question that should concern us. The key issue is the evidence used to decide who is involved and to determine what they ought to be charged with doing. If a DDoS action is deemed as always and under every circumstance unacceptable—always a tactic of chaos—this will in the short term result in excessive penalties; in the long term, an excessive clamp down, such as felony charges for those that stand accused, could stifle these tactics altogether on the internet.

This is damaging to the overall political culture of the internet, which must allow for a diversity of tactics, including mass action, direct action, and peaceful of protests, if it is going to be a medium for democratic action and life.

HOW THE

NDAA Threatens Average Americans

The NDAA Turns the U.S. Government Into a Dictatorship, the U.S. Military Into "Secret Police."

Journalists rarely take a vocal stand against legislation in order to remain objective, but sometimes new laws are such an egregious assault on our basic rights to democracy and freedom that we have a duty to speak up.

This is the case with the National Defense Authorization Act, which now gives the U.S. military the power to detain anyone without trial indefinitely, further criminalizing dissent and investigative journalism in the United States.

The NDAA Section 1021 gives the federal government the power to behave like dictators—to arrest individuals without warrant and indefinitely detain them in offshore prisons without charge and keep them there until "the end of hostilities."

The American Civil Liberties Union calls the law a "catastrophic blow to civil liberties." President Obama lied to the public and said he would veto the NDAA's indefinite-detention clauses. Instead, he surreptitiously signed the NDAA into law on December 31, 2011, while most Americans were distracted celebrating New Year's Eve.

The NDAA directly affects your everyday life because it is another violation of your rights to free speech and a fair trial. The NDAA also suffocates information that could expose the corruption that's rapidly destroying this country and affecting you financially.

The NDAA will prevent some whistleblowers from coming forward with information and documents vital to the public good out of fear the corrupt will pressure authorities to use the NDAA to detain the whistleblower indefinitely.

We need to reward, not instill fear in, our whistleblowers. They are vital to the survival of this nation. If we don't know what's broke, how can we fix it? What if more government whistleblowers had come forward before the start of the war to let the public know Saddam Hussein really didn't have weapons of mass destruction in Iraq?

Investigative Journalists Could Start Being "Disappeared" Under the NDAA

The NDAA frightens journalists because it turns us into criminals. There are no provisions within the law to protect journalists. As journalists, we take a vow to never reveal our confidential sources. If the U.S. government, or corrupt corporations pressuring authorities, want information on our confidential sources, the NDAA gives them the power to indefinitely detain us by saying the refusal to reveal sources is an act that is "aiding terrorists."

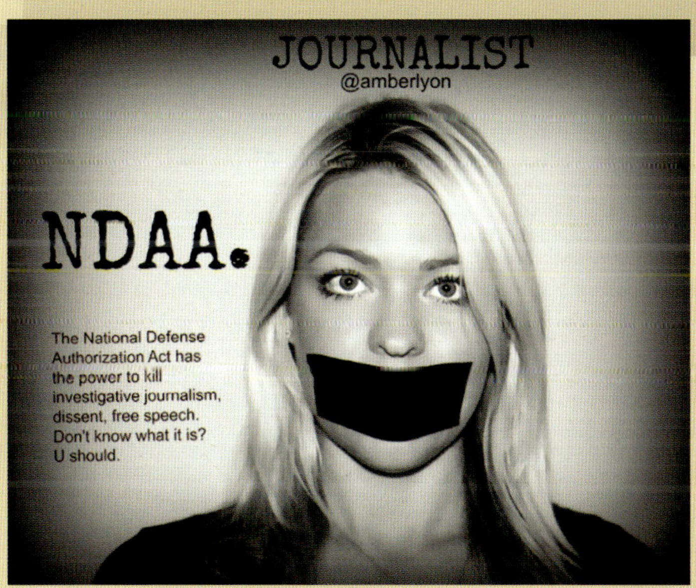

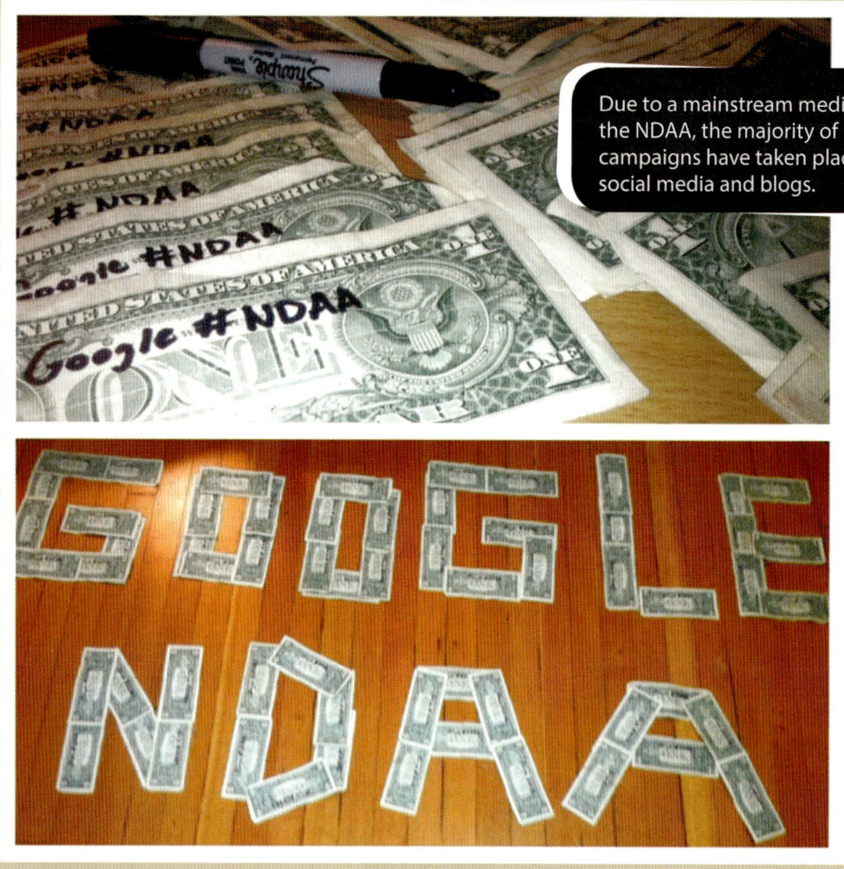

Due to a mainstream media blackout on coverage of the NDAA, the majority of NDAA protest and awareness campaigns have taken place online through the use of social media and blogs.

We Are All "Terrorists"

Another disturbing aspect of the NDAA is that it allows the government to imprison anyone suspected of or even associated with "terrorism." This power is open to wide interpretation under the law and can and will be abused.

Who in the heck is a terrorist anymore? We've witnessed the U.S. government and military-industrial complex mold the term "terrorist" to their subjective and financial goals too many times to trust any use of that word. Even Nobel Peace Prize winner Nelson Mandela was once considered a terrorist by governments worldwide and put on U.S. terrorist watch lists.

As Pulitzer Prize–winning journalist Chris Hedges told Democracy Now, the term "terrorist" is too loose so what the NDAA is really doing is setting up a legal mechanism to criminalize dissent.

"We saw an attempt to link the U.S. Day of Rage with Al Qaeda. Once they link you with a terrorist group, then these draconian forms of control can be used against legitimate forms of protest, in particularly the Occupy Movement," Hedges said. Corrupt corporations can use the NDAA to pressure the government to crush banking protests, environmental protests, strikes . . . it's a slippery slope.

The NDAA Will Be Used to Crush Protests

Possibly most disturbing is the NDAA's power to crush all dissent and protests in the United States, protests that are vital to free speech, change, the survival of democracy.

What will keep the government, possibly under pressure from banks, corporations, and the military-industrial complex, from starting to list various protesters and organizations as terrorists? What will happen when protesters stop voicing their concerns or hitting the streets because they fear they will "disappear" under the NDAA?

The systematic crushing of dissent through NDAA-esque powers is already happening in this country. The family of U.S. Marine veteran Brandon Raub says he was kidnapped by law enforcement after posting anti–U.S. government statements on Facebook.

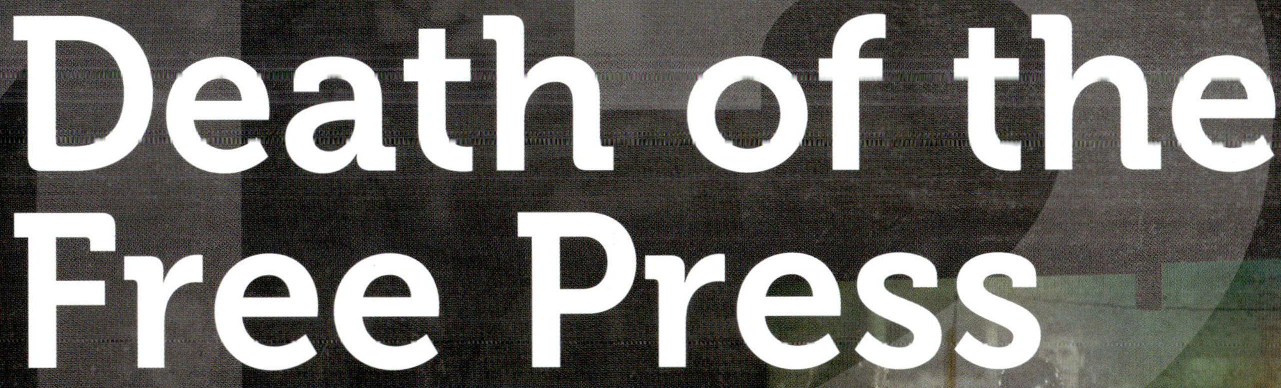

Death of the Free Press

The 2011–2012 period was one of the worst times for press freedom in the history of the United States. According to the journalism rights organization Reporters Without Borders, the United States dropped 27 rankings in 2011 on the annual Press Freedom Index to number 47, behind El Salvador. Reporters Without Borders blames a massive amount of journalist arrests during the Occupy protests for the decline.

One casualty of the struggle between the Occupy movement and the corporate state that continues its stranglehold on our democracy is freedom of the press. Enshrined in the American Bill of Rights, the right to a free and open press is perhaps one of our most cherished ones: the ability of journalists to keep power in check and to be critical of said power helps to ensure that people are able to have a clear and unfettered understanding of events. On a more basic level, journalists—especially during protests when activists and law enforcement go head to head on the streets—must be able to document abuse of power.

There can be no better recent example of curtailment of this basic right than that of journalists—be they live-streamers or more institutional press—being assaulted, intimidated, and arrested during protests. It is no exaggeration to state that there has been an unprecedented crackdown on journalists over the past year. It is documented by free-press advocate Josh Stearns, who maintains an ongoing effort to tally and document freedom-of-the-press violations in real time during protests, that as of September 17, 2012—one year to the day since the Occupy movement kicked off in Lower Manhattan—conservative estimates of journalist arrests total 90. The explosion of live-stream technology and use of Twitter to provide real-time coverage of Occupy protests also put not only institutional journalists' freedom and safety on the line, but a new generation of activist journalists as well.

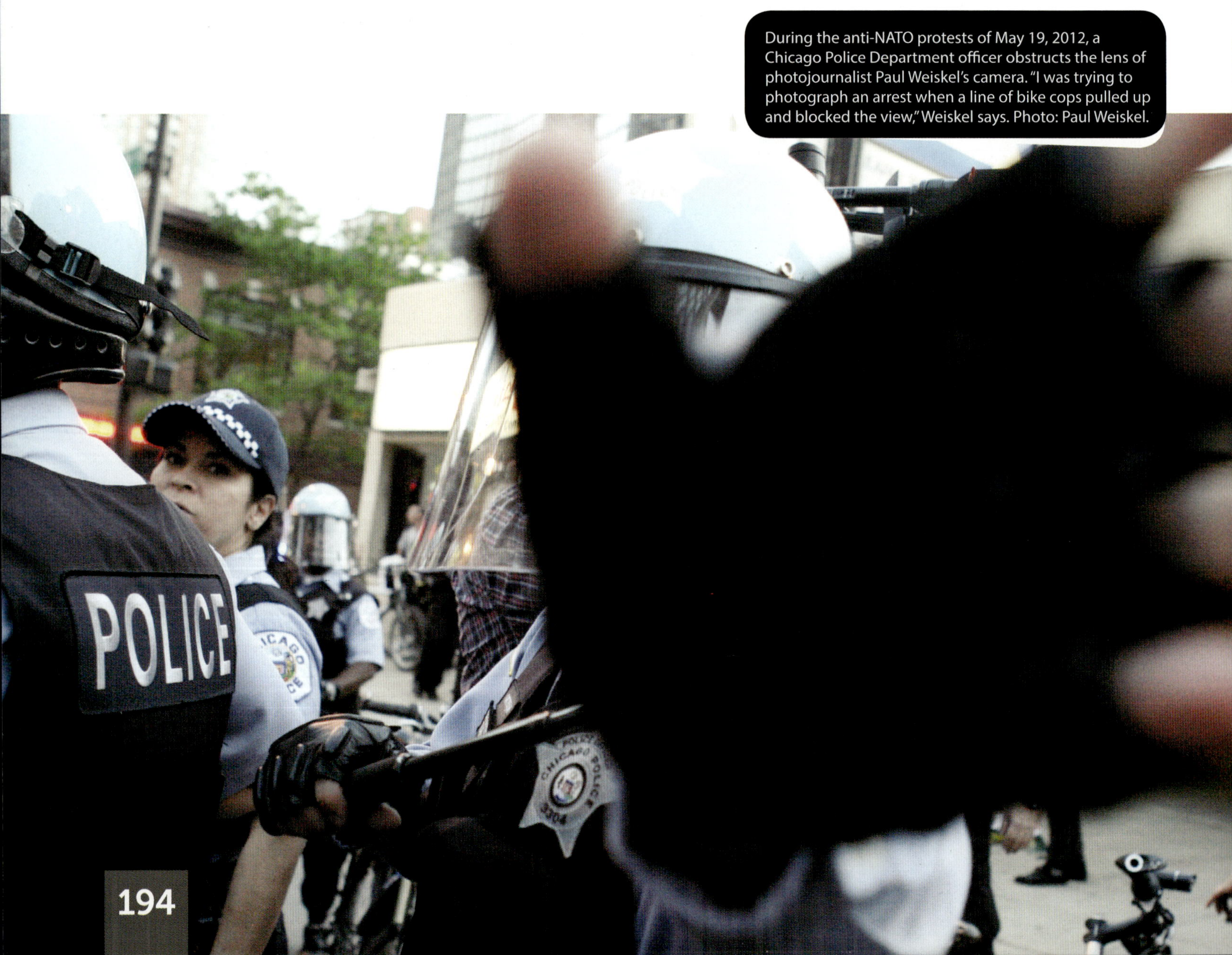

During the anti-NATO protests of May 19, 2012, a Chicago Police Department officer obstructs the lens of photojournalist Paul Weiskel's camera. "I was trying to photograph an arrest when a line of bike cops pulled up and blocked the view," Weiskel says. Photo: Paul Weiskel.

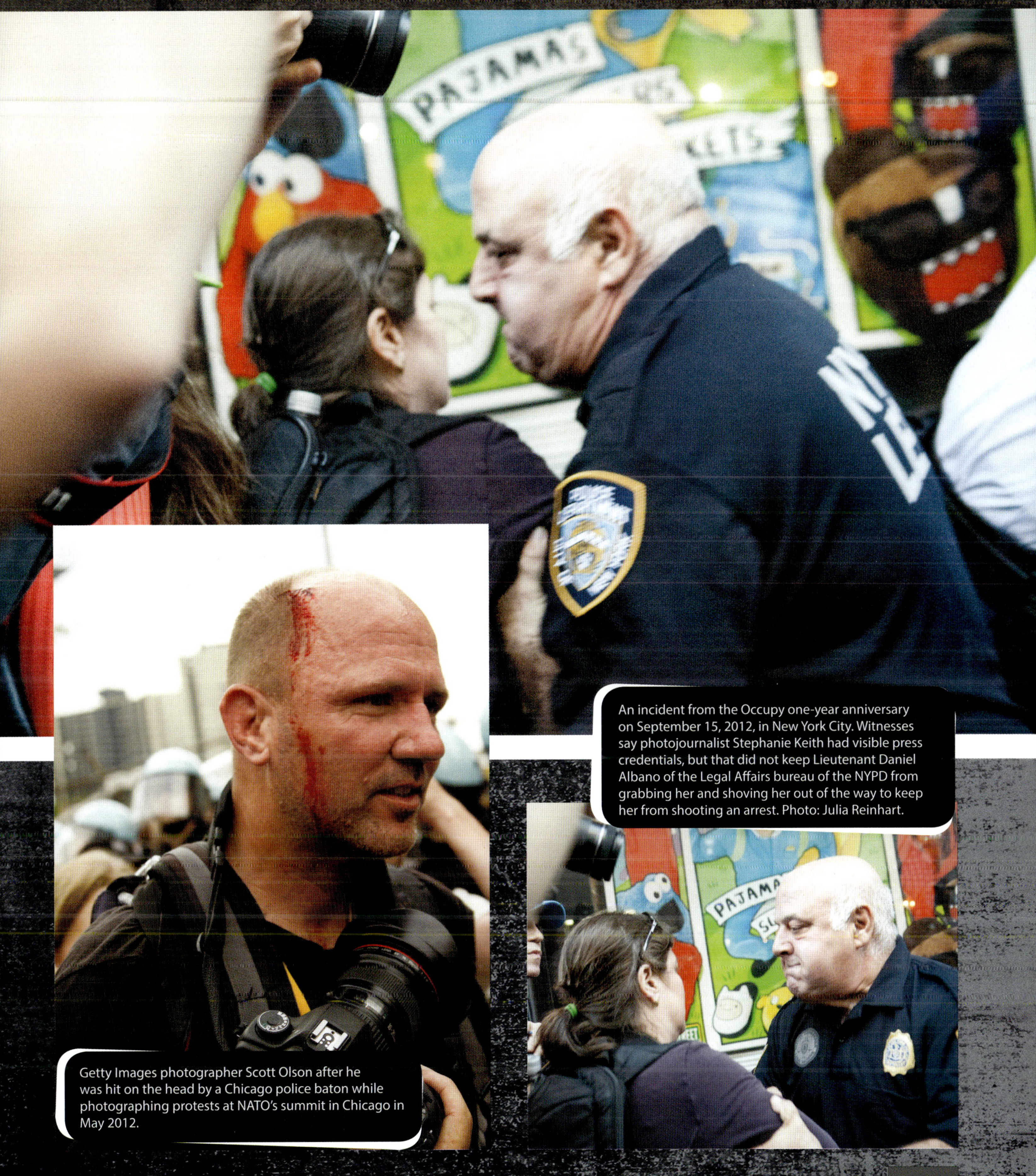

An incident from the Occupy one-year anniversary on September 15, 2012, in New York City. Witnesses say photojournalist Stephanie Keith had visible press credentials, but that did not keep Lieutenant Daniel Albano of the Legal Affairs bureau of the NYPD from grabbing her and shoving her out of the way to keep her from shooting an arrest. Photo: Julia Reinhart.

Getty Images photographer Scott Olson after he was hit on the head by a Chicago police baton while photographing protests at NATO's summit in Chicago in May 2012.

MY STATE-SPONSORED Assault, Courtesy OF THE NYPD

By John Knefel, freelance journalist

The first time I was arrested as a journalist covering Occupy Wall Street was a long and nightmarish journey through the intake procedure of what is mistakenly referred to as our criminal justice system.

The second time I was arrested—on September 17th, 2012, the one-year anniversary of Occupy—my time in custody was significantly shorter, but that was due to dumb luck, not a sudden respect for the press from the NYPD. My friend Jesse Myerson, also a journalist, often says that the fundamental question regarding the NYPD is whether they are driven more by stupidity or cruelty. Regardless of the specific proportions in my interactions with them, there has often been a healthy mix of both.

Shortly after 3:30 p.m., a march departed from the red cube across from Liberty Square with the goal of reading the People's Gong—a passionate declaration of resistance to the supremacy of capital—at or around the intersection of William and Wall Street, close to the New York Stock Exchange.

After a lively march that I characterized on Twitter at the time as possibly the most festive I had ever seen for Occupy Wall Street, the protesters ended up at the corner of Nassau and Pine. The "ringing" of the People's Gong commenced, and shortly afterwards I was on the ground with an officer telling me, "it's all right, it's over now."

At 0:37, you can see an officer grab John, who is clearly standing on the sidewalk, and pull him into the street. His sister Molly is standing directly behind him when he's grabbed.

My attorney has advised me not to describe the specifics of the arrest until my case has concluded, but I can safely say I was standing on the sidewalk at the time of my state-sponsored assault. The force with which I was thrown to the ground slid my glasses down the bridge of my nose, giving me the appearance of some sort of cartoonish professor. After being raised to my feet, a giant officer, softer around the edges than on the eyes, didn't simply push my glasses back up my nose for the nerd-assist; he took them off and put them in my pocket. He meant it as a kind gesture, I think, which only serves to show the complete submission the police expect from people they're charged with protecting. You're with us now; your sight is unnecessary.

Two of the seven protesters in the arrest van had blood covering their faces. I don't know the specifics of either arrest, but one, a traveler named Todd, had a nasty-looking cut above his left eye, and possibly a bruised eye as well. He works handing out Metro or AM New York newspapers in the subway in the morning.

"If I have to stay over night, I'm gonna lose my fucking job," he said as leaned his head back. Martina, a young Chilean woman, had also bled profusely from a cut above

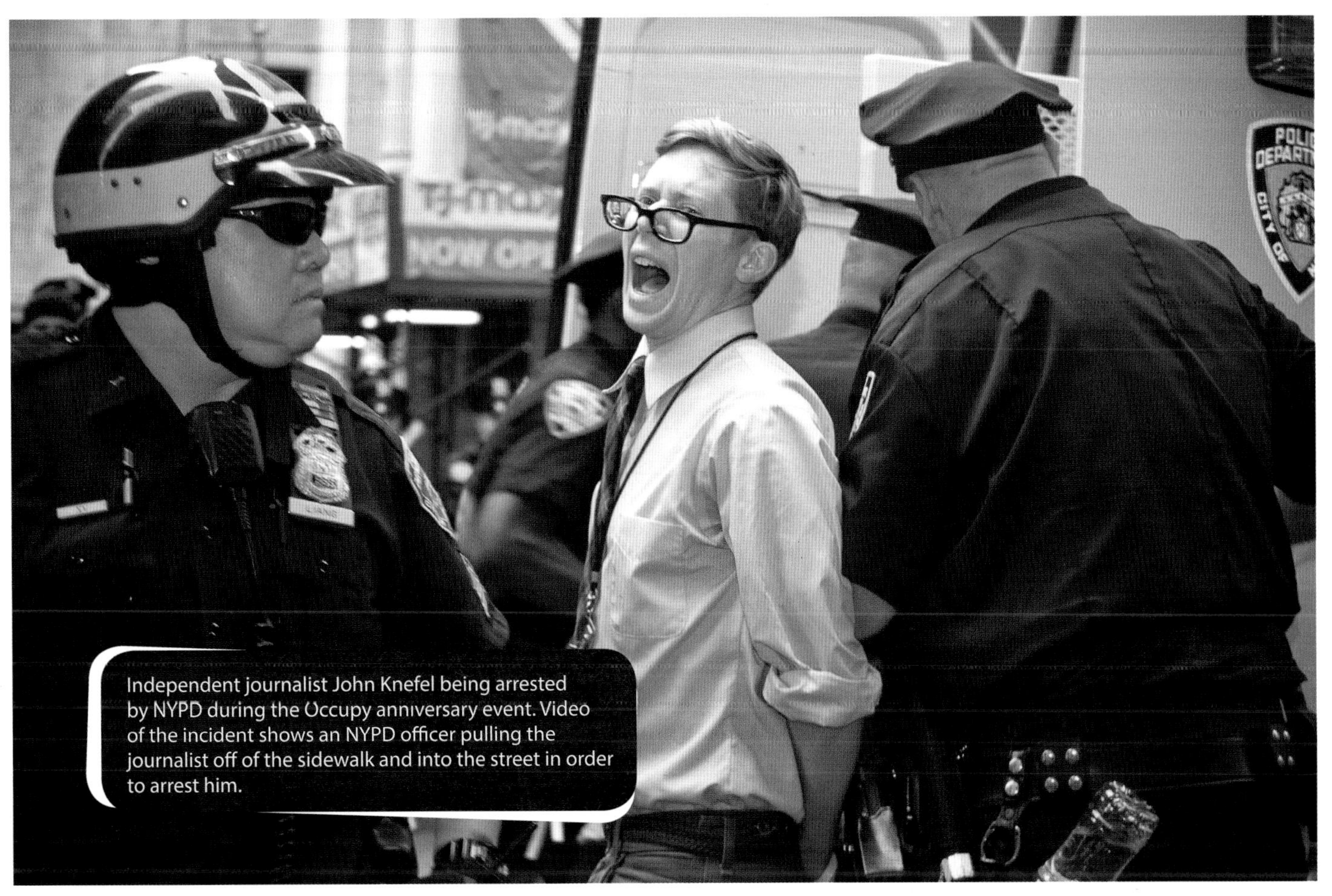

Independent journalist John Knefel being arrested by NYPD during the Occupy anniversary event. Video of the incident shows an NYPD officer pulling the journalist off of the sidewalk and into the street in order to arrest him.

her eye. She had a makeshift bandage on her head such as you might see in an amateur Civil War re-enactment. Her flex-cuffs were on so tight, her hands were turning purple.

"You gotta fix this woman's cuffs," yelled Derick, a member of the legal support group Mutant Legal. "Her hands are turning purple man."

A cop sat in the back corner of the van, taking down our names. "We'll get to it," he said. Derick told Martina to lean forward to help blood circulation, which she did.

"Hey, someone out there got a cutter so we can re-cuff this one?" the cop asked, nodding at Martina.

An officer standing outside said yeah, then walked away. A protester who had never been arrested before briefly joked about singing songs, as he'd heard that's what people do in this situation.

The cop suggested against it. "Your morale depends on my morale," he said, his voice empty of sarcasm, humor or empathy.

An officer standing outside slammed the door shut, and we proceeded to One Police Plaza for processing, with Martina, covered in blood, trying to keep quiet despite the pain in her hands.

When we got to 1PP, as it's called, the police there looked over Martina and determined she had to go to the hospital because of the injuries sustained during her arrest. Martina might have weighed 115 pounds, and has a somewhat bird-like quality about her

When they got to me, a thuggish bully named Czark looked at the non-NYPD-issued media pass hanging from a lanyard around my neck. He was a White Shirt, or high ranking officer, with between 15 and 20 years on the force, signified by the three arrows on his sleeve.

"You're press?"

"I'm a journalist."

"You're wearing this around your neck, like a press pass though, right?"

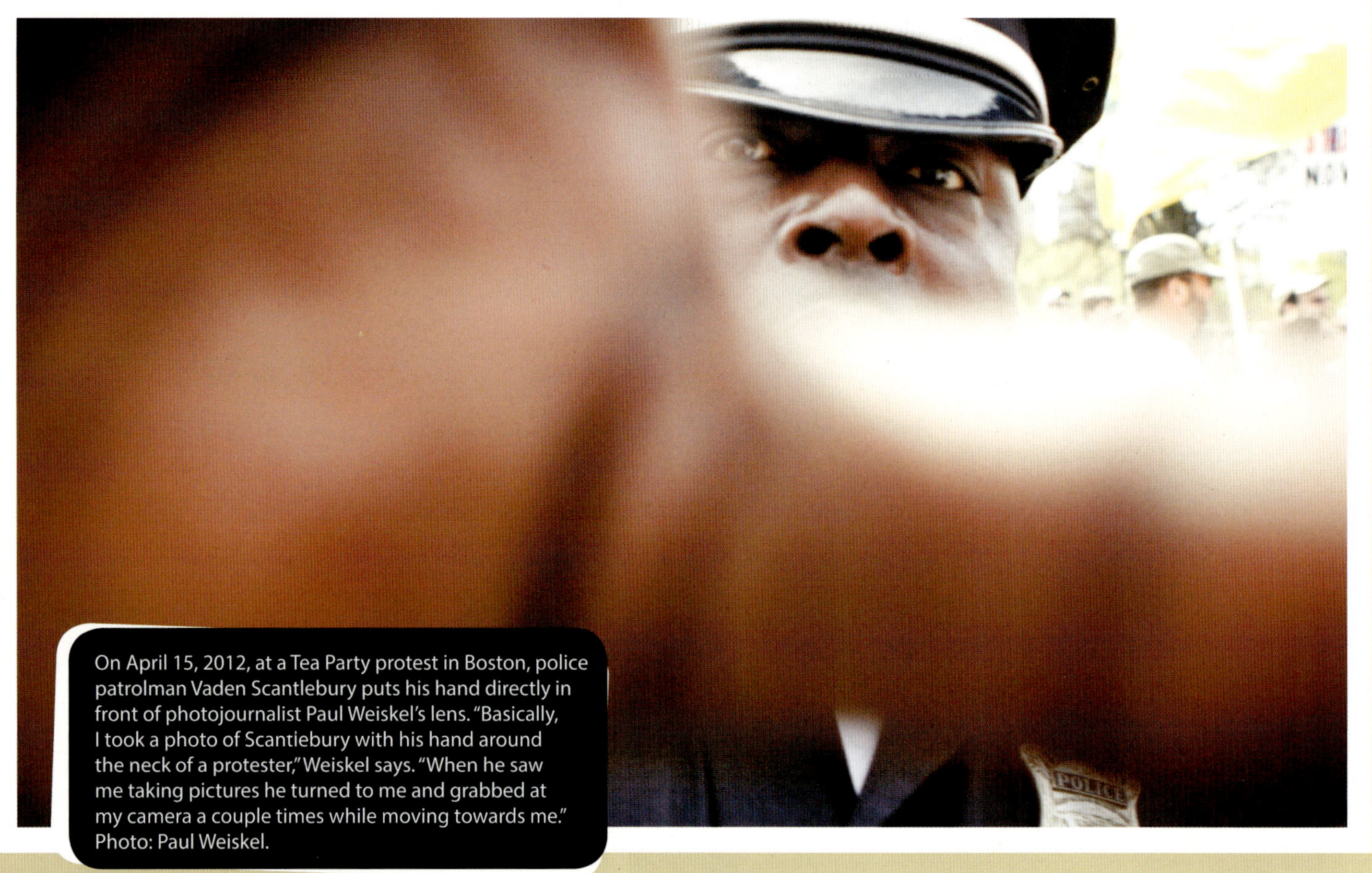

On April 15, 2012, at a Tea Party protest in Boston, police patrolman Vaden Scantlebury puts his hand directly in front of photojournalist Paul Weiskel's lens. "Basically, I took a photo of Scantiebury with his hand around the neck of a protester," Weiskel says. "When he saw me taking pictures he turned to me and grabbed at my camera a couple times while moving towards me." Photo: Paul Weiskel.

I informed him that I was a journalist and that I wasn't going to say anything else until I spoke with my attorney. He took the press pass off from around my neck.

"This is some bullshit, right? I mean, what, you make this yourself?"

I said nothing, although the pass had been issued by [radio station] WBAI.

He took the pass, which has my photo on it, told me to get back in the van, and said he was going to check with their press department to see if I was a "real" journalist. He returned shortly after to inform me that, "No, you're not in the database." He looked at the gentle young cop who would be referred to as my arresting officer and said, "Take him to that pen over there."

While a protester who had had several buttons popped from his shirt in his arrest and I were processed in our outdoor pen, a cop taking down Todd's information stopped, and looked around.

"Wait, we can't take this guy's picture," which they were doing on our intake. The cop pointed at Todd's bloodied face and gave a what-do-we-do-about-this shrug. I think Todd ended up going to the hospital, as I don't recall seeing him in the group cell later on, though I could be wrong.

The police had reserved a large group cell exclusively for Occupiers, as near as I could tell. The cell was actually two rooms, each about 20 by 25 feet, bisected with an open cell door and with a pair of disgusting toilets in the far corner. The cell was filled with about 40 protesters when I arrived.

Each person who entered was greeted with uproarious applause and hugs, and hey-they-got-you-too?s from friends who had missed the afternoon action. I saw a friend who had been arrested with me on December 12th and we hugged and shared a back-here-goddammit moment.

The criminal justice system relies on its victims having a lack of information about their rights. Because of my previous experience I knew that the iris scans the police tell you to take are optional.

The iris scans—which, I know, sounds creepy—are a two-step process, the stated purpose of which is to make sure you're the same person going to see the judge who was

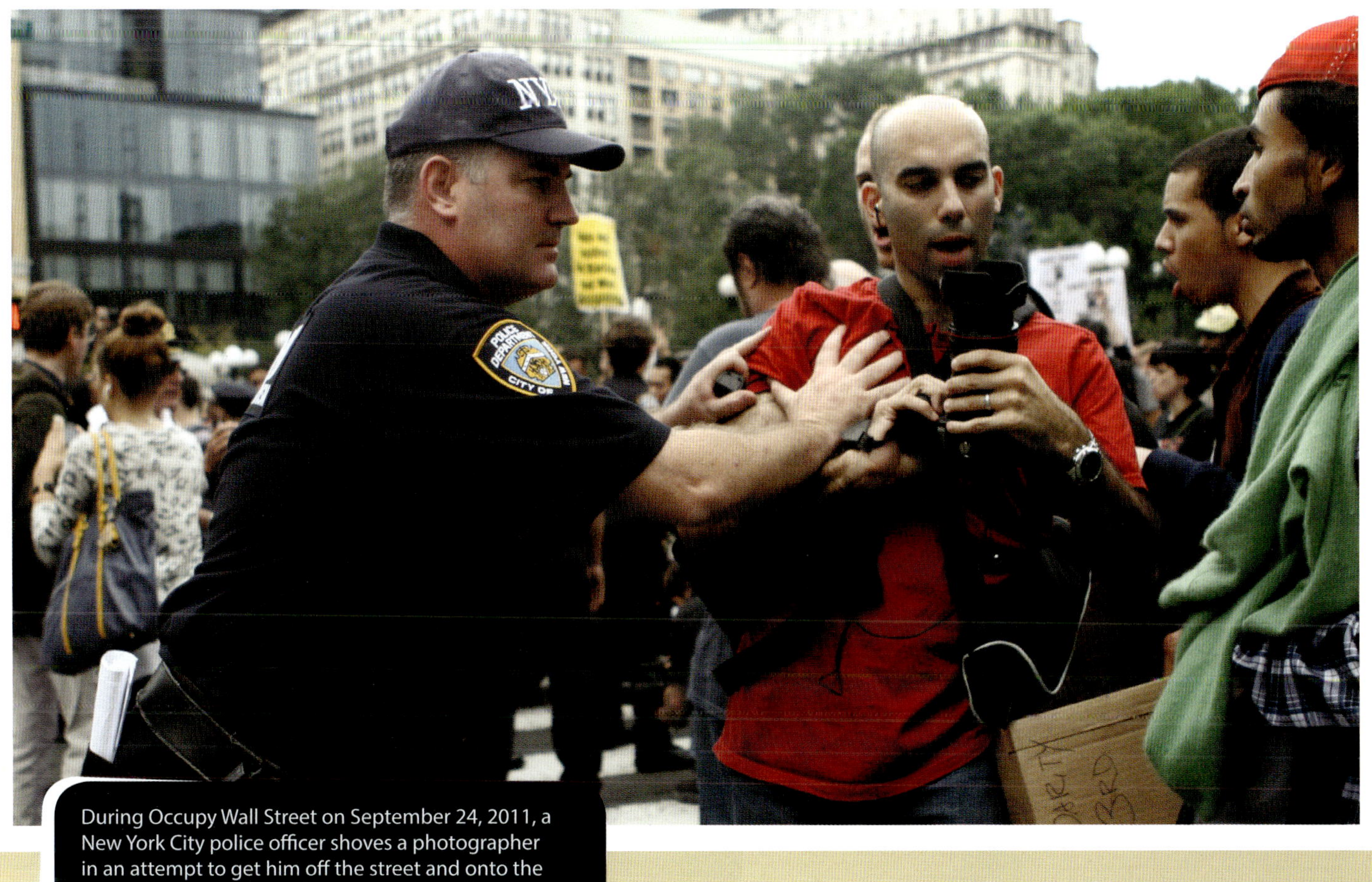

During Occupy Wall Street on September 24, 2011, a New York City police officer shoves a photographer in an attempt to get him off the street and onto the sidewalk. The photographer was covering the aftermath of an unpermitted march from Zuccotti Park to Union Square. Photo: Paul Weiskel.

brought in initially. They scan your eyes on intake, and then again at arraignment.

Their real purpose is to gain bio-metric data about you for their database, same as fingerprints. The first time I was arrested, several of us didn't consent to the first round of the eye scan. So, when it came time for the second round of the eye scan, right before we were set to see the arraignment judge, there was no first scan to compare it to. Despite this, we were threatened with an extra night in jail if we declined the second eye scan, even though its stated purpose—to match it with the first scan—was impossible.

I mic-checked this information to my cellmates, some of whom were familiar with it and some of whom weren't. Derick, the guy from Mutant Legal, added some other helpful information, and then went back to sleep. You can tell the old-hats because they don't get mad or shout or anything; they go to sleep.

I talked to Juan, from Puerto Rico, who was in the van with me. He and Martina kissed in the van in a few beautiful stolen moments—the only things stolen that day by activists—and I would've killed to get that shot.

"Martina's your girlfriend?" I asked.

"My wife."

"For how long?"

"Since Friday."

I burst out laughing and hugged and congratulated him, and told him I hoped Martina was okay.

"Yeah, I'm pretty worried about her."

I also talked to Jim, who told me that after crossing the street with the light and returning to the sidewalk, a White Shirt pointed him out to a rank and file cop, and said, "That guy."

At one point, a 17-year-old kid named Clay jumped up onto a bench to address us.

"When they took my information in the other room," he said loudly and clearly, "they told me I should be ashamed of myself. That my father isn't proud of me. But being in here

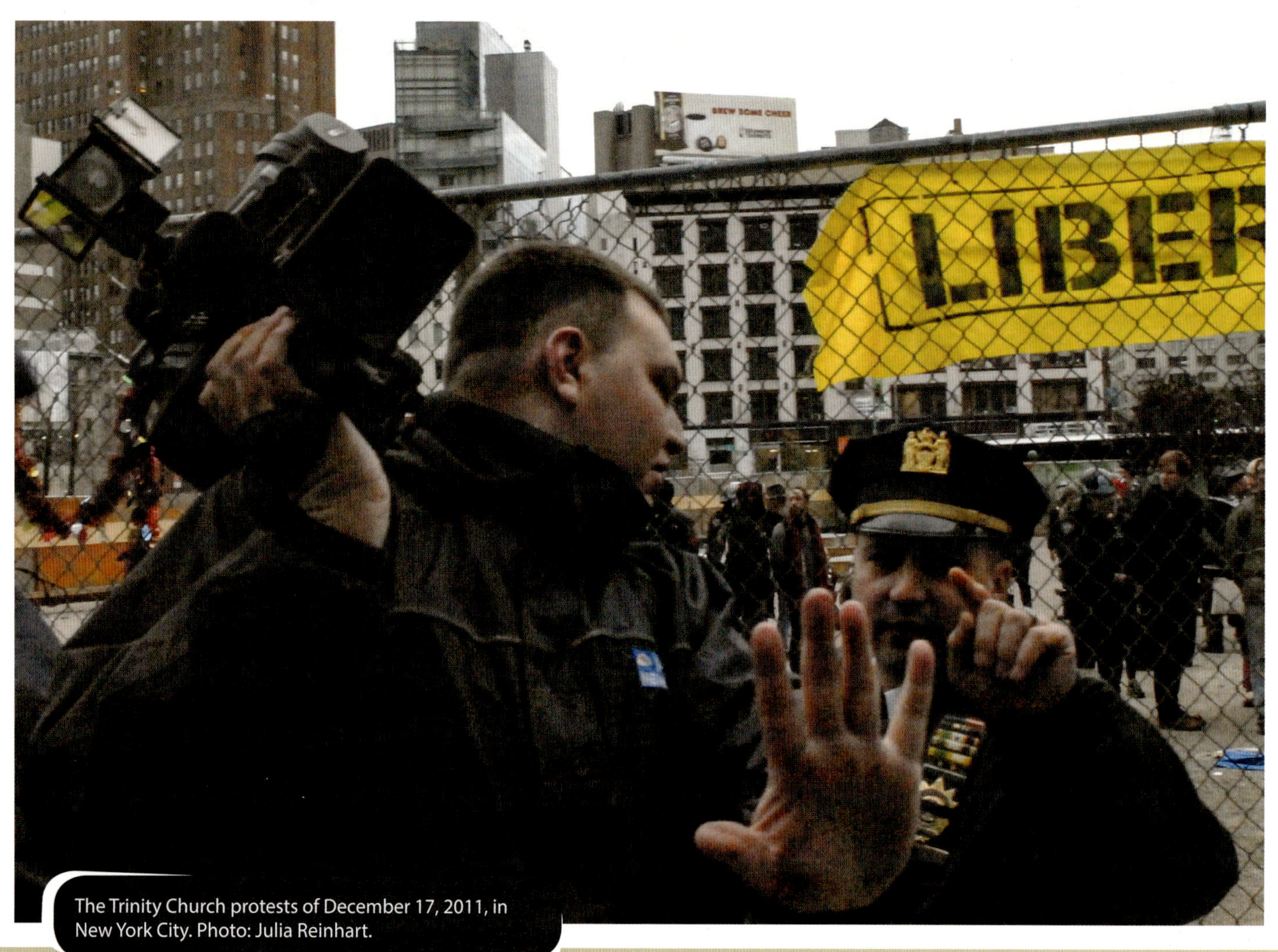

The Trinity Church protests of December 17, 2011, in New York City. Photo: Julia Reinhart.

with you guys, I just feel so much love and solidarity and it's really great."

Amid the applause, an old activist yelled, "Kid, your father's proud of you, I guarantee it."

Most of the Occupiers hung out in the front of the cell, near the door, so they could hear their name if it got called. One guy in the back, though, saw a TV on the other side of the cage.

"Hey, look!" he yelled. "We're on the news!" Several people rushed back to see a Chyron that read, "Over 100 arrested on Occupy Wall Street's Anniversary," and everyone burst into cheers like New Year's Eve.

I was only held for a few hours, given a Desk Appearance ticket, and allowed to leave. Thankfully I had an amazing group of friends, including my sister and co-host on Radio Dispatch, waiting for me at jail support. Being released to a torrent of well wishes in person and online certainly makes the whole experience more bearable.

But despite the relative ease of this detainment, there is an anger inside me that I can't shake. I can't begin to imagine how Jateik Reed must feel, or how Ramarley Graham's family must feel.

When you're the ward of the system, it strikes you that at every opportunity, every touch point, the person dealing with you just wants to be done dealing with you. Both times I've been arrested, it's been White Shirts who have grabbed me and thrown me to the ground, but they pass the paperwork off to some low level officer (both of whom have been quite nice in my cases) who, despite being identified as my "arresting officer," had nothing to do with my arrest.

Then, if they transfer you to the tombs, you become the Department of Corrections' problem. The DOC doesn't care what you did or who you are, they just want to get rid of you. The arraigning judge spends less than five seconds, literally, on you. It goes on and on like that.

Our entire justice system resembles nothing so much as a factory farm. Instead of chickens in cages, we put black and brown people in cages. The product isn't chicken nuggets, it's politicians who run on Tough On Crime, or the contracts businesses get to sell prison supplies, or the money made in the private prison industry, an industry whose incentives are so evil that they very nearly defy description.

The byproducts—the pink slime—is disenfranchisement, cheap labor and a culture that continues to treat black men as inherently dangerous, as one step away from being rightly locked up.

This is to say nothing of the Muslims who have been kidnapped and killed by the United States. Adnan Latif, whom I wrote about for AlterNet, had been repeatedly cleared for transfer back to Yemen, but he died in Guantanamo Bay because the despicable Obama justice department intervened. Will any establishment journalists ask Obama about the death of Adnan Latif, or the hundreds of others murdered while detained by US forces?

A form of authoritarianism has arrived in the US. I don't say this because I was arrested, but because to look over the past 11 years and arrive at any other conclusion is delusional. Police routinely pre-arrest activists before planned actions. Innocent men are held in cages with no hope of freedom. Elites are not only free from prosecution for their crimes, but are actively protected by the justice system and use the law as a weapon against those not in their class.

Trevor, who had been snatched up while taking pictures as a bystander, not a protester or journalist, is moving to California soon for undergrad.

"I had read about [Occupy] and the police and stuff, but I didn't really realize how bad it was until I saw it," he said, nervous like a young man who didn't expect to go to jail that day. "I mean, it's really, really bad."

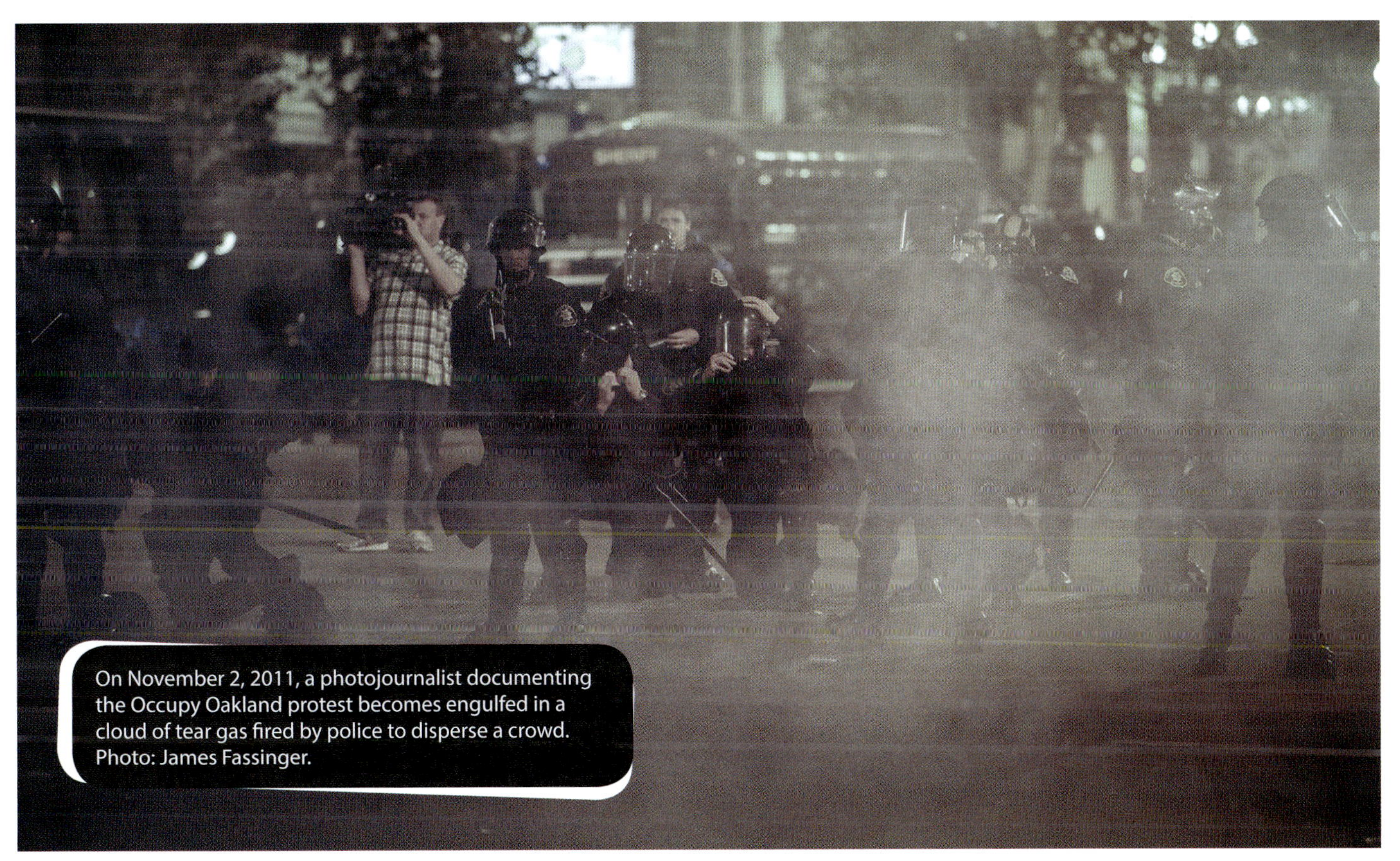

On November 2, 2011, a photojournalist documenting the Occupy Oakland protest becomes engulfed in a cloud of tear gas fired by police to disperse a crowd. Photo: James Fassinger.

Obama's War on Journalism

If when he promised "change" President Obama meant criminalizing journalism in the United States, then he's succeeded.

The investigative journalism that Obama has silenced could have exposed more corruption in the U.S. government, military, and banking industry—corruption that has caused anguish to numerous Americans. The reports that will never be heard, read, or seen on TV might have led to positive change.

The Obama administration is smothering investigative journalism at an alarming rate through the abuse of the Espionage Act of 1917, an act more prone to be used to protect government secrecy than national security. Before Obama took office, the act had been used only three times in total since 1917. The current administration has already used it six times to go after whistleblowers and the journalists to whom they leak information.

President Obama was bold enough to use the Espionage Act to subpoena New York Times journalist James Risen in an attempt to force him to give up information on a CIA whistleblower. Risen accused the administration of trying to silence journalists and refused to acquiesce, saying, "Can you have a democracy without aggressive investigative journalism? I don't believe you can, and that's why I'm fighting."

Risen predicted that Obama's attack against him would have an unprecedented chilling effect on mainstream investigative journalism in the United States. He was right.

I was on the receiving end of the Obama-generated censorship while employed at CNN as an investigative correspondent. My superiors and CNN's lawyers were quick to remind me that we needed to be extra careful because "President Obama has gone after more journalists and whistleblowers than any president in history." The decision of whether I was allowed to embark on future stories or even interview sensitive sources for potential investigations eventually became an "Obama subpoena risk assessment" and potential court cost calculation rather than a pure evaluation of the report's contribution to public good or our journalistic duty to cover the story.

As journalists we vow never to reveal our confidential sources, so to this administration we are criminals. It's time President Obama focused his time hunting down the real lawbreakers rather than attacking the messengers.

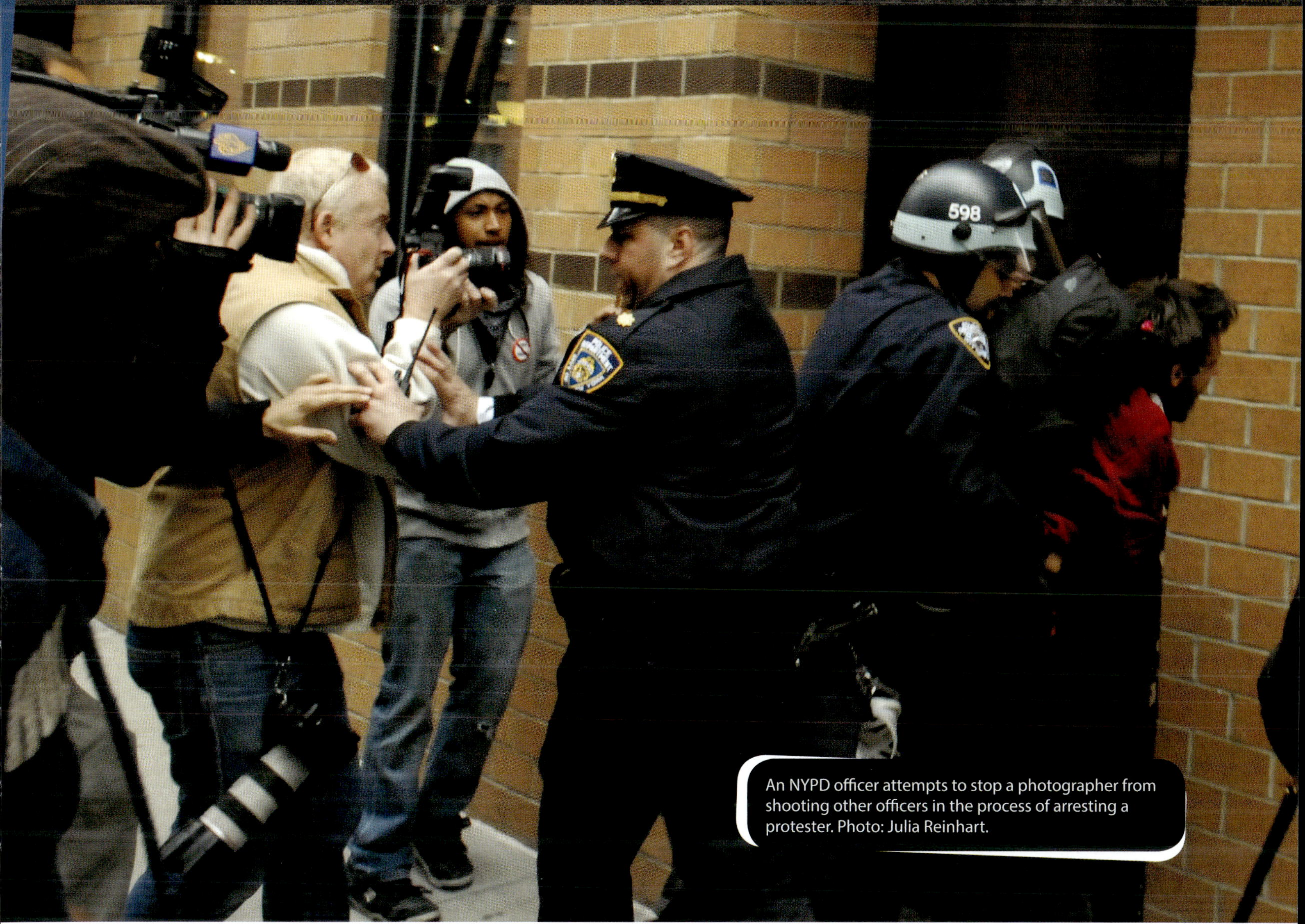

An NYPD officer attempts to stop a photographer from shooting other officers in the process of arresting a protester. Photo: Julia Reinhart.

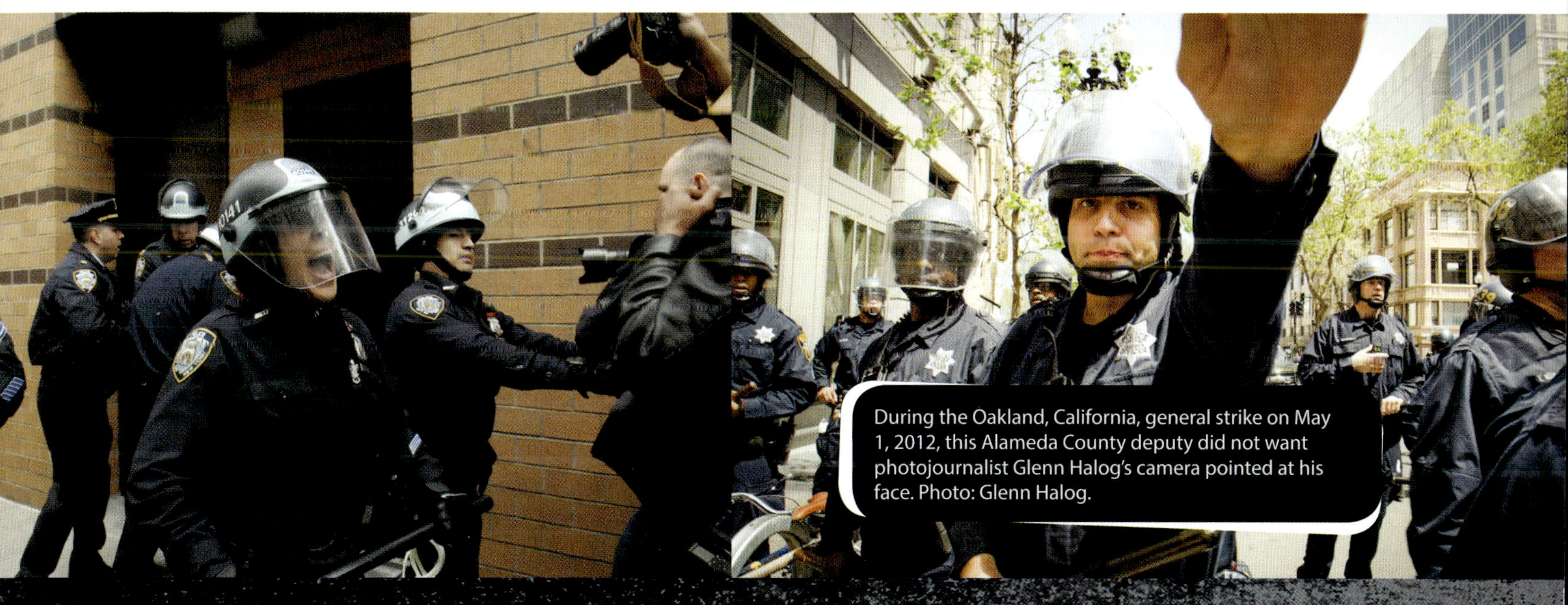

During the Oakland, California, general strike on May 1, 2012, this Alameda County deputy did not want photojournalist Glenn Halog's camera pointed at his face. Photo: Glenn Halog.

CONTRIBUTORS

DELL CAMERON, JOURNALIST

TWITTER: @DELLCAM

Dell Cameron is a writer, activist, and entrepreneur from Dallas, Texas. A contributing writer for SuicideGirls, he was campaign manager for David Seaman's run for Congress. Currently, Dell is the account director for Alomedia.net, a web development company that specializes in helping artists, musicians, and small businesses develop an online presence.

JAMES FASSINGER, PHOTOJOURNALIST

TWITTER: @STILLSCENES

WEBSITE: WWW.STILLSCENES.COM

The recent economic crisis in the United States has brought issues that were bubbling just below the surface for decades to the forefront of American life today. It has changed the very fabric of the nation and the way people of the country see their future and that of their fellow citizens. Photojournalist James Fassinger landed in the midst of this historic shift in 2008 when he moved back to the Detroit area, where he was raised, after more than 16 years living and working in former Czechoslovakia.

As he explains it, "It was only after living abroad for so many years that my eyes were opened to the immense influence the United States has over the rest of the world, both economically, socially and militarily, and how it has changed here at home in the years I was away. I see our country through different eyes, from a completely different perspective. Although I was born and raised here, I feel almost as if this is an entirely different place than where I spent my childhood and early adult life. I often struggle to discern whether I have changed so much or the country I thought I once knew has. I wonder whether things have always been this way, or was I simply unable to see them?"

Just as it was the possibility of witnessing and documenting historic change after the fall of communism that first drew James to Prague in 1992, so has the current situation in the United States. "I have the same sense here now as I did during the early 90s after the collapse of the totalitarian regime—that this is a time in history where monumental change is taking place. Back then, people in Eastern Europe took a stand and joined together against great odds to bring about a more just society, and this is similar to what we are beginning to see in the U.S. I am fortunate enough to be here, to try and capture what I can of our society as it pushes forward into what, I think, will prove to be one of the biggest periods of social and economic change since the late 1920s."

Now based in Detroit, James photographs assignment work throughout the Midwest and continues to pursue his passion for documenting social change sparked by his years photographing abroad. His work has appeared in the *Guardian* (U.S. and U.K.), the *Times of London*, the *Daily*, the *European*, the *National* newspaper, the Czech *Lidové Noviny* and *El Pais* of Spain. Limited editions of his hand-printed silver gelatin prints can also be found in collections throughout the United States and Europe. He is currently working on projects that document dissent in America and the movements that encompass it with the hope that his photographs will be preserved as a historical document of this time in American history.

CARLOS LATUFF, POLITICAL CARTOONIST

TWITTER: @CARLOSLATUFF

WEBSITE: HTTP://LATUFFCARTOONS.WORDPRESS.COM

Carlos Latuff is a freelance political cartoonist from Rio de Janeiro, Brazil. Latuff has been professionally creating cartoons that expose and infuriate dictators, kings, prime ministers, and corrupt elites since 1990.

Latuff uses his art as a vessel of communication with people around the world on topics of human rights issues, state terrorism, and police brutality mostly related to Brazil and the Middle East. Latuff has had a passion for drawing since he was a child.

NICOLE POWERS, JOURNALIST

TWITTER: @NICOLEPOWERS

Nicole Powers is a writer, photographer, conversationalist, armchair anarchist, and painfully polite protester. She has done time at occupations in New York, London, Chicago, and Los Angeles, and has engaged in creative activism both in the real world and online. She is a social media consultant and ghost tweeter for several forward-thinking organizations, and has written two chapters for the Demand Progress book Hacking Politics on the fight against PIPA and SOPA. She serves as editor-at-large for SuicideGirls, produces and hosts the weekly SuicideGirls radio show, and is developing Muckraker.com, a next-generation news site, with VICE contributor Dell Cameron and three-time Emmy Award–winning journalist Amber Lyon. Nicole was born in the United Kingdom and currently lives in the United States, but as a denizen primarily of the internet she imagines a world where there are no countries to live or die for (and no religion too). Her main goal in life is to live long enough to be able to upload her consciousness to the matrix.

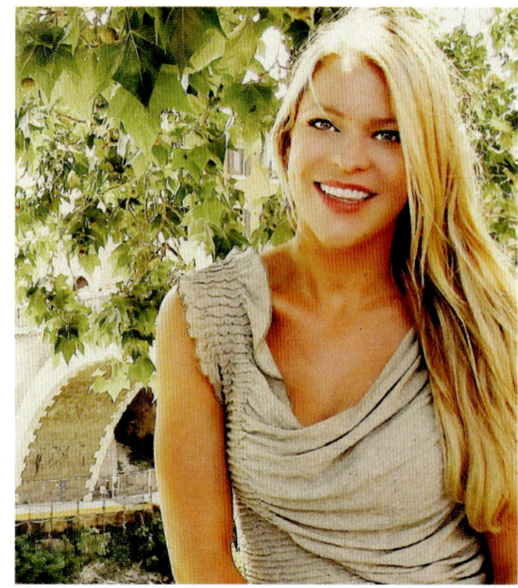

About the Author

TWITTER: @AMBERLYON

Amber Lyon is a three-time Emmy Award–winning journalist and photographer who grew up in St. Louis, Missouri. Formerly a CNN correspondent, she is the founder of the investigative news site Muckraker.com and has an obsession with covering hacktivists, human rights, and revolutions.

While at CNN, Amber was the only reporter to broadcast live while scuba diving in a hazmat suit from beneath the *Deepwater Horizon* oil spill to show viewers what was happening during the BP disaster. Her reporting contributed to CNN's winning a Peabody Award for coverage of the spill.

Lyon produced the documentary *Selling the Girl Next Door*, which gave viewers a raw look into the disturbing world of underage American girls caught up in the violent sex trade. For her documentary *iRevolution*, Lyon examined social media's critical role in galvanizing revolutions and exposing human rights abuse in Egypt, Tunisia, and Bahrain. She was honored with an Edward R. Murrow Award, received a Gracie Award for women in media, and was a Livingston Award finalist for her journalism.

Lyon continues to investigate ongoing cases of excessive use of police force against journalists and protesters in the United States. She has been crushed underneath a crowd in Chicago, directly shot at with less lethal weapons in Anaheim, and forced to inhale pepper spray more times than she can count. In February 2013, she was invited to speak at Harvard Law School about her experiences covering dissent.

Lyon often embarks on spontaneous adventures and lives by the adage "Well-behaved women seldom make history." You can learn more about her at www.AmberLyonLive.com.